GENERAL ROBERT F. HOKE

ALSO BY DANIEL W. BAREFOOT

Touring the Backroads of North Carolina's Upper Coast
Touring the Backroads of North Carolina's Lower Coast

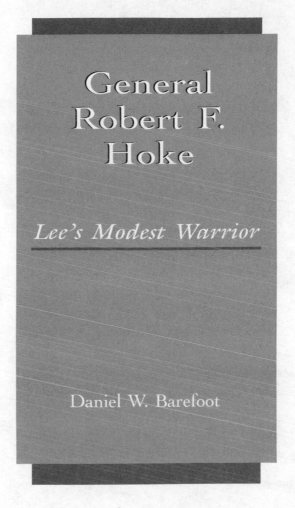

General
Robert F.
Hoke

Lee's Modest Warrior

Daniel W. Barefoot

John F. Blair, Publisher • Winston-Salem, North Carolina

*The paper in this book meets the guidelines
for permanence and durability of the
Committee on Production Guidelines
for Book Longevity of the Council
on Library Resources.*

Library of Congress Cataloging-in-Publication Data
Barefoot, Daniel W., 1951–
    General Robert F. Hoke : Lee's modest warrior / Daniel W.
Barefoot.
        p.   cm.
    Includes bibliographical references and index.
    ISBN 0-89587-150-5 (alk. paper)
    1. Hoke, Robert F. (Robert Frederick) 2. Generals—Confederate
States of America—Biography. 3. Confederate States of America.
Army—Biography. I. Title.
E467.1.H57B37   1996
973.7'42'092—dc20
[B]   96-2702

Design by Liza Langrall.

Photographs courtesy of author, unless otherwise noted.

Once again, to Kay
and Kris, with love

Contents

Preface

Young as the youngest who donned the Gray,
True as the truest who wore it . . .

FATHER ABRAM J. RYAN
POET-PRIEST OF THE CONFEDERACY

Although the Civil War ended more than 130 years ago, public interest in the history of America's bloodiest war has perhaps never been greater. My interest in Civil War history was born with the nation's centennial observance of that war. It was also during that 4-year observance that I first learned of and became interested in Robert Frederick Hoke. During the 1964–65 school year, I and countless other seventh-graders throughout North Carolina saw the likeness of Hoke flanked by those of Robert E. Lee and Stonewall Jackson in the state-prescribed textbook on North Carolina history. To be pictured in the company of the two most famous generals of the South gave some hint of the greatness of Hoke.

Two decades were to pass before I could begin a serious study of the man who has been described by prominent historians as "the most distinguished soldier of North Carolina," the state's "most distinguished son," and "the most commanding figure North Carolina has given to the world." It did not take long for my study to reveal that here was a genuine American hero, not only of war but of peace, whose story needed to be told to and preserved for future generations of Americans.

In the twilight of his long life, Hoke was once asked what words of wisdom he would offer young people. His response was simple and direct: "Strict attention to all duties of life." If ever a man heeded his own advice to others, it was Hoke. Throughout his life, he never shied away from duty; rather, he looked for and performed it with determination, dispatch, and modesty.

Born into a family that had already distinguished itself in state and national affairs, Hoke was never content to rest on the achievements of his forefathers. When hostilities between the North and the South appeared inevitable in the spring of 1861, Hoke saw as his first duty the need to defend his family, his home, his state, and the South. As a twenty-three-year-old second lieutenant, he was among the first troops North Carolina sent into the Civil War. His subsequent rise up the chain of command was meteoric: in less than three years, he was a major general, the youngest man to hold that rank in the Confederate army.

Hoke was one of only a handful of soldiers who fought in the first battle of the war, at Bethel, and subsequently laid down his arms in the last significant surrender after Appomattox. All along the way, from the beginning to the end of the war, Hoke led Confederate soldiers with uncommon bravery and skill on virtually every important battlefield of the Eastern theater. And still whispered today in North Carolina is the longstanding but heavily challenged tradition that Hoke was Lee's choice to become the commander of the Army of Northern Virginia in the event of Lee's death or disability.

Once the great war was over, it was over forever for Hoke. Although he returned home a hero, the young major general was unwilling to use his hard-earned fame for economic, personal, or political gain. A legend in his own time, he was offered most every honor, including the governorship, within the grasp of the people of North Carolina, but he refused

Preface

them all. Instead, he set about tirelessly and modestly rebuilding the industry and economy of his native state and the war-devastated South. Without fanfare and with great reserve, Hoke became a champion of the economic rebirth of the South, just as he had been of its war effort.

Why, then, have more than eighty years passed since the death of this citizen-soldier without a biography of his life? The most obvious answer lies with the greatest of Hoke's qualities of character—his sincere modesty. Not only was Hoke adamant in his refusal to have his name or reputation used for profit or advancement, he steadfastly refused to write or talk, much less boast, of his achievements in war and in peace. As a result, historians have found a paucity of first-person narratives by Hoke. There are no wartime letters to friends or family. There are few postwar accounts of military activities as related by Hoke. There are no memoirs.

Some military scholars have ignored or neglected Hoke because he served the first eighteen months of the war as a colonel or officer of lesser rank. His youth and relative obscurity as a junior officer in 1861 and 1862 have rendered him a military subject difficult to study.

Hoke was a mortal man. His brilliant military career was not without defeats, failures, quarrels, and shortcomings. His postwar life, dedicated to family and the revitalization of the South, was so self-effacing that he was often unrecognizable in a crowd. That is how Hoke wanted it. He never set out to become a hero. And once he was, he never sought or enjoyed the attendant fame and attention.

In a speech delivered in 1921, nine years after Hoke died, Secretary of the Navy Josephus Daniels made an appeal to the youth of America: "Get you a hero, and I give you Gen. Robert Hoke . . . as an ideal in peace and war." Now, more than three-quarters of a century later, Hoke is a forgotten American hero whose life is worthy of study and emulation.

I suspect that the ever-modest general would be embarrassed by this intimate portrait of his life. But it is an important chapter of American and North Carolina history that has been left untold for far too long. What follows is the story of a good life of a great man. It is a story of which even Lee's modest warrior would be proud.

Acknowledgments

People who know the author will readily testify that this book has been my cause célèbre for a half-dozen or more years. In all my professional life as an author, attorney, and speaker, I have never undertaken a project with more willingness, zest, energy, excitement, and enthusiasm than the biography of Robert F. Hoke. Researching and chronicling the life of this man of singular greatness has been a rewarding endeavor, but Lee's modest general did not make the task an easy one.

Hoke's aversion to speaking and writing about himself made the research for this book much like a giant jigsaw puzzle. Had it not been for the assistance and support of many individuals, the puzzle would have never been put together. To properly thank every individual who contributed to a book of this magnitude would be impossible, but there are some special people who deserve recognition.

General Robert F. Hoke

Research for this book was conducted in libraries and repositories in many places. At each location, I was treated with courtesy. My primary and most extensive research was conducted at the Wilson Library (Southern Historical and North Carolina Collections) at the University of North Carolina at Chapel Hill, the Perkins Library at Duke University, the Joyner Library at East Carolina University, the North Carolina Division of Archives and History, and the National Archives. The staffs at each of these institutions merit special commendation.

The transformation of my manuscript into a book is due entirely to the professionalism and hard work of the dedicated staff at John F. Blair, Publisher. Carolyn Sakowski, president of Blair, was receptive to the idea of a Hoke biography when I first proposed it to her, and throughout the project, she has taken a great personal interest in it. Steve Kirk, my editor, is the consummate professional. He has gone the extra mile to make sure that this is a quality book. His advice, suggestions, compliments, and patience have been of inestimable value to me. Debbie Hampton, Liza Langrall, Anne Holcomb, Anne Schultz, and all the other employees at Blair have done a masterful job in making this book a reality.

For the many people across North Carolina who encouraged me to press on with this project by saying time and time again, "I can't wait to read it," I hope the finished project is worthy of your words of inspiration.

Ed and Sue Curtis of Salisbury tirelessly promoted the need for a Hoke biography. They have been among my strongest supporters in the project.

Henry Mintz of Columbus County, the home of two of my great-great-grandfathers who gave their lives fighting on the same battlefields as Hoke, chased down an important letter and was always on the lookout for information that might be of interest to me. He is a true friend to all Civil War historians of North Carolina.

Selby Daniels and Larry Walker, my friends and fellow members of the Piedmont Civil War Round Table in Charlotte, shared their expert knowledge and important information with me.

Patricia Monte and my friends in the Washington County Historical Society in Plymouth provided assistance and encouragement from the early stages of my work on Hoke.

Acknowledgments

W. T. "Hank" Jordan of the Historical Publications Section of the North Carolina Division of Archives and History offered guidance, advice, and suggestions. He generously shared materials and critiqued much of the manuscript. Perhaps no living person knows more about North Carolina's participation in the Civil War than Hank Jordan.

Dr. Charles V. Peery of Charleston, South Carolina, graciously allowed me to quote from a letter in his private Civil War collection.

In my hometown, which was also Hoke's hometown, a multitude of friends came to my aid. The late judge John R. Friday never wavered in his support for me and this venture. Sadly, he did not live to see this book in print, but his memory and his example were and remain a guiding force in my efforts.

Leslie Levine, head librarian at the Lincoln County Library, allowed my wife to photocopy a little-known daybook kept by Hoke in 1861. Mary Dellinger was always ready to be of service at the library.

Horace Rhyne, whose parents at one time managed Hoke's Lincoln Lithia Inn, loaned photographs and written records of that historic hostelry. Sue Ramseur and her late husband Jack, Neil and Linda Ferguson, and Paul Dellinger allowed me to copy photographs from their extensive files. Harold Ford permitted me to examine and copy original letters written to Hoke's father in 1844. Judson Crow, a great admirer of Hoke, provided materials, assistance with reproduction of photographs, and constant moral support.

Hazel Andrews opened the doors to and the resources of the building where the youthful Hoke attended school. Her confidence in me has been a source of great strength. Dorcas Taylor graciously took me on a tour of her home, where Hoke was born in 1837. Likewise, Tom Wilson and his late wife, Jane, shared their house, in which Hoke died in 1912.

No one could find a better friend than I have in Darrell Harkey. Always willing to do anything to assist in the project and anxious to find new information about Hoke, he has gone beyond the call of duty to encourage me and promote my endeavors.

Cognizant of the kindness and generosity of spirit Hoke exhibited throughout his life, I should have expected the same from his descendants.

But I have been overwhelmed by the assistance, encouragement, and friendship extended to me by each member of the Hoke family it has been my honor and pleasure to meet.

The general's granddaughter, Anne West, and her husband, Robert, of Warsaw, North Carolina, were the first to "adopt" me into the Hoke family. Never have I encountered a kinder, more gracious couple. Two of the general's grandsons, R. F. H. Pollock of Southern Pines and Van Wyck Webb of Raleigh, opened their homes to me and generously provided access to family records and artifacts. From the Ukraine, Hoke's great-grandson Michael Hoke McGehee expressed excitement about my efforts and sent information about other family members. His aunt and the general's granddaughter, Lydia Hoke Jastram of Rehoboth, Massachusetts, shared in the enthusiasm. Not only did she offer insight into the life of her father, Dr. Michael Hoke, but she provided copies of family photographs.

Almost as soon as I met Hoke Kimball of Raleigh, I came to admire in him many of the same qualities possessed by his great-grandfather. He welcomed my family into his home and into the Hoke family; he introduced me to other family members; he shared family records and photographs; he joined me for research at the National Archives; and he assisted me in countless other ways. In Hoke Kimball, I have found a friend for life.

Finally, the Barefoot family is owed a debt of gratitude which I can never repay. My parents instilled in me at an early age a love and appreciation of history. With my sister, they have remained among my biggest supporters.

This book would not have been possible without my wife, Kay, and my daughter, Kristie. They gladly welcomed Robert F. Hoke into our home and our everyday lives. Without complaint, Kristie spent innumerable hours beside her father in academic libraries and archives on beautiful days when she could have been at play and leisure. Most of my hard-to-read handwritten manuscript was put into the computer by Kristie. She is my pride and joy.

No one deserves more credit for the culmination of the project than my wife. From the outset, she was firmly convinced that this book was meant to be. With each new discovery about Hoke, she would say with a pleasant

Acknowledgments

smile, "Dan, the general is looking over your shoulder." She was right. An avid reader and lover of good books, Kay has been my sounding board. She has read and reread the manuscript to improve its quality. Above all, over the past twenty-five years, she has been my constant source of love, kindness, encouragement, and praise, even in the times I probably didn't deserve it.

ROBERT F. HOKE'S FAMILY TREE

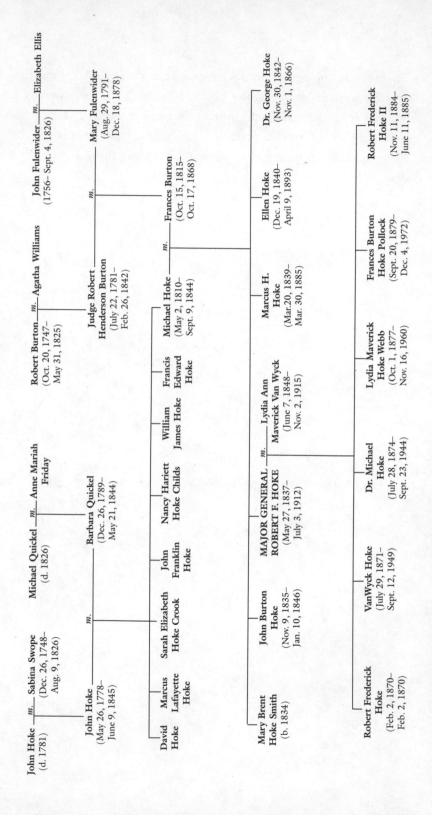

GENERAL ROBERT F. HOKE

> "If ever a child was destined for greatness based solely upon family roots, it was Robert Frederick Hoke."

CHAPTER 1

Roots of Greatness: A Lineage of Distinction

On Wednesday morning, July 3, 1912, seventy-five-year-old Robert Frederick Hoke woke briefly from a diabetes-induced coma. Now virtually robbed of sight by the disease which had brought his life to its lowest ebb, Hoke feebly gazed up from his deathbed in his summer cottage in Lincolnton, in the foothills of western North Carolina. Recognizing his oldest son, Van Wyck, he asked, "Van, are they all here?" in an obvious reference to his wife and four children.[1]

Van informed his father that the entire family was gathered by his bedside, and General Hoke seemed pleased and relieved. He remained conscious only a few minutes longer;[2] somehow, the aged Civil War hero who had fought so many desperate struggles knew that this final battle would not be won.

General Robert F. Hoke

At 10:20 A.M., the fight was over, and so ended the life of the man who was eulogized as the "most distinguished son" of North Carolina and "the State's wisest man" by Josephus Daniels, the famed newspaper editor who would serve as secretary of the navy and United States ambassador to Mexico. Hoke died in a house that stood just two and a half miles from the family home where he had been born.[3]

If ever a child was destined for greatness based solely upon family roots, it was Robert Frederick Hoke. As the son of Michael and Frances Burton Hoke, Robert had the good fortune to be born of gifted parents whose prominent families had established a tradition of service to North Carolina and the young American nation. Dr. Joseph G. D. Hamilton, eminent historian of North Carolina, noted that Robert's grandparents "for several generations were eminent, cultivated, educated people of character, intelligence, and refinement." Samuel A. Ashe, another respected North Carolina historian, concluded that Robert's "ancestry was such as has been most productive of men with those characteristics that have led to intelligent, persistent and courageous action, resulting in distinction in various walks of life."[4]

The first of Robert's name to arrive in America was Michael Hoke, a Palatine immigrant from Alsace-Lorraine who came to New York in 1709. In the succeeding years, the Hoke family settled in York County, Pennsylvania, and it was there that Robert's great-grandfather John, a Lutheran minister, married Sabina Swope, a woman of "great strength of character, energy, and perseverance."[5]

Reverend John Hoke died in 1781, leaving his widow and five children. In 1797, Sabina and her children did as many other residents of Pennsylvania did during the last third of the eighteenth century—they migrated to the North Carolina Piedmont, an area that had been the exclusive domain of the Cherokee and Catawba Indians until 1750.[6]

Sabina settled her family in Lincolnton, a small but significant outpost on the South Fork River, a sizable tributary of the Catawba. Lincolnton had been created, incorporated, and established as the county seat of Lincoln County by the North Carolina General Assembly in 1785. Both town and county were named for General Benjamin Lincoln, the distinguished

Revolutionary War officer whom George Washington purportedly selected to receive the sword of surrender of Lord Charles Cornwallis at Yorktown, Virginia.[7] Ironically, this small village, the birthplace of four generals who would take up arms against the United States, was the site of the crucial Battle of Ramsour's Mill, which helped turn the tide in favor of the American colonies during the Revolutionary War.

With but a single church, a small frame courthouse painted red, and shops and homes scattered about its dusty streets, the Lincolnton in which the Hoke family settled at the close of the eighteenth century was small. When noted French botanist François André Michaux visited Lincolnton in 1802, he noted that the town "was formed by the junction of forty houses, surrounded by the woods like all the small towns of the interior." Whatever Lincolnton lacked in size, the town and surrounding countryside had great economic potential. Not only was the area blessed with an abundance of powerful rivers and creeks and arable fields, but some of the nation's richest iron-ore deposits had been discovered in Lincoln County in the last quarter of the eighteenth century.[8]

John Hoke, Robert's grandfather, was the youngest of Sabina's children; he was nineteen years old at the time of his arrival in Lincolnton. Despite his youth, John possessed great business acumen, and he quickly established himself as a successful merchant. Over the next twenty years, he not only foresaw the economic potential of the local natural resources, but he parlayed those resources into great wealth for himself and his children.[9]

In 1817, John Hoke, Michael Schenck, and Dr. James Bivens built the Lincolnton Cotton Factory approximately two miles south of town. Boasting three thousand spindles, the facility was the first cotton factory ever constructed south of the Potomac. This imaginative enterprise represented the birth of the textile industry not only in North Carolina but in the entire South. The immediate success enjoyed by the Lincolnton factory led to the construction of cotton mills and factories in other parts of the state.[10]

Schenck and Bivens ultimately sold their interests in the factory to John Hoke, who operated it until his death in 1845. John's interest and success in manufacturing led to his acquisition of a paper mill and a facility for the production of linseed and cottonseed oils during the second quarter of the nineteenth century.[11] A pioneer industrialist in the South, John saw his empire grow, and he acquired extensive real-estate holdings and slaves.

On January 10, 1808, John married a local woman, Barbara Quickel. To this union, eight children—six boys and two girls—were born. The children grew up in an elegant three-story brick mansion which their father built in downtown Lincolnton in 1815.[12] John's second child, Michael, destined to become Robert's father, was born in Lincolnton on May 2, 1810.

Because of his family's affluence, Michael was afforded an excellent education for a boy who grew up on the fringes of the North Carolina frontier. After attending the local academy, he enrolled at Captain Alden Partridge's Military School in Middletown, Connecticut, in 1827. Among Michael's North Carolina contemporaries at the school were Thomas Bragg and Paul Cameron, who like Hoke later left their imprints on state history. In 1829, Michael began legal studies with Judge St. George Tucker of Virginia, and he subsequently completed his legal education with Judge Robert H. Burton in Lincoln County. A noted jurist and legal scholar, Burton had served as a judge of the superior court. In 1830, the legislature elected him state treasurer, but he declined the office.[13] It was as a result of the student-teacher relationship between Hoke and Burton that Michael became acquainted with and engaged to Burton's daughter, Frances.

Burton, a native of Granville County, North Carolina, first visited Lincoln County with his brother, Alfred, while they were students at the University of North Carolina. The Burton brothers were descendants of families distinguished in the affairs of Virginia, North Carolina, and the young American nation. As soon as their father, Robert, a young attorney and planter, had moved to North Carolina from Virginia in 1775, he had begun to establish a sterling record of military and civic service. During the Revolutionary War, he served as an officer with the Continental Artillery until he was appointed quartermaster general of North Carolina with the rank of colonel. Following the war, he was elected to two terms in the Continental Congress and subsequently served numerous terms on the Governor's Council, acting as president of that body on three occasions. In 1813, he was appointed to the commission which established the southern boundary of North Carolina. Owner of more than six thousand acres in North Carolina and Tennessee, the elder Burton once sold a horse to Daniel Boone.[14]

Robert H. and Alfred Burton settled in Lincoln County after marrying two sisters, Mary and Elizabeth Fulenwider, daughters of John Fulenwider. Fulenwider had settled in Lincoln County after fighting with the Whig forces at Ramsour's Mill and Kings Mountain. Exploiting the rich iron deposits in Lincoln County, he developed an extensive manufacturing business. Among his innovations were the first nail machine in America and the first rolling mill in the South. When he died, Fulenwider left a substantial estate consisting of twenty thousand acres of land and large amounts of capital, all of which was divided among his family. Fulenwider's wife, Elizabeth, was the aunt of John Willis Ellis, the governor of North Carolina in the first year of the Civil War.[15]

In June 1830, Michael Hoke was granted a license to practice law in the state of North Carolina, and he promptly embarked upon a legal and a political career that, while tragically short, acquired him a reputation as one of the most gifted North Carolinians of his day. Noted for "ease of manners, brilliancy of oratory, and acquirements in his profession," he soon won a "troop of friends" and a highly successful law practice. About Hoke's gift for public speaking, Samuel Ashe concluded that Michael "was so powerful in public debate that his oratorical powers were regarded by his contemporaries as extraordinary."[16]

Michael Hoke married Frances Burton on May 8, 1833, at her parents' elegant mansion on the Catawba River at Beattie's Ford in eastern Lincoln County. Following the ceremony, the newlyweds settled in Lincolnton. Later that same year, Michael completed an elegant, two-story H-plan Greek Revival residence for his bride. Built on a high lot within sight of the Ramsour's Mill battleground, the house would be the birthplace of Robert and his five siblings.[17]

On August 7, 1833, John Hoke, Michael's father, was elected clerk of superior court of Lincoln County, pursuant to legislation of 1832 that had made the office an elective one. John, a Democrat, ran unopposed for the position, but when he sought to claim it, Lawson Henderson, long an influential citizen in the county, maintained that the office belonged to him. And thus unfolded a series of events that caused a lasting rift between two of the most prominent families in Lincoln County and drew statewide attention. Henderson, a Whig who enjoyed great influence in local politics, had been appointed clerk of superior court "for life," and as a result, he maintained that he did not have to run for the position. Ultimately, the legal controversy surrounding the dispute made its way to the North Carolina Supreme Court, where the court upheld Henderson's position. The decision did much to split North Carolinians along party lines and did little to quell the burning animosity between the Hoke and Henderson families.[18]

For Michael and Frances Burton Hoke, 1834 was a year of promise. Their first child, Mary Brent, was born. Nineteen years later, Mary married Professor Hildreth Hosea Smith, and to that union was born Michael Hoke Smith, who would become a United States secretary of the interior, a United States senator, governor of Georgia, and owner of the *Atlanta Journal*. For Michael Hoke, 1834 marked the beginning of a stellar, albeit brief, career in politics. At the age of twenty-seven, he was elected by the voters of Lincoln County to the first of a half-dozen terms in the North Carolina House of Commons. In Raleigh, the young legislator promptly gained the respect and admiration of his colleagues, which led to his appointment to important committees on education, privileges and elections, and rules of order, as well as to the Board of Trustees of the University of North Carolina.[19]

It was into this world of prominence, wealth, politics, public service, and industry that Robert Frederick Hoke was born on May 27, 1837. Just four days later, another Lincolnton family welcomed a new baby, christened Stephen Dodson Ramseur. Dodson, as he was known to family and friends, became Robert's playmate, lifelong friend, and fellow major general in the Confederate army. They were two of the quintet of Confederate generals born in Lincoln County. The other three, all relatives of Robert Hoke, were Major General John Horace Forney (1829–1902), Brigadier General William Henry Forney (1823–94), and Brigadier General Robert Daniel Johnston (1837–1919).[20]

Less than three months after Robert's birth, the specter of open hostilities between the feuding Hoke and Henderson families became reality. Marcus LaFayette Hoke, the twenty-four-year-old brother of Michael and uncle of Robert, encountered Lawson Henderson on the main street of downtown Lincolnton on the morning of August 19, 1837. Abusive language and insults were traded, and bystanders who overheard the heated exchange reported it to Lawson Henderson's hot-tempered eighteen-year-old son, Logan. Infuriated by the public humiliation of his father, the younger Henderson set out in search of Marcus Hoke with the "intention of threatening Hoke" with a cane. When the two met near Court Square, Henderson landed several blows to Hoke's head, and a fight with a pistol and bowie knives ensued. Hoke was stabbed in the abdomen and died of the severe wound thirteen hours later.

A subsequent criminal trial in Rutherford County resulted in a guilty verdict on the reduced charge of manslaughter. After the presiding judge shocked the courtroom and the Henderson family with a sentence of six months in prison and the branding of Logan's hand with the letter *M* for murderer, subsequent appeals by Lawson Henderson saved his son from the pain and shame of branding. Logan ultimately joined his older brother James Pinckney Henderson, also a Lincoln County native, in Texas, where the elder brother was later elected the first governor of that state.[21]

From an early age, Robert Hoke was afforded an excellent education in his hometown. Although public schools were in the distant future when Robert reached school age, the leading citizens of Lincoln County had taken steps thirty years earlier to educate their youth. In response to a local initiative, the state legislature had chartered Lincolnton Male Academy, or Pleasant Retreat Academy, as it was later known, on December 10, 1813. Among the original board of trustees for the institution were several local ministers and civic and business leaders, including both of Robert's grandfathers, John Hoke and Judge Robert H. Burton, and his great-grandfather John Fulenwider. Housed in a large, two-story brick building on a four-acre lot located a stone's throw from the John Hoke mansion and from Robert's boyhood home, the school educated the sons of Lincolnton's prominent families. Among its earliest students were Michael Hoke, James

Pinckney Henderson, and William Alexander Graham.[22]

By the time Robert enrolled at Pleasant Retreat, the academy had earned an outstanding reputation in the western part of the state. Robert, Dodson Ramseur, Robert Daniel Johnston, and the other students of the 1840s and 1850s were challenged by a curriculum that included grammar, logic, mathematics, chemistry, Greek, Latin, and the classics. Robert's report card dated June 13, 1845, revealed grades that were slightly above average.[23]

Throughout the latter half of the 1830s, Michael Hoke had grown into the shining star of the Democratic Party in North Carolina, and by 1840, he was one of the foremost Democratic politicians in the entire state. It was little wonder, then, that the Democratic state convention, meeting in Raleigh on Thursday, December 14, 1843, nominated him as its candidate for governor of North Carolina in 1844. Michael was the unanimous choice of the convention delegates, who counted among their number many influential North Carolinians, including three future governors. Preliminary county meetings throughout North Carolina had already made Michael the hands-down choice for the nomination.[24]

A week before the Democrats named their standard-bearer, the Whig Party, also convening in Raleigh, selected another Lincoln County native (and an intimate friend of Michael), William Alexander Graham, as its gubernatorial candidate. Graham, also a descendant of an aristocratic family, had established a law practice in Orange County after completing his legal education.[25]

Of the two candidates, one historian noted,

> Never in any campaign in this or any other state, for any position, were two political antagonists more evenly matched. Both were in the very prime of life. Hoke was only thirty-four and Graham forty years of age. Both were strikingly handsome men, tall, well-formed, and graceful, with manners as polished as a Chesterfield, and tempers as placid as a theological student, characters as pure as a maiden, and habits as free from guile as those of a bishop. While possessing all these amiable qualities when it came to the advocacy of the principles of their respective parties or assailing those of the other they exhibited the courage of a Washington and the aggressiveness of a Jackson. The dignified

and majestic presence of Graham was formidably rivaled by the matchless manners and ready humor of Hoke, and no two were ever more enthusiastically supported by their partisan followers. It was a battle of giants.[26]

Samuel Ashe described the two political adversaries in glowing terms: "Both men were of superior character, and finely educated. They were of the highest type of manhood and were alike ornaments of society and exemplars of virtue and honor."[27]

The campaign of 1844 proved to be one of the most exciting in state history and was conducted by both men in a dignified manner. Because of his attractive personality and his integrity, Michael Hoke maintained the respect of his political foes all over the state. For example, during the contest, North Carolina Whigs referred to Democrats as "Locofocos," but they did not use that term for Michael Hoke. The *Raleigh Register*, the leading Whig publication in the state, best summarized the feelings of the opposition about Hoke when it told its readers, "We had as soon have him chosen as any man in his party in North Carolina."[28]

Following Graham's recovery from a serious illness, then the national political conventions in late May, the campaign swung into full gear. The Whigs had nominated Henry Clay for president on May 1 at their convention in Baltimore, and the Democrats had nominated dark horse James Knox Polk in the same city on May 27. A series of debates between the gubernatorial candidates was arranged where each man espoused the platform of his national party. Without question, the hottest item of debate was the issue of the annexation of Texas. Hoke seized upon the pro-annexation stance of the Democratic Party, which played well in eastern North Carolina. When he traveled to western North Carolina, where Whig strength was the greatest, the Democratic nominee discussed local issues and attempted to convince the mountain people to vote for a westerner. Historian John Wheeler described Hoke's manner of campaigning: "Such was the fairness of his conduct, his open, generous temper, his elevated mode of argument, that even in high excitement party spirit forgot its rancor; and he won, as he deserved, the regard and respect of all parties."[29]

Personal tragedy, a dark portent of things to come, befell the Hoke family while Michael was on the campaign trail in eastern North Carolina. In a letter dated May 21 and addressed to the Democratic candidate at Kenansville, a friend wrote, "This morning (Tuesday) about eight o'clock, your worthy and esteemed Mother departed from this world." Barbara Quickel Hoke was buried in a cemetery just south of Court Square in the Hoke family plot, where her son Marcus had been laid to rest seven years earlier.[30]

In late July, the gubernatorial campaign came to an end, and when voters went to the polls in August, they cast 42,586 votes for Graham and 39,433 for Hoke. Although Hoke and the Democrats lost the election, his effective campaign and strong showing dealt the first major blow to Whig supremacy and paved the way for the election of the state's first Democratic governor in 1850.[31]

In the wake of his first political defeat, Michael Hoke came home to Lincolnton to resume his law practice. His broken political dreams soon became a nightmare for his family. Despite his youth, the grueling state-wide campaign had taken its toll on Hoke. On September 9, he was in the middle of a trial in Charlotte when he fell seriously ill from malaria, to which he had been exposed during his political travels in eastern North Carolina. Death came quickly, and Hoke was buried in Lincolnton near the graves of his mother and brother.[32]

All of North Carolina mourned the loss of its young, talented statesman. Peter Ney, who taught school in Lincoln County in 1842 (and the man who some historians believe was Marshal Michel Ney, the French military officer who led Napoleon's troops at Waterloo), penned an epitaph for the fallen political hero from Lincolnton:

> Among the manly, Hoke was foremost found
> Of mind capacious and of morals sound.
> In public spirit, in private worth
> His State ne'er gave a nobler being worth.
> All mourn the exit of his prime
> But all must yield to the decree Divine.[33]

Roots of Greatness: A Lineage of Distinction

For the grieving Frances Burton Hoke, a widow at the age of twenty-eight, an arduous task lay ahead—she had six young children to rear and educate. In addition to Mary and Robert, there were John Burton, born in 1835; Marcus, born in 1839; Ellen, born in 1840; and George, born in 1842. But Frances was equal to the challenge. Described as "a woman of strong character, inheriting intellect from both her parents and singularly gifted in mental endowments," she used her talents and the privilege and affluence of her birth and marriage to nurture her children.[34]

For seven-year-old Robert, the traumatic loss of his father would have lasting effects on his long life. A staunch Democrat for his entire adult life, he maintained a strong disdain for politics even though he was virtually offered the state's highest office, which his father had literally died trying to attain.[35]

Tragedy struck the Hoke family again less than a year later when Robert's grandfather John Hoke died on June 9, 1845. Under the terms of his will, dated March 17, 1843, his large estate was divided equally among his children. Michael's children received land, cash, slaves, and an equal share of John's business properties.[36]

Seven months after John Hoke died, death came calling in Robert's home. On January 10, 1846, his older brother, eleven-year-old John Burton Hoke, was killed in a gun accident while playing with a cousin from the Fulenwider family.

Despite the cloud of sorrow that seemed to linger over the Hoke family from 1844 to 1846, Robert enjoyed a happy and playful childhood. The forests, fields, and creeks surrounding Lincolnton provided the perfect landscape for the Hoke brothers and their friends, including Dodson Ramseur and David Schenck, to hunt, fish, explore, and perfect their horsemanship.

Schenck, the son of a local physician and grandson of textile pioneer Michael Schenck, maintained a childhood diary that chronicled his daily activities with his friends. On one occasion in 1849, he provided a glimpse of Robert's boyhood days of fun and exploration: "Bob and Mark Hoke and I went out to the Mill Branch to get canes and we got after a squirrel but couldn't get him, as we were coming home we *all* got on one horse and he threw us all and the way we had fun wasn't slow." A Saturday morning in August 1852 was spent in the following manner: "I stopped at the store, coming back, and met Dod, who proposed to ride to the mill branch and loaned me a horse (Brimmer). We met Bob and Fran's Hoke who also went with us. We found the branch very full and got across only by getting soaked, it ran over the horses. We had some fun running a rabbit, which we frightened so bad by hollowing at it, that it stopped and let the dogs take it. . . . We returned home glutted with pleasure, and soaked with water."[37]

Robert's boyhood home actually overlooked the Revolutionary War battlefield at Ramsour's Mill, a gristmill on Clark's Creek just north of Lincolnton. This great drama of American history was played out on June 20, 1780. At first light on that fog-shrouded morning, Colonel Francis Locke and a force of four hundred patriots from Lincoln, Mecklenburg, and Rowan Counties surprised and routed an army of thirteen hundred loyalists that had assembled on the hill above the mill in anticipation of joining Cornwallis's approaching British army to achieve a final victory for the Crown. After the smoke cleared from the battlefield, more that seventy men lay dead and more that a hundred were wounded. And although the Revolutionary War raged on for another year, the Whig victory in Lincolnton temporarily stemmed the tide of British aggression in the South and paved the way for the critical victory that soon followed at Kings Mountain.[38]

The battleground held a special allure for Robert. No doubt, he spent countless hours of play on the historic grounds reliving the heroism of his ancestors[39] who had participated in the battle. Little did he know during those days of innocent make-believe that he would one day play a prominent role in the war which would divide the union created from the sacrifices made at Ramsour's Mill in 1780.

As a "city dweller," young Robert enjoyed the amenities and amusements of downtown Lincolnton. By 1845, the town, by virtue of the local textile, iron, and related industries, had become one of the most important in all of western North Carolina. It boasted a newspaper, four hotels, four grocers, a bookbinder, a jeweler, a cabinetmaker, a coppersmith, a watchmaker, three tailors, two hat makers, two shoemakers, five coach factories, two tanners, and five blacksmiths. When the Motz Hotel was completed in Lincolnton in 1852, it immediately ranked as the leading hotel in western North Carolina.[40]

Militia muster days brought particular excitement to the city streets, as Robert and his friends watched their relatives and local citizens drill about Court Square. During the pageantry, Robert and the onlookers purchased cakes and other sweet treats from Hiram Rhodes Revels, a barber and baker whose shop stood on Court Square. Born in Fayetteville, North Carolina, in 1822, Revels was the son of a Baptist minister of African and Indian blood and a white indentured servant of Scottish ancestry. He moved to Lincoln County during his youth and became a barber who shaved and groomed Michael Hoke and other local notables. Many times, Robert, Dodson Ramseur, and David Schenck were lifted into his chair for haircuts. In the mid-1840s, Revels left Lincolnton for Indiana, where he enrolled in a Quaker college and became an ordained minister in the AME Zion Church. Following the Civil War, Revels was working in Mississippi with the Freedmen's Bureau when he was selected as the first black United States senator in the history of the nation.[41]

Court sessions, religious meetings and services, and boyhood games and activities also occupied Robert and his comrades downtown. They reveled in pistol shooting, draughts, and sliding down a hill between Pleasant Retreat Academy and Robert's home.[42]

Cognizant that her fifteen-year-old son had advanced as far as the curriculum at Pleasant Retreat allowed and desirous for Robert to obtain a higher education, Frances Hoke enrolled him in Kentucky Military Institute in the fall of 1852. Founded in 1845, the school had quickly acquired a reputation as one of the most prestigious military academies in the country. By the time Robert was admitted, the school was attracting bright young men from all over the South who were interested in military careers. Located at the old Scanlan Springs resort about six miles from Frankfort, the school maintained a faculty of West Point graduates. One of Robert's fellow students at the school later reflected, "An able faculty made this one of the best and most-thorough institutions in the United States. It ranked side by side for years with the Virginia Military Institute and other like institutions of the first class. The military instruction and discipline were copied rigidly from that maintained at West Point."[43]

In her first letter to her son after he arrived at the Kentucky school, Frances Hoke expressed her mixed emotions about Robert's absence from home:

> I have missed you so much my dear boy—but I trust my loss will be your great gain. Hourly, constantly, my prayers ascend for your guidance and protection. God has promised to care for the widow and fatherless. My son must ever make his duty to God his first object, then all other duties will be fulfilled. Think of how your course may determine that of your younger brothers. If correct habits are yours, they will imbibe them. I do not doubt you dearest, I know you will strive to be all I can wish, my comfort and stay if I live to see you grown.[44]

Robert's course of study included Vergil, Latin composition, English grammar, and American history, as well as science and mathematics. Robert had a fondness for and excelled at engineering and mathematics. In addition to the academic training, the young cadets were drilled in military tactics and physical exercises.[45]

Circumstances in Lincolnton prevented Robert from graduating from Kentucky Military Institute. After completing one year of study, he was summoned back home in 1853 to assist in the management of the vast Hoke family manufacturing enterprises. Sixteen-year-old Robert assumed responsibility for the daily operation of an industrial complex which David Schenck had described two years earlier: "There is a Cotton Factory, Oil Mill, Blacksmith Shop, Brass Foundry and other machinery there and it is like a little town." The cottonseed oil mill at the Hoke complex was the first ever established in the country.

On the home front, Robert became the oldest child in the house with the marriage of his sister Mary to H. H. Smith on May 19, 1853.[46]

Robert successfully managed the family business interests until 1860, when the time came for him to complete his formal education. In the year before the nation would be torn apart by war, Robert made his way to Washington, D.C., where he studied law at night and worked at the United

States Census Bureau during the day. At an adjoining desk at the bureau sat friend and coworker Nelson Appleton Miles, the twenty-one-year-old son of a Massachusetts farmer. Less than a year later, both men would trade their pencils and paper for guns and sabers in opposing armies. Like Robert in the Confederate army, Miles would ultimately be promoted to the rank of major general in the Union army.[47]

As ominous political and war clouds began to spread about the country, there was a growing concern among Southerners for the safety and well-being of their elected representatives in the halls of Congress and on the streets of Washington. In response to tensions in the nation's capital, an organization of a hundred Southern men was formed in Washington with the avowed purpose of protecting the statesmen of the South. Among the membership of the "Minute Men" were two tall, handsome young men who had become close friends in Washington—John Hatcher of Virginia, six feet six inches tall and weighing 220 pounds, and Robert F. Hoke, six feet tall with dark hair and dark eyes.[48]

Uneasiness grew in Washington following the election of Abraham Lincoln as president of the United States. On March 4, 1861, the day Lincoln was inaugurated, Hoke, Hatcher, and several other members of the "Minute Men" found themselves among the multitude of people who had assembled to shake hands with the new chief executive. Robert intimated to his friends that they should take their place in line to greet Lincoln. All were receptive to the proposal except Hatcher, who allowed that he "would not shake the hand of old Lincoln." Robert implored, "We are going to shake hands with Mr. Lincoln; and I will wager you the finest suit of clothes to be purchased in this city that you cannot pass by Mr. Lincoln and carry out your purpose."[49]

Hatcher accepted his friend's wager, and the group assumed a place in line, with the resolute Hatcher in the lead. When the men reached the outgoing president, James Buchanan greeted Hatcher with a warm handshake and asked his name. When Buchanan turned to introduce him to Lincoln, Hatcher abruptly dropped his right hand to his side and attempted to make his way forward in the line without greeting or looking at Lincoln. Perceiving Hatcher's discomfort, Lincoln moved to the right, extended his arm to halt the young man's progress, and said with a grin, "No man who is taller and handsomer than I can pass by me today without shaking hands with me." The two shook hands cordially, and Lincoln invited Hatcher and his friends to stand near him for the duration of the reception.

Upon leaving the White House, Robert remarked to Hatcher, "John, I have won the suit of clothes."

Hatcher responded, "Yes, but who could refuse to shake hands with a man who would leave his position and put his hand in front of you and use such complimentary language as Mr. Lincoln did?"

Robert replied, "I have won the suit of clothes fairly, but I will not take the wager because you surrendered like a courteous Southern gentleman and shook the hand of our new President, as all Americans should do."

Soon thereafter, the young friends would bid each other farewell and return to their respective homes. Their friendship would be renewed a year later on a bloody battlefield called Malvern Hill, Virginia.[50]

For Robert F. Hoke, there were pressing matters to attend to in Lincoln County. Family and business affairs had to be put in order promptly because the maelstrom, long foretold by historians, was growing more inevitable day by day.

CHAPTER 2

Sabers Rattle:
The First Lifeblood Is Spilled

When Robert Hoke returned to Lincoln County in the wake of Abraham Lincoln's inauguration, he came home to a county and state whose loyalties were being severely tested. David Schenck, Hoke's childhood playmate who would soon represent Lincoln County at the North Carolina Secession Convention, had his finger on the public pulse when he noted in his diary on March 11, "Every hour and day brings some startling news. . . . Men, women and children look anxiously for the mails and fireside conversation is confined to the great issue of the day—'Will there be Civil War?'"[1]

When Confederate batteries opened fire on Fort Sumter on April 12, even the most ardent anti-secessionists in North Carolina lost all hope that the state could remain in the Union for long. William Alexander Graham, the Lincoln County native who was now one of the state's most respected statesmen, expressed the despondency that suddenly gripped Unionists: "Truly indeed, may it be said that madness rules the hour." Three days later, the secession issue came to a head in North Carolina. On that day, President Lincoln, through Secretary of War Simon Cameron, telegraphed a request to Governor John Willis Ellis for two regiments of troops, which was to constitute North Carolina's quota of the seventy-five thousand soldiers needed by the president to put down the Southern "insurrection." Ellis was outraged, and he promptly fired his state's first shots for the Confederacy, albeit verbal ones, when he telegraphed an acrimonious response back to Cameron:

> Your dispatch is recd. and if genuine which its extraordinary character leads me to doubt I have to say in reply that I regard the levy of troops made by the administration for the purpose of subjugating the states of the South is in violation of the Constitution and a gross usurpation of power. I can be no party to this wicked violation of the laws of the country, and to this war upon the liberties of a free people. You can get no troops from North Carolina.[2]

Robert Hoke and most other North Carolinians had no taste for taking up arms against their Southern neighbors, and Lincoln's call for troops became a rallying cry. Tar Heels were now anxious to defend their borders against invading armies. Citizens quickly closed ranks, and political differences were cast aside.

No one typified the sudden change of attitude in North Carolina more than Zebulon B. Vance, the young North Carolinian who in less than a year would be fighting beside Hoke in eastern North Carolina and who would subsequently serve with great skill as the wartime governor of the state. Vance, the quintessential Unionist, recalled his conversion to the cause of secession: "For myself, I will say that I was canvassing for the Union with all my strength! I was addressing a large and excited crowd . . . and literally had my arm extended upward in pleading for peace and the Union of our Fathers, when the telegraphic news was announced of the firing on Sumter and the President's call for seventy-five thousand volunteers. When my hand came down from that impassioned gesticulation, it fell slowly and sadly by the side of a Secessionist."

Although North Carolina would officially remain a part of the Union for more than a month after Lincoln's request for troops, a virtual "condition of war prevailed" in the state by mid-April, as Governor Ellis promptly set about marshaling forces and preparing his people for the conflict that now was inevitable. He immediately ordered seizure of the Federal military installations in the state. Two days later, when Virginia seceded, Ellis scheduled an emergency session of the legislature to deal with the pressing matters at hand: he called for thirty-thousand volunteer troops, and he established a military training camp in Raleigh. On April 19, Robert Hoke's uncle, North Carolina adjutant general John F. Hoke, directed Daniel Harvey Hill to come to Raleigh to organize the First North Carolina Volunteers. Hill, a graduate of the West Point class of 1842, was the superintendent of North Carolina Military Academy in Charlotte at the time he was called to Raleigh.[3]

In counties all over the state, men answered Ellis's call to arms with a flurry of activity. Lincoln County was no exception. On Monday, April 22, the very day Ellis received a request from Confederate secretary of war Leroy P. Walker for a regiment of North Carolina troops, Robert Hoke and ninety-six other men assembled in Lincolnton at the county courthouse to organize the Southern Stars military company. On that date, Hoke began making brief entries in a daybook that would offer a limited personal glimpse of the activities of his company and regiment for the remainder of the year.[4] Other than the daybook and the official reports subsequently written by him as a colonel or general, Hoke left few wartime accounts of his military activities. Moreover, his lifelong reluctance to discuss or write about the war has made it difficult for historians to conduct a detailed study of the life of this extremely modest man.

Hoke's first entry listed the names of the officers elected on that date: William J. Hoke, Robert's thirty-five-year-old uncle, captain; W. M. Reinhardt, first lieutenant; and Robert F. Hoke, second lieutenant. Included among the privates was Robert's eighteen-year-old brother, George.

Over the course of the week that followed, the men drilled about the streets of Lincolnton on a daily basis in preparation for acceptance into the First North Carolina Volunteers. On April 23, Adjutant General John F. Hoke reported to Governor Ellis from Wilmington that another Lincolnton native was rushing to the aid of the state. Stephen Dodson Ramseur, a graduate of West Point in 1860, had resigned his commission in the United States Army and was making his way from Montgomery to Raleigh, where he would take command of Ellis's personal artillery battery.[5]

In the meantime, the ladies of Lincolnton had formed a society for the purpose of making clothing for the Southern Stars, and by April 24, Second Lieutenant Robert F. Hoke had a uniform. A day later, the company received orders to prepare to leave for Raleigh. On Sunday, April 28, Hoke, cognizant of the uncertainties of the future, attended worship services at his church, St. Luke's Episcopal, in Lincolnton. The Southern Stars spent their final full day in Lincolnton on Monday in drills and in preparation for their departure for Raleigh.

When Hoke and his comrades gathered downtown on Tuesday, they were greeted by a "multitude of people" who had assembled to send their heroes off in grand style. A local newspaper reported, "It was the day, on which our brave volunteers, had to take, may be the eternal farewell from their parents, wives and children, brothers, sisters and friends, and face an unmerciful foe, on the verge of invading the South and desolating our homes." During the send-off ceremonies, a flag crafted by the ladies of the town was presented on their behalf by Hoke's minister, the Reverend C. T. Bland. Then the Reverend Robert N. Davis, the Presbyterian minister, offered "an appropriate address," and the homemade banner was accepted for the company by Sergeant L. J. Hoyle with "thanks and gratitude in a most excellent speech." Hoyle then placed the colors in the care of Ensign A. A. Ramseur, who "pledged himself to return it with honor, or make it his winding sheet." True to his word, Ramseur returned the flag with honor, only to subsequently lay down his life at Gettysburg.[6]

Following the presentation of the flag, Bland, Davis, and the Baptist and Methodist ministers offered prayers and the citizens lifted up their voices in hymns. Then it was time for the soldiers to go. Described by the local press as "the elite of our town and county," the Southern Stars marched to the depot, followed by the crowd. "Amid the congratulations of friends, tears of relations, with high hopes," Hoke and his fellow soldiers boarded a train for the 180-mile trip to Raleigh via the Wilmington, Charlotte, and Rutherford Railroad. Accompanying them to the state capital was the Lincolnton Brass Band.[7]

After their train pulled into Raleigh on May 1, the Southern Stars marched into the heart of the city, where they were temporarily quartered in the basement of the new First Baptist Church. Troops were now beginning to mass in the capital city as cheering crowds greeted trainload after trainload of volunteers from all sections of the state. An early observation of these soldiers produced an accolade in the *Charlotte Democrat* on May 1: "This regiment is said to be the finest looking body of men ever assembled in the State."[8]

Hoke and the members of his company quickly joined the other volunteers at Camp Ellis, a makeshift sixteen-acre military installation located at the state-fair grounds in the eastern suburbs of the city. Over the next sixteen days, Hoke used but one word in each daybook entry to describe his activities: "Drilled." While he and the other green soldiers were being fashioned into a well-disciplined regiment, they were reminded of the reason that they were at Camp Ellis by the posted proclamation of "Uncle" John F. Hoke: "The decree of our subjugation has gone forth; the time of our trial has come; the blow will soon fall; we must meet it with the whole energies of the State; we must show to the world that North Carolina will maintain her rights at all hazards." On May 7, Uncle John issued General Orders No. 7, whereby the election of officers for the First North Carolina Volunteers was set for May 11.[9] Finally, the regiment was taking shape.

On the prescribed day, the regimental election was held, and Daniel Harvey Hill, as expected, was elected colonel. Charles C. Lee, a West Pointer who would be killed in action a year later while leading the Thirty-seventh North Carolina, was elected lieutenant colonel; and James H. Lane, a V.M.I. graduate destined to fight as a general at Gettysburg and Appomattox, was elected major.[10]

On Monday, May 13, the First North Carolina Volunteers were officially mustered into state service. The ten companies constituting the regiment were given alphabetical designations and assigned a permanent order. The posts of honor—the right and left flanks—went to the Edgecombe Guards and the Southern Stars, Company A and Company K, respectively.[11]

As the junior officers of the ten companies drilled and paraded their soldiers about the streets of Raleigh during the first three weeks of May, many citizens of the city and visitors from afar were afforded an opportunity to observe and evaluate the regiment. Filling the ranks as privates were many distinguished men, including doctors, lawyers, and editors. In retrospect, one observer concluded that the regiment could boast "probably the highest average order of men ever mustered for war." From his residence on Capitol Square, former United States senator and secretary of the navy George Edmund Badger delighted in watching the troops as they went about their drills. Of the many soldiers he observed, Badger singled out one of their number as the likeliest of them all to attain high command—Second Lieutenant Robert F. Hoke. On one occasion when Hoke was among a group of officers, Badger pointed to him and remarked to a friend, "There is a man who will make his mark before this war is over."[12]

Exciting news on Friday, May 17, served to break the tedium of constant drilling. Three companies of the First North Carolina—the Lafayette Light Infantry, the Fayetteville Light Independent Infantry, and the Southern Stars—received orders to prepare for movement to Richmond. The following morning, the soldiers of these companies were issued two days' rations of bread and meat. Then, amid the hearty cheers of their comrades at Camp Ellis, the men of Companies F, H, and K marched down Fayetteville Street to the train station, where a spectacle awaited. Most of the populace of the city had assembled to applaud these brave soldiers, the first of more than 125,000 men and boys that North Carolina would send into battle. As the crowd roared and band music filled the air, Hoke boarded the special train waiting to carry him into a war which would consume the next four years of his life.[13]

When the North Carolina troop train pulled into Petersburg on the evening of May 18, the Tar Heel warriors were on Virginia soil not as Confederate soldiers, but simply as allies of their neighbor to the north, for North Carolina had not yet joined the Confederacy. As they passed through the city en route to Richmond, Hoke and his fellow soldiers drew rave reviews from the *Petersburg Express*:

> Three companies of the First Regiment of North Carolina Volunteers—the Fayetteville Independent Infantry, Captain Huske; the Fayetteville Light Infantry, Captain Starr; both from Fayetteville, and the Southern Stars, Captain Hoke, from Lincoln County—arrived in this city by a special train from Raleigh at 7:30 o'clock on Saturday evening. Each company had its full complement of one hundred and nine men, thoroughly armed and in the best spirits. If we may form an opinion of the whole regiment by the material and appearance of the above three companies, we should unhesitatingly pronounce it to be one of the finest in the world.[14]

At 11 P.M. on May 18, the grueling trip ended when the three companies reached Richmond. The troops set up camp at Howard's Grove, a wooded hill above the James River just outside the city limits. Over the next two days, they prepared the encampment for the other seven companies that were scheduled to soon arrive from North Carolina.[15]

Back in Raleigh on May 20, the balance of the regiment began receiving orders to move to Richmond. However, much of the attention in the state that day was directed to the State Capitol, where the secession convention had convened at 11 A.M. on the very day when, in 1775, North Carolina revolutionaries had signed the Mecklenburg Declaration of Independence, thereby declaring themselves "a free and independent people." Suddenly, about 6 P.M., a white handkerchief was waved from a window on the west side of the State Capitol, and Major Graham Davee, an aide to Governor Ellis, leaned out to relay a message to the young artillery captain in command of the battery of brass cannon at the west portico of the building. Instantly, the six guns of Ellis's Light Artillery boomed. Stephen Dodson Ramseur, Hoke's friend from childhood, enjoyed the honor of giving the order for the hundred-gun salute that hailed the exit of North Carolina from the Union. When news came from the building that the convention had adopted the Constitution of the Confederate States of America, Ramseur offered another salute from his guns.[16]

General Robert F. Hoke

The balance of the First North Carolina Volunteers arrived in Petersburg on Tuesday, May 21, to more rave reviews from the local press. Meanwhile, at Howard's Grove, Hoke was selected "officer of the guard," the first of many military honors he would earn in Virginia. When the troop train pulled into Richmond after midnight, Hoke's fellow North Carolinians were delighted to find tents already set up for them by the three advance companies. At dawn the following morning, the regiment awakened to reveille, and Colonel Hill formed his troops for a manual of arms. Throughout May 22 and 23, the regiment remained at Howard's Grove as the encampment swelled with soldiers, tents, and flags of other states.[17]

Hoke and his compatriots had come to Richmond at a time when Virginia needed all the troops it could get. To quickly crush the "rebellion," General Winfield Scott had made the state the object of a four-prong invasion. Union troops from Ohio, the Cumberland Valley, Washington, D.C., and Fortress Monroe would push toward the new Confederate capital of Richmond. Commanding Hampton Roads at the mouth of the James River, Fortress Monroe was not only one of the largest military installations in the world, but a strategic fortification from which the Union army could easily raid Richmond. Union gunboat movements up the James and York Rivers in April and early May served to make the threat of attack on Richmond very real. When, on May 23, a Federal regiment demonstrated against Hampton, three miles from Fortress Monroe, Confederate officials realized that measures had to be taken immediately to defend the peninsula against further Yankee incursions. Consequently, the First North Carolina Volunteers, "the crack regiment of the day," was ordered to Yorktown, a "post of danger and of honor."[18]

On May 24, the regiment broke camp and took the railroad to West Point, where the soldiers were crammed aboard the steamboat *Logan* for the trip down the York River. After sailing most of the day, they arrived at Yorktown after dark and set up a hasty camp near the waterfront. Hoke, however, did not spend his first night in the camp. Rather, he stayed "in the last house on the left Main Street."

When the North Carolinians awoke the next morning, they caught their first glimpse of the enemy. Although Fortress Monroe was almost thirty miles distant, a Federal warship was plainly visible in the waters offshore of the encampment.

To fortify the Confederate position at Yorktown and to ensure that the troops were ready to meet the enemy, Colonel Hill and his commander, Colonel John Bankhead Magruder, ordered the regiment to begin entrenching and drilling, a daily routine that continued for the next ten days. Known as "Prince John" because of his flamboyant dress and fondness for lavish entertainment and female companionship, Magruder was challenged to defend the plain of Yorktown, a strategic portion of his native state, with but twenty-five hundred troops.[19]

As they dug entrenchments at Yorktown, the men of the First North Carolina Volunteers were able to trace the outline of the defense works erected by Lord Charles Cornwallis in the twilight of the Revolutionary War. In the course of their travail, the Southern soldiers retrieved relics from the very ground where the fight for American Independence had been concluded.[20] Yorktown and its historic artifacts held a special irony for Hoke and the other members of the Southern Stars, for it was Benjamin Lincoln, the namesake of their home county, who had accepted the British surrender just eighty years earlier.

On Saturday, May 25, Hoke moved to the encampment at Yorktown, located "in the rear near a marsh." The next day being the Sabbath, Colonel Hill, a devout Presbyterian who had married the daughter of a Presbyterian minister in Lincoln County, deployed only the troops necessary to provide security for his position. For Hill, worship was the order of the day. Chaplain Edwin Yates preached to the remainder of the regiment after the soldiers had united their voices in an opening hymn personally selected by the colonel. Hill's expectations for a day of peace and tranquility were shattered, however, by the long roll. Hoke noted "Fight expected" in his daybook, but there was no encounter with the enemy.[21]

Hoke's twenty-fourth birthday, on May 27, was less than serene, as the long roll once again drew the men to their arms. Like the day before, he noted "Fight expected" in his daily entry. There was no appearance of the enemy. During the next day, the men devoted their full attention to their embankments and drills, Hoke noting, "All quiet." About 5 P.M. on May 29, an alarm was sounded, and the men were forced to sleep in their clothes and "on arms all night." A day of "all quiet" followed, but on the last day of May, a large portion of the regiment was ordered to proceed in a southwest direction toward Hampton, which was now controlled by the enemy. After a three-hour march of ten miles, the eight companies returned to Yorktown without having sighted the enemy.[22]

Colonel Hill, as if anticipating battle, called the regiment together at 4:30 A.M. on June 1 to drill before breakfast. Later in the day, he organized his command for combat. His important flank units, the Edgecombe Guards and the Southern Stars, were assigned as skirmishers, while the other eight companies, B through I, were divided into four battalions. On Monday, June 3, Colonel Magruder ordered Company K to march toward Newport News, but after three and a half miles, the Lincoln County soldiers were notified to fall back. Tuesday and Wednesday were days of "all quiet," offering a short period of calm before the storm, for on the following day, June 6, orders were issued by Colonel Magruder to pack three days' rations and prepare to march.[23]

At 12:30 P.M., the First North Carolina Volunteers broke camp and proceeded southwest toward Big Bethel Church, some fifteen miles distant. In addition to Hill's 800 North Carolinians, the expedition included 208 men from the Third Virginia, 150 assorted Virginia infantrymen, 150 men in a Virginia artillery battalion, and 100 men in Virginia cavalry companies. Tramping along trails in the dense, swampy terrain, the soldiers endured an exhausting march made even more difficult by a late-afternoon rain. Hoke noted that the soldiers ended their march "about dark." For the first time since their arrival in Virginia, Hill's soldiers were forced to camp without tents. With Hampton less than ten miles away, his men knew the enemy was close by, and as Hoke recorded in his daybook, they would "lay" on arms all night.[24]

Big Bethel Church, an isolated, unpainted clapboard building, was located adjacent to Sawyer Swamp Road, which led south to the last Confederate outpost, Little Bethel, a few miles distant, and then into enemy territory. Just south of the church building, a flat wooden bridge spanned the slow-moving northwest branch of Back River. A grove of trees and a swamp thicket surrounded the church on the west and south, and an open field was located just across the road on the east.

On Friday, June 7, Colonel Hill ordered his soldiers to throw up breastworks in a zigzag fashion on the east and west sides of the church and to construct a redoubt on the south near the bridge. Hoke described the works as "banks in a square." Although the work was plagued by a paucity of picks, shovels, and other implements, one soldier recorded that the works were erected in "a most scientific manner." As had been the case at Yorktown, the remains of Revolutionary War entrenchments were discovered as the men struggled to fortify their new position.

While the soldiers were laboring to finish the works on the morning of June 8, an alarm was sounded, causing the men to throw down their tools for their rifles. Throughout the afternoon, reports came in that enemy raiders were within miles of the camp. Several companies, chosen for their stalking and hunting abilities, were sent out to chase the enemy away. Lieutenant Colonel Lee and Major Lane volunteered to lead Companies F and E, respectively, in their search for Union soldiers. Lane's group clashed with the enemy near Hampton, and after wounding a number of Federals, the mountaineers of Company E returned to camp from their "hunting party" with a prisoner. Described as "a stout, ugly fellow," the unfortunate New Yorker told his captives that "he had nothing against the South." However, the walls of Big Bethel Church bore graffiti inscribed by the captive's comrades in arms, words that expressed much different sentiments from those of the prisoner: "Down with the Rebels! Death to the Traitors!" Later in the afternoon, Company K was dispatched across the Back River in search of the enemy. Colonel Hill subsequently concluded that these forays into enemy territory brought on the battle that took place June 10. By the time Colonel Magruder arrived on the evening of June 8, the immediate crisis had passed.[25]

A badly needed shipment of tools for use in completing the earthworks arrived on June 9, a sweltering Sunday. Due to the proximity of the enemy, sentry duty was of paramount importance on this day. Company A and a piece of artillery were sent forward on patrol. Nonetheless, there was time set aside for worship, and the regiment heard a sermon by the

Reverend Adams, a Baptist minister from Hampton. Hoke rated the sermon as "good."[26]

At 3:00 A.M. on June 10, the stillness of the camp was broken by a loud bugle calling the North Carolinians to prepare to march. Colonel Magruder, anxious to determine the strength and location of the enemy, ordered Colonel Hill to march the First North Carolina in the direction of Fortress Monroe. Accompanied by the cavalry and a battery of artillery, the foot soldiers set out down the road toward Hampton before dawn. Magruder did not instruct Hill how far to go, and little did either officer know that a large Federal force had left Hampton the previous evening and was now advancing rapidly toward Big Bethel. In effect, the two armies were on a collision course.[27]

After chafing about the recent Confederate incursions toward Hampton for several days, General Benjamin Butler, the Union commander at Fortress Monroe, had decided to surprise the Southerners at Little Bethel at daybreak on June 10 and then attack the main body of their forces at Big Bethel. His immense forty-four-hundred-man assault force consisted of troops from the First, Second, Third, Fifth, and Seventh New York, the First Vermont, the Fourth Massachusetts, and the Second United States Artillery.[28]

Not far into the march, Colonel Hill received cavalry reports of the Union approach, but there was still no information about the size of the enemy attack force. After the regiment had marched approximately three miles, Hill came upon a local woman whose husband had been taken prisoner by the Federals. She identified herself as Mrs. Hannah Tunnell and informed Hill that "the foe, in large force, was within a few hundred yards of us." Lieutenant Benjamin R. Huske of Company H noted that "it was through her coolness that their large number was learned." Hill wasted no time in ordering a quick retrograde march to Big Bethel. By 5 A.M., the regiment had reached its fortifications, and the companies were deployed into battle formation. On the south side of the Back River, outside of the works, Hill placed Companies A and C, as well as some artillery. On the other side of the river and north of the works, Hoke and his fellow skirmishers in Company K were stationed in a grove of trees. The remainder of the companies were positioned near or inside the works. Artillery was strategically located to protect the fortifications and the roads.[29]

As the new day dawned with a cloudless sky, Hill's untested soldiers nervously fingered the triggers of their rifles. Their colonel, a veteran of the ferocious fighting in Mexico at Monterey, Vera Cruz, and Chapultepec, paced about the men, reassuring them. In a calm voice, he said, "When you hear the bugle you may know the enemy is in sight."

Hours passed without sign of the adversary, and the bright June sun cast its hot rays on the waiting North Carolinians. Suddenly, about 9 A.M., a column of "dark blue figures" carrying the colors of the United States of America burst from the woods south of the bridge. Although the enemy soldiers were yet more than a half-mile away, the gleam of their bayonets was clearly visible to the Confederates. Artillery major George W. Randolph, the grandson of Thomas Jefferson and a man who would later serve the Confederacy as secretary of war, did not wait for the Federals to offer fire. As commander of the Richmond Howitzers, he personally aimed a Parrott gun and sent forth the shot which threw up the curtain on the first battle of the Civil War. Randolph's aim was true, as his shot hit the earth just in front of the approaching Yankees and ricocheted. One Confederate soldier noted that the enemy troops "fell away from the road like a mist before the sun," while Colonel John E. Bendix of the Seventh New York reported, "Before we had got ready for action the enemy opened their fire upon us, striking one man down by my side at the first shot."[30]

Union artillery vigorously responded to Randolph's initial offering, and over the next three and a half hours, the artillery and infantry of both armies ushered in the grim combat that would engulf America for four years. Union attacks on each flank were handsomely repulsed. Throughout the fight, Colonel Hill instilled confidence in his troops as they were receiving their baptism under fire.[31]

After failing to force his way around either flank, General Ebenezer Pierce ordered a second attack on the Confederate right. Observing the renewed assault on his wing, Colonel Magruder expressed fear that the North Carolinians were about to give way and run. Major Randolph scampered across the field under heavy fire, only to find the Tar Heels "waiting in the trenches for a chance at the rascals, and Col. Hill smoking a short pipe as calmly as if sitting in his tent." Randolph reported back to Magruder, "Colonel, the North Carolina boys are doing the prettiest kind of work." Magruder responded, "Then, sir, they [the enemy] are whipped." However, the battle was not yet over.[32]

During the renewed attack on the Confederate right, Colonel Hill expressed concern about a house south of the bridge that afforded shelter for a regiment of Zouave sharpshooters. Private Henry L. Wyatt and four other members of Company A volunteered to make their way across the field to set fire to the structure. Armed with only matches and hatchets, the quintet scrambled over the breastworks and raced toward the house. A volley greeted the soldiers from the left, and Wyatt fell mortally wounded. One of his companions on the mission, John H. Thorpe, later described the scene: "He never uttered a word or a groan, but lay limp on his back, his arms extended, one knee up and a clot of blood on his forehead as large as a man's fist." Thus, the twenty-year-old became the first of many thousands of Tar Heels to lay his life down for the Confederate cause.[33]

Thwarted once again on the right, Pierce launched a final attack about 1 P.M. This time, he sought to push around the left flank, protected by the Southern Stars. During the offensive, Major Theodore Winthrop, General Butler's personal secretary, was killed while bravely leading a charge of several companies from the First Vermont and the Fourth Massachusetts.

As Winthrop's attempt to pierce the Confederate left was falling apart, Hill's North Carolinians exuded confidence. Hill described their high spirits in his official report: "The three field officers of the regiment were present, and but few shots were fired without their permission, the men repeatedly saying, 'May I fire? I think I can bring him.' They were all in high glee, and seemed to enjoy it as much as boys do rabbit-hunting." When a howitzer landed a shell into the house that Wyatt had tried to burn, the Yankees were finished. "Completely discouraged," they withdrew from the field and began the retreat to Hampton. Colonel Hill, concerned about enemy sharpshooters that might be lingering in the woods on the left, sent the Southern Stars to clear them out. After Captain William J. Hoke had "thoroughly explored them" and had given the "assurance of the road being clear," Magruder gave the order to pursue the fleeing Federals, who in their haste "threw away hundreds of canteens, haversacks, overcoats, &c.; even the dead were thrown out of wagons."[34]

After some five hours, the first battle of the war was over. Fourteen hundred volunteer soldiers, with no more than three hundred in action at any one time, had soundly defeated an army three times as large. Confederate losses were virtually nil: one dead and ten wounded. Among the wounded was Private William White of the Southern Stars. On the other hand, the Federals suffered significant losses: eighteen killed and seventy-six wounded. As the victorious North Carolinians surveyed the battlefield, one of their officers recalled, "The scene was one of perfect rout, horrible beyond description, men with limbs shot off, brains oozing out and every imaginable horror."[35]

Although the fight at Bethel was small, almost minuscule, when compared to the great battles that Robert Hoke would later fight on Virginia soil and elsewhere, it had far-reaching implications. In both the North and the South, the press had a field day. Some Northern papers called on President Lincoln to make peace with the Confederacy, while others called for the removal of General Butler. Newspapers in Virginia were particularly lavish with their praise for the First North Carolina. In Richmond, the *Examiner* urged its readers, "Honor those to whom honor is due. All our troops appear to have behaved nobly at Bethel, but the honors of the day are clearly due to the splendid regiment of North Carolina, whose charge of bayonets decided it, and presaged their conduct on many a more important field." At Petersburg, the *Express* proclaimed, "All hail to the brave sons of the Old North State, whom Providence seems to have thrust forward in the first pitched battle on Virginia soil in behalf of Southern rights and independence."[36]

In Raleigh, the North Carolina Secession Convention passed a resolution that expressed appreciation for "the valor and good conduct of the officers and men" of the regiment and "authorized said regiment to inscribe the word *Bethel* upon their banner." However, it was the praise from their commanders that was most treasured by the Tar Heels. In his congratulatory address, Colonel Magruder exclaimed, "North Carolinians! You have covered yourselves with glory, not only as undaunted in the presence of an overwhelming force bearing yourselves with a bravery resistless, but above all with a perfection of discipline in an exciting conflict that was unequalled." Colonel Hill, in his official report on the battle, wrote of his North Carolina soldiers, "Their patience under trial, perseverance under toil, and courage under fire have seldom been surpassed by veteran troops. . . . They have done a large portion of the work on the intrenchments at Yorktown, as well as those at Bethel. Had all of the regiments in the field worked with the same spirit, there would not be an assailable point in Virginia."[37] Although he was just a junior officer in the regiment, Hoke had caught the attention of Colonel Hill, who noted in his official report, "Lieutenant Hoke has shown great zeal, energy, and judgment as an engineer officer on various occasions."

But on the afternoon of June 10, there was little time for Hoke and the other members of the First North Carolina Volunteers to wait around for praise and reviews. About an hour after the Union army took flight from the battlefield, the Zouaves of the First Louisiana Battalion, attired "in red pants with about three times as much cloth in them as necessary," appeared on the scene to reinforce the Tar Heels. But no sooner had they arrived than the Zouaves, as well as the North Carolinians, were ordered to march back to still-vulnerable Yorktown. As Hoke and his fellow North Carolinians set out from the field where the honor of the South had first been successfully defended, they proudly joined their voices in "The Old North State."[38]

After reaching Yorktown on the night of June 10, the regiment made camp and began a ten-week stay in the historic town. A visitor to Yorktown noted that Hoke's tent "was hard by the historic Nelson house and the line of defenses constructed by Cornwallis." Although the regiment would move to several different locations on the peninsula over the coming months, the remainder of its six-month enlistment was relatively free of hostile encounters with the enemy and was, according to the historian of the regiment, "uneventful."[39]

On Tuesday, June 11, Hoke recorded in his diary, "Rested all quiet." However, work was resumed on the fortifications and continued through-

teers moved once again. This time, on October 8, the soldiers marched in the rain to Camp Rains, located a few miles south of Camp Fayetteville. A week later, an alarm was sounded, and Company K was dispatched two miles toward Big Bethel in a fruitless search for the enemy. Sickness continued to plague the Southern Stars; Private J. G. Rudisill of the company died on Wednesday, October 16. On the rainy Thursday that followed, he was laid to rest in the Virginia landscape.[45]

Growing concerns about a possible enemy advance caused the regiment to be moved from Camp Rains to Big Bethel on Sunday, October 20. At the latter place, the long roll was sounded, forcing the men to "lay out all night." Consequently, the tents were removed from Camp Rains to Camp Bethel the following day. On October 22, the regiment "was ordered to look for an attack by land and water," but the enemy did not show. A subsequent report that a Federal attack on Yorktown was imminent forced the North Carolinians to move again. At 3 A.M. on October 24, the men were roused and ordered to strike the camp. At 7 A.M., they marched into Yorktown, where they camped on the "old ground." Again, there was no sign of the enemy. The regiment was hurried back to Camp Bethel via Camp Rains on October 25. Over the next week, scouting parties were sent out in the direction of the enemy on a daily basis, but there were no clashes.[46]

On the last day of October, the regiment bade farewell to Big Bethel, where it had earned a place in the history books. With Major Hoke in the lead, the North Carolinians made their way back to Yorktown one final time. Because the six-month regiment had but two weeks left on its enlistment, the men enjoyed a period of relative inactivity. There was a grand review of the troops by Magruder, who was now a major general, on Friday, November 8. Hoke was the proud officer of the day. After the review, a detachment of four companies of the regiment left Yorktown for Richmond en route to their homes. Similar detachments departed on November 9 and November 11. Hoke arrived in Richmond via steamer on November 11, where he remained until November 14.[47]

The First North Carolina Volunteers had come to the end of their road. The regiment was mustered out of Confederate service on November 12 and out of state service the following day. Its short term of service had been authorized by state authorities in "recognition of the remarkable character of its rank and file." Indeed, Brigadier General Gabriel J. Rains, the West Pointer who was the munitions wizard of the Confederate army, described the First North Carolina Volunteers as "the best regiment he had ever seen." Hoke and his fellow Tar Heels had built a lengthy record of accomplishments during their relatively short stint: they had defeated the enemy on the first field of battle of the war; one of their members had been the first to lay his life on the altar; they had protected the historic plain of Yorktown against enemy incursion; and they had helped to raise the spirits of the Southern people in the early days of the war. But perhaps the most significant contribution of the regiment was that it served as a "nursery school" for a vast number of distinguished officers of the Confederate army. From the ranks of the First North Carolina Volunteers came four generals, fourteen colonels, ten lieutenant colonels, eight majors, twelve adjutants, fifty-seven captains, thirty-seven first lieutenants, and forty-three second lieutenants.[48]

For most soldiers of the regiment, their joyous homecoming would be brief. They were destined to promptly volunteer for the many regiments that their state had fielded since the first regiment had been raised in Raleigh. And so it was with Hoke. Before he left Richmond for home, he was appointed major of the Thirty-third North Carolina.

Hoke arrived in Lincolnton on Friday, November 15. He spent the next week at home attending to family and business concerns. On November 20, he and the other members of the Southern Stars were feted at a dinner given in their honor by the community. By November 23, Hoke was back in Richmond, where he stayed a week in order to wrap up regimental affairs. Except for a few days at Camp Mangum in Raleigh, he spent the entire month of December at home before joining his new command. As 1861 drew to a close, Christmas Day offered Hoke the simple pleasures of home that would be sorely missed over the next twelve months.[49]

Hoke had emerged from the first year of the war with a reputation as a solid soldier, an able young officer of promise. As one of the rising stars of the Confederate army, he would soon have his opportunity to shine.

CHAPTER 3

A Rising Star

When Hoke joined his new regiment in Raleigh in early January 1862, forces were at work that would soon require his presence in coastal North Carolina.

After gaining its first significant victory of the war at Hatteras Inlet on August 29, 1861, the Union high command was anxious to achieve a strong foothold on the North Carolina coast in order to threaten the vital railroad link between Richmond and the port of Wilmington. Accordingly, the "first major amphibious force" in American military history was assembled at Fortress Monroe on January 6, 1862. After moving to Annapolis, Maryland, the expeditionary force of eighty ships and twelve thousand soldiers under the command of General Ambrose Burnside set sail for North Carolina on January 9. After overrunning and occupying

Roanoke Island, the amphibious force was to move south on Pamlico Sound and up the Neuse River for an attack on New Bern. Not only was this historic city one of the most commercially vibrant on the North Carolina coast, it also served as a vital link in the railroad running between the port at Beaufort and Goldsboro.[1]

As the massive amphibious assault force was being assembled in Virginia, reports of its creation poured into Raleigh from Richmond. Because New Bern was known to be an attractive target for the Union expedition, efforts were quickly made to fortify and defend the town. Consequently, Hoke and the Thirty-third North Carolina were transferred to New Bern on January 8.

Much like Hoke's old regiment, the Thirty-third North Carolina was composed of companies raised in all parts of the state, from Hyde County in the east to Wilkes County in the west. Organized in Raleigh at the state-fair grounds in September 1861, the bulk of the regiment had remained in the capital city until its deployment at New Bern. Commanding the regiment was Colonel Lawrence O'Bryan Branch, a Princeton-educated attorney who had resigned from the United States Congress at the outbreak of the war. For the first eight and a half months of 1862, Hoke would serve under and learn from this distinguished North Carolinian.[2]

When the regiment arrived in New Bern, Lieutenant Colonel Clark M. Avery was second in command. Like Hoke and Branch, he was descended from a family of distinction; his grandfather, the first attorney general of North Carolina, once accepted a challenge to a duel with a young firebrand named Andrew Jackson. A graduate of the University of North Carolina, Avery left his ancestral home in Burke County in western North Carolina in May 1861 to serve as commander of Company G of the First North Carolina Volunteers. As such, he had served with Hoke through the triumphs and tragedies of that regiment on the Tidewater peninsula.[3]

The Thirty-third North Carolina had been in New Bern less than ten days when, on January 17, Colonel Branch was promoted to brigadier general and given command of the four thousand troops assigned to defend New Bern. On the same day, Avery was appointed colonel and Hoke lieutenant colonel of the regiment. William Gaston Lewis, another young veteran of the First North Carolina Volunteers, became the new major.

While these organizational changes were being made, James G. Martin, who had taken over as state adjutant general in the early days of the war, dispatched a staff officer to New Bern to inspect the works and the troops available to defend the city. On his tour, the inspector was accompanied by engineering officer Robert F. Hoke, who told him that "unless greater energy was displayed in the near future than in the past the place could not be defended."[4]

Fortunately for the Confederates, there was a delay in the Union attack on New Bern. Although Roanoke Island fell with relative ease on February 8, Burnside would not threaten New Bern for another five weeks. In the meantime, General Branch was anxious to improve the defenses that Hoke had deemed so inadequate.

Branch inherited an elaborate system of works that had been constructed prior to his arrival. Situated at the mouth of Otter Creek on the Neuse River ten miles below the city, Fort Dixie represented the first line of defense. Stretching three-quarters of a mile west from the small fort into a dense swamp was the Croatan Works, a line of entrenchments considered by Branch to be the strongest element of the defense system. Four miles closer to New Bern stood Fort Thompson, "the usual type of sand and sod-revetted fort of that day"; positioned directly on the Neuse, the fort mounted thirteen sizable siege guns, only three of which bore on the land approaches to the city. A line of defense works stretched west from the fort to the Atlantic and North Carolina Railroad. On the west side of the railroad stood the kiln for Wood's Brickyard, which would prove to be the fatal flaw in the Confederate defenses. Because of the kiln, engineers were forced to drop the line back a distance of 150 yards west of the railroad. To protect the resulting gap, Branch ordered the kiln to be "loopholed." Instead of constructing a contiguous line of entrenchments west of the railroad and the brickyard, the Confederates fabricated a series of redans that extended to Weathersby Road at the edge of a swamp near Bullen's Creek. Closer to New Bern, there were several small, insignificant forts.

Because this system of defense works was surrounded by three sizable bodies of water—the Neuse River, the Trent River, and Brice's Creek ("an

impassable stream" flowing into the Trent River)—the only means of retreat for the Confederates were the 1,840-foot-long railroad bridge near
the confluence of the two rivers and a private wooden bridge spanning the
Trent west of the railroad bridge.[5]

At 2 P.M. on March 12, Burnside's expedition left Pamlico Sound and
entered the mouth of the Neuse en route to New Bern. As soon as the
approach of the enemy was detected by Confederate outposts along the
river, the news was hastened to General Branch, who received it about
4 P.M. by a series of bonfires built along the river. By nightfall, Branch
dispatched the Thirty-fifth North Carolina, under Colonel James Sinclair,
south toward Fishers Landing near Otter Creek with orders to resist any
landing attempt by the enemy. However, the Confederates were too late,
for by 9 P.M. on the bright, moonlit evening, the fleet had anchored at the
mouth of Slocum Creek, twelve miles south of New Bern by water and
seventeen by land. Twelve hours later, the first wave of the eleven-thou-
sand-man army began making its way ashore under the cover of Federal
gunboats. As a result, the Thirty-fifth North Carolina and the cavalry and
artillery forces that had subsequently been sent south to thwart the landing were recalled to the primary defensive line at Fort Thompson.[6]

After the Federal amphibious forces splashed their way ashore, they began their trek toward New Bern. With the gunboats out front, the bluecoats
marched four miles through "open piney woods" to the Croatan Works,
which, much to their surprise and delight, had been abandoned by the
Confederates. As the exhausting march continued, heavy showers fell
throughout the day and night, making the muddy roads difficult for soldiers and artillery. At 8 P.M., the Federals bivouacked within a mile and a
half of Fort Thompson.[7]

General Branch spent the night of March 13 making final preparations
for the battle that was to take place the following morning. To repel the
invaders, he had approximately one-third of their number under arms. From
Fort Thompson to the railroad, a distance of one mile, he stretched four
of his six regiments. The left wing of this line—commanded by Colonel
Charles C. Lee, another of Hoke's fellow officers from the First North
Carolina Volunteers—was anchored by the Twenty-seventh and the Thirty-

seventh North Carolina. Colonel Reuben P. Campbell of the Seventh North Carolina was in command of the right wing, which consisted of Campbell's regiment and the Thirty-fifth North Carolina. A. C. Latham's six-gun battery and four guns from Thomas H. Brem's battery were also placed on the east side of the railroad. Just across the railroad, the vulnerable gap at the brickyard was to be defended by Captain Brem's remaining two guns and the local militia battalion commanded by Colonel H. J. B. Clark. Drafted for service just two weeks earlier, the militiamen had no uniforms and were armed with hunting rifles and shotguns. For the mile and a half of defensive line that extended from the gap westward to Weathersby Road, Branch had a force of fewer than a thousand men, composed of Colonel Zebulon B. Vance's Twenty-sixth North Carolina and several companies of unattached dismounted cavalry and infantry. Some parts of the line west of the railroad had to be left unguarded. Beyond the gap, there were but two pieces of Confederate artillery, located on the far right on Weathersby Road. Branch located his headquarters on the east side of the railroad at a position where he could observe action along the length of the works. Although he intended to superintend the entire line, the general's primary battle command would be the center of the line and his reserves. Branch's lack of troops meant that he could keep only a single regiment in reserve, the Thirty-third North Carolina. These soldiers were positioned behind Branch, about four hundred yards to the rear of the brickyard. But on the morrow, Avery and Hoke and their reserves would quickly find themselves on the front line in the thick of the fight for New Bern.[8]

Despite a slow, steady rain that continued throughout the night, the heavily outnumbered Confederates, many of whom were green troops, were "anxious to feel the fire of the enemy" and "were spoiling for a fight." The historian of the Thirty-third North Carolina recorded, "There were no complaints, no murmuring. Every one seemed to be anxious to do his duty to his country and to his God."

By daybreak on the foggy morning of March 14, Avery and Hoke had the men of the Thirty-third North Carolina fully awake and ready for combat. As soon as the regiment was formed, the soldiers were ordered to remove their knapsacks so that they might "be ready to move with quickness to any point." Colonel Avery then stood before his soldiers and offered a short, well-received speech "full of fire and enthusiasm." Closer to the front, all along the Confederate line, the North Carolinians were in a state of readiness, "eager for the fight." On the Confederate right, the men of the Twenty-sixth North Carolina had just now picked up their rifles and put down their digging implements, having completed the last redans during the night.[9]

At his position south of Fort Thompson, Burnside was just about ready to strike at the Confederates. He had divided his army into three columns: Brigadier General John G. Foster was to move his brigade up Beaufort Road and hit the Confederate left; Brigadier General Jesse Reno was to advance his brigade along the railroad and hit the enemy's right; and Brigadier General John G. Parke was to hold his brigade in reserve, ready for action where needed.

All these brigade commanders were on their horses by 6:00 A.M. An hour later, the Federal columns began their advance on Branch's lines. Around 7:20 A.M., General Burnside almost became the first casualty of the battle when he and several aides rode ahead to a point in the woods some 350 yards from the Thirty-seventh North Carolina. As the general attempted to monitor the Confederate line on the gray, misty morning, he was spotted by Lieutenant Wheeler of Latham's Battery. A shell from one of the Confederate Parrott guns suddenly exploded near the general's party, scattering the Yankee horsemen and opening the first battle for New Bern.[10]

General Foster promptly launched a vicious attack on the Confederate left. From the rooftops of their homes, the residents of New Bern watched with a mixture of awe and terror as the guns of Fort Thompson and the Federal fleet roared. For some two hours, Foster was able to make little progress in the face of "incessant and very severe" infantry fire. Moreover, the three land guns of the fort were most effective, mowing "gaps in the Yankee line at every discharge."[11]

While Foster was having his troubles, Reno was likewise making no progress against the Confederate right. Colonel Edward Ferrera of the Fifty-first New York described the fighting on the west side of the railroad: "A continuous fire was then kept up on the enemy, which they returned with great vigor and making sad havoc in our ranks." Yet Reno was able to score one early, telling success. He saw the gap at the brickyard and immediately sent the Twenty-first Massachusetts, commanded by Lieutenant Colonel William S. Clark, in to flank the militia. Combatants on both sides reacted with surprise. Clark reported, "At the first volley from Company C the enemy, in great astonishment, fled from the road and the trench to a ravine in the brick-yard. General Reno now ordered the color-bearer, Sergeant Bates, to plant his flag upon the roof of a building within the enemy's intrenchments." Though the battle raged for more than three additional hours, it was decided by the penetration of the Twenty-first Massachusetts at 8:45 A.M.[12]

When the flight of the militia revealed the presence of enemy troops on the flank of the Thirty-fifth North Carolina, Colonel James Sinclair "in much excitement" reported the news to his wing commander, Reuben P. Campbell. Colonel Campbell ordered Sinclair to charge with bayonets, but the soldiers of the Thirty-fifth North Carolina "left the field in confusion." Reacting quickly, Campbell dispatched men from his regiment to temporarily stem the enemy advance.

Seeing the center of his line give way, General Branch sent for his reserves about 9 A.M. Just after the Thirty-third North Carolina moved forward about a hundred yards to the rear of Branch, Hoke, in command of the right wing of the regiment, was ordered to occupy the entrenchments on the right of the railroad with five companies. Hoke rushed his soldiers through the woods and down the ravines "in order to protect the men as much as possible." He halted the advance in a ravine. No sooner had one company been placed in position than Hoke was ordered to return to Branch with his command. As he was making his way back with four companies, Colonel Avery and Major Lewis were rushing forward with the left wing. Avery told Hoke to join them, "and the regiment moved up to the scene of action in fine style." With Hoke in command of the right, Avery the center, and Lewis the left, the soldiers were ordered to fire before they reached the entrenchments, since the enemy was firing upon them in full force from a hill immediately across the swamp. Much to Branch's delight, "the whole ten companies opened a terrific fire from their Enfield rifles."

For an instant, the tide of battle seemed to shift once again. Hoke noted, "Our fire seemed to have great effect as the enemy scampered."[13]

At the brick kiln near the gap that had allowed Reno to exploit the Confederate line, Major Lewis used the left wing to repulse "the enemy time and time again, and twice charged them with detachments of companies, and each time made them flee." This furious fighting subsequently provided Hoke with his first opportunity to write an official report of an engagement. His first battle narrative, like all the others he would write over the next three years, revealed Hoke's willingness to extend credit to, and offer praise to, fellow officers and soldiers who excelled in combat. Of Major Lewis at New Bern, Hoke reported, "No one could have behaved with more coolness, bravery, and determination than he, and he deserves the praise of every true countrymen for his actions." In the center of the Thirty-third North Carolina, men under Lewis's immediate command offered "very destructive" fire.[14] Two years later, Hoke and Lewis would again collaborate in the same theater of action.

Of Avery, his colonel, Hoke wrote, "He was perfectly cool, and never did man act better upon the battlefield than he." In the heat of battle, when Avery received a shot through the top of his hat, he continued to cheer his men on, calling out, "Boys, they liked to have gotten me."[15]

While Avery and Lewis were stemming the tide at the brickyard, Hoke was doing a masterful job of fighting on the right. He used two companies to plug a gaping quarter-mile hole that had developed in the line adjacent to the Twenty-sixth North Carolina. Until well past noon, the Thirty-third and Twenty-sixth North Carolina fought stubbornly to maintain the integrity of Branch's right. General Reno described the stiff resistance he faced there: "The battle now became general along one whole line, and raged fiercely for about three and a half hours." Branch later praised the Thirty-third North Carolina for its stand: "As the Thirty-third Regiment was under my command it is proper for me to say that its conduct was all I could desire. It moved into action with as much promptness and steadiness as I ever saw in its ranks on dress parade and its fire was terrific. . . . Colonel Avery, Lieutenant Colonel Hoke, and Major Lewis did their duty fully against an overwhelming force."[16]

Despite the heroics on the Confederate right, the hole left by the flight of the militia and the Thirty-fifth North Carolina could not be filled, and reinforcements from General Parke's reserves were ordered up to flood the gap. At the same time, General Foster charged the Confederate left. Branch now realized that the fight could not be won: "Seeing the enemy behind the breastwork, without a single man to place in the gap through which he was entering and finding the day lost, my next care was to secure the retreat."[17]

While the broken regiments on the Confederate left fled the field across the river bridge toward New Bern, Branch dispatched two couriers to Colonel Vance and two to Colonel Avery with orders to fall back. Somehow, none of the couriers reached their intended destinations, and the men of the two beleaguered regiments steadfastly maintained their posts against the combined firepower of three Union brigades. In his official report, Lieutenant Colonel Clark of the Twenty-first Massachusetts wrote that the Thirty-third and Twenty-sixth North Carolina "were the best-armed and fought the most gallantly of any of the enemy's forces." Clark continued, "Their position was almost impregnable so long as their left flank, resting on the railroad, was defended, and they kept up an incessant fire for three hours, until their ammunition was exhausted and the remainder of the rebel forces had retreated from that portion of their works lying between the river and railroad."[18]

Hoke and his fellow officers and men of the Thirty-third North Carolina continued their fight in the face of overwhelming odds until they could fight no more. Just past noon, the battle was all but over. Hoke recalled, "At 12:15 o'clock I saw the United States flag flying upon one of our works, but saw Colonel Avery still fighting, and I, being very busily engaged with the enemy, did not know that Colonel Avery and Major Lewis had fallen back until I saw the enemy upon my left. . . . I then saw for the first time we were driven back, and ordered the men under my command to fall back, but to do so in order."[19]

Under heavy enemy fire, Hoke intended to unite with Avery and Lewis, but he could find neither. Unknown to Hoke at the time, Avery and two hundred of his men had been cut off in their retreat and were forced to surrender to General Foster. Lewis and his wing, separated from Hoke by enemy forces, were a bit more fortunate but "had to run the gauntlet" to avoid capture. Hoping to join the remainder of the regiment at the Trent River, Hoke was dismayed to find no familiar faces at the bridge, which was now burning.

With all avenues of retreat into New Bern closed or destroyed, there was no escape other than Brice's Creek, a deep, wide waterway. At the creek, the lieutenant colonel located a boat, which was used to ferry some of the soldiers across. Even in this desperate hour of retreat, there was still time for courage and valor. Particularly moving to Hoke was the sacrifice of Private H. Dolehite, who threw "away his clothing in order to swim the creek and save his gun." Hoke noted, "He is a boy of sixteen years of age."

In the meantime, Colonel Vance used the boat that Hoke had located and several others supplied by a local resident to get the men of the Twenty-sixth North Carolina across the creek, which was, as Vance had learned the hard way, "too deep to ford." North Carolina almost lost its future war-time governor when Vance, in an attempt to instill confidence in his men, spurred his horse into the creek. When the animal refused to swim, the colonel, weighed down by his accouterments, began to sink into the deep, dark waters. After he was pulled to safety, Vance swam the creek to search for the boats he subsequently employed in the crossing.[20]

On the opposite side of the creek, Hoke and Vance were no doubt pleased to find each other. They joined forces and took the road to Trenton, some twenty-five miles southwest of New Bern. "Stopping at no time for more than four hours," the Confederates marched day and night. When they arrived in the riverside town, Hoke and Vance learned that the remainder of Branch's brigade had fallen back to the safety of Kinston. Wasting no time in Trenton, the Confederates crossed the Trent River and hastened toward a reunion with their comrades.[21]

Hoke noted that the "march of 50 miles in about thirty-six hours" came to an end at 10 A.M. on Sunday, March 16. At Kinston, his "footsore and weary" band was greeted with "a cordial welcome and shelter and food." Over the course of the war, Kinston would play an important part in Hoke's military career, but it was the reception he received in March 1862 that forever enshrined Kinston in the young officer's memory. For the next seven weeks, the men of the Thirty-third North Carolina and the other survivors of the fight for New Bern camped in and around the city, where they "found the cheer and rest they sorely needed."[22]

While the battle-weary troops mended their wounds, news of the defeat shocked and outraged North Carolinians. The Confederate debacle resulting in the Union capture of New Bern was extremely costly to the state. Much of the upper and central portions of the coast were now subject either to Federal occupation or raids. Before April was over, Newport, Carolina City, Morehead City, Beaufort, and Fort Macon were under Union control. Plymouth and Washington fell soon thereafter. Blockade running north of Wilmington was virtually stamped out. In the wake of the loss of New Bern, Robert E. Lee remarked to President Jefferson Davis that another "disaster" on the North Carolina coast "would be ruinous."[23]

During their sojourn at Kinston, the North Carolina regiments were divided into two brigades—the First and Second Brigades. General Robert Ransom was given command of the First Brigade and General Branch, who most observers believed had done as well as could be expected at New Bern, was assigned command of the Second. In addition to Hoke and the men of the Thirty-third North Carolina, Branch's new command included the Seventh, Eighteenth, Twenty-eighth, and Thirty-seventh North Carolina. When the Second Brigade was subsequently transferred to Virginia, it was known as the Fourth Brigade until the Confederate War Department ordered brigades to bear the names of their commanders.[24]

For Hoke, the fight at New Bern was a learning experience, his first real taste of combat, Bethel notwithstanding. At New Bern, Hoke witnessed the first men under his command sacrifice their lives in battle. His regiment suffered three times as many casualties as any other Confederate regiment at New Bern. Of the 64 Confederates killed and 101 wounded, 32 and 28, respectively, were from Hoke's regiment. There was no dispute that Hoke had been in the hottest part of the fury and borne the brunt of the final Union assault. The intensity of the fight near Hoke's position on the front line was best measured by the graphic description provided by a member of the Twenty-first Massachusetts: "The saddest sight I saw was some Rebel officer's splendid gray charger, both of whose forelegs had been carried away at the knee by a cannon ball, standing immobile and silent upon the stumps—a sickening monument to man's barbarity."[25]

During the fighting—about which one survivor noted, "I myself had a variety of experiences in battle . . . but I was never engaged in anything quite so peppery as the battle of New Bern"—Hoke not only served as a gallant front-line participant in his first full-scale engagement, but also made good use of his first opportunity to shine as a combat leader. He "won his spurs." As the Confederate right had begun to give way under the weight of a full Union assault at midday on March 14, the lieutenant colonel skillfully extricated the soldiers of his command from a position of imminent peril and possible capture, thereby rendering a glimpse of the military genius that would stand him in good stead over the next three years. Hoke's mastery of command continued to be evident throughout the retreat. With the enemy in hot pursuit, he commanded an orderly movement across a dense swamp and over a major creek swollen to flood stage by recent rains. John W. Graham, the son of William Alexander Graham and a member of General Richard C. Gatlin's staff, accurately described Hoke's performance in the "disastrous defeat." In a letter to his father, Graham noted that Hoke "distinguished" himself.[26]

New Bern provided Hoke with his first taste of defeat in the war. Once lost to Union control, the city would never again be in Confederate hands; however, it would forever be a favored target in Southern attempts to reestablish a foothold on the central portion of the North Carolina coast. On two future occasions, Hoke would return to the city as a major player in Confederate ventures to wrest New Bern from the enemy. Twice he would fail, each time coming within an eyelash of success.

But at Kinston, Hoke had no time to dwell on the Confederate failure at New Bern or on any future glory he might attain. Colonel Avery remained a Union prisoner, and the command of the Thirty-third North Carolina had devolved to the lieutenant colonel. During the stay at Kinston, the new commander labored diligently to rebuild the regiment and to prepare it for any field of battle to which it might be called. In early May, rumblings in Virginia indicated that Federal offensives could soon be expected in the Shenandoah Valley and on the peninsula where Hoke had first fought the enemy. In response to the threats, Branch's brigade entrained on May 4 for Virginia,[27] where Hoke's mettle as a regimental commander would be severely and frequently tested.

Hoke and his men reached Gordonsville in north central Virginia on the night of May 5. They remained there for the next ten days while the remainder of Branch's brigade arrived. On Friday, May 16, the entire brigade was ordered to move to reinforce Stonewall Jackson in the valley. One adjutant of the brigade recounted the beginning of the march: "Every foot moved with a light and steady step and the expression of satisfaction was on the countenance." However, when the brigade reached Massanutten Gap at the foot of the Blue Ridge Mountains, Branch was ordered to move his soldiers back to Gordonsville. After the return, the brigade was quickly sent by train to Hanover Court House, some fourteen miles north of Richmond. At their new post, the North Carolinians performed picket duty, maintaining a watch on Federal armies threatening the Confederate capital and Fredericksburg. On Sunday evening, May 25, as if a portent of combat, Latham's Battery reported to Branch for duty. Unfortunately for the Confederates, the artillery contingent arrived "with the guns and with horses entirely untrained."[28]

On May 26, Branch moved his camp south from Hanover Court House to Slash Church, the site of an ancient church and settlement named for a common pine that thrived in the swamp environs. Branch's movement was designed to position him "at the mouth of a road leading to Ashland" and to provide him with a route of retreat in the event he was attacked by General Irvin McDowell from the north or General George B. McClellan from the south. Although the North Carolinians marched through rain and mud that was almost knee-deep, they were "cheerful and confident" en route to Slash Church.[29]

Soon after Hoke awoke on Tuesday, it became apparent that he and his men would be busy with the enemy on his twenty-fifth birthday. Early that morning, after Branch received a report that Federal soldiers were advancing on the road to Taliaferro's Mill, he sent the Twenty-eighth North

Carolina and some artillery in that direction. About the same time, an attached Georgia regiment was sent on patrol for the enemy near the railroad at Ashecake. Then, in the middle of the day, McDowell threw his twelve-thousand-man right wing, commanded by General Fitz John Porter, against the four thousand men of Branch at Slash Church. After an exchange of artillery, Branch moved forward a mile and a half until he found the enemy "strongly posted across the road."

Branch quickly developed a battle plan: the Thirty-seventh North Carolina under Colonel Lee was to strike the right flank of the enemy battery; the Thirty-third North Carolina under Hoke and the Twelfth North Carolina under Colonel Wade, after sweeping through the woods as previously ordered, were to strike at the left flank; and the Eighteenth North Carolina under Colonel Cowan was to make a direct frontal assault.

Hoke and Wade got the best of a sharp skirmish in the woods, taking six prisoners and eleven horses, but the fight prevented them from attacking the left. Instead, Hoke was hurried in to reinforce Colonel Lee on the right, where the Thirty-third North Carolina "rendered admirable service, and [added] no little to the fighting reputation it had already acquired." As his brigade waged a spirited fight against a full division in its front, Branch received a number of cavalry reports of a heavy enemy force passing around the Confederate right. Ultimately, there was only one decision the general could make. He explained, "Finding I could remain no longer without being surrounded, and hearing of no re-inforcements, . . . I determined to draw off." The subsequent retreat was carried off with relative ease. Unlike New Bern, Branch retired from the fight at Slash Church without suffering a defeat. However, his losses—66 killed and 177 wounded—were heavy.[30]

Slash Church represented the first test for the soldiers in Branch's new brigade, and it "was only a prelude for their heroic conduct on every other field." Robert E. Lee offered his compliments to Branch and his troops for their efforts at Slash Church in a letter to the general on June 3: "I take great pleasure in expressing my approval of the manner in which you have discharged the duties of the position in which you were placed. . . . I beg you will signify to the troops of your command which were engaged

A Rising Star

on that occasion my hearty approval of their conduct, and hope that on future occasions they will evince a like heroism and patriotic devotion."[31]

During the month following Slash Church, Branch's brigade did picket duty along Brook Turnpike just north of Richmond. In early June, the brigade was incorporated into the division formed for A. P. Hill, who had been promoted to major general on May 27. At its formation, the division was assigned to Stonewall Jackson's corps. Hoke and the soldiers of the Thirty-third North Carolina would be conspicuous players as Hill's soldiers won renown as the famous Light Division in the grim, bloody fighting that embraced Virginia, West Virginia, and Maryland throughout the summer and autumn of 1862.[32]

Robert E. Lee had been in command of the army he fondly called "the Army of Northern Virginia" less than a month when he planned a grand strategy to drive McClellan's 100,000-man army away from the Confederate capital. Preparatory to the opening of Lee's campaign, Branch was ordered on June 24 to move his brigade the following evening to Half Sink on the Chickahominy River, about eight miles north of Richmond. On June 25, prior to moving, Branch called Hoke and the other commanding officers together for a council of war, during which he explained the manner of attack. Hoke, who had five companies on picket duty at Crenshaw Bridge, was ordered to take command there, while the other five companies of the Thirty-third, under Major Robert V. Cowan, were to march with the brigade, which was to cross the river at the telegraph bridge in the wee hours of June 27. Once the brigade was across, it was to move down the river toward Mechanicsville and sweep the enemy from its position. Hoke was to cross the river and attack in the rear once he heard gunfire. Branch's movement was predicated upon the receipt of a signal from Stonewall Jackson that he had crossed the Central Railroad on the left.[33]

Hoke relayed orders to the men of the Thirty-third to pack three days' rations, and then he addressed them in a pre-battle pep talk, telling his soldiers "that the time had come for the great battle to be fought and he expected every man to do his whole duty."

At 3 A.M. on June 27, Hoke, with his command at Crenshaw Bridge, was "ordered to be ready to march at a moment's warning." However, it was late morning before Branch could begin his movement, because Jackson was some seven hours late in crossing the railroad. Hoke moved his command at noon and at 1 P.M. joined the brigade, the first of the Light Division to cross the Chickahominy. Hoke immediately went to work to assist the brigade in clearing the way for the crossing of the remainder of the Light Division. During the skirmishing, Branch's forces captured an enemy flag. About an hour before sunset, the brigade reached Mechanicsville during "the progress of a severe engagement." Hoke recorded that he entered the battle "under a most terrific shower of shot and shell." One of his junior officers, forty-two-year-old second lieutenant Richard F. Epps, chronicled the battle in a letter to his wife and children: "The first fight . . . lasted until about 10 at night we had taken one of their Batteries drove them from one of their strong positions but the Battle was not ended." There was little rest throughout the night, as the men of the Thirty-third North Carolina "were ordered to lay on our arms in the open field under the ene[m]ys guns."[34]

At 3 A.M. the following day, Hoke was ordered "to be ready to move at a moment's warning," but the Yankees were not yet finished. Second Lieutenant Epps described the resumption of the battle at Mechanicsville: "About day Break on Friday morning the 27th we fired a signal gun to inform us that the work of Death was about to commence again in a few minutes our whole line was in a blaze the whole work was soon over th[e]y were driven from the Position which Resulted in a complete Route."[35]

Once the enemy fled the field and retreated east toward Gaines' Mill (Cold Harbor), the Confederates gave chase. Lee now had McClellan on the run, and he intended to keep up a hot pursuit with forty thousand soldiers. Hoke took up the line of march at noon and four hours later reached Gaines' Mill, where the fifty-thousand-man enemy army held a position of "immense strength." General Porter deployed his forces about a plateau that terminated on the northwest side of an eighty-foot bluff. Bordering the position was a moatlike stream ten feet wide and six feet deep. Artillery surmounted the heights. Below, the infantry was protected by their lines of entrenchments.

When the Thirty-third North Carolina arrived at Gaines' Mill, Hoke found "heavy fighting going on," and he was "ordered immediately into the engagement." Second Lieutenant Epps described the sights and sounds that followed: "The Roar of Artillery the Bursting of Shell the Rattle of Musketry and the Sharp Crack of our Rifles could be heard the whole line the Groans of the Dying the Shreaks of the wounded far surpassed a[n]y thing that the mind of man can sieve." For more than four hours on the front line, Hoke's soldiers waged a bitter fight. At dusk, the enemy began giving way on the Confederate right as a result of the severe pressure by the brigades of Branch and Pender. Advancing in the face of "murderous fire of artillery," the North Carolinians screamed the "defiant Rebel Yell," and line after line of Federal troops gave way, causing the artillery to join "in the general tumult." From the ranks of the Thirty-third North Carolina, Epps observed "heaps on heaps the Slaughtered yankees lie they Sleep in death and hear the wars no more far above the Roar of artillery the Shouts of our victorious Boys could be heard as they would charge Battery after Battery until the ene[m]y work in confusion and dismay leaving their killed and wounded on the field the fight was kept up until nine o'clock at night."[36]

Suddenly, the Battle of Gaines' Mill was over. The Yankees had been driven back two miles. McClellan had been dealt another staggering defeat. Following the battle, described as one of the most strenuous of the war, "nearly 7,000 Federals lay dead and wounded." But in human terms, the Confederates, with almost 9,000 casualties, paid a heavier price. Branch had two colonels down. Colonel Reuben P. Campbell of the Seventh North Carolina was killed just after seizing the colors from the hands of a fallen flag bearer. Colonel James H. Lane of the Twenty-eighth North Carolina was wounded in the head.[37]

At the conclusion of the battle, Hoke reported to Branch, who instructed him to bivouac his regiment and give his soldiers some rest. No doubt, Hoke considered the rest well deserved, for he lauded his troops for their performance: "This was a very hard-fought battle, and the men deserve great praise for their coolness and firmness on this occasion."

All was quiet on June 28, as the regiment remained in camp on the battlefield. Much of the day was consumed in the work of "burying the many dead upon the field and gathering the trophies of war." Additional casualties loomed on the horizon when Hoke was "ordered to prepare two days' rations and be ready to march at daylight."[38]

After the setback at Gaines' Mill, McClellan's army crossed to the south bank of the Chickahominy and made haste into the White Oak Swamp en route to the James River. Taking up the chase on Sunday, June 29, Hoke marched the Thirty-third North Carolina twelve to fifteen miles, crossing the Chickahominy in the evening. Hurrying down the river the next day, Hoke reached Fraser's Farm, near Glendale, about 3 P.M., where Lee promptly hit McClellan with the divisions of A. P. Hill and Longstreet. Stonewall Jackson was again late in arriving, as were Magruder and Benjamin Huger. Consequently, the two Confederate divisions that took the field suffered greatly in the face of the "heavy firing of shot and shell" from a "strongly posted and well defended" enemy. Roaring artillery announced the opening of the battle. Posted west of the Union army, Branch ordered his regiment in battle formation. Moving at double-quick, the North Carolinians poured across an open field for more than five hundred yards without protection. About the charge, Hoke reported, "We at the same time were enfiladed by grape shot; neither fire upon the front or flank at all stopped the men, but on they pressed and soon silenced the fire upon them. They seemed not to heed the falling of friends by their side, but had the great duty of defeating the enemy foremost in their minds."

Once across the field, the Thirty-third North Carolina was divided, as Hoke put it, "by the interference of a brigadier general, unknown to me, who had ordered the left of my regiment to march to the left." Late in the afternoon, the stiff resistance in the center of the Union line was overcome by Hill's division, and the Yankees again retreated. Confederate pursuit was not fast enough, as the fleeing army was able to reach the relative safety of Malvern Hill and the protection of the United States Navy gunboats on the nearby James River.[39]

Again, Confederate casualties, estimated at 3,615, outnumbered Union losses of approximately 2,853. Hoke reported that his losses were heavy, "not so much in killed as in wounded." Fraser's Farm cost Branch another commander and Hoke a close friend from the Bethel Regiment—Colonel Charles C. Lee of the Thirty-seventh North Carolina. Lee was killed by a cannon blast while charging an enemy battery. When he was hit, he was within a hundred yards of the battery, and as he fell, he cried out, "On, my brave boys!"[40]

Even though the Federal army had "escaped" to Malvern Hill, Lee was not ready to let up on his relentless pursuit. In the late afternoon on July 1, he ordered a full frontal assault on General Porter at Malvern Hill by the divisions of D. H. Hill, Huger, and Magruder.

While the Confederate lines were being formed, Hoke was pleasantly surprised to run into an old friend. After offering a salute, Hoke greeted John Hatcher, now an artillery lieutenant, with a memory from the past: "We are shaking hands with Mr. Lincoln today very differently from the manner in which we shook hands with him as President on the day of his inauguration in 1861." As the two officers waited for the time to advance, they discussed their combat experiences and the uncertainties of war. Before they parted, they agreed that after each battle in which both were involved, the first one that could do so would make his way to the other's command to determine the well-being of his friend. They further agreed that if one was killed or wounded, the other would make sure that relatives were notified.[41]

At 6 P.M., when the battle began, Hoke was ordered up to support D. H. Hill. Although the Thirty-third North Carolina was not heavily engaged during the sanguinary combat at Malvern Hill, the soldiers were subjected to continuous, heavy fire of shot and shell from land batteries and gunboats. By nightfall, the fighting was over. Disjointed, uncoordinated Confederate assaults had caused Southern soldiers to fall in clusters, their bodies riddled by murderous artillery fire. More than fifty-three hundred Confederates fell, while Union losses totaled just over thirty-two hundred. Among the severely wounded was Hoke's hometown friend, Colonel Stephen Dodson Ramseur of the Forty-ninth North Carolina.[42]

Following the battle, Hoke made his way to Lieutenant Hatcher's battery to check on his friend. There, he found his gallant comrade "cold in death, lying face downward, his head toward the enemy's line, with his sword firmly grasped in his hand." After John Hatcher was buried on the battlefield, Hoke dispatched the grim tidings to his friend's parents.[43]

Malvern Hill brought to an end the famous Seven Days' Battles, "the greatest series of battles ever known to American history." Though the Union army effected its escape at Malvern Hill, General Lee, during the week of fighting, saved Richmond from capture and drove McClellan back to his base at Harrison's Landing on the James River. As Second Lieutenant Epps put it, "The great McCleeland the young Napoleon now like a whiped cur Lies on the banks of the James River crouched under his Gun Boats."[44]

As to who should receive credit for the Confederate success in the "seeries of the grandes[t] Battles that was ever fought on the American continent," Epps had an opinion: "The Result of their Battles was not the Result of the Scill and experience of our Generals or the Brave Men but through the direction and guidance of Almighty God." Branch chose to give credit to his regimental commanders, including Hoke, indicating in his official report that they merited "special commendation." Two of his five colonels were dead and two wounded. Of the five regimental commanders, only Hoke had come through the week unscathed. In saluting his brigade, Branch enumerated its superlatives in the Seven Days' Battles: "In the late operations below Richmond you were the first brigade to cross the Chickahominy; you were the first to start him on that retreat in which the able combinations of our General-in-Chief allowed him to like no rest until he found shelter under the guns of his shipping."[45]

From the bivouac at Malvern Hill, the Thirty-third North Carolina joined with other Confederate forces to pursue the Federals on July 2 and 3. The enemy was invited to fight but refused. Over the next two days, the regiment received a welcome respite from combat and an opportunity to bind its wounds. Despite almost daily appearances on the front line for a week, regimental losses had been relatively light—eight killed and fifty-two wounded. While still in camp at Malvern Hill, Hoke exclaimed to his soldiers, "I am proud of the 33rd."

About July 6, Branch's brigade moved to a camp near Richmond, where it remained for the next three weeks. During that time, Lee organized the

Army of Northern Virginia into two corps, commanded by Jackson and Longstreet. Hill's vaunted Light Division was assigned to Jackson. There was cause for the men of the Thirty-third North Carolina to celebrate on July 29 when General Branch issued General Orders No. 6, whereby the brigade quartermaster was instructed to supply a new flag to Hoke's regiment, with "New Berne, Slash Church, Mechanicsville, Gaines Mill, Frazier's Farm, and Malvern Hill" proudly inscribed.[46]

On Tuesday, July 29, Branch's brigade was moved back to Gordonsville to monitor the activities of General John Pope, who was threatening the Confederate railroad network. While on this duty, the troops suffered from the hot weather and a lack of food. But good news was forthcoming for Hoke when, later in the month, he was promoted to colonel effective August 5, in recognition of his distinguished service as a regimental commander since New Bern.

On August 9, the Light Division was rushed to the aid of Jackson at Cedar Mountain. Earlier in the day, Jackson had attempted to crush an isolated corps from Pope's army, but stiff resistance by the Union forces left the Confederates on the precipice of defeat. With Branch's North Carolinians leading the way, Hill's division reached the battlefield at 3 P.M. "after a long, rapid, and weary march." Immediately, the Thirty-third North Carolina was ordered into action on the left of the road leading to Cedar Run. While moving to the front to support Jackson's first line, Hoke and his soldiers encountered the celebrated Stonewall Brigade, "fleeing as fast as they could." According to Jackson, "At this critical moment, Branch's Brigade met the Federal forces, flushed with temporary triumph, and drove them back with terrible slaughter through the wood." The troops of the Thirty-third, Thirty-seventh, Twenty-eighth, and Eighteenth North Carolina surged forward through dense undergrowth "in perfect order as on dress parade" and turned a sure Confederate defeat into victory. In the fierce struggle, Hoke lost six killed and thirty wounded.[47]

In his journal, Branch left no doubt about who he thought had won the Battle of Cedar Mountain: "We gained a splendid victory and the credit of it is due to my brigade." While Branch's opinion might otherwise be condemned as subjective, Stonewall Jackson affirmed it in one of the more moving scenes of the war. Following the battle, Jackson, by himself, rode up to Branch's brigade, and as he slowly made his way along the line to the hearty cheers of the North Carolinians, the general "dropped" his hat in silent tribute to the men who had saved the day for him. In one of the great ironies of the war, it was some of these same soldiers who would mistakenly bring Jackson down with a fateful volley at Chancellorsville less than a year later.[48]

The North Carolinians camped on the battlefield at Cedar Mountain until the evening of August 11. They were then returned to the Gordonsville area, and for the next two weeks, the Thirty-third North Carolina bivouacked near Orange Court House.[49]

On Sunday, August 24, the Thirty-third and the Twenty-eighth North Carolina were moved near Warrenton White Sulphur Springs to support the artillery batteries of Carter Braxton and Greenlee Davidson, which were there to prevent the destruction of the bridge over the Rappahannock River. Throughout the day, the two regiments were exposed to a "severe and protracted cannonade." The following day, Stonewall Jackson began a diversionary movement with the ultimate goal of flanking Pope, who was now on the north side of the Rappahannock. Participating in the maneuver, Branch's brigade, with "nothing to eat but roasting ears," crossed and recrossed the Blue Ridge. In the early-morning hours of August 27, the North Carolinians and other elements of Jackson's corps reached Manassas Junction, an important supply depot for the Union army. Shortly after their arrival, Hoke's men spotted Brigadier General George W. Taylor's New Jersey brigade in the distance, approaching in a line of battle. Any hope of capturing the Federals by surprise was lost when the Confederate artillery "fired too soon." Once the big guns thundered, the "entire command broke and fled precipitately," and Branch promptly ordered his regimental commanders to pursue the fleeing enemy. Capturing "a large number of prisoners" in the process, Branch's soldiers chased the Yankees for several miles until they took refuge in a swamp beyond Bull Run.[50]

A day later, after Branch marched the brigade through Centreville and across Bull Run, he was ordered to deploy his men in a wooded area that fronted on an open field at Manassas Plains. An artillery battery was planted in the field and "rendered very efficient service." None of Branch's regiments was "actively engaged that day, and about nightfall the whole command was moved into the woods into the railroad cut," where the soldiers slept upon their arms.

The following morning, the Battle of Second Manassas opened in earnest when Pope struck Jackson's army with a frontal assault. Branch was ordered to support Maxcy Gregg's brigade on the extreme left of the Confederate line. About the time the Twenty-eighth and the Thirty-third North Carolina sighted Gregg's soldiers in some woods on the right, a large force of enemy soldiers "opened a deadly fire." Branch rushed his other regiments to the scene, and during the melee that followed, "many hand-to-hand fights took place." Federal troops "came on like the waves of the ocean," but they were repulsed time and again by Branch's battle-tested veterans. When ammunition grew short, Branch sent out details to retrieve cartridges from the boxes of his fallen soldiers.

As the sun began to set, the fighting came to a halt. Branch had successfully driven the Federals back in complete disarray. Colonel James H. Lane, another of Hoke's fellow officers from the old First North Carolina and the man who would soon succeed Branch as commander of the brigade, saluted its soldiers: "Never have I witnessed greater bravery and desperation than was that day displayed by this brigade." Of Hoke and the men of the Thirty-third North Carolina, he wrote, "The Thirty-third, under Colonel Hoke, . . . fought well in the woods . . . and once gallantly advanced into the open field in front and drove the enemy back in disorder." Ecstatic over the performance of his brigade, Branch humbly told his troops, "Burnside whipped us at New Bern, but we have whipped him this evening."[51]

Heavy firing from Union artillery annoyed Hoke's skirmishers on the morning of August 30. Late in the afternoon, the regiment joined in the Confederate chase of the retreating enemy, but a heavy rain hampered the pursuers. Another battle had been won, and the last day of August was spent in burying the dead and caring for the wounded. Miraculously, Hoke had but a single man killed and seven wounded at Second Manassas. Later in the day, the brigade crossed Bull Run at Sudley Ford and camped for the night near Little River Turnpike. With the wagon train in the rear, the soldiers had nothing to eat, and a nighttime rain added to the misery.[52]

As Pope pushed his demoralized army back toward Washington, D.C., on September 1, Lee ordered Jackson to cut him off at Ox Hill (Chantilly), near Fairfax Court House. Late in the afternoon, as low, threatening clouds hovered above the two armies, Jackson struck Pope near a country mansion on Little River Turnpike. What followed was "one of the severest engagements of the war." Branch formed his brigade parallel to the pike to block the enemy. As his regiments charged the Union lines, a violent thunderstorm erupted. Strong winds swept sheets of cold, blinding rain into the eyes of the North Carolinians, and crackling thunder drowned out the roar of the dueling field guns. Heavy rain continued to fall throughout the battle. Hoke's regiment, though drenched to the skin, "fought with its usual intrepidity." His soldiers, like the others in the brigade, found that the driving rain caused their rifles to choke and fire badly. Nonetheless, the brigade expended every round of ammunition during the fierce battle, causing Branch to order his troops to hold their position with the point of bayonet. About dark, the Federals withdrew. Branch's regiment, after bearing the brunt of the fight, fell back to a field in the rear of a wooded area, where it made camp on the cold, wet night. Again, Hoke had suffered light casualties—one killed and sixteen wounded.[53]

Following the indecisive engagement at Ox Hill, Lee eschewed further attempts to flank Pope, and instead decided to move his army into Maryland. As Branch prepared his brigade to take leave of Virginia, he took stock of its unheralded accomplishments, pointing out, "I would not have believed without actual experience that flesh, blood and muscle could stand what we have stood—marching, fighting, and starving, almost incessantly night and day. No brigade in the service has been in as many battles, and done so much hard service as mine."

But more tough days were to follow. On September 3, Hoke marched his men through Leesburg, and two days later, they bid adieu to Virginia when they crossed the Potomac. On September 6, Branch's brigade made its way into Frederick City, Maryland. For the next several days, it camped nearby on the banks of the Monocracy River. In dire need of food, the soldiers eagerly obeyed Stonewall Jackson's order to make their way into a cornfield and fill their haversacks with roasting ears.

Worried about the Federal garrison at Harpers Ferry, Jackson prepared orders on September 9 for an attack on the town at the confluence of the Shenandoah and Potomac Rivers. Accordingly, Hoke moved out on September 11, marching his troops north to Williamsport, where they once again crossed the Potomac. Hurrying south toward Martinsburg, the Light Division quickly cleared the West Virginia town of enemy troops on September 12. On the following day, A. P. Hill's brigades could see the Bolivar Heights at Harpers Ferry. Hoke took his men down the road between Winchester and Harpers Ferry on the evening of September 14, and later that night, the brigade succeeded in driving the enemy from the cliffs of the Shenandoah. Throughout the evening, the North Carolinians lay on their arms, "ready and eager for the order to assault." When the next morning dawned, the Federal garrison, though well entrenched, found itself completely surrounded. With the Light Division on its rear, John G. Walker's division on Loudoun Heights, and Lafayette McLaws's division on Maryland Heights, the Union command was completely surrounded. "Rapid and well-directed fire" from Jackson's artillery promptly produced a number of white flags. Without further resistance, the town fell, and Hoke and his regiment proudly witnessed the surrender of eleven thousand Union soldiers, who marched out and stacked their arms.[54]

Once Jackson's capture of Harpers Ferry was a certainty, Lee decided to make a stand in Maryland at Antietam Creek, near Sharpsburg. Leaving the Light Division to protect the newly claimed prize, Jackson rushed the rest of his corps north into Maryland, where Lee assembled his army on September 15 and 16. At dawn on Wednesday, September 17, Major General Joseph Hooker stormed Lee's left at Sharpsburg, thus ushering forth the single bloodiest day of fighting on either of the American continents. For eight hours, Lee's forty-thousand-man army fought gallantly against McClellan's seventy-five thousand soldiers, but by 3 P.M., the Union army had a victory in its grasp. From a knoll near his headquarters, Lee watched in despair as his officers attempted in vain to rally their faltering commands. When he gazed beyond the field of death, Lee saw columns of troops approaching from the south, and at that moment, he believed the battle was lost. Noticing that Lieutenant John Ramsay had a telescope, Lee called him over and inquired, "What troops are those?" Ramsay offered his telescope to the general, but Lee held up his bandaged hands and remarked, "Can't use it." Dismounting from his horse, the lieutenant used the glass and reported, "They are flying the United States flag." These were the troops of Burnside, who had finally made their way across Antietam Creek. Lee pointed at a second body of troops, clad in blue uniforms and marching at right angles to Burnside's men. Fearing a similar response, he asked, "What troops are those?" Ramsay again focused his telescope and reported, "They are flying the Virginia and Confederate flags." With confidence and elation, Lee exclaimed, "It is A. P. Hill, from Harpers Ferry."[55]

Indeed, the biggest and best division of the Army of Northern Virginia had arrived in the nick of time to spare Lee and the Confederacy a disastrous defeat. In response to Lee's desperate plea for help, Hill had set the soldiers of the Light Division, many dressed in captured Union uniforms, on the march from Harpers Ferry to Sharpsburg less than an hour after McClellan had launched his assault. Covering seventeen miles at double-quick speed, the nine-hour forced march proved to be one of the most famous marches of the war.[56] As one of the officers who hastened the troops toward Sharpsburg, Hoke would forever remember the march and would use the lessons learned from it to mastermind a similar feat in May 1864.

Upon Hill's arrival, Lee was so overcome with joy that he embraced the hero of the day. Without rest from the fatiguing march, Branch's brigade was rushed onto the battlefield and fought "with courage and tenacity rarely equalled and never surpassed." Hill directed the Twenty-eighth North Carolina to repel Burnside's skirmishers, who were approaching through a cornfield. At the same time, the Thirty-third, Thirty-seventh, and Seventh North Carolina worked on Burnside's flank, three times driving the enemy back. In the heat of the action, forty-two-year-old general Lawrence O'Bryan Branch fell mortally wounded. Of the many Confederate casualties at Sharpsburg, none was more significant than the loss of Branch.[57]

When Branch fell, his senior colonel, James H. Lane, assumed command of the brigade. After sunset, he found Hoke and the other two regiments with him posted behind a stone fence. The bloodbath was over; the Confederate line had held. Although Union sharpshooters annoyed the Confederates throughout the night, the Federals "had been so roughly handled" that they were not about to attack. For most of September 18, Hoke's soldiers lay low behind the stone wall on the field that had claimed more than twenty-three thousand casualties in less than twelve hours. With three killed and sixteen wounded, Hoke's losses were minimal, considering the dreadful fight in which his regiment had been involved.

Lee's army began retiring across the Potomac that night, but Hoke did not cross until late the following day because Branch's (Lane's) brigade constituted part of Lee's rear guard. Although their position was fraught with peril, the North Carolinians saw every wagon and ambulance safely over the river. While protecting the retreat, they rescued some wounded Georgia soldiers who had been abandoned by their command. Finally, when the time came for Lane's men to cross the river into Virginia near Shepherdstown, Union artillery rained shells upon them.[58]

Once across the river, there was still no time to rest. On Saturday morning, September 20, Lee ordered the Light Division back to Shepherdstown, where Federal cavalry and infantry forces were threatening to pursue the retiring Confederates. Artillery batteries on each side of the river were booming when Hill arrived. He immediately sent the brigades of William Dorsey Pender, Gregg, and Edward L. Thomas to the front line to face the onslaught of Porter's two divisions. Pender was suddenly flanked, and Lane rushed his brigade forward. On the "extremely hot" day, Hoke and his comrades entered the battle "in the face of a storm of round shot, shell and grape." Upon reaching the top of a hill near the river ferry, they "roared a yell and poured a deadly fire into the enemy who fled precipitately and in great confusion to the river." Though "exposed to the heaviest cannonading of the war" and the flaming muskets of Union sharpshooters, the Tar Heels followed up on their advantage and secured the riverbank. Many fleeing Federals either drowned or were shot as they attempted to cross back over the river on an old dam just above the ferry. In the skirmish, none of Hoke's men were killed and only ten were wounded.[59]

Hoke's battle-weary warriors were now due a long period of rest and relaxation. This they received. With Lane's regiment, they went into camp first at Snicker's Gap and then at Bunker Hill, near Winchester, with the rest of Jackson's corps.[60] In a span of six months, the men of the Thirty-third North Carolina had been transformed from green troops to the most battle-tested soldiers in the Army of Northern Virginia. The man who had masterminded this transformation was Colonel Robert F. Hoke. He had gallantly and skillfully led his regiment in a dozen major battles and engagements. As commander of the Thirty-third North Carolina, he had demonstrated that he could lead and motivate fighting men under the most adverse of circumstances.

But while his troops were in camp during the autumn of 1862, the time came for Hoke to bid them farewell. Colonel Avery had been released from the Union prison at Johnson's Island and was about to be exchanged and returned to his old command. Accordingly, Hoke was transferred to the command of the Twenty-first North Carolina. New challenges awaited this bright young star of the Confederacy. In the coming months, he would be equal to those challenges, and a wreath would be added to the three stars that now adorned his collar.

CHAPTER 4

"How Are You, General Hoke?"

When Hoke arrived at the camp of the brigade of Isaac R. Trimble in October to assume command of the Twenty-first North Carolina, he found himself thrust into a new role—brigade commander. At Second Manassas, an exploding bullet had severely mangled the leg of Brigadier General Trimble, thereby incapacitating the sixty-year-old Marylander for many months. Consequently, although Hoke was a newcomer to Trimble's brigade, he was its ranking officer and accordingly took temporary command. A mixed brigade, Hoke's command contained soldiers from several states. In addition to the Twenty-first North Carolina, the brigade included the Twelfth Georgia, the Twenty-first Georgia, the Fifteenth Alabama, and the First Battalion North Carolina Sharpshooters. Most of the soldiers in these regiments were by this time battle-tested veterans, having experienced the same triumphs and hardships as Hoke on the bloody battle-fields of Virginia and Maryland.[1]

Like the other troops encamped at Bunker Hill, Hoke's men engaged in "eating, sleeping, and frolicking" throughout October, a month free of combat. But there was yet time for activities of a serious nature. Gratified that their lives had been spared during a summer of almost constant warfare, humbled by the ultimate sacrifices of their comrades in arms who would never fight again, and not yet hardened by the grim spectacle of the barbarity and inhumanity of war, the Confederate soldiers directed their attention to matters spiritual during the mild, bright days of early autumn. A great religious awakening took hold in the many brigade camps in the forests of the valleys of Virginia. Trimble's (Hoke's) brigade was reported to be among the first to hold the nightly services that drew large audiences of fighting men. A frequent visitor to the revival meetings in Hoke's camp was Stonewall Jackson himself. Making his way through the woods from his headquarters, the devout Presbyterian elder would quietly take a seat on a stump or a log and listen as "hundreds of strong, manly voices poured out a volume of rich melody on the evening air."[2]

After Burnside replaced McClellan as commander of the Army of the Potomac on November 8, it took Lee but a week to surmise that the Federals aspired to attack Fredericksburg. Despite the looming offensive by Burnside, Hoke's troops and the other soldiers in Jackson's Corps spent most of November much the same way they had October—in athletic games, revivals, and "frolicking and courting." Over the last ten days of the month, Jackson hurried his divisions toward Fredericksburg in order to prevent Burnside from slipping across the Rappahannock en route to Richmond.[3]

When Jackson's forces reached Fredericksburg on December 1, the general posted the division of Major General Richard Ewell, under the command of Brigadier General Jubal A. Early, at Buckner's Neck, located just north of Port Royal and eighteen miles southeast of Fredericksburg. Joining Hoke's four regiments in Early's division were Alexander Robert Lawton's brigade of Georgians, commanded by Colonel E. N. Atkinson, Early's brigade of Virginians, commanded by Colonel J. A. Walker, and the Louisiana Tigers of Brigadier General Harry T. Hays. The division monitored activity along the river. About the same time, Burnside deployed his three grand divisions under Edwin V. Sumner, William B. Franklin, and Joseph Hooker along the north bank of the Rappahannock parallel to Fredericksburg. Union artillery batteries enjoyed the benefits of Stafford Heights, located close enough to the bank to offer a commanding position. Located on the south side of the river, the city rested on a narrow strip of lowland backed by a number of hills and ridges, most notably Marye's Heights and Lee's Hill. Below Fredericksburg, the river bottoms gradually widened to almost two miles in front of the range of hills. Two canal-like water courses—Hazel Run and Deep Run—flowed through these bottoms just south of the city.[4]

Before dawn on December 11, signal guns thundered the news that the Union army had begun to move. Burnside's forces started laying pontoon bridges across the Rappahannock at Fredericksburg in preparation for their offensive. General Lee was quick to conclude that "no effectual opposition could be made to the construction of bridges or the passage of the river." At the city, the river, although navigable to steamboats, was extremely narrow—no more than three hundred yards wide at any point. Moreover, the Union artillery high above the north shore posed great danger to any Confederates who attempted to contest a landing. As a result, Lee decided to fight it out with Burnside after he made it across.[5]

Jubal Early received orders from Stonewall Jackson on the afternoon of Friday, December 12, to promptly move his division to Hamilton's Crossing, a point on the Richmond, Fredericksburg, and Potomac Railroad approximately four miles below the city. A dense fog hovered over the river as Early rushed his brigades north throughout the long, cold night that followed. Dry cedar fence rails were set ablaze on both sides of the road to Fredericksburg to afford light and heat during the march. Hoke rode at the head of his brigade with Captain A. S. Hamilton, who at the time was the temporary commander of the Twenty-first Georgia. With battle looming, Hoke was anxious to learn about the fighting characteristics of his new command. Turning to Captain Hamilton, he remarked, "I am a stranger to your brigade. They have the reputation of being good fighters but I wish to know whether they are impetuous or stolid in action." In a most direct response, Hamilton quipped, "We dash right into them; we either promote our commanders or get them shot. I hear Burnside is crossing the river. If you are the right kind of stuff and will lead, we will make you Brigadier General Hoke tomorrow, or get you killed." Never one to shirk a challenge, Hoke remarked, "That's the kind of talk I like to hear."[6]

Hamilton's remarks proved ever so accurate. Using the low-lying fog to their advantage, the Union commanders sent their soldiers over the pontoons and into the streets of Fredericksburg throughout the miserable night and the next morning. To counter the advance, Lee put Longstreet's corps on the left and Jackson's on the right. Longstreet's position was located on the heights behind the city, while Jackson's line protected the wide, flat plains below the city.

About two hours before daybreak on December 13, Hoke and his men arrived at Hamilton's Crossing, where they halted and stacked arms after being informed that Early's division would form a part of the second line. On the front line facing Franklin's fifty-thousand-man assault force were the men of Hoke's old division, that of A. P. Hill. To the rear of Hill, Early deployed Hays on his right on the west side of the railroad. To the left of Hays were Atkinson and Walker. Still farther to the left on the second line was Jackson's division, commanded by Brigadier General W. B. Taliaferro. Hoke's position rested upon the railroad immediately behind Hays. Directly across the railroad from Hoke was the reserve division of D. H. Hill.[7]

As the December Saturday dawned, the thick fog refused to yield its grip, and neither army could see the other. After marching all night, some of Hoke's men were attempting to catch a few winks of sleep before the onslaught when the big Union guns atop Stafford Heights suddenly began to loosen up, thereby heralding the Battle of Fredericksburg. One of Hoke's junior officers, Captain James C. Nisbet of the Twenty-first Georgia, complained that the barrage woke him "from a deep dream of peace." Initially, the shot and shell from the blazing Yankee field guns passed fifteen or twenty feet over the heads of Hoke's soldiers, but when the enemy artillerists lowered their aim, the Confederates were forced to lie prostrate in hopes of avoiding the murderous blasts. Even then, Hoke reported that he "lost a number of men in this place." After being pinned down for more than two hours by the furious shelling, Major Rufus Wharton, First Battalion North Carolina Sharpshooters, reported that "under such circumstances the order to advance was a welcome one."[8]

When the fog began to lift shortly after 9 A.M., Lee could see "a large force moving in line of battle against Jackson." Major John Pelham opened up the batteries of Stuart's Horse Artillery against the "dense masses," causing the Federals "to waver and retreat in confusion." In the early afternoon, the Federals, under cover of a furious cannonade, charged Jackson's front line with three waves of troops. This time, the Confederate artillery could not scatter them, and they pressed on into the face of A. P. Hill's waiting infantrymen. Lee noted that the ensuing "contest became fierce and bloody." The brigades of J. H. Lane and J. J. Archer from Hill's division successfully repulsed the frontal assault against them, but a gap between their lines allowed enemy penetration. Couriers were dispatched from the front with urgent pleas for reinforcements. Early, who had just been ordered by Jackson to ready his division to move to the right, responded to the emergency by sending Atkinson's brigade to Archer's aid. Learning that still another brigade was needed to seal the gap, Early ordered Walker forward. Hoke was then moved ahead to man Early's left flank, adjacent to Hays's brigade. As Atkinson and Walker were rushing forward, Lane's entire brigade and Archer's left were giving way. Brigadier General Maxcy Gregg's brigade, also moving to seal the gap, was thrown into confusion, but Gregg was able to rally his men. No sooner had Hoke pulled his brigade in place beside Hays than he was ordered to the front to support Archer, obliquing to the right as he moved.[9]

Atkinson and Walker advanced rapidly and with success, driving enemy columns out of the woods and across the railroad. As Hoke rushed forward to join the desperate attempt to turn the tide of battle, General Gregg took a bullet which passed through his spine. Though the wound robbed him of speech and proved to be mortal, the forty-eight-year-old South Carolinian pulled himself up by a sapling and urged his men forward by waving his hat as life ebbed from his body.

When Hoke arrived on the front line, he found Federals atop a hill

from which Archer, without ammunition, had been driven. In an instant,
Hoke chased the opposing brigade from the hill and into a long, deep
railroad cut. Then, in Captain Nisbet's words, "Colonel Hoke ordered a
charge of the whole brigade, which he led gallantly." Of the charge, Hoke
wrote,

> I saw that it would not do to allow them to remain in the rail-
> road as that point commanded a large portion of our
> intrenchments at the edge of the woods, and that I would lose
> from their sharpshooters; so I immediately ordered a charge,
> and drove them from this place, killing about 200 and wound-
> ing a large number, 100 of whom fell into my hands. I must
> have wounded quite a number of the enemy at this point who
> were able to make their escape, as I was immediately upon them.
> I also captured about 300 prisoners.[10]

Hoke's men were now flushed with victory, and it was difficult to stop
them. One of his Alabama officers, William C. Oates, recounted, "The
brigade swept everything before it in handsome style. . . . We had men in
front a-going, and there was no halting. The charge was kept up for a
quarter of a mile, just as though we were going through Burnside's lines
to the river until we reached a ditch and a fence in close range of quite a
number of federal batteries."

This fearless charge by Hoke almost became his last, as all at once, enemy artillery opened up a heavy fire. Hoke was riding about his lines when
a shell glanced off his mount's head, nearly severing the animal's ear. Startled
by the missile, the horse fell to its knees, causing Hoke to fall. There was
no chance for him to recover as the panic-stricken steed began to run with
Hoke's foot caught in the stirrup. Before he was seriously injured, however, some of his soldiers grabbed the bridle and ended the ordeal. Though
he "seemed addled for the moment by his fall," Hoke "recovered his self-
possession" just in time to realize that he had gone too far to the front.
Fearing that an enemy brigade fast approaching down the river road would
flank him on his right, Hoke ordered his brigade to retire. Impressed with
his young colonel's presence of mind in the face of peril, Jubal Early noted,
"He advanced his brigade to a fence some distance in front of the railroad,

but perceiving his danger of being flanked by the enemy, who had brought up large, fresh columns, I sent an order to him to fall back to the original line, which order, however, he anticipated by retiring in good order, leaving two regiments and a battalion in the railroad, and occupying the trench on the crest of the hill with the two other regiments."[11]

Hoke and Walker maintained their positions on the front line until darkness fell over the battlefield. All seemed quiet at sunset when Jubal Early was surprised to see D. H. Hill's division being moved toward the front. Upon encountering Hill, Early was informed that Jackson had issued orders for the advancement of the whole line. Early spurred his horse and galloped over to Hoke's position, where he found General Jackson, who confirmed his intention to advance. Anxious to destroy Burnside's army, Lee and Jackson had decided to launch a night assault. However, before the necessary guns could be put in place, Union artillery renewed its fire and, according to Jackson, "so completely swept our front as to satisfy me that the proposed movement should be abandoned."[12]

After the orders for the night attack were countermanded, Jackson instructed Early to pull his division back and to provide rest and rations for his combat-weary soldiers as soon as A. P. Hill's division returned to the front. However, relief was not immediately forthcoming. Until just before daybreak on December 15, Hoke kept his brigade on the front line at the position it had occupied at the close of the battle. Although there were some skirmishes and artillery fire on Sunday, December 14, the two armies spent a day of relative quiet under a flag of truce tending to their dead and wounded. Union casualties totaled 12,653, while Confederate losses were less than half that total. Hoke's brigade reported 8 killed and 98 wounded.[13]

When D. H. Hill's division moved forward to relieve Early in the predawn hours of December 15, Hoke was delighted to see his old friend and former commander, Major General Hill. Two days earlier, Hill had been with Jackson when Stonewall hurried to Hamilton's Crossing upon learning that his line had been broken. There, the two had watched Hoke's masterful charge. Hailing the young officer whom he had watched grow into a soldier at Bethel, Hill now called out, "How are you, General Hoke?" Taken aback, Hoke responded, "General Hill, you are poking fun at me."

In a tone and manner that evinced sincerity, Hill replied, "No, I am not. Jackson witnessed that charge!" Nothing would be official, however, for more than a month. Nevertheless, at Fredericksburg, Hoke had demonstrated his ability to handle a brigade on a regular basis. Lee complimented Hoke's "short and decisive charge." Jackson praised Hoke for his "courage and patriotism," while Early touted his "coolness, courage, and intelligence."[14]

On the night of December 15, Burnside's army crossed to the north side of the river and pulled up its pontoon bridges. The fighting was over for the winter. With the enemy moving away from Fredericksburg, Early was ordered on the morning of December 16 to move his division to Port Royal to monitor the movements of the Federal army. Soon, his brigade settled into its winter quarters on the banks of the Rappahannock sixteen miles south of Fredericksburg.

In a letter to Confederate secretary of war James A. Seddon dated December 29, 1862, Jubal Early officially recommended Hoke for promotion:

> I respectfully recommend Colonel Robert F. Hoke of North Carolina, who is colonel of the 21st North Carolina Regiment for promotion as Brigadier General in the Provisional Army of the Confederate States. Colonel Hoke has had command of Trimble's Brigade in this Division since about the 1st of October last, and has shown himself eminently qualified to command a Brigade, both in camp, on the march, and in action. He is an officer of great energy and industry, and attends most diligently to his duties on all occasions. In the late action at Fredericksburg, he led his Brigade against the enemy who had broken through our front line on the right, driving him back, and capturing several hundred prisoners, and took and held a position in advance of the position first held by our troops. In this action he displayed the most conspicuous personal gallantry and coolness, and the ability to command of a very high order. It gives me great pleasure to be able to recommend this officer.[15]

Stonewall Jackson heartily endorsed Early's recommendation: "Respectfully forwarded and recommended. Col. Hoke is an officer of great promise. He behaved very gallantly in the last battle and has been in command of the brigade."

Official action was forthcoming. January 19, 1863, was a warm Monday. It was Robert E. Lee's fifty-sixth birthday, and he gave Hoke a special present. On that day, the commander of the Army of Northern Virginia issued Special Orders No. 19, whereby he reorganized his army and made official a number of promotions. Specifically, Hoke was promoted to brigadier general. Thus, in just twenty-one months, Hoke had steadily ascended the ladder of command, holding almost every rank on his climb. He had gained each promotion not through political influence or favoritism, as did some officers during the war, but by skill, devotion to duty, courage, boldness in battle tempered by modesty off the field, and meritorious leadership. When the news of Hoke's promotion reached Lincolnton, his friends, full of pride, hurried to break the grand tidings to his mother. They found her busy knitting at the Hoke homestead. She received the joyous announcement quietly and after a long pause placidly remarked, "Bobbie always was a good boy." She then went back to her knitting.[16]

About the time Lee announced the changes in his army, Burnside was beginning another unsuccessful attempt to advance across the Rappahannock. Less than a week later, his "Mud March" ended in abysmal failure, and Abraham Lincoln replaced him with Joseph Hooker as commander of the Army of the Potomac. With Union forces now completely demoralized, Hoke was able to turn his attention to the organization of his new brigade. Isaac Trimble, still recuperating from his leg wound, had been raised to major general, and Hoke had been given permanent command of his brigade. However, the composition of the brigade changed dramatically as a result of Lee's special orders. Hoke's new brigade was an all–North Carolina unit made up of the Sixth, Twenty-first, Fifty-fourth, and Fifty-seventh North Carolina and the First North Carolina Battalion Sharpshooters. Between January 23 and 25, the old brigade was broken up, and the regiments of the new brigade were ordered to make their way to Hoke's headquarters, located fourteen miles downstream from Fredericksburg.[17]

Soldiers in the regiments that were leaving and coming to Hoke had mixed emotions about the changes. Some members of the three North Carolina regiments just assigned to Hoke did not relish a march of "over

20 miles thru the mud" to reach their new camp. Colonel Isaac Erwin Avery, the younger brother of Hoke's immediate commander at New Bern, was opposed to the transfer of the Sixth North Carolina. Although he did not doubt Hoke's valor, Avery questioned his youth and expressed reservations about joining him: "Bob Hoke was appointed a Brigadier a few days since. I do not want to leave this tent, I do not want to leave this Brigade (to go there) & I am dead against leaving this Division, and I must say I do not care to join 'old Jack's foot cavalry.'"[18]

On the other hand, soldiers of the Twenty-first North Carolina, the only holdover regiment in Hoke's brigade, were saddened by the departure of the regiments with which they had fought on many battlefields. Captain William J. Pfohl of Company L of the Twenty-first North Carolina lamented, "The old regiments were very averse to leaving us, as an attachment had been formed cemented by the many bloody fields on which we had stood up for each other side by side, & an effort was made to keep them here with us but without success."[19]

The men in Hoke's new regiments were battle-tested veterans—many members of the Sixth North Carolina had served in the army since First Manassas. Like good soldiers, and despite any lingering reservations, they trudged through the rain and mud to Hoke's camp. There, they began to forge a close relationship with their new commander that would grow over the next sixteen months while the brigade shared in the triumphs and disasters of the Army of Northern Virginia. Hoke not only possessed the sterling qualities of character that would inspire his new command, but he had the "looks" of a general, as one flattering description at this time revealed: "Gen. Hoke is nearly six feet in height, stands erect, has dark hair and dark eyes, and is noted as a high-toned Christian gentleman, having been for several years as a communicant in the Protestant Episcopal Church. He is a pious, praying man. We record this fact with pleasure, and on it we wound our hope of his rising still higher, and endearing himself to the people of North Carolina and the whole Confederacy."[20]

As the fortunes of war would dictate, Colonel Avery and General Hoke would serve together for less than four months and would fight together in just one battle. Nevertheless, in that short time, Avery came to admire in Hoke all the qualities that had led to his stellar rise in the army. And the time would come when Avery proved himself willing to lay down his life in his commander's stead at the head of the brigade he reluctantly joined.

The rainy weather that had made the march to Hoke's camp muddy and miserable continued to plague the soldiers as they went about building shelter in their new camp. On Wednesday, January 28, the weather grew more harsh, as "it snowed all day long." When the soldiers awoke the next morning, ten inches of snow were on the ground. Three clear, sunny days including "a pritty spring day" followed.

As the snow melted, the resulting mire made sanitary conditions in the army camps south of Fredericksburg almost intolerable. Soap became a precious commodity. Its scarcity was a problem in all the brigades. Hoke's quick actions demonstrated his concern for the well-being of his soldiers and did much to gain the respect of the newly arrived regiments. Always resourceful, Hoke dispatched a detail of his soldiers to Lincoln County to pick up a quantity of pots and utensils. When they returned, Hoke used his background in industry to convert the dead animals around his camp into a vast quantity of soap. Upset about Hoke's oversupply of soap and unaware of how it had come about, a Texas general lodged a protest with General Lee, claiming that the authorities were showing partiality to Hoke. When Lee summoned Hoke to his headquarters for an explanation, the young general invited his commander to ride over to his camp. Lee accepted the invitation, and when the two generals reached Hoke's head quarters, the "secret" source was revealed. Hoke informed Lee that he had more soap than he could ever use and expressed a willingness to send wagonloads of the product to other brigades. Delighted with Hoke's ingenuity, Lee returned to his tent, where he issued orders for the complaining general to report to Hoke for a lesson in soap making.[21]

Throughout February, Hoke kept his brigade at the camp on the river just north of Port Royal. Winter passed quietly without the imminent threat of combat, and picket duty along the south shore of the Rappahannock was the closest his troops came to engaging the Union army. Snow fell frequently during the month—on February 5, 10, 11, 17, 22, and 23. Hoke's men, as did the soldiers of the other brigades, took advantage of

General Robert F. Hoke

the snow to wage a "winter war" on friendly camps. Even Jubal Early, now a major general, got into the act as official reporter of the snowball fights that occurred within view of his headquarters. With a deep snow on the ground, Hoke's brigade, well armed with snowballs, launched a strike on Lawton's brigade. Personally leading his warriors, Hoke advanced against the Georgians, commanded by Colonel Clement Evans, and enjoyed initial success against the larger brigade. Early reasoned that the Georgians, recently up from Savannah, were not accustomed to snow and that Hoke's men were more experienced. Making a bold dash, Hoke joined his North Carolinians in the "rebel yell" as they mercilessly pelted Evans's men with well-pressed balls of ice and snow. Parodying the reports he had written after many a battle, Early noted in his memoirs that "Evans's men gave way in utter confusion and rout." But once Hoke took possession of the "enemy" camp, it was time for the Georgians to re-form and regain their former position. A vigorous counterattack sent Hoke's soldiers on a fast retreat. Hoke was taken prisoner, and though "Evans's men did not deem it prudent to press their victory too far," they did not release the general until he had "been well wallowed in the snow."[22]

On the "beautyfull" day of March 3, Hoke began moving his regiments back to Fredericksburg, where they set up camp "about 3 miles" below the town and "about 1¼ miles" from Hamilton's Crossing. The fun and games of February gave way to more serious picket duties throughout March and April. As they manned the riverbank in the cold rain and snow that fell periodically until mid-April, the Confederates could see Hooker's army massing on the north side of the river. Telltale signs of a coming enemy offensive were apparent: hundreds of troop tents continued to spring up; Union supply trains rumbled in; drums pounded; and observation balloons ascended over the river.[23]

As soldiers were prone to do in times of uncertainty, Hoke's men looked to their faith for strength and comfort in the early spring of 1863. Religious services were well attended. On Saturday, April 18, Hoke welcomed Stonewall Jackson's chaplain, the Reverend Beverly Tucker Lacy, to the brigade camp. Lacy preached to the North Carolinians from the third chapter of Hebrews: "Today if ye will hear his voice, harden not your hearts."

"How Are You, General Hoke?"

Hoke's soldiers spent much of Sunday, April 26—the eve of the commencement of Hooker's spring offensive—in religious services. A chaplain from a Virginia regiment provided evening inspiration from the eighteenth chapter of Proverbs: "There is a friend that sticketh closer than a brother."[24]

When Hooker put his massive army on the move in drizzling rain at sunrise on Monday, April 27, he had at his disposal 134,000 soldiers. Lee's army, depleted because a portion of Longstreet's corps had been detached for service elsewhere, consisted of no more that 60,000 troops. Hooker's complicated plan called for three corps under the command of Major Generals Oliver O. Howard, Henry Slocum, and George G. Meade to cross the river at the narrows north of Fredericksburg. Once across, most of these troops were to march west to a crossroads in the wilderness called Chancellorsville in hopes of striking Lee's rear. In the meantime, Major Generals John Sedgwick and John Reynolds would move their corps over the Rappahannock in a feint against Marye's Heights. In addition, Major General George Stoneman would use his 10,000 cavalrymen to get behind Lee to sever communication and supply lines.[25]

As had been the case in mid-December, fog shrouded the Rappahannock at Fredericksburg during the nights and early mornings of late April. Under cover of the fog, a Union brigade rowed across the river in the predawn hours of April 29 and overwhelmed the men of the Fifty-fourth North Carolina, who were on picket duty near the mouth of Deep Run. Bridges were promptly laid, and a Federal division with artillery was quickly across the river. A lone horseman galloped through Hoke's camp to spread the alarm. Private Bartlett Yancey Malone of the Sixth North Carolina described the urgency of the moment: "It was not meney minutes untill the man come back and sais Boys you had better get up we will have a fight hear to reckly and I commenced geting up and before I got my close on they commenced beating the long roal and it was not but a minnet or too until I herd the Adgentent hollow fall in with armes."[26]

After dispatching news of the crossing to Jackson, and without awaiting orders, Early rushed Hoke and his other brigades to the front near where his division had fought in December. He positioned the troops in a line along the railroad extending from Hamilton's Crossing on the right to

Deep Run on the left. Three regiments of skirmishers, including Hoke's Fifty-seventh North Carolina, were moved farther to the front on River Road. Overcoming stiff resistance offered by the Thirteenth Georgia, Sedgwick's forces effected a second crossing one mile to the south after 10 A.M. As waves of Union troops poured ashore throughout the day, additional divisions from Jackson's corps were brought forward. Although the invading forces made no offer of battle on April 29, "the pickets fought sum . . . and a good deal of canonading was don," according to Private Malone. All the while, Hooker's army was crossing the river in force to the north en route to its showdown with Lee at Chancellorsville.[27]

Rain started to fall again that evening and continued until noon the following day, adding to the misery of the tense soldiers. Before daylight on April 30, the Fifty-seventh North Carolina was relieved from the skirmish line and joined the rest of Hoke's brigade behind the breastworks. Union artillery began to loosen up about 10 A.M. and maintained its fire until nightfall. However, there was little fighting between the infantry forces. With large masses of Union troops fast approaching on his left flank and rear, Lee ordered Jackson to dispatch most of his army toward Chancellorsville that afternoon. To hold the line at Fredericksburg, Lee and Jackson left behind Early's division, Brigadier General William Barksdale's brigade of Mississippians, and General W. N. Pendleton's reserve artillery. Before he left for Chancellorsville, Lee implored Early to keep the enemy at bay and to conceal the weakness of the Confederate army.[28]

Alone at Fredericksburg, Early faced a formidable task. With forty thousand Federals in two corps in his front, Early was forced to defend the town and a six-mile line with Hoke's forces and the other four brigades left behind. Barksdale's brigade occupied Fredericksburg and the heights behind the town. To support the Mississippians, artillery was placed on Marye's Heights and Lee's Hill. Early stretched his division down the long line south of Fredericksburg, but he was forced to leave a gap between Deep Run and the foot of Lee's Hill.[29]

When the fog lifted on Friday, May 1, Hoke's pickets from the Sixth North Carolina found that "the Yankees had a very strong line of Scirmishers

[with]in about 5 hundred yards of ours." Despite the proximity of the enemy, "there was no fighting with small arms but right smart cannonading at our right near Hamilton crossing" on this "very warm" spring day. During the calm before the storm, some of Hoke's men "had a fine time frying and eating" herring. Optimism prevailed in the camp during the evening. In his diary, Private Samuel W. Eaton of the Fifty-seventh North Carolina recorded, "The troops seemed to be in good spirits that night, there was a great deal of holering along the lines." While Early's brigades settled down for what proved to be a quiet night at Fredericksburg, little did they know that Lee and Jackson were holding their fateful council of war in a wooded area at Chancellorsville where the crucial decision was made to split Lee's army.[30]

Saturday, May 2, broke clear and was, according to Private Malone, "a very pretty day." About daybreak, the Sixth North Carolina returned from picket duty and rejoined the remainder of the brigade in the breastworks. At 11 A.M., Colonel R. H. Chilton of General Lee's staff arrived at Lee's Hill with a verbal order directing Early to immediately move his entire force, less one brigade and Pendleton's artillery, toward Chancellorsville. Chilton had misunderstood Lee's orders, and as a result, Hoke's brigade and two others were sent on a wild-goose chase in the direction of Chancellorsville. Eight miles into the march, Early was informed that the enemy was advancing in great numbers against the heights at Fredericksburg. In an instant, he decided to return to aid the beleaguered troops on the Rappahannock, and he promptly dispatched his adjutant general to inform Lee of his decision.[31]

By 10 P.M., Early had all of his forces back in position at Fredericksburg. During his absence, Sedgwick had brought the remainder of his corps across the river. Confederate skirmishers were sent forward, but the night passed without incident. However, before daybreak on May 3, Barksdale rode out from his position at Marye's Heights to inform Early that the enemy had laid pontoons across the river and that troops were pouring into the town. In response to Barksdale's plea for assistance, Hays's brigade was ordered to support the Mississippians on the right.

As the new day dawned, Early saw that he had other problems—the north shore of the river was now devoid of enemy troops, and a heavy force of Federals was crossing below the mouth of Deep Run. Just after first light, the Yankees began a strong demonstration against Early's left, anchored by Hoke. Combined guns from the Confederate artillery and infantry served to silence the demonstration. Thereafter, Hoke's position at Deep Run was relatively quiet for most of the day. Private Eaton described the action: "We took a pop at them occasionally so did they at us when we took a peep at them from our breastworks."[32]

Early, however, had problems upriver. After gallantly repulsing several Federal assaults, Barksdale and Hays were overpowered at Marye's Heights and forced to retreat to a position approximately two miles behind Lee's Hill. Sedgwick began to push toward Chancellorsville at 2 P.M., but two hours later, he came face to face with four brigades under Major General Lafayette McLaws and the brigade of Brigadier General Cadmus M. Wilcox at Salem Church, four miles west of Fredericksburg. Dispatched by Lee to reinforce Early, McLaws and Wilcox stung Sedgwick and halted his advance. More Confederate reinforcements were on the way as Lee took advantage of Hooker's hesitation at Chancellorsville. Hoke was able to maintain his position until evening, when Private Eaton reported, "We retreated double quick across the bottom towards our camp, but halted at the woods. It was in consequence of the enemy taking the heights and some pieces of artillery & was supposed to have them ranged upon us." After his retreat, Hoke rejoined the division, where Early was maturing his plans to retake Marye's Heights and his position at Fredericksburg on the morrow.[33]

Monday, May 4, was to be a bittersweet day in the military career of Robert F. Hoke. Late in the afternoon, he would lead a searing charge against Sedgwick that would help ensure Lee's victory over Hooker, but that charge would almost end his days as a Confederate officer.

The day started well. Hoke and Hays moved across Hazel Run to flank Major General John Gibbon at Marye's Heights, while Early, with Barksdale and two other brigades, offered a direct assault. Private Eaton posted the results: "The Mississippians took the heights back again in the morning & did it without much fighting & but little loss." Another of Hoke's soldiers in the Fifty-seventh North Carolina oversimplified the ease of the recapture of Marye's Heights: "We . . . marched back to Fredericksburg where we built fires all over the woods and gave the Rebel Yell so loud that it frightened the Yankees away."

Positioning the brigades of Barksdale and William Smith to hold his gain, Early marched the brigades of Hoke, Hays, and John B. Gordon "in a line of battle through the bushes, & over hills and hollows" and deployed them "at the foot of a hill & at the edge of some woods" adjacent to the right flank of Major General Richard Anderson's division, fresh from Chancellorsville. By the afternoon, the Confederate line stretched west from the heights of Fredericksburg in a semicircle to Salem Church. Hoke was positioned on Early's left flank adjacent to the Georgia brigade of A. R. Wright along an unfinished railroad near the south end of the semicircle. Sedgwick's forces, now slightly outnumbered, were located to the north in a smaller semicircle.[34]

At 6 P.M., about sunset, the Confederate offensive against Sedgwick began. At the sound of the long-awaited signal, Hoke led his men up a slight ridge at Downman's Farm, where he was greeted by "a strong line of sharpshooters occupying the crest of the ridge and the house and fencing around Downman's yards, with heavy batteries in the hills in their rear." One of Hoke's chaplains, the Reverend John Paris, chronicled the onset of the brilliant charge: "Hoke's brigade moved to the attack with great gallantry under a most destructive fire of infantry and artillery. The prospect before them seemed to be that of certain destruction and death; but like true Carolinians they know how to bleed and still fight. On they rushed through the fearful storm of fire, assailed and scattered the enemy's first line in the wildest confusion and disorder and took the position thus yielded."[35] Jubal Early also recounted the gallantry of the charge: "Hoke moved at once across the plateau in his front between Downman's house and Hazel Run, then down the slope, across the valley, and up the steep ascent of the next ridge towards the Plank road, driving the enemy's skirmishers before him, while the guns at Guest's house played upon his advancing line without disturbing his beautiful order."[36]

On the approach to the Union earthworks, Hoke, on horseback, led his troops forward at a "determined pace." As they closed in on the enemy, the North Carolinians lifted up a yell "so well known to Confederate ears," offered a round of musketry, closed ranks, and charged with bayonets. All along Hoke's line, cheers of joy rang out as the Federal lines gave way, causing confusion in their rear. According to one account, General Lee, who was supervising the overall attack, witnessed Hoke's charge and asked "who the young man was leading that gallant brigade."

The charge was beginning to take on the appearance of a general rout when suddenly Hoke was shot from his horse. In the heat of the fight, the seriously wounded general continued to rally his men. Without realizing the gravity of his wound, he remounted and pushed his forces forward until he found himself far ahead of any other Confederate brigades. Weakened by the loss of blood, he fell to the ground. A minie ball had shattered his shoulder bone near the joint.[37]

After Hoke fell, his brigade, "without anyone to direct its movement at that particular crisis," came into contact with Hays's brigade. Confusion resulted, and although Colonel Avery assumed command of Hoke's troops, both brigades temporarily lost their organization. Early arrived to reform his line and dispatched the two brigades to reinforce other positions.[38]

The Battle of Chancellorsville and the attendant fight at Fredericksburg were over on the night of May 4. Within two days, Hooker's defeated army would be gone. In the wake of the Confederate victory, Hoke's soldiers counted their casualties. In a letter written on the battlefield, Private William F. Wagner told his wife, "Dear, I never saw such a time since God made me I hope and pray to God they soone will quit it we routted them completely. Dear we lost a good many men on Boothe sides." The brigade's casualties totaled 35 killed and 195 wounded.

Among the most seriously wounded was the general himself. After he was transported from the battlefield for medical care, surgeons were called in. Upon their examination of the wound, they found that the ball had "entered the lateral portion of the left clavicle, passed through the shoulder joint, smashed the head of the humerus and acromion process of the scapula" and "exited in the area of the scapula." Citing the high potential for gangrene, the physicians told Hoke that it would be necessary to amputate his arm in order to save his life. Hoke adamantly refused, and though he won the battle with the surgeons, his recuperation from the wound and surgery would be ever so slow. As soon as he was able to travel, Hoke was transported home to Lincoln County, where he would remain for almost three months.[39]

When the news that Hoke had been shot at Fredericksburg reached Lincolnton, it was reported that he had been killed. Once the heartbreaking revelation was delivered to his mother, she penned the following prayer:

> Almighty God, thou who alone canst see the whole extent of my misery, canst alone cure it. Give me, I implore thee, the faith, the hope, the love, the Christian courage that I need. Enable me ever to raise my eyes to thee, the all powerful, who will give to thy children only what is for their everlasting good, and to Jesus Christ thy Son, who is our example in suffering.
>
> Raise my heart O my Father: make it like his, that I may be self denying and may fear only thy displeasure and eternal sorrow. O Lord, thou seeth the weakness and desolation of the creature of thy hand. It has no resource in itself; it wants every thing and seeks in thee with confidence the good it cannot find elsewhere.[40]

CHAPTER 5

Frustration and Heartbreak

The life-threatening wound sustained by Hoke at Fredericksburg was the first of a series of events that would keep him separated from his brigade for much of the remainder of 1863. During that frustrating eight-month period, Hoke would not be on hand when his veteran soldiers fought with distinction yet suffered heartbreak and heavy losses at Gettysburg and Rappahannock Station.[1]

Although the death of Stonewall Jackson on May 10 was an omen of the great tragedies that would befall Hoke's brigade and all of the Army of Northern Virginia in the coming months, the collective spirits of Lee's troops remained high throughout May. Following the Battle of Chancellorsville, Hoke's brigade spent the remainder of the month in relative peace and quiet at its camp near Fredericksburg. Buoyed by their recent victory, the North Carolinians were, however, spoiling for "another opportunity to measure arms with the yankees," who for the time being had left forces on the north side of the river.[2]

By the end of May, as Lee matured his plans "to transfer the war into the enemy's country" and "to compel" Union forces "to withdraw from Virginia," it became apparent that Hoke, whose shoulder was on the slow mend, would not be ready or able to lead his brigade in the ambitious expedition to his ancestral homeland. On May 27, Hoke quietly passed his twenty-sixth birthday while temporary command of his brigade devolved to his senior colonel, Isaac Erwin Avery, who had led Hoke's soldiers since the general's fall.

Avery was the consummate field officer. Descended from a prominent Burke County family that produced five Confederate officers, four of whom died as a result of the war, the thirty-four-year-old bachelor had left his plantation in western North Carolina at the outbreak of the war to assist his business associate, Colonel Charles Fisher, in the organization of the Sixth North Carolina. Receiving his baptism under fire at First Manassas, Avery, then a captain, witnessed Fisher lose his life while leading the Tar Heels into the fray at a crucial moment. Almost two years later, the time would come when Avery would be called on to make the same sacrifice. Following First Manassas, Avery was promoted to lieutenant colonel of the regiment, which proudly earned the nickname "the Bloody Sixth" because of its ferocious fighting ability. On June 18, 1862, he became colonel of the Sixth North Carolina, replacing William Dorsey Pender, who had been promoted to brigadier general. On the eve of the invasion of Pennsylvania, Isaac Erwin Avery was given the opportunity to command a brigade. Over the course of the month that followed, he would demonstrate that he was equal to the challenge and that he was ready to step up to the next level of command. A number of prominent generals, including Early, Hood, Pender, and Law, recommended Avery for promotion to general, but the cruel fate of war was to intervene all too soon.[3]

Around 11 P.M. on Thursday, June 4, Hoke's brigade struck its camp at Hamilton's Crossing and joined the other brigades in Early's division on the long march north. The invasion of the North was under way![4]

General Robert F. Hoke

On June 13, Early's division hurried to Winchester to participate in the investment of the town, which was defended by the five-thousand-man division of Major General Robert H. Milroy. During the two days of fighting that followed, Avery's command was not heavily engaged. In the early-morning darkness of June 15, Milroy slipped away, but he left behind some four thousand Federals, who quickly became captives. Faced with an immense number of prisoners, Early detached the Fifty-fourth North Carolina to assist in marching the Union soldiers to Staunton. Consequently, this regiment would not be with Avery when the brigade resumed its march toward Pennsylvania. About the same time, the brigade was further depleted when the First Battalion North Carolina Sharpshooters was assigned as provost guard for Ewell's corps.[5]

Early and Avery left Winchester with Hoke's reduced brigade on Thursday, June 18, and caught up with the rest of the division near Sheperdstown the next day. Crossing the Potomac there on June 22, the division marched into Maryland and passed through the streets of Sharpsburg, where Lee's previous northern offensive had come to a halt less than a year earlier. A day later, an important milestone was achieved: Avery and his North Carolinians defiantly crossed the Maryland state line into Pennsylvania.[6] The war was now to be waged on the soil of the enemy.

At daybreak on Sunday, June 28, Avery broke camp near East Berlin and put his men on the march for York, a city located a dozen miles away and about the same distance from the birthplace of Hoke's paternal grandparents. When the column entered the downtown streets around noon, church bells were tolling as groups of well-dressed citizens walked along the sidewalks to services. As they passed the curious onlookers, the soldiers of Hoke's and Harry T. Hays's brigades heard some children question their father, "Why Papa I thought the Rebs had horns, where are they?" Responding to the comment, the Confederates jabbed their bayonets and scoffed, "Here are our horns!"[7]

On the morning of July 1, Early was pushing the division toward Heidlersburg when he received a dispatch from Ewell directing him to move swiftly to Gettysburg. Marching seven miles in the direction of the town at a rapid pace, Hoke's soldiers could see its spires to the south by noon. As Avery and his officers discussed the booming artillery that was by this time clearly audible, John W. Daniel, Early's young adjutant general and a future United States senator, galloped up with an order to make haste to the battle raging on the west and northwest sides of town. Dropping their blankets and other unnecessary encumbrances, the North Carolinians "took up the quick step." Within a mile of Gettysburg, they could see a cloud of smoke hovering over the town and hear the raging battle. The last mile of the march was covered at double-quick speed. Upon reaching the northern suburbs, Early's division was deployed on the Confederate left. Avery placed his men on the extreme left of the division. When they halted for a well-deserved ten-minute rest, Hoke's veterans enjoyed a great vantage point from which they could watch almost the entire battle unfold before them. Colonel Hamilton Jones recalled, "From our position we could see the Confederate and Federal lines arrayed one against the other in open ground, no breastworks, no fortifications, but they stood apart in battle array and were in plain view for two miles except where the line was lost in the depression of the hills."[8]

About 3 P.M., as a refreshing mist began to fall, the order was given for Early's division to advance. Avery's three brigades moved out slowly in the face of an enemy protected by stone fences on a hill on the northeast side of town. Separating the warring factions was Rock Creek, "a small, sluggish stream" with "abrupt and rugged banks." When Hoke's soldiers reached the creek, just 200 yards from the Federal position, Union artillery opened up on them. Avery gave the order to charge, and his men scrambled through the water and surged up the hill to the stone wall protecting the enemy. On this day, Hoke's warriors were unstoppable. Captain John A. McPherson of Company E of "the Bloody Sixth" praised his comrades in a letter to Avery's father on August 3, 1863: "I never saw men fight better or act more gallant than the men of our Brigade. Col. Avery rode up and down the lines and some of the time he was in front of the Brigade gallantly leading and cheering on his Brigade. He rode up to within 30 or 40 yds of the enemy before we broke their lines but at last they broke and we drove them to the town."[9]

General Early was overwhelmed by the Confederate success, calling it "a brilliant victory." Colonel Jones proclaimed, "It looked indeed as if the end of the war had come." However, the Union forces that escaped capture took refuge on Cemetery Hill and the surrounding heights, and Ewell failed to follow up on the Confederate advantage. Hoke's soldiers settled down for the night in a wheat field in a ravine near the base of East Cemetery Hill.[10]

As the new day broke, the Southerners at the base of the hill discovered that their adversaries had done a miraculous job in strengthening their position at the summit. The Union artillery batteries of Michael Wiedrich, R. Bruce Ricketts, and Gilbert H. Reynolds, well placed behind newly constructed breastworks, lined the hill. German immigrants in Leopold von Gilsa's New York brigade formed a strong skirmish line, protected by the artillery and the stone fences and trenches at the crest of the hill. These skirmishers maintained "a galling fire" during the morning and afternoon, forcing the North Carolinians and Louisianians to remain prone in the wheat field under a sweltering sun.[11]

About 4 P.M., Confederate artillery on both flanks of Early's division opened fire on the Union strongholds on Cemetery and Culp's Hills, thus signaling that the long wait for the infantry was about over. Hoke's soldiers were anxious for another chance to smash the Union lines, and when the enemy artillery offered a response, Major James F. Beall of the Twenty-first North Carolina noted that it "fell like music upon our ears." Soon after the artillery duel began, Ewell ordered Early to prepare to move the brigades of Hoke and Hays against Cemetery Hill while Edward Johnson's division attacked Culp's Hill. By this time, the sun "was low" in the western sky. As Avery readied the brigade for combat, he decided to lead his troops on horseback in the attack up the hill. Avery's mount at Gettysburg was Hoke's big black war-horse, San Jose, or "Old Joe," as he was fondly referred to by Hoke. The animal had been loaned to Avery for the Northern campaign after Hoke realized that he would not be able to participate.[12]

There was little light left when Johnson's division became "warmly engaged" at Culp's Hill. Suddenly, the Confederate batteries facing Cemetery Hill fell silent, only to be replaced by the blare of Confederate bugles.

The two small brigades—Hays had but twelve hundred men and Avery nine hundred—quickly came to attention. To the surprise of the Union forces defending the heights, the twenty-one hundred Confederates rose, moved forward at double-quick speed from behind the low ridge that had been protecting them, and marched into open view. It took more than an hour for the North Carolinians to make their way across the seven hundred yards of rocky Pennsylvania landscape that separated them from the base of the hill. Onward they came in the face of a murderous shower of grape and canister from sixteen big guns atop Cemetery Hill and another half-dozen on Culp's. Lines of well-entrenched sharpshooters, firing from behind the stone walls on the incline, took a deadly toll. But the charging Confederates were undaunted.[13]

Just as the advance commenced, Avery was quick to realize that the Union batteries he was assigned to take were positioned to the right of his right flank and in front of Hays's brigade. Colonel Archibald C. Godwin of the Fifty-seventh North Carolina was in the thick of the action as Avery ordered his brigades to wheel to the right—a movement which, according to Godwin, "none but the steadiest veterans could execute under such circumstances."

To make this sudden and dangerous movement, Avery shouted, "Forward, guide right!" Those were the last words Captain McPherson heard his commander utter. As the only mounted officer in the charge, Avery proved to be a perfect target for the enemy skirmishers near the base of the hill. A bullet pierced his neck on the right side and plowed "its way through the great blood vessels and nerves that supplied the upper extremities." Critically wounded, he slumped off "Old Joe" to the ground. As he lay bleeding to death far from his home in western North Carolina, Avery managed to pull from his pocket a pencil and a scrap of Confederate notepaper. With his right arm paralyzed, the colonel used his left to scrawl a few words to his hometown friend and junior officer, Major Samuel M. Tate. His usually beautiful penmanship was now reduced to indistinct characters, but Avery's last words, though jumbled on the small bit of paper, presented a clear message that would be heard and uttered time and time again beyond the bloody battlefield at Gettysburg: "Major: Tell my father

I died with my face to the enemy. I. E. Avery."

When litter bearers reached the unconscious colonel, they found the bloodstained note beside his hand. Decades later, Lord Bryce, the British ambassador to the United States, happened to notice a dingy piece of Confederate notepaper on display at the North Carolina Department of Archives and History in Raleigh. Deeply moved by Avery's last official act as commander of Hoke's brigade, Lord Bryce remarked, "The message of that soldier is the message of our own race to the world."[14]

Few, if any, of Avery's men saw their commander fall, because the darkness and the dense, acrid smoke from the guns that blazed about the hillside greatly reduced visibility. They surged forward, drove back the soldiers manning the enemy's main line of works, and made their way up the hill. Indeed, Tate and fewer than seventy-five men from his regiment, aided by some soldiers from the Ninth Louisiana, reached the summit, silenced and spiked the guns there, and planted the colors of the Sixth North Carolina atop Cemetery Hill. General Hays noticed the sudden quiet: "At that time, every piece of artillery that had been firing at us was silenced."

For a fleeting moment, the soldiers of Robert F. Hoke occupied the hill on the outskirts of Gettysburg which would forever represent the apogee of the Confederate war effort. Captain Ray of the Sixth North Carolina proudly proclaimed, "We had full possession of East Cemetery Hill, the key to Meade's position, and we held it for several minutes." Celebrated historian Glenn Tucker subsequently pointed out the significance of the accomplishment of the Tar Heels on the night of July 2, 1863: "Here was a high point, possibly the high point, of Lee's invasion of the Free States." Walter Clark, the youngest commissioned officer in the Confederate army and a man who later served as chief justice of the North Carolina Supreme Court, termed it "undisputed fact that on the evening of the second day Hoke's brigade . . . together with Louisianians from Hays's brigade, climbed Cemetery Heights, being farther than any other troops ventured during the three days."[15]

The desperate pleas for assistance for the small band of Confederates atop the hill brought no help. Accordingly, by 9:30 P.M., the troops from the two brigades who could make it down the hill were back near the positions they had held during the morning. For a second night in a row, Lee's army had failed to follow up on its advantage and had frittered away a golden opportunity—as it turned out, its last opportunity—to win the war.

When news trickled back to Lincoln County about the events of the evening, Hoke could take great pride in the accomplishments of his soldiers, for in the estimation of the men who had witnessed their heroic stand, the entire Battle of Gettysburg would have been won had Hoke's brigade received timely reinforcements. Major Beall claimed the soldiers of Hoke and Hays had "victory in their grasp." About the inability of the Confederates to hold Cemetery Hill, Union general Carl Schurz opined, "The fate of the battle might [have hinged] on the repulse of their attack."[16]

Following two days of difficult fighting, Hoke's brigade was spared from heavy combat for the remainder of the battle. About 2 A.M. on the morning of July 4, Godwin, who had assumed command when Avery fell, was ordered to move the brigade, this time one mile to the west of Gettysburg. For the duration of the birthday of the divided nation, the North Carolinians maintained their position of relative safety, from which they watched the lead elements of Lee's army set out on the retreat to Virginia.[17]

A torrential rain was falling in the wee hours of Sunday, July 5, when Hoke's brigade and the remainder of Early's division were awarded the ever-dangerous "post of honor," the rear guard, in the retreat across the mountains toward Hagerstown, Maryland. On July 6, Robert Rodes's division replaced Early's as the rear guard, and on the next day, Godwin marched his three regiments into Hagerstown, where they labored for five days building fortifications. The brigade received badly needed reinforcements when the Fifty-fourth rejoined it at Hagerstown on July 10. Near Williamsport in the early-morning hours of Tuesday, July 14, Godwin began sending the first of his men across the rain-swollen Potomac back into Virginia. About 2 P.M., as the men of the Fifty-seventh North Carolina were making the crossing, they distinctly heard the volley that fatally wounded Brigadier General James Johnston Pettigrew, the native North Carolinian who had been so conspicuous in the grand charge on July 3. Once on Virginia soil,

Hoke's brigade spent the next two weeks in hard marching over the mountainous country near the northern tip of the state.[18]

By the end of July, Hoke was recovered sufficiently to return to action. While the brigade was encamped near Madison Court House on the east side of the Blue Ridge Mountains on Wednesday, July 29, Hoke rode into camp and was "received with great cheering." On the "extremely hot" day that followed, his exhausted soldiers "were allowed" to spend the day "washing and sleeping." At 1:30 P.M. on August 1, Hoke set the men out on a difficult march over "very bad" roads and under a searing sun toward Orange Court House. Crossing the Rapidan, the brigade halted for the night four miles south of the river. Exhaustion and the intense summer heat continued to plague the brigade; at the conclusion of the march, Hoke's men "threw themselves down upon the grass in a few moments, and went to sleep." On the next evening, they were at Orange Court House in anticipation of an enemy advance. Chaplain John Paris observed that the troops of his regiment were in "a state of collapse." One of them, Private Wagner, recorded his emotional fatigue: "I am the worst out of heart I Ever was." Three days earlier, he had expressed his pessimism about the ultimate success of the Southern war effort: "I don't Believe we Ever can whip the north." Relief came on August 3 when the brigade set up camp nearby at Rapidan Station, where it would remain for more than a month. The long march that had begun on June 4 for most of Hoke's soldiers was finally at an end.[19]

Shortly after resuming command of his brigade, Hoke called on General Lee to pay his respects. He found Lee busy writing at a table. When Hoke remarked that he did not want to disturb his commander, Lee replied, "Be seated, General." Lee then began to reflect upon the failed Gettysburg campaign. He told Hoke, "I am just preparing my report of the battle of Gettysburg. I have taken all the blame; but had General Stuart kept me informed as he should have done, all would have been different. He stopped to capture a wagon train; and what was a wagon train compared with the tremendous issues that we had at stake?"[20]

Despite the pride Hoke held for his brigade because of its outstanding performance at Gettysburg, he was dismayed at the heavy losses it had sustained there. Casualties had totaled 434—39 killed, 246 wounded, and 149 missing. All of the field officers of the Twenty-first North Carolina save Colonel William Whedbee Kirkland, who would later serve under Hoke as a brigadier general, had been killed or wounded. The ranks had been greatly reduced by the invasion of the North, and it quickly became apparent to the general that his brigade would have to be replenished. A recruiting mission to North Carolina looked to be necessary. Forces were already at work, however, that would require Hoke's return to his native state to be double duty.[21]

In early September, Hoke would be sent to North Carolina to recruit his diminished ranks, but that was to be his secondary purpose; his primary mission would be to round up deserters and quell disloyal uprisings in the western and central counties of the state. As early as April 1863, Lee had complained to Secretary of War Seddon, "There have already been frequent desertions from the North Carolina regiments." By late summer, desertion of North Carolina soldiers from the Army of Northern Virginia had become an alarming problem. In a letter to his wife on August 15, Private Wagner pointed out that Hoke's brigade was not immune to the desertions that were plaguing North Carolina companies, regiments, and brigades: "Dear I hope and trus if they dont soone End it some way they solegers will End it by Runing a way for that is a bout all the way they will End it there is lost of them a runing a way and some sais they want fite not more and I cant Blame them for it 2 run a way out of our company last week and more talks a bout it."[22]

Many of the deserters made their way down the mountains of Virginia in armed bands. Once back in their home state, the "outliers," as they were called, located in areas where they could elude the home guard, the militia, or any other force that might be sent forth to seek them out. The mountains of western North Carolina proved to be a popular destination for the deserters. Others fled to the rural areas of Randolph, Chatham, and Moore Counties in central North Carolina. Zebulon B. Vance, who had been elected governor of North Carolina while still on the battlefields of Virginia in 1862, pointed out the extent of the problem to Secretary Seddon: "A large number of deserters, say 1,200, are in the mountains and inaccessible wilds of the west. I have found it impossible to get them out, and they are plundering and robbing the people."[23]

Confederate officials, the loyal people at home, and many of the soldiers who remained committed to the cause blamed the desertion problem on the growing peace movement in North Carolina. William Woods Holden, attorney, political kingpin, and editor of the *Raleigh Standard*, was viewed as the leader of those who sought an "honorable peace." Holden, long a force in the state's Democratic Party, had prior to the war used his editorials to champion populist causes including equal suffrage, internal improvements throughout the state, labor issues, and universal education. At the outbreak of the war, Holden had been an anti-secessionist, and although he had supported Vance for governor in 1862, he evolved into an outspoken critic of the Confederate administration on both the state and national levels.[24]

By September, the desertion problem in North Carolina had reached the boiling point. After making a thorough study of the problem, Lieutenant Colonel George W. Lay issued a report on September 2 to Colonel J. S. Preston, the superintendent of conscription at Salisbury. In the report, Lay sounded an alarm: "Desertion has assumed . . . a very different and more formidable shape and development than could have been anticipated." He proceeded to document a camp of some five hundred deserters in Wilkes County, and he cited as the source of all the trouble "the newly developed but active intrigues of political malcontents, having the *Raleigh Standard* for their leader." Lay reported that the deserters were "determined to kill in avoiding apprehension" and "in revenge." According to Lay, the citizens of the affected areas in North Carolina expected "a reign of marauding and terror," and he urged that an "effective force . . . from the main army" be deployed in North Carolina "to occupy the infected districts, surround the traitors, bring the disloyal to punishment, fortify the loyal, and decide the wavering."

One week before Lay's report was issued, Governor Vance had dispatched a plea to Richmond for military assistance to deal with the growing problem. Vance told Seddon that his militia and home guard were no longer effective against the ever-increasing number of deserters in the western counties, and he ended his letter with a suggestion and a demand: "If General Lee would send one of our diminished brigades or a good strong regiment to North Carolina, with orders to report to me, I could make it increase his ranks for more than the temporary loss of his brigade, in a very short time. Something of this kind must be done."[25]

Seddon referred Vance's letter to General Lee on August 29. Lee responded on Tuesday, September 1, with a directive to Longstreet that one of the young generals from Lincoln County be selected for the job: "I wish a small regiment from the brigade of Hoke or Ramseur, as I think a good opportunity will be presented of filling its ranks to the legal standard, and I desire whichever of these officers thinks the best and most suitable for the duty to be selected." Hoke was chosen for the assignment, and the force to accompany him to North Carolina was composed of the Twenty-first North Carolina, the Fifty-sixth North Carolina (from Brigadier General Matt W. Ransom's brigade), and a cavalry squadron from Brigadier General A. G. Jenkins's brigade.[26]

About the time Hoke was consulting with Lee and Vance to obtain final instructions for the mission, the importance of the expedition was accentuated by John A. Campbell, the assistant Confederate secretary of war, who concluded on September 7, "The condition of things in the mountain districts of North Carolina, South Carolina, Georgia, and Alabama menaces the existence of the Confederacy as fatally as either of the armies of the United States." Jefferson Davis, keenly aware of the problems in North Carolina, was confident that Hoke could take care of the situation. On September 8, the day Hoke arrived in Guilford County to begin his mission, the president noted, "The orders to Brigadier-General Hoke anticipated the proposed remedy."[27]

After assembling his troops in his home state, Hoke moved the Twenty-first North Carolina west to Salem, the Moravian settlement in Forsyth County. There, Hoke set up camp on the night of September 8. A party was held in the village that evening for the Confederate officers. One of the ladies of the town, much taken with Hoke at the gala, reported to her husband in a letter the next day that the general was "a gallant officer" who possessed "very pleasant manners, fine conversational powers, and is very handsome." Hoke, ever mindful of Lee's admonition "not to speak of the character of his duty," was mum about his presence. His admirer at the party, however, could sense the reason for his sudden return to North Carolina: "Their place of destination I know not, but I think their business is to arrest deserters, & if possible quell the union feeling in the western part of the state."[28]

On the very day of Hoke's arrival, the need for his presence was demonstrated by a heated skirmish in northern Iredell County between a band of "some two hundred deserters and traitors" and fifty-six Confederate troops from an instructional camp in Raleigh. In order to prevent further episodes of violence and insurrection, Hoke began his movement to the western counties the following day. Governor Vance had specifically charged Hoke "to capture the deserters and conscripts, and break up and disperse any organized bands of lawless men to be found there resisting the authority of the Government." Accordingly, he temporarily divided his command. Colonel Paul F. Faison was ordered to take the Fifty-sixth North Carolina into Randolph, Moore, Chatham, and the other "problem" counties in central North Carolina, while Hoke and his own Twenty-first North Carolina concentrated on the troublesome west. However, the heavy concentration of deserters in the western counties and the threat of a battle with them in Wilkes County required the deployment of the Fifty-sixth North Carolina there as well.[29]

Faison's troops reached Iredell County on September 10, and Hoke's entered Yadkin County a day later. Both regiments then converged on Wilkes County, which by September 17 was "full of troops." Hoke camped his men in northern Wilkes County at Trap Hill, a stronghold for local dissidents. County residents expected a fight with deserters there, but no engagement was in the offing. On September 18, Private Thomas Francis Price of Company I of the Fifty-sixth, himself a native of western North Carolina, wrote of Hoke's determination to successfully complete his mission: "We hant catched but about 5 of the Runaways yet and we have to hunt for them night and day. . . . [We] are under the command of general Hoke . . . and he says that he intends to stay up here till he catches them if he has to stay till it comes a Snow and then track them like rabbits."[30]

Several days later, Hoke moved his troops to Wilkesboro, where he established his headquarters for the operations that would last for most of the remainder of the year. Rather than provoke conflict with the deserters, the general decided to use more subtle approaches. For example, as to the troublemakers at Trap Hill, Hoke decided to give them some time "to reflect & Come in & behave themselves," but if they did not do so, he would "sweep the Country." As his troops fanned out through Wilkes and Yadkin Counties, many deserters turned themselves in after Hoke promised furloughs in order for them to take care of their affairs. His efforts began to reap fertile results, and by October 21, Colonel Faison was able to report that in excess of five hundred deserters and draft dodgers had been rounded up in Wilkes County and put into the ranks.[31]

There was, however, a dark side to Hoke's campaign in the mountain counties. Not all of the deserters and insurgents were given amnesty after their capture or surrender. Some of the most militant leaders were dispatched to Castle Thunder prison in Richmond. Of even greater concern was the wide variety of abuses to which the citizenry was exposed during the campaign. Crops were pilfered and burned; homes and farms were plundered; and some men mistaken for "outliers" were executed. While many of the outrages were committed by members of home guard units seeking to extract a measure of revenge, Hoke's soldiers were not entirely blameless. In a letter to his father, Major John Washington Graham of the Fifty-sixth North Carolina admitted that a company of the Twenty-first North Carolina "was doing a good deal of harm, in indiscriminate plunder of property to deserters families . . . and depredations on property of good citizens."[32]

During November, Hoke's troops devoted much attention to the central counties. This area posed serious problems for the soldiers because many of the inhabitants, particularly in Randolph County, were Union supporters. Major Graham complained that his work in Davidson County was "the most disagreeable business I have ever been engaged in." He indicated to his father that there was but one way to capture the deserters: "There is very little use in hunting the rascals, the only way to get them is to seize their property and keep it until they surrender." Although Vance deplored the practice, Hoke approved of and encouraged it. According to the general, "This had a fine effect upon them."[33]

Although Hoke found himself detached from his brigade less than six weeks after he had rejoined it, he maintained an intense interest in the activities of his men while he was on special assignment in North Carolina. From mid-September until October 9, Hoke's three regiments in Virginia, under the command of Colonel Godwin, spent most of their days on picket and skirmish duty along the Rapidan River. Falling back across the Rappahannock, the division, including Hoke's brigade, made camp east of Brandy Station around October 18.[34]

With cold weather fast approaching in northern Virginia, Hoke attempted to obtain new uniforms for his soldiers. At least a hundred members of the Sixth North Carolina had returned from the grueling Gettysburg campaign without blankets, coats, or trousers. Although he was busy with his duties in North Carolina, the general felt it was his obligation to see that his soldiers received clothing because, as he put it, "Col. Godwin . . . will not think of it."[35]

As if Hoke and his brigade had not endured more than their share of casualties, hardships, frustrations, and disappointments from spring until fall, tragedy loomed on the horizon as Hoke's three regiments in Virginia began to set up winter camp two miles west of Brandy Station on Sunday, November 1. Excitement prevailed in the camp when orders were given to construct winter quarters. A false sense of security pervaded the camp as the soldiers anticipated "a long rest and cessation of hostilities." Joy abounded. Thanks to Hoke's efforts, new clothing and equipment were delivered. On November 6, there was more good news, perhaps the best news of all. For the first time in five months, the soldiers were paid. Unfortunately, many of them would never have an opportunity to spend any of their hard-earned money.[36]

About 2:00 P.M. on November 7, the long roll sounded, and Colonel Godwin moved his soldiers five miles at double-quick speed to the Rappahannock, where Meade's skirmishers were advancing on the "tete-de-pont," or bridgehead, at Rappahannock Station. When Lee and Early arrived on the scene about 3:00 P.M., the only Confederate forces on the north side of the river were the Louisiana Tigers of Harry Hays, protected by a four-gun battery. Godwin and his troops made it to the bridge at 4:30 P.M. Despite heavy artillery fire from the enemy, the three North Carolina regiments were sent across the bridge to plug a gap in Hays's line to the left of the bridge. Deployed on Godwin's left were the Seventh and Fifth Louisiana, and on his right were the Eighth, Ninth, and Sixth Louisiana.[37]

After Federal skirmishers successfully drove in their counterparts in Hays's and Hoke's brigades, the artillery unleashed a fierce barrage on the Louisianians and North Carolinians. Darkness had begun to envelop the river when Meade's twenty-thousand-man attack force started a cautious advance against the eighteen hundred Confederates on the north side of the river. According to Chaplain Paris, the Union force slowly extended its lines in the form of a half-moon, so as "to envelop our forces entirely, his right and left resting on the river below." The Federals, who had never attacked the Army of Northern Virginia at night until this occasion, went on the offensive. On the south side of the river, the Confederates, because of darkness and poor angles of fire, were forced to helplessly stand by as their embattled comrades grimly fought against waves of attackers. Following the seesaw fight, the beleaguered troops were overwhelmed.[38]

Godwin and his men were soon cut off, and it suddenly became every man for himself. Many Confederates were captured, while others attempted to escape. Samuel M. Tate, who had been promoted to lieutenant colonel on July 3, and some of his men in the Sixth North Carolina were able to dodge bullets as they ran across the bridge. Others were not so lucky— they fell with bullets in their backs. Early waited as long as he could before firing the bridge, but fearing that the Yankees would advance over it, he ordered it burned. Consequently, some of Hoke's men were forced to swim the ice-cold waters of the Rappahannock. Some of the swimmers drowned in the darkness; others were shot by Union marksmen. Among the few who successfully swam the river was Hoke's gallant adjutant, Captain James Adams, who stepped ashore almost naked.[39]

Adams joined the fortunate few from the two brigades who had escaped death or capture. Chaplain Paris recorded the dreadful news about Hoke's veteran fighting force: "The brigade is almost annihilated." Indeed, the losses were staggering: Colonel Godwin, the brigade commander, and Colonel Robert Webb of the Sixth North Carolina had fallen into enemy hands. According to Early, no more than 150 of Hoke's soldiers made it back across the river. In his official report, he wrote, "In the regiments of Hoke's brigade . . . the loss was very nearly three-fourths of the men present with the army." When Lieutenant Colonel Tate was finally able to rally the survivors of the disaster, the three regiments counted a total of 275 soldiers present for duty. That head count included some soldiers who had not been involved in the affair at the bridge; they had been away from camp gathering timber for winter huts when the alarm sounded. Hoke lost 928 men and Hays 702 in the disaster. In contrast, Federal casualties included 83 killed, 330 wounded, and 6 missing. Walter Taylor, Lee's loyal aide, called the event the "saddest chapter in the history of this army."[40]

Following the stunning defeat, Lee pulled his army back to its former position on the south side of the Rapidan River. Lieutenant Colonel Tate was in command of the remnants of Hoke's brigade as the soldiers made their way to a point two and a half miles from Raccoon Ford, where they set up camp for November. Snow fell when they once again began work on winter quarters there on November 9. Despite the harsh weather and the fresh memories of the tragedy at Rappahannock Station, the morale of the North Carolinians was surprisingly high. Chaplain Paris explained, "This is a serious disaster, so far as our feelings are concerned, but it does not shake our hopes as to success."[41]

When news of the Confederate nightmare on the Rappahannock reached Hoke, he was in Salisbury, North Carolina. Anxious to learn the fate of his men, he telegraphed Governor Vance on November 11, "What is reliable concerning my brigade?" A day later, Hoke received the heartbreaking details in a personal letter from Robert E. Lee:

> I regret to inform you that in the recent advance of the army at Rappahannock Bridge, that part of your brigade which is here sustained a loss of 3 killed, 19 wounded, and 906 missing, most of whom were taken prisoners. . . .
> This unfortunate affair reduces your brigade, leaving only 29 officers and 257 men for duty. . . . I hope you will endeavor to

procure some additional regiments from the Governor to fill up your brigade, as it could not be spared from the army, and I shall be glad to see you back again as soon as possible, with your command at least as strong as before.[42]

As soon as he was able to take temporary leave of his duties in North Carolina, Hoke hurried to Virginia to check on his men. On Sunday evening, November 22, he arrived to a hero's welcome at the brigade camp, where he was "serenaded by the band of the 6th at night and cheered by the crowd." During his four-day stay, the general provided glowing accounts of the progress of his work in North Carolina. On November 24, a rainy Tuesday, Peter W. Hairston recorded Hoke's observations about his campaign against deserters: "Hoke says he had some rich scenes in No. Ca. He caught a conscript dressed up in woman's clothes. He says Wilkes is now the truest & most loyal county in the State. He had cleared it of deserters & disloyal men. . . . He worked very hard and sent off 3000 deserters & conscripts and was the cause of a great many more coming back voluntarily."[43]

Hoke's small brigade grew excited as the general prepared to return to North Carolina to seek permission from Governor Vance to send his men home on a recruitment mission. On November 25, the day before Hoke left for Raleigh, he enjoyed a sumptuous feast with Early and his staff officers. Hairston commented about their fare, "The dinner did not look much like starvation among the rebels as we had fine veal mutton &c." After Hoke departed, his soldiers' dreams of an imminent trip home were shattered, as they soon became involved in the Mine Run campaign. After a week of skirmishing in the cold of late November and early December, the brigade returned to its winter quarters at Raccoon Ford. In the cold, harsh days that followed, picket duty was the order of the day. The expected trip to North Carolina would have to wait until the new year.[44]

Upon returning to his native state, Hoke worked to tie up the loose ends on his campaign against deserters and to recruit his brigade. Concerned about abuses and misconduct committed by his soldiers during the expedition, the general launched an investigation into the matter. At Salisbury on December 8, he penned a letter to a physician in Wilkes County wherein he stated his determination to see justice served: "I am exceedingly anxious to ascertain the names of the officers and men who have acted in this manner and also those of the persons who sustained the losses in order that I may have all damages paid for." Hoke requested that the physician serve as a member of a committee appointed to investigate the charges against the troops.[45]

By the middle of December, Hoke was in Richmond, his mission in North Carolina complete. Though he may have been overly optimistic in his estimation of the effects and extent of his work in the state, he had tackled a most difficult problem and brought a large measure of relief to his state and nation. Moreover, he had demonstrated to Lee and the administrations in Richmond and Raleigh that he was well able to handle an independent command.

Despite the series of tragedies and disappointments that had plagued Hoke's brigade over much of the last half of 1863, the year ended on a positive note with the completion of the general's successful campaign in North Carolina. A new year would soon be at hand, and Hoke would be presented with exciting opportunities to render service in his native state. Because opportunities were fast becoming a scarce commodity for the Confederacy, it would be of tantamount importance for Hoke to take full advantage of those that came his way.

CHAPTER 6

The Promise of a New Year

Snow blanketed the Richmond landscape as Jefferson Davis pondered a letter from Robert E. Lee dated January 2, 1864. Written at Lee's winter headquarters on the forested southern slope of Clark's Mountain, the letter revealed the general's ardent desire to commence a campaign in eastern North Carolina: "The time is at hand when, if an attempt can be made to capture the enemy's forces at New Berne, it should be done. I can now spare troops for the purpose, which will not be the case as spring approaches. . . . A large amount of provisions and other supplies are said to be at New Berne, which are much wanted for this army, besides much that is reported in the country that will thus be made accessible to us."

If ever two great minds were on the same wavelength, such was the case with Lee and Davis in the first weeks of 1864. For several months, the

North Carolina coast had been a source of great concern for the president. While taking autumn-afternoon horseback rides around the Confederate capital, he and his nephew, Confederate navy commander John Taylor Wood, had frequently discussed the problems resulting from Union occupation of that region. Taylor reasoned with his uncle that as long as enemy forces had control over the North Carolina sounds, the Union blockade would continue to effectively operate against the vital port of Wilmington.[1]

Davis was also cognizant that the Federal stronghold at New Bern represented a serious threat to the vital supplies and recruits that poured into Virginia from North Carolina. From New Bern, Federal forces had launched damaging raids against important Confederate towns in the North Carolina coastal plain throughout 1863. Not only had Kinston, Greenville, Tarboro, Rocky Mount, and other Confederate enclaves been hit, but so had Weldon, a key station on the Wilmington and Weldon Railroad. Goldsboro, another important stop on the railroad, had become increasingly vulnerable to potential attack from New Bern.[2]

Lee's overture of January 2 prompted Davis to send for Hoke, who had just returned from his special service in North Carolina. Davis was anxious to learn more about the conditions in North Carolina and to question the general about what he thought could be done in his native state. Although Hoke's most recent assignment had taken him to western and central North Carolina, he had read newspaper accounts and talked with citizens about the alarming state of affairs in the eastern portions of the state under Union control. Consequently, Hoke shared the concerns of many Tar Heel citizens.

Over the two-year period that New Bern and the upper coastal plain had been in Union hands, the citizens of the area had suffered many depredations at the hands of the occupying army. Moreover, "Buffaloes," native Union sympathizers, had continued to terrorize their neighbors who had remained loyal to the South. Few plantations and farms in the region were spared from the "unchecked rapine and pillage" of Union troops and lawless "Buffaloes." As a member of the Federal garrison at New Bern, a soldier of the Tenth Connecticut wrote of the nearby countryside, "This whole country for purposes of maintenance of man or beast, for the next twelve months is a desert and hopeless as 'Sahara' itself." A Confederate scout who observed the waste laid to the counties surrounding New Bern proclaimed, "If every person in the South could witness the useless ruin that the Yankees have caused in Jones and adjoining counties, the name and sight of the Yankee soldier would be hated throughout all eternity, and it would help to show what an abandoned and Godless foe we have to contend against."[3]

Fueling the fires of dissatisfaction in North Carolina was editor William Woods Holden, who continued to use his newspaper to call for peace. Thus, when Davis questioned Hoke about what should be done in North Carolina, the general initially said, "Arrest Holden and send him out of the country." Davis responded, "Oh no! I can't do that." The president then suggested to Hoke the possibility of a military expedition to New Bern. Although the general had not fully recovered from his wound at Salem Church, he was anxious to tackle New Bern, and he departed his conference with Davis filled with excitement.

Hoke then set about drafting a "carefully prepared" plan for the capture of New Bern, which was "approved most heartily and authorized" by Lee. So important was the expedition to Davis and the Confederate war effort that the president proposed that Lee personally lead the campaign. Lee disdained the offer, saying on his fifty-seventh birthday, "In view of the opinion expressed in your letter, I would go to North Carolina myself, but I consider my presence here always necessary, especially now, when there is such a struggle to keep the army fed and clothed." As his substitute, Lee proffered Hoke, but Davis was resolute in his conviction that the campaign should be led by an officer of higher rank. Therefore, Major General George E. Pickett was given nominal command of the mission. Nonetheless, Hoke would be a major player, and it was upon his plan that the campaign was based.[4]

Despite Hoke's successful recruitment campaign in North Carolina the previous autumn, his brigade remained greatly diminished because of the disaster at Rappahannock Station. In an effort to strengthen the brigade for the New Bern expedition, Lee saw to it that the Twenty-first Georgia and the Forty-third North Carolina were temporarily assigned to Hoke.

General Robert F. Hoke

The addition of both regiments was a boon to Hoke and his brigade. Hoke was particularly fond of the Twenty-first Georgia. Not only had he commanded the men of that brigade and been witness to their valor and fighting ability, but he would never forget that many of these Georgia soldiers had helped to win his general's wreath at Fredericksburg. Just before the campaign in eastern North Carolina was launched, Hoke made a personal appearance before the Twenty-first Georgia. Most of the soldiers he knew by name, and he proceeded to compliment them for their past deeds of gallantry. Then he explained to the Georgians that they "needed recreation" and that he was going to give them a "fine time" in his home state rounding up deserters. Following Hoke's presentation, the troops, who "all adored" the general, sent up "loud, lusty, cheers" in hearty approval of the "frolic with 'Our Bob'." In the days to come, the Georgians' enthusiasm would be tempered when they learned of their true mission: a desperate fight to capture New Bern.[5]

To ensure the success of Hoke's plan, Lee was willing to commit a sizable fighting force from his army. He was well aware of the challenge his troops faced in North Carolina. Union major general J. G. Foster, who had served as commander of the Department of North Carolina for most of the time that New Bern had been under Federal occupation, had done much to make the place "one of the best fortified towns in the United States." An armored train patrolled the tracks to protect the railroad and the garrison at New Bern, estimated by Confederate officials at approximately four thousand soldiers on the eve of the January 1864 expedition.[6]

To prosecute the campaign, Lee authorized a force of thirteen thousand troops from the brigades of Hoke, Seth Barton, Montgomery Corse, Thomas L. Clingman, Matt W. Ransom, James L. Kemper, and other commands. In addition, Commander John Taylor Wood would lead a naval force of three hundred handpicked sailors and marines.[7]

January was two-thirds gone when Lee and Davis were satisfied that the mission to North Carolina should proceed. In a letter dated January 20 that Hoke personally delivered to Pickett at Petersburg several days later, Lee outlined the basics of Hoke's plan. General Barton was to lead a column south of the Trent River, where he would surprise the Union forces at Brice's Creek, then take command of the railroad so as to cut off the possibility of enemy reinforcements from Morehead City and Beaufort, and finally take "the town in reverse." Hoke was to proceed down the Trent and Neuse Rivers, where he would surprise the enemy at Batchelder's Creek, then "silence the guns in the Star fort" and other fortifications on the Neuse, and finally make his way into New Bern from the northwest. A third column was to attack Fort Anderson in order to lighten the load on Hoke. On the evening prior to the three-pronged attack, Commander Wood was to lead a commando raid down the Neuse River, during which the Union gunboats protecting the city would be captured. In conjunction with the assault on the city, Major General William Henry Chase Whiting was to send a force from Wilmington to threaten the Swansboro area in order to draw the attention of the Union forces at Morehead City.

Although Pickett was given permission to modify the plan "according to circumstances developed by investigation and your good judgment," Lee's confidence in Hoke was apparent. "General Hoke is familiar with the vicinity of New Berne, has recently returned from a visit to that country, and it is mainly upon his information that my opinion has been formed. He will hand you this letter, and explain to you the general plan, which, at this distance, appears to me the best."[8]

In his letter to Pickett, Lee stressed that secrecy was of tantamount importance during the expedition. Pickett was cautioned to "commit nothing to the telegraph" that might reveal his intentions. Not only was the enemy to be deceived, but so was the civilian population. Lee suggested that Pickett explain the sudden concentration of Confederate troops in North Carolina to be the result of "apprehension of an attack from New Berne." As to Hoke's return to North Carolina, Lee explained, "General Hoke will give out that he is going to arrest deserters and recruit his diminished regiments." Urging Pickett to carry forth a successful campaign, Lee noted that it would "have the happiest effect in North Carolina and inspire the people."[9]

On the same day, Lee issued marching orders to Hoke, instructing him to proceed to Petersburg the following day, where he was to deliver to

Pickett the orders and "explain to him fully the plan of operations." At 3 P.M. on January 20, the men of Hoke's brigade received the news of their long-anticipated return to North Carolina. Hoke ordered them "to cook two days rations and prepare to march at a moments notice." Indicative of the significant role Hoke was to play in the operation, Lee personally took steps to expedite rail transportation for Hoke's soldiers from their winter headquarters to Petersburg. Consequently, at 7 P.M., the two regiments temporarily assigned to Hoke, the Twenty-first Georgia and the Forty-third North Carolina, were loaded on the train at Gordonsville for the trip to North Carolina.[10]

At 4 A.M. on Thursday, January 21, the excited soldiers of Hoke's brigade embarked on a fourteen-mile march from the banks of the Rapidan to Orange Court House. They boarded a train for Richmond at dusk, but their journey was interrupted for six hours when the engine ran off the tracks. Over the next two days, the troop train slowly chugged its way south to Garysburg, North Carolina.

When Hoke delivered Lee's orders and explained the operational plan to Pickett at Petersburg on January 23, Pickett was less than enthusiastic about Hoke's strategy. Later, in the wake of his failure to capture New Bern, Pickett reported, "The present operations I was afraid of from the first, as there were too many contingencies." While he was conferring with Pickett, Hoke was under the expectation that Corse's brigade would arrive in timely fashion; however, he learned that Corse could not deliver his troops until January 27. Therefore, the start of the campaign in North Carolina was postponed until January 29. During his visit to Petersburg, Hoke took care of various arrangements for the expedition, including the collection of artillery. It was placed on cars as if to be shipped to Richmond, in order to deceive the enemy.[11]

From Petersburg, Hoke hastened to Kinston ahead of his troops. Upon learning that the enemy at New Bern was quiet, he returned to Weldon "to give the shipment of my troops my personal attention." In a letter to John N. Whitford, colonel of the Sixty-seventh North Carolina, dated January 23, Hoke related that his troops were now arriving at Garysburg without causing "the slightest suspicion." Filled with optimism, the general

The Promise of a New Year

told Whitford that "everything was working firmly." Over the next five days, Hoke's brigade remained in the Weldon area, awaiting the late arrival of Corse's brigade. At the same time, Hoke busied himself with final preparations for the mission. On January 25, Brigadier General Seth Barton, whose role in the offensive was vital, met with Hoke in Goldsboro, where the details of the operation were explained to him.[12]

On January 28, the first of the Confederate troops were entrained at Weldon for the trip to Kinston, where the expeditionary force was to be assembled. To Hoke's dismay, it took several days to move his brigade. Despite this irritation, he was of the opinion that "everything so far was working fairly." During the heavy troop movement, the secrecy of the ultimate destination of the mission was maintained. Chaplain Paris of the Fifty-fourth North Carolina noted the uncertainty among Hoke's soldiers when he recorded in his diary on January 29, "Took the cars at 11 o'clock for we know not where. . . . Travelled all night at a slow pace." In the meantime, at Wilmington on January 28, Major General Whiting had dispatched portions of the Seventeenth North Carolina and the Forty-second North Carolina, under the command of Brigadier General James G. Martin, on the mission to divert the attention of enemy forces south of New Bern and to disrupt railroad traffic from Morehead City.[13]

By January 30, Pickett's army was fully assembled at Kinston. That afternoon, Hoke marched his personal column, which included his brigade, several regiments from the brigades of Clingman and Ransom, and some troops from Corse's brigade, down Dover Road toward New Bern. The column bivouacked for the night "without tents" some four to six miles south of Kinston.[14]

The last day of January, although "moderately cold," broke "fair and pleasant" as Pickett put his army on the move. At 6 A.M., Hoke's brigade took the lead position in the column as it began a forced march toward Batchelder's Creek, a 14-mile waterway that entered the Neuse River 3½ miles northwest of New Bern. The route took Hoke's soldiers through the Gum Swamp and through what Chaplain Paris described as "15 miles of the most dreary part of Carolina I ever saw." After following the railroad for 6 miles, the column turned onto a country road near Sandy Ridge, the site of a skirmish between the Forty-ninth North Carolina and Union forces a year earlier.

In order to maintain the element of surprise, the Confederates arrested all with whom they came in contact during the twenty-three-mile march. In the course of his rapid movement into New Bern, Hoke and a group of his officers encountered a Federal courier who unwittingly galloped right up to the Confederate general and his lieutenants. In an instant, the courier put a piece of paper in his mouth, which prompted Hoke's aide to put a pistol to the Union soldier's head and say, "If you swallow that I will kill you." The captive obliged his capturers and spat the paper out. It turned out to be a dispatch about the movement of a Union regiment and four pieces of artillery. With the information, Hoke's forces were subsequently able to capture the Federal detachment.

After the long, exhausting march, Hoke's column camped near Stevens Fork, approximately ten miles from New Bern and two miles from the nearest Union outpost. Because of the proximity of the enemy, "no fires were allowed to be kindled" on the dark and rainy night that ushered in the new month.[15]

While Hoke was making his approach on January 31, Barton's sizable column, composed of his brigade, Kemper's brigade, most of Ransom's, and cavalry and artillery detachments, made a rapid twenty-one-mile advance en route to its intended backdoor attack on New Bern. At Trenton, the soldiers crossed the Trent River and camped for the night about twelve miles from New Bern. To this point in the campaign, Barton had brilliantly carried out his assigned tasks. However, his toughest challenge lay just ahead: on the morrow, his soldiers would be expected to make the primary thrust toward New Bern.[16]

In the wee hours of Monday, February 1, all was ready for the Confederate assault. Hoke, whose main responsibilities on this day were "to create a diversion and draw off the enemy," ordered his soldiers to attention at 1 A.M. Chaplain Paris recorded what happened next: "The Army marched at 2:00 o'clock A.M. It was very dark. At 15 minutes before 3 the vanguard fell in with the enemy's pickets and firing began." Hoke was able to sweep all of the outposts in front of him, and he rushed his soldiers "with all speed" in the predawn hours so they might cross the seventy-five-foot-long bridge at Batchelder's Creek before their presence was detected by the enemy. However, his pickets had alerted the strongly fortified Union forces at the creek, and by the time the first wave of Hoke's troops arrived at the bridge, it had been taken up. Dismayed by the turn of events, Pickett ordered Hoke to halt his advance until morning. Lieutenant Colonel William Gaston Lewis sent word to Hoke that the bridge could be repaired if planks from the pontoon train could be sent forward. This was done, and when daylight broke, Hoke rushed a detail forward to fell some trees across the creek for use as a temporary bridge. Over this span advanced two regiments under the command of Colonel John Mercer of the 21st Georgia. They attacked the enemy on the rear and flank as other Confederate soldiers, exposed to heavy fire, effected repairs to the bridge. Federal reinforcements had been hurried forward on the nearby railroad, and an iron-clad steam car moved along the tracks in support of the defenders. Shells were poured into the Confederate lines, and the Union soldiers manning the blockhouse and the redoubts at the creek offered steady musket fire. According to Chaplain Paris, the "battle was furious." Colonel P. J. Claassen of the 132nd New York later recalled that the veteran Confederate soldiers "admitted that the Batchelder's Creek fight was about as hot as they ever had it from the damned Yankees."[17]

As he pushed his soldiers within two hundred yards of the repaired bridge, Hoke suffered significant casualties. Despite the stiff Union resistance, the showdown at Batchelder's Creek was over by midmorning, when the Federals "gave way in confusion," thereby allowing the Confederate soldiers to capture the Federal outpost and some prisoners. Pickett noted in his official report that Hoke forced passage across the bridge "in most gallant style." His troops stormed across in pursuit of the fleeing Federals, who were being driven toward town. Major W. J. Pfohl of the Twenty-first North Carolina lamented, "We followed them up, but as usual they were too fast for us & most of them succeeded in getting to New Bern." Pickett attributed the failure to catch the Federals to the lack of cavalry and the fatigue of the troops. Nonetheless, once across the creek, Hoke again displayed the military genius which had earned the confidence of Davis and

Lee. As he noted, "They made my anticipated move, which was to throw troops by cars across the creek on the railroad, and came in our rear. This was what we wanted." At double-quick speed, Hoke rushed a portion of his army six miles in a desperate race to capture the train. The lead elements of this column, primarily soldiers from the Forty-third North Carolina and the Fifty-sixth North Carolina, were within twenty yards of the armored train when it pulled away. Had his men been able to capture the train, which Major Pfohl described as "containing stores, & having a mounted battery of 3 guns attached to it," Hoke planned to load his soldiers aboard and roll into town with the United States flag flying and guns blazing.[18]

Although he just missed capturing the train, Hoke seized several hundred prisoners who were retreating down the railroad. Among these and the other captives taken by Hoke on February 1 were a number of Confederate deserters who had taken up arms with the Union forces. Several days later, Hoke would be involved in the disposition of these "special" prisoners. True to his word, the general had taken the Twenty-first Georgia on a mission to capture deserters. But as one member of that regiment later recounted, Hoke had not told the Georgians that the deserters "were in the Yankee army and that we would have to fight like blue blazes to get them."[19]

Pickett ordered Hoke and Clingman to continue their advance toward New Bern, then halted their approach in the afternoon. By that time, Hoke was within a mile of downtown. A reporter for the *New York Herald* described the scene in the Union lines: "The rebels are in sight of the city, and can be seen from Fort Totten by the naked eye. Our forces are resting on their arms day and night, waiting for the assault, on the city." While Hoke was told to meet any offensive launched by the Federals, Clingman was instructed to cross the Trent to intercept retreating enemy soldiers from an outpost at Deep Gully. Clingman, unfamiliar with the area, was unable to reach Trent Road. Hoke noted that Clingman's failure "was extremely unfortunate, as during the evening at different times 500 infantry and 400 cavalry passed into the town panic-stricken, leaving their camps in wild confusion."[20]

The Promise of a New Year

Pickett had stopped his column "to await the sound of Barton's guns from the opposite side of Trent River." He and Hoke waited in vain for a sound or a signal. Suddenly, there was an indication of problems on the other side of town. Hoke explained, "Much to my amazement, I saw two trains come into town from Morehead City, which proved clearly that Barton had not reached the point of destination." Indeed, Barton had failed in his quest. Capturing by surprise several enemy outposts, one of which had but a single soldier awake, Barton had enjoyed success during his early-morning approach. As his soldiers moved closer to Brice's Creek, they could see the steeples and housetops of New Bern; as Captain Henry Chambers of the Forty-ninth North Carolina noted in his diary, "We all knew that Newbern was just before us." But Barton saw more than the outline of civilian buildings when he, General Ransom, and Colonel William A. Aydlett reconnoitered the area near the eighty-yard-wide waterway. Suddenly confronted by what he perceived to be difficult terrain and an almost endless complex of Union forts, blockhouses, and breastworks, Barton lost his appetite for the offensive. "Forced to the conviction" that the obstacles before him were insurmountable, he promptly dispatched "several messengers, scouts, and couriers" to inform Pickett of "the posture of affairs" and to seek further instructions.[21]

While awaiting word from Barton, Pickett, his staff officers resting on the ground around him, paced impatiently under a tree at a spot that afforded a splendid view of New Bern. As the sun began to set behind the treetops, the major general was nervously fiddling with his sword knot and biting his fingernails when the news of a Union movement toward his right wing was received. Suddenly, looking in the direction of Trenton, Pickett saw Hoke approaching. Once he dismounted, Hoke gave Pickett the details of the Union advance. Pickett responded in absolute terms: "They must be driven back!" Then he asked Hoke, "Can you do it?" Hoke replied in the affirmative: "Yes, with my own brigade." He promptly disappeared, and in less than a half-hour, the Union artillery was no longer heard. Not only had Hoke silenced the guns, but he had chased the Federals back into their works.[22]

Afternoon faded into evening, and while he waited for tidings from

Barton, Pickett summoned a council of war. Clingman, who had just shaken off a slight shrapnel wound, urged the commanding general to demand an unconditional surrender, and if rejected by the Federals, to launch an immediate frontal assault. Hoke, anxious for his plan to be given a chance for success, objected. Pickett likewise was opposed to Clingman's idea. Instead, his soldiers lay on their arms throughout the night.[23]

Just before midnight, Wood's commandos headed for their raid on the New Bern waterfront, where only one enemy ship, the *Underwriter*, was anchored. Weighing 325 tons and measuring 186 feet long, the side-wheel steamer was one of the largest warships operating in the North Carolina sounds. Like the swashbucklers of old, the Confederate raiders boarded the *Underwriter*, and fierce hand-to-hand combat ensued. Slowly, the boarding party gained the upper hand, and the surviving Union crewmen sought the protection of the hurricane deck. Soon thereafter, they cried, "We surrender!" After briefly plundering the ship, the Confederate tars were challenged by the guns of Fort Stevenson. Unable to get up enough steam to move the captured ship, Wood loaded his prisoners into his boats and set fire to the *Underwriter*.[24]

Wood's triumph on the New Bern waterfront in the wee hours of February 2 was followed that afternoon by the unqualified success of General Martin's operations at Newport Barracks, where a series of well-supplied fortifications protected the railroad midway between New Bern and Morehead City.[25]

While Martin was overrunning the Federal positions south of Seth Barton, and while the Union commander at New Bern was entertaining thoughts of surrender, the fortunes of Barton himself had not improved. His skirmishers kept the Federals in check, but Barton remained reluctant to move against the defense works. Twice he had sent forth cavalry details to cut the railroad, and twice these detachments had failed. It was not until the morning of February 2 that his courier reached Pickett with a message stating that Barton had "found the work laid out for him impracticable." Although he kept his anger to himself at the time, Hoke was livid at Barton's failure. Pickett was also incensed. Convinced that he could take New Bern with the whole force, Pickett, over Hoke's vehement objections, decided to attempt to take the city through a *coup de main*. Captain Robert A. Bright of Pickett's staff made haste to Barton with instructions for him to bring his troops around for a consolidated attack. So strong were Hoke's protestations against the modification of the original plan that Pickett threatened him with court-martial and arrest.[26]

When the unfortunate Barton received Pickett's instructions, he was again in a quandary. "By the nearest practicable route," he was some twenty-four miles from Pickett and Hoke. While Pickett waited for a response from Barton, he received reports from his cavalry commander, James Dearing, that he had found the Union defenses at Fort Anderson too formidable to take. Pickett reasoned that the element of surprise had now been lost; and moreover, as he concluded, "we were making the fight single-handed." Therefore, before Barton's column could make its way across the Trent en route to a rendezvous with Hoke's column, the angry and frustrated Pickett called off the expedition on the night of February 3 and ordered his entire army to march back to Kinston.[27]

Throughout that night and over the course of the next day, the Confederate troops struggled to return to Kinston. Along the route, pine trees, boxed for their turpentine, were set ablaze to light the way. Men, horses, and mules stuck fast in the quagmire; some of the animals had to be killed.[28]

Pickett lingered but a short time in Kinston, choosing instead to make his way north to Weldon and Petersburg. As commander of the expedition, he refused to shoulder any of the blame for the bungled operation. Instead, he cited "lack of cooperation" and, more particularly, the failure of Barton to carry out his part of the plan. Pickett called for an investigation of Barton's conduct. In his official report of the campaign, Barton joined in the request: "The press and common rumor have been kept busy in casting censure upon my course. If my superiors entertain similar opinions, I request that a court of inquiry be called to investigate the matter." Lee subsequently ordered the investigation, but there is no record that a court of inquiry was ever convened. Hoke likewise pointed an accusing finger at Barton. "Being a junior officer," he noted, "it does not become me to speak my thoughts" of Barton's failure to carry out his part of the program.[29]

Pickett, however, could not escape personal criticisms about his failure to take New Bern. Commander John Taylor Wood criticized Pickett's decision to call off the attack. From the opposing navy came the opinion of Admiral David D. Porter: "Had the enemy attacked the forts, the chances are that they would have been successful, as the garrison was unprepared for an attack on the river flank, their most vulnerable side." Junior officers in the Confederate army who had taken part also derogated Pickett's handling of the mission. Captain Robert D. Graham of the Fifty-sixth North Carolina later recalled, "It seemed the general opinion that a determined assault would have been crowned with success." Lieutenant Thomas D. Roulhac concurred: "That New Bern could have been taken in a short time and without any considerable loss, if any vigorous pressing had undertaken by our troops on either side of the river, is now well ascertained."[30]

On the other hand, Hoke's efforts at New Bern generally drew praise. Laudatory comments could be found in the pro-Confederate newspapers in the state. For example, the *Raleigh Daily Confederate* told its readers that Hoke's "rout of the enemy, the pursuit of the fugitives, and the advance of the brigade to within range of the fortifications around the town, were successful exemplifications of the ardor and courage of our troops when well-handled." Of the general officers involved in the New Bern campaign, only Hoke was praised by Lee. In a letter to Hoke on February 11, Lee wrote, "I am glad to see that you and your gallant brigade accomplished your part of the work, while I regret very much that success did not attend the whole expedition." Indeed, by this time, Lee had come to see Hoke as he was described by Major John W. Moore of the Third North Carolina Battalion (artillery): "He was still a youth, but a gravity beyond his years, cojoined with judgment, discretion and serenity amid danger, marked him for command and the conduct of great enterprises."[31]

There were many who were of the belief that had Hoke been in supreme command of the mission, it would have succeeded. The daring John Taylor Wood, grandson of President Zachary Taylor, expressed that belief to Jefferson Davis upon his return to Richmond. Private W. R. Burwell of the Forty-third North Carolina wrote, "If Genl Hoke had had command of the last expedition to Newbern it would certainly have been in our hands now." According to one civilian, Hoke was the "moving spirit" behind the operation.[32]

By February 5, Hoke and his brigade were back in Kinston, "still eager for new adventures." Bitterly disappointed over the lack of success that had attended the recent campaign, Hoke reflected on the lost opportunity: "Our surprise was most complete, and had all parties done their duty our hopes would have been more than realized. We know the place was within our grasp, which was seen before leaving the front of town. The enemy were thoroughly routed and demoralized."

Despite his lingering frustration and regret, Hoke was most optimistic about the future. Overall, Confederate losses at New Bern had been relatively light, and the spoils had been significant: 300 prisoners, 2 flags, several field guns, a variety of wagons, 103 horses and mules, and a large quantity of stores and provisions. Hoke was enthusiastic about the mental and physical condition of his soldiers when, several days after his return to Kinston, he wrote, "My men are in good health and fine spirits. The troops do not look upon our campaign as a failure, as the real object was not known to them and the capture of several rich camps pleased them wonderfully."[33]

Hoke's spirits and confidence were buoyed by the fact that he and his brigade were authorized to remain in North Carolina in anticipation of another attempt at the Federal strongholds in the state. Lee had intimated as much in his January 20 letter to Hoke: "Upon completing the business concerning which you have oral instructions, you will take some convenient position in North Carolina and recruit your regiments." As for his eagerness to tackle a new engagement on the coastal plain, Hoke wrote in a report to Lee's trusted aide, Major Walter Taylor, on February 8, "I assure you I found matters more favorable than I expected. The work could have been done, and still can be accomplished."

The prospects for a subsequent campaign against the Federals in eastern North Carolina improved substantially on February 11 when Lee, in an attempt to put the New Bern expedition in the past and look toward a new offensive, told Hoke, "It is difficult in a combined attack to regulate and harmonize on an extensive field all the operations, but much was accomplished, and I hope the information will secure future success. I hope you will also do all in your power for the comfort of your men, as well as render them as strong and effective in the approaching campaign as possible." Lee's words only served to stoke the fire in Hoke, who was more anxious than ever to deal a death blow to Union domination of the upper coastal plain of North Carolina.[34]

Both Lee and Hoke knew that much of the success of any future offensive in eastern North Carolina hinged on the availability of the two Confederate ironclads being constructed on the Roanoke and Neuse Rivers. On January 20, Lee had lamented to Jefferson Davis that neither ship would be available for the attempt to take New Bern. After the expedition failed, Pickett warned, "I would not advise a new movement against New Berne or Washington again till the iron-clads are done."

Fortunately for Hoke, both of the vessels were nearing completion in February. To the north, near Hamilton on the Roanoke River, the CSS *Albemarle* was being forged into a formidable naval weapon, while at Kinston, her sister ship, the CSS *Neuse*, was also beginning to take on the appearance of a gunboat and battering ram after a history of frustrating delays. Hoke, who had supervision over both projects as they rushed toward completion, hoped to have the two ships available for service by March 1. From his headquarters at Kinston, he paid particular attention to the *Neuse*. By February 8, he had assigned ninety-five carpenters and mechanics and fifty laborers from his brigade to aid in the completion of the vessel. Hoke's words on that day not only expressed the importance he placed on the project, but his great determination as well: "In the mean time I will remain here, where I have already made my men comfortable, and push forward the work, and at the same time give the boat protection, which is absolutely necessary. . . . There is no doubt of success in this undertaking, and we cannot and must not stop."[35]

Throughout February, Hoke also worked to fill the ranks of his brigade and procure provisions for his men. Lieutenant Colonel Samuel M. Tate of the Sixth North Carolina was sent to the western and central portions of the state to locate recruits. Meanwhile, Hoke was forced to deal with the unpleasant duties of his command. During the unhappy retreat from

New Bern, Pickett had happened to be near a group of the Union soldiers captured during the campaign. An officer of the Sixth North Carolina remarked, "They belong to my company." Overhearing the comment, Pickett was enraged. He screamed, "You damned rascals, I'll have you shot, and all the damned rascals who desert." As the prisoners were led away, Pickett told those around him, "We'll have a court martial on those fellows pretty soon, and after some are shot, the rest will stop deserting." Almost as soon as the retreat was over, Pickett ordered a court-martial, composed of Virginia officers, to convene at Kinston. Twenty-two of the prisoners, all members of the First and Second Regiments, North Carolina Union Volunteers, were hurried before the tribunal. Charged with desertion, the men were convicted and sentenced to die by hanging. Pickett summarily approved the death warrants, and Hoke was ordered to execute the sentences.[36]

While awaiting their execution, the condemned men were confined in the courthouse dungeon at Kinston, where their friends and families were allowed to visit them. On February 5, Hoke requested that Chaplain Paris visit two deserters who were destined to be the first hanged. Paris found the captives to be the "most hardened and unfeeling men I ever encountered." These two men, known as William Haddock and William Jones, were hanged publicly in the presence of Confederate soldiers and civilians. One of Hoke's soldiers described the impression that the executions made upon him: "I suppose you heard of Genl H. hanging some deserters who were caught near Newbern. I saw two hung the first men I ever saw hung in my life and the last I ever intend to see if I can help it."

Over the course of the month, the other twenty condemned men were taken to the gallows. Before each execution, Hoke sent Paris to counsel them. On Monday, February 15, the chaplain baptized eight of the prisoners. Noting that the distress of their wives and children was "truly great," Paris recorded that thirteen men were arranged on a single scaffold and "ushered into Eternity at a given signal."

After all of the death sentences had been carried out, the chaplain deemed it appropriate to deliver a sermon about the executions to Hoke's brigade. In his discourse on Sunday, February 28, Paris asked Hoke's soldiers, "But who were those twenty-two men whom you hanged upon the gallows?

They were your fellow-beings. They were citizens of our own Carolina. They once marched under the same beautiful flag that waves over our heads, but in an evil hour, they yielded to mischievous influences, and from motives or feelings base and sordid, unmanly and vile, resolved to abandon every principle of patriotism, and sacrificed every impulse of honor, this sealed their ruin and enstamped their lasting disgrace."[37]

Hoke's personal sentiments about the executions were manifested when Bryon McCullom called on the general to seek an order for the body of his brother-in-law, in order to bury it. When Hoke asked if he wanted to bury the executed man in a Yankee uniform, McCullom responded in the affirmative. Hoke then expressed surprise that "so respectable a man would bury his brother-in-law in a Yankee uniform."[38]

News of the hangings was greeted with outrage in the North, and the ensuing controversy would survive the war and be a source of great concern for Hoke during the early days of Reconstruction.[39] But in February 1864, he had little time to dwell on the matter.

By month's end, Hoke brought his brigade up to full strength. His fighting machine now boasted 1,664 officers and men. For Hoke, the new year continued to hold great promise. And in the eyes of the North Carolina delegation in the Congress of the Confederate States of America, Hoke held great promise for the cause of Southern independence. Consequently, the entire delegation submitted a joint recommendation that Hoke be promoted to major general. Although Jefferson Davis was receptive to the proposal, he pointed out, "The merit of General Hoke is fully recognized. The question of a vacancy first presents itself—without which promotion would be a withdrawal from active duty." Secretary of War Seddon concurred: "There is no vacancy at present for the gallant officer."[40] Forces were already at work, however, that would soon cause both Davis and Seddon to quickly find a vacancy for Hoke.

"The Battle of Plymouth
was over. Hoke had just
dealt Union forces their
first substantial defeat in
North Carolina . . ."

CHAPTER 7

"Heaven Has Crowned Our Efforts with Success"

In March, a whirlwind of political and military considerations on both the state and national level swept Hoke into the vortex as the dominant player in the significant events that would unfold in North Carolina over the next two months.

Despite the overall failure of the Pickett operation at New Bern, Jefferson Davis remained convinced that Union forces could be driven from eastern North Carolina. Nonetheless, Pickett's inept handling of the New Bern offensive forced Davis to reassess the military leadership for the campaign. As a result, Pickett was recalled to Virginia and Lee's original nominee for the project, Hoke, was placed in command of the Confederate forces in North Carolina. And although Lee was steadily growing more apprehensive about the impending spring offensive by Union forces in Virginia, he expressed confidence that Hoke would be successful. In late March, Lee noted in a letter to Davis, "I have delayed calling for Genl Hoke, who besides his own brigade, has two regiments of another of this army, under the expectations that the object of his visit to North Carolina might yet be accomplished."[1]

In early 1864, Governor Vance faced complicated political and domestic problems on the state level that required assistance from Richmond. Less than a week after Vance opened his reelection campaign for governor in late February, William Woods Holden, the editor of the *Raleigh Standard*, announced his candidacy, based on a platform of "peace at all costs." So concerned was Davis with the peace movement in Raleigh that he ordered Hoke's brigade near the capital for a brief time in March to guard against civil unrest.[2]

Davis chose to solve Vance's "headaches" in North Carolina by military means. The president was cognizant that much of northeastern North Carolina had been under Union control for two years and that, as a consequence, the Confederacy and the state had lost control of some of its most vital waterways and fishing grounds, as well as the fertile agricultural lands along Albemarle Sound and other sounds. As Davis saw it, returning this region to Confederate control would not only materially help the war effort, but also would quell the growing disaffection in North Carolina.[3]

As the man selected to effect Davis's military solution, Hoke spent the month of March with a single goal in mind: to rid his native state of enemy troops. With the exception of the brief emergency service near Raleigh, his brigade remained at its camp in Kinston. Early in the month, the major decision confronting Hoke and the Confederate high command was where to strike the enemy first. Essentially, the Confederates had two choices: they could hit the Federal forces at New Bern for the third time in a year, or they could launch a three-stage offensive that would begin with the Union stronghold at Plymouth and, if successful, proceed south to Washington and New Bern.[4]

Even though the Confederate presence at Kinston was well known to the enemy, the uncertainty as to its ultimate destination kept the Federals strung out between Plymouth and New Bern and prevented a consolidation of forces against the impending offensive. Ultimately, the Confederate decision as to whether to begin the new campaign at Plymouth or New Bern was based upon the completion of the first of the two Confederate ironclads being constructed in the region. To ensure success for Hoke's campaign, the cooperation of at least one of the ironclads was considered a necessity. Although Hoke had directed his personal attention to the project throughout much of February, the CSS *Neuse* was behind schedule and could not be counted on to sail down the river of the same name in mid-April for a confrontation at New Bern. In a letter to his brother dated March 10, Private William R. Burwell of the Forty-third North Carolina, which was temporarily assigned to Hoke, reported, "There is a gun boat being built here and from what the workmen say, some of whom are of this Regt., it will not be finished before the first of May although everyone seems to think it will be done in a month or six weeks." On the other hand, and opportunely for Hoke that March, the sister ironclad, the CSS *Albemarle*, was quickly being readied for duty at Hamilton, about thirty-five miles up the Roanoke River from Plymouth.[5]

Thus, by March, Plymouth looked to be the most logical target for the Confederate offensive. During the second week of the month, Hoke traveled to Richmond to confer with Davis. There, he unveiled his proposed campaign to expel all enemy troops from North Carolina. Davis listened as the general explained that with his brigade and two others, and with the assistance of the *Albemarle*, he believed he could capture Plymouth, Washington, and New Bern. Following the presentation, the president posed many questions about the Federal strongholds in eastern North Carolina, and particularly about the feasibility of an expedition against Plymouth. Hoke assured Davis that if he were instructed to attack Plymouth or any other place in his home state, there would be a fight. Davis ended the conference by telling Hoke that he was delighted to know that someone still thought something could be done. Hoke left with assurances that he would be provided with the necessary forces to accomplish his purpose in North Carolina.

During his stay in Richmond, Hoke attended a church service with a host of Confederate generals including Robert E. Lee, James Longstreet,

Braxton Bragg, W. H. C. Whiting, and Thomas Lanier Clingman. With her acerbic pen, diarist Mary Boykin Chesnut proclaimed, "Somebody counted fourteen generals in church and suggested that less piety and more drilling of commands would suit the times better."[6]

On his return trip to North Carolina, Hoke took a freight train at Weldon in order to rejoin his command. At Nahunta (now Fremont) in Wayne County, the train was delayed on a siding so that a passenger train might pass. While they waited, Hoke and two passengers who were bound for Raleigh on business departed the train and built a fire to warm themselves on the chilly night. As the three talked, it was revealed that the two Raleigh-bound men were from Plymouth. Hoke did not introduce himself, he was not wearing any indication of rank, and the men did not know or recognize him. Therefore, he was able to direct innumerable questions to them about Plymouth. In the course of the conversation, the two men complained of the many depredations committed by Union forces. They told Hoke that many blacks were fleeing to the Federal lines from the farms near the Plymouth fortifications. One of the men noted that he had lost ten blacks in such a manner and would give one to any person who recovered the other nine for him.[7]

While specific plans were being formulated in Richmond, the soldiers in Hoke's command were being readied for the coming combat. Mary Chesnut's words were not meant for the troops in Kinston, because drilling was the order of the day throughout March and early April, not only for the new recruits Hoke and Lieutenant Colonel Samuel M. Tate of the Sixth North Carolina had brought to Kinston, but for the veterans as well. Second Lieutenant William Beavans of the Forty-third North Carolina noted in his daybook, "Busy drilling; all day, nothing but drilling." Beavans's compatriot, Lieutenant George Wills, did not associate the continuous drilling with combat readiness, but saw it as a lack of discipline in Hoke's brigade: "The officers of this Brig. are generally so loose that they had to go to drilling to keep the men from plundering the country." Beavans echoed Wills's sentiments about the general's manner in running his camp: "Gen. Hoke is not very strict." Private Burwell complained about the site of the camp: "We are encamped about the same place we were this time last year and what a doleful and dreary looking place it is. Nothing but pine thickets and swamps as far as you can see. We are on the opposite side of the Neuse River from Kinston and about a half mile from the river."[8]

Despite the complaints about camp geography and drilling, March found Hoke's men "well and hearty and i[n] fine spirits," for there was now time for fun while the brigade enjoyed a brief break from combat. The fair weather of early March provided the opportunity to fish in the numerous creeks and swamps near the camp. By mid-month, the temperatures dropped, and a week of intermittent snow and sleet replaced the sunny skies. This change yielded a landscape for recreational snowball warfare similar to what Hoke had enjoyed in the Shenandoah Valley. On March 23, the day after a storm of heavy sleet and snow, Chaplain Paris noted in his diary, "Gen. Hoke at the head of his Brigade Attacked Gen. Corse's Brigade of Virginians in a Snowball fight, and was whipt. Corse attacked us in camp and got whipt in turn."[9]

After Jefferson Davis approved Plymouth as the first target of the campaign in eastern North Carolina, he apparently left the final planning and troop assignments to his newly appointed chief of staff and military advisor, General Braxton Bragg. Both Bragg and Hoke were cognizant of the vital role that the *Albemarle* would play in the coming campaign. To ensure perfect coordination between land and water forces in the attack, Hoke insisted that the commander of the ironclad be placed under his command. Davis initially demurred to the request, citing the potential for discord between the Navy Department and War Department, but he ultimately acceded to Hoke's wishes and issued an appropriate order.

Toward the close of March, Hoke traveled to Hamilton to inspect the *Albemarle* and confer with its commander, James W. Cooke. Like Hoke, Cooke was a native North Carolinian who welcomed an opportunity to drive the enemy from his state. Hoke found the ironclad in the final stages of completion. When he informed Cooke that he would need the gunboat for a mid-April attack at Plymouth, he was told that it would be impossible to have the ram ready by that time. But Hoke was insistent; he explained that the front in Virginia would not remain quiet for long, and that the opportunity would soon pass. Finally, Hoke's entreaties wore Cooke down, and the general got the reply he wanted: the ram would be ready "in fifteen days, with ten additional mechanics." Upon Hoke's return to Kinston, he dispatched the needed carpenters and workmen from his brigade to Hamilton.[10]

Although the ram Hoke inspected in late March lacked much of its exterior metal plating, it had at last taken on the appearance of a warship. Just days before, it had been floated two miles down the river from Edwards Ferry, where it had been constructed over the past year. Gilbert Elliott, the nineteen-year-old marine engineer from Elizabeth City awarded the design and construction contract for the vessel, said, "No vessel was ever constructed under more adverse circumstances." Because the "shipyard" at Edwards Ferry was nothing more than a cornfield beside the river, the ram earned the nickname "Cornfield Ironclad." Despite that unsophisticated sobriquet and the primitive working conditions at the site where its keel was laid, the *Albemarle* was to be a mighty vessel. Designed to destroy ships by ramming them with an eighteen-foot prow, it was mounted with a deadly armament of two eight-inch Brooke rifles.[11]

While Cooke was striving to armor the *Albemarle* for a showdown at Plymouth, time was running out for the Hoke expedition as March faded into April. Disappointed that neither ironclad was combat-ready and increasingly anxious about the massing Union forces around Richmond and Petersburg, Lee urged Bragg on April 7 to return Hoke's brigade to him. Several days later, he was a bit more adamant in a letter to George Pickett: "As far as I can judge, the Army of the Potomac will advance as soon as the roads will permit, and I shall require all the re-inforcements I can get. I therefore request you to forward Hoke's command as soon as you can."

Although Confederate authorities had "tactfully disposed of" Pickett after the New Bern fiasco, he apparently harbored no ill feelings over being supplanted by Hoke in North Carolina. In fact, he continued to support the Hoke campaign even after Lee began to call for Hoke's return to Virginia. Nevertheless, when Bragg sent copies of Hoke's marching orders to Pickett on April 12, he carefully worded his communiqué so as to not offend the displaced general: "Inclosed I send you copies of instructions to Brigadier General Hoke and Brigadier General Ransom, both sent direct to save time, which is an essential element in the operations contemplated. . . . The conduct of this expedition is intrusted to Brigadier Hoke, so as not to withdraw you from a supervision of your whole department at this critical time." A day earlier, Bragg had notified Lee of Davis's decision to proceed with the Plymouth campaign. He noted that Hoke was "being employed in an important expedition which may add materially to our sources of supply for the subsistence of your command."[12]

Amid the correspondence among Lee, Pickett, and Bragg, Hoke was recalled to Richmond for consultation with the Confederate high command. There, he learned that the days of indecision and planning were over: he was to proceed with the Plymouth campaign. On April 12, Hoke returned to Kinston exhilarated and anxious to proceed with the great mission. His attitude was infectious. William Beavans noted in his diary on the day of Hoke's return, "Quite an excitement about moving." Rumors were rampant about the destination of the mission. On April 13, Chaplain Paris sounded an ominous note: "Our ambulances and horses started at 4 o'clock A.M. where we know not."[13]

From Confederate headquarters in Richmond came Hoke's much-awaited orders under date of April 12. In part, they read,

> GENERAL: You are assigned to the special command of the land forces for an expedition against Plymouth, &c in Eastern North Carolina. Your force will be . . . immediately assembled at Tarborough. . . . As soon as you are prepared to move from Tarborough you will notify the commander of the gunboat *Albemarle*, and inform him at what time you propose to make your attack, so that he may co-operate as nearly as possible. . . . In your movement on Plymouth, success will depend in great measure on celerity and secrecy, but great confidence is reposed on your well-known activity and energy. . . . Should you succeed in the first step, in capturing Plymouth and opening the river, then your attention should be immediately directed to Washington and New Bern.[14]

When Hoke's brigade entrained for Tarboro on Thursday, April 14, it exhibited a new makeup. The Fifty-fourth and Fifty-seventh North Carolina were detached temporarily; they remained at Kinston with Corse's brigade to defend the city and to keep the Federals worried about a possible attack on New Bern. These two regiments were replaced by the Forty-third North Carolina. Because Hoke was in charge of the entire campaign, the command of his brigade—now composed of the Sixth, Twenty-first, and Forty-third North Carolina and the Twenty-first Georgia—evolved to John T. Mercer of the Twenty-first Georgia. In 1854, Mercer had graduated fortieth in a class of forty-six at West Point, where his class had included many noted future general officers of both armies, including G. W. C. Lee, Thomas H. Ruger, Oliver O. Howard, John Pegram, Jeb Stuart, Stephen D. Lee, and William Dorsey Pender. Though described as "brave as the bravest and a splendid military officer," Mercer had not risen above the rank of colonel, to which he had been appointed by Jefferson Davis on July 19, 1861.[15]

At 3 P.M. on April 14, the brigade arrived at the staging area in Tarboro where most of the remainder of Hoke's assault force was being assembled. To ensure the success of the expedition, Davis and Bragg had provided Hoke with an impressive array of troops. In addition to his own brigade, Hoke's little army included Matt W. Ransom's brigade, composed of the Eighth, Twenty-fourth, Twenty-fifth, Thirty-fifth, and Fifty-sixth North Carolina; James L. Kemper's brigade (commanded by Colonel William R. Terry of the Twenty-fourth Virginia), composed of the First, Third, Seventh, Eleventh, and Twenty-fourth Virginia; Colonel James Dearing's regiment of cavalry; and an artillery force of some thirty-five guns in the batteries of Branch and Reid of Virginia, Miller of North Carolina, Lee of Alabama, and Bradford of Mississippi. John Taylor Wood accompanied the expedition as an advisor to Hoke. In all, the Confederate forces under Hoke numbered about seven thousand, and the expeditionary force resembled a large division.[16]

In Plymouth, Hoke and his superiors had chosen an attractive target. Not only was the town a vital outpost for continued Union domination of the upper Albemarle region of North Carolina, but it served as an important supply depot for Federal land forces operating in the tidewater part of the state. Moreover, official correspondence recently intercepted by the Confederates indicated that the Federals proposed to send a strong force up the Roanoke River to Weldon to sever the railroad to Richmond—and thus Lee's "lifeline." Consequently, Hoke's mission was of singular importance in North Carolina.

But at Plymouth, the young general faced a formidable challenge. Located on the south bank of the Roanoke River approximately three miles west of its mouth on Albemarle Sound, the highly sought-after prize presented a wide assortment of geographic barriers that made Hoke's task most difficult. Vast, virtually impenetrable swamps were on the north side of the river and the south side of town. On the west side, the invading army would encounter Welch's Creek and a woody marsh that extended around the southwest corner of town. On the east, a series of swamps and Conaby Creek posed logistical problems for Hoke.[17]

Three important roads—Washington Road from the southwest, Lee's Mill Road from the south, and Columbia Road from the east—made their way into town. However, none of these routes was open to Hoke's army; instead, each was protected by the extensive system of Union defenses in and around Plymouth. Over the year and a half that the town had been under Union control, it had been transformed into a veritable Gibraltar. The mastermind behind the intricate fortifications was Brigadier General William H. Wessells, a fifty-five-year-old West Point graduate who had assumed command at Plymouth on May 3, 1863. During his tenure, "every appliance of engineering skill and yankee industry with pick and spade had been exhausted for a twelve months' labor to make Plymouth a Sebastopol."[18]

Fort Gray, the outermost of the earthwork forts protecting the Union stronghold, was located two miles upriver on the south shore of the Roanoke. Named for Colonel Charles O. Gray, who had fallen in previous fighting in eastern North Carolina, the diamond-shaped fort was isolated from and out of sight of Plymouth on Warrens Neck, a spit of land created by two creeks. Armed with several big guns with a range of over a mile, the fort was designed to protect the town from approaching enemy riverboats. Nearby and just downriver was Battery Worth, one of the numerous redoubts constructed to augment the forts. It mounted a two-hundred-pound rifled gun. South of this installation, a line of breastworks extended to the southwest corner of town and then proceeded east along the southern boundary of Plymouth. In the town, "the fortifications were somewhat in the shape of a parallelogram, the longest side parallel to the river," according to Major John W. Graham of the Fifty-sixth North Carolina. Fort Williams, the strongest and oldest of the defense works, served as the headquarters of General Wessells and guarded the southern approach to town. Located along the breastworks between Washington and Lee's Mill Roads, the fort projected a half-dozen heavy siege guns and three field guns from its commanding elevation. It was enclosed on all sides by a stockade and surrounded by a moatlike ditch crossed by a drawbridge. Fort Wessells (also known as Fort Sanderson), located less than a mile southwest and just outside the breastworks, was a smaller fort with a similar moat-and-drawbridge defense; also known as the Eighty-fifth Redoubt, it mounted two guns. And even though General Wessells surmised that an attack from the east was highly unlikely because of the natural barriers there, two small installations, Fort Comfort and Conaby Redoubt, were constructed adjacent to Columbia Road. Together, the forts and batteries were armed with approximately thirty cannon.[19]

In the spring of 1864, Wessells's 2,834-man garrison included the 85th New York, the 16th Connecticut, the 101st and 103rd Pennsylvania, two companies of the 2nd North Carolina Union Volunteers, two companies of the 2nd Massachusetts Heavy Artillery, the 24th New York Independent Battery of Light Artillery, and two companies of the 12th New York Cavalry. To further solidify the defenses of Plymouth, Lieutenant Commander C. W. Flusser of the United States Navy patrolled the Roanoke River with a small flotilla which included four gunboats (the *Miami*, the *Southfield*, the *Whitehead*, and the *Ceres*) and one transport (the *Bombshell*). Flusser, a native of Kentucky who was known as an "officer of rare intrepidity and merit," sought to thwart the approach of enemy gunboats by placing mines, sunken vessels, and other obstructions in the river at Thoroughfare Gap near Warrens Neck.[20]

By late March, Union authorities in North Carolina had begun to pay special attention to the intelligence trickling in about the Confederate buildup in eastern North Carolina. Information from deserters and "loyal"

North Carolinians indicated that not only was the *Albemarle* nearing completion, but that Confederate forces were beginning to mass near the Union strongholds. From Plymouth, Edward Nicholas Boots, quartermaster of the 101st Pennsylvania, expressed a defiant, confident attitude in a letter to his sister on March 30: "We are making preparations for receiving a visit from a ram that the rebels have built up the river. . . . So you can see we think ourselves in a fit state to receive the rebel sheep whenever it chooses to honor us with a visit."[21]

Within a week, the garrison at Plymouth was shocked into the realization that a fight was close at hand. On April 9, a drizzle fell during the entire day, and the gray skies only served to heighten the gloom, frustration, and despondency resulting from the cancellation of all veteran furloughs, due to "the continued threat of the enemy." More than thirty years later, a Union veteran from the 103rd Pennsylvania was still complaining when he wrote Hoke, "You deprived me of a furlough home and sent me instead to Andersonville Prison."[22]

Despite the discouraging news that no assistance was forthcoming, Lieutenant Commander Flusser was determined to ready the river for the approaching ironclad. In addition to placing river obstructions, he lashed the *Southfield* and the *Miami* together with spars and chains in a V-shaped formation. Flusser's plan was to lure the *Albemarle* into the V, where it would be captured or destroyed by shore guns at Fort Gray and Battery Worth. Cautiously confident, Flusser was heard to say, "If I can bring the ram to close quarters, I will sink her, or by Goddamn, I will sink myself." His statement would prove prophetic.[23]

About the same time, Hoke garnered praise and encouragement from the press for his attention to affairs in eastern North Carolina. Just before his attack on Plymouth, a Raleigh newspaper credited the general with changing "the public sentiment of the area" by acting as a "terror to tyrants and traitors [and an] unflinching advocate of justice." Using rhetoric that sounded like a pre-battle pep talk, the newspaper told its readers, "Whatever [Hoke] does he does with all might [and] he fearlessly pursues the path of duty."[24]

By mid-April, the time was at hand for Hoke to prove himself worthy of the confidence reposed in him by Davis, Lee, Bragg, and the entire Confederate nation. At 10 A.M. on the rainy morning of Friday, April 15, with regimental flags flying and bugles blowing, Hoke set his expeditionary force in motion. The Confederate quest to liberate eastern North Carolina was under way. As the Southern soldiers began the first leg of their three-day, sixty-five-mile march to Plymouth, Kemper's brigade took the lead, followed by Ransom's, and then Hoke's (headed by Colonel Mercer). After a difficult fifteen-mile march through a steady rain and over muddy roads, the army made camp about two miles west of Hamilton. During the night, a torrential rain soaked the soldiers as they tried to sleep. Bad weather notwithstanding, Lieutenant Colonel William Gaston Lewis of the Forty-third North Carolina expressed the high morale of Hoke's army in a letter to his wife written as the drenching rain fell: "We are all in good spirits and have no doubt of our success."[25]

On Saturday, April 16, the army, with Ransom's brigade now in front, resumed its trek east. While in the Hamilton area, Hoke made one final call on the *Albemarle* and Commander Cooke, who again assured the general that the ironclad would participate in the assault on Plymouth whether it was completed or not. Upon rejoining his army, Hoke, cognizant of Bragg's mandate to maintain secrecy, swung his army south of Williamston to avoid the Union patrols that he knew frequented the area. In his diary, Second Lieutenant Beavans noted that even though the rain continued during the morning, the "roads [were] very good for the country." At nightfall, the march was halted at Fosters Mill, some five miles south of Williamston. Local citizens told Hoke that the adjacent creek could be easily forded; however, upon close examination, the general found it to be six feet deep and ordered pontoons laid. Consequently, the army made camp for the night in the vicinity of the creek.[26]

At 5 A.M. on Sunday, April 17, Hoke broke camp for the final leg of the march. Although Plymouth was just sixteen miles distant, the route Hoke was forced to take covered twenty-two miles. The new day dawned, according to Second Lieutenant Beavans, "very pretty, pleasant and warm," and despite the recent rains, the roads were "tolerably good." At Plymouth, a surgeon from the Eighty-fifth New York agreed with Beavans's assessment of the weather, describing April 17 "as one of the loveliest of spring days, even for the South." During the Confederate march, which passed through Jamesville, Hoke's army was completed with the arrival of Dearing's cavalry, the Thirty-fifth North Carolina, and the artillery.

By 4 P.M., Hoke was within five miles of Plymouth, and at that point, he made his first strategic move in preparation for laying siege to the town. He divided his army, sending Kemper's brigade, Colonel Dearing, most of the cavalry, and some pieces of artillery to attack Fort Gray two miles away, while he and the remainder of his force continued on the road to Plymouth. They turned right at a creek four miles from town. Finding the bridge down, the soldiers hurried across a mill dam and made their way to the junction of Jamesville and Washington Roads, about two miles from town. There, a detachment of cavalry scouts surprised Union pickets, capturing nine and killing two. However, two blue-clad soldiers escaped the skirmish and sounded the alarm. One of them, Lieutenant Robert J. H. Russell of the Twelfth New York Cavalry, rode into Plymouth "severely wounded and barely clinging to his horse" just as the garrison was preparing for a dress parade. Suddenly, Wessells's soldiers heard the long roll instead of the expected bugle and drum call for parade. Plymouth was under attack![27]

Wessells's forces rushed to action. As Union haversacks were packed with hardtack and their owners made their way to defensive positions in the trenches, Wessells sent an urgent dispatch to Union authorities in New Bern informing them that the Confederate attack had been commenced by as many as five brigades. But Major General John J. Peck, the commander of Union forces in North Carolina, was under the false impression that Washington was being attacked and felt he could not render assistance. In what was most likely a ruse developed by Hoke, two planted "deserters" turned up at Peck's headquarters just about the time action was beginning in Plymouth. They informed Peck "that General Corse was in front of the outposts at Batchelder's Creek with a large force of all arms, and that General Pickett would attack Little Washington on Tuesday."[28]

While the Union survivors of the cavalry affray were making their way into Plymouth to sound the alarm, Hoke and the main body of his troops were learning of the initial encounter with the enemy. James C. Elliott of the Fifty-sixth North Carolina captured the moment: "As they brought prisoners back, we noticed one horse shot in the nose, and a little further on a dead Yankee in the road."

For Hoke, it was now apparent that the element of surprise had been lost. Accordingly, his artillery fired a few well-placed shells into Plymouth. One "hissing, rushing, screeching" shell found its way into the guard-house of the Eighty-fifth New York. Another exploded in the quarters of Company F of the same regiment. Forthwith, an avalanche of shells from the Union guns, particularly from Fort Williams, was directed toward the two Confederate brigades on the south side of town, but the projectiles fell harmlessly short. Hoke's batteries stood by without reply as the general put his forces into battle formation. Mercer's brigade, about four hundred yards in front, was deployed on both sides of the road. Ransom, who urged Hoke to "advance at once," was placed to the right of the road. A Confederate soldier writing under the pseudonym of "Lone Star" told readers of the *Raleigh Daily Confederate*, "The march had been long and rapid; and the men were much fatigued, but eager to advance at once, and entering the place with pickets; take it by *coup de main*, and render effective the surprise." Disdaining Ransom's advice, Hoke chose a more deliberate course of action in anticipation of the arrival of the *Albemarle*.[29]

All the while, Hoke and his soldiers could hear the roar of Dearing's guns to the left on Warrens Neck. From a distance of fifteen hundred yards, Dearing used a cannonade to effect damage at Fort Gray. With deadly accuracy, the Confederate shells ripped away the garrison's flagstaff and disabled the gunboat *Ceres*. Under cover of the artillery, sharpshooters advanced toward the compound and offered such withering fire that Fort Gray's artillerists responded with wild shots from their guns. With the fort under siege, Dearing and Terry refrained from an attempt to storm it, fearing heavy losses.[30]

Almost simultaneously with the commencement of hostilities in Plymouth, the *Albemarle* slipped its moorings at Hamilton for its rendezvous with destiny downriver. At 3 P.M., just one hour after the ram had been commissioned, Cooke gave the order, "Cast off all lines." Resembling a large turtle adrift in the river, the ship had mechanics scrambling about its decks to complete the armor plating on the port side. The inexperienced crewmen, described as "long, lank Tar Heels . . . from the Piney woods," were volunteers from Hoke's brigade. Not long after the voyage downstream began, a small steamer arrived alongside to deliver to Cooke a detachment of twenty Confederate sailors and an officer from Charleston. At 10 P.M., a drive-shaft coupling broke, causing an eight-hour delay while blacksmiths worked to fashion repair parts.[31]

Back at Plymouth, Hoke, confident of initial success at Fort Gray, sent forward Mercer's and Ransom's skirmishers. The infantrymen streamed through the pine forests toward the entrenched Union positions. By nightfall, except for "an occasional interchange of shots between the skirmishers," the fighting ceased. Under a flag of truce, Hoke made a demand for the surrender of Plymouth. Wessells responded indignantly: "Take it." In a reply that foretold the coming hostilities, Hoke retorted, "Remove all non-combatants within twenty-four hours." Wessells ordered his men, who now realized they were surrounded by enemy forces, to sleep on their arms. And although little or no action took place along the lines after the sun went down, "great commotion existed through the night in Plymouth."[32]

In the predawn hours of Monday, April 18—during the calm before the storm—Hoke moved Mercer's brigade forward and farther to the left of Washington Road in anticipation of an attack on Fort Wessells. At 2:30 A.M., the Fifty-sixth North Carolina was called up to a position just behind the skirmishers. Until dawn, a detail of 250 men from the regiment was deployed in throwing up breastworks for Branch's guns in advance of the main Confederate line. At daylight, a new detail was brought forward to complete the breastworks, and the Twenty-fifth North Carolina took over skirmishing duties and extended the line farther to the right.[33]

Meanwhile, up the river at Fort Gray, Colonel Terry advanced Kemper's brigade through knee-deep swamp water to within eight hundred to a thousand feet of the fort. Two companies of the Eleventh Virginia made their way four hundred feet closer, well within musket range of Gray's defenders, and were forced to endure the "dogs of war . . . shells, grapeshot, canister, and minie balls." Dearing's artillery could not provide effective cover, and the Virginians retreated with a loss of two dead and thirty wounded. The reduction of Fort Gray would have to wait until the main assault on Plymouth was completed. Nevertheless, during the artillery exchange at Fort Gray in the early-morning hours of April 18, there was one significant success for the Confederates: the dispatch boat *Bombshell* sustained serious damage below the waterline and went down in the river several hours later at a wharf on the Plymouth waterfront.[34]

By midmorning, Hoke was prepared to open his offensive in earnest. With his artillery now in place, the batteries opened up on Fort Wessells and were countered with return fire from that fort and Fort Williams. The fire from Fort Wessells was quickly silenced, although the big guns of Fort Williams continued booming throughout the day. About 5 P.M., Hoke positioned his troops for the assault on Fort Wessells. He selected his own brigade and one artillery battery for the attack.[35]

To keep Fort Williams occupied, Hoke ordered Ransom to use his brigade and fourteen pieces of artillery to demonstrate against that fort. With his artillery out front, Ransom's line advanced toward the enemy in the face of twenty pieces of artillery and two gunboats raining down "every grade of shell from 200-pound gun to the 12-pound Napoleon." While bravely manning the big guns at Fort Williams, some of the Union gunners paid a horrible price. From 6 P.M. to 10 P.M., the North Carolinians inched to within eight hundred yards of the fort. Major John W. Graham described the advance: "It was splendidly done, the skirmishers running the enemy over his breastworks, some pieces of our Artillery firing over 200 times, and the Infantry advancing in admirable order." A correspondent for the *Richmond Examiner* identified only as "R" described the nighttime fighting around Fort Williams in picturesque terms: "The action commenced about sunset, the night being perfectly clear with a full moon, every object was visible. The sight was magnificent—the screaming, hissing shells meeting and passing each other through the sulphurous air, appeared like blazing comets with their burning fuses, and would burst with frightful noise, scattering their fragments as thick as hail."[36]

Ransom's soldiers realized they were only acting as decoys; the real attempt to take Fort Williams was yet to come. Correspondent "Lone Star" reported, "Three times we advanced, each time nearer, until within good charging distance; but the artillery had it all to themselves. This movement was merely a demonstration for Hoke's attack upon Fort Wessells, which after a short but sharp resistance, fell before the superior powers of Hoke's brigade; and that night's work was done."

Indeed, Ransom succeeded in diverting the Union forces' attention, for while the artillery battle raged at Fort Williams, Hoke's brigade, led by Colonel Mercer, emerged from a swamp near Welch's Creek to assault Fort Wessells. From the compound, which contained no shelter for the garrison of forty-two enlisted infantrymen and twenty-three enlisted artillerymen, came fire from the fort's two guns, a small six-pound field piece and a thirty-two-pounder mounted on a ship's carriage. Mercer countered with three rifled guns that were moved within 250 yards of the fort. Suddenly, under cover of darkness, Confederate infantrymen poured out of the woods "yelling like so many wild beast[s]." Despite the galling artillery and musket fire, the abatis was penetrated. However, hand grenades from the fort took their deadly toll, and the Southern soldiers were temporarily repulsed. Three more times they charged, and in one of the charges, Colonel Mercer, at the head of Hoke's brigade, fell mortally wounded with a bullet in his skull. Lieutenant Colonel William Gaston Lewis of the Forty-third North Carolina then assumed command.[37]

In addition to the dead and wounded, a number of Confederates were taken prisoner during the charges against Fort Wessells. Consequently, Lewis shifted his position, then opened up on the fort with guns located on a knoll 250 yards from the south wall and others hidden in the nearby swamp. At 9:30 P.M., the guns found their mark—a small arsenal building in the center of the fort. An explosion rocked the fort and sprayed shrapnel through the air. Captain Nelson Chapin, the commander of the fort, received one of the deadly missiles. Union gunboats in the Roanoke attempted to aid their beleaguered comrades, but most of their shells either flew harmlessly over the Confederates or fell within the fort, causing more misery and damage. Recognizing they held the upper hand, the Confederates ceased firing and demanded a surrender. As he lay dying, Captain Chapin conferred with his junior officers. The decision was made to surrender the fort.[38]

Hoke's casualties in the attack on Fort Wessells totaled twenty killed and fifty wounded. With the reduction of the fort, he took the first step toward the capture of Plymouth, because a significant Union flank position had been removed. Despite the elation over the fall of the fort, there was cause for concern in Hoke's camp. The *Albemarle* was nowhere in sight! Moreover, when Ransom's brigade, save the skirmishers, was pulled back about midnight, many of the soldiers were demoralized after enduring what Major Graham of the Fifty-sixth North Carolina described as "the heaviest dose of Iron I ever took." Graham expressed the low spirits of his fellow soldiers when he noted that they were "bitterly disappointed at our gun-boat not making its appearance as expected, thinking that if what we had gone through with was only a demonstration, what must a fight be?" As Graham and his compatriots rolled into their blankets on the chilly spring night, they "fell to sleep, deeming it more probable that the morrow would bring orders for Tarboro, than for Plymouth."[39]

While Hoke's land forces were launching their attacks on the Union fortifications, Commander Cooke was doing all he could to get the *Albemarle* to Plymouth. But the going was not easy. After getting under way once more at 4 A.M. on April 18, trouble struck two hours later, when the rudder head shattered. Again, the *Albemarle* was dead in the water while mechanics, blacksmiths, and carpenters scurried about to effect repairs. After a delay of four hours, the ironclad set forth on the final leg of its journey to Plymouth. A farmer who witnessed the activity aboard the ram from the riverbank remarked, "I never conceived of anything more perfectly ridiculous than the appearance of the critter as she slowly passed by my landing."[40]

By 5:00 P.M., Cooke determined that he was as ready as he could be for the showdown at Plymouth. Accordingly, he put the remaining carpenters and materials ashore, cleared the decks, and made final preparations for combat. Finally, as the river began to widen, the ram was turned so that it would meet the enemy bow-first. About an hour before Fort Wessells surrendered, the *Albemarle* was within three miles of Plymouth. Uncertain of the success of Hoke's land forces and concerned about river obstructions, Cooke dropped anchor to assess the situation. Gilbert Elliott, the builder of the *Albemarle*, aboard the ship as a volunteer aide, was convinced "that it was then or never" and so persuaded Cooke to allow him to take a small boat down the river to determine its navigability. Elliott returned about two hours later with good news: "To our great joy it was ascertained that there was ten feet of water over and above the obstructions." He reported to Cooke "that it was practicable to pass the obstructions provided the boat was kept in the middle of the stream." Basing his decision on Elliott's observations, Cooke ordered all hands to take a short rest in anticipation of the naval assault on Plymouth that would begin at 2:30 A.M. on April 19.[41]

A full moon over the Roanoke aided Cooke as he sent the *Albemarle* into battle. As the menacing hulk became visible to the gunners at Fort Gray, they unleashed a heavy barrage of shot and shell, which ricocheted off the metal plating and sounded to those aboard "no louder than pebbles thrown against an empty barrel." Arrogantly failing to answer the fire, the ram steamed past the fort toward Plymouth. As dawn began to reveal its first light on the horizon, lookouts on the ram sounded the alarm that two enemy gunboats lay just ahead. Although he did not at first recognize the booby trap Flusser had fashioned with the *Miami* and the *Southfield*, Cooke quickly recovered, moved his ship close to shore, and turned it into the middle of the river. Suddenly, the deadly prow of the *Albemarle* crashed into the *Southfield*, ripping a gaping hole in its hull that sent it to the bottom of the river. Aboard the *Miami*, Flusser was killed by a ricocheting shell. Thus, the naval battle (described by a Federal officer as a contest between "the bull-dog and rabbit—the crunching of bones and all was over") ended almost as quickly as it had begun. The surviving Federal fleet steamed downriver, away from the deadly prow and guns of the ironclad. As Union corporal Nathan Lanpheur saw it, "The ram was the master of the situation."[42]

Confident that he had control of the Roanoke, Cooke anchored the ram a mile below Plymouth until he received further orders. Gilbert Elliott volunteered once again and made his way to shore, where he could consult with Hoke. Although Hoke believed he could take Plymouth without the ram, he was jubilant upon its arrival. Through Elliott, he relayed messages to Cooke to open fire on the Union fortifications in order to soften them up for an infantry assault. Throughout the day and night of April 19, the two Brooke rifles offered deadly fire against the enemy.

At the same time, Hoke used his land-based artillery to add to the enemy's misery. After morning reconnaissance dissuaded the general from launching an attack from the direction of Fort Wessells, he prepared his final plan of battle. Realizing that the wilderness of Welch's Creek on the west would prevent a Confederate retreat, Hoke reasoned that the main attack should be from the east. During an afternoon conference, he ordered Ransom to move his brigade across Conaby Creek. Under Hoke's scheme, Ransom's assault from the east would be supported by the brigades of Kemper and Hoke (Lewis) on the south and west. As Hoke and Ransom parted company in the late afternoon, Ransom agreed to signal his commander with a rocket as soon as the brigade was in place.[43]

Following a detour that took his men four or five miles to Columbia Road, Ransom reached Conaby Creek after dark. En route, his soldiers came to the realization that they would bear the brunt of Hoke's grand assault. Major Graham of the Fifty-sixth North Carolina made the following observation:

> That intuitive perception, with which the private soldiers could often foretell that intent with which a move is made, now comes into play, and through the brigade the feeling becomes universal that it has been determined to make the final assault from the east side of the town. . . . Laughing and joking almost all the way, and a grim determination to do all that could be expected seems to pervade the ranks. Although marching at will, there is no straggling, and the companies close up and each soldier is glad to feel the touch of a comrade's elbow.[44]

Once at Conaby Creek, Ransom sent forward skirmishers, who reported that the bridge was down and the enemy was strongly fortified on the opposite side of the creek. A brave volunteer from the Twenty-fourth North Carolina swam across in the face of heavy rifle fire and brought back a skiff with which to effect a landing on the west side of the creek. Pontoons were then hurried forward, and the resulting bridge allowed the bulk of Ransom's brigade to pour across to a position within a mile of the Union

"Heaven Has Crowned Our Efforts with Success"

fortifications.

By the time Ransom notified Hoke that he was ready, it was 1 A.M. on Wednesday, April 20. Consequently, Hoke decided to delay the attack until first light, and Ransom's soldiers were given a pleasant command: "Stack arms; lie down, and rest until daybreak." On this night of "sharp and piercing" cold, the troops fell asleep on the bare ground "covered with blankets in groups of two or three."

In the meantime, under a full moon glowing in a cloudless sky, Hoke convened a council of war, in which he provided last-minute details to his regimental field officers. One eyewitness at the conference noted of Hoke, "His confidence, coolness, and resources seemed to inspire them thoroughly with his own self-reliance." At the conclusion of the meeting, Hoke placed artillery in the rear of his infantry, an ingenious move that caused the enemy guns to overshoot the Confederate lines in the assault that took place just a few hours later.[45]

April 20 was a day of "very pretty weather." General Ransom was in the saddle as the moon was going down, and his troops were awakened by his ringing voice: "Attention, brigade!" Soldiers scrambled from their blankets and took their places in the ranks as field officers paced up and down the lines calmly and quietly telling their men, "North Carolina expects every man to do his duty. Pay close attention to orders, keep closed up, and press forward all the time. The sooner we can get into the town the better for us." Suddenly, a signal rocket was sent up to notify Hoke that all was ready. Out front, Ransom's skirmishers were already feeling out the enemy when the Confederate lines all around Plymouth received the command, "Fix bayonets! Trail arms! Forward march!" Major Graham described the beginning of the magnificent charge: "At first we start in quicktime, the gunboat steaming up on our right. Soon it becomes double quick, and 'yells' break from the whole line, which are answered by Hoke's brigade, on [the] other side." A newspaper correspondent characterized the charge as "the wildest gust of tornado as it prostrates the forest, or the mad fire as it dashes through the prairies, it was a thunderbolt."[46]

The Federals were besieged from all sides. From the east stormed Ransom's screaming North Carolinians, from the west came Hoke's Tar

Heels and Georgians, from the south charged Terry's Virginians, and from the north came the destructive fire of the *Albemarle*. Ransom temporarily dispatched the Eighth North Carolina, the Thirty-fifth North Carolina, and a portion of the Twenty-fourth North Carolina to silence Fort Comfort and the Conaby Redoubt. With the remainder of his brigade and the Forty-third North Carolina from Hoke's brigade, Ransom pushed forward into town, as "Lone Star" reported, "slowly and carefully . . . clearing the enemy from every street, yard, and house." Fleeing for the relative safety of Fort Williams, the Federals poured out of "houses, cellars, and bombproofs like a colony of prairie puppies, or ground hogs on the 2nd of February," according to Major Graham. The Confederate success was infectious, causing "Lone Star" to proclaim, "Nothing could check our progress."

However, in the midst of the excitement, an unauthorized charge against Fort Williams by overly exuberant members of the Eighth North Carolina was handsomely repulsed by the Federals and drew a rebuke from Hoke, who saw it as a needless waste of life. Nevertheless, even in such a reckless charge, Hoke's soldiers died with courage and few regrets. One member of the regiment to fall in the charge was colorbearer Francis J. Perkins. Upon being carried to a barn where the wounded were being treated, the mortally wounded officer asked a fellow soldier what the men of the regiment thought of his conduct on the field. When told that he was being praised for his bravery, Ensign Perkins remarked, "If that is so, if it were not for my sister, I would not mind dying."[47]

Anxious to gain his prize without further bloodshed, Hoke requested and was granted an interview with Wessells. In a manner described by Wessells as "courteous and soldier-like," Hoke demanded an unconditional surrender of the Plymouth garrison in consideration of its "untenable position, of the impossibility of relief, and that the defense had been highly honorable to all concerned." Because Hoke was a civilian officer, the West Pointer requested that he be allowed to negotiate with General Pickett, who he had been informed was in the area. Hoke made it clear that he, not Pickett, was in command. Wessells refused Hoke's demand, insisting that he be allowed to "march out with his colors, the officers retaining their side arms."

According to Lieutenant Leonidas L. Polk of the Forty-third North Carolina, who was among a group of "brave and excited" Confederate soldiers surrounding the two generals, Wessells was reluctant to surrender without the approval of his government, because otherwise it would appear "that he had surrendered a force and strong garrison without damage." Hoke replied "that if to be damaged was what he desired, he could readily be gratified, but that the dictates of humanity and discretion alike demanded that he could spare further effusion of blood, or loss of life, but intimated to him in plain terms, that if he were compelled to assault the fort, which was now completely surrounded, the responsibility of the terrible consequences must rest on his head."

Wessells comprehended Hoke's words to be a threat of indiscriminate slaughter. As if to accentuate Hoke's ominous tone, the *Albemarle* threw a shot into Fort Williams about the time the garrison suddenly lowered its flag. Wessells continued to maintain, however, that "he would not surrender." As Hoke suggestively gazed upon his artillery, poised to fire on Wessells's stronghold, he gave his opponent a bit more time to change his mind. But Wessells would have none of it. He went back inside the fort and proceeded straight to Sergeant J. W. Whitehill, who manned the only operable gun. Wessells told Whitehill, "Sergeant, commence firing. We will have to stand it a little longer."[48]

Hoke countered with twenty pieces of artillery and the blazing guns of the *Albemarle*. "Lone Star" graphically described what followed: "This was a case for the artillerist, and the guns of the captured forts were soon turned upon their stronger brother, fighting as the result shows, better for us than they had against us. Capt. Cooke too, of the *Albemarle*, dropped some of his 90-pound shells among them." It did not take long for Wessells to recognize the futility of the situation. He later noted in his official report of the battle, "I was now completely enveloped on every side, Fort Williams an enclosed work in the center of the line, being my only hope. This was well understood by the enemy, and in less than an hour a cannonade of shot and shell was opened upon it from four different directions. This terrible fire had to be endured without reply, as no man could live at the guns."[49]

Wessells made the decision to capitulate just after a Confederate shell burst directly on the fort's powder magazine. Of his helpless situation, he remarked, "This condition of affairs could not be long endured without a reckless sacrifice of life, no relief could be expected, and in compliance with every officer, I consented to hoist a white flag, and at 10:00 A.M. of April 20 I had the mortification of surrendering my post to the enemy with all that it contained."[50]

No sooner had the white flag been raised than Confederate soldiers of the Thirty-fifth North Carolina scaled the fort to pull it down. Lieutenant A. E. Wright described the special moment of joy: "With the assistance of a comrade, I helped Major [Simon B.] Taylor up the parapets of the fort, and then someone kindly helped me up; so he and I went side by side when the white flag was put into his hands. He waved it high, so it might be seen by the gallant boys in gray who had made the charge, not surpassed by any that was made in the most heroic of wars." What followed was best described by Lieutenant Leonidas L. Polk: "Then one long, wild, prolonged shout went up from the army, and never was a flag of truce more eagerly and heartily greeted during the war." From his position atop the fort, Lieutenant Wright watched as Wessells made his way out to meet Hoke. Wright later recalled, "I saw General Wessell and his staff, all mounted, Wessell on a coal-black horse, ride up to General Hoke and staff, General Hoke on a bay horse, and General Wessell handed his sword to General Hoke."[51]

Soldiers on the ground near the generals noted that Hoke was magnanimous in victory. One eyewitness, Captain Robert D. Graham, observed, "The writer was near General Hoke when he received General Wessels, accompanied by his officers, as his prisoner. There was everything in his courteous and considerate bearing to lessen the sting of defeat. Dismounting from his horse and clasping the captive's hand, he assured him of his respect and sympathy and added, 'After such a gallant defense you can bear the fortune of the war without self-reproach.'"

No doubt, Hoke sympathized with his adversary, a career army officer more than twice his age who had been looking forward to retirement. Wessells extended his sword to Hoke and dolefully remarked, "General

Hoke, this is the saddest day of my life." The hero of the day responded, "General, this is the proudest day of mine!" Then Hoke graciously handed the sword back to Wessells with words of praise and comfort: "General Wessells, you are too brave a man to part with your sword; take it back! Have you any request to make?" Wessells replied, "I have but one request to make, General, and that is that my men are not robbed." Hoke quickly responded, "Your request is granted."

A soldier from the 103rd Pennsylvania later reported, "This promise of Gen. Hoke's was faithfully kept." Almost fifty years after the surrender, another Federal soldier confirmed the considerate treatment that he and his comrades received from the victorious general at Plymouth: "We had been doing garrison duty there for about a year and a half. We were very comfortably situated and our personal property was considerable. General Hoke gave permission for each man to take as much of his property as he could carry in getting to the railroad, I think about several miles away. It was a remarkable boon and for me at least it was of great service in smoothing my prison experience."[52]

Immediately following the surrender formalities, the Confederate soldiers applauded their commander. Private James Evans of the Eighth North Carolina recalled many years after the war, "We boys took occasion to cheer General Hoke. In my imagination I can see that noble General just how he looked, as holding the reins of his horse in his left, with his right hand, he raised his hat and said, 'Men, cheer General Ransom; he is the man that most deserves it.'" That gesture by Hoke in his own hour of glory left a lasting impression on Private Evans, who observed, "It is the nature of great men (and especially brave men) in time of battle to be ready and willing to divide honors with their comrades and brother warriors."[53]

Fighting around Fort Gray continued throughout the morning of the surrender. Suddenly, Colonel Dearing's soldiers noticed that the firing down the river had ceased. One of them, William H. Morgan, chronicled the drama of the moment at Warrens Neck: "The men began to say, 'They are cheering--sh! sh! Listen!, listen! See which side is cheering!' It was not long before the 'Rebel yell' was recognized, then all knew the day had been won, when the troops above sent up a mighty shout in answer to their comrades."[54]

The Battle of Plymouth was over. Hoke had just dealt Union forces their first substantial defeat in North Carolina; he had masterminded "the cleanest, most competent victory" that the Confederacy would ever earn on the soil of his native state; and he had successfully commanded "one of the best combined land-sea attacks by the Confederates during the war."

Indeed, the spoils of his victory were sweet. Although reports of the captured men, materiel, and supplies varied, the *Raleigh Daily Confederate* of May 3, 1864, published an extensive list that included 2,437 prisoners, 1,000 barrels of flour, 150,000 rations of pork and beef, 50 or 75 bags of coffee, 20 barrels of ground coffee, 10,000 pounds of sugar, a large quantity of coal, a machine shop with tools and 12 forges, 40 pieces of artillery, 25 wagons and teams, 200 horses, a good supply of ammunition, and "the best fortifications in the State." Other reports noted the capture of 5,000 stand of small arms. Little time was wasted in sending the bulk of the desperately needed booty to Tarboro for transport to the railroad at Weldon, where it was rushed to Lee's army.[55]

Likewise, the smoke had scarcely cleared from the battlefield when the telegraph operator at Plymouth relayed the joyous news to Richmond. Hoke wired Bragg with the happy results. John Taylor Wood followed suit with a telegram to his uncle, Jefferson Davis, exclaiming with glee, "Heaven has crowned our efforts with success."

As the news spread, there was excitement throughout North Carolina and all of the Confederacy. The *Raleigh Daily Confederate* of April 23 lavished praise upon Hoke: "We only add for the present, that this is not the first field on which General Hoke has written his worth as a man, his bravery as a soldier, his skill as a General and his entire consecration to the cause of his country. May the Ruler of all worlds and armies preserve his life and may his adoring country prove itself worthy of his sublime exploits." To many observers in eastern North Carolina, Hoke's victory marked the end of Union domination in that region. From the city where the great expedition had begun, the editor of the *Tarboro Southerner* proclaimed, "The people of eastern North Carolina now breathe more free and hope that the time is near at hand, when that lovely portion of the state will be rid of the insolent threat of an insidious foe."[56]

In Virginia, the victory at Plymouth raised the eyebrows of influential editors. At Petersburg, where Hoke would save the day less than two months later, the *Daily Register* of April 23 reported, "General Hoke has struck a most effective blow for the redemption of his native State." A day later, in the Confederate capital, the *Richmond Examiner* sang Hoke's praises: "General Hoke, who commanded the expedition, though only 27 years of age, may well rank with our ablest division commanders in the service. He has wonderful tact, force, activity, and endurance that despises fatigue: handles troops with great ease and celerity, and has their unbounded confidence."

Arguably, there was no place in all the Confederacy where the news of Hoke's success was received with greater relief. While Hoke had been waging his battle at Plymouth, President Davis had been seriously contemplating the removal of the capital from Richmond. John B. Jones, a clerk in the War Department, chronicled the crisis in Richmond in his diary. On April 21, Jones made the following notation: "A report was circulated and believed that the President resolved yesterday to remove the government to South Carolina or Alabama, and the commotion was great." Just a day later, Jones's words expressed the change in fortune that Hoke had brought the Confederacy:

> APRIL 22D—A bright day and warmer. Cherry-trees in blossom. We have the following war news:
>
> PLYMOUTH, N.C. April 20th
>
> TO GEN. BRAGG.
>
> I have stormed and captured this place, capturing 1 brigadier, 1600 men, stores, and 25 pieces of artillery.
>
> R. F. HOKE, Brig. General
>
> The President has changed his mind since the reception of the news from North Carolina, and has determined that all government shall not leave until further orders. . . . The news is said to have had a wonderful effect on the President's mind, and he

hopes we may derive considerable supplies from Eastern North
Carolina. So do I.[57]

Jefferson Davis expressed his gratitude in a telegram to Hoke dated
April 23: "Accept my thanks and congratulations for the brilliant success
which has attended your attack and capture of Plymouth. You are promoted to be a major-general from that date." Thus, one month before his
twenty-seventh birthday, Hoke became the youngest man ever to hold the
rank of major general in the Confederate army. Moreover, his battlefield
promotion to that rank was the only one of its kind in the Southern army
during the entire war. Other honors were forthcoming. A joint resolution
of thanks to Hoke and Commander Cooke was passed by the Confederate
Congress on May 17. The North Carolina General Assembly did likewise.

Robert E. Lee, ever mindful of Hoke's absence from his army, advised
Davis on April 28, "I am glad of General Hoke's promotion, though sorry
to lose him, unless he can be sent to me with a division." And while drilling his troops for the coming fight at Spotsylvania Courthouse, Virginia—
the great battle that would make him the youngest West Pointer to hold
the rank of major general in the Confederate army—Dodson Ramseur expressed the hope that the brilliant victory at Plymouth by his close friend
would bring more good news from their home state.[58]

On the Union side, the tidings from Plymouth caused shock, disbelief,
and pessimism. Among the most surprised was General Benjamin Butler,
who had been confident that Plymouth could withstand a sixty-day siege;
on the very day of the surrender, Butler suggested, albeit too late, that
Plymouth be abandoned by the Federals. For several days after the Union
capitulation, the editors of the New York newspapers refused to believe
and report the story. Finally, on April 26, the *New York Tribune* broke the
news with the following observation: "What a Blue Monday! thought most
people, yesterday, and no wonder. The skies were moist, the streets muddy,
and the atmosphere muggy enough to make most folks melancholy. Added
to these the news of another battle lost. . . . It was but natural to turn to
the gloomiest aspect of affairs."[59]

In the aftermath of the battle, Hoke felt obliged to allow his soldiers to
enjoy themselves after four days of hard fighting. Not long after the sur-

render ceremony, Hoke praised his troops by saying, "My men, my confident expectations in you have been fully realized in this fight." He then told them that they could "help themselves to whatever might please their fancy except the horses and wagons." Private James C. Elliott noted, "As soon as the surrender was made, all our troops were turned loose to help themselves to anything they wished—grocery and dry goods stores richly stocked to select from." Another soldier added, "Our little army lived high for a few days, literally feasting on the fat of the land." Some looting of the few residences that had survived the artillery battle occurred, but Hoke's officers quickly quelled any lawlessness. Hoke himself received one souvenir from the victory—Wessells's garrison flag.[60]

After their "shopping trip," Hoke marched most of his soldiers approximately a mile south of town on Washington Road, where they made camp for several days of rest and relaxation while their general took stock of the victory and plotted his next course. During this respite, some of the soldiers penned letters to the folks back home detailing the good news. Major John Graham spoke of a "glorious victory," while Captain William H. S. Burgwyn of the Thirty-fifth North Carolina deemed the battle "one of the most brilliant victories of the war." John K. Walker told his father back in Alamance County, "It was one of the completest victorys during the war. . . . We all got just what we wanted."[61]

Hoke was not immune to the merrymaking that abounded among his troops. Upon receiving the news of his promotion, he enjoyed a congratulatory serenade from the soldiers. And while taking care of administrative details with neighboring civilians, the general enjoyed a good laugh at the expense of an earlier acquaintance. One of the citizens who appeared before Hoke seeking the return of property was the man who had unwittingly provided the general with information on that chilly March night at Nahunta. When the man identified his property, he sought an order to take his ten runaway blacks home; however, he was informed that he could have only nine because of a promise he had made at Nahunta. Suddenly, the man realized that the person he had talked to at the railroad siding was Hoke. Not yet willing to give up on a bit of mischief, Hoke informed the man that he had come to Plymouth for the express purpose of getting the

black he had been promised. The man departed well satisfied after informing Hoke that he would vote for him for president of the Confederacy.[62]

Amid the pleasure generated by his success, Hoke was forced to come
to grips with the problems resulting from the victory. In human terms,
Plymouth had exacted a heavy toll: casualties amounted to about 10 percent of Hoke's total force. More than 160 men had been killed and another 550 wounded. Many of the dead were buried with military honors
on the night of the victory. Union casualties were much lighter; most estimates placed the number at fewer than 200. However, Hoke had more
than 2,400 prisoners on his hands. Anxious to press on with his important
business to the south, he supplied the prisoners with four days' rations and
put them on a march to Tarboro under heavy guard at 2 P.M. on April 21.
During their day of captivity under Hoke's command, the Union soldiers
described the Confederates as "every inch soldiers, and very gentlemanly
in their conduct toward us." Once they reached Tarboro, most of the captives were entrained for Andersonville Prison.[63]

There was but one blemish on the record of Hoke's troops during the
campaign: the so-called Plymouth Massacre. In the wake of Wessells's surrender, an untold number of black Union troops and "Buffaloes" fled into
the surrounding swamps fearing for their lives. Dearing's cavalry pursued
the runaways, and the sound of Confederate rifles could soon be heard
from the swamps. Estimates of the number of men killed have ranged as
high as seven hundred, but the most thorough study of the matter has put
the number closer to fifty. Unlike other incidents of purported Confederate savagery, such as the Fort Pillow Massacre and the hangings at Kinston,
there was never a congressional investigation into the Plymouth matter.
On April 26, 1864, Lincoln's cabinet discussed the incident, but "the hor-
rid story [was] . . . not believed." No evidence has ever been discovered
that would suggest Hoke either ordered, knew of, or acquiesced in the
incident.[64]

For Hoke, there was no time to rest on his newly won laurels. Even
greater prizes—Washington and New Bern—lay before him, and he aimed
his sights at those two targets, knowing full well that if he hit the bull's-
eye at each place, the enemy would be banished from North Carolina.

But memories of that most rewarding victory at Plymouth would long burn brightly in Hoke. Many years after the war, Dr. Joseph G. D. Hamilton happened to run across Hoke and his son-in-law at a restaurant in Raleigh. As the men sat together on the porch before dinner, Hoke rested quietly, gazing off into the distance. In a tone designed not to arouse the reticent old soldier, Hamilton began to relate a newspaper story about an event that had occurred after the surrender of Plymouth. A Federal chaplain who had been denied officer's privileges and "his" library called on Hoke, who responded favorably to his pleas. After the chaplain left, the general noticed two large wooden boxes. When he inquired about the contents, a soldier responded, "They are the books of that Yankee chaplain." Hoke noticed that the top of one of the boxes was broken, so he removed a book. It bore the bookplate of Josiah Collins of nearby Somerset Place in Washington County. When the boxes were torn open, it was seen that all the books were likewise marked. The chaplain was immediately summoned to Hoke's headquarters, where the general dressed him down and stripped him of all privileges.

At the conclusion of the story, Hamilton sparked laughter from his listener, which in turn drew the attention of the general. Hoke inquired, "What are you boys laughing about?" His son-in-law responded, "Hamilton is telling tales on you, General." Hoke turned and tersely asked, "Mr. Hamilton, what are you telling?" Rather sheepishly, Hamilton replied, "I was telling him about your interview with that chaplain." For a brief moment, Hoke's face displayed a stern look, which soon gave over to "a smile of retrospective enjoyment." With great enthusiasm in his voice, the general replied in a manner that seemed to summarize his entire campaign at Plymouth: "*Didn't* I give him hell?"[65]

"One more day was all
Hoke had needed. But it
was not to be for him or
the Confederacy."

CHAPTER 8

From Triumph
to Disappointment

Sunday, April 24, was a warm and pleasant spring day in coastal North Carolina; it was the last full day in Plymouth for Hoke and his army. Buoyed by his own boundless confidence and the continued support of the Confederate high command, the general spent the day in last-minute planning as he prepared to send his troops to capture Washington and New Bern and complete his mission in North Carolina. In the course of but one week, he had done much to lift the spirits of the Southern people. Ecstatic over the triumph at Plymouth, Robert E. Lee had told Braxton Bragg on April 22, "I am profoundly grateful to the Giver of all Victory for our success in North Carolina. I trust it may continue, and that the end may be as favorable as the beginning."[1]

Despite the encouragement for the successful completion of his mission from many quarters, Hoke faced one major limitation: time. Indeed, Hoke was ever mindful that his army was desperately needed to the north and was subject to recall at any time. In his April 22 communiqué to Bragg, Lee had sounded a note that would grow more ominous over the coming days: "I desire Hoke's brigade be sent to me as soon as practicable."

Moreover, Hoke now had an immediate commander who initially did not approve of the Confederate initiative in eastern North Carolina. On April 22, General Pierre G. T. Beauregard had arrived at Weldon to assume command of the Department of North Carolina and Southern Virginia, which included that portion of Virginia south of the James and Appomattox Rivers and all of North Carolina east of the mountains. Almost immediately upon his arrival in North Carolina, Beauregard had dispatched telegrams and letters to Richmond expressing alarm about a possible enemy attack on Petersburg and intimating a lack of readiness for such an assault. In a telegram to Bragg, he questioned the prudence of the continuation of Hoke's campaign, noting, "Every indication is that Burnside will attack Richmond via Petersburg. Are we prepared to resist him in that direction? Can the forces of this Department be concentrated in time? are questions worthy of immediate consideration by the War Department." Accordingly, Hoke felt compelled to move at once toward the two remaining objectives south of Plymouth, and he issued marching orders on the evening of April 24 as a heavy rain fell.[2]

At 10 A.M. on April 25, another "very pretty, warm, and pleasant day" in eastern North Carolina, the Confederate column began its southern movement toward Washington, thirty-five miles distant. General James G. Martin's brigade of North Carolinians, fresh on the scene, was left behind to protect Hoke's newly won prize. After a dusty march of eleven miles, the expeditionary force camped for the night near Jamesville, described by one of Hoke's officers as a "dilapidated town."

While the Confederate soldiers were making their way to Washington, the Union command in North Carolina was undergoing change. At New Bern on April 25, Major General John J. Peck issued General Orders No. 70, whereby he announced that he had been relieved of command in the state and had been replaced by Brigadier General Innis N. Palmer, a graduate of the famous West Point class of 1846. Palmer had rendered distinguished service in North Carolina since December 1862 and was well respected by many of the civilians in the Washington–New Bern area.[3]

Early on the warm morning of Tuesday, April 26, Hoke's forces resumed the march over dusty roads to the looming showdown at Washington. As the grueling trek began to take its toll, "a good many men fell out" before the army camped seven miles from town. As the soldiers bedded down for the night, the expedition continued to enjoy the countenance of Richmond, despite Beauregard's protestations. Earlier in the day, Bragg had intimated its importance in a response to Beauregard: "The movement under Major-General Hoke, if prompt and successful, will enable us to concentrate a formidable force to meet Burnside."

As the Confederates were drawing near their second target, General Palmer was wasting little time in making his first strategic move as district commander. Although he did not believe the enemy was near, Palmer issued instructions at 11 P.M. to Brigadier General Edward Harland, the Union commander at Washington, to begin the evacuation of the town. Harland was urged to "speedily, but as secretly as it is possible" move his garrison, stores, and guns to New Bern. Palmer noted that the decision to evacuate Washington was made because the town was "of no strategic importance" and was "not worth the expense which is required to hold it." Nonetheless, Harland was admonished to "keep up the idea that there is no intention of evacuating Washington, and even after the guns and stores have all been removed a small force must be kept in the works." The town that Harland was ordered to evacuate had been under Federal control for just over two years, and more than two-thirds of its prewar civilian population of twenty-five hundred had long fled into the interior of the state.[4]

On the "very fair and pleasant" morning of April 27, the Confederate army approached within two and a half miles of Washington, and General Hoke personally made his way "in front of the town." The Federal evacuation had not yet begun or at least was not apparent, because Hoke described the place to Beauregard as "much stronger than expected." Well-armed Union gunboats operating about the Washington waterfront posed a special problem for the Confederates, who could not count on the *Albemarle* or the *Neuse* in the operations against the town.

At this juncture, the general was forced to make a tactical decision. He notified Beauregard that if Washington could not be taken without attack, he would move immediately against New Bern, the fall of which, Hoke reasoned, would ensure the fall of Washington. As it turned out, Hoke would have done well to bypass Washington and move directly to New Bern. Had he known about the impending Federal exodus from Washington, had he been able to foresee the exigencies of war that would abruptly force him back to Virginia ten days later, he no doubt would have let events follow their natural progression at Washington and move south.

However, on April 27, Hoke was anxious to have one or both of the ironclads on hand when he took on the Federal forces at New Bern. In order to buy the time necessary for the rams to be ready for duty at the third and final target of his campaign, the general decided to lay siege to Washington. From his headquarters at New Bern, General Palmer dispatched news of the beginning of this action: "This morning, however, heavy firing has been reported in the direction of Little Washington, and it may be that they are attacked there."

As siege was being laid to the town on April 27, the *Neuse*, a boat to which Hoke had devoted much personal attention, got under way from Kinston on its maiden voyage. Navy lieutenant B. P. Loyall commanded the ram as it headed downriver toward New Bern to "take the city and sink the gunboats without much trouble." But less than a half-mile from its home port, the ironclad smashed into a sand bar and was grounded. Loyall and his crew frantically did all they could to free the vessel, but their efforts were in vain. As day turned to night, the ironclad stood four feet out of the water, useless to the Confederate war effort. Thus, Hoke's grand strategy was dealt a severe blow on the first day of the siege. After sustaining "shelling a good portion of the day," Hoke decided about 8 P.M. to move his wagon train back about eight miles west on Greenville Road.[5]

Over the next three days, while Hoke waited for his siege to claim Washington, the fleeing Federal troops took the time to wantonly burn and pillage the town. As the continuing evacuation became more evident, Hoke grew more confident that Washington could be taken without bloodshed. Accordingly, he began to move a portion of his army away from town. Before daylight on April 28, the wagon train was packed and moved fifteen miles toward Greenville in anticipation of the New Bern offensive. Although Lee again called for the return of Hoke that same day, President Davis and Bragg were still of the opinion that Hoke's quest should not be disturbed or halted. Davis noted, "The attempt should be made with all vigor to improve our condition in the manner indicated, and in the plan adopted for the campaign of General Hoke."[6]

Frost covered the landscape on the chilly morning of Friday, April 29, as Hoke put the bulk of his army on the move. His troops passed through what one officer described as "a lovely farming country," and by day's end, they camped three miles from Greenville. Beauregard, now convinced that Richmond was determined to see Hoke's mission to fruition, decided to counsel Hoke on the attempt to take New Bern. That evening, Beauregard left Weldon for Kinston, where he planned to confer with Hoke.[7]

During their conference at Kinston on April 30, Hoke offered command of the New Bern offensive to Beauregard, but the offer was refused. Instead, Beauregard used the opportunity to exchange ideas and to offer a detailed plan of his own. In a post-conference memorandum to Hoke, he explained, "Having no authority to interfere in your proposed movement on New Berne, your instructions having been received direct from General Bragg, I avail myself of your desire that I should command the expedition to offer you the following suggestions, resulting from information received or collected since my arrival here." Both generals concurred that the participation of the *Albemarle* in the assault would help ensure its success. Beauregard exuded confidence about the ironclad in a telegram to Bragg following the conference: "With its assistance I consider capture of New Bern easy. Without it sacrifice of life must be very great."[8]

Just as it appeared that Hoke had gained Beauregard's backing for the attempt on New Bern, cracks began to surface in the once-solid support in Richmond on April 30. While Beauregard and Hoke were conferring in Kinston, Bragg issued a directive with foreboding overtones: "A dispatch from General Lee to the President, just received, reports Burnside certainly moving rapidly to join Meade, and General L. urges the movement of all assistance practicable to his front. The Secretary of War concurs with me in the following: Urge the expedition of General Hoke to an issue at once, so that his force may join General Lee."[9]

Hoke knew that his days in his home state were numbered, but there was yet time to put all of eastern North Carolina under Confederate control if he acted quickly. Fortunately for him, several developments on April 30 worked in his favor. At New Bern, General Palmer was uncertain about the intentions of the Confederate army. Believing Beauregard would lead an attack on New Bern, Palmer was less than confident when he dispatched a request for reinforcements with the words, "I think we can hold out." Of more importance to Hoke, however, was the bloodless capture of Washington on April 30. Without the loss of a single man, the city fell into Confederate hands on the "warm and pleasant Saturday," as the last of the fleeing Federals boarded a steamer for the relative safety of New Bern.[10]

When the Southern soldiers entered town in late afternoon, they were appalled by what they found. Although General Palmer's evacuation orders had directed that not "a particle of property of any description" be destroyed, hordes of Union soldiers had gone on a lawless rampage throughout the city soon after receiving notice of the evacuation. No building or civilian was safe from the mayhem.[11]

At 10 A.M. on April 30, about six hours before the last of the Federal troops departed Washington, they perpetrated one last act of terror, setting fires throughout town. The wind swept flames soon engulfed the buildings along the waterfront and spread to the residential areas north of the river, leaving "houseless and homeless hundreds of poor women and children." After the arrival of the Confederates, the conflagration spread when an accidental fire broke out. When the flames were finally quelled, more than half of Washington lay in ruins.[12]

The devastation witnessed by Hoke's men in Washington proved a source of motivation for them to finish their task. From the captured town, James Evans, Jr., wrote his father, "A new Era seems to have dawned upon North Carolina. The *Day* of *Retribution* seems near at hand from the Reports we hear. Woe! be unto the Yankees at Newberne and *Everywhere else* in N.C."[13]

On May 1, Hoke notified Bragg that Washington had been evacuated, and he urged that Confederate agents be sent to nearby Hyde County to obtain corn and bacon for his troops and the hapless civilians of Washington. Incensed by the atrocities of the enemy at Washington, Hoke grew more determined to wrest New Bern from Union control. After stationing the Sixth North Carolina in Washington to restore order and defend the shell of a town, the general sent Dearing's cavalry in pursuit of the fleeing Federals and consolidated the remainder of his land forces at Greenville. There, Hoke lost valuable time while he waited for the arrival of Confederate marines and pontoons from Richmond. During the delay, Hoke, ever mindful of the significant role that naval assistance had played in the victory at Plymouth, was anxious to gain assurances that the ironclads would be able to make their way to New Bern for a coordinated assault. However, on May 1, Beauregard relayed the disappointing news that the *Neuse* remained grounded and would not be available. Consequently, Hoke conferred with Commander Cooke, who, although painfully aware of the difficulties and dangers inherent in the naval mission, again promised the general that he could count on the *Albemarle*.[14]

Confident of naval assistance and deeply concerned that his opportunity in North Carolina was passing, Hoke set his army in motion toward New Bern via Kinston on the "warm and fair" morning of Monday, May 2. Crossing the Tar River at Greenville, the army made its way to Contentnea Creek, a tributary of the Neuse River approximately sixteen miles south of the city. There, the Sixty-seventh North Carolina joined the assault force. Although his expectations of success at New Bern were high, Hoke was anxious to receive even more reinforcements. Many of his best soldiers had been lost in the ferocious combat at Plymouth; moreover, enemy troop strength at New Bern was projected to be far greater than what Hoke had faced in the battle along the Roanoke.

In anticipation of Hoke's arrival at Kinston in the early afternoon on May 2 for a final pre-attack conference, Beauregard tactfully made a request for additional manpower through a telegram to General Samuel Cooper, the Confederate adjutant general: "Please state what troops of all arms shall move with General Hoke, and whether they shall march or go by railroad." In Richmond, Bragg saw the telegram and promptly responded to Beauregard, offering no prospect for more troops: "You can send with Hoke any and all the forces in your department as you may think best. The movement requires the greatest possible expedition." Cooper's response, which followed, was more absolute: "Dispatch received. By General Hoke's force was meant that which he took with him to Plymouth."[15]

After a difficult march of twenty-two miles on May 2, Hoke's army made camp on Kinston Road just north of Kinston. Rations were now very short, and a hard rain during the night only served to heighten the discomfort of the soldiers. Early on May 3, the expedition resumed. Approximately twelve miles east of Kinston, the troops hurried across the Neuse over a pontoon bridge. In the meantime, Beauregard had made his way to Goldsboro, where he wired Bragg that Hoke had commenced his movement toward New Bern a day earlier. In the telegram, he warned Bragg, "Four or five days may be required by him."

As his army was completing its twenty-five-mile march on May 3, Hoke grew more confident of success upon learning from Confederate naval authorities that the *Albemarle* was in shipshape condition and would "be around on Thursday." Hoke's growing optimism was shared by Private James Evans of the Sixth North Carolina, who told his father in a letter on May 3, "The many prayers which have been offered in the past 2 years for the deliverance of this Portion of the good old North State from the hands of our ruthless Foe are now being answered." When they made camp on the night of May 3 along Trent Road some twenty miles from New Bern, Hoke's soldiers shared this enthusiasm.[16]

Although the plan he had personally prepared for the reduction of New Bern had failed just three months earlier, during the Pickett expedition, Hoke remained of the opinion that it was sound. And this time, he was in command. Thus, on the morning of May 4, he began to put his grand scheme into action by sending his army down Upper Trent Road. Once again, there would be a three-pronged attack, which would issue as follows: one portion of his army would strike Fort Anderson and the other Union defenses on the north side of the Neuse above New Bern; a second, more substantial attack force would assault New Bern's inner works after surprising the Federals at Batchelder's Creek northwest of town; and the third prong, led by Dearing's cavalry and some artillery, would cut the railroad and telegraph lines to Morehead City and then work its way north into New Bern on the railroad bridge.[17]

While Hoke's soldiers were marching down the dusty roads on the morning of May 4 toward their first encounter with the defenders at New Bern, little did the general know that this day would be the beginning of the end for his mission in North Carolina. At Kinston, Beauregard received an urgent message from President Davis: "Unless New Bern can be captured by *coup de main* the attempt must be abandoned, and the troops returned with all possible dispatch to unite in operations in North Virginia. There is not an hour to lose. Had the expedition not started I would say it would not go. Have all practicable arrangements made to transport the troops to this place with dispatch." By 4 P.M., the die had been cast: Beauregard had decided to recall Hoke. He promptly wired Davis, "One of my aides will leave this evening with special orders to General Hoke. Utmost dispatch will be used."

Unaware of the fateful decision, Hoke enjoyed his first success of the New Bern attack when advance elements of his old brigade surprised enemy pickets at Deep Gully, a tributary canal of the Trent about eight miles west of New Bern. The Sixty-seventh North Carolina was placed at Deep Gully to protect the position while the remainder of the brigade hurried to catch up with the main body of Hoke's army, which had made camp on the north side of the Trent near Pollocksville, some twelve miles south of New Bern.[18]

To ensure that Hoke received his peremptory orders, Beauregard dispatched no fewer than five couriers with the communiqué. But none was able to reach the general until late on the night of May 5. Hoke used the entire day to capture the outer defense works and sever the railroad and telegraph links with the Federal enclave at Morehead City.

Early in the day, the Confederates crossed to the south side of the Trent well below the city near Evans Mill on Brice's Creek. The Federal outpost at Evans Mill consisted of a blockhouse supported by a redoubt with one heavy gun mounted at an elevated point, so as to allow the small garrison to keep a large force at bay. When Hoke and his staff rode up to reconnoiter the defense works, they attracted the attention of the enemy. A journalist accompanying Hoke described the greeting that followed: "Very soon a puff of smoke announced the salute intended for us, and almost instantaneously a twelve pound solid shot ricocheted in front, and sped at a few feet above our heads, to seek the earth some distance in the rear." Hoke immediately ordered Colonel John A. Baker of the Third North Carolina Cavalry to deploy skirmishers in the woods to flank the outpost and protect the artillerymen. Two Napoleons were rushed forward into an open field several hundred yards in front of the works and soon unleashed a steady barrage of well-directed fire. As soon as the skirmishers made their way through a nearly impassable bog, the Federals "took to their heels." Soon after the encounter, a bridge spanned Brice's Creek, and Hoke's troops poured across and headed in the direction of New Bern.[19]

While Hoke was enjoying success at Evans Mill, Dearing was endeavoring to do the same at Croatan Station, located along the Atlantic and North Carolina Railroad about twelve miles south of New Bern. In the predawn hours of May 5, Dearing's forces had crossed the Trent and, through the use of a trusted guide, made their way through a treacherous swamp. About 7 A.M., Dearing encircled the fort, which was garrisoned by the Fifth Rhode Island Artillery. Without the loss of a single Confederate soldier, the issue was decided quickly when the Federals raised the white flag. Thus fell the outpost that General Seth Barton had described as impregnable just two months earlier. For his efforts, Dearing came away with sixty prisoners and a piece of artillery.[20]

While struggling through the wilderness to reach Fort Croatan, Dearing had just missed another prize—the train making its way from New Bern to Morehead City. Nonetheless, he promptly set about his primary mission, destroying the rail and telegraph links between the two cities. Soon, dense columns of dark smoke signaled that Dearing had accomplished his purpose. Hoke then hurried forward his artillery, placing it within two miles of the city. As morning melted into afternoon, Hoke's soldiers continued their advance from the south along Evans Mill Road toward the railroad.

General Robert F. Hoke

Once the approach of the Confederates was detected, the Federals opened a heavy fire from a railroad monitor and their gunboats in the river. For more than an hour, the artillery duel raged, but the Confederates suffered only light casualties.[21]

As the spirited fight continued, Hoke made a personal reconnaissance of the Federal defense works and pronounced them "pretty strong." In the process, he was slightly wounded in the arm. A nearby soldier promptly produced a treasured silk handkerchief from his pocket and handed it to the general to bind his arm. Despite his wound, all had gone well for Hoke during the day. He now commanded the outer works, and the town was under siege.[22] But where was the *Albemarle*?

True to his word, Commander Cooke had cast off at Plymouth at noon on May 5 en route to New Bern. On this voyage, the ram was escorted by two steamers, the refloated *Bombshell* and the *Cotton Plant*. But Cooke knew the mission was fraught with peril. Before he could even reach Hoke's new battleground and the enemy vessels waiting there, Cooke would be forced to negotiate not only the Roanoke River, but Albemarle, Croatan, and Pamlico Sounds as well. Then he would face obstructions in the Neuse River on the final leg of his voyage. Cooke was also mindful that somewhere along his route, he was almost certain to encounter a formidable fleet of Union warships.[23]

When Cooke headed the ram into Albemarle Sound on the afternoon of May 5, he encountered and engaged a fleet of nine enemy gunboats, sinking one, disabling two more, and sending the others fleeing. However, in the aftermath of the affray, the *Albemarle* was in no shape to proceed toward New Bern. Instead, her smokestack full of holes and her steering mechanism badly damaged, the ram limped back to Plymouth fueled by bacon and lard.[24]

As Thursday night fell on New Bern, Hoke "had fully matured his plans" and was confident that he would occupy the town by Sunday even without the assistance of the ironclad. Once again, he knew that the town was almost in his grasp. Years after the war, Hoke noted about his effort at New Bern in early May 1864, "I had no doubt of its success." His confidence was infectious. Colonel Thomas Kenan of the Forty-third North

From Triumph to Disappointment

Carolina noted that "the capture of the town seemed probable." Lieutenant Colonel Rufus Wharton of the Sixty-seventh North Carolina termed Hoke's capture of New Bern "almost a certainty." Captain William H. S. Burgwyn of the Thirty-fifth North Carolina noted that the planned assault had "every prospect of success." As he witnessed Hoke making his final preparations on the evening of May 5, the editor of the *Raleigh Daily Confederate* concurred with the officers, writing a few days later, "The project was sure of success, and before this day, General Hoke would have occupied Newbern."[25]

To some Confederate observers at New Bern on the eve of the planned attack, the Federal garrison appeared to lack the will or the ability to beat back the challenge. Colonel John T. Kennedy and Lieutenant W. F. Parker of the Seventy-fifth North Carolina (Seventh Cavalry) concluded, "The city of New Bern was not well supplied with troops and was ready to capitulate." The *Raleigh Daily Confederate* agreed: "The fact is there was no fight in them. Their terror was apparent; and we have not a doubt that forty-eight hours would have given us the place."[26]

During the evening of May 5, Hoke took final steps to make sure his troops could get across the Neuse to bring the "storm" to New Bern the following day. Preparations were made to lay a pontoon bridge under the protection of the artillery. On the north side of New Bern, some of Hoke's soldiers were separated from town by a canal that had been cut by the enemy from one river to the other. They were so enthusiastic that they were willing to swim the waterway to join in the planned attack. Every soldier in the Twenty-first Georgia stepped forward as a volunteer. Among this group was lanky private George Petty, who stood six feet four inches tall. One of his comrades called out, "Why, George, what are you stepping out for; you can't swim." Private Petty responded, "I know that, but I can wade like hell." The soldiers shed their clothes, tied their cartridge boxes on their heads, and waited for an order to swim the canal—an order that never came.[27]

At the worst possible moment, Beauregard's special messenger, Lieutenant Chisolm, arrived in New Bern with an urgent order for Hoke, who was "to repair forthwith to Petersburg, no matter how far his operations might have advanced against Newbern." Long after the war, Hoke recalled, "The recall was one of the greatest disappointments I ever had." Nonetheless, he wasted no time in carrying out his orders. As night turned to morning, Hoke prepared marching orders: his army was to proceed with all haste to Kinston, where Beauregard had collected trains to transport the soldiers to the battlefields of Virginia via the Wilmington and Weldon Railroad. His old brigade was ordered to be ready to march at 10 A.M. on Friday, May 6. Most of his soldiers, anxious to drive the Federals from New Bern, were dismayed when their commanders sent them in the direction of Kinston, rather than into the face of the enemy.[28]

Before turning his back on the prize he desperately coveted, Hoke decided to play "one round for the game" on the morning of May 6. This final piece of strategy almost paid off handsomely for the retreating Confederate army. Under a flag of truce, Hoke demanded that General Palmer surrender New Bern. Palmer immediately summoned his officers for a council of war that lasted three hours. Not until the "pale and depressed" council received cavalry reports of the Confederate retreat did Palmer decline Hoke's demand. A day later, when enemy forces were nowhere in sight, the emboldened general noted in his official report of Hoke's attempt on New Bern, "Yesterday morning a flag of truce came in with one Major Read, who stated verbally that he had come by direction of General Hoke, to demand the surrender of the place, as they had possession of the Neuse River, the railroad, etc. I directed one of my aides-de-camp to go to Major Read and say to him that his delicate jest was duly appreciated by me, but that he must leave in one-half hour, or we should fire upon him. He left immediately, and I have heard nothing from him since."[29]

As he hurried his army from New Bern to Kinston, Hoke inspired his soldiers to make "one of the hardest forced marches of the war." During a twelve-hour period, the distance covered by the Forty-third North Carolina, including the running fight toward New Bern and the retreat to Kinston, was thirty-seven miles. Plagued by a lack of drinking water, dusty roads, and blistered feet, the soldiers endured great suffering and fatigue "without scarce a murmur." Most expressed but one regret—that they had not been permitted to "finish the job." Not only was the march one of the hardest during the war, but it was long taught at the United States Military Academy as one of the most rapid troop movements on record.

Many years after the war, General Carle A. Woodruff of the United States Army related a West Point story that told of the Hoke modesty, the hallmark of the general's life. In 1866, Hoke had occasion to be in New York and happened to visit West Point. As he was strolling about the grounds and buildings, he made his way into the rear of one of the recitation rooms where a class was in session. As fate would have it, the instructor was lecturing the cadets on rapid troop movements, and he cited Hoke's march from New Bern to Kinston as one of the most brilliant during the Civil War. Hoke heard the comments but did not make himself known to the instructor or the students. Rather, he left the classroom as quietly as he had entered.[30]

In the aftermath of his campaign in eastern North Carolina, Hoke had little time to reflect on just what he had accomplished in his native state. In but three weeks, he had reclaimed Plymouth and Washington for the Confederacy and had come within an eyelash of taking New Bern. He departed North Carolina without having been defeated on the battlefield. With seven thousand soldiers, he had succeeded where Daniel Harvey Hill and George Pickett, both with much larger armies, had failed.

For Hoke, the expedition was a classic case of what might have been. Had Richmond been willing to gamble one more day in New Bern, the wager would have reaped untold returns. All of eastern North Carolina, with its valuable waterways, vast fishing grounds, and fertile agricultural lands, would have been returned to Confederate control. Almost as important as the tangible rewards would have been the psychological effects. North Carolina and all of the Confederacy would have received the badly needed impetus for the impending battle in Virginia, which Confederate War Department clerk John B. Jones predicted would "probably end the war."

Conversely, the loss of the region where Union forces had won their very first victory of the war would have cast a pall over Grant's spring offensive around Richmond and Petersburg. One more day was all Hoke

General Robert F. Hoke

had needed. But it was not to be for him or the Confederacy. In a moment of retrospection after the war, the general relived the bitter frustration he had experienced at New Bern and on many other fields: "So many times we failed of success by such a narrow margin that it seems it was not intended that we should succeed."[31]

*The **Hoke House**, birthplace and boyhood home of Robert F. Hoke, Lincolnton, N.C., as it appeared in 1996. Hoke was born on the first floor room on the right on May 27, 1837.*

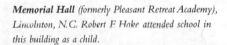

Frances Burton Hoke (1815–1868), mother of Robert F. Hoke. Photo courtesy of Hoke Kimball

Memorial Hall (formerly Pleasant Retreat Academy), Lincolnton, N.C. Robert F. Hoke attended school in this building as a child.

Report card of Robert F. Hoke, dated June 13, 1845. Photo courtesy of Southern
Stars Chapter, UDC, Lincolnton, N.C.

Colonel Robert F. Hoke, 1862. Photo
courtesy of Lydia Hoke Jastram.

General Robert F. Hoke. Other than the photograph on the front jacket, this is the only surviving photograph taken of Hoke when he was a general. Photo courtesy of Hoke Kimball.

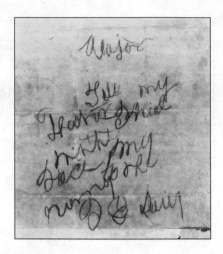

Colonel Isaac Erwin Avery (1828–1863). Colonel Avery was mortally wounded while leading General Hoke's brigade up Cemetery Hill at Gettysburg on the evening of July 2, 1863. Colonel Avery rode Hoke's horse on the assault. Photo courtesy of the North Carolina Department of Archives and History.

Dying message of Colonel Isaac Erwin Avery, found near his hand on the battlefield at Gettysburg on July 2, 1863. "Major Tell my Father I died with my face to the enemy I. E. Avery." Photo courtesy of the North Carolina Department of Archives and History.

Lydia Ann Maverick Van Wyck Hoke (1848-1915), wife of General Robert F. Hoke

*Wedding photograph of **Mr. and Mrs. Robert F. Hoke**. General Hoke married Lydia Van Wyck in New York City on January 7, 1869. Photo courtesy of Hoke Kimball.*

Downtown Lincolnton, N.C. *as it appeared in the early part of the 20th century. At the time, Hoke was busy developing his enterprises at the nearby Lithia Inn. Photo courtesy of Paul Dellinger.*

Robert F. Hoke (exact date unknown, but most likely in the early 1900s). It was at this time that Hoke greatly resembled Robert E. Lee. Photo courtesy of Southern Stars Chapter, UDC, Lincolnton, N.C.

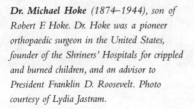

Dr. Michael Hoke *(1874–1944), son of Robert F. Hoke. Dr. Hoke was a pioneer orthopaedic surgeon in the United States, founder of the Shriners' Hospitals for crippled and burned children, and an advisor to President Franklin D. Roosevelt. Photo courtesy of Lydia Jastram.*

General Robert F. Hoke, sitting on the porch of Lincoln Lithia Inn, 1911 or 1912. Photo courtesy of Mr. and Mrs. Jack Ramseur.

Postcard photograph of Hoke's **Lithia Inn**. The inn remained in operation more than 25 years after the death of the general in 1912. Photo courtesy of Horace Rhyne.

Photograph of the **Hoke family** or. the front porch of the Lithia Inn, shortly before the death of the general. Standing: Van Wyck Hoke. Sitting in chairs: Robert F. Hoke and wife, Lydia Van Wych Hoke. Adults sitting on porch (left to right): Alexander Webb, Lydia Hoke Webb, Laurie Harrison Hoke, Dr. Michael Hoke, Frances Hoke Pollock, William D. Pollock. Photo courtesy of R. F. H. Pollock.

The Hoke Cottage at the Lincoln Lithia Club, Lincolnton, N.C. as it appeared in 1996. Hoke died in this house on July 3, 1912.

Grave of General Robert Frederick Hoke, Oakwood Cemetery, Raleigh, N.C.

CHAPTER 9

Spring Bloodbath

As Hoke pushed his troops from New Bern toward Kinston throughout the night of May 6, he was beginning the first leg of a desperate race to beat the Army of the James to Petersburg, for at the same time, Union major general Benjamin Butler was assembling his thirty-nine-thousand-man army at Bermuda Hundred, a thirty-square-mile neck of land formed by the James and Appomattox Rivers. Protected by Union gunboats pa trolling the waterfront and a natural topography featuring deep ravines at the foot of the peninsula, Butler's new base not only provided security for his forces but also served as a strategic staging ground for his assigned tasks in the planned spring offensive. Because of its location—fifteen miles southeast of Richmond, seven miles northeast of Petersburg, and just three miles from the vital railroad link between the Confederate capital and the lower South—Bermuda Hundred presented Butler with a variety of attractive targets. However, because Grant was at the time locked in a fierce struggle with Lee in the Wilderness, Butler chose to direct his initial efforts toward the destruction of the Richmond and Petersburg Railroad and the capture of Petersburg.[1]

Beauregard, who had assumed command of the Petersburg defenses on May 5, remained in North Carolina for the time being. Although he was physically ill, the fiery Creole labored to collect trains for the transportation of Hoke's soldiers and the other troops being sent north to Virginia. In Beauregard's absence on the front at Petersburg, George Pickett assumed immediate command of the lone regiment on hand to defend the city and the railroad.[2]

In advance of the arrival of Hoke's soldiers, the South Carolina brigade of Johnson Hagood—soon to become an integral part of Hoke's division—and the Tennessee brigade of Bushrod Johnson made a determined stand on May 6 and 7 against Butler's forces, which advanced from City Point on the south side of the James to the railroad junction at Port Walthall, just a few miles north of Petersburg. Despite the heroics of the two brigades, the question posed on May 6 by Major General W. H. C. Whiting to Beauregard—"Can you save Petersburg?"—was unresolved.[3] In both the short term (the next ten days) and the long term (the next six months), Hoke would help Beauregard and Lee answer Whiting's query in the affirmative.

On the afternoon of Saturday, May 7, Hoke's troops began pouring into Kinston after their fatiguing textbook march. In order to expedite their movement to Petersburg, they were quickly loaded onto waiting trains. Bad luck and delays would plague the trip north. For example, later the same day, one of the troop trains derailed en route to Goldsboro.[4]

While trainloads of Hoke's troops passed through Weldon on May 8, the Confederate high command, in consideration of Beauregard's recent illness, was on the verge of heaping even greater responsibilities on the young North Carolinian who had been a major general less than a month. In a dispatch to Bragg, President Davis intimated, "If General Beauregard's health disqualifies him for field operations, it would be well to order Hoke to proceed in advance of his troops and take command of the forces in front of Petersburg." Later that day, however, Beauregard reported to Bragg from Weldon that the water "had improved" his health to such an extent that he would be able to depart for Petersburg the following morning.[5]

Hoke arrived in Weldon on the night of May 8. On the eve of his departure from North Carolina, he thought back to what might have been at New Bern. In a letter to his friend and able Confederate comrade James Cooke, Hoke expressed his mixed emotions: "I had taken the River Road and had command of the river and the enemy completely surrounded when I had my orders to proceed to another field, which I deeply regret, but the summers work can still be accomplished and I hope with the aid of the Almighty to do it as soon as my troops are not wanted elsewhere." Hoke was mindful of the new challenge before him. With great resolve, he told Commander Cooke, "Everything is being concentrated around Richmond where the big fight of the war is to take place, and with the aid of the Almighty we must be successful." And because he was to be away from the site of his greatest triumph for an indeterminate time, Hoke made one request of Cooke: "Take care of Plymouth."[6]

On May 9, as the troop train lurched closer to its destination, Captain Cary Whitaker recorded the immediate concerns of the soldiers: "I was uneasy all the time as I know how easy it would be for the enemy to throw the train off the track and attack us and throw us in confusion and probably kill a good many of us." Soon after the train rumbled across the state line into Virginia that day, some of Whitaker's fears were realized. Hoke's soldiers were forced to scramble out of the cars when it was discovered that Federal cavalry raiders had cut the railroad just below Jarratt's Station and burned two bridges over the Nottoway River. William Gaston Lewis was able to march Hoke's old brigade into Petersburg by nightfall, but it would be the following day before the bulk of Hoke's troops reached the city. Yet for the meager Confederate forces defending Petersburg, the news of the impending arrival of Hoke's division from North Carolina and Robert Ransom's division from Richmond was a great morale booster.[7]

After the trains were halted on May 9, Hoke's soldiers marched parallel to the tracks for as much as twenty miles before settling in for the night.

Captain Robert D. Graham of the Fifty-sixth North Carolina recalled that the "weird hooting of great owls in the swamps" along the route "was almost human in its intonations." These sounds evoked ominous predictions from the men in the ranks: "That is a bad sign boys: hard times in old Virginia, and worse a' coming." Bivouacking for the night near Stony Creek, the troops, with loaded guns, were put aboard trains the following morning and delivered to Petersburg throughout the morning and afternoon. As one train pulled into town about 11 A.M., the sounds of nearby fighting were evident. Private James C. Elliott of the Fifty-sixth North Carolina noted, "As soon as our train rolled in we could hear the popping of musketry on suburbs, and the greatest excitement prevailed."[8]

Beauregard arrived in Petersburg via a special train on May 10 just before 9 A.M., and Hoke followed in the early afternoon. With bayonets gleaming in the bright spring sunshine, Hoke's troops marched through city streets lined by cheering townspeople. Private Elliott described the warm reception: "Beautiful ladies showered bouquets of flowers upon us as we marched the streets, with such exclamations as 'We are safe now. There are the brave North Carolinians who have driven the enemy from their own State and have come to defend us. These are the brave boys that took Plymouth.'" Setting up camp on the comfortable grounds of Poplar Lawn Hospital a few miles outside the city, the soldiers were delighted by the "generous hospitality" of the citizenry. Private Elliott recalled, "As soon as we were settled the white ladies and colored aunties began to pour in upon us with great baskets of everything good to eat and gave us a bountiful feast."[9]

While the North Carolinians enjoyed a brief, well-deserved rest, Beauregard was busy organizing the forces available to him and devising a strategy to defend Petersburg and launch a strike against Butler. New temporary divisions were created by Beauregard for Pickett and Hoke, who had been given command of the north side of the Appomattox by Bragg on May 9. Assigned to Hoke were the brigades of William Gaston Lewis, Johnson Hagood, Thomas Lanier Clingman, and Bushrod Johnson. Before the night was over, however, Pickett, thoroughly exhausted from the defense of Petersburg, collapsed from the strain to which he had been exposed over the past week. Command of his division would soon devolve to Major General William Henry Chase Whiting, a brilliant officer destined to be a key player—or, as it were, nonplayer—in the upcoming offensive against the Federals.[10]

While the Confederates were struggling to reach Petersburg from North Carolina, Butler had been slow to move and had in effect frittered away a golden opportunity to take lightly defended Petersburg. Upon the arrival of Hoke and his veteran soldiers, Butler decided to pull back to the line of entrenchments his army had constructed across the narrowest point of Bermuda Hundred. Jefferson Davis, Braxton Bragg, and Secretary of War Seddon saw the movement as a prelude to a strike against Richmond. Beauregard viewed Butler's apparent lethargy as an invitation to take the offensive.

Bragg, however, provided instructions for defensive operations in a telegram received by Beauregard around 3 A.M. on May 11. Under the dictates of the telegram, Hoke and all the forces that could be spared from Petersburg were to hasten north to join the division of Robert Ransom at Drewry's Bluff, located between Richmond and Petersburg on the south shore of the James. Hoke's movement was to be a swift, defensive one; he was to engage the enemy only if it blocked the turnpike toward Drewry's Bluff. The Confederate administration was confident that the two major generals from North Carolina could defend the capital from advances by Butler's infantry and Phil Sheridan's cavalry.[11]

Although Beauregard wired Ransom, through Bragg, at 7 A.M. that Hoke was on his way, three hours would pass before the actual advance commenced. When he put six brigades and eight artillery batteries in motion at 10 A.M., Hoke was under orders from Beauregard that varied from what the Louisianian had received from Richmond in the wee hours of the morning. Beauregard was anxious to hit Butler hard, so he instructed Hoke to make a "forced reconnaissance" in the direction of Bermuda Hundred to ascertain if the enemy had retired to that place. In the event that Hoke found the enemy reembarking, he was to attack.

Under a bright sun that sent temperatures soaring into the upper nineties, each of the half-dozen brigades marched in columns of four. Field batteries, ordnance wagons, and ambulances followed each brigade. According to Private Elliott, cavalry details moved parallel to the infantry, "rubbing against the enemy on our right with frequent brisk skirmishes." Several miles outside Petersburg, the soldiers observed grim reminders of the valiant stand made by Hagood's brigade just a few days earlier. Elliott recalled, "The thickets were shattered and remnants of equipments were scattered about, and the bloody places where many had fallen were still visible."[12]

Beauregard had forwarded a telegram at 8:00 A.M. informing Bragg of the change in Hoke's orders and his willingness to rescind the orders if the War Department objected. By noon, he had a response from Seddon: "Division of your forces is earnestly objected to. It is decidedly preferred that you carry out the instructions given last night, and endeavor to unite all forces." As a consequence, Beauregard dispatched a communiqué to Seddon at 12:45 P.M. that Richmond's wishes were then being carried out.

As Hoke turned his course north for Drewry's Bluff, a war of words began to rage between Beauregard and the Confederate capital. Before receiving Beauregard's early-afternoon message, Seddon had fired off a telegram containing sharp-toned verbiage: "This city is in hot danger. It should be defended with all our resources to the sacrifice of minor considerations." This telegram was received at Beauregard's headquarters at 2 P.M., but before the short-tempered general could react to it, a message from Bragg expressing approval for Hoke's forced reconnaissance arrived. Now, bombarded with contradictions from Richmond, the outraged Beauregard threatened a personal course of action that could have very well led to Hoke's assumption of the command of the defense of Richmond. In a strongly worded dispatch to Seddon, Beauregard requested that he be relieved of command if his course of action was not approved.[13]

Throughout the night, both Seddon and Jefferson Davis tried to soothe Beauregard's irritation with complimentary telegrams. Seddon applauded the general's "past services, patriotism, and reputation," and Davis termed the "order for a forced reconnaissance . . . entirely appropriate." In the meantime, at 5 P.M., Hoke led the advance column of his sizable force to a rendezvous with Ransom's division two miles south of Drewry's Bluff.

Spring Bloodbath

Violent thunderstorms threatened on the western horizon as the long procession of troops stretched for several miles. Hoke's arrival was welcome news for the authorities in Richmond, but he brought with him rather grim tidings. During the day, Federal forces had moved past his rear, thereby threatening the ability of expected Confederate reinforcements and Beauregard himself to move from Petersburg to Drewry's Bluff. Nevertheless, Beauregard telegraphed Hoke at 7 P.M. that he would leave for Drewry's Bluff the following day with the brigades of James C. Martin and Alfred Colquitt.[14]

As Hoke's soldiers bedded down for the night near Proctor's Creek, there was much anxiety and discomfort in camp. Because the enemy was nearby, the Confederates were forced to sleep on their arms. Hoke was deeply concerned that his men might be called upon to fight during the night. Earlier in the evening, Ransom had relayed to Bragg Hoke's urgent request for ammunition. At the time, Hoke had but forty rounds of ammunition for eleven thousand muskets. To further heighten the gloom, the heavy rain that had arrived with thunder and lightning about dusk continued to fall throughout the night.[15]

While the Confederates attempted to catch some sleep on the wet ground, Butler was making ready to end his period of relative inactivity. The next morning, he would attempt to flank the Confederate forces and either capture them or drive them into their defenses at Drewry's Bluff. His lead elements moved out at 4 A.M. on the rainy morning of May 12. However, Hoke's soldiers had been awake for several hours, ready for action. Private Elliott noted, "About 2 A.M. the rain falling in our faces woke us, and soon our pickets close by commenced firing."

A few hours later, both armies, separated by just a few miles, were marching north in a miserable rainstorm. Second Lieutenant William Beavans of the Forty-third North Carolina expressed the common sentiments of Hoke's men: "Expect to meet the Yanks." Meanwhile, Major General Ransom and two brigades departed for Richmond. In Ransom's absence, Hoke assumed command of all of the troops in the vicinity of Drewry's Bluff. Beauregard sent a message to Hoke instructing him to follow the wishes of the War Department. This dispatch was intercepted by the enemy, but Hoke subsequently learned of its existence and contents from captured Yankee soldiers.[16]

When several of Hoke's brigades reached the Half-Way House, a local landmark, they engaged the enemy in heavy skirmishing throughout the morning. That afternoon, Hoke labored to move the brigades up from the Half-Way House to the defense works at Drewry's Bluff. In the course of the afternoon's work, Hoke received orders to send two more brigades to Richmond. Once his old brigade under Lewis and James L. Kemper's brigade under William R. Terry were dispatched toward the capital, Hoke was left with but five brigades to withstand the "terribly strong force" in his front. William "Baldy" Smith had positioned his Eighteenth Corps of the Army of the James on the south side of Proctor's Creek in the face of the Confederate defenses on the other side. As field guns from both armies engaged in an artillery duel, rain continued to pour in torrents, and Hoke began to worry about an attack not only from Smith but from reported forces of ten to twelve thousand men under Major General Quincy A. Gillmore and Brigadier General A. V. Kautz, moving to the Confederate right and rear from Chesterfield Court-House. Hoke courageously wired Bragg, "I shall fight them if met from all sides."[17]

Fortunately for Hoke, Smith reasoned that his line was stretched too thin to launch an effective assault, and Gillmore's forces arrived on the scene too late to reinforce Smith. Thus, the infantry fighting during the afternoon and evening was limited to heavy skirmishing. There was no letup in the downpour as the gray skies gave way to night. By 10 P.M., Hoke was cautiously optimistic. Almost simultaneously, he sent two telegrams which evinced his mixed emotions. He told Bragg, "I will do all in my power to destroy the enemy, but think prudence should be used on account of this position." On the other hand, he showed himself ready to proceed with an offensive movement when he wired Robert Ransom, "The strength of the enemy in my front prevents a division of my forces. If you could join me here and we drive them immediately in my front, it would protect this place and Richmond, and at the same time would cut off the retreat of the enemy . . . and also be of advantage to Petersburg." Three days would pass before Ransom returned with his forces to Drewry's Bluff.[18] In the meantime, it would be up to Hoke to keep Butler at bay.

The rain continued to fall as Friday, May 13, broke dark and bleak. Surprisingly, "all was quiet on the lines" throughout the morning. By afternoon, however, a serous problem developed on Hoke's extreme right, where Matt Ransom's brigade of North Carolinians anchored the line at Wooldridge's Hill. Private Elliott described the scene: "We were stretched out single file to cover the ground. The enemy was drawing our attention down the railroad towards Petersburg by firing some shells at us, all of which were falling a little short. We were in fine spirits, hoping to see the enemy advance to the open in front, but it had been discovered that the enemy had outflanked us and a force gone around."

At approximately 4 P.M., the Third New Hampshire from Gillmore's division poured into the rear of Ransom's brigade. Only moments before, Hoke and Ransom had dismounted and gone into a nearby farmhouse for consultation. When the enemy attack commenced, the two generals emerged and narrowly escaped capture. They immediately remounted and rode along the line, shouting instructions to the North Carolinians and urging them to rally against the attackers. In an instant, the soldiers of the Fifty-sixth, Forty-ninth, and Twenty-fifth North Carolina responded by jumping over to the other side of the earthworks. Captain Robert D. Graham recalled the behavior of his comrades in that moment of crisis: "The perfect discipline of the command was evinced by there being no sign of a panic." The Confederates made a determined stand; marksmen offered a well-directed fire at the enemy while their fellow soldiers in the trenches below "handed up their rifles as rapidly as they could be reloaded."[19]

Although Ransom's men were able to repulse every assault of the first wave of attackers "with telling effect," Yankee reinforcements—primarily the Twenty-fourth Massachusetts and the Seventh New Hampshire—forced Ransom to pull his forces back from Wooldridge Hill toward the inner line of defenses. Confederate losses during the skirmish were moderate: 13 killed and 30 wounded. Union casualties totaled 140.[20]

Throughout the afternoon, Hoke fretted about his ability to hold the fragile line that separated the enemy from the Confederate capital. Determined to do everything he could to check Butler's advance until Beauregard and Ransom arrived with reinforcements, the general called for his division scout, Halifax Richards Wood. With darkness fast approaching, it was time, Hoke reasoned, to use some guile. And "Fax" Wood was just the man to pull off an elaborate ruse.[21]

Born in Virginia, Wood had spent much of his youth in North Carolina. Two months before his fifteenth birthday, he had volunteered for service in the Twenty-first North Carolina in May 1861. Thereafter, while a member of the First Battalion North Carolina Sharpshooters, the teenager had rendered distinguished service as personal courier for Hoke, earning the utmost confidence of the general. When Hoke was promoted to major general, Wood was the logical choice for his scout.[22]

When the seventeen-year-old veteran reported to Hoke at twilight on May 13, his commander asked if he was willing to risk his life to save Richmond. Hoke knew the answer before he posed the question, for he had never met "a man of such cool daring and faithfulness to perilous duty." Wood did not hesitate to accept the dangerous mission offered him at Drewry's Bluff. In an instant, he donned the uniform of a Yankee cavalryman and rode off with specific orders from Hoke: he was to first make his way to the Federal rear, then "ride boldly, as if coming from the river" to Butler's headquarters, where he would report that the Confederates were disembarking in large numbers on the James River. Finally, Wood was to leave the enemy camp as quickly as he had arrived in order to avoid "too many questions."[23]

As twilight turned to darkness, Hoke grew apprehensive about the safety of his scout and the success of his mission. But he could ill afford to ponder the fate of a single soldier on a mission of deception, as he had to deal with the growing crisis facing his five brigades. With Butler's massive army drawing ever closer, Hoke hoped that the night would bring relief in the form of fresh troops. At 7:15 P.M., he wired Bragg, "Do you know anything of General Beauregard's movements?" Fifteen minutes later, Hoke sent telegrams to Bragg and Robert Ransom informing them of the sizable enemy forces threatening him. To Bragg, he noted, "I still hold the outer line, but the force of the enemy is so great that they can go entirely around it, and have done so. My force is not sufficient to fill up the entrench-ments, and I cannot leave them to fight, as Drewry's Bluff has to be pro-tected." Cognizant that he had no feasible alternative, Hoke then evacu-ated the outer line "with all possible secrecy" and withdrew his forces to the relative safety of the second, or inner, line.[24]

As he watched and waited for the enemy to make another approach, Hoke was astonished to see Fax Wood gallop up to his headquarters. Saluting the general, Wood informed Hoke that he "had carried out his instructions to the letter." Although there is no record that Union au-thorities were taken in by Wood's subterfuge, the Army of the James, for whatever reason, chose not to follow up on the advantage it had gained on Hoke's right that afternoon.[25]

Throughout the long night, Hoke prepared his heavily outnumbered brigades for an expected attack on his front and right the following morn-ing. Unaware of the tenuous position of the Confederates at Drewry's Bluff, General Lee had urged Davis on May 13 to send Hoke to him: "If General Hoke with fresh troops can be spared from Richmond, it would be of great assistance." More than two weeks would pass before Hoke was free to come to Lee's aid on another field.[26]

Beauregard arrived at Drewry's Bluff in a cold rain at 3 A.M. on May 14 after riding around the Federal line in the company of Alfred Colquitt's twelve-hundred-man brigade. Upon being briefed about the events of the previous day, Beauregard proposed that Lee move his forces into the Rich-mond defenses after sending fifteen thousand men to Drewry's Bluff. Beauregard would promptly dispose of Butler and then turn his twenty-five-thousand-man army toward Richmond to join Lee in an orchestrated attack against Grant. Jefferson Davis, however, expressed his disapproval of the plan.[27]

In the meantime, Butler had pushed his army into the exterior defense works abandoned just hours earlier by Hoke. In the early morning, skir-mishing broke out all along Hoke's two-mile line. The Federals took shel-ter where they could find it; they ducked in and out from behind tree stumps and occupied the huts that had been built as barracks between the inner and outer works. Fighting was particularly severe along Matt Ransom's portion of the line. About 9 A.M., Ransom, who according to Private Elliott exposed himself "unnecessarily," went down with a serious wound to his left arm. For the remainder of the day, the Yankees, some armed with seven-shot Spencer carbines, "kept up an incessant fire" while artillery from both armies pounded away with destructive force. Hoke's well-positioned batteries in Fort Stevens produced the most telling results.[28]

By nightfall, the intensity of the fighting decreased significantly. Yet for Hoke's soldiers deployed as pickets outside the works in pits and holes, the night was one of terror. Private Elliott reported, "The bullets were striking the ground around us with a noise as if they were as large as goose eggs." Among Hoke's casualties on the "dangerous and trying" picket line was Captain Thomas Jarvis of the Eighth North Carolina. Though Jarvis's right arm was permanently damaged, he recovered to later serve as governor of North Carolina, United States senator, and United States minister to Brazil.[29]

When the new day broke, the weather was a bit better; three days of constant rain had given way to occasional showers. In the morning light, Beauregard was taken aback by the growing strength of the enemy position at Drewry's Bluff. Based upon his observations and the realization that Robert Ransom's division would return later in the day, Beauregard concluded, "I saw how important it was to attack Butler the very next morning."[30]

Beauregard's "fragmentary army" was divided into three divisions (right, left, and reserve) under Major Generals Hoke and Ransom and Brigadier General Colquitt. Hoke's large division of seven thousand men included the Virginia brigade of Montgomery Corse, the North Carolina brigade of Thomas L. Clingman, the Tennessee brigade of Bushrod Johnson, the South Carolina brigade of Johnson Hagood, the Third North Carolina Cavalry, and the Washington Artillery. Under the terms of Beauregard's plan, which Hagood described as "ingenious," Ransom was to drive back Butler's right flank and separate the Yankees from their fortified base at Bermuda Hundred. Meanwhile, Hoke was to demonstrate against Butler's left side until Ransom turned the right. At that moment, Hoke would launch his attack. And despite the objections raised earlier by President Davis, Beauregard issued orders at 10:45 A.M. on May 15 to Major General Whiting to use the forces at Petersburg to attack Butler in the rear as he attempted to fall back to the safety of Bermuda Hundred. Colquitt's demi-division, consisting of his brigade and Matt Ransom's, would be held in reserve at Drewry's Bluff for use when and where needed.[31]

In the early afternoon, Hoke and his fellow division commanders assembled for a pre-battle conference with Beauregard. There, they were given a circular containing written instructions as well as additional oral details as to the plan of attack, "so that none could be taken by surprise." Following the meeting, Hoke returned to his headquarters, where he pored over the plan for the action scheduled to begin before dawn the next morning.

All along Hoke's lines, the fire from Federal infantry and artillery annoyed the Confederates. Colonel William Clarke, who had replaced the wounded Matt Ransom as commander of the Fifty-sixth North Carolina a day earlier, fell prey to a Yankee bullet. Yet even though the troops were weary from the tedium of the trenches, they exuded confidence on the eve of the battle. Under the nighttime sky, Beauregard rode along the lines and breastworks to Hoke's cheering soldiers. He asked the men if they were not tired of "this sort of fighting," and in response to his own question told them he "would change it for them." Captain Cary W. Whitaker of the Forty-third North Carolina expressed the fervent hope in the hearts of many of the soldiers as they waited anxiously for the fight that was now just hours away: "Every body seems to think if we can drive the Yankees back this time that they will give it up, at least that the crisis of the country will have been passed and that most of the fighting will be over."[32]

At 10 P.M., as fog billowing up from the river began to veil the would-be field of death, Hoke summoned his brigadiers to his headquarters, where he thoroughly reviewed the battle plan with them. Soon, all was in a state of readiness. The divisions were now properly deployed along the lines. On the Confederate left, Ransom's brigades were positioned behind the trenches on Kingsland Creek, a watercourse that ran on an easterly course not far from Drewry's Bluff. Hoke's right wing manned the intermediate line of fortifications running from Fort Stevens across the Richmond-Petersburg Turnpike to the railroad. To the rear of Hoke, centered on the turnpike, were the reserve forces of Colquitt.[33]

General Robert F. Hoke

All along the Confederate lines, officers roused their soldiers just after midnight on Monday, May 16. Heavy fog covered the entire landscape at Drewry's Bluff. At 2 A.M., Ransom began to pull his troops from the trenches in anticipation of his attack against Butler's right, which was generally considered the weakest point in the Union line. Three hours later, Beauregard, in the first of many telegrams he would send to Bragg throughout the day, announced the opening of the bloody conflict: "The battle has just commenced. Our trust is in God, the valor of our troops, and the justness of our cause."

Although troop movements were "retarded by almost perfect obscurity of the densest fog," Ransom began his general advance at 5:45 A.M. Within fifteen minutes, his division carried the breastworks in his front and began to turn Butler's right flank. After enjoying this brief success, Ransom halted his forward probe in the fog because his "lines had become confused and required readjusting" and his "ammunition had to be replenished throughout." In his moment of peril, Ransom called for assistance.[34]

"At the earliest dawn" on the Confederate right, Hoke ordered his batteries to limber up and sent forth his skirmishers in a broad sweep. From left to right, his brigades were employed thus: Hagood, Johnson, Clingman, and Corse. After waiting an hour for Ransom's advance to begin, Hoke supposed that the commander of the left wing had met with success even though "dense fog" allowed him to see "nothing of the movement." Accordingly, he sent forward Hagood and Johnson with some artillery. Upon encountering the enemy in heavy force along the outer line of entrenchments, the two brigades were unable to retreat. Hagood's soldiers stumbled over telegraph wire as the fog hung close to the ground, but Hoke ordered him and Johnson to attack. According to Hoke, the charge was "gallantly and handsomely done." Hagood captured five pieces of artillery and a number of prisoners.[35]

In response to Ransom's plea for help, Colquitt's reserves were rushed forward to his assistance, but about 7:15 A.M., they were moved to relieve Hoke, for "on his front the enemy had been allowed to mass his forces by the inaction of the left." As the morning wore on, Hoke handled his command, according to Beauregard, "with resolution and judgment for which he was conspicuous." Enemy resistance on the Confederate right was most stubborn, but Hoke's brigades gradually cleared their front. On several occasions, the Federals charged Hoke in vain attempts to retake their lost works and artillery, but these charges were "most handsomely repulsed."[36]

Even though the Army of the James was on the defensive all day, the early-morning confusion on Ransom's wing caused by the fog added significance to Major General Whiting's role. At 9:00 A.M. and again at 9:30, Beauregard sent urgent requests to Whiting: "Press on and press over everything in your front, and the day will be complete." Hours passed, and the guns Beauregard heard to the south proved not to belong to Whiting.[37]

During the brutal fighting that raged for more than twelve hours on May 16, Jefferson Davis was on hand at Drewry's Bluff, where he joined Hoke for a portion of the battle. In Hoke's estimation, "No braver man than Jefferson Davis ever lived." At no time during the war was Hoke more impressed with the president's courage under fire than on that spring day in 1864 on the south side of the James. Hoke recalled, "He rode all day without flinching under as terrible a fire as I ever saw. Some of us who had been used to that kind of thing for a long time didn't relish that day's experience too well."[38]

By 4 P.M., Beauregard was no longer entertaining the prospect that Whiting was going to participate in the offensive as he had been ordered. Consequently, he abandoned all hope of capturing or destroying the Army of the James and promptly turned his attention to "a vigorous pursuit of Butler and driving him into his fortified base." Hoke was ordered "to send Corse and Clingman forward along the Court-house Road, to take the enemy in flank and establish enfilading batteries in front of the heights west of the railroad." Further Confederate advances were impeded, however, by a "heavy and prolonged storm of rain" and approaching darkness.

After consulting with Hoke and Ransom, Beauregard decided to halt the fighting. Leaving their unburied dead on the field, the Federals retired toward Bermuda Hundred. Hoke's hungry soldiers "feasted that night upon the unwonted luxuries of coffee, sardines, and canned meats, with which his [the enemy's] abandoned camps were abundantly supplied." Beauregard could not be certain of the enemy's intention, but he was anxious to press his advantage. Preparations were made to resume the pursuit on the following morning, and orders were sent to Whiting instructing him to meet Hoke's right wing the next day.[39]

At first light on May 17, Beauregard took up the chase again. Hoke's troops found the turnpike "drenched with blood" and observed many Yankee soldiers scattered about—"the debris of a broken army." Even the most war-hardened veterans were appalled at the slaughter. By midafternoon, Butler's army had been chased back to its entrenched position across Bermuda Hundred Neck. The Battle of Drewry's Bluff was over! For the time being, Richmond was safe.

Beauregard proclaimed the gains achieved by his victory: "We had defeated Butler and forced him to take refuge within his fortified lines. The communications south and west of Richmond were restored. We had achieved the main object for which our forces had encountered the enemy." Indeed, Butler was locked between the James and Appomattox Rivers—as Grant put it, he was corked in a bottle. Nonetheless, Beauregard realized that his success was incomplete. Johnson Hagood concluded that Beauregard's plan would have "annihilated his antagonist, had not two of his division commanders failed him." Beauregard concurred. Of his three major generals, all of whom were North Carolinians, Beauregard pointed the finger of blame at two of them: Whiting and Ransom.[40]

Only Hoke maintained, and even built upon, his reputation at Drewry's Bluff. Beauregard praised him for his "judgment and energy." Many of the findings set out on May 25 in Hoke's first official report as a major general were adopted by Beauregard in his report on June 10. All things considered, Hoke had performed well in his first real test as a division commander. He had handled new brigades in the heat of battle with great skill and played an instrumental role in defending the Confederate capital. His soldiers had fought gallantly, and many of them had paid the ultimate price. In the fighting on May 16 alone, 208 of Hoke's soldiers had been killed and 903 wounded.[41]

On May 17, Kemper's brigade of Virginians replaced Johnson's brigade in Hoke's division. At the same time, Bushrod Johnson was given command of Ransom's division upon the transfer of Ransom back to Richmond. A day later, Colquitt's brigade was assigned to Hoke.

The Confederate lines were steadily advanced by skirmishers on May 18 and 19 despite heavy shelling from Union gunboats operating in nearby waters. About 7 P.M. on May 19, the Federals assaulted Hoke's skirmish line in force, but the Southern riflemen repelled the attack. Severe fighting took place for most of the day on May 20 at Ware Bottom Church, where Beauregard launched a furious assault on Butler. A soldier from the Seventeenth North Carolina described the results: "Our boys poured such a sheet of fire into them that no living thing could withstand it. . . . The ground was covered with their dead and wounded." At the close of the day's fighting, the Union line had been pushed back up to a mile along most of its length. Indeed, Butler was now completely "bottled up."[42]

Once hostilities subsided at Bermuda Hundred, the formal organization of a permanent division for Hoke was announced. As a result, Hoke was blessed with four excellent, well-qualified brigadiers: James Green Martin, Thomas Lanier Clingman, Johnson Hagood, and Alfred Colquitt. Each of these gifted men had entered the war with a record of distinguished public service.

Like Hoke, General Martin was descended from a prominent family in North Carolina. After graduating fourteenth in the West Point class of 1840, he had rendered conspicuous service in the Mexican War and lost an arm at Churubusco. His subsequent military service took him throughout the United States. After the outbreak of the Civil War, he succeeded Hoke's uncle as adjutant general of North Carolina troops. His excellent administrative skills allowed North Carolina to send forth the best-equipped and best-organized soldiers of the Confederacy. After putting his native state's war machine on solid footing, Martin accepted an appointment as a brigadier general in 1862. Known affectionately to his soldiers as "Old One Wing," Martin became a source of anxiety for Hoke when Beauregard organized the permanent division on May 21. Hoke was most reluctant to assume command over a veteran officer almost twenty years his senior. Martin, however, insisted that his brigade be a part of Hoke's division, and so it was until the war's end.[43]

General Clingman likewise was much Hoke's senior. Born in northwestern North Carolina in 1812, he had graduated from the University of North Carolina at the head of his class twenty years later. As a young attorney, he was elected to the United States House of Representatives in 1843. Except for a two-year period, Clingman served in either House or the Senate from 1843 until the beginning of the war, when he resigned his seat in the Senate. An ardent Confederate, Clingman entered the war as a colonel and was promoted to brigadier general in August 1862. After the war, he devoted much of the remainder of his life to scientific studies and the exploration of western North Carolina, which he had begun prior to the war. Clingman's Dome, the highest peak in the Great Smoky Mountains, was subsequently named for him. Clingman was once described as "the best-informed man North Carolina has ever produced."[44]

Although he was eight years older than Hoke, Johnson Hagood was the youngest of the major general's brigadiers. Born in Barnwell County, South Carolina, he had practiced law after graduating from South Carolina Military Academy. Hagood participated in the reduction of Fort Sumter and went to First Manassas as colonel of the First South Carolina. He was promoted to brigadier general in the summer of 1862. Once the war was over, Hagood played a prominent role in South Carolina politics. In 1880, he was elected the fifty-first governor of his native state.[45]

General Colquitt, the son of a United States senator, was born in Walton County, Georgia, in 1824. Educated at Princeton, Colquitt had been trained in law, but he temporarily gave up his books for the sword when war with Mexico erupted. After attaining the rank of major as a citizen-soldier, Colquitt returned to his law practice and was elected to the United States House of Representatives in 1852. He entered the Civil War as colonel of the Sixth Georgia and fought with Hoke in the grim warfare of the Seven Days' Battles and Sharpsburg. On September 1, 1862, he was promoted to brigadier general. He resumed his political career after the war. When he was elected governor of Georgia in 1876, his vote total represented the largest majority in the history of the state to that time. Following a six-year stint as governor, Colquitt was elected to the United States Senate, where he served until his death twelve years later.[46]

Except for the replacement of Brigadier General Martin (for health reasons) with Brigadier General William Whedbee Kirkland later in 1864 and the addition of the North Carolina Junior Reserves in 1865, the organization of Hoke's division remained unchanged for the duration of the war. This stability, coupled with the quality of the general officers, field officers, and soldiers in the command, enabled Hoke to mold his division into a cohesive fighting machine which in time would be regarded as among the best in the Army of Northern Virginia.[47]

Although Lee had frustrated the Army of the Potomac throughout May at the Wilderness, Spotsylvania, and North Anna, Grant was convinced as the month neared its close that he could successfully conclude his Overland Campaign by turning Lee's flank and stepping between the Army of Northern Virginia and Richmond. In a communiqué to Chief of Staff Henry W. Halleck on May 26, Grant exuded confidence: "Lee's army is really whipped. The prisoners we now take show it, and the action of his army shows it unmistakably. . . . Our men feel that they have gained the morale over the enemy and attack with confidence. I may be mistaken, but I feel that our success over Lee's army is already insured." In but a week, Grant would find out how terribly mistaken he was, for he was set to sustain his worst defeat of the war. And one of the key players in that debacle would be Hoke.[48]

Grant put his army on the march south before sunrise on May 27. A day later, four corps of the Army of the Potomac crossed pontoons over the Pamunkey River near Hanovertown. By nightfall on May 29, the Federals began to arrive on the banks of slow, swampy Totopotomoy Creek, approximately ten miles due north of Richmond. Lee, suffering from a diarrhetic illness that had decimated his entire army, was meanwhile attempting to keep pace with the rapid Union advance by pushing the starving men in his three corps in a line parallel to the enemy. When the Confederate soldiers arrived on the evening of May 29 to form a line of battle on the opposite bank of the marshlike watercourse, many had not had food for two days.[49]

By noon on May 30, with three of the Federal corps across Totopotomoy Creek, Grant's left flank had been extended to the Chickahominy. To make matters worse for Lee, the sixteen thousand men from Smith's Eighteenth

Corps of Butler's army had been unloaded at White House Landing at 11:30 A.M. and were pressing toward Cold Harbor, just sixteen miles away. Lee reasoned that his thin line could not stretch as far south as Cold Harbor.[50]

At Bermuda Hundred on May 30, Beauregard pondered reports that a corps from the Army of the James had been moved to aid the Federal forces massing to the north. He queried Hoke, "How in the world can we discover whether Grant has recalled those troops?" In a response that evinced the major general's cleverness, Hoke remarked, "Have all our cannon heavily shotted. Let all the troops be in line, and station officers at given intervals to observe the enemy's works. At the same moment fire the cannon and let all the men give the Rebel yell in concert. The head of every Federal soldier will show above the works." Beauregard put Hoke's plan in action, and as the heavy guns thundered in unison with thousands of Southern voices, the heads of the enemy troops popped above their works. It was evident that the size of Butler's army had been greatly reduced, and the reports of reinforcements being sent to Grant were thus verified.[51]

Desperate for reinforcements, Lee bypassed Richmond on the afternoon of May 30 by sending a telegram directly to Beauregard. Although not as resolute in his refusal as on the previous night, Beauregard responded, "War Department must determine when and what troops to order from here." For Lee, there was no time to lose. In a 7:30 P.M. dispatch to President Davis which contained ominous language never before used by Lee, the commander of the Army of Northern Virginia stated the division he needed to save Richmond: "General Beauregard says the Department must determine what troops to send for him. He gives it all necessary information. The result of this delay will be disaster. Butler's troops (Smith's corps) will be with Grant tomorrow. Hoke's division, at least, should be with me by light tomorrow."[52]

Lee's use of an absolute such as *disaster* spurred Davis, Bragg, and Beauregard to action. Between 10:15 and 10:30 P.M., telegrams crossed the wires between Richmond and Bermuda Hundred with the same message: Hoke's division would be sent to Lee immediately. Once again, a frantic race was on. This time, the finish line was Cold Harbor, and the opponent was Major General William "Baldy" Smith.[53] The prize was a big one: the Confederate capital.

By 5:15 A.M. on Tuesday, May 31, Hoke began loading Clingman's brigade onto a train at Chester Station for the trip to Richmond. Forty-five minutes later, Hagood's soldiers were the last to be pulled from the trenches. Five trains were on their way north by 9:00 A.M., with two more soon to follow. The real race would not begin, however, until the trains reached Richmond. Once in the capital, Hoke would have to put his soldiers on a forced march to beat Smith to the vital crossroads. At best, Hoke had the odds of a long shot.[54]

By midday, the last of Hoke's soldiers had arrived in Richmond. Like his fellow brigadiers who had preceded him throughout the morning, Hagood quickly moved his soldiers directly through the city and onto Mechanicsville Turnpike. On this day of excessive heat, Hoke's soldiers moved toward Cold Harbor on dusty roads jammed with artillery and wagons. With the men "suffering greatly" from a lack of water and shade, there was little alternative but to halt the march at times to allow them to rest. Nevertheless, by the time Hagood hit Richmond, the lead brigade under Clingman was within two miles of Gaines' Mill and fast closing in on Cold Harbor. As the afternoon wore on, it became apparent that Hoke was going to win the race. Due to miscommunication with Grant and poor directions, Smith overshot Cold Harbor and would not arrive until midday on June 1.[55]

Yet serious problems erupted for the Confederates at Cold Harbor before the first soldier from Hoke's 7,656-man force could get there. Fitzhugh Lee had been posted by his uncle to hold the crossroads pending Hoke's arrival. In midafternoon, the Confederate horse soldiers were attacked by one of Phil Sheridan's cavalry divisions under the command of Brigadier General Alfred Torbert. Armed with Spencer repeaters, the brigades of George Armstrong Custer and Wesley Merritt charged Lee without success. By late afternoon, the Federals began to have their way, and some of Fitzhugh Lee's exhausted soldiers started fleeing their works just when the lead elements of Clingman's brigade were making their appearance. About thirty minutes later, the remainder of the cavalrymen broke, and the North

Carolinians joined in what they assumed was a general retreat from Cold Harbor.[56]

Cold Harbor had fallen to the Federals, but Sheridan, cognizant that more and more soldiers from Hoke's division were arriving to form a strong line midway between Cold Harbor and New Cold Harbor, was convinced that he could not hold his position. In reporting his success on the afternoon of May 31, Sheridan pointed out, "Since then the second brigade, of Hoke's division, has arrived. I do not feel able to hold this place, and have directed General Torbert to resume his position of this morning." Thus, despite the temporary setback at the crossroads, Hoke had not only beaten Smith to Cold Harbor but, more important, had dissuaded Sheridan from pressing his advantage.[57]

While Sheridan worried about the growing Confederate presence in his front, Hoke formed his division in a line of battle. By nightfall, he had three brigades in position, "his right extending a little beyond Cold Harbor and his left a little this side of Beulah Church." Hoke's ground would not change during the critical events of the next three days, and it would prove to be a position vital to the successful strategy of Robert E. Lee. Hagood's brigade reached the front at 3 A.M.[58]

Always anxious to surprise the opposing army, Robert E. Lee decided to move from defense to offense. On the afternoon of May 31, he directed Lieutenant General Richard Anderson to move his three divisions to Cold Harbor, where they would join Hoke's forces. Lee reasoned that his four divisions under the overall command of Anderson could strike Sheridan's outnumbered cavalry in the early-morning hours of June 1 and turn the left flank before Federal infantry appeared in strong numbers. As Anderson marched his troops toward Cold Harbor, Lee moved his headquarters to Shady Grove Church so he might be closer to the events on a day that he hoped would alter the course of the war. Though he was physically stronger, he still could not ride a horse and had to be transported by carriage.[59]

Lee assumed that Anderson, upon his arrival at Cold Harbor, would personally instruct Hoke that the Confederate assault on June 1 was to be of a general, coordinated nature. Instead, Hoke understood that he was to attack only after Anderson, whose divisions were posted on Hoke's left, had launched an assault on the Union flank. As Hagood understood it, "Kershaw's division was to lead the attack, and when Kershaw sent Hoke word that he had reached a certain point (Beulah Church) on the road, Hoke was to advance." As might be expected, the misunderstanding was destined to spell doom for the opening of the Confederate offensive.[60]

In accordance with his orders, Anderson commenced his attack at sunrise on June 1. Leading the Confederate advance was a battle-tested brigade belonging to Major General Joseph B. Kershaw. Although Anderson selected a veteran brigade for the vanguard of the assault, the charge was led by Colonel Lawrence M. Keitt of the Twentieth South Carolina. Both the colonel and the regiment were green. Keitt fell mortally wounded with a bullet to the liver at the beginning of the attack. Panic engulfed his troops, and they broke. After Keitt fell, Anderson's advance halted almost as quickly as it had started. Hoke, still waiting for a signal from Anderson, had not moved. In his memoirs, Hagood explained the reason for the inactivity: "During the morning, firing from Kershaw was heard on Hagood's left front, and afterwards a courier to General Hoke announced that the attack was foregone. . . . This, with perhaps other reasons, to the writer unknown, stopped the attack."[61]

The failure of Anderson's early-morning offensive provided Grant with the opportunity to rush his infantry forward to Cold Harbor. H. G. Wright's Sixth Corps wheeled into position to replace Sheridan's men on the front line about 10 A.M. Two hours later, the ten thousand men of Smith's Eighteenth Corps arrived. As the Confederates braced for an attack by the massing Federals, the men of Hoke's division dug furiously to fortify their position. In the afternoon, Hoke ordered Hagood to send out skirmishers to "feel for the enemy."[62]

About 4 P.M., the Federals began a concerted effort to turn Hoke's right. To beat back the attempt, Hoke marched the brigade of Hagood and Martin to the extreme right of the Confederate right, to "the field on which the battle of Gaines' Mill had been fought in McClellan's campaign." On his way to the fight, Hagood observed grim reminders of the battle two years previous: human bones exposed from imperfect burials. By the time the two brigades reached their position, the Confederate cavalry guarding the flank had been routed. Skirmishers were instantly sent forward, and the advancing Federals were handsomely driven back. By quick action, Hoke saved the Confederate right. Hagood later put the importance of the stand by Hoke's soldiers in perspective: "The point now held by these two brigades was the tactical key of Lee's position. The field was a high plateau, with Watt's Hill behind it, and commanded most of the line now being taken up by the Confederates for the impending battle. . . . Had the position been seized by the enemy at this time, it was probable that Lee would have been forced across the Chickahominy and into the lines of Richmond without a general engagement. It was a race for it, won by a few minutes."[63]

While Hagood and Martin were able to avoid a general assault on the right, Hoke was not so fortunate on his other flank. About 5 P.M., Smith's corps slammed into the right flank of Anderson's corps and the left flank of Hoke's division at the point from which Hagood had been withdrawn. Clingman's North Carolinians manned the position, which was separated from William T. Wofford's brigade of Kershaw's division on the left by a seventy-five-yard gap at a branch.

As the Federals suddenly made their way down a hill toward the Tar Heels, Captain Fred R. Blake of Clingman's staff cried out, "Here they are, as thick as they can be!" Clingman could count the flags of four regiments as the advancing Yankees closed in. In a loud voice, he exclaimed, "Aim low and aim well!" Just as he uttered the command, "a tall and uncommonly looking officer" at the head of a Federal column looked Clingman directly in the face, removed his cap, waved it about his head, and urged his men forward. No sooner had the officer returned his hat to his head than one of Clingman's soldiers sent a ball into his forehead, causing the gallant Federal to fall backward into the path of two of his comrades. Lee's artillery wizard, Edward Porter Alexander, described the ferocious fighting that ensued: "Soon a perfect tornado of fire broke out in front of Hoke & Kershaw, & every thing on the line turned loose in reply, guns & musketry." All along Clingman's line, the Union advance was met with a deadly resistance described by a New York artilleryman as hell "turned up sideways."[64]

After Smith's forces had been driven back on Hoke's left, the soldiers "cheered all along" the lines. But before the smoke cleared, Federals began to pour into the gap between Clingman and Wofford. Reinforced by the brigades of Colquitt, Eppa Hunton, and John Gregg, Clingman was able to seal the hole as darkness fell over the battlefield. By 10 P.M., the fighting was over for the day. Thereafter, Clingman vehemently denied reports that his brigade had at any time given way. He admitted, however, that "the thick woods and dusk of the closing evening allowed the enemy to rest within fifty yards of our left." Hagood noted that the enemy had lost two thousand men in the afternoon and evening assault but "had gained . . . some advantage of position."[65]

Although both armies had suffered disappointments at Cold Harbor on June 1, their respective commanders had reason for optimism. Despite the heavy casualties sustained in the late-day assault, Grant was heartened by the hole that had been briefly exploited in the Confederate line. He ordered Winfield Scott Hancock's Second Corps to move into position alongside Wright on the extreme left of the Union line. Once Hancock was in place, Grant reasoned, he could launch an early-morning attack on June 2 using Smith, Wright, and Hancock to pierce the weak spot between Hoke and Kershaw and thus tear the Confederate lines apart. To the north, two additional corps—those of Gouverneur K. Warren and Burnside—would be available if needed.[66]

Lee had arrived at the scene on the afternoon of June 1 in time to confer with Hoke concerning his movements to save the right flank. He set up his headquarters "in the field of the right of the Cold Harbor road, just west of the crossing of Powhite Creek at Gaines' Mill," directly behind Hoke's line. His army had failed to take advantage of the opportunity before it when the day began, but Lee offered no recriminations against Anderson or Hoke. Instead, he praised both for their efforts in repulsing the afternoon attack. In order to strengthen and lengthen his line south to the Chickahominy, Lee ordered the divisions of John C. Breckinridge, William Mahone, and Cadmus M. Wilcox to move quickly to man the Confederate line to the right of Hoke. With these reinforcements, Lee believed that he might be able to find an opening on the Union right.[67]

General Robert F. Hoke

Things did not go as Grant had planned on June 2. Hancock's corps failed to reach Cold Harbor until 6:30 A.M., an hour and a half after the time scheduled for the assault on the Confederates. After marching in oppressive heat and dust throughout the night, the soldiers were completely exhausted. Accordingly, Grant postponed the attack until 5:00 P.M. In the meantime, Breckinridge, Mahone, and Wilcox all arrived in the early afternoon to take their places on the Confederate right. Sometime after 4:00 P.M., the skies opened up and heavy rain drenched the opposing armies. Because Hancock's soldiers had not yet recovered from their nine-mile forced march, Grant decided to delay his attack until 4:30 A.M. the next day.[68]

Up early on Friday, June 3, a day that broke gray, misty, and cool, Lee had many concerns. With Richmond just eight miles behind him, there could be no retreat. Because Hoke's division had been organized less than two weeks and its brigades had not fought together as a unit until June 1, Lee was particularly anxious about its ability to hold the portion of the line which was likely to be hit the hardest. Accordingly, Lee sent an aide, Colonel Charles Venable, to ask Hoke to come to his tent. Hoke replied that he could not leave presently, as he was expecting an attack at any moment, but that Lee should not be apprehensive about that position of the line.[69]

As the time for the great Union assault neared, the Yankees began to pull themselves out of their muddy trenches for a charge that many believed was nothing more than a death march. Stretching for nearly seven miles, the Confederate line was manned by upwards of sixty thousand soldiers. Across the way, more than a hundred thousand Federal troops had been deployed by Grant. At some points along the line, no more than a hundred yards separated the opposing armies. At Hoke's position on the line, all was in a state of readiness. To his right, John Breckinridge, the presidential candidate of 1860, had entrenched his troops. Kershaw remained on the left. In his own division, Hoke had deployed Martin, Colquitt, and Hagood from right to left. Clingman was placed in reserve.[70]

Suddenly, at 4:30 A.M., waves of bluecoats began pouring toward the entrenched Confederates. Roaring artillery, the crash of musketry, and the cheers and screams of thousands of soldiers created a din that could be heard in Richmond. Nowhere along the line was the Union attack more furious than in front of Hoke and Kershaw. In less than ten minutes, the initial assault was over there. The advancing Federals had been slaughtered. Lieutenant Colonel Martin T. McMahon of Wright's Corps reported, "In that little period more men fell bleeding as they advanced than in any other like period of time throughout the war." From Martin's brigade, Captain Charles G. Elliott reported, "The slaughter was terrific. I did not see one man on our side falter. It was a great victory from the start. . . . No men or officers ever made a braver charge than did these Federals on 3 June. But the flame of continuous fire from Martin's Brigade was too much for them or any men to overcome, and our line would not yield an inch. . . . Never will the inspiring sight be effaced from my memory."[71]

So rapidly was the attack against Hoke repulsed that Hagood did not realize the Yankees had mounted a general assault. In his memoirs, he confessed, "It may sound incredible but it is nevertheless strictly true, that the writer of these Memoirs, situated near the center of the line along which this murderous repulse was given, and awake and vigilant of the progress of events, was not aware at the time of any serious assault having been given." Chaplain Paris described the rout in his diary: "At daylight a furious battle was opened on our center. The attack was upon the divisions of Hoke [and] Breckinridge. The battle raged until 10 o'clock. The enemy was repulsed with great slaughter at all points." Second Lieutenant Wilson G. Lamb, an officer in Clingman's brigade, was appalled by the carnage: "In its front the enemy's dead were so thickly strewn that one could have walked on their bodies its whole extent."[72]

Reports of the early Confederate success soon began to make their way to Lee's headquarters. One of Lee's aides, Walter Taylor, vividly remembered the report received from Hoke: "I well recall having received a report after the assault from General Hoke—whose division reached the army just previous to the battle—to the effect that the ground in his entire front, over which the enemy had charged, was literally covered with their dead and wounded; and that up to that time he had not a single man killed." Lee was ecstatic at the news. At 8:45 A.M., he relayed the good tidings to Richmond: "About 4:30 A.M. to-day the enemy made an attack upon the right of our line. In front of General Hoke and part of General Breckinridge's line he was repulsed without difficulty. . . . Our loss to-day has been small, and our success, under the blessing of God, all that we could expect."[73]

Although some fighting would continue until 1:30 P.M., when the merciful orders were handed down by Grant that all offensive operations were to be suspended, the Battle of Cold Harbor was over by 8:00 A.M. After the first assault failed miserably, General Meade sent orders to his corps commanders to renew the attack, but as the orders made their way down the lines, the survivors of "the bloodiest repulse of the Federals known in the history of the war" remained motionless, refusing to obey the commands of their superiors. William Swinton, the historian of the Army of the Potomac, recorded that "no man stirred, and the immobile lines pronounced a verdict, silent, yet emphatic, against further slaughter." Walter Taylor empathized with the soldiers in the opposing lines: "No wonder that, when the command was given to renew the assault the Federal soldiers sullenly and silently declined to advance."[74]

About the grim bloodbath, Grant later lamented, "I have always regretted that the last assault at Cold Harbor was ever made." And well he should have. He lost approximately ten thousand soldiers in the debacle, and for all of the lives spent, he was no closer to Richmond than McClellan had been two summers earlier. In a thirty-day period, Grant had lost more men than Lee had in his entire army; for every mile of his spring offensive, the commander of the Army of the Potomac has lost a thousand men. But the debacle at Cold Harbor taught Grant a valuable lesson, one that would serve him well during the last year of the war. Instead of further attempting to whip Lee on the battlefields in Virginia, Grant decided to stretch his lines so as to weaken Lee's and to substitute deadly attrition for rifles, bayonets, and field guns.[75]

After the immediate crisis had passed on the morning of June 3, Hoke called on Lee at his tent as his commander had earlier requested. Buoyed by encouraging reports about the battle, described by Colonel Venable as "the easiest victory ever granted to the Confederate armies by the folly of Federal commanders," Lee was on his cot sitting up when Hoke entered.

Despite his recent illness, Lee was, according to Hoke, "bold and with the spirit of a game cock." As the two generals discussed the momentous events of the morning, little did either realize that this battle, in which Hoke had played such a pivotal role, would be the last great field victory for the chieftain of the Army of Northern Virginia.[76]

Skirmishing between the two armies continued into the next day. But the sounds of musket fire paled in comparison to the heart-wrenching cries of the wounded and dying on the battlefield. Not before June 5 did Grant propose to Lee that arrangements be made to provide for treatment of the wounded and burial of the dead. For some of Hoke's men, the sound of "Water!" resonating over the battlefield from the thirsty mouths of men suffering from loss of blood was too much to bear. Dozens upon dozens of Hoke's troops ran from the ranks to kneel beside the wounded enemy soldiers and provide them water from their canteens. Just minutes after they began providing aid, the Federals opened fire on the men of mercy. Hoke was outraged by this response, and he forthwith directed that no other soldiers leave his lines.

Thereafter, the general lay down under a tree for some shade on the hot day. While he was resting, two of his soldiers approached him with a salute and said, "General, a wounded Yankee is lying out in front and he wanted to know whether there are any Masons among us. We told him that there were, whereupon he gave the sign of distress and begged us to go out and bring him into our lines. We replied that we had been fired upon while helping his companions, and because of that you had issued strict orders against our passing outside." His attention aroused, Hoke responded, "Are you Masons?" When the soldiers answered in the affirmative, the general asked, "Do you know that it is almost certain death for you to try to give any help to that poor fellow?" The Masons responded, "We do; but he had made the Masonic appeal to us, and we only await your permission to try to bring him in." Hoke told the two, "Then go, in God's name. I do not stand in the way of such courage as that." In an instant, the men were running through a hail of bullets to aid their Masonic brother. Without faltering, they rescued the fallen soldier and returned safely with him to Hoke's line.[77]

General Robert F. Hoke

During the ten days that followed the great battle in front of the Confederate capital, the soldiers of Hoke's division skirmished with enemy troops and strengthened their fortifications. Near the end of that period, Lee sent his engineering officer, Major General Martin L. Smith, to Hoke's line to call upon Brigadier General Martin. Friends from the old army, the two officers greeted each other as "Smith" and "Martin." Smith explained that Lee feared another assault by Grant on Hoke's line, and that Lee was concerned that Martin's brigade, which was comparatively new, might not be able to withstand the assault.

In response, Martin told the messenger, "Smith, say to General Lee, with my compliments, that my men are soldiers, and he has no brigade in his army that will hold this place any longer than they will. . . . But tell him further that, in my judgment, he is mistaken. Grant is withdrawing his army from our front and going to City Point, and General Lee should at once return Hoke's Division to General Beauregard for the defense of Petersburg. Grant is going to attack Richmond from the rear."[78]

Major General Smith argued with Martin about his observations and questioned his judgment about Union intentions; however, by dawn on June 13, Grant had pulled his army from the trenches at Cold Harbor. A day later, as Grant's troops moved toward a crossing of the James, a new race was about to begin for Hoke.[79] In a little more than a month, he had twice raced to a battlefield to save Richmond. Now, as he was to be called on again, one question loomed large: Would the third time be a strike or a charm?

CHAPTER 10

Summer Siege

No sooner did Robert E. Lee discover that Grant had disappeared from his front at Cold Harbor on the morning of June 13 than Hoke had his division on the march. Hagood's brigade was pulled from the trenches at 8 A.M., and the other three brigades promptly followed suit, as Lee sought to monitor the movements of Grant and determine his intentions. Just twenty miles separated Richmond from Petersburg. For Lee, that distance was now a logistical nightmare. With an opposing army of nearly a hundred thousand men moving in the direction of either city, the commander of the Army of Northern Virginia did not have the manpower to adequately defend both Richmond and Petersburg and the line of defenses between the two. Accordingly, for two days, Hoke's race would necessarily be deliberate, until Lee could ascertain where Grant intended to strike next.[1]

After crossing the Chickahominy, Hoke's column continued its march south on June 13, a hot, dry day, until it bivouacked three miles from Malvern Hill, a place all too familiar to Hoke from the gruesome fighting two years earlier. For much of the next day, the division remained in camp. While awaiting orders, Hoke gathered with Lee and a number of other generals, including A. P. Hill, Henry Heth, Cadmus M. Wilcox, and Alfred M. Scales, to watch several of Hill's brigades fight a prolonged, heated skirmish on the roads leading from Fraser's Farm toward Malvern Hill. In the meantime, Smith had reported to Grant and Butler at Bermuda Hundred with his Eighteenth Corps, which had arrived by water transport. By noon, Lee perceived that Grant had designs on Petersburg.[2]

Less than three hours later, Lee advised Davis and Bragg that he was sending Hoke to a point above Drewry's Bluff. From all the information available, it appeared that Grant had targeted Petersburg, but Lee remained cautious. As to Richmond, he could ill afford to drop his guard. By deploying Hoke near Drewry's Bluff, Lee reasoned that the division would be in a position to be rushed to the defense of either the Confederate capital or Petersburg. Accordingly, around 5 P.M. on the afternoon of June 14, Hoke ordered his brigades to commence an eight-mile march to the north banks of the James River near a pontoon bridge in the vicinity of Drewry's Bluff.[3]

While Lee spent June 14 in circumspection, Beauregard, at his headquarters just north of Petersburg, grew more and more desperate. Convinced that an attack was imminent, Beauregard had begun his pleas for additional manpower early in the day. The alarm in Beauregard's early-morning dispatches was real, not perceived. Petersburg was virtually defenseless. To protect the city against attack, Beauregard had but twenty-two hundred men: the twelve-hundred-soldier brigade of Henry A. Wise; two cavalry regiments under James Dearing, recently promoted to brigadier general upon Hoke's recommendation; and the local militia. According to Beauregard's best estimates, some twenty-five thousand troops were needed to man the extensive line of fortifications designed by Confederate engineers to rim the city from the lower to the upper Appomattox.[4]

Beauregard continued to warn Lee and Bragg of the growing crisis at Petersburg with telegrams throughout that day and night. Although these dispatches brought no immediate relief, Bragg offered the promise of help in a message to Beauregard at 9:10 P.M.: "He [Lee] has sent Hoke's division to Drewry's Bluff, with a view to re-inforce you in case Petersburg is threatened."[5]

Wednesday, June 15, would prove one of the red-letter days of the war, for on that day Petersburg would either fall, opening the back door to Richmond to Grant's massive army, or remain in Confederate hands and thus prolong the war. At daylight, Beauregard's worst fears were realized when the advance elements of Smith's sixteen-thousand-man corps slammed into Dearing's cavalry and Captain Edward Graham's four-gun artillery battery near Baylor Farm on the west side of the city. For two hours, the badly outnumbered Confederates stubbornly held their own, thereby giving Brigadier General Wise precious time to get his forces ready for the coming fight. But by 8 A.M., the ever-growing number of Union troops forced Dearing to retreat into the primary fortifications of the city. According to Beauregard, captured Union prisoners told the story, "They say it is 'on to Petersburg' and more force behind." With the Second Corps of Winfield Scott Hancock moving behind Smith's corps, Petersburg was suddenly "in imminent danger of capture." The city was now at the mercy of the Union army.[6]

Only a miracle, a stroke of luck, Federal incompetence, an influx of Confederate reinforcements, or a combination of the same could prevent Grant from gaining Petersburg. Fortunately for the Confederates, all of the deciding factors would work in their favor in this time of crisis.

Beauregard wasted no time in sending for the help he desperately needed. At 9:30 A.M., he notified Bragg that he had ordered Hoke to move to Petersburg. Lee subsequently informed Bragg that he had issued a similar order. Hoke dispatched a telegram to Bragg at 11:30 A.M. to assure him that he was moving to Beauregard's assistance: "I have just received orders to cross the river and report to General Beauregard. My troops are on the march." Abruptly, the pace of Hoke's race quickened. His veteran soldiers held the key to the survival of Confederate Petersburg. About Hoke's division, Beauregard expressed to Bragg the collective thoughts of the Confederate nation: "Hope it will get there in time."[7]

By 11 A.M., Hoke had the four brigades on the march. After crossing the James at Drewry's Bluff on the relatively cool day, the men hit the turnpike to Petersburg. The forced march was fatiguing, and the soldiers sought relief any way they could find it. Major J. H. Rion of Hagood's brigade pulled out a flask of French brandy he carried for just such situations. As he imbibed, the wind spread "the most fragrant scent a weary soldier ever inhaled." A nearby officer remarked, "I believe the smell did me as much good as the dram did for him."

When the division reached Chester Station, about eighteen miles from Petersburg, in late afternoon, Hoke discovered that "partial transportation" had been arranged for him. The first to board the waiting train—consisting of but an engine, a tender, and two cars—were soldiers from the Seventh South Carolina Battalion of Hagood's brigade. When the call went out for two companies to board the tiny train, Major Rion stepped forward with orders: "The whole battalion will go." Eight companies totaling five hundred soldiers were soon packed aboard, "standing and sitting, inside and outside, on engine, tender and cars." First Lieutenant William M. Thomas forever remembered his ride aboard the engine: "I was on top taking in the scenery and the pine smoke from the engine. I was a dirty white man before we started, but by the time we arrived in Petersburg I was black." Additional trains arrived to pick up the remainder of Hagood's brigade and that of Colquitt, but Clingman and Martin were forced to continue their movement on foot by "the shortest cut, through fields and dirty roads."[8]

Beauregard arrived in Petersburg about 6 P.M., not far in advance of the trainloads of Hoke's men, which pulled in about sundown. As Hagood's South Carolinians jumped off the cars and formed in the streets, it became evident that Hoke had arrived none too soon. Wise's gallant soldiers, after holding their position for most of the day with "unsurpassed stubbornness," were now fleeing their lines.[9]

Marching across the Pocohontas Bridge and up Main Street, the first of Hoke's arrivals encountered the retreating Confederates, many without hats, shoes, or guns. Fearing a Federal occupation, citizens were busy moving household goods. Upon seeing the South Carolinians, women on the sidewalk called out, "What brigade is that?" Lieutenant Thomas proudly responded, "Hagood's brigade." Bowing down on their knees, the grateful women cried out, "We are safe now." Hagood reported to Beauregard's headquarters, where he learned that an early-evening attack by Smith had carried Battery No. 3 through Battery No. 7. Hagood was promptly ordered to move the brigade eastward on City Point Road and form a new defensive line to check the advance of the Federals. As his men filed out of the city, grateful residents waved handkerchiefs and exclaimed, "God bless Hagood and his South Carolinians."[10]

Notwithstanding the optimism of the citizens of Petersburg, the fight for the city was just beginning, and the ability of the Confederates to hold on was very much in doubt. Indeed, had it not been for delays occasioned by a "series of tragicomic staff-work blunders involving faulty maps, contradictory orders, and a failure to apprise key commanders and subordinates of plans," Petersburg would have fallen before Hoke arrived.[11]

Despite Smith's reluctance to press on with the 7 P.M. attack that had scattered Wise's men, neither Beauregard, Hoke, nor any of the Confederate brigade commanders was privy to the enemy's overabundance of caution. Whether Smith planned to attack in the dark of night or the light of the morrow, there was no time to lose for the Southerners. Darkness, unfamiliarity with the terrain, and conflicting information from guides hampered Hagood as he attempted to make his way to his assigned position. At length, a courier from Beauregard's staff engineer delivered a map to Hagood, which the South Carolinian used to determine his assigned position. Placing his left on the Appomattox at Batteries No. 1 and 2, Hagood extended the brigade south along the heights above the west bank of Harrison's Creek at Battery No. 15. Hoke favored the position because it looked down over a cultivated valley, through which the enemy would have to attack.[12]

Colquitt followed on Hagood's heels. Hoke positioned that brigade to the right of Hagood across Prince George Court House Road. The two North Carolina brigades were necessarily slower to reach Petersburg because of their march. When the soldiers of Martin and Clingman poured into Petersburg just after midnight, the entire city was lighted. Elderly men too old to fight, women, and children peered from windows as the Tar Heels marched through the streets. An enfeebled voice belonging to an old man cried out, "What troops?" The troops responded, "It is Hoke's Division." In a melancholy tone, the old man proclaimed, "Too late! Too late! General Wise was defeated, and there have been no armed soldiers between Grant's army and this city since sun-down." As the Confederate procession turned onto Bolingbroke Street, some of the mothers and wives of the city came out of their homes in great distress and cried out, "Do drive them back! My husband (or my son) was with Mahone, or Pickett, or Imboden's cavalry." According to one soldier, "We marched on, and there was no sound except the soldiers' tramping, and the wail of the women who wept." After the North Carolinians made their way to the rest of the division, Hoke continued the southerly progression of the line by placing Martin adjacent to Colquitt and Clingman adjacent to Martin.[13]

Though Hoke had arrived in time to improve Beauregard's ability to stave off Butler's first advance, the danger facing the beleaguered Confederates was readily apparent at the front. Once Martin's brigade was in position, Hoke and Captain Charles G. Elliott walked down a ditch to a point close to the Federal pickets. From their vantage point, the two officers could not see a single Confederate soldier. Beauregard was cognizant of the peril, and as the last of Hoke's soldiers were struggling to make their way to the city, the decision was made to sacrifice the line at Bermuda Hundred in order to bring Johnson's division to Petersburg.

Johnson would not arrive until the following morning, but Beauregard wrestled with the possibility of sending Hoke on a counterattack to regain the lines captured by the Federals earlier in the day. Lieutenant Thomas recalled, "Three times during the night we were drawn up in line of battle to charge, and the order was countermanded." Another of Hagood's soldiers indicated that the anticipated "orders at any moment, the clanking of a sword, passing down toward the left of the 21st regiment, suggested that the expected was about to happen." Instead, the weary soldiers fortified their lines "with bayonets, swords, tin plates, etc." Close to morning,

Hoke's soldiers, protected by pickets out front, "fell asleep upon the ground from sheer exhaustion."[14]

Early in the morning on June 16, Hoke ordered the Seventh South Carolina Battalion to attempt to occupy two nearby forts abandoned by Wise the previous evening. This sudden movement by the Confederates was greeted with hot and heavy fire from Federal artillery and skirmishers. Matt Ransom's brigade arrived about 8 A.M. and Johnson's division two hours later. But for every Confederate reinforcement, there were ten Federals joining the assault forces mushrooming at Petersburg. By late afternoon, the numerical odds were worse for the Confederates than they had been in the morning. Burnside's Ninth Corps had come on the scene, bringing Union troop strength to sixty-six thousand. Hoke, Johnson, Wise, and Ransom could field but ten thousand.

About 5:30 P.M., Union batteries unleashed a short, thunderous assault against the Confederate lines. As soon as the big guns finished their deadly work, thousands upon thousands of bluecoats rose up and began rushing forward to break through the sparsely manned lines separating the Union army from Petersburg. Hoke faced a heavy assault all along his lines, but the Federals made little, if any, headway. All four brigades reported similar results. Two attacks were made on Clingman, "both of which were repulsed." Portions of Clingman's and Martin's brigades were used to seal a temporary breach in Wise's line. In the words of Second Lieutenant W. G. Lamb of the Seventeenth North Carolina, "The Federals were driven out and our line re-established." As with Clingman and Martin, Colquitt's pickets were driven in, but the Federals could not storm his main line. Johnson Hagood reported, "About dark a feeble effort at assault was made upon my center, none getting nearer than seventy-five yards to our line. It was kept up for an hour or more, but they were kept at bay without trouble." By 9:00 P.M., the fighting stopped, and the Federals retired, having wasted another golden opportunity to take the city.[15]

Throughout the night, the Fifth Corps of Major General Gouverneur K. Warren marched into the Union camp, raising the Federal effectives to ninety thousand. Most of Lee's army was yet a day or so away, so when June 17 dawned, Hoke and his comrades found themselves outnumbered nine to one. Heavy shelling and skirmishing started early on Hoke's front, and thus began "another day of strife, attack and recoil, noise and bloodshed." As the conflict started anew, Clingman's aide-de-camp, Captain Hal S. Puryear, stopped on his way to visiting Hoke's headquarters to purchase an early edition of a Petersburg newspaper. As he continued his journey, Puryear was delighted to read high praise for the division of which he was a member: "Hoke's Division stood last night like a rock wall and saved the city. They may be overrun, but no power on earth can drive them from a position."[16]

Meade's corps commanders at Petersburg simply lacked the aggressiveness necessary to finish the job that Friday morning. Many of the exhausted Confederates were asleep with arms in their hands when a dawn attack was launched against Johnson's division on the Confederate right. Throughout the morning, the Federals continued the advance until they were within striking distance of the city, but the assault lacked direction and failed. Nevertheless, Butler exuded confidence when he wired Grant at 10:10 A.M., "There is nothing now in Petersburg save Hoke's division, Clingman's brigade, and Johnson's division." About noon, Hoke began to experience Federal pressure on the Confederate left. Lieutenant Lamb recalled, "Three times were the Federals repulsed but as often resumed the offensive." In a failed assault against Clingman and Wise at 2:00 P.M., Hoke's adversary was an old friend and coworker from his Washington, D.C., days—Brigadier General Nelson A. Miles.[17]

In late afternoon, Burnside began massing the fresh division of J. H. Ledlie on Hoke's center and right. H. T. J. Ludwig, a drummer in the Eighth North Carolina, noted, "It was evident that a heavy assault on our line was contemplated." At 6 P.M., the Federals charged forward over the bodies of their comrades who had fallen during the past two days. A withering fire from Confederate artillery and muskets staggered the first line, but on came the second wave over almost three hundred yards of open ground. Clingman's line yielded a bit but did not break. To the right, Wise's Virginians gave way; however, five companies from Clingman's Fifty-first North Carolina joined Ransom's brigade in a savage fight to seal the breach. Second Lieutenant A. A. McKethan of the Fifty-first North Carolina recounted the action: "At the signal these two commands charged front and rushed forward with fixed bayonets, and soon recaptured the lost ground, but at a fearful loss. . . . In this contest the bayonet and butts of guns were freely used, as there was not time to load and fire."[18]

While Hoke's right was repelling the attack by Burnside's troops, Hancock moved against Hoke's center by sending the division of Francis C. Barlow toward the position manned by Colquitt. From his position on the left, Hagood watched as the Yankees approached the Confederate breastworks, only to be repelled "with considerable slaughter." In a scene reminiscent of the final day at Cold Harbor, the Federal troops refused orders to charge a second time. To the right of Hoke, the arrival of the Alabama brigade of Archibald Gracie during the evening enabled Bushrod Johnson to hold his line. Nevertheless, the fighting continued until the approach of midnight.[19]

Late on June 17, there was little reason for the Confederates to be optimistic, notwithstanding their heroic stand against an overwhelming army for three straight days. As one Confederate officer put it, "The evacuation of the town seemed inevitable." Beauregard remained convinced that his lines must be drawn closer to the city if his troops were to have a chance. During the fighting that day, Hoke and Johnson had sent their officers to Beauregard's headquarters to familiarize themselves with their new positions, which would be eight hundred yards nearer to Petersburg. About 1:30 A.M. on June 18, Hoke's soldiers quietly began slipping back to the new interior line. Once at their position, they immediately set about fortifying the new defenses. Little did they know that the line was destined to be their home for the coming three months.[20]

As the fighting was drawing to a close on June 17, Meade issued orders for an all-out assault against the entire Confederate army at 4 A.M. the following morning. The Battle of Petersburg would be brought to a head. Assigned to carry the fight to Hoke were the Second, Sixth, and Eighteenth Corps. At daylight, as the endless waves of Federals advanced and discovered the abandoned Confederate lines, they lifted up "vociferous cheers." But as they continued toward the waiting Southerners, their line of battle halted and heavy skirmishing commenced. Meanwhile, Meade reconnoitered the new front and decided to attack selected parts of the line, instead of pursuing a general assault as originally planned. Fearing that reinforcements from Lee might be nearing Petersburg, he pushed his commanders throughout the morning to finish the job.[21]

Hesitation by the Federals gave the Confederates just what they needed. At 7:30 A.M., the advance column of Lee's army, Kershaw's division, marched across the Appomattox and into Petersburg, to the cheers of the townspeople. Before 10:00 A.M., the division of Charles Field streamed into town. While these reinforcements were being deployed on the Confederate right, the Federals struck with vengeance against Hoke. H. T. G. Ludwig provided a stirring account of the attack: "It was in the forenoon, in the light of a brilliant June sun, that the lines advanced in a clear open field. If there had not been other and more serious things to consider, the military display might have been looked upon as a grand one. But we were not there to look at military displays. The business our men had in view was to spoil such display. This they proceeded to do."[22]

At 2 P.M., the assault on Hoke's line was renewed. On Hagood's front, the Federals stormed unimpeded across fields of grain until they came within three hundred yards of the South Carolina rifles. Suddenly, the guns blazed, and the Yankees could advance no more than fifty yards farther. Hagood plainly heard the voices of the Federal officers as they attempted to rally their men in the face of the hot lead. Despite their efforts, the Federals "were repulsed in confusion and with heavy loss." Soldiers from the Twenty-seventh Massachusetts dropped to the ground whether wounded or not. Those who were able sought protection in the furrows and behind the bodies of the dead and wounded. Some of the hapless Yankees fashioned a "human breastwork by throwing dirt against their bodies."

Lieutenant William M. Thomas of Hagood's brigade recounted the Union nightmare: "Lincoln's pets, 1,950 strong, the Maine battery, charged us, and went back with 250. I can realize that this was so, for, except at Cold Harbor, I never saw such slaughter." In reality, 850 men of the First Maine Heavy Artillery joined in the assault against Hoke's line in late afternoon, and for ten minutes, the field on which they advanced was "a burning, seething, crashing, hissing hell, in which human courage, flesh, and bone were struggling with an impossibility, either to succeed or to return with much hope of life." When Hoke's riflemen finished their deadly work, 632 of the Maine soldiers were killed or wounded. The casualty rate was one of the highest sustained by any Union regiment during a single battle in the war.[23]

While the Confederates were beating back the last of the disjointed late-afternoon assaults, the troops of A. P. Hill's corps were funneling into Petersburg. Cognizant that Lee's soldiers had been arriving throughout the day, Meade came to the realization that further efforts to break through the enemy lines would be futile. Grant was briefed on the grim results later that evening. Union losses over the four days of fighting were staggering. Upwards of twelve thousand Federal soldiers were dead, wounded, or missing. Confederate losses hovered around four thousand.[24]

Despite his disappointment over the inability of his army to take Petersburg by force, Grant concurred with Meade's assessment of the events of June 18. His telegram to Meade at 10 P.M. that night hinted at a change in the grand strategy designed to destroy Lee's army: "Now we will rest the men and use the spade for their protection until a new vein can be struck." Over the past month and a half, Grant had been unable to beat Lee's troops on the battlefield; Union losses had been exceedingly heavy; and Confederate resolve to win the war had not been weakened. Accordingly, Grant decided to lay siege to Petersburg and attempt to destroy the vital supply lines to the city. If he could not destroy the Army of Northern Virginia with guns, he would do so by starvation. Grant reasoned that starving humans did not make good soldiers.[25]

Much like the three hundred Spartans of old, the Confederates had pulled off a miracle at Petersburg. Beauregard masterminded the defense, but on the field, Hoke and his division played the vital role. From the time they arrived in the defenseless city to the final shots three days later, Hoke's soldiers had kept the enormous Federal forces at bay by repelling every attack.

There was, however, no time for Hoke to enjoy the victory. The makeshift Confederate line needed much work to withstand a siege. For several days after the battle, Hoke suffered numerous casualties from the fire of

Union sharpshooters. Picks, shovels, spades, and axes quickly became complements to the soldiers' guns.[26]

On June 23, Hoke's division was abuzz as the Federals began to shell the city and its civilian population. Hagood recalled, "The portion of it within range was soon abandoned by the inhabitants, though many of the poorer class remained, taking refuge in their cellars, when the bombardment was heavy." As the shelling began, Hoke was briefed on a plan devised by Lee and Beauregard to strike at a weak section of the Union line between the river and City Point Road. Because Hoke manned the section of the line opposite the perceived vulnerable spot, his soldiers were chosen to lead the offensive. However, the plan of battle was such that only Hagood's brigade could participate. Charles Field's division from Richard Anderson's corps was assigned to support Hoke in the offensive. On the north side of the river, Edward Porter Alexander had assembled a mighty artillery arsenal to enfilade the Federal defenders.[27]

Through Beauregard, Lee issued written details of the plan. At daylight on June 24, Alexander's guns were to commence a thirty-minute barrage on the Federal lines, to be followed by a five-minute lull, which was to serve as a signal for Hoke to begin his movement. Simultaneously with Hoke's advance, the Confederate right was to make a serious demonstration. Hoke was then to take the flank of the first and second lines of the enemy and recapture the old Confederate line. Anderson was ordered to put Field's brigades in the best position "to support Hoke's attack and protect his left flank." Once Hoke was in position to hit the Federals on the east side of the Norfolk Railroad, Bushrod Johnson's division would "take the offensive and attack boldly the forces of the enemy."

Unfortunately for the Confederates, Hoke and Field comprehended the orders differently. As Hoke understood the plan, Field was to advance as soon as Hoke's men had driven the enemy pickets from their rifle pits. On the other hand, Field believed that he was to advance only "after Hoke had gotten entire possession of the first line of the enemy" and "to attack wherever and whatever I found best."[28]

"Fearing that by some means the enemy might learn our intentions and prepare for us," Hoke discussed the intended advance with no subordinate other than Johnson Hagood; on the eve of the assault, Hagood "was made sufficiently familiar with the mode of attack to make the necessary arrangements." Hagood welcomed the opportunity to "inflict such a blow as would raise the siege if not put an end to the campaign." According to the South Carolinian, the prevailing moods in both armies were conducive to the offensive: "The morale of the Confederate Army was at its highest, that of the enemy at probably its lowest during the campaign, and the great disparity of losses endured by Grant's sledge hammer style of fighting had brought the two armies at this time to the insurmountable inequality of numbers, other conditions being favorable."[29]

At dawn on Friday, June 24, Hoke provided Hagood with detailed instructions about the plan of attack. While the two officers were in consultation, a courier from Brigadier General James P. Anderson of Field's division reported that Anderson had his brigade in position to support the attack. Like clockwork, "the artillery opened precisely at 7 A.M. and ceased precisely at 7:30 A.M." As to Alexander's firepower, a writer for the *New York Tribune* reported there was no time during the war except Gettysburg that so many guns were concentrated upon a single point and fired so rapidly for so long. Hoke recorded that the mighty artillery assault commenced "as soon as the morning's mist had cleared away, and continued its fire with great accuracy, but no exception, for half an hour."

At 7:20 A.M., in the midst of the firestorm, Hagood notified Anderson that he "would move in exactly fifteen minutes." When Alexander opened up at 7:35 A.M., Hoke grew apprehensive about the effect of the guns: "Indeed I fear we were injured more than we gained by the use of our guns, as it notified the enemy of our intended advance." Moreover, the opening of the assault was delayed for seven minutes while Hoke waited to receive notice that Anderson was dispatching troops to fill the entrenchments soon to be vacated by Hagood. Both Hoke and Hagood anxiously waited in vain for "Anderson's approach advancing over the hill." Hagood was willing to wait longer, but Hoke sent an aide with orders for the advance to begin.[30]

Hoke divided Hagood's assault force into two lines. The first was composed of 400 handpicked skirmishers under the command of Lieutenant

General Robert F. Hoke

Colonel Patrick H. Nelson. Hagood assumed personal command of the 550 men in the second line. At 7:42 A.M., when Hoke's aide delivered the order to advance, Lieutenant Colonel Nelson, without speaking, "drew his handkerchief from his breast" and waved it about. Instantly, his gallant South Carolinians poured over the top and charged across the field while offering up the "rebel yell." Hagood's men followed close behind. Hoke noted that "the enemy became extremely uneasy along his entire line when the attack was made." Robert E. Lee was also on hand to watch "as the first line gallantly entered the entrenchments of the enemy and did their duty nobly. . . . [They] succeeded not only in breaking the enemy, but drove them from their works."

Yet when the supporting line of battle failed to appear, Hagood's second line did not advance beyond the enemy's rifle pits. Hagood recalled, "My men, under orders, laid down in the oats about half way between the two entrenchments to await Anderson's advance and then go with him." Hoke immediately sought out Field and pleaded with him "to order General Anderson forward, as a moment's delay would be fatal." Field obliged, but a delay—estimated by Hoke to be an hour in length—did indeed ensue before two of Field's brigades were ready to advance. By that time, it was too late, for as Hoke recorded, "I advised against it, as the enemy had had ample time to make all preparations for us, which they had done, and I felt assured they would sustain a very heavy loss and accomplish nothing. At this time orders were received from General Lee for me to report to him in company with General Field, who abandoned the attack after hearing the position of affairs."[31]

Both division commanders were reluctant to accept blame for the failure of the assault. Field blamed Hoke, complaining, "Instead of getting credit for doing much more that I was ordered to do, ignorant persons . . . took it for granted . . . that the failure was mine, whereas it was because I was active and exceeded my instructions that people supposed that it was I and not Hoke who was ordered to carry the place. So much for being too enterprising and ambitious."

Hoke was more diplomatic. He termed the plan of attack "good" but admitted it "failed in execution." He expressed regret that he had attempted

the attack "without full command of all forces which were to participate."
In his official report, Hoke appeared to be ready to face criticism for his
performance: "It is not my desire to place blame or responsibility on any
one (for I fear neither) in making the foregoing statements, but merely
give facts to the best of my knowledge, after which the commanding general may draw his own conclusions, as I have learned that both I and my
command were censured by the commanding general."[32]

In reviewing the affair, Lee believed that Field could not have moved
forward until Hoke made room for him, even though Hoke and Hagood
both contended that the trenches were empty when the call went up for
Anderson. Whatever the reason for the failure, Lee put it aside without
further criticism by noting, "There seems to have been some misunderstanding as to the part each division was expected to have performed." As
to Hoke's suggestion that he and his command were about to be censured, Beauregard wrote, "General Hoke is mistaken." The Creole went
on to adopt portions of the reports of Hoke and Hagood to buttress his
opinion that "the success would have been most brilliant had the skirmishers been properly supported."[33]

Darkness covered the battlefield before Hagood and his men limped
back to the Confederate lines. Brigade casualties were extremely heavy: 25
killed, 73 wounded, and 208 missing. Hoke praised the spirit and gallantry of his brigadier: "General Hagood did everything in his power to
give us success, and desired to push forward when in my judgment it appeared hazardous." Hagood referred to the episode as "a bitter experience" and claimed that his men were "uselessly sacrificed." He agreed with
Hoke that the plan was "a brilliant and entirely practical design" and that
it failed because the supporting troops were not "under the same command as the attacking line." But for Hagood, there was "another and more
palpable cause of failure manifest"—Brigadier General James Patton Anderson. In his memoirs, Hagood wrote, "On the record here given, there is
but one comment to be made, and that the obvious one—Anderson should
have been shot."[34]

In the wake of the "fiasco" of June 24, Hoke and his troops returned
to a life of grim trench warfare which would be theirs for many weeks.

Hagood explained that the line "was at first a simple trench with the parapet on the farther side of it, and though it was afterwards amplified it retained the general character of a trench, and was always known as 'The Trenches,' in distinction from the original portion of the works held by us."[35]

After fighting on two of the bloodiest battlefields the war had known, it would seem that Hoke's soldiers might have welcomed a respite from the countless marches, the attacks, and the terrible slaughter that had become all too common since mid-May. But Major T. J. Brown of the Forty-second North Carolina pointed out about life in the trenches, "All the hardships through which the men had to pass were far greater and more disastrous than the battles they had fought. It was simply awful." Adjutant George H. Moffett of the Twenty-fifth South Carolina eloquently described the misery that he and his comrades in Hoke's division faced on a daily basis: "Seldom are men called upon to endure as much as was required of the troops who occupied the trenches of Petersburg during the months of June, July, and August. It was endurance without relief; sleeplessness without excitement; inactivity without rest; constant apprehension requiring ceaseless watching." Hagood echoed the comments of these junior officers: "It is difficult to convey to one who has never had a similar experience an idea of the actual reality of the labors and suffering of the men who for these long, hot summer months held without relief the trenches of Petersburg."[36]

Soldierly duties were particularly harsh for Hoke's men in the trenches. From an hour before sunrise until well past dusk, the troops were detailed to man the lines or labor with the pick and spade to repair the works, which were knocked down regularly from almost ceaseless shelling and gunfire. They were forced to stay below ground, as it was dangerous for a man to show his head given the proximity of the two lines. In a macabre form of humor, some of the soldiers would place their hats on the tips of their bayonets and raise them above the works; by the time the hats were lowered, they had been pierced by numerous bullets. Casualties from the "spiteful hissing bullets" and artillery bombardment were a daily occurrence, because there was no safe place on the lines.[37]

Other than an occasional oilcloth stretched on four upright stakes, there was no shelter from the scorching sun or the infrequent rain. Men slept with arms in hand in the wet, filthy trenches, where vermin abounded and the stench from latrines was overwhelming. Safe drinking water was a rare commodity. Food could not be cooked on the front; rather, it was either eaten raw or prepared at a cook yard some miles distant and brought forward in bags on the shoulders of soldiers. One pound of pork and three pounds of meal were rationed for each man every three days. Coffee, sugar, vegetables, tobacco, and alcohol were virtually unheard of. On the rare occasion when a box of food from home made it to the trenches, Hoke's soldiers were filled with sentiment and gratitude.[38]

No one left the trenches without permission. Company officers lived with the soldiers, while field officers and brigade staff had pits six yards behind the trenches. Hoke's headquarters were located approximately a third of a mile to the rear.[39]

Deadly attrition quickly became a most difficult problem. Soldier after soldier fell prey to grievous wounds—primarily to the head or upper body—from Union shot and shell. Notably, Captain Joseph Morrison, the brother-in-law of Stonewall Jackson, was crippled for life by an exploding shell while spending the night at Hoke's headquarters. But many soldiers who were able to dodge the enemy fire fell victim to a variety of insidious diseases invading the trenches: malarial fever, diarrhea, scurvy, and dysentery. Poor rations, exposure, fatigue, and unsanitary conditions weakened once-strong bodies that had marched countless miles and fought on many a bloody field. Digestive organs became impaired; legs and feet swelled to the point that shoes could no longer be worn; and dust, dirt, mud, and grime gave once-handsome soldiers the appearance "of inmates of a miserably conducted poor house." At one time, five hundred of the soldiers in Hagood's brigade were in the field infirmary.[40]

Not only did the disease and wounds of trench warfare take from Hoke many of his veteran soldiers, but they also robbed him of valued officers. By late June, forty-five-year-old brigadier general James G. Martin "showed severe strain and exposure" and at his own request was relieved of command and transferred to less rigorous duty in western North Carolina. Robert E. Lee took time to express the sentiments of the soldiers who had served with Martin: "General Martin is one to whom North Carolina owes a debt she can never repay."

Until Brigadier General William Whedbee Kirkland arrived in August, Hoke was forced to assign junior officers to command the brigade. At one point, the brigade adjutant was down to one staff officer "and the brigade was commanded by one of the Junior Captains of the Seventeenth Regiment, all the field officers being '*hors du combat*.'" To remedy the situation, Hoke sent a colonel from Colquitt's brigade to assume temporary command. Hagood's brigade suffered from a similar attrition of officers. Hagood reported, "For some time, during July, not a field officer was present with the brigade for duty, and four out of the five regiments were commanded by lieutenants."[41]

Despite the deprivations and casualties, Hoke and the men of his division ably manned the trenches and carried on the duties of war during the hot, dry summer. At some places, Hoke's line was as close as sixty-three yards to the enemy, and at no point were the opposing lines separated by more than three hundred yards. Picket lines were within speaking distance of each other, "and when the officers would permit it," conversations were held between the lines. An odd fraternity developed, and at least in the early stages of the fight for Petersburg, the warriors were allowed to trade precious commodities such as newspapers and tobacco. On one occasion, when an order was issued to cease fraternizing with the enemy, one of Clingman's North Carolinians yelled across the lines, "Hide out, you Feds, we have orders to commence firing, and we are going to begin."[42]

A field return for the Army of Northern Virginia on June 30 revealed that Hoke's division was still relatively strong, with 373 officers and 4,936 men present for duty.

On the night of July 2, John Taylor Wood called on Lee at his Petersburg headquarters to discuss an upcoming secret expedition that promised substantial rewards for the Confederacy. Wood, with the approval of President Davis, planned to launch an amphibious attack on July 12 against the Union prison at Point Lookout, Maryland, which at the time held twenty thousand Confederate prisoners of war. The daring naval officer looked to include in his mission only officers known for their bravery, competence, and celerity. In response to Wood's visit and the president's request for an officer known to the prisoners expected to be released by the attack, "to have charge of them, and to organize them, inspire confidence, and put them quickly in motion," Lee replied to Davis, "The only officer here whom I could recommend for the duty is Genl Hoke. If he was taken from his division in the present emergency I would not know what to do with it. I am afraid it would be lost to us." A week later, Davis canceled the expedition."[43]

Although service in the trenches from June to September "was trying to the last degree," most of Hoke's soldiers "stood all their sufferings with unflinching endurance." Grant had hoped that siege warfare would destroy the will to continue the fight. However, from the trenches on July 6, John Cherry wrote to his sister back in North Carolina, "The day is past for Grant taking Petersburg. And he seemes aware of it." Cherry had but two complaints: "We are suffering greatly for rain. . . . I have and am now suffering some with diarrhea." Of Cherry and his fellow soldiers in the trenches, Major T. J. Brown recorded, "Their endurance was most severely tried, but they displayed the Fortitude so characteristic of the North Carolina troops." By July 21, Cherry had grown even more optimistic: "Our Army is getting along much better now since the rains. I hope the[y] may continue to improve. We are confident of success in the end. Though the campaign may last much longer even till the 1st of October . . . Grant will be as far if farther from Richmond than now."[44]

In a spectacular attempt to end the siege, Grant authorized his forces to spring a powerful mine under the Confederate works to the right of Hoke's position at daylight on July 30. When the fuse ignited the four tons of powder, there was "a slight quake of earth," followed by "an erupted mass of earth," and then a "roar appalling." Showering from the sky came "a kind of stone, earth, wood, and mangled bodies." Some 275 South Carolina soldiers from Bushrod Johnson's division were killed instantly by the blast, which opened a chasm measuring 170 feet long, as much as 97 feet wide, and 30 feet deep. Known thereafter as "the Crater," the incident was "perhaps the most prominent event of the siege," according to Hagood.

In the aftermath of the blast, several Union divisions charged the

Confederates in an attempt to permanently breach their lines. Some of the attacking forces unwittingly fell into the enormous hole, but many succeeded in opening a gap in Johnson's line. At the same time, Hoke was being threatened. In his "General Order and Letter Book," he recorded, "All my troops were then in my front line, on which there were two salients, closely approached by the enemy, which I had reason to believe might at any time be blown up, to be followed by a charge." Nevertheless, Hoke sent at least four regiments—two from Clingman, one from Hagood, and one from Colquitt—to help close the break in Johnson's line. By 1 P.M., the Federals had been chased back to their lines, and there ended a grand experiment which Grant termed a "stupendous failure."[45]

Like the Federals, the Confederates did their share of tunneling under the works of the enemy. Zigzagging their way under the lines, these tunnels were as deep as thirty feet below the surface. Many of the shafts excavated by Hoke's soldiers were elaborately crafted with planked ceilings and acoustic holes, designed to allow "miners" to monitor the activities of the enemy. Small rooms six to eight feet square were often located at the end of the tunnels, so that powder could be exploded upon the approach of the enemy. Hoke kept sentries in the shafts at all times, and although duty in the cool, quiet underground aisles was much preferred to life in the trenches, "there was something in the dark stillness . . . suggestive of the grave."[46]

After the Union disaster at "the Crater," the armies returned to three weeks of uneventful trench warfare. During the first twenty days of August, nothing "occurred with us to break the monotony of life in the trenches, such as it was," according to Hagood. Colquitt's brigade was permanently returned to Hoke on August 2. On August 19, Hoke's command was weakened by the temporary detachment of the brigades of Colquitt and Clingman. Assigned to Major General William Mahone, the two brigades took part in Lee's unsuccessful three-day effort to dislodge the Federals from the Weldon and Petersburg Railroad. On the last day of the fight, Hagood's brigade was also sent to Mahone. Of the 681 officers and men Hagood sent into the battle, only 292 emerged unscathed. General Clingman was seriously wounded in the leg on the first day of the engagement and was lost to Hoke for the remainder of the war.[47]

Several days after the setback, two of the three brigades were returned to Hoke. Because of deadly attrition and the casualties sustained on August 21, Hagood asked that he be allowed to take his survivors "to some quiet camp where rest and access to water might recruit their physical condition." His request was granted by Lee. When the 740 frail soldiers of his command emerged from the Petersburg trenches on August 20, they represented just a third of the complement that had entered the works sixty-seven days earlier. The brigade inspector was delighted when a local citizen offered his forty-acre estate in nearby Chesterfield County for a camp site. Swift Creek, "a bold, and handsome stream with precipitous banks," ran through the tranquil park and spread into "a deep, dark pool."[48]

In mid-September, Hoke was granted permission to pull his other weary brigades from the trenches and take them to the utopia being enjoyed by Hagood's men. Of the twenty-two hundred soldiers on hand when Brigadier General Martin put his soldiers in the trenches, seven hundred "living skeletons" scrambled out under the command of Brigadier General Kirkland on Thursday, September 15.

For ten days, Hoke and the worn and jaded men of his division enjoyed overdue pleasures. In a letter to his sister, Lieutenant Edward J. Williams of the Thirty-first North Carolina expressed the excitement that abounded: "The most pleasant topic amongst us—I mean Hoke's Division—is that we are at last clear of the ditches, shells, & balles of every description & are lying at ease on a beautiful hillside washing our faces at least once per day and no work to do. You can't imagine how highly we appreciate such treatment. Since the 15 of June we have held a portion of the works in front of Petersburg & have never been relieved until now."[49]

The brief respite from war ended all too soon on September 28, when the men returned to the trenches. As a climax to the period of rest and relaxation, the division was honored with a grand review by General Lee on September 26. Many citizens from Petersburg attended the review, turning it into a "gala occasion." Lee, dressed in full uniform with a yellow sash, was atop Traveller as he rode past the remnants of Hoke's four brigades. Hagood noted that even the general's famous gray horse "looked as if he thought it was all foolishness." Nevertheless, it was the "only review or military display" Hagood witnessed during the campaign of 1864.[50] Indeed, the special review of Hoke's command that September day was the beginning of a close association that was to develop between Lee and Hoke over the months to follow.

> "Never was an assault
> made more gallantly or
> against greater odds.
> The Light Brigade
> at Balaklava did no
> more."

CHAPTER 11

The Autumn of the Confederacy

Several weeks of quietude in an idyllic setting removed from the grim realties of war did little to make the soldiers of Hoke's division eager to return to the deadly trenches of Petersburg in late September. When the veterans, attired in "fine new uniforms," filed back into their disease-ridden subterranean homes on September 28, it was with the expectation of another long, harsh stay. Their return was greeted by the enemy with "a most brilliant pyrotechnic display," the heaviest mortar fire during their service at Petersburg.[1] Surprise, relief, and bewilderment were the reaction in the trenches less than twenty-four hours later, when Hoke received orders to remove the division to the north side of the James. But hopes that this new deployment would lead to another break from combat were to be shattered before the month drew to a close.

General Robert F. Hoke

Hoke's hasty removal from Petersburg was occasioned by Grant's sudden capture of Fort Harrison on September 28. Located just eight miles south of the Confederate capital, the earthwork installation was part of the fortified camp that enclosed Chaffin's Bluff on the river two miles west. Because the fort was strategically situated near the junction of the outer and intermediate defense lines of Richmond, Lee was alarmed that its capture might open the door to the city. Anxious to quell this new threat to the security of the Confederate capital, he promptly laid plans to retake the fort. On September 29, he moved his headquarters to the area and began marshaling the forces he felt were necessary to carry out his plan. Brigadier General William Porter Alexander and his artillery accompanied Lee, and marching orders were issued for the divisions of Hoke and Field.[2]

Field began his movement on the morning of September 29, but Hoke could not pull his soldiers from the trenches until 3 P.M. that sultry day. Darkness had fallen before the last of the troops, Hagood's brigade, left Petersburg by rail. To facilitate the troop crossing to the north side of the James, Lee ordered a special pontoon bridge to be laid. Clingman's brigade, the vanguard of the division that day, arrived at Chaffin's Bluff at 10 P.M., but the other brigades did not make their appearance until the wee hours of the next morning. Throughout the night, the Federals "diligently strengthened" the defenses at Fort Harrison.[3]

Lee had contemplated a night attack designed to hit the enemy before it could become strongly entrenched. Field importuned the Confederate chieftain to strike the Federals under the veil of darkness, but Lee ultimately eschewed the idea, deciding instead to await the arrival of Hoke's division. Once all of the Confederate forces were gathered for the attack on the morning of September 30, Lee could count on approximately sixteen thousand effectives, while Butler could field twenty-one thousand of the twenty-four thousand men Grant had supplied him for the successful assault on Fort Harrison.[4]

At 6 A.M., Hoke began moving his division closer to Fort Harrison. Clingman's brigade was again in the lead. Most of the soldiers in the other brigades were extremely weary, having received little or no sleep during the movement the past night. By the time the rear guard of the division reached the vicinity of Fort Harrison at 9 A.M., Lee was on the ground and "it was evident an effort was to be made to recover the lost work." According to Lee's plan of attack, Alexander's artillery would open the battle by offering thirty minutes of fire against the fort. Field's division, located to the left of and at an obtuse angle to Hoke's, was to begin the attack. Once Field's soldiers were ready to storm the fort, Hoke was to unleash his warriors.[5]

The task assigned Hoke and Field was a most difficult one. Their soldiers would rush across open ground into a compact line of Union skirmishers posted behind a rail fence. If the skirmish line were broken, the fort would have to be stormed. Before the Confederates could scale the towering earthen walls, they would encounter thousands of sharp wooden spikes and stakes positioned in front of the works. All the while, heavily massed ranks of Union soldiers armed with Spencer repeaters would be issuing a withering fire from their protected position.

Hoke's heart was not in the offensive. Because of the danger to his men, he reasoned with Lee that the attack should not be made. Hoke believed that such an attempt would be "impracticable" and "would result only in loss of life without accomplishing any good end." As he saw it, rather than storming the fort, Lee could build a new line of defenses near the place where Hoke's division was now positioned, just two hundred yards from the fort.

Second Lieutenant A. A. McKethan of the Fifty-first North Carolina, who subsequently participated in the attack, concurred with Hoke: "To have attempted its recapture under such circumstances was a mistake, and as carried out a terrible blunder on the part of some one." Colonel Hector McKethan, the commanding officer of Clingman's brigade, and other officers on the ground who saw "the impossibility of success and the heavy loss that we must sustain" protested against making the assault, "but being ordered by superior officers to go forward, nobly offered themselves and their comrades as sacrifices for their country." Artillery chief William Porter Alexander offered a similar view: "It was, however, almost a hopeless task to try & drive superior forces from works so strong as these now were."[6]

General Robert F. Hoke

Lee would have none of the pessimism, protestations, or alternate plans. Rather, his unfailing confidence in his soldiers convinced him that the attack could be successfully carried out. Thus, around noon, Hoke formed his division in a ravine two hundred yards from the fort. Clingman's brigade was placed in front, with Colquitt's just behind. Because Field's division would be forced to charge an additional five hundred yards to reach the fort, his men were to open the infantry attack. Field selected the brigade of James P. Anderson to lead the charge, and he ordered Anderson to move his men as close as possible to the fort, where they were to lie down until Hoke's men joined the charge. Unfortunately for Lee and the Confederates, Anderson failed to inform his troops that they were to wait for Hoke.[7]

All was ready by 1 P.M., and Alexander opened with his guns in anticipation of the infantry charge. Once more, Hoke voiced his troops' objections. To the artillery commander, he shouted, "I had rather you would not fire a shot from your guns, sir! You will demoralize my men more by your shells falling short and bursting among my men, than you will inflict damage on the enemy. If you will bring your guns up to my line and charge with my troops you may do some good, but not otherwise." In response, the artillerist remarked, "But my horses will all get killed." Hoke replied, "Yes, and my men are going to be killed. Are your horses of more value than the lives of my soldiers?"[8]

Hoke lost the argument, and the Confederate guns roared. According to Captain William H. S. Burgwyn of Clingman's brigade, "The ground shook with the mighty concussion, the smoke enveloped the field, and the enemy retreated under the protection of his earth works." For thirty minutes, Alexander's guns sent forth their blazing ordnance, masking the two lines in thick, acrid smoke. As the barrage neared its end, Field ordered Anderson to move forward. About 1:45 P.M., the brave Georgians poured out of the woods just as the clearing smoke revealed a Federal position that was virtually undamaged. Instead of halting to wait for Hoke to join the attack as Field had ordered, the brigade rushed headlong toward the fort and was bitterly repelled.

Although both Field and Hoke had been ordered not to start the attack before 2 P.M., Field sent forth the brigades of John Bratton and William F. Perry as soon as he discovered that Anderson had been thoroughly routed. All three of Field's brigades were quickly thrown into confusion and could make no headway against a hail of musketry that, according to Colonel James R. Hagood of Bratton's brigade, "would appall the stoutest heart." Colonel Hagood remarked about the deafening sound of the Union rifles greeting the charging Confederates, "The noise sounded like the magnified roar of a thousand kettle drums."[9]

During the fifteen-minute premature attack by Field, Hoke did not move. Prior to the battle, he had been cautioned not to attack before the appointed hour for fear of outdistancing the left wing. As the clock ticked toward 2 P.M., twenty-nine-year-old colonel Hector McKethan of the Fifty-first North Carolina lay on the ground among his troops, waiting for the order to charge. He was about to lead Clingman's brigade into battle for the first time and was "supremely anxious the men should acquit themselves creditably in the trying ordeal."

Despite his misgivings about the impending charge and his shock at the collapse of Field's division, Hoke gave the command for McKethan, then Colquitt, to charge the fort at the scheduled time. H. T. J. Ludwig of the Eighth North Carolina described the moment: "It was a charge in open day, over open ground, about two hundred yards to the fort. When the order to advance was given the men moved forward with a rapid run. The order was not to fire until the fort was reached." Maintaining their alignment until "as one man the enemy flashed his defiance from a thousand guns," the dauntless North Carolinians continued their charge. Captain Burgwyn, who was captured while leading the Thirty-first North Carolina, chronicled the slaughter:

> I . . . found the Yankees had massed their troops in the works right in our front having virtually vacated the works to their left and I suppose they were three lines deep behind their works and as they were all armed with seven shooters the fire was awful. By the time we got in about seventy yards of their works our line was entirely broken not from falling back but literally from the men being cut down by piles by the brigade's fire and our

General Robert F. Hoke

support, Colquitt's Brigade, having returned behind the hill being appalled at the sight of the mortality and fire.[10]

Some of Hoke's soldiers made it to the stockade near the fort. Second Lieutenant McKethan recorded their fate:

> To retreat was death, so the only choice was to throw down their guns and pull up these obstructions, which the men at once attempted, but a double line armed with repeating rifles posted in front of their works, and a deadly fire from the garrison in the fort, said to have been several lines deep, and the concentration of all artillery upon them, made the position untenable and the task impossible, so that the few left were forced to seek shelter offered by two buildings near the works. Never was an assault made more gallantly or against greater odds. The Light Brigade at Balaklava did no more.[11]

When Hoke sent the two brigades forward, he had been assured by Brigadier General John Bratton that the attack on the left would be simultaneously renewed. However, when Bratton saw how badly the North Carolinians were repulsed, he refused to attack again.

As the bloodied survivors of the failed charge struggled back to the safety of Hoke's lines, they were surprised and elated to see General Lee, who had been supervising the overall conduct of the battle. Aboard Traveller, he waved his hat, causing the Tar Heels to offer up a great cheer on his behalf. Explaining the importance of the recapture of Fort Harrison to the Confederate cause, he beseeched Hoke's soldiers to make another charge. One eyewitness to the battlefield meeting of commander and troops recalled, "I had always thought General Lee was [a] very cold and unemotional man, but he showed lots of feeling and excitement on that occasion; even the staid and stately Traveller caught the spirit of his master, and was prancing and cavorting while the General was imploring his men to make one more effort to take the position for him."

In response to Lee's adjuration, Hoke's men charged again when the order was given, only to be driven back with still heavier losses. Lee made yet another plea, and once again the ever-thinning lines shouted their readiness to enter the tumult. For a third time, the Federals rained death and destruction on the attackers, and when the lucky few who had cheated death returned to Hoke's position in near panic, Lee realized that it was time to cease for the day. No effort was forthcoming from the Federals to follow up on the crushing defeat they had dealt.[12]

The usually stoic Lee was visibly shaken by the debacle at Fort Harrison. William Porter Alexander, the man who had provided the artillery cover on the fateful charge at Gettysburg on July 3, 1863, noted that Lee "was more worried at this failure [at Fort Harrison] than I have seen him under similar circumstances." Upon his return to his headquarters at Chaffin's Bluff, Lee dispatched the grim news to Richmond. John C. Pemberton, the one-time lieutenant general who had resigned his commission after surrendering Vicksburg, called on Lee the evening of the disaster to discuss the events of the day. When questioned about whether he would attempt to retake the fort at any cost, Lee responded with words that hinted of the position urged by Hoke earlier in the day: "General Pemberton, I made my effort this morning and failed, having many killed and wounded. I have ordered another line provided from that point and shall have no more blood shed at the fort unless you can show me a practical plan of capture."[13]

By charging across the field three times, Clingman's brigade had suffered the heaviest losses. In a letter written on October 2, Lieutenant E. J. Wilkins, the only officer of the Thirty-first North Carolina to emerge from the battle unscathed, told his mother, "The brigade is literally cut to pieces; another such a fight will certainly wipe us out." With the possible exception of Rappahannock Station, at no time during his career as a general officer had Hoke suffered such brigade losses. At Rappahannock Station, many of the losses had been through capture, but at Fort Harrison, most came from bullets.

As night fell over the battlefield, the North Carolinians who were yet able to walk used the cloak of darkness to hobble back to their lines. Those less fortunate, the bleeding and dying men who helplessly lay on the killing ground where they had fallen, were taken prisoner by a large body of Union soldiers who poured out of the works to scour the field. Of the

911 men Colonel McKethan had led forward in the early afternoon, only 383 were present for roll call that night. Three of the four regimental commanders were down, as were 27 of the 40 company commanders. One soldier in the Eighth North Carolina reported that "the regiment was almost annihilated." It had gone into battle with 175 officers and men, but by the close of the day, it could count only 25 soldiers commanded by a lieutenant. None of the eight brigade flags survived the disaster. Memories of that last day of September 1864 would linger with Hoke's veterans for many years to come. For as long as he lived, Colonel McKethan, the brigade historian, "never could speak of this day without quivering lips and moistened eyes when he described the fearful slaughter of his brave men in so hopeless an undertaking."[14]

In the aftermath of the failure at Fort Harrison, Lee decided to leave the divisions of Hoke and Field on the north side of the James. For almost three months, Hoke and his soldiers would man the line of defense works between Darbytown and Charles City Roads in order to defend Richmond, monitor the movements of Grant, and prevent him from sending additional manpower to assist in the ongoing siege at Petersburg.

During the first five days of October, the troops busied themselves in throwing up breastworks and strengthening their position. In the meantime, Lee decided to take the offensive against Grant on Darbytown Road. Hoke and Field were ordered to pull their divisions from the works on the night of October 6 for an attack that would begin at daylight the next day. Under Lee's plan, the cavalry brigade of Harvard-educated M. W. Gary was to move down Charles City Road and drive in the Federal right flank. At that point, Field, moving down Darbytown Road, would join the fight. Hoke was to act as the reserve. If all went as Lee had planned, the Union forces holding the abandoned position of the exterior line north of Fort Harrison would be driven away.[15]

Early in the morning on Friday, October 7, the divisions of Hoke and Field massed on Darbytown Road. All went well initially for the Confederates. At sunrise, Gary attacked "with vigor," and Field followed suit. In twenty minutes, the Union cavalry division of German-born A. V. Kautz was thoroughly routed. Leaving sixteen pieces of artillery behind, the dismounted cavalrymen fled two miles to the rear, where their infantry and artillery forces were being massed behind breastworks protected by abatis. Field, eager to follow up the advantage he had gained, pressed on toward the Union position. At this point, Hoke's division moved from Darbytown Road and followed to the right of and behind the advancing line of Field and Gary.

As the Confederates neared the "strongly manned" and "rapidly re-enforced" enemy lines, there were two available courses of attack, according to Johnson Hagood: "First, to make a direct assault, or second, to bring Hoke before this line, and, feeling to the left with Gary and Field's command, turn it. Hoke's position was such that he could have replaced Field in thirty minutes." The first option was selected, and Field was under the impression that Hoke "was to assault simultaneously" with him.[16]

Field described what happened next: "My gallant fellows, led by the brigade commanders on foot, rushed forward and penetrated to the abatis, facing a most terrific fire, delivered . . . from those new repeating Spencer rifles. Hoke, for some unexplained cause, did not move forward. The consequence was that the whole fire was concentrated on my fellows. We were repulsed with heavy loss." The Confederates were finished for the day. Lee withdrew his forces and positioned them behind Cornelius Creek in order to cover New Market and Darbytown Roads.[17]

Hoke's failure to move in support of Field subjected him to immediate criticism. In addition to Field, William Porter Alexander questioned Hoke's role in the affair: "Hoke's line on his right never moved. I never knew why. . . . It would seem that the attack should have been by both or neither." Johnson Hagood came to the defense of his major general. As Hagood saw it, Lee had directed Hoke's movements during the fight: "Why General Lee did not put in his reserve is not known. . . . General Lee was, however, present with the reserve during most of the day, and just before and during the last assault he was with us. This settles the fact that the part borne by Hoke was under the immediate direction of the commander-in-chief." Hagood speculated that Lee chose not to deploy Hoke because his division stood between the enemy and Richmond throughout the battle.[18]

Hagood's explanation notwithstanding, Hoke's failure to move forward on that occasion is an example of the one major flaw that, according to some historians and scholars, plagued his performance as a major general. Douglas Southall Freeman and Richard J. Sommers, among others, have criticized Hoke for his failure to cooperate with other divisions during the engagements of the spring, summer, and fall of 1864. In his three-volume treatise, *Lee's Lieutenants*, Freeman cited five instances of Hoke's failure to cooperate. In addition to the incident on Darbytown Road, Hoke's performance at Drewry's Bluff on May 16, at Cold Harbor on June 1, at Petersburg on June 24, and at Fort Harrison on September 30 was called into question.

Yet the record on each of those occasions reveals that Hoke's actions were either proper or at least defensible under the circumstances existing at the time. Not only at the action on Darbytown Road but at Fort Harrison on September 30 as well, Robert E. Lee personally directed the movements of Hoke's troops. Of the three major generals assigned to the offensive at Drewry's Bluff on May 16, only Hoke garnered praise without criticism from Beauregard in the aftermath of the battle. At Cold Harbor on June 1, the Confederate offensive was called off before Hoke could begin to cooperate with the divisions of Richard Anderson. And while Lee refused to fault either Hoke or Charles Field for the failure of the Confederate attack at Petersburg on June 24, Johnson Hagood, whose brigade bore the brunt of the action that day, attributed the failure to the soldiers of Field's division. As Freeman admitted about Hoke, "Neither his State nor his command loses faith in him."[19]

Upon the return of Hoke's division to its lines on the evening of October 7, the soldiers settled in for a long stay that was characterized by daily entrenching, occasional skirmishing, and infrequent demonstrations against the enemy. An unidentified soldier described the routine: "We have to ly in our trenches day and knight Rain or Shine Hot or Coald. [T]hair is some killed or wounded moar or less evry day by morter shells or Sharp Shooters."[20]

For several hours almost every day during the autumn of 1864, Hoke found himself in the saddle riding with Lee about the Confederate lines on the north side of the river below Richmond. Hoke forever cherished this association with his commander. In a rare interview after the war, the major general recalled the events that led to the special relationship between the two officers:

> The first time I ever saw General Lee was at Yorktown a few days after the first battle of the war, that of Bethel, early in June, 1861. I was a lieutenant in the First North Carolina Regiment of Volunteers. . . . I thought that I had never seen a more superb figure of a man than General Lee, as he made a thorough inspection of our regiment and then reviewed us. Little did I think that high rank would come to me and that later in years I should have the honor and privilege of riding with General Lee for nearly three months, in the autumn of 1864. But time passed and I was given high rank, and it was my good fortune to be in the saddle with General Lee several hours each day. It was on the north side of the James River and we were guarding Richmond from an attack by General Butler. We had only two divisions. . . . My division had been fighting hard all the year, and though reduced in numbers was a perfect fighting machine, ready for anything and afraid of nothing. And I will tell you a fact— General Lee did not think his soldiers could be whipped. He never did think so, and his confidence in their success was simply limitless.[21]

As fall passed, Hoke came to admire in Lee many of the sterling qualities that soldiers and—in the postwar years—civilians saw in Hoke. When asked about Lee the man, he responded,

> General Lee was, in fact, a perfect man, of infinite nobleness of nature and without a single bad habit. He was an inveterate tease, and all of us, no matter what our rank, came in for teasing, this being always absolutely good natured. There was this peculiarity, however, that General Lee must not be teased. He could tease us, but we must not tease him, and we knew this well. He enjoyed a laugh as well as any man I ever knew, and his laughter was hearty and infectious. He has teased me often, and his quizzing of his staff was frequent and amusing.[22]

Hoke was of the opinion that Lee, as a military officer, had no equal.

Lee was always ready to listen to a battle plan "which had merit and good sense behind it." Hoke praised Lee's "wonderful grasp of military matters and strategy" and his "wonderful quickness of eye." As a soldier, Lee "loved to fight." As Hoke put it, "Surely no man was braver." From his wartime association with the Virginian, Hoke came away with a lasting impression:

> One thing always struck me in regard to General Lee, this being in all our times of fighting together and when I was with him daily, on the battlefield, riding together here and there through the country, in conferences at his headquarters, in fact everywhere, the impression I formed of him that day in June, 1861, when he reviewed my old regiment, that he was the grandest man I had ever seen, was never effaced or in fact lessened a particle, but on the contrary, was increased. . . . To sum it all up, General Lee was a perfectly-rounded man, and no greater ever lived than he.[23]

On October 10, Lee directed Hoke and Field to advance their line four hundred yards, so as to cut off the portion of the exterior line that had been abandoned. They were able to do so without opposition, and retrenchment began immediately. Three days later, the enemy advanced its skirmishers against the new line and attacked along Darbytown Road. Making no progress, the Federals retreated with a loss of twelve hundred. Hoke's losses, according to Hagood, were "inconsiderable."

On October 19, Lieutenant General James Longstreet, having partially recovered from a critical wound sustained at the Wilderness, returned to active duty and was assigned the command of Lee's 20,000-man left wing, which included Hoke's division. Under Longstreet's defensive scheme, Field was positioned between Charles City and Darbytown Roads and Hoke was deployed from Darbytown Road to New Market Road. Returns from the field showed that Hoke had 336 officers and 3,787 men present for duty. Southwest of Hoke's position, the defenses surrounding Chaffin's Bluff, which included Fort Hoke (named in honor of the major general), were manned by detachments of the Confederate navy and the local militia.[24]

On the same day that Longstreet assumed command of Southern forces along the James, Hoke's close friend Stephen Dodson Ramseur was mortally wounded as he fearlessly rode up and down his lines exhorting his division to hold the line against Phil Sheridan's massive counterattack at Cedar Creek, Virginia. The fallen general was taken prisoner and carried to Sheridan's headquarters, where a captured Confederate surgeon, Dr. James Gillespie, and the chief medical officer of the Union army labored to save his life. They soon concurred, however, that the bullet, which had plowed its way through both lungs, had produced a fatal wound.

Still on the lapel of the dying general's frock coat was a white flower pinned there by Ramseur in honor of the birth of his first child. Just hours before the battle that was to take Ramseur's life, an officer of the Confederate signal corps had delivered to the general's headquarters a cryptic message informing him of the birth of the child back in North Carolina. As Ramseur drifted in and out of consciousness on his deathbed, he was visited by former classmates at West Point who were now Union officers— George Armstrong Custer, Wesley Merritt, and Henry A. DuPont. As life ebbed from his body, the twenty-seven-year-old general spoke of his desire to see the newborn child just one time before he died. But at 10:27 A.M. on October 20, Ramseur drew his last breath without ever knowing that his only child was a daughter. Among his dying words was a message for that fellow Confederate general whose life had begun just four days before his own in the peaceful town in the foothills of North Carolina: "Tell General Hoke that I die a Christian and have done my duty."[25]

After deploying his division along New Market Road, Hoke set about building a line of ten-foot-high breastworks that stretched some four miles. Because Butler's army was much larger than the Confederate forces on the north side of the river, Hoke attempted to deceive the Union commanders about the size of the Confederate army behind the high embankments by double-quicking his troops back and forth on a regular basis.

On Wednesday night, October 26, Hoke detected the preliminary enemy movements for what was to be his last significant engagement on Virginia soil. He described the scene:

> I and my staff went out in front of our works, and keeping
> perfectly quiet, listened for noises. The night was still and frosty,

and you know that on such nights you can hear noises an incredible distance, for instance, talking a couple of miles or so.
We heard the rumbling of artillery and all other noises which
showed that General Butler was on the move, and I soon arrived at the conclusion that he was going to attack at that part
of our works immediately across the Newmarket road. Action
was taken and our force was massed there, with plenty of artillery, with shell and canister shot arranged for close work.[26]

Very early on the morning of October 27, General Lee left his tent and
rode over to consult with Hoke. On this occasion, Hoke noticed in Lee an
emotion he had never before observed and would never again see in his
general: nervousness. In a "quicker way" than Hoke had ever heard him
speak and "in a tone which betrayed his anxiety," Lee asked, "What will
they do, General Hoke?" Hoke recognized the emotion as uneasiness rather
than fear, later noting, "He did not know the meaning of the latter word."
Many years after the war, Hoke recalled his response to his anxious commander: "I told General Lee that General Butler had massed his attacking
force directly in front of us and that he was going to try and take the
Newmarket road." Soon thereafter, Butler unleashed an attack as Hoke
had predicted. According to Hoke, "That instant General Lee was himself
again, all uncertainty gone, and full of the fire of battle."[27]

Hoke's men were ready for Butler's attack. A soldier of the Sixty-sixth
North Carolina recorded the results: "With a shout and cheer the enemy
was easily repulsed, leaving a large number of dead and wounded in our
front, and not a man in our whole line hurt." Again and again the Yankees
charged, but after several hours of failure, they retired. Hoke was proud of
the readiness of his troops behind the "high and heavy intrenchments." If
only Butler had cooperated, Hoke felt he would have severely damaged
the Army of the James that day: "Had he tried, by dividing his force, to
attack there and then the flank at the same time, we would have advanced
from our works, and by assaulting his troops in our front compelled him
to bring the other to their aid, and then would have beaten the entire
force."[28]

Hoke's success on New Market Road brought the two armies on the north side of the James to a stalemate. For now, the Confederate capital was safe. Johnson Hagood concluded, "This campaign had shown clearly that it was impregnable to attack."

As the pace of the war around Richmond slowed dramatically, the two armies prepared for the coming winter. Over the last three days of October, the weather was exceptionally pleasant, thereby affording Hoke's soldiers the opportunity to push toward the completion of their works, which had proven invaluable just days before. Hoke's newest brigadier, William Whedbee Kirkland, proved of great assistance in the construction of the new works.[29]

Kirkland was the last of the distinguished men permanently assigned to Hoke's division as a brigadier general. Born and reared in Orange County, North Carolina, Kirkland had attended the United States Military Academy for three years. He left West Point in 1855 before graduation in order to accept a commission in the United States Marine Corps. A career military officer, he offered his services to the Confederacy long before his native state seceded. Through dedicated service and solid fighting, Kirkland had risen up the chain of command in the Confederate army from the rank of captain.[30]

As work on the lines neared completion, Hoke's men set about constructing their winter quarters. Comfortable pine-pole cabins equipped with clay chimneys soon replaced the tents and trenches to which the soldiers had long been accustomed. The lull in combat and the more cheerful labor buoyed the spirits of the officers and men. As November opened, Johnson Hagood expressed the confidence that abounded in Hoke's camp: "On the lines before Richmond to Lee's army, erect and defiant, there appeared no reason why the war should not last another four years." Soldiers who had earlier left the division because of sickness and wounds began to return, so that by November 1, Hoke could count almost five thousand men present for duty.[31]

Over the three and a half years of the war, Hoke had been witness to the first Confederate battle death and had seen literally thousands of compatriots make the ultimate sacrifice on the conflict's bloodiest fields. Yet it was on Thursday, November 3, 1864, that the great tragedy of war had its

most profound effect on the major general. On that day, Hoke was notified that a Union army detail under a flag of truce had appeared outside
the Southern lines of Richmond with Dodson Ramseur's coffin. Hoke
hurriedly rode out to meet the detail and then escorted the coffin bearing
the body of his fallen friend into the city. It lay in state in the Confederate
capital until the next morning, when Hoke detailed Major James Adams, a
staff officer, to accompany the body of the youngest West Pointer to attain
the rank of major general in the Confederate army back to North Carolina
for burial in Lincolnton.[32]

There was time for some long-overdue rest and relaxation for the officers of Hoke's division during the break in fighting in late October and
early November. On two occasions, the officers enjoyed magnificent fetes
with a "distinguished party of ladies" from Richmond. For these grand
affairs, a farmhouse far removed from the lines was decorated with flags
and arms and made ready for dancing. The Eutaw Band from Hagood's
brigade was detailed to provide musical entertainment. Division ambulances
were sent to Richmond to pick up the guests, who brought with them
"the edibles of the feast." Upon their arrival, the ladies took "charge of
the festivities." General Hagood recorded of them, "It was a charming
circle; refined, intelligent and accomplished, and the times had added to it
the least dash in the world of the freedom of bivouac. They were admirable specimens of high bred Southern women, as the war developed
them."[33]

Throughout November, rumors were rampant in both armies that Hoke's
division was about to be moved. When the frequent but unfounded stories made their way through the lines that the division was to be sent to
North Carolina, "a shout along the whole line would be raised and Gaston's
grand old song, 'The Old North State', could be heard from every North
Carolina soldier in the division." George M. Rose, the adjutant of the
Sixty-sixth North Carolina, described the disappointment that followed the
momentary elation: "On more than one occasion, however, instead of going
to North Carolina as a division, the order was given to 'Unsling knapsacks
and go over the breastworks' upon some demonstration, or to engage in
some skirmishing to direct Grant's attention in that direction." On No-

vember 24, enemy troop movements on the south side of the James forced Lee and Longstreet to prepare Hoke and Field for any movement neces-' sary to prevent a new offensive.[34]

Hoke and his soldiers spent their last days in their cozy camp without seeing heavy action. On the frigid night of Friday, December 9, with sleet pouring down, Hoke received orders to have the division ready to march at daylight the following day. The next morning, the division took part in its last active mission on Virginia soil when it began a reconnaissance around the enemy's right flank. After a rather uneventful day, the Confederates returned to camp that evening. With harsh winter weather fast approaching, it had become all too apparent to the high command of both armies that the ultimate fate of Richmond would be decided on fields of battle far removed from the Confederate capital.

As Sherman began bearing down on Savannah, Beauregard notified Jefferson Davis on December 19 that the Georgia coastal city would have to be "evacuated as soon as practicable." Beauregard made a desperate plea for troops to aid in the defense of Georgia and South Carolina. He specifically asked for Hoke, but Lee had already determined that his young major general was to be sent elsewhere. There was one last race that Hoke was to run for Lee, and as Lee saw it, this race would most likely determine whether the Confederacy was to survive.[35]

CHAPTER 12

The Fate is Sealed

On the night of Tuesday, December 20, Hoke ordered his division to prepare to move in heavy marching order with three days' rations. As it would turn out, the long-anticipated return to North Carolina was about to unfold. Once again, this urgent movement was occasioned by a Federal threat against a vital Confederate position—the port of Wilmington.[1]

That Wilmington would be the object of a concerted Union offensive had been common knowledge in Richmond and Washington and even in foreign capitals for some time. On November 15, 1864, the *London Times* reported, "There is abundant cause for thinking that Wilmington is the great thorn in the flesh of the Federals at this moment." From the outset of the war, Wilmington had been one of the most important cities of the Confederacy, but during the last half of 1864, it emerged as the only major Southern port "to and from which blockade runners could ply with any degree of safety." C. B. Denson, a Confederate engineering officer, observed about Wilmington, "It was, in fact, the second capital of the Confederacy."

After Union admiral David Farragut achieved his strategic victory at Mobile Bay in August 1864, Robert E. Lee realized that the fate of the entire Confederate nation might well lie with Wilmington. In a letter to Governor Vance on August 29, Lee acknowledged the importance of the port city by remarking "that every effort should be made to defend it." As 1864 drew to a close, Lee's dependence on Wilmington continued to grow. His army, with less than a month's rations on hand, was receiving half its food supply through the blockade at the North Carolina port.[2]

Geography favored Wilmington as a haven for blockade runners. Located twenty-eight miles upstream from the mouth of the Cape Fear River, the port was inaccessible to the deep-draft warships of the United States Navy. On the other hand, the river offered two attractive inlets for the sleek vessels which slipped through the blockade. At its mouth near the mainland town of Smithville (modern-day Southport), the river opened into the Atlantic between Bald Head Island and Oak Island. On the north side of Bald Head, New Inlet provided a second gateway between the island and the tip of a peninsula known alternately as Confederate Point and Federal Point. Only six miles separated the two inlets. However, located between these river entrances was the southernmost of North Carolina's treacherous capes: Cape Fear. Its deadly Frying Pan Shoals forced the Federal blockading fleet to patrol a fifty-mile arc around the inlets giving access to Wilmington.[3]

To protect the inlets at Cape Fear and defend the upriver port, an extensive system of forts had been constructed or confiscated by the Confederates. Guarding the mouth of the river were Fort Holmes on Bald Head Island and Fort Caswell and several lesser forts on Oak Island. Fort Johnston stood on the riverfront at Smithville, and Fort Anderson, a large earthwork installation, loomed on the west bank of the river fifteen miles north of that town. Chief among the Cape Fear forts, however, was Fort Fisher. Known as the "Gibraltar of the Confederacy" and the "Malakoff Tower of the South," the fort was named for Colonel Charles Fisher, a North Carolina hero who had fallen at First Manassas. Located one mile north of Confederate Point, the L-shaped fort protected New Inlet, the favored passageway of blockade runners.[4]

Colonel William Lamb, the commander of the fort, and Major General W. H. C. Whiting, the commander of the Cape Fear defenses, were the masterminds behind the design and construction of Fort Fisher, which was not only the largest earthwork installation of the Confederacy but the strongest seacoast fortification in the South. Lamb had one purpose in mind: "I determined at once to build a work of such magnitude that it could withstand the heaviest fire of any guns in the American Navy." He was successful in that end. Major General A. A. Humphreys, who commanded the Corps of Engineers after the war, called Lamb's handiwork "the greatest piece of engineering on this continent."[5]

Stretching more than a half-mile across the peninsula, the walls of the fort's land face featured a series of fifteen traverses, or mounds, that were twenty-five feet thick, thirty feet high, and angled at forty-five degrees. Twenty heavy guns were mounted along this northern wall. To further fortify the land face, a ditch and a palisade fence were constructed just outside the fort proper. The field beyond the wooden fence was laced with some two dozen "torpedoes," connected by wires to a crude electric battery inside the compound. The traverses of the sea face extended southward down the beach for more than a mile. Immediately south of the Northeast Bastion stood the Pulpit Battery, Lamb's combat headquarters. Twenty-five heavy guns were mounted along the sea face, which terminated at the sixty-foot-tall Mound Battery. Constructed for the most part from sand, earth, and marsh grass, the tall, thick walls could withstand the largest artillery rounds of the day. Located at the extreme tip of the peninsula and separated from the fort by a mile of beach, the towering Battery Buchanan mounted four guns overlooking New Inlet and the river.[6]

Despite the formidable nature of the fort, there arose a clamor in Washington after the Union victory at Mobile Bay to close the port of Wilmington. Secretary of the Navy Gideon Welles noted in his diary on August 30, 1864, "Something must be done to close the entrance to Cape

Fear River and port of Wilmington. . . . Could we seize the forts at the entrance of Cape Fear and close the illicit traffic, it would be almost as important as the capture of Richmond on the fate of the Rebels, and an important step in that direction."

The tacit approval for an attempt was finally obtained from Secretary of War Stanton and General Grant on September 2, 1864. Admiral David D. Porter was tapped to command the massive naval fleet to be assembled for the operation, and Major General Benjamin Butler was given command of the soldiers to be used in the attack. The selection of Butler came as a surprise to the would-be participants, including Porter, who like so many Union military officials intensely disliked the cockeyed general. Without doubt, Butler was the most controversial general in the Union army.[7]

Jefferson Davis followed the example provided by Washington. When rumors of an attack on the Cape Fear defenses reached Wilmington in mid-October, the Confederate president ordered his close personal friend, his chief military advisor, and the most controversial general in the Confederate army—Braxton Bragg—to North Carolina to assume command of the Department of North Carolina and the defense of the Cape Fear in particular.

The assignment of Bragg to his native state was a source of bewilderment to the people of the Confederacy. In its edition of October 31, the *Wilmington Journal* reported, "We suspect that General Bragg is going to Wilmington. Goodbye, Wilmington." From the enemy camp, Admiral Porter explained the distress suffered by many Southerners: "Bragg's name had once been a household word in the United States, but he was not so well thought of by some of the Southern politicians. It was a foregone conclusion then that Fort Fisher would fall, under his management of affairs."[8]

On December 7, Butler began assembling his sixty-five-hundred-man army at Bermuda Hundred. Two days later, he notified Porter that he was ready to proceed with the campaign against Wilmington. Troop transports set sail from Hampton Roads on December 13 and arrived at a rendezvous point about twenty miles off New Inlet on December 15. There, Butler waited for Porter, who arrived with his vast armada of more than fifty warships late on the night of December 18. Suddenly, the weather at sea changed for the worse, forcing the transports back to the Union-held port of Beaufort and thus delaying the attack for almost a week.[9]

In the meantime, Confederate telegraphers kept the lines busy with the news that the great Union fleet had appeared off the North Carolina coast. Throughout the afternoon and evening of December 18, it became apparent that the reports from North Carolina were true. Knowing the stakes, Lee now had no choice but to send troops to aid the defenders of the Cape Fear, which at that very minute might be under attack. He had recently informed Colonel Lamb that "Fort Fisher must be held or he could not sustain his army; that the Cape Fear was the last gateway to the world." Lee noted that if "Forts Fisher and Caswell were not held, he would have to abandon Richmond."

Upon receiving "a midnight order for me to send Hoke to Wilmington," Longstreet promptly responded to Lee, "General Hoke's division is ordered to be ready, as I have no better troops." Lee was extremely reluctant to part with Hoke's well-oiled fighting machine, for it comprised just over a twelfth of the Army of Northern Virginia. Earlier that day, Lee had rejected a desperate plea from Beauregard for Hoke to be sent to South Carolina and Georgia to stop Sherman. But Wilmington was a different matter. Now was clearly the time when Lee's best were needed on a field far from Richmond. Thus, he decided to hinge the fate of the Confederate nation on the shoulders of his young major general and the 6,155 veteran soldiers in his division. President Davis concurred in Lee's selection, noting that Hoke was "distinguished by service on other fields."[10]

Each day from December 21 through December 23, Hoke put a brigade on the move. Kirkland was in the vanguard, followed by Hagood. The weather in the Richmond area was miserable; freezing rain stuck to the troops as they marched over muddy roads toward the city and the train depot. As the first of Hoke's regiments (the Seventeenth, Forty-second, and Sixty-sixth North Carolina) marched through the Confederate capital for the last time, they enjoyed a hero's welcome. One of Kirkland's officers recorded the scene: "Having been recruited in winter quarters the command made a fine appearance marching through the streets of the capital, with three brass bands and three drum and fife corps, its steady step and fine bearing eliciting cheers from the people. . . . Officers and men felt the thrill which comes to the young soldier's heart from the 'pomp and circumstance of war', and approving smiles of woman."[11]

Meanwhile, Bragg sent official notice of the arrival of the enemy fleet to Richmond. Davis promptly responded, "Hoke's division is under orders to re-enforce you. One brigade has gone. The rest will follow as rapidly as railroad transportation permits."

By the time the first of Hoke's troops made their way through Richmond and over the river to Manchester to the train depot, the freezing rain gave way to snow and sleet. Hoke was about to begin the most important and most challenging race of his military career. Time was quickly running out for the Confederacy. But try as he might to win the race to Wilmington, delays plagued him from the outset. Kirkland's North Carolinians were forced to endure several hours of freezing temperatures without shelter while waiting for transportation back to their home state.[12]

Southern railroad service, now in a state of deterioration, was symbolic of the fortunes of the Confederate war effort. Because the route from Petersburg to Weldon was closed, Hoke had no alternative but to send his men via Danville, Greensboro, and Raleigh. "In the severest bitter cold we had ever experienced," the men of Kirkland's brigade were placed on and in flatcars and boxcars on a train that made its way ever so slowly south.

Though the exact destination was kept secret, speculation was rampant among the troops. Soon after the train got under way, the North Carolinians "were very enthusiastic" when they learned "they were going to defend the soil of their native state." Despite the heartwarming news, there was little to warm the bodies of the soldiers as they were transported in the unheated cars. A soldier in the Sixty-sixth North Carolina chronicled the misery of his regiment: "There was no opportunity to have fires, no way to keep ourselves warm and the train worked its way along, the men frequently having to get off and run alongside of it to keep themselves warm, and to fill the tender with water, by buckets, from the mud holes on the side of the track, and to gather wood to keep the fire in the engine burning." With temperatures approaching zero, the men of the Forty-second

North Carolina survived by building fires in the center of the cars, closing the doors, and enduring the smoke-filled compartments.[13]

When Hagood's brigade boarded the train for Danville at 11 A.M. on December 21, the frigid weather had not improved. High winds blew as the wet soldiers lay motionless in the cars. Hagood noted, "The suffering was intense." After some of his soldiers froze to death en route to Danville, Hagood broke out a barrel of apple brandy that he had secured for his men before the train pulled away at Manchester.[14]

Frequent delays along the route were a source of frustration and anger for Hoke. Not only was the division being detained from its vital mission in North Carolina, but the misery of his soldiers was prolonged by the snail-like train service. Following a long wait in Danville, Hagood's brigade was packed aboard a train late on December 22 for the forty-eight-mile trip to Greensboro on the Piedmont Railroad. However, it took three days for the brigade to reach Greensboro, and then only after Hagood seized the engine and commandeered the train. Exasperated, Hoke pulled the soldiers to the rear off their train and marched them down country roads; they beat the train to the next junction by several hours. Hagood suspected "treachery," concluding, "It is hard to say whether there was design or only criminal mismanagement in the delay."[15]

Hoke was red-hot by the time he reached Greensboro. There, he decided to go to the top with a desperate request for action to save the vital transportation network of the Confederacy. In a dispatch to Lee, Hoke detailed the delays and utter chaos he had encountered, urged seizure of the railroad, and sounded an ominous warning: "The delays on the Piedmont Railroad from this place to Danville are such as will cause much suffering in the Army of Northern Virginia for supplies this winter, and unless change is at once made cars cannot pass at all. . . . My troops are now wanted in Wilmington, where they should have been two days ago. No one but yourself can make the above and much wanted change." Ironically, Hoke's plea was intercepted by the enemy, then recaptured, and finally placed in Lee's hands on January 9, 1865.[16]

Once the trains were in North Carolina, the delays were less frequent, but the bitter weather continued to plague the fatigued troops. Disturbed by the suffering of his men, Colonel John E. Nethercutt of the Sixty-sixth North Carolina sent a telegram ahead from Greensboro to Raleigh informing Governor Vance "that it was necessary that some stimulant be furnished his troops for them to stand the bitter cold." When the train carrying Kirkland's brigade pulled into the state capital on December 23, the soldiers were delighted to find "a barrel of corn, persimmon, or some other sort of 'juice' ready for their consumption." Soon after the train began chugging its way on its southeastern route, the troops "left nothing in the barrel but 'an empty sound', and a more jolly crowd from there to Goldsboro . . . was never seen in North Carolina."[17]

By the time the train bearing the lead elements of Hoke's division was on the last leg of its trip to Wilmington, the word was out that the major general had been sent to the Cape Fear. Union intelligence reported to George G. Meade on December 22 that Hoke had left Virginia bound for Wilmington.

Throughout the Confederacy, there were manifestations of the confidence the Southern people had in Hoke. On December 22, the *Richmond Examiner* told its readers, "The Confederacy is not, we apprehend, about to be deprived this time of its chief port of entry for foreign commerce." Crowds gathered to cheer the trainloads of Hoke's troops along the route. Deeply moved by the welcome, Adjutant George Rose of the Sixty-sixth North Carolina wrote, "All along the line from Goldsboro to Wilmington, especially at Magnolia and Mt. Olive, the ladies hearing of our coming, had such provisions as they could spare from their scanty store to give to the regiment as it passed by." At his headquarters in Wilmington on December 23, Major General Whiting, while "waiting in much anxiety Hoke's arrival," noted that "if we can hold until Hoke arrives all may be well."[18]

Fortunately for the defenders of Wilmington, the weather off the North Carolina coast remained tempestuous until December 23, making it impossible for Butler's troop transports to return to the Cape Fear until late on Christmas Eve. This "special intervention" provided Hoke with just the opportunity he needed. Personally, he was yet between Danville and Greensboro striving to push the troop trains along, but the first waves of his division—the Seventeenth North Carolina and portions of the Forty-second and Sixty-sixth North Carolina—began pouring into Wilmington around 1 A.M. on December 24. Commanding these thirteen hundred troops was Kirkland, a savvy soldier who knew what was expected of him.[19]

After being fed by "the patriotic ladies" of Wilmington, the brigade took up the line of march in the direction of Fort Fisher. In accordance with orders received from Whiting, Kirkland halted his march between Wilmington and Fort Fisher in the predawn hours of December 24 so his travel-weary soldiers might receive a few hours of sleep. Meanwhile, Porter readied for battle "the largest collection of combatant ships ever assembled under the American flag" to that date. At dawn, the admiral began moving the "most powerful naval force ever assembled by the United States" into a semicircle about a half-mile from the fort.[20]

Soon after sunrise, Kirkland had his soldiers on the march again. The horses and wagon trains had not arrived, and Kirkland was one of the few officers who had a mount. He rode ahead to scout developments near the fort. His troops were still hours away at 11:30 A.M. when Porter issued the command to unleash the fury of six hundred guns of the massive fleet on the fort. Colonel Lamb vividly recalled the opening of the naval assault: "This was the commencement of the most terrific bombardment from the fleet which war had ever witnessed." Hoke's soldiers could distinctly hear the explosions as they drew ever nearer.[21]

At 1:00 P.M. on December 24, Kirkland arrived at Sugar Loaf, a massive, sixty-foot-tall sand dune on the east shore of the river seven miles north of Fort Fisher, in advance of his troops. His men, "much jaded," arrived at 4:30 P.M. In the absence of Hoke, Kirkland was anxious to follow the orders issued by Bragg at Wilmington earlier that day: "Maj. Gen. R. F. Hoke, or the senior officer of his division, will command the troops on the sound and the entrenched camp at Sugar Loaf, and will make the necessary dispositions to prevent any landing of the enemy between Masonborough and Fort Fisher."

As his troops continued to make their way to Sugar Loaf, Kirkland rode several miles south to Battery Gatlin, an earthwork outpost, where he found a piece of artillery, a small contingent from the Tenth North Carolina, and

The Fate is Sealed

approximately twelve hundred boys and men from the North Carolina Junior and Senior Reserves. Shells were beginning to drop all around the general when he turned his horse back toward Sugar Loaf. There, Kirkland took measures to prevent the landing of enemy troops. He deployed several companies from each of the three regiments on hand to Battery Gatlin and Battery Anderson, a similar earthwork fortification two miles farther down the beach. In response to an appeal from Whiting, the Junior Reserves and most of the Seventeenth North Carolina were dispatched to Fort Fisher. The bulk of Kirkland's brigade was positioned in an entrenched line extending across the peninsula from Sugar Loaf.[22]

Butler's transports arrived too late on Christmas Eve to begin the amphibious assault, so Porter pulled his fleet out of range of Lamb's guns. Both sides settled down for the night. The waiting game had begun. Whiting, Lamb, and Kirkland could only hope that Hoke would arrive with the rest of his division before the Federals decided to attempt a landing. Without help, Hoke's single brigade on the peninsula would face insurmountable odds in fending off a landing by six thousand troops supported by the awesome armada.[23]

As Porter's big guns ushered in Christmas morning in coastal North Carolina, Kirkland was anxious to monitor the activities of the enemy. He ordered Captain Charles G. Elliott to make his way down the beach to look for any sign of troop landing. Elliott located a pony at an abandoned farmhouse and galloped off. Finding "no indication of landing," he made his way back to Sugar Loaf with the good news. However, a short time later, a soldier came running up virtually out of breath with a report that the Federals had landed and captured some of Kirkland's soldiers at Battery Anderson. Kirkland and Elliott then rode through the woods to a point where they could observe a large mass of enemy soldiers on the beach and more approaching in boats. Kirkland promptly sent forward the two regiments at Sugar Loaf as skirmishers. At the general's direction, Elliott "rode down the line and told the men to keep up the fire upon the enemy and cheer as much as they could."[24]

Leading the first group of Union soldiers ashore were twenty-nine-year-old Major General Godfrey Weitzel, the commander of the landing forces and chief engineer of the Army of the James, and twenty-nine-year-old Colonel Newton M. Curtis, a six-foot-four citizen-soldier. As the afternoon wore on, additional troop landings supported by Porter's fleet took place without significant resistance.

From Fort Fisher, Whiting issued an appeal: "Tell General Kirkland or General Hoke if they can attack we will arrest those fellows between them and us." Kirkland attempted to comply by pushing his thin skirmish line forward against the three enemy brigades ashore. Concerned that he might be flanked, Kirkland concluded, "It would have been madness to have advanced farther, besides I was fearful the enemy would land a force at Gatlin and push up the Wilmington Road, which was covered by but one regiment." Instead, he ordered his forces back to his line at Sugar Loaf, where he could better defend against enemy movement up the peninsula. In a telegram to Bragg, who was still in Wilmington, Kirkland promised to keep up the resistance while he waited for Hoke: "I am fighting them; my ammunition is very short. . . . I will fight to the last." One of his soldiers reported that "a lively Christmas was spent" on the peninsula.[25]

By 4 P.M., Weitzel had almost three thousand men on the beach, and Curtis had advanced his brigade of New Yorkers to within fifty yards of the fort. While Curtis anxiously awaited the order to assault, Butler fretted inside the comfortable confines of his stateroom. Outside, an angry sea was quickly developing; the heavy surf threatened to prevent further troop movements to and from the shore. In his moment of hesitation, Butler received an unnerving report from an interrogation of one of Kirkland's soldiers: Hoke and his large fighting force were expected on the peninsula presently. Suddenly, the general began to panic: "Knowing the strength of Hoke's division I found a force opposed to me outside of the works larger than my own." As he saw it, there was only one course of action. He must retreat.

On the beach, Weitzel concurred, reporting to Butler "that it would be butchery to order an assault on that work under the circumstances." But Weitzel's soldiers, many of whom had to remain on the beach in freezing temperatures with sleet pouring from the sky before they could be rescued, openly cursed Butler as they began their retreat. Admiral Porter shared their wrath. In one of his several highly critical reports of Butler, he wrote, "There was never a fort that invited soldiers to walk in and take possession more plainly than Fort Fisher."[26]

On the afternoon of December 26, Hoke arrived in Wilmington with a portion of Hagood's brigade. After consulting with Bragg, he hurried toward Sugar Loaf with six hundred of Hagood's men and a group of home guards. Reaching Kirkland's line at 8 P.M., Hoke sensed that the emergency had not yet passed. Although Butler had loaded most of his troops back onto the transports, the Federal fleet loomed within striking distance. Whiting shared Hoke's concern. Even if the enemy decided to forgo another attempt at Fort Fisher, it was poised to strike at the other entrance to the river. Consequently, Hoke began to fortify the Confederate position at Sugar Loaf. He put his small band of soldiers to work constructing a strong line of entrenchments that ran eastward from the river at Sugar Loaf to the strand at present-day Carolina Beach. During the evening, the remainder of Hagood's brigade reached Wilmington, where it was put aboard a steamer for the trip downriver to Hoke's position.[27]

Early in the morning on Tuesday, December 27, Porter set about retrieving the last of Butler's soldiers. By midday, all of the men were safely aboard the transports, and Porter ordered the entire fleet to set sail north. Even as the last of the great warships passed over the horizon, all the officers charged with the defense of the Cape Fear save Braxton Bragg were of the opinion that the Federals would be back, and soon. The quick and relatively easy victory at Fort Fisher lulled Bragg into a false sense of security. Although he promised Richmond that his forces would "be much better prepared for the enemy in any future effort near this point," he brashly suggested that the Federals would not be in a hurry to attack again at Cape Fear.

Believing that a second attempt to take the fort was imminent, Hoke appealed to Bragg to allow him to construct a continuous line of earthworks from the head of Masonboro Sound, at the north end of the peninsula, to Fort Fisher. Such a defensive line had been proposed in 1861 by Captain J. C. Winder, the original engineer assigned to defend Confederate Point. Bragg refused Hoke's request; nonetheless, Hoke set about doing

General Robert F. Hoke

all he could to ready the peninsula for another battle.[28]

By December 28, all of Hoke's troops had arrived in Wilmington, and Bragg, convinced that "all immediate danger is passed," ordered his young major general to hold Clingman's brigade in Wilmington, to maintain Kirkland's and Hagood's at Sugar Loaf, and to deploy Colquitt's at Battery Anderson. A day later, a grand celebration was held at Fort Fisher.[29]

Hoke had a right to be pleased with the part his division had played in the victory at Fort Fisher. Granted, neither he nor three of his brigades had been able to reach Wilmington in time to prevent the Federal landing; however, his lead brigade had rushed to the scene as the battle began. Although heavily outnumbered by the landing forces, Kirkland's soldiers had blocked the road to Wilmington and kept the Federals at bay until Butler gave up. Even after he was captured on the beach on Christmas Day, Captain Jacob H. Koontz of the Forty-second North Carolina immeasurably aided the Confederate cause by feeding Butler inflated figures of Hoke's troop strength. Indeed, Hoke could take pride that it was the news of the approach of his division that led Butler to cancel the attack. Respected as "the largest and best division" in Lee's army by the Union high command, Hoke's men by reputation alone had helped to keep the South's last major port open—for the time being, at least.[30]

Nothing, however, could destroy Bragg's state of euphoria on the eve of the new year. Excited by the celebration at the fort and satisfied that Confederate Point was no longer in danger, Bragg decided that Hoke's presence at Sugar Loaf was no longer needed. Accordingly, on December 31, Hoke was ordered to move the division back to Wilmington. Remembering the reason that Lee had sent him to North Carolina, Hoke protested Bragg's order, to no avail. Reluctantly, Hoke put his men on the march. Captain Elliott of Kirkland's brigade recalled, "We marched, with colors flying and bands playing, into the city, and were enthusiastically received by the people as their victorious defenders." The division went into camp near Green's Millpond at Camp Whiting, just east of the city. There, the soldiers would remain for the next twelve days.[31]

On the same day Hoke moved to Wilmington, Whiting requested that Bragg "authorize General Hoke to furnish suitable details for guard duty"

251

The Fate is Sealed

at Fort Fisher and Masonboro Sound. In a curt response from Bragg's headquarters, Whiting was advised, "Hoke's division is held for a special purpose, and it is not deemed advisable to use it as indicated." Bragg now had a special mission for Hoke, and it was not at Fort Fisher. Rather than making preparations for another Federal assault at Cape Fear, Bragg was anxious to send Hoke on a secret expedition to capture New Bern. At one point during Hoke's stay at Camp Whiting, Bragg went so far as to order the troops to prepare three days' rations in anticipation of the campaign.[32] But forces were at work in the first days of the new year that would wreck Bragg's plans.

Despite the abysmal failure of the recent expedition to Fort Fisher, Grant was willing to promptly make another attempt to reduce the fort and capture Wilmington. By taking possession of the port, Grant would not only sever Lee's primary source of supplies, but would also have a coastal base to aid Sherman in his forthcoming campaign in the Carolinas. Again, Admiral Porter would command the naval operations. However, a change of command in the army forces had become a priority, for, as Porter noted, "Grant had made up his mind to do so the moment he heard of Butler's failure." On Monday, January 2, 1865, Grant appointed a citizen-soldier, Major General Alfred H. Terry, to lead the eight-thousand-man attack force. To prevent the Confederates from gaining advance warning of the operation, absolute secrecy was maintained. According to Grant, Terry was already at sea when his orders were unsealed.[33]

During the first week of January, Hoke was occupied with administrative matters. On January 3, efforts were made to obtain badly needed shoes for the division from the quartermaster general of the Confederacy. A day later, Brigadier General Hagood left the division on a twenty-one-day leave to his home in South Carolina; in his stead, Hoke assigned Colonel Robert F. Graham of the Twenty-first South Carolina to command the brigade.

Meanwhile, the Federal mission to Fort Fisher was in a state of readiness. Transports loaded with Terry's soldiers pulled away from the docks at Bermuda Hundred on January 5 and rendezvoused with Porter's fleet at Beaufort three days later. There, the ships remained at anchor for four days while the two commanders put the finishing touches on plans for the "first modern amphibious assault in history."[34]

On January 8, the opposing armies received intelligence reports of varying credibility. Five Confederate deserters incorrectly advised Union officials that Hoke was concentrating his forces near Kinston. On the other hand, Colonel Lamb obtained information that the troop transports had joined Porter at Beaufort. Bragg either disbelieved the report or ignored it, because on January 12, the very day that Porter's fleet set sail for Fort Fisher, the commander of the Department of North Carolina ordered Hoke to assemble his division for a grand review in Wilmington. While the enemy was nearing its destination, Bragg, dressed "in a new suit of uniform presented to him by his admirers in Wilmington," paraded with Hoke's troops through the city streets.[35]

On the afternoon of January 12, a Mr. McMillan observed the approach of the enemy near Topsail Sound, located between Beaufort and Cape Fear. He immediately attempted to communicate his discovery to General Bragg by telegraph. However, "the operator was not in a condition to send the dispatch," so McMillan was forced to relay the urgent message to Wilmington via courier. It was midnight before Bragg received it. At that time, according to eminent Cape Fear historian James Sprunt, "the band of Hoke's division was in town serenading, the officers were visiting, and the men scattered about—Bragg, no doubt, asleep in fancied security." Immediately upon receipt of the report, Bragg sounded the alarm to Hoke: "The general commanding desires you will put one brigade of your command in motion immediately . . . to move by water to Sugar Loaf; the rest of the division will march without a moment's delay to the latter point. The enemy's fleet has appeared again off Fort Fisher."

The long roll broke the early-morning stillness at Camp Whiting. Within two hours of the notice from Bragg, Hoke had not only assembled the division but put it on the move "to confront the enemy." Incredibly, Bragg did not see fit to relay the news of the return of the enemy to Colonel Lamb. But Lamb actually knew before Bragg, because the colonel was personal witness to the arrival of the eighty-ship fleet: "At night on January 12, 1865, I saw from the ramparts of the fort the lights of the great armada, as one after another appeared above the horizon."[36]

At 1 A.M. on January 13, as Hoke was scrambling to ready his troops for movement to Sugar Loaf, he received another dispatch from Bragg. This one provided Hoke's immediate assignment on the peninsula: he was expected "to make every effort to prevent a landing of the enemy." Some twenty miles now separated him from Fort Fisher. The great race against the enemy was about to be resumed. Once again, Kirkland's brigade served as the vanguard. The North Carolinians began to arrive at Sugar Loaf just before dawn, but by that time, Terry had commenced his preparations for a landing midway between the fort and Sugar Loaf. Porter had arranged the warships of his mighty armada into three lines of battle. Two of his frigates, the *Minnesota* and the *Wabash*, together had more firepower than all the guns at the fort. Inside the compound, Lamb had just eight hundred men, a hundred of whom were unfit for duty, to face a landing force ten times larger.[37] For the Confederates, the situation was grim.

Hoke made it to Sugar Loaf about 8 A.M. on January 13, well in advance of his other three brigades. At that very moment, two hundred launches filled with blue-clad soldiers were making their way to a landing spot near abandoned Battery Gatlin. Hoke quickly moved forward, only to find that a landing had been effected. Facing deadly fire from Porter's big guns, he decided it was "impracticable" and "very injudicious to attack." Admiral Porter explained the reason for Hoke's decision:

> The most important matter to the Confederates was to prevent a landing by the Federal troops, or to dislodge them as soon as they got on shore, and drive them into the sea, but this had been anticipated by having a line of sixteen or seventeen gunboats anchored inside of the transports within one hundred yards of the beach. . . . Before a single boat was allowed to leave a transport, there was opened all along the line such a tremendous fire from the vessels reaching as far as Cape Fear River, about a thousand yards distant, that no troops could withstand it five minutes.[38]

Upon discovering the landing, Hoke telegraphed the news to Bragg in Wilmington: "I arrived here at 8 o'clock and found the enemy landing at

Battery Gatlin. . . . Our brigade is in position, and the others are just coming up. The enemy, apparently, is preparing to attack me." While anxiously awaiting the remainder of the division, Hoke deployed Kirkland's soldiers under the cover of scrub forest and sand hills along the Sugar Loaf line "with a view to giving battle upon any attempt of the enemy to advance." As Bragg saw it, "Nothing was left but to post our troops to watch their movements, which was judiciously done by Major-General Hoke."

Thousands upon thousands of Terry's soldiers poured ashore while Hoke, pinned down by the fierce shelling from the gunboats and separated from the landing site by a swamp, was forced to watch, wait, and hope for the arrival of the remainder of his men. Some of the North Carolinians in Hoke's thin picket line, then positioned in the woods looking out on the landing site, wondered aloud why they were not ordered to open fire at the soldiers wading through the breakers.

All the while, Fort Fisher was undergoing a "storm of shot and shell which caused both earth and sea to tremble." Greatly alarmed by the large number of Federal soldiers massing several miles up the beach, Colonel Lamb issued a telegraph of anguish: "Where is Hoke? The Yankees are landing a heavy force." Whiting and his staff entered the fort after arriving by river steamer at Battery Buchanan and then moving by foot from Confederate Point through a barrage of exploding shells. Greeting the colonel, Whiting said, "Lamb, my boy, I have come to share your fate. You and your garrison are to be sacrificed." Lamb responded with optimism, "Don't say so, General, we shall certainly whip the enemy again." But Whiting had brought doleful news from Wilmington: Bragg was busy removing his supplies and ammunition and searching for a place of retreat.[39]

Hoke had his full division with him at Sugar Loaf in the afternoon, but as one soldier recorded in his diary, "[We] found the Yankees had landed in full force and were entrenching. We immediately went . . . to work and threw up dirt that really took the shine of ground mole and gopher." Indeed, by 3 P.M., some eight thousand well-equipped Union soldiers were ashore and busy throwing up a strong defensive line between Hoke and the fort. Making up the ground forces were the divisions of Brigadier Generals Adelbert Ames and Charles J. Paine and a detached brigade under the command of Colonel Joseph C. Abbott. Most of the soldiers in Paine's division were Negroes.[40]

Bragg arrived at Sugar Loaf later in the afternoon and joined Hoke at the latter's headquarters. After conducting "a free conference" with Hoke, Bragg "fully approved his disposition." Throughout the afternoon and evening, Whiting sent telegrams to Bragg with stern language: "You must attack them at once." Dissatisfied with Bragg's inaction, Whiting decided to go over his commander's head, only to receive a stern rebuke from Secretary of War Seddon: "Your superior in rank, General Bragg, is charged with the command and defense of Wilmington."

Whiting and Lamb particularly feared a night attack and accordingly urged Bragg and Hoke to take the offensive on the night of January 13. Bragg, however, had a defensive mind-set and was unwilling to divide Hoke's division or risk the loss of the fortified position at Sugar Loaf by launching a preemptive strike in the darkness. Rather, Hoke's troops, under heavy shelling, "lay upon their arms all night, ready to move to the attack or towards the fort if the enemy did so."[41]

During the night, the Second South Carolina Cavalry—assigned by Bragg to protect Hoke's right flank, to stay between the enemy and the fort, and to monitor Federal troop movements—allowed a strong force of Federals to thread its way through the thick undergrowth and marshy terrain to the river. When Hoke awoke early on Saturday morning, January 14, he found a strong line of Union breastworks extending from Battery Anderson on the beach across the peninsula to a point near the river. He promptly reported the unsettling development to his commander. Bragg was livid, complaining that "not a word had been heard from our cavalry, and they had evidently withdrawn from their position in the night and did not themselves know what occurred." Lamb, however, was not surprised. Complaining about Bragg's strategy, he later said the Union entrenchment might have been discovered by "a reconnaissance that an officer could have made on foot within an hour. To those familiar with the Carolina sea coast at night, and how a man on horseback looms like a dromedary in the desert, it will not be surprising that these horse-marines, not wishing to become targets for the Federal sharpshooter, followed the example of General Bragg and his army, and retired for the night."[42]

Bragg instantly ordered Hoke to assail the fortified line and drive the enemy from its works. Whiting was notified of the action and instructed to scout his front and flanks. Hoke obeyed Bragg's directive and personally moved the division forward into a line of battle. Riding ahead in the face of enemy fire to assess Federal strength, Hoke and his brigadiers concluded "that their troops were unequal to the task"; it was at this point that Hoke and his generals formed the opinion that a Confederate offensive had little chance of success and would likely result in devastating casualties for the attackers.

After reporting his observations to Bragg, Hoke invited the general "to examine the present conditions on his front." Bragg agreed and rode out to his left. At the same time, Hoke and his staff reconnoitered in the direction of the fort and received fire from the Confederate cavalry. Bragg noted, "My knowledge of the ground was good, as I knew General Hoke's to be, both of us having been over it." Upon completing his personal examination of the Federal lines, Bragg again consulted with Hoke and concurred with "the opinion already expressed." As a result, the order to attack was rescinded, and Bragg reported his decision to Lee: "His line has been closely examined by myself and General Hoke, and he considers it too hazardous to assault." In Bragg's estimation, the enemy "had landed and assumed a most precarious position" without horses or artillery. Deserters and prisoners had assured him that one repulse by the fort would cause Terry's troops to repeat the retreat of Christmas Day. In response to appeals by Whiting for reinforcements at the fort, Bragg ordered Hoke to send a thousand of Hagood's soldiers to Fort Fisher by steamer. Supremely confident, Bragg concluded, "I did not feel the slightest apprehension for the fort. . . . With this garrison I considered the fort *perfectly safe*, and capable of standing any length of siege."[43]

Sunday, January 15, broke clear, cold, and bright. Throughout the morning, Lamb watched as Curtis moved the Union skirmish line close to the minefield in front of the land face. Ames's full division was not far behind. At the same time, Porter's landing force could be observed working its way down the beach. All the while, the guns of the fleet continued their deadly labor against the fort.

In the early afternoon, 350 of the men dispatched from Hagood's brigade made it to the fort out of breath, disorganized, and demoralized. Following their landing at Battery Buchanan, the soldiers had dodged exploding shells during their run in the sand to the fort. Lamb realized that the soldiers were in no condition to fight, so he sent them into a bombproof. Braxton Bragg, apparently oblivious to the crisis at the fort, was ready to assign its command and trust its defense to one of Hoke's brigadiers who was unfamiliar with the installation. At 1 P.M., Bragg notified Whiting, "General Colquitt, assigned to the immediate command of Fort Fisher, will be down to-night. General Bragg directs you report in person at these headquarters this evening for conference and instructions."[44]

About an hour later, Whiting began a series of desperate appeals to Bragg: "Is Fisher to be besieged, or you to attack? Should like to know." Twenty minutes passed, and Bragg responded, "Hoke is moving on enemy, but I am confident you will repel him with your infantry." However, Hoke had no orders at the time to attack Paine's division, which held the line between him and the fort. Bragg's response to Whiting was being relayed to the fort at 2:30 P.M. when one of Lamb's lookouts, Private Arthur Muldoon, called out, "Colonel, the enemy are about to charge." Lamb reasoned that there was yet time to save the fort, but he would have to have help. Whiting wired another plea to Bragg: "The enemy are about to assault; they outnumber us heavily. . . . Attack! Attack! It is all I can say and all you can do." Bragg was not yet stirred to action. But when Hoke reported to him at 3:00 P.M. that "the enemy was moving apparently to assault the fort," Bragg directed him to advance against Paine. At that time, the Federal forces nervously waiting near the fort had not received the order to charge. Terry had agreed upon 3:00 P.M. as the time for the attack, but that moment passed, and both armies continued to lie in wait for each other inside and outside the fort.[45]

It was precisely 3:25 P.M. when Porter signaled from the *Malvern* for the fleet to cease fire. For a brief moment, an eerie stillness pervaded Cape

Fear. Suddenly, the tranquility ended as quickly as it had come. Every ship in the great armada sounded its steam whistle in a unified call to attack. Regimental flags unfurled as Union soldiers and sailors raced forward to storm the fort.

Lamb's soldiers leaped out of their bombproofs with wild abandon, sprang upon the parapets, and mounted a stout defense with rifles, bayonets, gun butts, knives, swords, hand grenades, and the few big guns that could still be used. From the outset of the attack, the soldiers inside the fort, although heavily outnumbered, held the upper hand, and the battle took on the early appearance of a rout by the Confederates. In the meantime, Porter, angered by the repulse, resumed his naval barrage, but his vessels were now directing their fire away from the northern wall of the fort to the lower sea face.[46]

Back at Sugar Loaf, Bragg took the resumption of Porter's fire as a sure sign "that the assault was successfully repulsed." Nevertheless, the brigades of Kirkland and Clingman were sent forward by Hoke to probe Paine's defensive line and drive in his pickets so Hoke might "make reconnaissance of the enemy's position." According to Captain Elliott of Kirkland's brigade, "We easily drove in the enemy's skirmish line, occupied their rifle pits, and our skirmishers were making their main line keep their heads down behind the entrenchments."

Exposing himself to great personal danger, Hoke spurred his horse through the dense undergrowth to the skirmish line to survey the situation. When he returned to report to Bragg, there were "two balls in his clothes, between the left arm and breast." A young lieutenant leading Kirkland's skirmish line never forgot the appearance of Hoke on the front line: "The writer recalls the calm and heroic bearing of the modest and gallant Hoke who withdrew from the reconnaissance with two bullet holes through his coat." At headquarters, Bragg took notice of Hoke's close call.

The moment of decision was now at hand. While Bragg mulled over the matter, Hoke rode away to join his troops and await orders. His warriors were ready for an attempt to break the line separating them from the battle raging down the peninsula. Captain Elliott later recollected the anticipation of many of the soldiers: "We confidently expected to run over the troops in our front and drive them in confusion upon Terry's attacking column." But Bragg was not of that opinion. He considered Paine's line too formidable for Hoke: "Their line was impracticable for his small command, and I did not hesitate to recall him. *He could not have succeeded.*" Elliott was dismayed: "When we all expected an order to charge a courier came to Hoke from Bragg advising him to withdraw to Sugar Loaf." Bragg had made his decision: Fort Fisher would stand or fall on its own.[47]

At the fort, the Confederates had gained what Lamb termed a "Pyrrhic victory." Scores of Yankees fell, but on came others, and the colors of the 117th New York suddenly appeared atop the works, followed by the banners of other Federal regiments. Lamb and Whiting were appalled by the swift reversal of fortune. They wasted no time in rallying their forces, the Southern soldiers accosting their foes with whatever weapon they could find. Soon, both Lamb and Whiting were seriously wounded, but the fierce battle inside and outside the fort raged on. Close to 8 P.M., Bragg received one last message from the beleaguered outpost, this one from Major J. H. Hill: "We still hold the fort but are sorely pressed. Can't you assist us from the outside?"[48]

With both Lamb and Whiting down, command of the fort devolved to Major James Reilly, the ranking officer still on his feet. Reilly pledged to Lamb that "he would continue the fight as long as it was possible." Fearing that his wounded commanders might be captured in the fort, Reilly ordered that Lamb and Whiting be transported on litters to Battery Buchanan. As the general and the colonel were carried out of the bombproof, "spent balls fell like hail-stones" around them. Not far behind the stretchers bearing the two wounded officers were columns of retreating Confederate soldiers.

Reilly hoped to make a stand at Battery Buchanan, but upon his arrival there, he found several hundred of his unarmed and demoralized men milling about. At the base of the battery, Lamb was enduring excruciating pain and agonizing over the apparent loss of Fort Fisher when he looked up to see the face of a Confederate general. It was Hoke's brigadier Colquitt, who, accompanied by two nattily attired aides, had come down to the outpost from Sugar Loaf by small boat to assume command. Lamb recalled the meeting that took place amid the chaos: "I was accosted by Gen. A. H. Colquitt. . . . I had a few minutes conversation with him . . . and I assured him that if Bragg would even then attack, a fresh brigade landed at Battery Buchanan would retake the work." During the conversation, a wounded soldier, inebriated from whiskey and enraged by the gall of the three "reinforcements," raised his pistol and took aim at one of Colquitt's dapper aides. His hand was knocked away at the last moment. One of Colquitt's boatmen suddenly appeared and announced that the Yankees were fast approaching. Lamb's hope of saving the fort was gone. There was no time left. Colquitt and his aides disappeared into the night. Left behind to fall into the hands of the enemy were Whiting and Lamb.[49]

By 10 P.M., Major Reilly knew there was no chance to win the battle. Accompanied by Major Hill and Alfred C. Van Benthuysen, a wounded Confederate marine officer, Reilly moved up the beach with a handkerchief atop his sword. Upon encountering Captain E. L. Moore of Abbott's staff, Reilly ended the battle (which Whiting described as "unparalleled in the history of war") with two simple words: "We surrender." Ironically, Reilly had been the United States Army officer who surrendered Fort Johnston, just across the river, to zealous Confederates back in 1861.[50]

More than ninety minutes had passed since the surrender when Bragg sent a directive to Brigadier General Louis Hébert, the Confederate commander at Smithville: "General Bragg directs you send the most reliable man you have in boat to communicate with Fisher, and ascertain facts. Let him say to commander of Fort Fisher General Bragg orders him not to surrender." Meanwhile, after witnessing the disaster unfold before him, Colquitt was eager to alert Bragg. In definite terms, he telegraphed the bad news: "Fort Fisher evacuated; troops rushed in confusion to Battery Buchanan. . . . I will report to you to-night. There is no mistake in this information."

By 1 A.M., Bragg was finally convinced that the calamity was real, for at that time he sent a dispatch to Lee, Davis, and Vance: "I am mortified at having to report the unexpected capture of Fort Fisher." Davis responded, "The intelligence is sad as it was unexpected. Can you retake the fort?"

The Fate is Sealed

Bragg was not about to face the wrath of Porter's guns, and he promptly so notified the president: "The enemy's fleet alone would destroy us in such an attempt were we unopposed by the land force. The most we can hope to do will be to hold this line."[51]

As soon as the news of the surrender spread among Terry's land forces, three resounding cheers were sent up from the shore. Sailors aboard the ships in the vast fleet were drawn into the victory celebration. Fireworks turned night into day at Cape Fear. At Sugar Loaf, Hoke and his soldiers watched in utter dismay as the "rockets and roman candles" illuminated the otherwise dark January sky. Captain Elliott recorded, "Sad was the sight when the rockets from the ships and display of colored lights and blowing of whistles announced the surrender of the fort."[52]

When Porter proudly proclaimed that the battle "did more damage to the Confederate cause than any that took place during the war," he expressed a view widely held in both the North and the South. Alexander Stephens, the Confederate vice president, agreed: "The fall of the fort was one of the greatest disasters which had befallen our Cause from the beginning of the war." Colonel Lamb echoed Stephens's opinion: "The capture of Fort Fisher . . . was followed so quickly by the final dissolution of the Southern Confederacy that the great victory was not fully realized by the American people."[53]

And so it was that Hoke turned out to be a key player—or nonplayer, as it were—in one of the most pivotal events of the entire war. Controversy inevitably followed. In Hoke's hometown, his friend David Schenck wrote, "The heart sickens to record our continued disasters. . . . Bragg was in command and his ill luck has not forsaken him—with Hoke's division [of] 7000 men outside the fort, not a gun was fired in its relief and loud complaints are made against both of these officers. It seems to be the crowning disaster." Johnson Hagood admitted, "The defense is a page in the history of the war that redounds little to our credit. . . . Without the fort, there was inefficiency and indecision, and as a result a strong supporting force did nothing from first to last commensurate with its strength." One of Hoke's men in the Sixty-sixth North Carolina bemoaned, "The soldiers of Hoke's Division had to grind their teeth and bear the humiliation of not having been there." Colonel Lamb opined, "Had General Hoke attacked the enemy resolutely at 3:00 P.M., he would have saved the fort."[54]

Most of the criticism for the fall of Fort Fisher was reserved for Braxton Bragg, and rightly so. After all, he had been the supreme commander during the battles. Whiting was the most caustic in his criticism. Just three days after the fort fell, while a prisoner of war, he penned a scathing letter wherein he charged Bragg with "neglect of duty," and he demanded, "in justice to the country, to the army, and to myself " that an investigation be conducted as to Bragg's conduct. Just before he died in prison at Governors Island, New York, on March 10, 1865, the embittered Whiting wrote a friend, "That I am here, and that Wilmington and Fisher are gone, is due wholly and solely [due] to the incompetence, the imbecility, and pusillanimity of Braxton Bragg."

In the January 17, 1865, edition of the *Wilmington Daily Journal*, editor James Fulton told readers, "There is no doubt but there is strong excitement against Gen. Bragg. There can be no doubt either, that Gen. Bragg has attached to him the prestige of bad luck. Unfortunately, he always has that prestige. Permanent luck means permanent bad management, somewhere. A man with this prestige ought not to have been sent here." Hoke's longtime chaplain, John Paris, declared that Bragg "manifested as much timidity as the Yankees did boldness."[55]

Since the fall of Fort Fisher, a debate has raged among historians as to whether Bragg made a grievous error when he withdrew Hoke from his advance on the Federal line on the afternoon of January 15, 1865. More than 130 years later, the question begs to be answered: Could Hoke's division have saved Fort Fisher that day? There seems to be no definitive answer. Even the participants in the events at Cape Fear differed in their opinions. In 1901, one of Hoke's most trusted field officers, Captain Charles G. Elliott, maintained, "I believe our charge would have been successful because the troops in front were *blacks*." However, Elliott conceded, "The impartial reader of history must decide."

Some Union soldiers believed Hoke would have been successful. In a letter to Colonel Newton M. Curtis, who had his left eye blown away and his face ripped open in the charge against the fort on January 15, a fellow soldier concluded in 1897,

> Hoke with 5,000 to 6,000 men made a vigorous attack on our rear line. Suppose that part of our force which were defending those lines had been withdrawn to support you, and Hoke had come on, or suppose Hoke had captured that line, as he probably would have done if he had been equal to the emergency, . . . and had there pressed forward with his 5,000 comparatively fresh veteran troops, disaster must have logically followed because our more or less disorganized and scattered battalions, worn out with 4 hours tough fighting, would have been hemmed in between Whiting and Hoke with 5,000 men ambitious to maintain that great stronghold.[56]

Conversely, one Confederate soldier confided to friends back home, "It is a sad blow to lose Fort Fisher but I suppose it could not be held." A Federal soldier agreed, stating that Hoke "showed his wisdom" in not attacking, "for he would have got terribly thrashed." Years after the war, when Elliott questioned Hoke about Bragg's decision to cancel the attack on January 15, the major general told Elliott that "he concurred with Bragg."[57]

Most soldiers and contemporary journalists were reluctant to criticize Hoke in the Fort Fisher debacle. Colonel Lamb pointed out, "General Hoke was not an officer to disobey the command to keep the enemy engaged." On January 18, 1865, the *Wilmington Daily Journal* reported, "The officer in command who was ordered to make the attack after carefully reconnoitering the position declined." However, the editor was quick to inform readers that he did not want to "tarnish the fame of Hoke," nor did he believe the major general would "derelict his duty." A week later, the *Raleigh Weekly Conservative* wrote about Hoke, "From the character of this officer, and the distinguished services he has heretofore performed for North Carolina in the field, we feel assured that his declination was the result of honest convictions of the hopelessness of the attempt. We know the officer personally, having served with him in the field, and feel perfectly satisfied that it would have been idle for any other men to attempt what he would decline."[58]

The use of "decline" and "declination" by wartime journalists is misleading. While Hoke's personal reconnaissance of the enemy position on January 14 and 15 convinced him of the ultimate futility of a Confederate assault, there is no evidence that he at any time declined or refused to move against the enemy. To the contrary, he and his men were ready and willing to strike Paine's line on the afternoon of January 15 had the order come down from Bragg.

In the final analysis, it seems that the most egregious error committed by Bragg in the defense of Fort Fisher was his movement, over Hoke's objections, of the division to Wilmington after the Federal failure on Christmas Day. As a consequence, Hoke's soldiers were not where they should have been when the Federals came ashore three weeks later. Hoke greatly feared another landing by the enemy and was anxious to bear the burden Lee had placed on him. On the day before Terry effected his landing, Hoke requested that Bragg allow him to send a brigade back to Sugar Loaf. Instead, Bragg held his glorious review in Wilmington with Hoke's full complement of troops.

Like the major general, Hoke's soldiers were perplexed by the curious conduct of Bragg on that occasion. Said Second Lieutenant A. A. McKethan of the Fifty-first North Carolina, "Why we should have been stopped in Wilmington, thirty miles from Fort Fisher, I have never understood. Had General Hoke and his division been put in supporting distance of Fisher, the enemy could not have made their landing, and without this the capture of Fisher, was in my opinion, impossible." An officer of the Sixty-sixth North Carolina shared the same opinion: "If Hoke's division had been where, it seemed to the officers, it ought to have been, the landing of troops could never have been made and there never would have been a land attack upon Fort Fisher."[59]

There will always remain some doubt as to whether Hoke's division—even if it had been in place at Sugar Loaf on January 12—could have prevented the landing and saved Fort Fisher. Admiral Porter firmly held to the belief that Hoke's division was no match for the firepower of his fleet: "To do justice to Bragg, the best general in the Southern Confederacy could not have held Fort Fisher, with the forces he had, against the terrific fire that was poured upon the works by the Federal fleet."

The Fate is Sealed

After surviving the fall of Fort Fisher, B. L. Blackmore, a member of the Thirty-sixth North Carolina, was of a similar opinion: "Gen. Bragg might have displayed bad generalship in refusing to order Gen. Hoke to attack the federal forces while landing, or afterwards, but at the same time he displayed a wonderful sense of humanity when he refused to sacrifice the lives of Hoke's division in an already hopeless cause, because Porter's fleet could have destroyed a large army before they could have got in shooting distance of the federals while landing, or after they did land, and no doubt but Gen. Bragg was aware of this."[60]

CHAPTER 13

"We Will Dispute Every Point"

Whatever mistakes Braxton Bragg made at Fort Fisher, he compounded them in the initial phase of the defense of Wilmington after the fall of the fort. These subsequent mistakes greatly impacted Hoke's ability to keep the Union army away from Wilmington. Johnson Hagood, who returned to duty ten days after the fort fell, offered scathing remarks about Bragg's post–Fort Fisher strategy: "Bragg, with independent command of North Carolina, remained in Wilmington, until he was pushed out, flittering away his strength in skirmishes, and letting the dry rot of desertion unchecked by vigorous action gnaw into his army until in a few weeks he had no troops but Hoke's division and a regiment of cavalry."[1]

On the evening of Monday, January 16, Bragg notified Lee that he was abandoning Fort Caswell, Fort Johnston, and the other forts protecting the mouth of the river. Suddenly, the defense system of the Cape Fear, for so long deemed impregnable by both sides, was in shambles. With each of the entrances to the river undefended, both banks were subject to enemy operations and movements toward Wilmington. Moreover, the river was now open to the small gunboats of the United States Navy.

Following the fiasco at Fort Fisher, Bragg seemed determined to make a stand upriver. To that end, he concentrated Hoke's forces and the remnants of the commands from the abandoned forts at Sugar Loaf and Fort Anderson. Atop Sugar Loaf itself, Hoke positioned Kirkland's brigade, as well as Lieutenant Alfred Darden and the seventy men of the Third North Carolina Battalion. Posted around the massive dune were the North Carolina Junior and Senior Reserves, under the command of Colonel James K. Connolly. Manning Hoke's fortified line east of the hill were Company A of the Third North Carolina Artillery, Clingman's brigade, and Colquitt's brigade. To protect the west bank of the river, Hagood's brigade was moved across to Fort Anderson, where it was joined by the evacuated garrisons from the forts to the south.[2]

In the wake of the crucial victory at Fort Fisher, Grant was intent on taking Wilmington. Yet he realized that it was one of the best-defended cities in the South. Consequently, he summoned Major General John M. Schofield and a portion of the Twenty-third Corps from the Western theater. Because the bulk of Schofield's forces would not arrive at New Inlet until the second week of February, the Federal forces at Cape Fear were content to limit their engagements with Hoke to skirmishing and occasional naval shelling until that time.[3]

During the three-weeks following the fall of the fort, Hoke did all he could to strengthen his position and boost the morale of his troops. He was resolute in his desire to preserve the last major Confederate port, and he felt good about his defensive position. Others shared his optimism. For example, the Richmond press held out hope that Wilmington might still be saved. On January 19, the *Richmond Examiner* pointed out, "The capture of the town is not a necessary . . . consequence."

Nevertheless, there were clouds of doom on the Confederate horizon. Amid miserable living conditions at Sugar Loaf, some of Hoke's soldiers had already begun to sense that the loss of Wilmington was inevitable. Yet in the bleak days of January, most of the men remained ready to fight. Adjutant George Rose of the Sixty-sixth North Carolina detailed life on the peninsula at the time: "The division, after the fall of Fort Fisher, remained on the Sugar Loaf lines, strengthening the same, living amidst sand and dust and on unsifted cornmeal and spoiled Nassau bacon until life became almost unendurable, but the spirit of the troops never flagged; they were always willing to do their full duty, and always glad to see the enemy in their front." In order to better feed his army, Hoke sent an urgent request to Bragg's headquarters on January 21: "An increase of the ration is respectfully asked and extremely advisable."[4]

In order to keep an "edge" on his army and monitor the enemy's movements, Hoke continually sent out scouting parties. On January 19, he warned Bragg, "I am inclined to think that the enemy will fight to-day." At 2 P.M., Brigadier General Louis Hébert, in command of the forces at Fort Anderson during the continued absence of Hagood, reported, "General Hoke seems to be attacked." There was, however, no significant advance by the enemy, and by the next morning, Hoke could report that the Federals had "returned to their entrenched camp last evening." On the west bank of the river, it was a different story. Union forces took possession of Smithville the same day, thus clearing the way for a future land advance against Fort Anderson. Fearful that Federal gunboats were now free to make their way up the river to shell Fort Anderson as well as his position at Sugar Loaf, Hoke urged Confederate authorities to lace the river with "torpedoes."[5]

Bragg persisted in his defensive mind-set. On January 20, he provided Hébert and Hoke with evacuation plans in the event of an enemy attack against Fort Anderson. Hoke was more aggressive. Satisfied that the Federals were content to remain stationary while awaiting reinforcements, the young major general advocated an offensive: "If the governor would collect a force for the protection of Wilmington we would be able to move against Terry."[6] But there would be no such collection of forces and no offensive.

In Wilmington, Bragg was busy removing Confederate stores and defending his honor in the face of the mounting criticism of the Fort Fisher campaign. Hoke was aware of the condemnation of Bragg by the press, but he was eager to get on with matters at hand—the defense of Wilmington. On January 18, Hoke told Colonel Archer Anderson, Bragg's assistant adjutant general, "I am sorry General Bragg allowed himself to be all disturbed about the article you refer to. My views about the matter are not changed, and I care nothing for what is said in a newspaper. My only desire is to have my superior officer satisfied." Despite Hoke's assurances, Bragg instructed the major general on January 25 to provide him "a report of his troop movements against the enemy on January 13, 14, and 15." The dispatch to Hoke ended with an ominous statement: "If you consider the responsibility of our not making the attack designed in case of the enemy's endeavors to extend across Confederate Point Neck rests upon the part of your force, charges should be preferred against the officer in command."[7]

Hoke had not the time or the inclination to join in the recriminations against Bragg. The major general faced problems of his own at Fort Anderson. Although Bragg had denied Hagood's request for an extension of his furlough on January 19, the South Carolina general did not reach the west bank of the Cape Fear until January 26. On the day before Hagood's return, Bragg ordered Hoke to visit Fort Anderson to inquire into reports that "large numbers of Hagood's brigade are represented as straggling off home, plundering indiscriminately as they go." At the time, Hoke was in great physical pain, reporting, "I have been unable to get about much on account of a carbuncle on my face."[8]

On January 25, Bragg reported to Governor Vance that Porter's heavy fleet was gone, leaving twenty light gunboats. Upon his departure from Cape Fear, Porter spread alarm in New Bern when he reported that Hoke was preparing to attack that city. The admiral's report was untrue, because the only movement of the division that day was the temporary transfer of Colquitt's brigade to Wilmington. When that brigade returned to Hoke at Sugar Loaf on January 28, it marched in without Colquitt, who had been granted a leave.

Even with the return of Hagood, Hoke was now suffering a crisis of command at the brigade level. Clingman had been missing for months, due to the serious wound he had sustained in Virginia. Down two briga-diers at a critical time, Hoke made a number of pleas to Richmond to obtain the appointment of Collett Leventhorpe as temporary commander of Clingman's brigade. Leventhorpe, born in England in 1815, was a briga-dier general of North Carolina troops. Two months were to pass before Hoke's request received final approval. But despite the need for brigade commanders and the desertion problems in Hagood's force, Hoke's divi-sion remained strong at the close of the first month of 1865. At that time, he had 368 officers and 4,706 men present for duty.[9]

Hoke's respite from the imminent threat of attack ended on February 7, when Schofield's infantry began arriving at New Inlet. Three days later, there were twenty thousand Union soldiers at Cape Fear, and Hoke's forces were outnumbered almost four to one. But Hoke was not yet ready to concede Wilmington. In anticipation of the coming fight, he canceled all furloughs for his Georgia soldiers on February 8. The same day, he re-ceived instructions from Bragg concerning his duties in the face of a stron-ger enemy. Specifically, Hoke was to keep a constant vigil on Schofield, who was now in command of the Union forces at Cape Fear, and to keep Bragg posted on all developments. Bragg cautioned Hoke to resist "by all means" any attempt by Federal gunboats to pass Fort Anderson. Planning for the worst however, Bragg warned Hoke, "We must be prepared to move also."[10]

On Thursday, February 9, Bragg left Wilmington for high-level confer-ences in Richmond. In his absence, Hoke assumed temporary command of the Department of North Carolina. Union skirmishers, primarily from the Seventh Connecticut and the Third New Hampshire, commenced bold demonstrations against Hoke the following day, making some headway by driving in the Confederate pickets. On the river, gunboats moved alarm-ingly close to Fort Anderson. Hagood opened up the fort's Whitworth gun on the wooden vessels, causing them to back off. In their stead ap-peared an ironclad, which opened up on the fort. Hagood's soldiers watched helplessly as their guns returned fire with little effect. From the fort, Lieu-tenant David A. Buie noted with frustration, "Our balls would bound from it like shooting marbles against a brick wall."[11]

With the enemy making aggressive moves in his front, with Bragg in Richmond, and with mounting evidence that Grant was preparing to "transfer his movements to a very considerable degree to our state," Hoke sent a telegram to Governor Vance on February 10 requesting that the two men meet in Goldsboro to discuss the growing crisis. The meeting did not take place, due in part to the Union offensive launched against Hoke the next day.

Moving toward the Confederates at Sugar Loaf, Schofield pushed Terry's eight-thousand-man force, supported by the forty-five-hundred-man division of Canadian-born major general Jacob D. Cox, to "a new position, close enough to the enemy's line to compel him to hold the latter in force." Hoke was able to check the oncoming Federals, and no assault was made against his fortified line. Instead, Schofield began to lay plans to turn Hoke's left flank with a joint land and water attack. An attempt on February 12 was called off, owing to gale-force winds and heavy surf.

In the meantime, Hoke, as the supreme Confederate commander in North Carolina, was forced to divert his attention to other matters. He denied a request that troops from North Carolina be sent south. And as heavy skirmishing was taking place along his lines on February 13, he engaged in a verbal war with the Confederate War Department over a plan to make Wilmington a depot for a large number of Federal prisoners of war. At 5 P.M., Hoke warned J. A. Campbell, the assistant secretary of war, that "it will not do to make this a depot for prisoners." But the problem would only grow over the next week. Schofield made a second attempt to flank Hoke at Sugar Loaf on February 14, but once again he was forced to countermand the order, this time because delays threatened to alert the Confederates of the movement.[12]

Disgusted with his inability to make significant progress against Hoke at Sugar Loaf, Schofield decided to shift his attention to the west bank of the river, where he "would not have to contend with difficulties of both land and sea." He dispatched Cox's division by steamer to Smithville on February 16. The following morning, the Federals began their march toward Fort Anderson, first encountering Confederate pickets three miles north of Smithville. Throughout the afternoon, as troops inched their way closer to the fort, a monitor and seven gunboats maintained heavy fire against Hagood's garrison. Before sunset, Hagood was chagrined to learn that all of the ammunition for the Whitworth gun had been exhausted. After a ten-mile march, Cox camped his soldiers just two miles from the fort.

As if the enemy advance against Hagood were not enough, Hoke received an avalanche of disturbing reports from other parts of the Confederacy on February 17. From Charlotte, his uncle, Colonel William J. Hoke, reported, "The enemy hold Columbia. Arrangements should be made to hold Charlotte." From Goldsboro, Brigadier General L. S. Baker notified Hoke that the corps of Union major general George H. Thomas was then arriving at New Bern. Hoke also had in his possession an "intercepted order" from Schofield to Terry indicating that "Schofield with part of his corps is now at Morehead City."

In an immediate dispatch to Lee, Hoke warned the Confederate commander in chief of the grand Union strategy that would unfold in North Carolina over the weeks and months to come: "Their design is against Goldsboro, and perhaps Greensborough in connection with Sherman." In an attempt to maintain the secrecy of the communiqué, Hoke ordered his aide to put "those letters underscored in cipher if you have a signal officer who understands it." In addition to the reports of enemy troop movements, Hoke was informed that the prisoners of war were to be brought to Wilmington despite his objections.

While Hoke was striving to stay abreast of Union strategy throughout February 17, the Federals were likewise keeping tabs on the Confederate major general. That same day, George G. Meade received an intelligence report which read in part, "It is understood that Beauregard has sent, insisting that Hoke's division shall be sent him from North Carolina, and that he has pledged himself to whip Sherman if it is sent."[13]

The situation at Fort Anderson grew from bad to worse on February 18. At 6:30 A.M., Federal gunboats opened a furious fire on Hagood while Cox advanced his skirmish line toward the fort. In less than three hours, Hagood was forced to pull his skirmishers back to a second line. Sharp fighting continued all day, as did the intense shelling from the gunboats.

Under cover of darkness, Hoke sent a staff officer to confer with Hagood about "the propriety of withdrawing from Fort Anderson." Hagood outlined his tenuous situation in a dispatch to Hoke. Upon its receipt, the major general queried, "What do you think best?" At 2:05 A.M. on February 19, Hagood replied, "I think this place ought to be evacuated and the movement commenced in half an hour." Hoke trusted the judgment of his brigadier and therefore took little time to send back his order to evacuate.[14]

Hoke directed Hagood to move his brigade north to Town Creek, a fifty-yard-wide tributary of the Cape Fear approximately seven miles from Fort Anderson. Upon his arrival at the new position, Hagood telegraphed Hoke for further orders. Hoke responded, "Future operations will depend on circumstances." The Confederate retreat to Town Creek was not disturbed, but the Federals took up the chase as soon as they discovered the fort had been abandoned. By 3:30 P.M., the Yankees appeared on the south side of the creek and opened fire on the Confederates, who were well entrenched behind breastworks on the opposite shore. About the same time, Union gunboats made their approach. To impede the progress of the advancing Federals, all bridges over the creek were burned. At 5:35 P.M., Hagood optimistically reported to Hoke, "Town Creek is a line can be held whenever occupied." Later in the evening, Hoke responded, "Hold Town Creek until you hear from me." By that time, however, Cox's skirmishers had begun to press Hagood.[15]

February 19 had been another dismal day for Hoke. Hagood's evacuation of Fort Anderson had far-reaching effects. As Federal gunboats now enjoyed full reign on the river, Hoke's position at Sugar Loaf was no longer tenable, because his right and rear were exposed to fire. As a consequence, he retreated up the east bank of the river to a point opposite Town Creek. Upon finding the line at Sugar Loaf abandoned, Terry's forces pushed ahead in Hoke's rear for six miles without encountering any Confederate opposition.

During the day, Lee expressed his concern to Hoke: "Can we ascertain Schofield's strength?" Bragg, in transit from his visit to Richmond, also telegraphed Hoke, informing him that he was leaving for Goldsboro. Unfortunately, Bragg did not offer the promise of good news: "Advise me there if anything important. We can look for no assistance." Hoke's soldiers began to question whether they could hold Wilmington. One concluded in a letter that "despair and death is the order of the day."

Meanwhile, Hoke's prisoner-of-war problem at Wilmington continued to grow. Some twenty-five hundred prisoners had arrived in the city, and he was forced to send a communiqué to the Union commander at Fort Fisher suggesting that a prisoner exchange take place at Fort Anderson.[16]

With the fate of Wilmington hanging in the balance on February 20, Hoke was still mired in the prisoner controversy. Because he had heard nothing from the Federals about the proposed exchange, he attempted to convince Confederate officials to refrain from sending more prisoners. In a blunt telegram to Brigadier General B. T. Johnson, the commandant at Salisbury Prison, Hoke directed, "Send no more prisoners here. Enemy refuses them." Likewise, Hoke made arrangements to ship the prisoners in Wilmington to Goldsboro. He reasoned that Confederate Wilmington was hanging by a thread and that all his attention should be directed toward its defense. Braxton Bragg certainly agreed that the city was in serious trouble. As he made his return trip to Wilmington to resume command in North Carolina on February 20, Bragg began disavowing any responsibility for the potential loss of the city.[17]

At daylight on February 20, Cox moved artillery into position at Town Creek and pushed forward a strong line of skirmishers. After locating a scow on the banks of the creek, the Federals began moving to the north side of the waterway. Hoke stayed in close contact with Hagood through a series of telegrams, pointing out early in the day, "You must move your command as you think best; at the same time recollect the importance of your communication with Wilmington. . . . I leave the matter to your judgment." A bit later, Hoke's directive was firmer: "Dispute their advance at every available point."[18]

Despite the worsening conditions on both sides of the river, Hoke maintained a strong resolve to keep up the fight. In a telegraph to Lee at Petersburg, he provided Schofield's troop strength and made a promise: "Schofield has 15,000 men. We will dispute every point." At 1:30 P.M., Bragg received a telegram that offered promise: "General Hoke holds his line confidently."

However, on the west bank, Hagood was in serious trouble. Just after 2 P.M., he was satisfied that the Federals were about to flank him, and "considering the overwhelming number opposed to him," made the decision to withdraw from Town Creek. With his troops scattered over twelve miles in the swamps and wilderness, Hagood issued an urgent request to Confederate headquarters in Wilmington: "Please send me the largest and most complete military map you have of the country north of this point. I would like, also, guides to the country north. . . . In case I am prevented from making a junction with General Hoke at Wilmington, I will have to cross the Cape Fear River higher up." Opportunely for Hagood, a detachment from the Confederate Engineer Corps had joined Hoke's command after the division was withdrawn from Sugar Loaf. Upon receipt of Hagood's request, Hoke issued an order directing that the maps and guides be provided to his brigadier.[19]

Throughout February 20, Hoke was pushed closer to Wilmington by the enemy on the east bank of the river. Adelbert Ames's division had rejoined Terry's army on the previous night to aid in the pursuit. Kirkland guarded the rear as the Confederates poured north closer and closer to the city. At Forks Road, approximately four miles southeast of the heart of Wilmington, Hoke determined to make one last strong stand. If he could not defeat the Federals, he could at least impede their progress and provide time for the evacuation of the city. In late afternoon on February 20, Terry's lead columns slammed into the waiting Confederates at Forks Road. Greeted by artillery and a hail of musketry, the Yankees were repulsed with heavy casualties. They promptly erected a defensive line, and heavy skirmishing continued throughout the night and into the next day in the Battle of Forks Road, known alternately as the Battle of Jumpin' Run.[20]

February 21 was the beginning of the end of Confederate control of Wilmington. While Secretary of War Breckinridge could report to Lee that "Hoke holds his position," the news on the west bank of the river was grim. Hagood and the head of his column made it to Wilmington in the morning not far in advance of the Federals. Just past noon, Cox's soldiers arrived at the Brunswick River within sight of their prize—the port city. Between that river and Wilmington were Eagles Island, manned by Confederate pickets, and the Cape Fear River. Hoke directed Hagood to position his "force on the causeway leading from the pontoon crossing to the city, so as to check any advance of the enemy if attempted, and give us warning of his approach."

However, Bragg was once again in command, and he was ready to abandon the city. He ordered Hagood to send his brigade, which had suffered 350 casualties in the retreat, to Hoke on the east side of town. In the meantime, Hagood was to remain in the city to monitor the approach of the enemy. From the island, the Confederates watched forlornly as Union soldiers cheered and danced upon receipt of the news of the fall of Charleston. Now, another Confederate port, the most vital of all ports, was on the verge of falling.[21]

With the Atlantic Ocean to the east and enemy forces at the west and south entrances of the city, Bragg had no place to go but north. Thus, he commenced the final stages of the evacuation of the city. Arrangements were made to burn cotton, naval stores, and other goods that remained in the port. In advance of the bulk of Hoke's army, the Federal prisoners were marched across the Northeast Cape Fear River. Throughout the night, Confederate supplies, including shoes, that could no longer be shipped by rail were distributed to Hoke's men. As he prepared to retreat through his hometown, First Lieutenant Zaccheus Ellis told his mother, "You have no idea, Mother, of my feelings knowing that our good old town was doomed. . . . You can imagine what they were, when I turned my back on our good old town, to see it no more, till after the war." Young Ellis was killed in action at Bentonville less than a month later.

At 10:45 P.M. on February 21, Bragg informed Lee of his decision to abandon Wilmington: "Holding one corps in Hoke's front, the enemy has thrown another to the west of the Cape Fear, which is now opposite the town. This compels me to cross the Northeast River or they will be in my rear to-morrow. Our small force renders it impossible to make any serious stand."[22]

Before daylight on February 22, the soldiers of Hoke's division were ready to march into and through the city. Hoke had orders to evacuate, and according to Second Lieutenant C. B. Denson, he "proceeded to execute it with soldierly care." When his cavalry notified him of the approach of the enemy, Hoke reported, "I will have everything in readiness. Will ride out to investigate it." With the North Carolina brigades serving as the rear guard, the division was put in motion. Despite the gloom that prevailed in the city, Hoke's soldiers remained loyal and duty-bound. Denson was proud at what he witnessed: "The troops never marched with more good order and quiet courage than when they filed through the city, with a section of light artillery at the end of each street facing the water, while masses of blue crowded nearer and nearer the opposite bank of the river."

Most of the Confederate soldiers had not lost their fighting spirit. One of Hoke's artillery batteries, positioned at the intersection of Front and Market Streets, greeted the leading column of the Sixteenth Kentucky as the blue-clad soldiers approached the city from Eagles Island. About the same time, one of Hoke's men observed an "enterprising" Yankee as he climbed to the top of a railroad building on Eagles Island to hoist the Stars and Stripes in the face of the fleeing Confederates; drawing a bead, the Southern sharpshooter picked him off before he completed his mission. When the last of the Confederate infantry made their way out of the city, only gray-cloaked cavalrymen remained. Up and down the city streets they galloped in the last frantic minutes before the enemy arrived. Soon, Hoke's horsemen vanished,[23] and so did the hopes of the Confederacy.

As Hoke looked back toward Wilmington, he could see that "a mass of black smoke had settled like a pall over the silent town; in its extent and density suggestive of the day of doom." The black cloud was a reminder that he had not been able to achieve the purpose for which Lee had sent him to North Carolina. But there were some consolations. His men, as always, had fought nobly, and were yet fighting on the retreat. The dark smoke above Wilmington was not the result of torching or shelling by the invading army, but rather of goods set afire by the fleeing Confederates. Hoke's defense of the Cape Fear River following the fall of Fort Fisher had prevented Federal gunboats or troops from laying ruin to the city. After Wilmington was evacuated, the *Raleigh Weekly Conservative* praised the defense of Wilmington: "The place was defended to the last and only evacuated when the pressure of an overwhelming force of the enemy rendered it necessary."[24]

Notwithstanding the horrendous setback at Wilmington, Hoke remained determined to keep the enemy at bay. He pushed his troops along the tracks of the Wilmington and Weldon Railroad to the Northeast Cape Fear River, some thirteen miles from the city. Infantry reserves had, as ordered, fired the railroad bridge just north of the city after the last of the Confederates crossed, but the Union pursuit was so rapid that the fire was put out. As a result, Hoke's rear guard was attacked on the "right, left, and rear" in frequent encounters with the enemy.

Captain Charles G. Elliott, who exhibited great personal courage in the rear-guard action, described the miserable conditions to which he and his men were exposed while skirmishing on the cold night of February 22: "Our campaign in the barren turpentine peninsula was very uncomfortable. Food was scarce, and we all got smutted by lightwood fires." Once the division reached the Northeast Cape Fear River, Hoke ordered his engineers to lay a pontoon, over which his soldiers safely crossed. However, by the time the last of the Confederates were across, the Federals had opened fire from the opposite shore. In order to prevent a rapid crossing, Hoke ordered the engineers to destroy the bridge. Because the pine boats of the pontoon were water-soaked, they could not be fired, so the engineers were forced to knock the bottoms out of the boats. They heroically did so under "the plunging fire of the enemy, part of which was armed with new repeating arms." Hoke's infantry offered supporting fire during the operation.[25]

After the grueling day, Hoke's men were in desperate need of sleep, but before he allowed them to set up camp, he "ordered a reconnaissance to see if Terry's troops had pontoons for immediate pursuit." Hoke gave his horse to his aide, Lieutenant George L. Washington, to carry out the perilous mission. Accompanied by Second Lieutenant Denson, Washington rode out into the night. They returned with good news, and the division settled down for the evening. Enemy skirmishers maintained a steady fire across the river throughout the night, but the Confederate encampment was for the most part out of harm's way.[26]

Well before sunrise on February 23, Hoke, anxious to keep the enemy off his rear, had the division on the march. To impede the progress of Terry's troops, he ordered his men to fire the woods. By the time the Confederates reached Rockfish Creek, twenty-five miles north of Wilmington, later in the day, it was apparent that the enemy was no longer in pursuit. Here, the division would remain encamped in relative safety for the next ten days. During the stay, Hoke was finally able to exchange the Federal prisoners that had caused him so much concern over the past week. A communication from Hoke to Schofield on February 22 had finally gotten the attention of the Union commander: "I beg leave to call your attention again to the condition of the Federal prisoners in my hands, and to urge upon you in the name of humanity to consent to their delivery. . . . They have been subjected to great suffering and considerable mortality by the delay."[27]

Other than the frequent rains that turned their encampment into a quagmire, Hoke's soldiers enjoyed their brief respite from the rigors of war. All the while, Hoke had to remain vigilant. Scouting parties were the order of the day. Of all his scouts, Hoke trusted none more than young Fax Wood. In recognition of Wood's many daring deeds beyond the call of duty, President Davis, upon the request of Hoke and his brigadiers, had approved an officer's commission for the eighteen-year-old veteran. Hoke was prepared to place the commission in the hands of his spy upon his return from a scouting expedition into enemy territory. In the course of the mission, Wood and the other five soldiers in his detail came upon a house filled with Federal soldiers on a stormy night. Wood was mortally wounded in the ensuing skirmish, but before he fell, he killed or wounded several Yankees.[28]

By the end of February, the final fight for the Confederacy was taking shape. Sherman was to be confronted by Joseph E. Johnston on North Carolina soil. On February 28, Lee gave Bragg the word: "Communicate with General Johnston at Charlotte. Unite with him as you propose for a blow on Sherman when practicable."[29]

That the denouement of the long war was to be played out in his native state provided Hoke the inspiration he needed as the Confederacy appeared to be crumbling around him. But even though the prospect of defeat was

General Robert F. Hoke

casting an ever-lengthening shadow over the Confederate war effort, Hoke was prepared to fight to the end. After all, he had been on hand when the first guns of battle were fired. Only recently had he promised Lee that he would "dispute every point." And citizen-soldier Hoke was not one to break a promise.

CHAPTER 14

The Last Grand Stand
of the Confederacy

When William T. Sherman's cavalry commander, Brigadier General Judson Kilpatrick, skirmished with Major General Joseph Wheeler at Phillips Cross-Roads just across the North Carolina line on March 3, the fears of many North Carolinians were about to be realized. Kilpatrick was charged with scouting a path for the entrance of Sherman's sixty-thousand-man army into the state. Sherman was intent on making his way to Goldsboro, where a store of supplies would be waiting for his campaign-weary troops. He was not anxious to do battle with the Confederates until he united with Schofield's thirty-thousand-man force in Goldsboro. He would then be in a position to join Grant, if necessary, to deal the final death blow to the Confederacy. But upon receiving the news that General Joseph E. Johnston had been placed in command of the Confederate troops in the Carolinas,

Georgia, and Florida, Sherman supposed that somewhere along the way to
Goldsboro, the road would be blocked by the Confederate army. His sup-
position was correct. Ultimately, that roadblock would be the division of
Hoke.[1]

Despite personal reservations, Jefferson Davis had reluctantly appointed
Johnston to the command of the Army of Tennessee on February 22.
Robert E. Lee, the man who had replaced Johnston as commander of the
Army of Northern Virginia, welcomed the appointment, as did most South-
erners, who believed that a miracle was now needed to save the Confederate cause. To many, Johnston represented that miracle. At the time of the
appointment, Johnston was living off-duty with his wife, Lydia, in Hoke's
hometown. Another Confederate citizen of note had also taken refuge in
Lincolnton. Diarist Mary Chesnut came into close contact with the Hoke
family during her sojourn there in February and March 1865. Upon
Johnston's return to duty, Chesnut recorded the comments of one of
Hoke's relatives: "Miss McLean said triumphantly: 'Sherman will be cut
off. Joe Johnston, Cheatham, Hoke, Beauregard, surround him.'" But
Chesnut was of a contrary opinion: "Dear, these are not the days of Jeri-
cho. Names won't do it—blowing horns does not come to much. Mere
waste of breath, indeed."

Joe Johnston was inclined to agree with Mary Chesnut. He was reluctant to accept what he correctly perceived to be an impossible task. Pride
had much to do with his reluctance. After all, Davis had relieved him of
command in the face of Sherman at Atlanta in July 1864. Moreover,
Johnston now held little hope for an ultimate Confederate victory. But
when he learned that he had the support and confidence of Lee, his spirits
brightened: "Be assured that Knight of old never fought under his King
more loyally than I'll serve under Gen. Lee."[2]

Johnston had little to work with to meet the challenge before him. The
battered remnants of the Army of Tennessee, approximately forty-five hundred men under the command of Lieutenant General Alexander P. Stewart,
were ever so slowly making their way eastward into North Carolina. Some
seventy miles southeast of Charlotte, Lieutenant General William Hardee
had fifty-four hundred infantrymen at Cheraw, South Carolina. In addi-

tion, Johnston could count on the depleted but skillful cavalry commands of Lieutenant Generals Wade Hampton and Joe Wheeler.[3]

Braxton Bragg was incensed by the sudden change. He strongly resented being placed under the command of the general he and Davis had sacked less than a year earlier. From Hoke's encampment at Rockfish Creek on March 5, Bragg dispatched to Davis a request that he be relieved from "the embarrassing position." However, Bragg was forced to grit his teeth, bear the humiliation, and move ahead with the task at hand.

On March 3, Johnston had urged Bragg to "interpose" Hoke's division between Schofield and Sherman in order to delay the union of the two armies. Fortunately, Bragg had time to comply with Johnston's request. Schofield's movement toward Goldsboro had been delayed because of transportation problems in Wilmington. As a result, he shifted his base of operations to New Bern. There, on March 6, Major General Jacob D. Cox put the divisions of Brigadier Generals I. N. Palmer and S. P. Carter on the march for Goldsboro. Major General Thomas H. Ruger commanded another division that was to follow. Cox's army counted thirteen thousand soldiers. Bragg, ever the defensive strategist, was ready to go on the offensive with Hoke.[4] Ironically, the two Confederate officers that had been criticized for their lack of aggressiveness at Fort Fisher were poised to strike the first blow in the last grand stand of the Confederacy.

In anticipation of blocking Cox's westward march, Hoke began entraining his division for Kinston on March 5. Two days later, Hagood's brigade was the last to leave. Only Hoke's cavalry remained behind to protect the rear in the wake of the news that Major General D. N. Couch had left Wilmington on March 6 with two divisions from the Twenty-third Corps bound for Kinston.

Although the trains to Kinston ran more smoothly than those from Richmond to North Carolina, the route from Rockfish Creek was not without problems. As the cars rumbled through eastern North Carolina, some of Hoke's soldiers, particularly the men of the Fifty-first North Carolina, were homesick as they passed by the places they had lived in better times. In order to prevent the temptation to leave the army in its hour of virtual hopelessness, the officers of the Fifty-first were ordered to put the local men in an "ordinary box car," to ride atop the car with sentries, and to "allow none of the men to get off as we passed through the section in which they lived."

Not far into the trip, two of the "best men" got off the train while it was stopped for water. When questioned about their violation of orders, one of them pointed to a lady standing in the doorway of a nearby house and identified her as his sister. He indicated that he was going to remain behind to see her, "but would be on next day." His immediate commander, Second Lieutenant A. A. McKethan, "did not have the heart" to stop him or others because "the enemy was closing in behind us and this would perhaps be their last chance to see their loved ones." Before he reached Kinston, McKethan lost "the greater part of my company," and at roll call on March 8, the "First Sergeant and myself represented the company." Later that night, all the men reported for duty. Each of Hoke's veteran soldiers was yet duty-bound to the war effort. As McKethan put it, "The cause was almost lost and he knew it, and immediately before him he could picture his fields laid in waste, his home plundered and his family exposed and suffering, yet even to the last roll call, he answered to his country's summons at the post of danger."[5]

Even though Bragg was willing to take on Cox, he believed he needed reinforcements to be successful. Johnston really had no troops to spare, but he was willing to do what he could. Accordingly, at 2 P.M. on March 7, he telegraphed Bragg, "I have instructed Major-General Hill, at Smithfield to join you with his troops for a battle." And so it was. Much like Johnston and Bragg, still another Confederate general had to swallow his pride as the ever-darkening cloud of defeat hovered over the Southern war effort. Johnston was cognizant of the longstanding feud between D. H. Hill and Bragg, but he urged Hill to consider the stakes: "Should General Bragg be about to fight join him for battle. . . . I beg you to forget the past for the emergency."[6]

Amid the backdrop of rivalry, jealousy, and dislike surrounding Johnston, Bragg, and Hill, Hoke was expected to bear the brunt of a crucial battle. He was the first of the four generals to arrive in Kinston, reaching the city on Monday, March 6. From Goldsboro, Bragg sent word to Hoke to be ready for a fight: "Push all to the front and be ready for a blow. . . . All arrivals will report to you. Move them to position immediately, that no time may be lost after I join." As his troops arrived, Hoke entrenched them on the west bank of Southwest Creek, a significant tributary of the Neuse about three miles east of Kinston. Long considered by the Confederates to be a key defensive position in eastern North Carolina, Southwest Creek was crossed by the railroad and all the major wagon roads leading to New Bern and Wilmington. The ensuing battle would take its name from Wyse's Forks, formed at Upper Trent and Dover Roads in the Gum Swamp.[7]

Throughout March 7, Cox moved his two divisions to the eastern fringes of the swamp at Wyse's Forks. Carter's division was deployed on the left to guard Dover Road. Two regiments under the command of Colonel Charles Upham were stationed at the intersection of Dover Road and British Road, a route that ran parallel to the creek. One mile south of Carter, Palmer's division was positioned on the Union right to cover the railroad. Although many of the bridges across the creek had been destroyed or taken down, the Twelfth New York Cavalry patrolled the creek in an attempt to prevent enemy crossings. From his new headquarters at New Bern, Schofield reported to Grant that Cox had arrived at Southwest Creek only to find Hoke. Confidently, he noted, "If Hoke's command alone is in our front, he cannot detain us long."[8]

Hoke likewise wasted no time in reporting the arrival of Schofield's forces to Bragg at Goldsboro at 11 A.M. on March 7. Bragg in turn relayed the information to Johnston with a promise: "No delay will occur in making an issue."[9]

At Kinston on the night of March 7, Hoke, Bragg, and Hill met at a local home to map out strategy for the coming attack against Cox. Hoke unveiled a bold plan which, if successful, would catch the Federals by surprise and result in the capture of a large number of prisoners. Hoke reasoned that a frontal assault could not be made until the "wedge" of Federal troops under Colonel Upham had been taken out. To both Bragg and Hill, the task seemed "too arduous," but Hoke's confidence in his veteran division "inspired the others to agree to the plan." By late evening, Hill's two-thousand-man command, which included the North Carolina

Junior Reserves and some veterans of the Army of Tennessee, arrived and encamped below Kinston. The stage was set for the battle.[10]

In the wee hours of March 8, Hoke put three brigades in motion. Hagood's soldiers would not arrive in Kinston until later in the morning, at which time they would be temporarily assigned to Hill. As Hoke's men quietly moved off the front line in the darkness, they were replaced by Hill's troops, who "so cunningly" kept the Yankee skirmishers busy while, according to one Union soldier, "the rebel commander . . . made a detour of 8 or 10 miles on one flank and rear, absolutely unseen by the Union scouts until the storm broke."

To get to the rear of the enemy for the surprise attack, Hoke had to make his way through a dense swamp and across the creek. Kirkland's North Carolinians were chosen to lead the division in the difficult, secretive move-ment. At the head of the column were Hoke and his local guide, William "Bill" Loftin, "a man who knew every foot of the ground over which he led the way." The going was tough. In the dark swamp, Hoke's soldiers were forced to hack their way through thick undergrowth and briers, trudge through mud, and wade through deep water. Colonel Upham reported that "much chopping was heard on our right and apparently near the creek," but Hoke's troops were not discovered. After successfully crossing the creek, Hoke moved quickly to get behind Upham. About 9 A.M., the Confeder-ate artillery and infantry on the west bank of the creek opened up to draw attention away from Hoke's preparation for attack. One Connecticut sol-dier recalled, "They made it as lively for us as they could without coming out of their works and charging us."[11]

By 11 A.M., Hoke had flanked Upham and was ready to hit the enemy in the rear. There was no indication that the Federals knew the swamp behind them was filled with Confederate soldiers. Before launching the attack, Hoke called his brigade commanders together for a final consulta-tion; the conference included about twenty mounted officers. Convinced that the Confederate presence had not been detected, Hoke decided to extend his line farther to the right.

However, Upham had just learned of the enemy's approach and rushed infantry forward to confront Hoke. As Hoke's men were wading in knee-deep water to extend the line, Upham's soldiers suddenly stood up from the bushes that concealed them and offered a blistering fire into Kirkland's brigade. One of Kirkland's officers described what happened next: "This sudden check to Hoke and his generals was startling, and here the Major-General displayed his genius. He did not order his division 'Forward to the line!' but raised his hat and shouted to those around him, 'Make all the men cheer!' Shout and cheer they did like a tornado among the pines and rushed with great spirit upon the enemy. Hoke thus prevented either his own troops or the enemy from seeing that he was for the moment himself surprised."[12]

Union soldiers began to drop "on every side," and the fury unleashed by Hoke's veterans quickly demoralized the Federals. They began to flee in utter confusion, as "from the front, the rear, the flank, a storm of lead, increasing every moment, was thinning their ranks." Hoke's swarming soldiers gave chase "with such yells as only a victorious force can produce."

As soon as Hill heard that Hoke was engaged, he advanced across the creek to hit the right flank of the enemy. Despite his inability to get the Junior Reserves to take part in the attack, Hill enjoyed initial success against the right battalion of Upham's Connecticut regiment and was ready to move toward Hoke when Bragg, upon Hoke's suggestion, ordered him to proceed to the intersection of British and Neuse Roads to intercept the retreating Federals. Hill complied, but upon his arrival at the designated spot at 4:30 P.M., there was no evidence of the fleeing enemy. Bragg soon advised him to return to the west side of the Creek "if too late to strike a blow." With Federal cavalry appearing in his front, Hill chose to move back to the other side of the creek. Once across, he was advised by a courier that Bragg wanted him to recross and effect a junction with Hoke.[13]

All the while, Hoke was capturing a multitude of prisoners. A member of the Fifteenth Connecticut who avoided the melee sent the sad news home: "I am obliged to tell that the brave Fifteenth are no more, they were nearly all taken prisoners. . . . They were surrounded by a Division of rebs and they fought bravely and were slaughtered at the onset. . . . It is rather a sad affair." By late afternoon, Hoke had captured more than a thousand prisoners. Lieutenant Colonel Henry Splaine, commander of the

Seventeenth Massachusetts and a witness to the Federal debacle, later re-marked, "If every general officer of the Confederate army had captured as many Northern soldiers as General Hoke did, there would have been no Union army left."

After taking time to reorganize his brigades, Hoke recognized that the Federals had entrenched their position. With dusk approaching, the division was ordered to retire for the evening and entrench on the east side of the creek in front of Cox. Riding out to meet the victorious general, who had completed a series of "brilliant maneuvers," Bragg passed the "trophies" as they were being herded into Kinston. He greeted Hoke by "baring his head" and "joining in the cheers and congratulations of the soldiers."[14] Little did anyone know that Hoke had just won one of the last—if not the very last—field victories that the Confederacy would enjoy. Indeed, Hoke and Hill, student and teacher at that first Confederate victory so long ago at Big Bethel, had teamed to teach the Yankees one final lesson on the soil of their home state.

By 7 P.M. Bragg had telegraphed the glorious tidings to Lee and Johnston. Lee in turn sent the report to Richmond, where every item of good news was welcomed: "We captured 3 pieces of artillery and 1,500 prisoners. The number of enemy's dead and wounded left on the field is large; ours comparatively small. The troops behaved most handsomely, and Major-Generals Hill and Hoke exhibited their accustomed zeal and gallantry."

Upon receipt of the report of the victory at Kinston, William Alexander Graham wrote home from Richmond, "This is cheering news, but the point of most solicitude is, whether a sufficient force can be concentrated to withstand Sherman, and arrest his invasion from South Carolina." Graham's observations were astute, for on the very day of Hoke's victory, the right wing of Sherman's massive army, commanded by Major General Oliver O. Howard, had moved into North Carolina. The left wing, under the command of Major General Henry W. Slocum, was not far behind. But for the moment, the Confederate army had a genuine victory.[15]

With Sherman now moving into North Carolina in force, it became imperative for the Confederates at Southwest Creek to delay Schofield, who had arrived on the scene on March 8, and Cox as long as possible.

But the task grew ever more difficult while the men in gray celebrated their victory on the opening day of the fight. Ruger's soldiers arrived just before nightfall and took up a position between Carter and Palmer. Schofield was not yet ready to force his way past the Confederates. He was willing to wait for the assistance coming from Wilmington, and he cautioned Cox "to maintain a watchful defensive."[16]

Hill united with Hoke about midnight. By early morning on March 9, their soldiers had completed one line of breastworks extending along British Road and another at right angles to it running from the railroad to the creek. Determined to remain on the offensive, Bragg ordered Hoke to lead an oblique assault against Cox. Hill was to "take up the attack" once Hoke "was fairly engaged." Bragg urged his generals to be aggressive: "The attack must be vigorous and determined, as success must be achieved." At daylight, Hoke pushed his brigades across the breastworks and moved to flank the Federals on the right. Finding Cox's forces strongly entrenched, he made little progress and returned to a position on the right of Hill in the afternoon.[17]

Despite the lack of success on March 9, Bragg remained confident that he could defeat Cox. Hoke was to make another try on March 10. Before daylight, his full division moved through swampy terrain in a cold rain in order to hit the Union right flank. For much of the morning, the Federals watched and waited anxiously without detecting any sign of the approaching enemy. Again aided by the element of surprise, Hoke's soldiers were positioned for an assault near Lower Trent Road around noon. Hoke planned to attack *en echelon* with the brigades of Kirkland and Colquitt on the front line. But on this day, the Confederates were rudely greeted by a strong skirmish line.

After the sharpshooters of his lead regiment, the Sixty-sixth North Carolina, reported stubborn resistance, Hoke, who was on the scene directing troop movements, ordered Kirkland to send his entire brigade forward "to feel the enemy, but not to attack the breastworks." Somehow, the orders were misunderstood or Kirkland was unaware that Federal breastworks were located in front of him. At any rate, his brigade launched an assault, contrary to the advice of its guide, who warned Charles G. Elliott, "Captain, your brigade has not gone far enough to the right, and Hoke is doing wrong to attack here." Through "very thick" woods the North Carolinians charged "with great spirit." A Massachusetts soldier recalled, "Out into the open they came, screaming . . . a great gray billowing, surging forward . . . through shell and canister . . . furious, determined, persistent." Federal skirmishers gave way, but Kirkland's soldiers soon found themselves confronted by "a very strongly intrenched line of the enemy, obstructed by trees . . . and supported by artillery." Facing a gallant fire, the Confederates were forced to lie down.

Captain Elliott rode back to inform Kirkland of the trouble. Kirkland responded, "Go back and hold our line and I will go to Hoke for help." Before help could be rushed forward, the brigade was forced to begin its retreat after suffering the South's first extensive casualties in the three-day campaign. Kirkland's losses were put at three hundred. Realizing that Kirkland's brigade had been "roughly handled," Hoke ordered the division to retire. Hill, who had advanced against skirmishers on the Federal front at the sound of Hoke's guns, was likewise ordered to retreat.[18]

Cox was delighted by the events of the day, and when he dispatched the results to naval authorities in Beaufort, he fell prey to unconfirmed and inaccurate reports from the field: "I repulsed them after a sharp fight, in which Hoke's division was routed and he is reported killed. . . . The enemy was severely punished." Although Cox greatly embellished the results of the fight on March 10, he had reason to celebrate. Because every available soldier in eastern North Carolina was now needed to face Sherman, Bragg could no longer remain in Kinston to delay the Federal advance. About midnight, Hoke began pulling his division back toward the city, where the soldiers camped for the evening. Praising Hoke and the other commanders for their "able, prompt, and gallant support," Bragg pronounced the withdrawal the culmination of a great victory.[19]

Unfortunately for Bragg, Hoke, and their soldiers, the terrible crisis facing the Confederacy diverted public attention from this last victory in North Carolina and tended to minimize its significance. Jefferson Davis remarked, "This success, though inspiring, was on too small a scale to produce important results." Had the victory at Southwest Creek been achieved at another time and place in the war, it would have drawn wide-spread acclaim. Assuredly, the Confederate performance there was impressive. Of primary importance, the engagements served to provide Joe Johnston the time he desperately needed to assemble an army to confront Sherman. Moreover, Cox suffered substantial casualties while inflicting only slight losses on the enemy. His soldiers had received a lethal reminder that the Confederate army was still full of fight.[20]

Under orders issued by Bragg, Hoke's division crossed the Neuse and set out toward Goldsboro on the morning of March 11. In advance of the marching column, Hoke sent his wounded soldiers and supplies by rail. Hill's troops were also moved by train. Hoke left Hagood's brigade in Kinston for several days to serve as the rear guard. All communication in the rear was destroyed as ordered. Covering the Confederate retreat was Hoke's old pet project, the ram *Neuse*.[21]

As Hoke pulled out of Kinston on March 11, Johnston remained uncertain whether Sherman intended to move to Raleigh or Goldsboro. The massive Union army had just taken possession of the former Confederate stronghold of Fayetteville, where Sherman's soldiers continued to employ his concept of total war. From the captured city, Sherman wrote Schofield, "We can live where the people do, and if anybody has to suffer let them suffer." With the showdown looming ever closer, Johnston was certain he could not defeat Sherman's entire army. Rather, he hoped that he could isolate, attack, and destroy one of the wings of the army before Sherman could regroup. So as to be in a position to strike a blow at Sherman wherever he went in North Carolina, Johnston concentrated his forces at Smithfield, located on the north bank of the Neuse River about halfway between Goldsboro and Raleigh.[22]

Because Sherman kept his army in Fayetteville through March 14, Hoke's soldiers were able to enjoy a pleasant five-day "march through a fine planting country of the valley of the Neuse." Joining Hoke's command on this march and for the duration of the war were the beardless boys of the North Carolina Junior Reserves. Created in 1864 because of the dwindling pool of manpower, this reserve force of boys under the age of eighteen had been pressed into active duty when the Federals first threatened Fort Fisher.

Governor Vance and President Davis referred to the young warriors as "the seed corn of the Confederacy." When Hoke had fought at Bethel in 1861, these youngsters were but thirteen years old. According to noted historian Glenn Tucker, "They were soldiers before they were citizens, volunteers before voters, and veterans before many of them doubtless had ever touched a razor to his face." By mid-March 1865, the Junior Reserves, with almost twelve hundred effectives, represented not only the largest brigade in Hoke's division but the largest that Johnston could field in his entire army.[23]

On March 15, the day before Hoke arrived in Smithfield, Johnston received a message of desperation from Lee: "If you are forced back from Raleigh, and we be deprived of supplies from East North Carolina, I do not know how this army can be supported. That you may understand my situation I will state that the supplies in Virginia are exhausted. . . . I think you can now understand the condition of affairs and correctly estimate the importance of resisting the further advance of Sherman." On that day, Sherman again divided his army and put it on the move. The eastern, or right, wing under Howard, composed of the Fifteenth and Seventeenth Corps, headed toward Sherman's destination of Goldsboro, while the western, or left, wing under Slocum, made up of the Fourteenth and Twentieth Corps, feinted toward Raleigh.[24]

When Hoke reached Smithfield on March 16, he crossed the Neuse and camped with the division outside town at Black Creek. There, he and his soldiers learned that Slocum's column had run into Hardee a day earlier at Averasboro, located between Fayetteville and Smithville. A heavy engagement ensued on March 16, ending when Hardee decided to disengage about 8 P.M. Though Hardee was forced to withdraw with casualties almost as great as the Federals, he created the opportunity Johnston needed. While Slocum was delayed at Averasboro, Howard's wing continued its march. The distance between the two wings had increased substantially, and the tight formation ordered by Sherman was no more.[25] One of the wings could now be isolated, and Johnston was positioned to implement the plan that carried with it the last hopes of the Confederacy.

Hoke kept the division at Black Creek on March 17. His 5,557 officers and men spent the uneventful day in well-deserved repose. In addition to

"Hoke's excellent division," Johnston now had with him at Smithfield the 4,500-man command of Alexander P. Stewart. Hardee was camped at nearby Elevation with his 5,400 soldiers, having retired there after the fight at Averasboro. The cavalry commands of Hampton and Wheeler were about the area on patrol and scouting duties.[26]

About midnight on March 17, Johnston asked Hampton for information about the location of the enemy and the best site for a confrontation. Hampton reported that Sherman's army, though definitely marching to Goldsboro, was badly strung out. Howard's right wing was considerably east of Slocum's left wing, and in Hampton's estimation, the two columns were separated by one day's march. Based on that information, Johnston decided to isolate and strike Slocum. Hampton suggested that Johnston choose to do battle with the Federals near Bentonville, the place from which the cavalry commander was reporting. Located twenty miles west of Goldsboro, the small village rested on the southeast side of Mill Creek, a tributary of the Neuse. The site selected by Hampton was outstanding. It was located on elevated ground along Goldsboro Road, the single road upon which Slocum's wing was moving. Surrounding the road were dense wooded areas called "blackjack," which contained a complex of marshy streams. Terrain and location were perfect to allow Johnston to spring a surprise on the approaching Federals.[27]

Upon receipt of the report from the cavalry, Johnston was quick to act. According to Hampton, "In a few hours a reply came from General Johnston saying that he would move at once to the position indicated, and directing me to hold it if possible." Hardee, Hoke, and Stewart were directed to move their troops to the site selected for the showdown. Hoke received his marching orders at 6:55 A.M. on Saturday, March 18: "The general commanding directs that you immediately put your command en route for Bentonville."[28]

While Hoke was pushing his troops on the thirteen-mile march to Bentonville, Sherman was riding near the head of Slocum's column on a collision course. At 2 P.M. on March 18, Sherman sent word to Howard that he thought "it probable that Joe Johnston will try to prevent our getting Goldsborough."[29]

General Robert F. Hoke

Hoke's soldiers arrived at Bentonville on the night of March 18 and camped in an area of "low, wet pinewoods, interposed with bay gulls and sluggish drains and having considerable undergrowth." They slept "without fires, on the wet ground, to prevent the enemy from learning the movement." Stewart's command likewise arrived during the night. One of Stewart's soldiers, Hiram Smith Williams, described the feelings that no doubt were shared by many weary Confederates on the eve of the great battle: "Should not be surprised if we were not in a fight ere long." Because of faulty maps and inaccurate information about the distance from Elevation to Bentonville, Hardee was forced to camp five or six miles away from the site selected for the battle.[30]

By all accounts, Sunday, March 19, dawned "clear and beautiful." Peach trees were in bloom, hinting that spring was about to make its arrival in eastern North Carolina. For the first time in weeks, the sun was shining brightly. Sherman departed Slocum's camp early in the morning in order to join Howard. During his six-mile ride, Sherman heard fighting, but a messenger from Slocum assured him that the trouble was nothing more than a skirmish with Confederate cavalry. Indeed, Hampton had deployed his dismounted cavalry in the predawn hours to give Johnston an opportunity to position his army. Sherman rode ahead, firm in his convictions that Johnston was not going to attempt to block his path: "All signs induced me to believe that the enemy would make no further opposition to our progress, and would not attempt to strike us in flank while in motion." But Sherman was badly mistaken. At that moment, a roadblock was being put in place on the route to Goldsboro. The opposing force was not Hampton's cavalry, as Slocum expected, but Hoke's division of experienced warriors.[31]

As Slocum put his left wing in motion at 7 A.M., thousands of Confederate soldiers were laboriously making their way through the thick forests that separated Bentonville and the battlefield, located two miles south of the village. To give Johnston time to deploy his infantry, Hampton's men offered stubborn resistance against the foragers of the Fourteenth Corps, causing the Federals to use an expression coined during the fight for Atlanta: "They don't drive with a damn." Once all of Johnston's troops were in place, the deployment would resemble a giant sickle, with Hoke's division representing the handle and Stewart's and Hardee's men the blade.[32]

Hoke's division, which comprised a third of Johnston's foot soldiers, was first on the battlefield at Bentonville. Initially, Hoke positioned the division across Goldsboro Road. The brigades of Hagood and Colquitt were placed on the front line, and the North Carolina brigades formed the second. When Hoke learned that the approaching Federals were moving to his left, he brought Kirkland forward and placed him on Hagood's left. This new line "was rather a crooked one," the left flank extending to the east edge of the Cole Plantation and the right stretching four hundred yards into the dense undergrowth south of the plantation. Hoke had the only Confederate artillery at Bentonville, and he placed it in the gap, which Hardee would fill upon his arrival later in the morning. As Hoke's troops began to reach their assigned position, Hampton pulled his cavalrymen from the front and aligned them to the right of Hoke.[33]

Johnston had laid his trap well. Brevet Major General Jefferson C. Davis, who had begun the war at Fort Sumter as a second lieutenant, was about to be ambushed by Hoke. When Davis's lead division, that of Brigadier General William Carlin, slammed into Hoke's skirmishers, Slocum's column had moved but three miles. Although Hoke had managed to block the road, his brigades were not yet fully deployed when the two armies encountered each other. Carlin enjoyed initial success by driving in the Confederate pickets, but when Hoke opened his artillery, the Federals scattered. Carlin pushed the brigades of Harrison C. Hobart and George P. Buell forward into a wooded ravine on the left, where they ran into Stewart's soldiers; Carlin also hurried his third brigade, commanded by Colonel David Miles, to the right of the road. Moments later, Miles's command came face to face with Hoke's well-entrenched soldiers. Repeated assaults by the three Union brigades were beaten back by Hoke and Stewart.[34]

Carlin quickly relayed the distressing news to Davis: "I attacked the enemy with Buell's brigade and half of Hobart's, but failed to drive the enemy. The same result attended the attack on the right by Miles's brigade. . . . My loss is not inconsiderable." When the report reached Slocum, the commander of the left wing "became convinced" that he "had to deal with something more formidable than a division of cavalry." Hoke fought a masterful battle throughout the morning. About the enemy, Hagood wrote, "He was handsomely repulsed, leaving a good many dead and wounded men and abandoned rifles in our front." Wade Hampton observed, "Hoke repulsed the attack made on him fully and handsomely."[35]

Though Braxton Bragg remained in nominal command of Hoke and his forces, it was Hoke who was in charge at Bentonville. As Wade Hampton explained, "Bragg by reason of his rank, was in command of this division, but it was really Hoke's division, and Hoke directed the fighting." There were two instances, however, when Bragg intervened. Both spelled trouble for Johnston and his army. The first occurred as Slocum was sending forward reinforcements to extricate Carlin on the morning of March 19. Fearing Hoke would be overrun, Bragg "applied urgently" to Johnston for assistance. Hardee, who had just appeared on the scene, was ordered to send the first of his divisions on the field, that of Lafayette McLaws, to Hoke. McLaws, delayed by poor guides and the wilderness, arrived just in time to see the repulse of the enemy by Hoke "after a sharp contest of half an hour, at short range." For the remainder of the day, the fighting power of McLaws's division was wasted, for it was placed in reserve until 6 P.M. Johnston forever lamented playing to Bragg's defensive mind-set. He later told Hoke, "I believe that Genl. Bragg's nervousness when you were first attacked at Bentonville was very injurious. It was great weakness on my part, not to send him to Raleigh on the 18th."[36]

Major General James D. Morgan's forty-five-hundred-man command "brushed by Hoke" and moved to the right of Carlin about 11:00 A.M. Shortly after noon, the fighting on Hoke's front ceased. Hoke had blistered Miles, and Slocum's command was gripped with concern. At 1:30 P.M., Slocum sent a message to Sherman requesting assistance. With reports of Johnston's troop strength at forty thousand, Slocum was concerned that he was heavily outnumbered. Rumors were rampant that Lee was orchestrating the fight in person.[37]

By midafternoon, Johnston was ready to launch a series of attacks that would mark one of the last major offensives the Army of the Confederate States of America would ever undertake. Johnston's ragtag army of fewer than twenty thousand men had been pieced together from all parts of the Confederacy. It was composed of three separate commands that had never fought together. But the soldiers knew what was expected of them. From Virginia to Texas, the soldiers of the South had hurried to a tiny hamlet in North Carolina to do their duty in the last grand stand of the Confederacy. Gray-bearded grandfathers stood side by side with beardless teenagers as the army formed for battle. The bright March sun cast its rays on gleaming bayonets shouldered by men and boys dressed in tattered uniforms.

Although Johnston suffered from a shortage of manpower, he was supported by an impressive array of generals. This galaxy of greatness included two full generals, four lieutenant generals, and a host of major generals and brigadiers. Throughout the four years of warfare, these officers— Johnston, Bragg, Hampton, Hardee, Stewart, Wheeler, Hoke, D. H. Hill, Loring, Taliaferro, Stevenson, McLaws, Bate, and many others—had skillfully led men on countless battlefields. But never before had they faced such a crisis.[38]

Johnston had hoped to strike the Federals with his full army earlier in the day. However, his offensive was delayed for several reasons: Carlin's attack on Hoke; Hardee's late arrival; and reconnaissance movements by William B. Bate and W. B. Taliaferro. This delay proved critical, as it provided Slocum with time to entrench and reinforce. Johnston finally launched his assault around 3 P.M., with Hardee, Stewart, and Hill leading the charge. Hoke, who had been busy all morning, did not take part in the attack. From their entrenchments, his soldiers watched the Confederate advance with pride and awe tinged with a bit of sadness: "Several officers led the charge on horseback across an open field in full view, with colors flying and line of battle in such perfect order as to be able to distinguish the several field officers in proper place. . . . It looked like a picture and at our distance was truly beautiful. It was gallantly done, but it was a painful sight to see how close their battle flags were together, regiments being scarcely larger than companies and a division not much larger than a regiment should be."[39]

Hardee smashed the left of the Fourteenth Corps, and the brigades of

Buell and Hobart were driven pell-mell into the forces of the approaching Twentieth Corps. One of Buell's soldiers remembered being flanked by the hard-charging Confederates: "Falling back we met a line of Rebs marching straight for our rear and in 15 minutes more we would have been between two lines of the buggers. . . . We showed to the Rebs as well as our side some of the best running ever did."[40]

By 4:30 P.M., the Confederates had regrouped and were ready to launch a second assault. Hoke, who under orders from Bragg had remained idle during the entire first assault, prepared to join in the renewed offensive.

Meanwhile, Morgan's division had been moved to plug the gap caused by Carlin's retreating brigades. Morgan's reserve brigade, led by Benjamin Fearing, encountered D. H. Hill's division and quickly began to retreat after being flanked. Hill then moved against the rear of Morgan's entrenchments. Fearing's retreat created a hole in Morgan's line, and Hoke saw the gap as a golden opportunity and looked to exploit it. However, Bragg, who was not even on the field at the time, sent a courier to Hoke with orders to launch a full frontal assault. Though he knew it was a mistake to do so, Hoke complied with Bragg's orders. His men made their way through a dense pine thicket until they came face to face with Morgan's entire line. In a rush, Hoke's veterans stormed the enemy. A soldier from the Forty-second Georgia who witnessed the charge related his observations to Hoke after the war: "It was at this point that your Div. was ordered forward and I have often remarked that it was one of the grandest charges made during the war. I can remember now, how the declining sun shown through the pine forest in the afternoon as the sun was going down and your gallant division came rushing over us in the last battle of the war. How grandly the officers and men looked like a whirl wind as they made that *last charge*."[41]

The combat on Hoke's front in the late afternoon on March 19 was some of the most fierce, desperate fighting that took place during the entire war. Some of Hoke's veterans termed it "the hottest infantry fight they had been in except Cold Harbor." A North Carolina officer added, "If there was a place in the battle of Gettysburg as hot as that spot, I never saw it." On the other side of the line, Lieutenant Colonel G. W. Grummond of the Fourteenth Michigan described the close fighting: "The enemy advanced steadily, firing rapidly until within thirty yards before I opened on them. . . . The men steadily rose as one man and poured into the enemy the most terrific fire I ever listened to, nothing could withstand it."

Hoping for the best, Major General Davis remarked to an aide, "If Morgan's troops can stand this, all is right; if not the day is lost." Hoke was in the thick of the fight. At one point, Grummond's commanding officer, Brigadier General William Vandever, reported, "The rebel General Hoke was also captured, but in the melee in sending prisoners to the rear through the swamp he effected his escape."[42]

McLaws moved forward late in the afternoon to take part in Hoke's frontal assault, but Morgan was nevertheless able to hold his line. In the meantime, Hill had been driven back by soldiers from the Twentieth Corps. By sundown, Slocum's wing had been battered and bloodied but not destroyed.[43]

Hoke's soldiers spent another miserable night on the wet ground without fires. Much time was devoted to building a strong defensive line and tending to the wounded. In the ill-advised frontal assault, Hoke had suffered extensive casualties. The Thirty-first North Carolina sustained losses of 50 percent, while the Thirty-sixth North Carolina lost 152 of 267 men. In all, Hoke lost 593 men—45 killed, 370 wounded, and 178 missing and presumed captured. Johnson Hagood blamed Bragg for the casualties and the lack of success in the field: "The loss in our division at least would have been inconsiderable and our success eminent had it not been for Bragg's undertaking to give a tactical order upon a field that he had not seen."[44]

Sherman received word of the near-disaster at Bentonville at Howard's camp, twenty miles from the battlefield. By 3 A.M. on March 20, Howard had the Seventeenth Corps moving to the rescue of Slocum. The Fifteenth Corps followed not far behind. Johnston was forced to realign his troops as Howard's approaching men posed a threat to Hoke's rear. The new V-shaped formation enabled Johnston to face the left wing on the west and the oncoming right wing from the east. There were, however, two serious drawbacks to the new alignment: Johnston could only escape by crossing

Mill Creek, and he did not have the soldiers to sufficiently man the long lines.[45]

Skirmishing was the order of the day on March 20. There was no heavy fighting except on Hoke's front. The new Confederate formation made it necessary for Hoke to establish a new line parallel to Goldsboro Road. Amid the morning's skirmishing, his soldiers fashioned new breastworks fortified with "logs filled with earth." By noon, nearly all of the Fifteenth Corps had reached the battlefield. It was obvious to the Federals that Kirkland's brigade had not completed fortifying its new position. Consequently, a number of fierce assaults were made against Hoke from noon until sunset.[46]

According to George Rose, adjutant of the Sixty-sixth North Carolina, Kirkland's men were engaged "in rolling together logs and making such defenses as they could" when Howard instituted his repeated attacks against Hoke. As the onslaught began, Hoke's soldiers were ordered to take cover "behind such obstructions as they could find, and to await the order to fire until the advance came very near to them." When the charging Federals were within a hundred yards, the Confederates were ordered to fire; to a man, Hoke's soldiers raised to their knees and offered a deadly hailstorm of bullets. Rose witnessed the carnage: "Their ranks were mowed down like wheat before the scythe. . . . When the line went forward, the whole front was covered with the dead and dying, and showed the effect of troops obeying the commands of their officers, to shoot low and wait until the enemy was near upon them."

Word that Hoke and Kirkland were being attacked spread to the rear of the lines, where Johnston was attempting to rest after the rigors of the past few days. An aide galloped up to the commander's position and exclaimed, "General, they are attacking Kirkland's Brigade." Johnston, exhibiting no sense of alarm, rolled over on his pallet and replied, "Let them attack. I know of no brigade in the Southern Army I would sooner they would attack." Johnston's confidence in Hoke's soldiers was borne out. He later wrote, "The Federal army was united before us about noon, and made repeated attacks, between that time and sunset, upon Hoke's division; the most spirited of them was the last, made upon Kirkland's brigade. In all, the enemy was so effectually driven back, that our infirmary corps brought in a number of their wounded that had been left on the field."[47]

In addition to Kirkland's soldiers, another of Hoke's brigades of North Carolinians played a key role in repelling the Federal assaults on the afternoon of March 20. The boys of the Junior Reserves stood firm against the veteran Union brigades. Commanding the skirmish line of teenagers was their veteran officer, seventeen-year-old lieutenant colonel Walter Clark. Just a year earlier, Clark had graduated first in his class at the University of North Carolina. Said to have been the youngest officer of his rank in either army, the gallant North Carolinian inspired the youngsters manning the front line during the engagement. In a letter to his mother after the battle, Clark described the savage fighting to which he was exposed: "I commanded the Skirmish line of our Brigade on Monday. It was in a good woods for skirmishing. . . . We had a regular Indian fight of it behind trees. They charged our line twice but were both times driven back. . . . General Hoke complimented our Brigade very highly."

Clark was right. Hoke, who as a major general was only ten years older than his boy soldiers, was indeed proud of the "unripe wheat," as they were sometimes called. Although Hoke was always reticent about discussing wartime experiences, he showed no hesitation in praising the Junior Reserves in 1890:

> The question of the courage of the Junior Reserves was well established by themselves in the battle below Kinston, and at the battle of Bentonville. At Bentonville, you will remember, they held a very important part of the battle field in opposition to Sherman's old and tried soldiers, and repulsed every charge that was made upon them with very meagre and rapidly thrown up breast works. Their behavior in camp, on the march, and on the battlefield was everything that could be expected of them, and I am free to say, was equal to that of the old soldiers, who had passed through four years of war.[48]

By nightfall on March 20, the fighting was over for the day. Sherman's army was united, and Johnston was surrounded on three sides by enemy troops. No longer was there an opportunity to deal Sherman a staggering blow. About sundown, the heavens opened up and a torrential rain fell upon the battlefield. Mill Creek was already swollen from recent heavy rains, and with the bridge over the creek offering the only avenue for Johnston's escape, many Confederates thought they would be leaving during the night. But Johnston was determined to remain another day.[49]

Morning broke on Tuesday, March 21, with Hoke manning the east side of the Confederate line in the face of Howard's wing. Hagood guarded Hoke's left flank and Kirkland watched the right. Rain continued to fall as Union skirmishers opened fire along the entire front, but for the most part, Hoke's line was spared heavy action.[50]

Though his hodgepodge army had fought gamely against a numerically superior enemy, Johnston was unable to achieve the result he sought. News that Schofield had reached Goldsboro left Johnston no alternative but to retreat from Bentonville. Throughout the night of March 21, all the Confederate wounded who could be moved were loaded aboard ambulances and sent across the creek. Rain added to the misery, turning the roads and camps into a quagmire. At 2 A.M. on March 22, the Confederate retreat began in earnest, but the muddy conditions made for slow going. By daybreak, the rear guard, composed of Hoke's infantry and Wheeler's cavalry, was still near the battlefield. But soon, these last Confederates turned their backs on Bentonville. One North Carolina soldier expressed the sentiments of many of Hoke's veterans as they began their retreat: "Many . . . saw the sun of the South rise in glory at Bethel, and set in its blood-sheen at Bentonville."[51]

Sherman's less-than-spirited pursuit of Johnston's army ended a few miles beyond the bridge, and Hoke's soldiers were able to enjoy a relatively peaceful march. Hoke set up camp for the night five miles outside Smithfield, where he could take stock of the momentous events of recent days. He and his men had been key players in the largest battle ever fought on the soil of his native state and, as it turned out, the last major battle of the war.[52] Sherman's massive army had been fought to a standoff, but that was now of little consequence. Victory, it seemed, was no longer to be had. Yet the time to surrender was not at hand. Hoke and his comrades could still hear the clarion call to duty.

CHAPTER 15

"But It Is All Over Now"

Following the disengagement of the two armies at Bentonville, Johnston moved his entire army north across the Neuse River and set up camp around Smithfield, some fifteen miles from the battlefield. Still anxious to impede Sherman's march to Virginia, Johnston viewed the Smithfield area as an excellent strategic position from which he could quickly make a move whenever the need arose.[1]

Rather than take up an immediate pursuit of Johnston, the Federals moved to Goldsboro, where the large store of supplies so long promised to the soldiers was located. For almost three weeks, Sherman rested his troops there while consulting with Lincoln and Grant about the future course of the war. In the meantime, twenty-five miles to the west, Johnston used Sherman's exercise in caution to his advantage. Buoyed by the arrival of several thousand troops from Georgia, he set about consolidating and reorganizing his patchwork army in an attempt to put it "into effective condition for further service." Johnston divided his forces into two commands: the remnants of the Army of Tennessee were placed under Lieutenant General Alexander P. Stewart, and the other three divisions—Hoke's, McLaws's, and Taliaferro's—were formed into a corps under Lieutenant General William J. Hardee. After Bentonville, Braxton Bragg, at his own request, had been relieved of field command.[2]

Soon after the retreat from Bentonville, Hoke encamped his division on the north side of Smithfield along the railroad tracks near present-day Selma. News soon arrived that Sherman had vanished. As one of Hoke's soldiers noted, "That was the last armed force that we saw in our front during the war." Like Johnston, Hoke was determined to use the lull in fighting to rehabilitate his division. The inability to bring in recruits and attrition brought on by disease, desertion, and battle casualties had greatly depleted the ranks of his division since its return to North Carolina. According to Johnson Hagood, "Brigades had become regiments, regiments companies, and some organizations had almost ceased to exist." A field return of Hardee's corps on March 26 revealed that Hoke had 3,919 effectives present for duty. That total was no doubt bolstered by the inclusion of formerly detached units such as the Fiftieth North Carolina, which had just been assigned to Kirkland's brigade. Hoke was aware that on paper there were sufficient men on his brigade rolls, and he believed that if all were returned to active duty, his vaunted division would once again be restored to its combat potential.[3]

Ready to continue the fight and reluctant to believe the war was lost, Hoke was determined to recover the soldiers who were absent from his command. To that end, he was willing to part with a veteran brigadier general. On March 30, he issued orders to Johnson Hagood to return to South Carolina to recruit his brigade. Hoke's efforts to rebuild his division were destined for naught. Time was fast running out for the Confederate war effort. Before Hagood's forty-day assignment came to a close, the war would be over.[4]

As the warm days of April replaced the gloom of March, Hoke remained at Smithfield, where he continued to prepare his charges as if there would be no end to the war. On a daily basis, his troops were drilled and inspected. His fortitude and example were infectious in the division. Lieutenant Colonel Walter Clark informed his mother in a letter, "While I am able for service I intend to stand by the cause while a banner floats to tell where Freedom and freedom's sons still support her cause."[5]

When Hoke's 4,126 men stood at attention during a general review by Johnston on Tuesday, April 4, they represented what was by far the largest Confederate division in the state. Visitors made their way to the Confederate encampment at Smithfield in an attempt to bring cheer to the troops. Brigadier General Clingman arrived on crutches, not fully recuperated from the serious leg wound sustained in Virginia. After visiting Hoke and the men of his brigade, Clingman called on Johnston to ask the Virginian for the honor of commanding the rear guard of the army. Observing that Clingman could not even walk, Johnston turned down the request. Clingman, like Hoke, still had the fire of the fight in his eyes and speech. He implored Johnston, "Sir, much has been said about dying in the last ditch. You have left with you here thirty thousand of as brave men as the sun ever shone upon. Let us take our stand here and fight the two armies of Grant and Sherman to the end, and thus show to the world how far we can surpass the Thermopylae of the Greeks." Johnston, who was growing increasingly tired of the war and more and more convinced of its futility, replied, "I'm not in the Thermopylae business."[6]

On April 5, rumors about the fall of Richmond spread throughout the camp. But before the gloomy reports could cast a pall over Johnston's army, events at the encampment a day later served to boost the spirits of the soldiers, the North Carolinians in particular. Many civilians, including ladies from Raleigh, accompanied Governor Vance and officers of the state and Confederate governments for a grand review of Johnston's army. One observer noted that the Confederates "once more . . . began to look like soldiers," while one of Hoke's soldiers proudly recorded, "The army presented a fine appearance and the men were in excellent spirits." Captain William H. S. Burgwyn of Clingman's brigade described a group of veterans not yet ready to lay down their guns: "It was a splendid body of American soldiers; survivors of a hundred battlefields; and they marched proudly in review before their General, they were conscious of duty nobly done and nerved for any further service that might be required of them in defense of their country." As the troops passed in review, the ladies sent up the loudest cheers for Hoke's soldiers.

Following the ceremony, Vance made his way to Hoke's headquarters, where the noted orator presented "one of his wonderful speeches" to the members of the North Carolina Junior Reserves. But the Confederate soldiers who assembled for the elaborate review that April day took part in the last great military rally for the flagging war effort.[7]

In the meantime, at Goldsboro, Sherman learned on April 6 that Richmond had fallen. Consequently, his role in bringing the war to a close was altered. No longer would he make his way to Virginia; rather, he would attack Johnston in the rear. Two days later, Sherman informed Grant that he was ready for the final push: "On Monday at daylight all my army will move straight on Joe Johnston, supposed to be between me and Raleigh, and I will follow him wherever he may go."

Sensing that Sherman was ready to begin pursuit, Johnston ordered Hoke and his other division commanders to have their wagons packed and their troops ready to march at reveille on April 10. As Hoke prepared his men for what would be their final march of the war, his forces, with 3,998 arms and 371,563 rounds of ammunition, were the most heavily armed Confederate division in the Eastern theater.[8]

Early on the morning of Monday, April 10, Sherman put his 88,948-man army on the march toward the state capital in pursuit of Johnston. Although neither Sherman nor his soldiers had received the news of Lee's surrender, they could sense that the end of the war was in sight, and the slow march to Raleigh was characterized by singing and jubilant shouting. Sherman was still businesslike in his approach, reporting to Grant that "I will push Joe Johnston to the death."[9]

With a massive army moving on his rear, Johnston had no alternative but to put his loyal band of 14,402 armed soldiers on the march. Hoke issued orders to prepare to move at 10 A.M. on April 10. A half-hour before noon, the division passed through Smithfield in a heavy rainfall that cast a pall over the business of the day. Hoke halted the division for the day about five miles west of Smithfield on Raleigh Road. Once again, the camp was rife with rumors, especially tales about the surrender of Lee in Virginia. Most of the soldiers were unwilling to believe the stories of the parolees who were now filtering into North Carolina after the surrender at Appomattox. A South Carolinian in Hoke's division wrote, "Major Cleland K. Hager of the artillery, upon today's march, intimated to me that General Lee had met with a disaster, a few hours later the army was filled with vague rumors upon the subject."[10]

As both armies began making their way toward Raleigh, the last significant state capital in Confederate hands, Governor Vance continued preparations to protect the city from destruction. He had already shipped a vast storehouse of supplies from the city westward to Salisbury. Now, with an enemy invasion of Raleigh imminent, Vance conferred with David L. Swain, the president of the University of North Carolina and a former governor, about the impending crisis. Swain convinced Vance to consider sending a commission to Sherman, with General Johnston's approval, for the purpose of seeking a suspension of military operations until the state could determine its future.[11]

At 1:00 A.M. on April 11, Johnston received a telegram from Jefferson Davis, then at Danville, "conveying the intelligence that an unofficial report had just been brought to that place, to the effect that General Lee had surrendered on Sunday, the 9th." All hope that Lee could bring his army to North Carolina was dashed upon receipt of the telegram, but Johnston did not immediately spread the grim news. He knew that he must maintain an orderly retreat; panic must not destroy his army. On April 11, Hoke marched his division fifteen miles even though the troops "were out of marching condition." Straggling became a problem before the division bivouacked approximately five miles east of Raleigh, near the site of the modern town of Garner. At 9:30 P.M., marching orders for the following day were issued by Johnston. Hoke was to move at 6:00 A.M. on a route that would take him through Raleigh toward the railroad bridge over the Haw River. It was then apparent that there would be no fight for the capital city of Hoke's native state.[12]

General Robert F. Hoke

Throughout April 11, Sherman moved his army into and took possession of Smithfield after encountering stiff resistance from the Confederate rear guard. There, he rested his soldiers for the night.[13]

In the early-morning hours of Wednesday, April 12, the pace of events quickened. At Raleigh, Vance prepared to dispatch his commissioners— William Alexander Graham and David Swain—for an interview with Sherman "for the purpose of conferring upon the subject of a suspension of hostilities, with view to further communications with the authorities of the United States, touching the final termination of the existing war."[14]

In the meantime, Sherman had received confirmation from Grant that Lee had surrendered. Within hours of the notification, the Union army was marching toward Raleigh. Before departing Smithfield, Sherman issued Special Field Orders No. 54, wherein he broke the good news to his soldiers and challenged them to finish the job: "A little more labor, a little more toil on our part, the great race is won, and our Government stands regenerated after four long years of bloody war."[15]

Throughout the morning and afternoon of April 12, Johnston's soldiers marched through the streets of Raleigh. As in the past, citizens watched with pride as bands played "Dixie" and other popular airs. But this time, the revelry was gone, for citizens and ragged soldiers alike knew that this was the "last hurrah" for both Raleigh and the Confederacy.

When Hoke and his division moved into the city around midday, it was all too apparent that the state capital was being "rapidly evacuated." Upon entering "the once proud Capital of North Carolina," one of Hoke's soldiers observed that "now all was wrapped in gloom, uncertainty and dread." As depressing as the scene was, Hoke remained proud of the soldierly discipline of the men and boys of his command. Watching the North Carolina Junior Reserves march through the city, Hoke was taken with their sense of duty in an hour of despair: "On the retreat through Raleigh, where many passed by their homes, scarcely one of them left their ranks to bid farewell to their friends, though they knew not where they were going and what dangers they would encounter." Likewise, Sherman's cavalry commander, Major General Judson Kilpatrick, was personal witness to the fight remaining in Hoke's soldiers. At 11:50 A.M. on

April 12, he reported, "They have a long wagon train and are fighting stubbornly."[16]

As the long gray lines continued through the city during the afternoon, Vance grew anxious when the commissioners failed to return. He had expected to see them by 4 P.M. at the latest. Vance later explained his cause for concern: "It was extremely important that they should return at that time, for the city of Raleigh was to be completely uncovered that night and the remaining of the Governor and all state officers in the discharge of their duties depended on the reply which was expected from General Sherman."[17]

While Hoke's soldiers pressed ahead to the place selected for the division encampment, a site about seven miles west of the capital near modern-day Cary, Hoke remained in the Raleigh area to monitor political and military events. Word about the city was that President Davis had authorized Hoke to arrest Vance, Swain, and Graham if it were determined that they were negotiating the surrender of North Carolina. Indeed, rumors concerning the crisis facing Raleigh and the state dominated talk on the streets as the last hopes of the dying Confederate cause marched toward the sinking sun with their backs to the city.

In the midst of the hubbub, General Johnston's adjutant general hailed Hoke on a downtown street and remarked, "Have you heard the latest news that Vance has surrendered the State of North Carolina to Sherman?" Hoke expressed disbelief, but he realized there was only one way to ascertain the truth. Accompanied by his orderly, Hoke promptly made his way to the steps of the State Capitol. Giving the reins of his horse to the orderly, Hoke dashed into the building and knocked on the door of the governor's office. Vance told him to enter, and upon doing so, Hoke discovered that the governor was embroiled in a debate with a group of noted Raleigh citizens, among them Bartholomew F. Moore, a distinguished jurist who had formerly served the state as attorney general; William Woods Holden, the editor who had enraged Hoke and many of his comrades with his diatribes for peace; Kenneth Rayner, a former United States congressman and the dean of the North Carolina bar; and Judge George Edmund Badger, who on a bright April day in Raleigh just four years earlier had foretold the military greatness of an untested soldier, Robert Frederick Hoke.

Anxious to talk with Vance alone, Hoke told the governor, "I want a five minutes' interview with you." Vance consented, and the two men walked out of the room and stood at the window of the office of the governor's secretary. Hoke wasted no time in getting to the point: "It is currently rumored upon the streets of Raleigh that you have surrendered the State of North Carolina to Sherman." Vance responded, "You see that bunch in there talking to me; they are trying their best to get me to do it, but all hell can't make me do it." Expressing delight at the governor's resolve, Hoke bid him farewell. But before leaving the building, the general sought reassurance: "I suppose I can depend this being your final action." Again Vance replied, "All hell cannot make me do it."[18]

Two years before he died, as he was walking past the spot where Johnston's aide had told him the rumor forty-five years earlier, Hoke vividly remembered his call upon the governor. He recalled his conviction on that day: "I left feeling very much relieved. I loved Vance as a brother, but I went there for the purpose, if he had made up his mind to do such a thing to arrest him and take him along with me and in that way prevent it."[19]

When darkness came to the capital city on the night of April 12, Vance was still present, but there was no sign of Swain and Graham. Some Confederate cavalrymen were still patrolling, and the last elements of Hoke's division, now the rear guard of the Confederate army, were passing out of the city.[20] Somehow, it was fitting that Hoke should command the last of the men in gray to leave the capital just before the great stage upon which so many American lives had been sacrificed was clothed in darkness. After all, Hoke had been in the first group of North Carolina soldiers to leave the city in 1861 as the curtain was about to go up on one of the greatest tragedies in American history.

The last train out of the city, loaded with state officials and records, pulled out of the station at 9 P.M. Vance remained behind, growing more fearful by the minute that his commissioners had been taken prisoner. Jonathan Worth, the state treasurer, appealed to the governor to wait and personally surrender the city to Sherman when he came. That was the dip-lomatic voice Vance heard during the hours of indecision on the night of April 12. But there was a military voice that sounded louder and clearer. Before leaving Raleigh earlier in the evening, Hoke had urged the chief executive to join him at his camp in order to avoid possible capture by the Union army. Cognizant that the governors of Georgia and South Carolina had escaped Sherman, Vance was determined to do the same. Finally, just before midnight, Vance penned a letter to Sherman informing the general that Mayor William H. Harrison was authorized to surrender Raleigh, and he again requested that the city and its buildings be spared. Arming him-self with a revolver, the governor mounted his horse and rode away into the night. He was escorted by only two volunteer aides, his staff officers having already fled. Vance later complained, "I rode out of Raleigh at mid-night without a single officer of all my staff with me! Not one. I shall hit the deserters some day, hard."[21]

When Vance left the capital city, he promptly made his way to the rela-tive safety of Hoke's camp, where he spent the night in the tent of his close friend the major general. Before retiring for the evening, the two men discussed fully the state of affairs facing North Carolina and the Con-federacy. Then Hoke faced a dilemma concerning his distinguished visitor: "I was very much troubled in securing a place for him to sleep, but after awhile secured a cot, as I was afraid for him to sleep upon the ground as we were; that it might make him sick, give him pneumonia."[22]

At 6:30 A.M. on Thursday, April 13, Hoke broke camp and resumed the march west toward Greensboro. Acting as rear guard for Hardee's corps, the division moved to within four miles of Chapel Hill before halting for the evening. As the members of the Eighth North Carolina crossed the railroad near the university town, they were excited to see Governor Vance on a westbound train. They called out, "Hello, Governor, where are you going?" Vance responded, "To the western part of the State to prepare a spout for you all to go up." Hoke marched the division another twenty-two miles on April 14. There was little straggling as the column continued west in the direction of Greensboro.[23]

During the day, Sherman received Johnston's request for a conference, and he promptly responded with an optimistic message: "I am fully empowered to arrange with you any terms for the suspension of further hostilities between the armies commanded by you and those commanded by myself, and I will be willing to confer with you to that end. . . . I really desire to save the people of North Carolina the damage they would sustain by the march of this army through the central or western part of the State." Although Sherman was anxious for a reply from Johnston, Kilpatrick and his officers were less than diligent in relaying their commander's letter through the lines. As a result, Johnston did not receive it until the morning of April 16.[24]

There was no rest for Hoke and his men during the delay in communications between the two commanding generals. Hoke had the division ready to march at 4:30 A.M. on April 15, but the column did not move until an hour and a half later. The misery of the rain-soaked early-morning march was heightened when the soldiers reached the bridgeless Haw River, much swollen by recent downpours. Strong currents washed some men away, but rocks near Ruffin's Mill allowed most of the troops to cross safely. One of Hoke's officers recalled the ordeal: "The water was generally waist-deep, sometimes when on a rock not so deep, then deeper as the rock was stepped off. It was rough wading."[25]

Further hardships were forthcoming as Hardee's corps neared Alamance Creek, which was flowing out of its banks. The entire column came to a halt. With the Union army in the vicinity of Chapel Hill, there was cause for alarm for the Confederate soldiers. The Union cannon fire heard by Hoke's troops was, according to H. T. J. Ludwig of the Eighth North Carolina, "the last hostile cannon that was fired in our part of the army." In order to get his men moving, Hardee ordered his leading teamster to attempt to cross the dangerous waterway. One of Hoke's officers described what happened next:

> With a crack of the whip, and a shout to his mules he is in and under, rises, struggles, and is swept away. Everything was again at a standstill, the rain was falling in torrents, the river was rapidly rising, something had to be done, and our lieutenant-general determined to try to swim another wagon and team across.

The order was given, and followed by the same result. Mules, wagon and teamster were swept down the stream, and it was hard to tell which was uppermost in the struggle with the flood. The general's resources seemed now exhausted and he ordered the destruction of the train.[26]

Before such drastic action was taken, however, Major General Benjamin Franklin Cheatham, whose division preceded Hoke's, tried his hand at advancing the column across the treacherous creek. When he ordered his troops to move forward, they "emphasized their determination with some pretty lively swearing" and "doggedly refused to move." Cheatham promptly grabbed the man closest to him, and the general and the soldier tumbled into the water. After the two struggled in the creek for a few moments, Cheatham came out and repeated the process. Soon, his soldiers were attempting to cross, until three wagons—one filled with bacon, one with hardtack, and one with guns—were swept away by the raging waters.[27]

Impatient with the delay and disturbed that his soldiers were in a vulnerable position in the rear, Hoke moved forward and received permission from Hardee to locate a more favorable place to effect a crossing. Four miles upstream near Holt's Mill, Hoke discovered such a spot. Once the soldiers moved to the new site, the major general revealed "the resources of a fertile brain." Describing Hoke's plan for crossing, Second Lieutenant J. C. Ellington of the Fiftieth North Carolina wrote, "He moved the head of his column to this point, directed one man to seize his horse's tail, and another to grasp this man's shoulder, and another and another until he had a long line, swam his horse across the narrow stream and discharging his cargo safely on the opposite bank, would quickly return for another. The rapidity with which the men were carried over was astonishing." In the estimation of Captain W. E. Stoney of Hagood's brigade, "the train was saved" by Hoke.[28]

Despite the method of crossing effected by Hoke, the swollen creek, which reached as high as the armpits on some of the men and boys, threatened to further deplete the dwindling ranks. Colonel Charles Broadfoot of the North Carolina Junior Reserves recalled that "many narrow escapes from drowning occurred, especially among the boys."

On that trying afternoon, a poignant drama involving one of Hoke's young charges was played out on the flooded banks of the creek. Lieutenant R. M. Furman of the Seventy-first Regiment, North Carolina Junior Reserves, who later served as auditor of the state of North Carolina, witnessed one of the smaller boys in Hoke's command disappear under the murky water, only to be pulled out by a taller, stouter soldier. But the boy dived into the stream a second and a third time. His fellow soldiers, fearing an attempt at suicide, brought the boy to dry land once again and asked him what he was doing. "Why," remarked the wet warrior, "my gun's down thar and I'm trying to get hit."[29] Even in the darkest of times, the troops remained true to their calling.

Once Hoke had his division safely across the creek, the soldiers made camp a half-mile from the water after "a most fatiguing march." As the men settled down for a well-deserved rest, hard news replaced the rumors that had been the talk of camp for the past several days. Colonel Olmstead of the First Georgia arrived in Hoke's camp with details of Lee's surrender on April 9. Captain Stoney expressed the mood upon confirmation of the story that many had doubted: "Great God! can it be true? I have never for a moment doubted the ultimate success of our cause. I cannot believe it."[30]

When the westward retreat resumed at 6:30 A.M. on Sunday, April 16, Hoke found that the rains had made the roads virtually impassable. In order to expedite his movement, the major general divided the wagon train. By day's end, the march covered twenty miles, and the soldiers set up camp at Redcross in northern Randolph County, some twelve miles southeast of Greensboro. Before they bedded down, Hoke issued instructions for the division to move at 4:30 A.M. the following day. However, the order was later countermanded, and the division remained in camp while Johnston met with Sherman at the farmhouse of James Bennett in Durham County on April 17.[31]

Most of the soldiers in Hoke's division, which by this time had dwindled to 385 officers and 2,857 men, realized that this day was the beginning of the end. Rumors abounded that the army was about to be surrendered, and confusion became the order of the day. In an attempt to confirm the

reports, Captain Stoney rode to Hoke's headquarters, where he encountered Majors Cross and Adams of the division staff. According to Stoney,
the two officers informed him "that beyond a doubt the army would be
surrendered" the following day. When Stoney asked Adams if the information could be made known to the men in the ranks, the major replied,
"Yes, and you can further say that any one who desires to leave can obtain
a written permit from division headquarters."

Stoney immediately rode back to Hagood's brigade and made the announcement, but Lieutenant Colonel J. H. Rion, the brigade commander
in Hagood's absence, pleaded with the men not to leave. He reasoned that
the army was now surrounded by the enemy and that "if any considerable
number left it might compromise the terms given to those that remained."
For the moment, most men were willing "to remain and abide the issue
where they were." But in the afternoon, when the cavalrymen passed
through Hoke's camp with the news that they "were going out," the officers lost control of the soldiers who had been willing to march into the
face of death on so many battlefields. Captain Stoney described the grim
scene:

> The infantry soon became almost frantic, and in every direction
> were rushing to beg, borrow, buy and steal horses. Disorganiza-
> tion was complete. Horses and mules were everywhere taken
> without the least regard to ownership. Trains were openly car
> ried off after plundering the wagons. The division supply train
> was thoroughly stripped. The flags of the brigade were burned
> by the men in the certainty of surrender. About dark an order
> came from army headquarters to keep the men together, but
> with that day the army perished—a mob remained.[32]

For Hoke, April 17 was the day he had hoped would never come. On
that day, not only was his heralded army falling apart, but the Yankees
entered and took possession of his hometown. Hoke could take some so-
lace in the fact that when Colonel John C. Palmer's cavalry brigade entered Lincolnton, they found the citizens "bitterly rebellious."[33]

When Johnston concluded his meeting with Sherman on April 18, the
Confederate general rode away cautiously optimistic that he had entered

into an agreement that would end the war. In the back of his mind, however, Johnston realized that he must keep his army together pending approval of the agreement. He expressed "great displeasure at the report" of surrender which had made its way to Hoke from Hardee's headquarters. At sunset, Hoke sent a staff officer to his brigades to inform them "that there was no truth in the reported surrender." But there was now little that could be said or done to restore the army to fighting condition. That evening, Captain Stoney wrote in his diary, "Demoralization, however, is utter and complete; there is no spark of fight left in the troops."[34]

Hoke and his men remained in their camp south of Greensboro on April 19. Amid the talk that day was "a strange rumor" that Lincoln had been assassinated. A circular received from General Johnston in the afternoon expressed regret at the report of surrender and informed the troops "that a suspension of arms had been agreed upon pending negotiations between the two governments." In the interim, both armies were to remain in their present positions. Some of the soldiers were heartened by Johnston's mention of "two governments," but most were displeased with the circular because it meant they would have to remain in camp a bit longer.[35]

Another day of watching and waiting followed for Hoke and his troops on April 20. There was little in the way of news, and the loyal soldiers who remained with the army had little to do but exchange opinions about the future course of events. The majority of men still in camp were "opposed to surrender" or "to anything like subdivision or reconstruction of the accursed Union." The most militant of the warriors started to drift away from camp in small bands with the intention of keeping up the fight at another place in another time.

A day later, Hoke returned from a visit to Greensboro with "various items of news." The story that Abraham Lincoln had been killed was no longer rumor. Also of particular interest to Hoke's soldiers were the terms of the proposed agreement between Johnston and Sherman. During his trip, Hoke had briefly directed his attention to family matters. He happened to meet Captain B. L. Ridley, and as the two officers discussed the state of affairs, they learned they were kinsmen. Ridley's paternal grandfather was the first cousin of Hoke's maternal grandfather, Judge Robert Burton. When Hoke was informed that Ridley's father had arrived for a visit, the major general saw to it that an ambulance was dispatched for his transportation.[36]

Over the next three days, there was little news flowing into Hoke's camp about the future of the army or the war effort. More and more soldiers began to leave the ranks. Captain Stoney reported, "The division is being rapidly reduced in this way. They are going in large bodies, and at all hours without an effort being made to stop them." A field return on April 24 revealed the loss of manpower Hoke was suffering. His seven-thousand-man division had been reduced to just under three thousand effectives.[37]

In the meantime, the agreement crafted by Johnston and Sherman a week earlier had been rebuked, scorned, and disapproved by the Andrew Johnson administration. Faced with the threat of a resumption of hostilities, Hoke issued orders for the division to be ready to move at 11 A.M. on April 26, the time when the truce was set to expire. So diminished were his ranks that Hoke was concerned about the ability of his division to continue the fight. One newspaper sarcastically reported that Sherman might have to lend the Confederate army some soldiers to surrender.[38]

Like Hoke, Johnston was greatly distressed about the ability of his army to fight. Consequently, he disregarded further directives received from Jefferson Davis and resolved to do all in his power "to bring about a termination of hostilities." A noon meeting was convened between the two generals at Bennett House. An hour before the conference started, the order was given for Hoke's men to march. An eyewitness was appalled at what he observed: "May I ever be spared such a sight as I witnessed when the order to move was given. Whole regiments remained on the ground, refusing to obey. In the last ten days desertion had reduced Kirkland's brigade from 1,000 to 300 men; Clingman's and the brigade of junior reserves from the same cause were each no stronger; Hagood's and Colquitt's brigades had suffered, but not so much. Now not more than forty men in each brigade followed Kirkland and Clingman from the ground."[39]

By the time Hoke halted the ten-mile march—the last the division would make together—near Centre Meeting House on Trinity College Road at Archdale in northern Randolph County, Johnston had formally surrendered to Sherman. Despite its weakened condition, the Confederate army was still respected by the men that had fought against it. Hoke's position on the south side of High Point and S. D. Lee's on the north side prevented Stoneman's raiders from damaging that city before the surrender was announced.[40]

Hoke's soldiers "remained quietly in camp all day" on April 27. At length, formal notice of the surrender was received in the form of General Orders No. 18. After detailing the terms of the surrender, Johnston explained the reason: "Events in Virginia, which broke every hope of success by war, imposed on its general the duty of sparing the blood of this gallant army and of saving our country from further devastation and our people from ruin."[41]

Over the next few days, Hoke's little army remained together to undergo the execution of the necessary paroles. It had been months since the soldiers were last paid, and Johnston took steps to remedy that grievance before the loyalest of the loyal took leave. Disregarding President Davis's instructions to send the thousands of dollars in silver held by the Confederate treasury agent, Johnston decided to use the money to make a final, token payment to each man in the army. In his opinion, the money remaining in the Confederate treasury belonged to the men who were about to leave for homes suffering from the effects of four years of war. He ordered that each man receive an equal share of the treasury regardless of rank. Thus, when Hoke called his men to attention on Friday, April 28, each soldier from general to private received one dollar and a quarter in silver. But in these dark last hours of the Confederacy, dissension arose concerning the final payment. Upon examination of a field return for Hoke's division, Major General Cheatham complained to Hardee that Hoke had drawn more money than he was entitled to. Hardee promptly settled the matter by accepting Hoke's return.[42]

By month's end, Hoke's camp was one of despair. Summarizing the conditions facing the troops, one soldier wrote, "Rumor seems to have tired of her occupation. The stern reality of accomplished defeat is upon us. Famine begins to threaten us." On the first day of the new month, Hoke, his brigadiers, and his colonels were summoned to High Point to receive paroles for the brigades and regiments of the division. In their absence, the camp was the scene of virtual lawlessness. Captain Stoney noted, "No right acknowledged now except might, no property safe which is not defended with pistol and rifle."[43]

When Hoke returned from High Point, his troops began making preparations to start for their homes. As the time to disband the division approached, Hoke offered his farewell address. Upon hearing it, one officer remarked, "It is full of feeling." Noted Civil War historian and author Glenn Tucker characterized Hoke's "ringing words" as the "finest sentiments at this dark hour."

Headquarters Hoke's Division
Near Greensboro, N.C., May 1, 1865

Soldiers of my Division:

On the eve of a long, perhaps a final separation, I address to you the last sad words of parting.

The fortunes of war have turned the scale against us. The proud banners which you have waved so gloriously over many a field are to be furled at last; but they are not disgraced, my comrades. Your indomitable courage, your heroic fortitude, your patience under sufferings, have surrounded them with a halo which future years can never dim. History will bear witness to your valor and succeeding generations will point with admiration to your grand struggle for constitutional freedom.

Soldiers, your past is full of glory! Treasure it in your hearts. Remember each gory battlefield, each day of victory, each bleeding comrade.

Think then of your future.

> "Freedom's battle, once begun
> Bequeathed from bleeding sire to son,
> Though baffled oft, is ever won."

General Robert F. Hoke

You have yielded to overwhelming forces, not to superior valor. You are paroled prisoners, not slaves. The love of liberty, which led you into this contest, burns as brightly in your hearts as ever. Cherish it. Associate it with the history of your past. Transmit it to your children. Teach them the rights of freedom, and teach them to maintain them. Teach them the proudest day in all your proud career was that on which you enlisted as Southern soldiers, entering that holy brotherhood whose ties are now sealed by the blood of your compatriots who have fallen, and whose history is coeval with the brilliant record of the past four years.

Soldiers, amid the imperishable laurels that surround your brows, no brighter leaf adorns them than your connection with the late Army of Northern Virginia!

The star that shone with splendor over its oft-repeated fields of victory, over the two deadly struggles of Manassas Plains, over Richmond, Chancellorsville and Fredericksburg, has sent its rays and been reflected wherever freedom has a friend. That star has set in blood, but yet in glory. That army is now of the past. The banners trail, but not with ignominy. No stain blots their escutcheons. No blush can tinge your cheeks as you proudly announce that you have a part in the history of the Army of Northern Virginia.

My comrades, we have borne together the same hardships; we have shared the same dangers; we have rejoiced over the same victories. Your trials and your patience have excited sympathy and admiration, and I have borne willing witness to your bravery. It is with a heart full of grateful emotions for your services and ready obedience that I take leave of you. May the future of each one be as happy as your past career has been brilliant, and may no cloud ever dim the brightness of your fame. The past rises before me in its illimitable grandeur. Its memories are part of the life of each one of us. But it is all over now. Yet, though the sad, dark veil of defeat is over us, fear not the future, but meet it with manly hearts. You carry to your homes the heartfelt wishes of your General for your prosperity.

My comrades, farewell!

R. F. Hoke,
Major-General.[44]

On May 2, Lieutenant General Hardee "quietly slipped off," but Hoke remained at his post of duty. Starvation was now threatening not only the livestock, but the soldiers as well. For more than a week, the horses had been fed only a quart of corn each day, and the mules had received no grain, only a handful of long forage. Although the soldiers had been promised rations from the Federal army, none had been received. Captain Stoney recorded the final decision that Hoke, the division commander, made: "No orders to leave have been received, but with famine staring us in the face, General Hoke consents to our starting. As it might, however, turn out a serious step, in the event of our not being able to get food on our route, the question of waiting for the Federal issue of supplies, or of starting now was submitted to the men. Of course, they voted to go."

Most of the North Carolinians took leave of the camp on May 2. With but thirty-six men left, the Fifty-first North Carolina disbanded; so did the Fortieth North Carolina. Each man set out on foot through a "devastated country, made so by the ravages of the enemy, until it was so poor that a 'jaybird' would starve flying over it, unless he ceased his rations."[45]

The Georgians and South Carolinians in the division left on May 3. At 8 A.M., Hagood's brigade fell in line for its final march. Its lead regiment, the Twenty-seventh South Carolina, counted seven men. Next came the Twenty-fifth South Carolina with five soldiers, and the Eleventh South Carolina guarded the rear with sixteen. As it made its way out of camp for the final time, the tiny contingent paused at Hoke's headquarters to pay their respects and offer their farewells. One of the participants noted that "Hoke and his staff seemed to feel the occasion deeply, and their expression of regard and good will were very grateful to us all."[46]

With his army now gone, with the cause now lost, and with the war now over, Hoke spent several days completing administrative matters before beginning the journey home. Though the Confederate war effort was in ruins, Hoke could take personal satisfaction that he had served his homeland with gallantry from the opening battle to the bitter end. As historian Samuel Ashe noted, Hoke was magnanimous in defeat: "As brilliant as his career had been, the spirit and brave heart he exhibited at the trying moment of irresistible disaster and subjugation were as credible to him as his proud bearing on any fields of glorious victory."[47]

General Robert F. Hoke

In advance of Hoke's homecoming, Captain Ridley arrived in Lincolnton on May 7 to call on his kinfolk. In his diary, Ridley recorded the details of his visit with the major general's mother: "She treated us royally; remembered to have met my father when he was only fifteen. Having lost our coffee pot in camp, she generously provided another."

Frances Burton Hoke had reason to be generous, for Captain Ridley brought joyous tidings. He had recently seen her son, Robert, and he was alive and well.[48] Soon, Mrs. Hoke's "Bobbie" would come home to Lincolnton a genuine Southern hero.

CHAPTER 16

Picking up the Pieces: A Half-Century of Reconstruction

As Hoke made his way home on "Old Joe" after four years of war, the hundred-mile trip yielded a glimpse of the miserable economic conditions in the North Carolina Piedmont. Because enemy activity had not come to the area until late in the war, the region had been spared as a battleground. Nonetheless, the harsh effects of the long-running conflict were obvious: fields usually green with grain and other crops were fallow; pastures once filled with livestock were empty; railroads and bridges were in shambles; some factories were burned, others were idle; and shops and stores were either depleted of stock or boarded up.[1]

When Hoke rode into Lincolnton, he found conditions much like those throughout the area. The once-mighty Hoke family industrial enterprises were no more; a fire had ravaged the complex in 1863. In recent weeks, town and country had been subjected to Stoneman's raiders. Yet the general returned home with hope. According to one account, "His hero-heart remained unconquered and unconquerable." There was promise in the land and in the people. A contemporary description of Lincolnton provided clues to Hoke's optimism: "This is naturally a beautiful place. . . . Topographically, it is quite elevated and its mineral water, proximity to the mountains, together with its salutorious atmosphere, render it quite a healthy climate.

" . . . There are about fifteen hundred inhabitants here, many of whom are industrious and enterprising citizens, who will doubtless improve the place very much, whenever circumstances are such as to admit their return to peaceful avocations."[2]

Unwilling to live in the squalor of defeat, the general promptly hitched Old Joe to a plow and began making a crop on family lands in Lincolnton during the spring and summer of 1865. His twenty-seventh birthday was spent accordingly. To townspeople and many of his neighbors, farm work seemed demeaning to a man who had achieved fame as "an acknowledged master of war." But Hoke saw it as the first step in the reconstruction of his town, North Carolina, and the South. It was to Hoke "the duty of the moment." The immediate task was not easy, however. As the same man and horse that had enjoyed the adulation of cheering crowds and the pomp of military reviews and parades struggled with a plow under the hot summer sun, a passerby called out, "Ain't you General Hoke?" Stopping to wipe his brow, the general responded, "Yes." Another question followed: "Ain't that thar the horse you rode in the army?" Hoke responded that it was. Overcome with emotion, the stranger exclaimed, "God Almighty, God Almighty." Without further comment, he buried his face in his arms and rode away.[3]

As to his labors behind the plow, the general once remarked, "I like this better than shooting Yankees." Assuredly, once the war was over, it was over forever for Hoke. When the final act of the great drama was played out near Greensboro, "he left the stage, never to return again." Over the next half-century, as the Southern people glorified, almost deified, their Confederate heroes, Hoke never attended reunions of veterans, never visited old soldiers' homes, never wore his uniform or sword, never returned to the battlefields where he had achieved military greatness, never made a speech about his battle experiences or his record of wartime achievement.

Some observers expressed surprise that Hoke refrained from participation in most postwar activities for veterans. When questioned about his reluctance to take part in "demonstrations given to honor the lost cause," he indicated that "he could not bear to see the old and infirm veterans, who were lusty and full of fire and dash in the days when he and they campaigned together." One of Hoke's contemporaries recorded, "His attachment to the cause for which he fought was profound—inexpressible. Seeing the faces of the comrades with whom he fought, remembering the faces of those who fell by his side, dwelling upon the vanished hopes of the past—all these would be too painful almost to be borne—far less to be sought."

On one occasion, Hoke remarked, "I have never seen Gettysburg . . . have paid no battlefield visits since we left them victorious or over-powered." Recalling the ultimate sacrifice of Colonel Isaac Erwin Avery at Gettysburg, the general observed, "I remember Gettysburg the more sadly for that brave man's death." Hoke's memories of the war were indeed painful. In countless battles, he had seen innumerable men and boys shot down in the prime of their lives. Over the war's last year, his division had reported 4,045 men wounded and 694 killed.[4]

Hoke's involvement in postwar efforts to perpetuate the glories of the war was limited to his work in associations that erected memorials to the leaders and fighting men of the Confederacy. On May 29, 1890, he served as a marshal in the gala ceremonies surrounding the unveiling of the statue of General Robert E. Lee in Richmond. Three years later, he was appointed one of the five members of the North Carolina committee selected to work with other state committees to erect a monument honoring Jefferson Davis. Two years later, he was appointed to a similar state committee established to plan and build the National Confederate Memorial in Washington, D.C.[5]

Not only did Hoke refrain from taking part in postwar Confederate activities, but he was extremely reluctant to write about the war or his role in it. He received numerous requests for military information and records in the years following the conflict, and more often than not, his response was similar to the one he sent a New Jersey resident in 1876: "I regret that I cannot comply with your request as I have none of the reports before me, made during the war." A year later, Hoke responded to a similar request: "All of my papers were burned after the close of the war." When Joseph E. Johnston and Pierre G. T. Beauregard wrote to Hoke for information about various aspects of the war, he was not forthcoming with the details they sought. On the rare occasion when he wrote about the war, it was to praise the men who had served under him or to correct an inaccuracy in print that reflected badly on one of his compatriots.

Neither was Hoke inclined to discuss the war, even with friends and family. One journalist wrote, "General Hoke, while he is known to be one of the greatest soldiers the State has sent to the front, is modest with it all. He has never even let it be known that he has fought a battle. What a contrast to some who have been singing their praises."

With grim reminders of the war all about him, there were times, however, when memories of his experiences evoked a comment or two. For example, on a postwar business trip to Washington, D.C., Hoke was in the company of three Northern businessmen as they walked down a busy street. When they spotted a blind Union veteran who had lost a leg and an arm in the war, the group passed without dropping any coins in his cup. Suddenly, Hoke stopped, returned to the beggar, and put some money into his tin. His behavior astonished his companions, causing one of them to remark, "Why did you do that? He was your enemy." With his customary wry sense of humor, the general replied, "That's the only condition I like to see a Yankee in."[6]

From his return to Lincolnton in the spring of 1865 through the rest of his days, Hoke never forgot his parting charge to his soldiers: "The past rises before me in its illimitable grandeur. . . . Fear not the future, but meet it with manly hearts." He believed that the gallantry of his fellow Southerners, their service, and their sacrifice should be honored not by mere words and not by dwelling in the past, but by looking to the future and rebuilding the South. Just as he had been a leader in war, he chose to become a leader in peace.

Hoke knew the character, industriousness, and ingenuity of the soldiers who had gone into battle time after time in the face of insurmountable odds. He realized that the hope of a reconstructed South lay in them. If he were to provide the example through leadership, hard work, and vision, the men who had followed him into the face of death would fight with the same determination to resurrect the Southern economy. Because of his family heritage, his excellent practical education, his early experience in business and industry, his proven ability to lead, his love of home, and the desire and spirit of his youth, Hoke was one of the returning soldiers most capable of leading the South into the Industrial Age and the twentieth century.[7]

Thus, quietly, modestly, Hoke set about leading his state toward a future as bright as the fighting record he had left behind. For the remaining forty-seven years of his life, he remained devoted to that cause, working to bring new prosperity to his state. He tilled the land and watched with pride as once again the fertile soil produced its "blossom and fruit"; he dug into the bowels of the earth to bring forth the metals and minerals so vital to the economic well-being of the region; he engineered new railroads and guided the development of a modern transportation system for the South; he restored confidence in a business climate clouded by gloom; and he served as advisor and counselor to the statesmen who shaped the destiny of North Carolina. As Josephus Daniels once remarked, "Hoke was the same patriot . . . in making a crop in the spring of 1865 on his Lincoln County farm, as when holding back superior forces around Richmond. . . . He was the same noble soul developing industrial North Carolina and aiding in rebuilding Southern fortunes." James T. Morehead, a Confederate officer, attorney, and business associate of the general, added, "From the hour that peace was proclaimed, his face was ever to the future, his eye, like the eagle's, watching for the rising sun."[8]

Before Hoke could turn his full attention to the revitalization of his homeland, there were military and personal matters to consider in the aftermath of the war. Some farewells were yet to be said. Among the soldiers who called upon the general to pay their respects during the summer of

1865 was James Longstreet, who was entertained at the Hoke home on his way south.

On a less pleasant note, Hoke was aware that he must apply for a pardon from the United States government. At Lincolnton on January 8, 1866, he penned his application for pardon to President Andrew Johnson. Two days later, he was in Raleigh, where he took the oath of allegiance and obtained the written recommendation of Jonathan Worth, the governor of North Carolina. In Washington on January 13, Lieutenant General U. S. Grant added his endorsement to the application: "I heartily recommend amnesty to R. F. Hoke late a general in the Southern Army. The wording of the written application in my opinion gives a good guarantee for the future, coming from an officer of the standing of Genl. Hoke." Nevertheless, approval of the application by the president would not be received for eighteen months.[9]

In the meantime, there were other troubling repercussions from Hoke's service in the Confederate army. By late 1865, there were rumblings in Washington, D.C., and Raleigh concerning the report of a three-officer board of inquiry impaneled in New Bern in October to investigate the hanging of the alleged Confederate deserters at Kinston in February 1864. In the report issued to Joseph Holt, judge advocate general of the army, on December 12, 1865, the panel recommended "the immediate appointment of a military commission for the trial of the parties implicated, especially General Pickett, who ordered the execution, General Hoke who was in charge of it."

Pickett had not waited for the results of the inquiry; he had fled to Canada in October. In the wake of the army investigation, congressional action followed. During the controversy, Hoke had begun his initial mining operations in the North Carolina mountains. When it appeared that he might be called on to account for his "act of military discipline," speculation spread throughout North Carolina. Fearing that her son might face drastic punishment, the general's mother rushed to the mountains to inform him of the developments and offer him money with which to flee the country. But Hoke assured her that he had done nothing wrong; rather, he had acted in accordance with applicable military law.[10]

Determined to settle the controversy, Hoke made his way to Raleigh and then hurried to Washington. There, he called on U. S. Grant, the commanding general of the United States Army. Hoke's calling card was sent into Grant's private office, and after some delay, the Confederate general was shown into the room, where he found the Federal commander sitting at a table. Grant motioned his caller to take a seat opposite him. Looking at the card in his hand, Grant read aloud, "Robert F. Hoke, North Carolina." He then inquired, "Are you any relation of General Hoke who commanded the Confederate lines at the Battle of Cold Harbor in 1864?" His association with Grant's greatest military calamity momentarily unnerved Hoke. However, he quickly regained his composure and responded, "Yes, General, I am General Hoke of North Carolina." Grant immediately stood up, moved around the table to Hoke, cordially shook his hand, and remarked, "Well, Sir, that was the worst drubbing I ever got. You may depend on me to look after you. I will see that no harm comes to you." As far as Hoke was concerned, the meeting with Grant concluded the controversy.[11]

Despite the satisfactory outcome in Washington, personal tragedy struck the Hoke family when the general's younger brother, Dr. George Hoke, died in Lincolnton on November 1, 1866. The young physician had served under his brother as adjutant and assistant surgeon during a portion of the war. Ill health, from which he never recovered, had forced him to resign from Confederate service in 1864.[12]

It was not until President Andrew Johnson visited his native state in the late spring of 1867 that formal action was taken on Hoke's pardon. After visiting Raleigh, his birthplace, the president, accompanied by an entourage that included Secretary of State William H. Seward, traveled thirty miles west to attend commencement ceremonies at the University of North Carolina. At one point during the visit to Chapel Hill, Johnson, Seward, and university president David L. Swain were enjoying the shade of one of the towering trees on the campus when "a bevy of lovely girls" made its way to Johnson, began to exchange compliments with him, and proceeded to beg him to pardon Hoke. Taking interest in both their pleas and their beauty, Johnson indicated his willingness to grant the pardon upon the condition that each of the girls kiss him. His young audience complied.

Once Johnson was satisfied that he had "missed none of the 'rosebud garden of girls,'" he instructed Seward to remind him upon his return to Washington to pardon Hoke.

At the White House on June 13, 1867, a notation was entered on Hoke's application for pardon: "The President directs that the warrant for the Pardon of Genl. Hoke be prepared and sent to his office." A day later, the pardon was granted. Included in the official record was a petition to the president on behalf of Hoke signed by some three dozen ladies of North Carolina. When Josephus Daniels once asked Hoke about the Chapel Hill incident, the general smiled and said that "every word of it was true."[13]

Hoke first met the woman he would marry and spend the rest of his life with in 1868. But his mother had met her four years earlier. Lydia Ann Van Wyck was fifteen years old when she visited Lincolnton in 1864 during a vacation from St. Mary's Episcopal School in Raleigh. In Lincolnton, she was the guest of a family acquaintance who had fled the ravages of war in Virginia. During her stay, she became acquainted with the general's mother, Frances Burton Hoke. Mrs. Hoke "took great fancy" to the teenager, who possessed "rich dark hair and bright eyes and . . . a dangerously winning smile." As the friendship between the two grew, Mrs. Hoke told Lydia about her son Robert, who "was far away fighting for freedom." Before Lydia returned to Raleigh, Mrs. Hoke remarked, "If he returns you two must meet. I would love to have you for my daughter."[14]

Described as "bright and intelligent, with pleasing manners, and possessing a rich, sweet voice, and so attractive as to draw all hearts to her," Lydia was a native of Pendleton, South Carolina. The daughter of William A. Van Wyck and Lydia Maverick Van Wyck, she, like her future husband, was born into a family of distinction. Her father was a renowned lawyer who had served on the board of aldermen in New York City in 1832. Her mother was the daughter of Samuel Maverick, a prominent landowner and businessman in South Carolina. Mrs. Van Wyck's brother, also named Samuel, was a Texas legend. Captured by Santa Anna during the Mexican War, he was a signer of the Texas Declaration of Independence. He ultimately acquired hundreds of thousands of acres of land and so many head of cattle that it was impossible to brand them all. His roaming, unbranded cattle became known as "Maverick's" or "mavericks." Thus, Lydia's uncle was the source of the Americanism *maverick*.[15]

Lydia was born on her grandfather's plantation, which stood adjacent to that of John C. Calhoun near present-day Clemson University. Her four older brothers were also men of distinction. William Van Wyck II, a Civil War soldier, graduate of the University of North Carolina, and attorney, married Mary Johnston Battle, the sister of the president of the University of North Carolina; Lydia spent some of her vacations from St. Mary's with William and Mary at their Chapel Hill home. Another brother, Dr. Samuel Van Wyck, served as a surgeon on the staff of Nathan Bedford Forrest and was killed in Tennessee. Two other brothers achieved fame in New York City. Augustus Van Wyck, an attorney and New York Supreme Court justice, was defeated in the race for governor of New York State in 1898 by just over seventeen thousand votes; the victor was Theodore Roosevelt. Like his brother Augustus, Robert A. Van Wyck was a noted attorney and jurist. He served as chief justice of the city of New York and was later elected the first mayor of greater New York City upon the consolidation of Brooklyn, Manhattan, Queens, the Bronx, and Richmond. When he died in Paris in 1918, Robert Van Wyck left an estate in excess of $2 million.[16]

When St. Mary's broke for summer vacation in 1865, Lydia returned home to South Carolina. She subsequently went to New York City, where she enrolled in a French boarding school at which her mother had been educated. Following the death of her father in 1867, the remainder of the Van Wyck family moved to New York City.

Mrs. Hoke had not seen Lydia since 1864 when she visited the young woman and her mother at the family plantation in South Carolina in March 1868. During her visit, Mrs. Hoke presented Lydia with an autograph album, which Lydia took with her to a gala masked ball for Southern notables at White Sulphur Springs, Virginia, on August 28, 1868.

Before attending the grand affair, Lydia and her mother returned to their New York home at the Fifth Avenue Hotel. There, Lydia welcomed a gentleman caller. Robert F. Hoke had made his way from Lincolnton with a letter of introduction. From the outset, it was a classic case of love at first sight. Lydia was captivated with the tall, dark, handsome Southern hero, and Robert was taken with Lydia's beauty. He later recalled his first impression of her: "She was the prettiest girl I've ever seen." During the visit, Robert and Lydia were descending the grand staircase of the hotel side by side when they saw their image in a great mirror. The general quipped, "Wouldn't we make a handsome couple?"

When the time came for Hoke to depart, he took a coach to the train station. According to his daughter, he was promptly arrested upon emerging from the coach for wearing the best coat he had—his Confederate frock coat. William Van Wyck II was summoned, and Hoke was soon released from jail.[17]

A contemporary account of the White Sulphur Springs gala contained a description of Lydia: "Miss Van Wyck formerly of South Carolina and now of New York, who as Helen McGrego, was clad in Black Velvet and Plaid. More than one admirer remained as if compelled to remain in the circle of her charm." Autographs set out in the album presented by Mrs. Hoke bore testimony to the distinguished guest list: Robert E. Lee, Alexander H. Stephens, George E. Pickett, and Pierre G. T. Beauregard.

In the days following the ball, Robert and Lydia became engaged to be married. The wedding took place at 7:30 P.M. on the evening of January 7, 1869, at the Church of the Transfiguration on Twenty-ninth Street in New York City. But Frances Burton Hoke, the woman who brought the couple together, was not in attendance; she had died in Lincolnton on October 17, 1868.[18]

After their marriage, Mr. and Mrs. Robert F. Hoke settled in Raleigh, where the general had witnessed both the sunrise and the sunset of the Confederacy. For the remainder of their lives, the capital city would be home for the couple, although the general would forever maintain a close association with Lincolnton. Over the last twenty years of his life, Hoke made his summer home in the town of his birth.

His initial business venture, as happened to be the case with a number of Confederate veterans, was in the insurance industry. As president of the Home Life Insurance Company, Hoke developed business contacts with men he had served under and with during the war. In 1870, he was appointed North Carolina agent for the Carolina Life Insurance Company, in which Jefferson Davis and Wade Hampton were principals. Hoke's initial foray into the business world was attended by success, as were his many subsequent ventures. Fred A. Olds, a noted historian who knew Hoke personally, once wrote, "Success and prosperity attended the kindly general everywhere."[19]

February 2, 1870, began as a day of great joy in the Hoke household with the birth of Robert Frederick Hoke II, but by evening, joy turned to grief as the couple's first child died.

Van Wyck Hoke arrived on July 29, 1871, and the birth of a healthy boy brought word from Jefferson Davis: "Accept my congratulations and present to Mrs. Hoke the cordial good wishes and affectionate remembrance in which I hold her. Hoping before the Fall to see the young soldier of the cause which like truth cannot be lost." Varina Davis followed her husband with a note to the general: "I have heard so often [of Mrs. Hoke] that I feel as though I have seen her, indeed have done so through my Husband's admiring eyes. I welcome you and her to the fraternity of parents of whom we have been so very long members." Van Wyck Hoke subsequently graduated from the University of North Carolina. An attorney, he worked with his father in a number of business ventures.[20]

During a family stay in Lincolnton, Hoke's third child was born on June 28, 1874. Michael Hoke, named for his paternal grandfather, graduated from the University of North Carolina, where he captained and starred as halfback on the first great football team in the history of the institution. Following a 26–0 victory by the 1892 team over the University of Virginia, a Confederate veteran hailed the Carolina captain as he was making his way off the field. "What's your name?" asked the veteran. "Hoke," replied the football star. "Any kin to General Hoke?" was the next question. "Yes, sir; his son," Michael proudly replied. "Well," responded the veteran, "you go back and tell your pa that I've seen the finest fighting today that I've seen since Chancellorsville."[21]

Michael Hoke subsequently graduated from the University of Virginia Medical School. After completing his internship and residency at Johns Hopkins University, Dr. Hoke studied another year at Harvard University. Following the advice of his father, he began the practice of general surgery in Atlanta in 1897. Three years later, he took a one-year leave to study under Dr. Joel E. Goldthwait, the first orthopedic surgeon in the United States. Upon his return to Atlanta, Hoke became the first physician to practice that specialty in Georgia; at that time, he was one of only a few orthopedic surgeons in the entire country. Although his pioneer work in orthopedic surgery was met with initial skepticism by some physicians, his successes soon began to attract national and international attention. His remarkable surgical techniques were named "the Hoke operations" by his peers.

From the outset of his career in orthopedic surgery, Hoke's passion was the treatment of crippled children. For many years, he performed services for these youngsters without pay. Hoke was instrumental in the establishment of the hospital for crippled children in Decatur, Georgia, that evolved into the world-famous chain of Shriners' Hospitals.

In late 1931, Franklin D. Roosevelt summoned Hoke to serve as surgeon in chief and director of the Warm Springs Foundation at Warm Springs, Georgia. At the facility, Hoke and his wife resided in the Little White House, vacating it only when President Roosevelt visited the foundation.[22]

Of the man who has been called "the father of modern orthopedic surgery," President Roosevelt once said, "He is a man who is dear to my heart because he is not above a logical experiment. He is also dear to my heart because in a larger percentage of cases than anybody else I know, his experiments work." During World War I, Sir Robert Jones, the chief orthopedic surgeon of the British army, described Hoke as "the greatest orthopaedic surgeon in the world."[23]

Two daughters were born to Robert and Lydia. Lydia Maverick Hoke was born in Raleigh on October 1, 1877. She married Alexander Webb, a member of the Raleigh Board of Aldermen and a businessman in the insurance and railroad industries. Frances Burton Hoke was born in Raleigh on September 20, 1879. When Jefferson Davis's body was moved from New Orleans for reinterment in Richmond in 1893, Frances was one of the four teenage girls selected to ride on the funeral carriage through Raleigh and serve as flag bearers. In 1905, she married William Durward Pollock, a Kinston attorney who served as superintendent of the Lenoir

County schools, mayor of Kinston, and aide on the staffs of North Carolina governors Charles B. Aycock and R. B. Glenn.

A sixth child, Robert Frederick Hoke II, was born to Robert and Lydia on November 11, 1884, only to die six months later.[24]

In February 1873, General Hoke seized an opportunity to begin in earnest the industrialization of his native state. During his early postwar mining activities in the mountains, he had become interested in the Cranberry Iron Mine, "the most noted iron mine in the state." It was located in Mitchell (now Avery) County in northwestern North Carolina in the "Cranberry Iron Belt," a vein that stretched more than twenty miles from the village of Cranberry to the Toe River, crossing the state line into Tennessee at several places. At the time Joshua Perkins had discovered the vein of magnetite iron ore in 1826, it was considered the richest deposit of its kind in the United States. During the Civil War, the mine was a source of iron for the Confederacy.

According to a local resident, when Hoke came on the scene, he was able to purchase the entire township "for a little gray mare and a rifle gun." On February 23, 1873, the Cranberry Iron Mine Company was chartered by the state of North Carolina. Two days later, Hoke was elected secretary of the corporation. Among his partners in the enterprise was Ario Pardee, a Philadelphian who dominated much of the coal and iron market on the East Coast.[25]

Hoke and Pardee realized that modern transportation was needed to efficiently and profitably move iron ore from the mountain mine to furnaces and markets. The solution to their dilemma was the East Tennessee and Western North Carolina Railroad Company, a defunct corporation chartered by the state of Tennessee in 1866. Hoke and his associates purchased the railroad for twenty-five thousand dollars on September 10, 1875; in time, Hoke would become president of the railroad. Work commenced immediately to construct a narrow-gauge line stretching twenty-four miles across the mountains from Cranberry to Johnson City, Tennessee. Consequently, Hoke not only launched a great mining enterprise but entered the railroad business, a field of endeavor that would maintain his interest for the rest of his life.[26]

In 1882, the first train puffed through the mountains on the railroad. However, work on the route would continue for many years. When the Linville River Railway was connected with the East Tennessee and Western North Carolina Railroad in 1894, it became the longest narrow-gauge railway in the world.

Hoke maintained ownership in the railroad and mining operations in the Cranberry area for several decades. In a letter to a Philadelphia businessman on June 6, 1890, he extolled the virtues of some of his mountain holdings: "The Iron property that I and some of my friends own is situated about 20 miles from Cranberry. This is one of the purest and richest ores I have ever seen, and I believe the vein will yield large quantities of ore. . . . If you desire a pure iron for your business, I do not know where you would go to get a better property. . . . If you wish to look into the property with a view to purchasing, I will arrange to meet you sometime this summer." From 1881 to 1931, more than 1.5 million tons of high-grade magnetic iron ore were hauled from the Cranberry Iron Mine.[27]

Although Hoke's narrow-gauge railroad vanished long ago, one of the engines from that old line still chugs along in the North Carolina mountains at the popular tourist attraction Tweetsie Railroad.[28]

Never one to pass up a chance to introduce a new enterprise to the North Carolina economy, Hoke embarked on an interesting venture near the Cranberry Iron Mine. He and several associates raised sheep for a time on the Old Fields of Toe. A Scottish shepherd and a sheepdog were imported to manage the flock of a hundred ewes, but Hoke's efforts at sheep raising proved unprofitable.[29]

Throughout his life, Hoke was adamant that his name not be used to further political causes. He was unwilling to use the fame he had gained during the war to reap profit in the business or civic world. Historian Joseph G. D. Hamilton observed, "He sought neither place nor honors, but shrank from them. The reputation he had won through his passionate devotion to a sacred cause was not to be used as a step to place and power. Honors and place were his for a word, but he remained silent." Although for many years he provided wise counsel to North Carolina officials, Hoke never aspired to public office, unlike many of the men who were leaders in the Confederate army.

There was, however, one major public position that Hoke could not turn down. In 1877, he reluctantly accepted an appointment by Governor Vance to the board of directors of the North Carolina Railroad Company, a railroad owned jointly by the state and private stockholders. Hoke saw the appointment as a magnificent opportunity to meet one of the South's greatest needs—the reconstruction of the railroads that the general had seen so badly damaged in the war. He served on the board as a gubernatorial appointee until 1893 and thereafter until his death as a director elected by the private stockholders.[30]

Hoke's desire to build and rebuild railroads was apparent from the close of the war, but a lack of capital and the prevailing postwar economic conditions prevented him from turning his dreams into reality until the Cranberry enterprise came along. Subsequently, Hoke used his position on the board of the North Carolina Railroad Company to aid the development of that quasi-public enterprise so vital to the birth of modern North Carolina. Bennehan Cameron, one of the most successful industrialists of the South during the first quarter of the twentieth century, served as president of the North Carolina Railroad Company at the time of the general's death. In a report to the stockholders, Cameron lauded the efforts of Hoke:

> Coming into the Board under the appointment of Gov. Vance, at the end of the Reconstruction period of our State's history, he found your property in a very dilapidated condition and your stock at a very low figure on the market.
>
> By the sagacious management adopted by him and his associates . . . they gradually lifted your company out of the slough of despond into a more healthy condition, until now its prosperity is surpassed by but very few companies in the United States. . . .
>
> Every policy advocated by Gen. Hoke resulted in benefit to your Company. . . .
>
> Well and truly did he serve this Company as a labor of love for the long period of 35 years, with profit to the Company, with credit to himself and honor to his State. For his devotion to the Company was only succeeded by his devotion to the State.[31]

General Robert F. Hoke

Hoke's abiding interest in agriculture never waned. In 1877, he accepted an appointment to a five-man committee charged with lobbying the North Carolina General Assembly for the establishment of an agricultural experiment station at the University of North Carolina. Hoke's fellow committeeman Kemp P. Battle, the president of the university, had provided ample evidence to Hoke and the public that the state's farmers were suffering significant losses from problems with fertilizers. The lobbying efforts of the committee were successful, and the station was subsequently established on the Chapel Hill campus.[32]

In 1879, Hoke launched his second great iron-mining enterprise with the incorporation of the Chapel Hill Iron Mountain Company. He joined four other principals—including Robert Rufus Bridgers, who had operated the High Shoals Iron Furnaces after the death of the general's great-grandfather John Fulenwider—to mine iron ore that had been discovered approximately one mile north of the university. Hoke was elected chairman of the board, and mining began in November 1880. At the time, the market price of iron had reached such a level that it was profitable to ship the ore to furnaces in Pennsylvania. Operations continued at the Chapel Hill mine until the early 1890s.[33]

From valuable lessons learned at Cranberry, Hoke understood that the success of the Chapel Hill Iron Mountain Company hinged on dependable rail transportation. Aware that an earlier attempt to build a line to Chapel Hill had met with failure, the general nonetheless believed that such a railroad connection could be successfully laid. While it would immeasurably aid his nearby mining operations, the railroad link would also do much to end "the poverty of the people of Chapel Hill and of the University."

A charter for the State University Railroad was granted by the general assembly. University president Battle served as president of the corporation and Hoke as superintendent of the project. Both men worked without salary. As Battle saw it, "Only wise and careful management could have succeeded. The prime mover was General Robert F. Hoke." Despite a shortage of funds, the railroad became a reality. In the years following its completion, Battle commented, "The road has been of great benefit to the

University and the town. The University could not possibly have increased so fast without it and valuable factories and new buildings owe their origin to its facilities."[34]

Following that project, Hoke embarked on the most ambitious of his railroad enterprises—the Georgia, Carolina, and Northern Railway Company. Designed, constructed, and managed by the general, the great railroad ultimately stretched from Monroe, North Carolina, to Atlanta. With Hoke as its president, the line was a success from its inception; in time, it became an integral part of the Seaboard Airline System. Hoke's friend Fred A. Olds described the manner of man who undertook the building of a four-hundred-mile railroad: "He was a large man, of most imposing figure, and dressing himself in the garb of the everyday countryman, with a big felt hat and mounted on a large horse, went over all the line of the proposed road, in his modest way making friends everywhere and securing rights of way. Then he built the road, being president of the construction company, and it passed into the hands of the Seaboard."[35]

As the decades passed, Hoke the beloved military hero came to be admired by the people of North Carolina and the South as a champion of a vibrant and growing economy. One contemporary journalist commented, "In the hearts of the people he held a first place. . . . General Hoke's life attained to that of the ideal. Brave, honest, courteous, modest as a woman, none knew him but to love and to admire. Deprecating any reference to his great record as an officer of the Southern army he spent his days since the war unostentatiously and quietly, yet as an active force in the industrial life of the State."

While laboring to build the Georgia, Carolina, and Northern Railway, Hoke received a letter from his nephew Hoke Smith requesting information for a story about the general to be printed in Smith's newspaper, the *Atlanta Journal*. In a most characteristic response, he told Smith, "I thank you very much for your favor of the 8th inst; but I do not desire to have my picture published in the *Journal* with a sketch of my life. I do not believe in such things as they create jealousies, and provoke opposition. What I desire to do is to go along and build the G. C. & N. and have as little said about it as possible. This course enables us to accomplish what we desire to do more readily than if our acts were daily published."[36]

A friend to rich and poor, young and old alike, Hoke never lost touch with the common man regardless of the fame and success he attained. From a newspaper report of the annual meeting of the directors and stockholders of the North Carolina Railroad Company, a telling description of the man emerged:

> This attention to General Hoke is not confined to the old veterans, for young men who have the honor of his acquaintance, instinctively recognize the genuine article when they get in his atmosphere and pay respectful, cordial homage to one of the best specimens of true, chivalrous manhood, combined with gentleness of heart and iron-nerve of purpose whether in war or industrial development. In his presence one feels certain that no thought of politics or design to use you as a boost, for some future prominence of self-glory has ever entered his honest old heart. There is a look in his eye, a feeling communicated by the touch of his old-fashioned hand clasp that banishes the too common greeting of "big men."[37]

Because Hoke shied away from the spotlight, he was not recognized by many citizens of his native state born after the war. In an editorial on December 11, 1903, the *Raleigh News and Observer* lamented about Hoke,

> He made reputation that entitles him to rank with the first soldiers of the War Between the States, and yet so great is his modesty and his aversion to appearing in public that half the young people in Raleigh fail to recognize that, here in the capital city, there resides a man more like Lee, in appearance and in military genius than any living man. If he lived in some far off spot, young people of this city would make pilgrimages to see him. But, living quietly among us, we forget the distinguished honor that is given to Raleigh to have a citizen so honored and so distinguished.[38]

That Hoke closely resembled Robert E. Lee in character and disposition was denied by no one who had met the two men. According to

Josephus Daniels, Hoke was "second only to Lee in poise, in equanimity, in virtue, and magnanimity." As Hoke matured in years, not only his character but his physical appearance became the double of Lee's. After his dark hair and close-cropped beard turned gray, Hoke became almost a mirror image of the beloved Confederate chieftain. In a speech at Plymouth on June 19, 1920, Daniels told his audience: "If you ever saw Lee you have seen Hoke. If you ever talked with Hoke, you have been in the light of Lee's company. No two men, not of blood kin, ever looked so much alike, and they were kin in spirit."[39]

On many occasions during the last two decades of his life, Hoke was mistaken in picture and in person for Lee. When Alfred Hamilton, the son of Dr. Joseph G. D. Hamilton, saw a portrait in the general's home, he remarked to Hoke's daughter that it was a fine portrait of Lee and was astounded to learn that the likeness was that of Hoke. Fred A. Olds, who for many years managed the forerunner of the North Carolina Museum of History, watched the reaction of many Confederate veterans when they encountered a portrait of Hoke in the facility. As they came face to face with the image, the old soldiers cried out in astonishment, "Why, there is General Lee!" When Olds mentioned the confusion to Hoke, the general commented "that he had a picture of General Lee made when the latter entered the United States Army, and that he found the likeness between this picture and one of his own, taken about the same age, was also remarkable."[40]

On one occasion, a gentleman boarded a train at Hickory, North Carolina, and as "the monotonous journey" began, his eyes gazed about the car until they fixed upon a singular subject: "There apparently seated before me and calmly reading his daily paper was none other than the greatest commander that the English speaking race ever gave to the world, Robert E. Lee. The resemblance to General Lee could not have been more striking and lifelike if one of the portraits of the mighty Southerner had stepped from its frame and became incarnate in the figure before me." When the passenger inquired about the identity of the man reading the paper, the conductor responded with evident satisfaction, "That is Major General Robert F. Hoke, C.S.A."[41]

Without question, the most amazing case of mistaken identity between

Hoke and Lee occurred many years after the war in Washington, D.C. During Grover Cleveland's first administration, Lee's daughter Mildred was touring the various federal departments when she happened by the office of Hoke Smith, the secretary of the interior. Noticing a photograph on Smith's desk, Mildred Lee exclaimed with pride and satisfaction, "Mr. Smith, I see you have a splendid photograph of my father." Smith replied politely, "I am a great admirer of your father, but that is a photograph of my uncle, General Hoke."[42]

From 1875 until the general's death, home for the Hoke family was a sprawling multistory white frame house near the corner of Edenton and Dawson Streets within sight of the State Capitol. The 1850-vintage dwelling stood until 1967, when it was demolished to make way for a modern hotel in downtown Raleigh. In the early 1890s, the Hokes had a brief taste of suburban living when they purchased a magnificent Victorian mansion replete with vertical cupolas and turrets, marble and oak floors, and mahogany banisters. But for Lydia Hoke, the elegant castle was "too far from the center of things," and the family returned to its downtown home after a year.[43]

In 1887, when Hoke began work on the last great business enterprise of his career, he turned to the beloved place of his birth. At about age fifty, Hoke was diagnosed as suffering from Bright's disease. After his physician advised him to drink lithia water for his condition, Hoke made his way to Lincolnton in search of the special water. There, he was attracted to the soon-to-be famous Lithia Springs, located a mile and a half from downtown Lincolnton. Hoke was among the first of many people to enjoy the relief the spring water offered for certain kidney and bladder ailments. A contemporary report on the therapeutic powers of the water noted, "The waters of this spring—their medicinal scope and efficacy considered—are unsurpassed if they are not incomparably superior to those found in any other part of the American continent."

Convinced that the water could be profitably marketed, Hoke purchased the property on which the springs were located. In 1887, Hoke, Benjamin N. Duke, and others organized the Lincoln Lithia Water Company in order to bottle, distribute, and sell the water. The general was the president and principal stockholder in the venture. Markets for the bottled water were quickly developed in major cities such as St. Louis and Atlanta. In time, the product, bottled on-site, was distributed nationwide.[44]

As the fame of the springs spread, the general decided to build a spa. By 1890, work commenced on a rambling, multistory hostelry of thirty rooms near the springs. While the hotel site was being excavated, Hoke became the first person to detect the presence of tin in Lincoln County. For a number of years thereafter, the only tin mine in the United States was operated near the inn.

Once the Lincoln Lithia Inn was completed, it remained a popular resort for more than fifty years. In a travel publication issued during the summer of 1896, Hoke's role in the operation was described: "This gentleman, though a native of Lincolnton, is a resident of Raleigh. He spends much time here, however, constantly elaborating and supervising new improvements. His whole heart is in the work, for he intends to make this resort second to no other in the United States."[45]

To avail himself of the healing waters and monitor the thriving enterprise, Hoke constructed a comfortable summer home near the inn around the turn of the century. It soon became his "favorite place to live." Though he was still heavily involved in the railroad business, the general spent much of the last decade of his life at the springs. He was devoted to his grandchildren, who began to arrive in the early years of the new century. Never disposed to excess recreation, Hoke enjoyed reading military history. His favorite subject of study was Napoleon.[46]

By 1909, the health of the seventy-two-year-old general had improved substantially. At the time, he was described as "active, erect and vigorous in mind and body." Eager to complete the development of the Lithia Springs property, he had just two years earlier incorporated the Lincoln Lithia Club. A plat prepared for Hoke by Biltmore Nursery of Biltmore, North Carolina in 1908 revealed a layout of streets and scores of lots surrounding the hotel.[47]

As Hoke entered the twilight of his life, he treasured the time spent at his summer home in Lincolnton. He enjoyed returning to the pursuit which had kept hunger from his door immediately after the war. In the Lincolnton countryside, he could keep his mules, cows, and chickens, and to the extent his health and age allowed, he tilled the earth that had been so good to him. His engineering skill enabled him to construct a corncrib that "was absolutely rat proof." Hoke was proud of his paradise and willing to share it. A hometown journalist described the Hoke hospitality: "No man, whether he was the poorest or richest ever set foot on the threshold of this hospitable place without receiving from him a cordial welcome—a hearty hand shake, and 'help yourself to all the lithia water you can drink.' It was a genuine welcome such as only this noble old gentleman knew how to give."[48]

Hoke last returned to his home in Raleigh in June 1912. While in the capital, the general called on Secretary of State J. Bryan Grimes, the son of a Confederate major general. Grimes pleaded with Hoke, as he had so many times before, to write his recollections of the war, but the general declined the request. Hoke "felt that it was too long ago and he had forgotten so many incidents that he did not feel that he could do justice to many gallant men who deserved special mention." When he departed the city for Lincolnton, his appearance "gave promise of a life longer than it was spared."[49]

Upon his return to Lithia Springs, Hoke grew gravely ill from diabetes during the last week of June. Day by day, life slowly ebbed from his body. By the end of the month, his children were summoned to Lincolnton. On Monday night, July 1, his condition "took a decided turn for the worse." Newspapers throughout the state began to publish daily bulletins about the general's deteriorating condition. On July 2, the *Charlotte Observer* reported, "The end seems to be near." After alternating "between stupor and consciousness" for three days, it was all over for Hoke at 10:20 A.M. on Wednesday, July 3: "Death came to the great soldier sweetly." Just as he had faced death in so many battles as a young man, Lee's modest warrior "met it calmly, died fearlessly."[50]

At 7:30 P.M. on July 4, Hoke's remains arrived in Raleigh via the Southern Railway. A large assemblage of citizens met the body and proceeded with it to the Hoke home on Edenton and Dawson Streets.

Statements of sympathy and tributes began to pour in from all quarters.

In Lincolnton, the local newspaper eulogized Hoke in the simplest of terms: "A giant has fallen." In Hoke's adopted hometown, the *Raleigh Times* noted, "By his work and his example and by his life long modesty and simplicity, he was as great in peace as in war." On behalf of Confederate veterans, Brigadier General William Ruffin Cox paid tribute to a fallen comrade: "In passing he leaves behind him in the admiration of our people, a light that illumines our State's records as among the first of her sister states for devotion to the right and cheerful sacrifices whenever honor leads the way." Hoke's associates in the North Carolina Railroad Company eulogized him as "the most commanding figure which our State has given to the world."[51]

On July 5, the flags atop the State Capitol were lowered to half-mast, and the Capitol and all public buildings were draped in mourning. In a fitting tribute to a great native son, the state legislature closed for the funeral. A multitude of distinguished citizens attended the service, held at 11 A.M. at Hoke's beloved Episcopal church, the Church of the Good Shepherd, located just around the corner from his home. Along the walkway outside the church stood a row of aged Confederate veterans quietly paying tribute to their compatriot and hero. Many people were forced to stand outside for lack of room. On the inside, the rows of active and honorary pallbearers were a who's who of North Carolina.

The service was as Hoke would have wanted: "The ceremonies were entirely without ostentation. They were as simple as they would have been had the dead been the lowliest private, instead of the military marvel of the latter days of the Confederacy. But for such prodigality of flowers and the presence of many distinguished men, nothing could have betrayed the character of burial to be solemnized."

After the choir offered up "Nearer My God To Thee," the pallbearers stepped forward to bear the casket out of the church. As they carried out their duty, the choir ended the service with "Thy Will Be Done." The time had come for Hoke's final march. Included in the long cortege to nearby Oakwood Cemetery was a long line of Confederate veterans who like Hoke had done their duty in a war that ended almost a half-century earlier. Hoke was laid to rest on a knoll in the historic cemetery, which contained the graves of many noted North Carolinians, as well as soldiers who had fought and died under Hoke's command.[52]

Fittingly, a final memorial service was held for Hoke in the town where his life began and ended. On Sunday afternoon, July 14, the large brick building where young Robert had attended school was filled to capacity by townspeople, who "came quietly and reverently to take part in the services in memory of the hero all delighted to honor." The Reverend W. A. Minter, the local Presbyterian minister and the nephew of Major General Stephen Dodson Ramseur, offered an address wherein he lauded Hoke for his devotion to the "cause of right, of honesty, of simplicity of life, and of peace when peace was honor."[53]

The Reverend Minter's stirring words rang out within earshot of the home where Hoke's life had begun seventy-five years earlier. In the intervening years, Hoke had spent much of his life away from the place where he was born and reared. But the values he had learned there during his formative years stood him in good stead all the days of his life. And when the end of that life drew near, Hoke chose to come home.

Of the many wonderful eulogies presented to memorialize him, Hoke no doubt would have been proudest of the words offered up in his hometown by historian Alfred Nixon on July 10, 1912: "In his death the State has lost one of its very greatest sons. His deeds are written in her history, and as the years pass coming generations will have pointed out his life as one fit for all emulation, for he was of the highest and best of Southern manhood."[54]

CHAPTER 17

Requiem for a Modest Man

During the Civil War, North Carolina, with but one-ninth of the population of the Confederate States of America, supplied more than 125,000 Confederate troops, a total that exceeded the voting population of the state. By doing so, North Carolina provided approximately one-sixth of all Confederate soldiers—more than any other state. Among those troops were many distinguished soldiers, including the much-heralded generals William Dorsey Pender and James Johnston Pettigrew.[1]

But of all the illustrious soldiers North Carolina gave to the Confederacy, Robert Frederick Hoke has been described as "the most distinguished soldier of North Carolina" and "the North Carolina Lee" by Samuel A. Ashe, noted author, editor, and attorney and the last surviving commissioned Confederate officer. Throughout the four years of the Civil War,

General Robert F. Hoke

Hoke won the praise, respect, and admiration of his commanders, fellow officers, subordinates, and even adversaries. Josephus Daniels noted, "The Marse Robert of the Confederacy was the only officer in an army distinguished for the lofty character of its generals who stood higher in the affection and admiration of his soldiers than Robert F. Hoke."[2]

At the top of the chain of command, President Jefferson Davis expressed his respect for Hoke and his military abilities in April 1864 by making him the youngest major general in the Confederate army. And from the time Hoke achieved regimental command in 1862 until the end of the war, he enjoyed the implicit confidence of Robert E. Lee. The *Official Records* reveal the numerous occasions over the last twelve months of the war when Lee repeatedly requested the services of Hoke and his soldiers.[3]

Brigadier General William Ruffin Cox, the officer whose troops fired the final shots at Appomattox and who elicited Lee's famous compliment "God Bless gallant old North Carolina," noted about Hoke, "He was . . . our State's most accomplished soldier in the War between the States." As a division commander, Hoke won accolades from the brigadiers who served under him. Johnson Hagood, who gallantly led one of Hoke's brigades during the final year of the war, characterized Hoke as a soldier "of good presence and agreeable manner; a good administrative officer, of undoubted personal gallantry, and possessed of habits of vigilance. His intercourse with his subordinates was always marked with good feeling on both sides."[4]

Officers of lower grade were equally lavish in their praise. Hugh H. Colquitt, a Georgian, wrote, "General R. F. Hoke was one of the finest soldiers in the southern army. . . . As a staff officer actively in the field, I had an opportunity to form a fair opinion of many division commanders, and I can say without hesitation that General Hoke was the best I ever came in contact with. We served under him during some very hard and trying times, and he was always the cheerful, active, attentive, and able officer. He was a modest and lovable man, a cool and gallant officer." Captain Charles G. Elliott, a staff officer of the Martin/Kirkland brigade, recalled, "Hoke, as a division commander, was the peer of any in the army. Conspicuous for his bravery, coolness, and good judgment, the youngest Major General in the army, his rapid promotion from the grade of lieutenant was due alone to his gallant and meritorious conduct and *fitness to command*." About Hoke's fitness for command, Lieutenant Colonel Walter Clark of the North Carolina Junior Reserves wrote in later years, "It is not too much to say that by common consent in the army Pender, Hoke, and Pettigrew were entitled to command Corps or even Armies."[5]

From the Confederate navy came the sentiments of Commander B. P. Loyall, who believed "there was not a more competent or brilliant officer of his rank in the Confederate Army" than Hoke. Major J. A. Weston, a member of the Thirty-third North Carolina who fought with Hoke at Malvern Hill, Second Manassas, and Sharpsburg, offered a similar tribute in 1901 by noting that "(if we except Lee and Jackson) there was no more gallant nor skillful officer in either army" than Hoke.[6]

Despite the suffering to which they were exposed during the four years of the war, the men who fought under Hoke never lost their confidence in or their esteem for him. Major James F. Beall of the Twenty-first North Carolina, who served under Hoke during the ferocious fighting at Fredericksburg, pointed out, "General Hoke held, in pre-eminent degree, the confidence of his men, being trusted and idolized by them, and they knew that he trusted them. His appearance in battle always inspired the greatest confidence and enthusiasm." Private James C. Elliott of the Fifty-sixth North Carolina concluded, "Among the younger officers none excelled General Hoke." Private James Evans, who shared in Hoke's triumph at Plymouth and the debacle at Fort Harrison, stated, "General Hoke was a noble commander, and we boys all loved him."[7]

Fred A. Olds, the beloved historian and newspaperman credited with putting together the collection that formed the basis of the modern North Carolina Museum of History, grew up in North Carolina during the Civil War and spent his entire adult life acquiring information and artifacts from Confederate veterans. A personal acquaintance of Hoke's, Olds wrote of the general in 1919, "It ought to be said, as showing the character of the man, that while he was an inflexible soldier, doing his duty always, he was invariably thoughtful of his men, and to this day has their undying love and regard. They appreciated his bravery and he appreciated theirs. I have heard them talk about him and have heard him talk about them many a time and oft, and so know both sides of the matter."[8]

From the enemy camp, Hoke received the ultimate accolade when Union intelligence reported to the headquarters of the Army of the Potomac in late December 1864, "Hoke's division is the only one sent south from General Lee's army, it being the largest and best division in his command."[9]

Many celebrated North Carolina historians in addition to Fred A. Olds, Samuel A. Ashe, and Josephus Daniels have lauded Hoke's character, ability, and record as a military leader. Dr. Joseph G. D. Hamilton, the long-time head of the history department at the University of North Carolina at Chapel Hill and the founder of the renowned Southern Historical Collection at that institution, characterized Hoke as "North Carolina's foremost soldier." The Reverend Joseph B. Cheshire, Jr., observed of Hoke's sense of duty, "He was a man of great force and of iron will, quiet in method, but immovable and inexorable in matters of duty. What had to be done he did; he did it at once, without hesitation or delay: in a sense, remorselessly, for he had no fear and no regrets, when he knew what his duty required of him."[10]

On a national level, Glenn Tucker described Hoke as "one of the greatest soldiers North Carolina ever produced," "great on any field," and "one of the foremost of all the great soldiers of the Civil War." And despite Douglas Southall Freeman's criticisms, as alluded to earlier, he described Hoke as "a tall magnificent young North Carolinian" who had "a certain ferocious quality of leadership" and who "manifestly knew how to fight."[11]

Hoke the man was highly respected as a kind, hardworking, humble Southern gentleman who maintained an abiding love of family, friends, and his native state. In 1912, State Senator Victor S. Bryant summarized Hoke's life and character: "He was a student and scholar, a soldier and a commander, a manufacturer, farmer, miner, railroad-builder, and a gentleman without reproach." Less than three years before the general died, an unidentified writer described Hoke as "a gentleman of the old school, companionable in spirit, thoughtful in speech, considerate of the weak and courteous to the strong. He comes nearer attending strictly to his own business and letting severely alone that of all others than any man I ever knew."[12]

Requiem for a Modest Man

In a Confederate Memorial Day address at Kinston on May 10, 1921, Josephus Daniels urged those in attendance, "Get you a hero, and I give you Gen. Robert Hoke . . . as an ideal in peace and war." He continued, "It is because of what General Hoke was—clean of mind, steady of purpose, clean in living, the very soul of courtesy and truth and courage that I offer him as the model to young men not only of the South, but to the young men of America."[13]

Hoke was respected throughout his life for his kindness and gracious manner. Reflecting upon the decent treatment he and his comrades received from Hoke after their capture at Plymouth, a former Union soldier heartily endorsed a remark he had once heard: "There is not a mean drop of blood in Bob Hoke's body." One observer concluded that the meanest thing he ever heard Hoke say was in response to being asked about a particular man who was extremely stingy and greedy. "Why," replied Hoke, "he is very careful with his money."[14]

But Hoke's kindness is best illustrated by a wartime incident when the general happened to be in Charlotte. At the same time, a frail but well-educated lady striving to rear six children received the doleful news that her husband had been seriously wounded while fighting with the Confederate army in the Western theater. Accompanied by her oldest child, who was scarcely in his teens, the woman came to Charlotte in a desperate attempt to reach her husband, who had been transported to a hospital in Macon, Georgia. While the lady was discussing her plight with a man in the telegraph office, a Confederate officer stepped to the counter, wrote out a telegram, and handed it to the operator. In the process, he overheard the lady's conversation. Without introduction, he proceeded to ask her about her condition of distress, then requested that she remain in her seat while he attended to some business. Shortly thereafter, the officer returned and placed in the lady's hands a large roll of Confederate bills. He then explained that because of heavy troop movements and the constantly deteriorating condition of the railroads, it would not be prudent for her to make the trip to Georgia. Instead, he persuaded her to locate a male neighbor too old for military service to travel to Georgia on her behalf. The officer promptly scrawled a note of introduction for the old gentleman to the authorities in Macon. To the note was affixed the signature of General Robert F. Hoke. Subsequently, the neighbor made the trip and returned with the wounded soldier, who survived the war for nearly thirty years.[15]

But of all of his good qualities, Hoke, much like Robert E. Lee, considered the greatest to be attention to duty. When asked in the twilight of his years what advice he would offer to the young, Hoke responded, "Strict attention to all duties of life."[16]

Hoke is also noted for his great modesty. Characterized as "the most modest commanding officer in the Confederate army" and "modest as a woman," he was the epitome of reserve throughout his life. Fred A. Olds observed, "No man was more modest than General Hoke." Dr. Joseph G. D. Hamilton concurred: "We can search long without success to discover so modest a character as General Hoke." He also noted, "His pride was great, but his modesty was greater." But no one described the quality that became the trademark of Hoke's life better than the editorial writer for the *Greensboro Daily News*:

> Since the close of the struggle in 1865 General Hoke has gone in and out before the people of North Carolina with a record for courage, ability, and fidelity that would have made an arrogant man the most conspicuous figure in the state. Not so with General Hoke. With modesty as gentle as a woman, with quiet reserve as tender and as becoming as the delicate purity of the fairest flower he refrained from the blare and glare of the dress parade, shrinking from the plaudits he knew could be his for a mere change of manner. He has lived a life as quiet and as free from show as if he had been the humblest soldier in the ranks of that titanic struggle. It required a big man and a brave man to live that way. He was master of himself. Fleeting show and glittering honors could not tempt him to come down from the lofty pedestal where his sterling manhood placed him. He maintained his beautiful poise with a quiet dignity that few men ever attain.[17]

The Hoke modesty was not a false one, like that exhibited by some Confederate veterans. Not only did he refuse to take part in postwar Confederate reunions, but he was extremely reluctant to talk or write about his military career. Fred A. Olds, the interviewer of many a Confederate veteran, lamented, "It was extremely difficult to induce General Hoke to talk about his war, or speaking that the war was over, experiences. . . . He had been pressed over and over again to talk for publication, but his extreme modesty invariably caused him to decline. . . . If General Hoke would only have talked, his reminiscences would have made a book of highest interest and value." Josephus Daniels, one of Hoke's most intimate friends in Raleigh, sounded a similar strain: "What a book he could write of impressions of the war if only he would do so, and what a feast of good things I could set before the North Carolina public if he would only allow me to put in print what he has many a time told me privately. But when he looks at you with that winning smile, and says, as he has almost invariably, 'You must not print what I say,' it is over."[18]

On the rare occasion when Hoke was persuaded or disposed to discuss the war, it was always in the company of a few good friends. He was described as a "charming conversationalist" who related a "story of a brilliant dash, a bloody struggle, a glorious battle, or a sorrowful defeat with a clearness" that seemed to bring the event to life. Almost without exception, when telling of a war event, Hoke emphasized "what my soldiers did" and left himself out of the story. Olds observed, "His memory was without fault and hence his personal recollections had a value beyond those of ordinary men."

When the rare opportunity presented itself, a journalist, with apologies to the general, might print the information related by Hoke to friends. From a meeting of the directors and stockholders of the North Carolina Railroad, it was reported, "The preceding quotations from some of his conversations intended only for private ears cannot possibly offend the tender sensibilities of so modest and reserved a gentleman as is General Hoke. Certainly not when he realizes that they will carry pleasure and comfort and approval to thousands besides the few to whom they were spoken."[19]

As time passed, Hoke's modesty drew gentle criticism on occasion. On December 11, 1903, the editor of the *Raleigh News and Observer* told readers, "North Carolina people who know him well have but one fault to find with Gen. Robert F. Hoke, who honors Raleigh by making it his home, and that fault is his extreme modesty and retirement. It is a fault that is rare and one that is easily forgiven." Josephus Daniels, the Raleigh editor who bestowed upon Hoke many superlatives including "the State's wisest man," declared in the 1921 speech at Kinston, "If any criticism could be made of General Hoke it would be that he was too modest, too reserved, and that he denied to his fellow citizens the privilege of calling him to the same high station in peace which he occupied in war. But that criticism stands out in relief when contrasted with the action of some of the soldiers of our day."[20]

Without question, Hoke, through his modesty and reserve, did a great disservice to Civil War historians and students of history. His unwillingness to write or speak about the war deprived future generations of Americans of personal stories about the general and invaluable eyewitness accounts of many of the most important battles and campaigns of the war. No doubt, some historical inaccuracies found their way into print and into public acceptance following the war because Hoke refused to speak out. Moreover, his lifelong silence not only kept him out of the limelight but also robbed many of his gallant soldiers of the public accolades that Hoke quietly held for them in his heart.

When Hoke died, he was hailed as "North Carolina's foremost citizen," "North Carolina's first citizen," and "the most commanding figure which our State has given to the world." In 1920, Fred A. Olds maintained, "No name in North Carolina is more honored than that of the late Major General Robert F. Hoke."

Olds's observation and the lofty sobriquets set forth in Hoke's obituaries may well have been accurate, but Hoke was honored throughout his life for the most part in name only. A decade before the general's death, Samuel Ashe bemoaned the lack of tangible honors: "If Gen. Hoke were a resident of some Northern city—or indeed of any other Southern State, what honor would be heaped upon him, what personal respect, I may almost say reverence, would be accorded him? . . . In England, France, Germany—how heads would bow in the presence of such a veritable hero." At the same time, Ashe realized that his lamentations were hollow, since the general himself had been unwilling to accept any gifts, titles, offices, or honors offered him. Ashe conceded, "Since like his immortal chieftain, Lee, he has sought no public office, he passes among us undistinguishable in the crowd. Such doubtless is his own desire. I do not question that it would be disagreeable to him to attract public attention. If we are ever to begin to cure our deficiency in regard to perpetuating the fame of our great men, we may well begin with Gen. Hoke."[21]

During Hoke's lifetime, practically every "honor within the gift of the people of North Carolina" was tendered to the general, but he remained resolute in his desire to gain no profit from his military career. "Honors and place were his for a word, but he remained silent," noted Dr. Joseph G. D. Hamilton. Hoke never aspired to any political office although "he was virtually offered the Governorship" of North Carolina. The *Richmond Virginian* reported, "Any public position of honor and profit—from that of the governorship down—could have been his for the asking, indeed, would have been forced on him (as was repeatedly attempted by admirers time and again) had he not so firmly protested and refused all political honors."

To some observers, Hoke's disdain for political office was curious. After all, his family had been prominent in state and national affairs since the country's birth. Not only had Hoke's father been one of the premier Democratic politicians in antebellum North Carolina, but his nephew Hoke Smith gained national political prominence as United States secretary of the interior and as governor of Georgia in the last quarter of the nineteenth century and first decade of the twentieth. Moreover, Hoke's brothers-in-law Augustus and Robert Van Wyck enjoyed political fame in New York.[22] No doubt, Hoke's reserve played a role in his distaste for political position, but perhaps the greatest reason why he shunned campaigns and elections can be traced to his childhood. The gubernatorial campaign of 1844 not only robbed the state of one of its most competent statesmen but took from seven-year-old Robert F. Hoke his father. Many years later, Hoke would have no desire for the office which cost his father's life—and one to which his father would have probably been elected had he not died before his prime.

A soldier who had served under Hoke inquired of the general many years after the war, "You take no active part in politics?" "No," he said. "I vote, that's all." However, Hoke maintained an abiding interest in the affairs of North Carolina despite his aversion to office. His strong roots in the Democratic Party did not prevent him from acquiring "friends in all parties." Politicians as well as civic and business leaders often sought his counsel, and he obliged them on the condition that he be kept out of the limelight. A week after Hoke's death, Josephus Daniels disclosed, "North Carolina has had no wise Governor in thirty years who has not benefited by the advice of General Hoke. No man was wiser than he or so well posted upon questions affecting the policy of the State." On a personal basis, Daniels later expressed his gratitude to Hoke for "his devotion to the public weal by placing his store-house of information and his large horizon of counsel at my disposal in more than one great contest and for the good of the people of his state. . . . The world needs more Hokes who give and give and ask no compensation, no approval, no applause. Could any youth select a nobler hero?"[23]

Outside the political arena, high honors were extended to Hoke, and prompt refusals usually followed. During the Spanish-American War, President William McKinley offered him an appointment as brigadier general in the United States Army. Such an offer was a great tribute to a man who had seen only four years of military service, and that more than thirty years earlier. The offer also disclosed that the wounds of the once-divided nation had dramatically healed. Nonetheless, the appointment was declined by Hoke, who maintained that his fighting days were over unless his country needed his services in a crisis. He did not believe that the conflict with Spain in the Caribbean posed such a crisis as to disrupt the life of a man nearing sixty years of age.[24]

On February 8, 1905, the North Carolina Senate and House of Representatives passed a joint resolution which read in part, "As an expression of the high appreciation of the personal worth and public services of Robert F. Hoke . . . the General Assembly of North Carolina hereby tenders to that distinguished citizen of the State, a reception, and invites him to name an evening when it will be convenient for him to meet the members of the General Assembly in the Hall of the House of Representatives." A committee of two senators and three House members was appointed "to visit on General Hoke" and present him a copy of the resolution. When the committee called, Hoke responded to their invitation by relating the story of Captain Jack, the chief of the Modocs, and an army chaplain. Captain Jack was visited daily by the chaplain while awaiting execution for killing General Edward R. S. Canby under a flag of truce. Day after day, the chaplain counseled Captain Jack on the heavenly rewards for the contrite at heart. Finally, one day just after the chaplain finished an enthusiastic description of the Creator's goodness, Captain Jack remarked, "You know Him, me don't. If that is such a happy land, you go there. Me give you nine ponies to take my place." "Now," said Hoke to his visitors, "I'll give you nine ponies to take my place." Thus, the reception was never held.[25]

There were other honors, both large and small, that Hoke could not refuse. For example, in 1899, the Salisbury chapter of the United Daughters of the Confederacy changed its name to the Gen. Robert F. Hoke Chapter. In an unsuccessful attempt to dissuade members from making the change, Hoke penned the following note to the recording secretary: "I appreciate most highly the honor you have shown me in changing the name of your chapter from Rowan to that of Robert F. Hoke, but I feel as if it should not have been changed from Rowan, as that county furnished so many gallant and brave soldiers to our war, whose noble deeds should be represented by the name of your chapter of the Daughters. They fought the battles and should never be forgotten."[26]

In June 1885, Hoke received a letter from a North Carolina veteran who had fought in his division as a member of Kirkland's brigade. The writer made a request for Hoke to forward a photograph of himself, for which the veteran would pay "what you charge." As to his plans for the photograph, he wrote, "I want to have it framed up so it will keep nice as long as I live and my son after me." The writer concluded his letter, "I have a son ten years old named after you." No doubt, the son was one of many born after the war who bore the general's name.[27]

During the first decade of the twentieth century, a clamor arose among residents of western Cumberland and northern Robeson Counties in the North Carolina sand hills for the formation of a new county. Proponents of the new political subdivision realized that if they were going to win legislative approval, the county would need to be named for a person popular with all members of the general assembly. Supporters selected Hoke as the namesake of the proposed county, but even they "may not have realized the power of Hoke's name." M. Delancey Haywood, a distinguished North Carolina historian, jumped on the Hoke County bandwagon by pointing out, "It seems to me that our state could not do better than confer upon it the name of one of its own gifted sons, Robert F. Hoke. As a soldier, citizen and gentleman, no North Carolinian—living or dead—is more worthy of such an honor, and the tribute to our State's last surviving Major General would be both graceful and just." And so, on February 11, 1911, more than a year before Hoke's death, the people of North Carolina conferred the honor of naming the state's hundredth and last county Hoke County. Ironically, Fort Bragg, the sprawling United States Army installation named for the Confederate general with whom Hoke was closely associated during the last eighteen months of the war, now covers much of Hoke County.[28]

Hoke County, however, was not the first place name on the North Carolina map to honor the general. In 1900, the people of the Washington County community of Long Ridge changed the name of their village to Hoke in honor of the general who liberated Plymouth, located seven miles north.[29]

For many years after Hoke's death, the honors continued. A highway historical marker was erected at his birthplace, and monuments and markers were placed at Plymouth, Southwest Creek, and Bentonville, where the general commanded troops with distinction. Hoke was also a front runner in the group of generals from which four were to be chosen to join the likenesses of Lee, Jackson, and Davis in the central group of Gutzon Borglum's bas-relief carvings at Stone Mountain, Georgia; in 1925, just two years after Borglum began his work, the project was left unfinished for lack of funds and dissension among various state historical groups and commissions. On May 4, 1943, the Liberty ship S.S. *Robert F. Hoke* was launched at Wilmington to join the Allied convoy fleets of the Atlantic.[30]

If a personal battle flag had been sewn for North Carolina's most honored soldier, it would have borne inscriptions for virtually every vital campaign in which the Army of Northern Virginia was involved—Bethel, the Peninsula, Gaines' Mill and Malvern Hill and the other Seven Days' Battles, Second Manassas, Harpers Ferry, Sharpsburg, Fredericksburg, Chancellorsville, New Bern, Plymouth, Drewry's Bluff, Cold Harbor, Petersburg, Richmond, Fort Fisher, Wilmington, Wyse's Forks, and Bentonville. Only the life-threatening shoulder wound at Salem Church kept Hoke out of Gettysburg. Assuredly, Hoke was conspicuous at most every place in the Eastern theater that has been deemed important by scholars. Despite the fact that he held the rank of general for less than two and a half years of the war, his name is mentioned in the *Official Records* (Army) more than a thousand times, an indication of his importance to the Confederate war effort.

Nevertheless, most eminent Civil War scholars and writers of the twentieth century have not considered Hoke a major player in the conflict. They have either neglected him altogether or relegated him to the ranks of the commanders of the second or third level who were promoted in the final years of the war not so much for merit but because of deadly attrition. Among the historians in the latter group are Douglas Southall Freeman and Shelby Foote. While Freeman takes more notice of Hoke in *R. E. Lee* and *Lee's Lieutenants* than does Foote in *The Civil War*, neither historian has accorded Hoke the prominence he enjoyed in the Army of Northern Virginia or acknowledged the services he rendered for the Confederate States of America, particularly during the last sixteen months of the war. Still more troubling is Bruce Catton's trilogy, *The Centennial History of the Civil War*, which fails to mention Hoke at all.

There are a number of possible reasons for the neglect of Hoke in scholarly studies of the Civil War in the twentieth century: his youth and his position as a junior officer during the early stages of the war; his status as a civilian soldier, a man lacking in military training, especially when compared to general officers of high rank educated at West Point or Virginia Military Institute; his lack of the flamboyance that characterized some of the generals in Lee's upper echelon and put them in the forefront of the press; his ability to carry out the duties of a high-ranking office without fanfare; his postwar modesty and his steadfast refusal to profit from or

General Robert F. Hoke

allow others to publicize his remarkable military record.

Whatever the reason, Hoke for the most part has not enjoyed the same notoriety as many Civil War generals of equal or of even lower rank. Nonetheless, there is yet one other honor—indeed, the "ultimate" honor—that must be examined to understand Hoke's importance to Civil War history. It is an honor that has never been authenticated to the satisfaction of many historians and scholars, an honor that has been dismissed by some Civil War experts as pure legend or fable, an honor that has been ridiculed by some students of the Civil War as akin to blasphemy, and an honor so controversial that it has been overlooked or ignored completely by many historians.

This disputed honor, taught to North Carolina schoolchildren throughout much of the twentieth century, was publicized to much of the world at Hoke's death in stories similar to the one that appeared in the July 4, 1912, issue of the *New York Tribune*: "General Robert F. Hoke, a Confederate soldier, said to have been the personal choice of General Lee to succeed him in case he was killed in battle, died to-day at his home in Lincolnton." Newspapers in Boston, Philadelphia, Pittsburgh, Newark, Baltimore, Washington, D.C., Norfolk, Raleigh, Greensboro, Charlotte, Atlanta, Jacksonville, New Orleans, Montgomery, Nashville, St. Louis, Indianapolis, Chicago, and San Francisco spread the shocking revelation throughout America. Headlines were absolute: "Gen. Lee's Favorite General Is Dead" in the *Boston Evening Herald*; "Gen. R. F. Hoke, Who Was Slated To Succeed Lee, Dies in Carolina" in the *Virginian-Pilot* of Norfolk; "Was Next In Rank to Gen. Robert E. Lee in Command of Confederate Forces" in the *Atlanta Journal*; "Confederate Officer Was Lee's Choice for Successor" in the *New Orleans Picayune*; and "Gen. Hoke, Picked by Davis to Succeed Lee, Passes Away" in the *New York Times*.[31]

Reports of this "ultimate" honor were first made public in North Carolina in 1905 through an unusual set of circumstances. Around 1896, Colonel (later General) Henry W. Lawton of the United States Army, a veteran officer who had defeated Geronimo in the Indian Wars, came to Raleigh to inspect the federal cemeteries in the city. One day during his visit, Lawton was chatting with William M. Russ, mayor of Raleigh, on the street near the State Capitol when Hoke passed by. As a courtesy to the city's most respected citizen, Mayor Russ doffed his hat, and Hoke did likewise. As Hoke walked on, Lawton asked Russ, "Who is that soldierly looking old gentleman?" Russ responded, "That is General Hoke." Lawton, who was subsequently killed in action in the Philippines in 1899, expressed his desire to meet the general, so the two men hurried up the street and caught Hoke. Lawton informed Hoke that while in Washington, D.C., he had discovered some Confederate records wherein it was noted that Lee had recommended Hoke be placed in command of the Army of Northern Virginia in case Lee was killed or incapacitated. Hoke's simple response was, "Yes, in 1864."[32]

No further reference was made of the matter until 1905, when Mayor Russ related the details of the meeting of Lawton and Hoke to Joseph J. Laughinghouse, a Civil War veteran who had fought under Hoke as a member of the North Carolina Junior Reserves. Laughinghouse promptly repeated the story to his son-in-law, J. Bryan Grimes, North Carolina's secretary of state and the son of Confederate major general Bryan Grimes. Intensely interested in the history of his native state, J. Bryan Grimes saw to it that the story was brought to the attention of the public. On Thursday, December 21, 1905, he informed those assembled at Centennial Elementary School in Raleigh for the North Carolina Day exercises that Hoke had been selected by Davis to succeed Lee as commander of the Army of Northern Virginia in the event Lee was wounded or killed.

Six days later, upon learning of Grimes's speech, Hoke asked the secretary of state for his authority for the statement. Once Grimes told Hoke the source of his information, the general verified the story was true. He provided but few details to Grimes: "While camped on the north side of the James River in the winter of '64, he was with General Lee almost everyday for several months. One afternoon General Lee asked him to ride with him and told him that it had been decided by President Davis that in the event that anything happened to Lee that Hoke had been selected to succeed him and take command of the army."

Hoke cautioned Grimes that only once before had he talked about his conversation with Lee, confiding in an old friend, R. E. Battle, who was extremely ill at the time. Battle had promised to keep the matter confidential, and Hoke likewise swore Grimes to secrecy because "some might feel that he was trying to claim credits which could not be ascertained by official records." Respecting the general's wishes, Grimes affirmed that he would not mention the conversation during Hoke's lifetime.[33]

But Grimes had no control over the press and word-of-mouth accounts in the wake of his speech. No mention of the matter had ever been made in the Hoke home. Accordingly, one of the most astonished readers of the newspaper stories that followed Grimes's speech was Dr. Michael Hoke in Atlanta. Dr. Hoke later recalled, "Father was the most modest of men and had never in his life referred to this matter in the home circles. It was just like him not having done so. He had a very great contempt . . . for the policy of some people who had been prominent in the Army for using a record, that to Father, should be considered almost as a sacred contribution to his country for political ends."

His curiosity aroused, the physician immediately dispatched a letter to his father. General Hoke responded with a letter of his own. Unfortunately, Dr. Hoke either lost or destroyed this letter, thus depriving the world of a written account of the story by the general himself. Thereafter, the physician relied on his memory when relating the contents of the letter to others. On April 8, 1924, Dr. Hoke recorded his recollection of the letter in his correspondence to Bennehan Cameron, a leading North Carolina financier and industrialist who was a longtime admirer of the general:

Dear Mike,

Yes, it is true that General Lee recommended to President Davis that I be placed in command of the Army of Virginia in the event of his death or if ill health or accident incapacitated him. It happened in the fall of 1864. General Lee called me to his tent and told me about it. My reply was that I thought it would be unwise because there were older men than myself in the army, of higher rank, whom I would remove. General Lee smiled and replied, "That is why I have made the recommendation, because I know you will do your duty as you see it." I do not care for you or any member of my family to ever make reference whatever to this event. It is on record somewhere, and some day will be known.

Your affectionate father,
Robert F. Hoke[34]

Following the revelation to Dr. Hoke, the general shared the story with his other children and also swore them to secrecy. Other family members received the news, but not from the general. From his law office on Broadway, Augustus Van Wyck wrote his brother-in-law on March 4, 1907, "It was a great compliment to have been selected by the Confederate Cabinet at Lee's suggestion to be his successor in case of accident. At the Banquet of the N.Y. City 'North Carolina Society' last week, one of the speakers, assistant Editor of *Baltimore Sun*, paid you a great tribute referring to the above matter. I was greatly pleased to hear it."[35]

In response to the press coverage of Grimes's speech, Captain Robert S. Park, the state treasurer of Georgia, wrote Grimes for confirmation. Grimes notified Park that Hoke had requested he not discuss the story further. Subsequently, on October 21, 1906, Park wrote Grimes that when he had seen General Hoke in Atlanta, Hoke confirmed the story. In order to get a record from Hoke, Grimes wrote the general on December 15, 1910, asking for a statement in writing. Hoke responded on December 20, "I thank you for your kind consideration, but I cannot comply with your request."[36]

When Hoke died, he took to the grave the remainder of the details of the matter. Almost as soon as obituaries and sketches of his life were published, skeptics began to challenge the story. In the September 1912 issue of *Confederate Veteran*, the editor observed, "The report seems unfortunate, as it would have reflected upon all of General Hoke's superior officers." Included in the same edition of the magazine were the skeptical comments of a reader from Arkansas: "It will also be interesting to Lee's old veterans to learn for the first time that Gen. Robert E. Lee desired to pass over all of the full generals and the brilliant corps commanders and have appointed to succeed him a young man who had but one rank above a brigadier general, and who was not with Lee's army at all during the latter part of the war."[37]

General Robert F. Hoke

To Douglas Southall Freeman, who penned the Pulitzer Prize–winning biography of Lee, the notion that Hoke was selected as Lee's successor merited nothing more than a brief discussion in a footnote. Freeman asserted that Lee would not "have dreamed" of selecting Hoke over generals such as A. P. Hill, Richard Anderson, Jubal A. Early, and others. Citing the lack of any contemporary record of the claim, Freeman concluded that "its improbability is so great that it may be dismissed as pure fable." Although he deemed speculation about Lee's successor "futile," Freeman surmised that Lee would have recommended Beauregard.[38]

In *Front Rank*, the highly acclaimed centennial history of North Carolina in the Civil War, Glenn Tucker was unwilling to reject the story. Acknowledging that it had been challenged, he concluded, "But there it is; and Lee could have made many less prudent choices."

Virtually every prominent North Carolina historian who knew Hoke personally had no doubt that the story was true. Josephus Daniels wrote that Hoke "was selected by Gen. Robert E. Lee to receive his mantle if the Virginian should lay it down." Fred A. Olds stated that Hoke "was slated to be General Lee's successor . . . General Lee having named him in this connection. I have never heard this story denied but once, but detail is useless since it is true in every respect." Samuel Ashe noted in his *History of North Carolina* that "the President had desired General Lee to indicate who should have command of the army. General Lee told General Hoke that he had recommended General Hoke to have the command." Dr. Joseph G. D. Hamilton concluded, "The fact that General Hoke admitted the truth of the story is conclusive to all who knew him or of him. . . . In light of all these facts it seems conclusive that the account is correct."[39]

Although family sentiments about the integrity of another family member are not highly valued in the court of public opinion, Dr. Michael Hoke, the eminent orthopedic surgeon who rivaled his father in modesty and lack of self-idolatry, expressed a conviction about the claim that no doubt turned some heads: "It is a fact because my Father could no more have made an untrue statement upon the matter than Jesus Christ would have made."

In the years after the general's death, Dr. Hoke was always protective of his father's name. He intimated his opposition to the nomination of the general for the Stone Mountain bas-relief if it were based on the "ulti-mate" honor. Dr. Hoke cautioned, "That would mean a lot of newspaper discussion and criticism and would subject his name to contentions, to which I do not care to have it subjected because I have too much rever-ence for his memory and I know exactly how he would feel about it if he were here. . . . I do not want any cheap skate who hankers after publicity and representation of this and that and the other thing to be taking pot shots at him, because if he did, I would very likely take some pot shots at him."[40]

At first glance, this "ultimate" honor seems highly suspect. No written wartime record has ever been found that bears out the claim. Like Dr. Hamilton and other historians, this author has combed the records at the National Archives in a vain attempt to locate documentation. Hamilton noted, however, that "the way in which the Confederate records were mis-handled for years, makes the destruction of the document not unlikely. But sometime it may turn up."[41]

Yet even though Civil War records that might substantiate the matter have not been found or do not exist, there are haunting aspects of the claim that make it credible. Henry W. Lawton, the winner of a Congres-sional Medal of Honor during the Civil War, had no reason to fabricate such a story when he happened to meet Hoke in Raleigh. Moreover, had the story been fiction, it seems that the ever-modest Hoke would have scoffed at Lawton's account rather than confirming it.

Perhaps the most credible piece of evidence is Hoke himself. Even the most egotistical of Confederate veterans would have been reluctant to claim the honor as Lee's successor, because such a claim would lead to ridicule, skepticism, and criticism. Thus, it would have been completely out of char-acter for Hoke, the archetype of reserve, to falsely claim what was probably the greatest honor to be bestowed upon a Confederate veteran, and invite the attending public attention, disbelief, and derision. Dr. Hamilton ob-served, "No man who removed himself from public notice as he did would have admitted it unless it was true, and his insistence of it not being made public only strengthens the authority of the story."[42]

But the worth of Hoke as a soldier and a civilian should not be judged on the basis of a single disputed honor. Rather, his greatness should be measured by his half-century of dedicated service to his state and the South. Of the many tributes Fred A. Olds paid to Hoke, an eloquent statement made in 1919 summarized the general's life: "Hoke was in the fight, always modest, always brave and zealous, doing the full measure of his duty, with all his heart a soldier and a gentleman through and through. What he then was he was to the day of his death—a typical American."[43]

Perhaps better than any other of the multitude of distinguished citizens North Carolina has produced, Robert Frederick Hoke exemplified the motto of his state—"*Esse Quam Videri*," or "To Be Rather Than to Seem." This quiet, humble man of few words let his noble deeds speak for him, and what an eloquent speech they made.

Endnotes

The following abbreviations are used in the endnotes:

DU Perkins Library, Duke University, Durham, North Carolina

ECU Joyner Library, East Carolina University, Greenville, North Carolina

LCL Lincoln County Library, Lincolnton, North Carolina

NCC North Carolina Collection, Wilson Library, University of North Carolina at Chapel Hill

NCDAH North Carolina Division of Archives and History, Raleigh

O.R. *War of the Rebellion: A Compilation of the Official Records of the Union and Confederate Armies*

O.R.N. *Official Records of the Union and Confederate Navies in the War of the Rebellion*

O.R. Supp. *Supplement to the Official Records of the Union and Confederate Armies*

SHC Southern Historical Collection, Wilson Library, University of North Carolina at Chapel Hill

CHAPTER 1
Roots of Greatness: A Lineage of Distinction

1. *Charlotte Observer*, July 4, 1912; *Lincoln County News*, July 5, 1912.
2. *Charlotte Observer*, July 4, 1912; *Lincoln County News*, July 5, 1912.
3. *Charlotte Evening Chronicle*, July 3, 1912. Daniels, a close friend of Hoke's and editor-owner of the *Raleigh News and Observer*, paid high praise in the editorial/eulogy published six days after the death of the general. *Raleigh News and Observer*, July 9, 1912; Marvin A. Brown and Maurice C. York, *Our Enduring Past*, p. 160.
4. William L. Sherrill, *Annals of Lincoln County, North Carolina* (hereafter cited as *Annals of*

General Robert F. Hoke

Lincoln County), p. 329. Dr. Hamilton met Hoke in the twilight of the general's life. After Hoke's death, Hamilton did extensive research on the military career and life of the general. J. G. D. Hamilton, "General Robert F. Hoke and His Military Career" (hereafter cited as "General Robert F. Hoke"), Robert F. Hoke Papers, SHC. Samuel A. Ashe, Stephen B. Weeks, and Charles L. Van Noppen, eds., *Biographical History of North Carolina* (hereafter cited as *Biographical History*), I:309.

5. Hoke family records in the possession of Hoke Kimball, great-grandson of Robert F. Hoke, Raleigh, North Carolina; Gilbert Ernest Swope, ed., *History of the Swope Family and Their Connections, 1678–1896* (hereafter cited as *Swope*), p. 185.

6. Swope, ed., *Swope*, p. 185; Sherrill, *Annals of Lincoln County*, p. 132.

7. Sherrill, *Annals of Lincoln County*, pp. 54–55; Brown and York, *Our Enduring Past*, p. 247; Alfred Nixon, "The History of Lincoln County," *North Carolina Booklet* 9 (January 1910): p. 113; William S. Powell, *The North Carolina Gazetteer* (hereafter cited as *Gazetteer*), p. 282; Edward L. Purcell, *Who Was Who in the American Revolution*, p. 294; Charles E. Hatch, *Yorktown and the Siege of 1781*, p. 31; Henry P. Johnston, *The Yorktown Campaign and the Surrender of Cornwallis, 1781*, p. 156. The claim that Lincoln received Cornwallis's sword has been challenged by some historians. Mark D. Boatner III, *Encyclopedia of the American Revolution*, p. 637.

8. Sherrill, *Annals of Lincoln County*, pp. 466–67; Guy M. Leedy and Carolyn M. Stroup, eds., *A Pictorial Walk through Lincoln County* (hereafter cited as *Pictorial Walk*); Reuben Gold Thwaites, *Travels West of the Alleghenies*, p. 291. Although Lincolnton was growing into a regional trade center at the close of the eighteenth century, it had a relatively small population—forty-eight whites and forty-four slaves. Brown and York, *Our Enduring Past*, p. 262.

9. Swope, ed., *Swope*, p. 185, 188; Sherrill, *Annals of Lincoln County*, p. 132; "The Hoke House (Inverness)," Lincoln County Library.

10. Using some machinery he brought from Providence, Rhode Island, Schenck had constructed two small cotton mills near Lincolnton in 1813 and 1816. Though subject to flooding, these mills were profitable and enticed Hoke, Bivens, and Schenck to build the first factory. Sherrill, *Annals of Lincoln County*, pp. 81–82; Leedy and Stroup, eds., *Pictorial Walk*. Shortly after the Schenck-Hoke-Bivens enterprise began, North Carolina could boast forty thousand looms that produced seven million pounds of cloth annually. William S. Powell, *North Carolina through Four Centuries*, pp. 315–16.

11. Sherrill, *Annals of Lincoln County*, p. 83; Hamilton, "General Robert F. Hoke," Robert F. Hoke Papers, SHC.

12. Swope, ed., *Swope*, pp. 188–89; "The Hoke House (Inverness)," Lincoln County Library.

13. Bragg, the brother of infamous Confederate general Braxton Bragg (under whom Hoke would serve during the Civil War), was elected governor of North Carolina in 1854 and 1856 and was elected a United States senator in 1859. He served for a brief period as attorney general of the Confederacy. Paul Cameron was the wealthiest man in North Carolina at both the outbreak and the end of the Civil War. Though he never entered the political arena, Cameron, like Hoke, was instrumental in rebuilding the railroad system of the state after the war. William S. Powell, ed., *The Dictionary of North Carolina Biography* (hereafter cited as *North Carolina Biography*), 3:165, 1:209, 312; Sherrill, *Annals of Lincoln County*, p. 126, 140.

14. While he was rearing his sons, Robert H. and Alfred, Robert Burton also reared his nephew, Hutchins Gordon Burton, who had been orphaned in 1777. Hutchins Burton was elected a

Endnotes

United States congressman in 1820 and governor of North Carolina in 1824. John Williams, the father-in-law of Robert Burton and grandfather of Robert H. Burton, was a noted Revolutionary War officer, state judge, state legislator, and delegate to the Continental Congress. Burton Family Papers, SHC; Ashe et al, eds., *Biographical History*, 3:39; Powell, ed., *North Carolina Biography*, 1:285–86.

15. Sherrill, *Annals of Lincoln County*, p. 126, 140; Ashe et al, eds., *Biographical History*, 1:311; Powell, ed., *North Carolina Biography*, 1:224, 2:247. Fulenwider's foundry at High Shoals, several miles south of Lincolnton, produced cannonballs for the United States Army during the War of 1812. During the Civil War, R. R. Bridgers of Edgecombe County operated the remnants of Fulenwider's iron forges, mills, furnaces, and foundries, which at the time were deemed the second most important in the South for the production of nails and rolled material. Robert F. Cope and Manly Wade Wellman, *The County of Gaston*, p. 47.

16. John H. Wheeler, *Historical Sketches of North Carolina*, 2: 246; Ashe et al, eds., *Biographical History*, 1:309–10. Sherrill, *Annals of Lincoln County*, p.102.

17. Nixon, "The History of Lincoln County," p. 135. Following the death of Mr. and Mrs. Burton, the large plantation, at which the Hokes were married, was acquired by John Hill Wheeler, eminent historian of North Carolina. While residing in Lincoln County, Wheeler wrote *Wheeler's History of North Carolina*, the first full history of the state written by a native North Carolinian and the most widely read history of the state until the twentieth century. Ironically, Wheeler was a potential contender for the 1844 Democratic nomination for governor, which Michael Hoke gained. Sherrill, *Annals of Lincoln County*, p. 106; Ashe et al, eds., *Biographical History*, 7:472–78. Still standing, the Michael Hoke House was moved in the late 1930s to a site several hundred yards west of its original site. Brown and York, *Our Enduring Past*, p. 160; *Charlotte Observer*, April 6, 1941.

18. Sherrill, *Annals of Lincoln County*, p. 107; Nixon, "The History of Lincoln County," pp. 138–39; *Gaston Observer*, May 5, 1994; Lawson Henderson to Beverly Daniel, December 8, 1837, William Henderson Papers, NCDAH.

19. Swope, ed., *Swope*, p. 234; Sherrill, *Annals of Lincoln County*, p. 157, 401; Powell, ed., *North Carolina Biography*, 3:165.

20. Swope, ed., *Swope*, pp. 205–13, 234; Powell, ed., *North Carolina Biography*, 3:166; Gary W. Gallagher, *Stephen Dodson Ramseur*, p. 6–7; Patricia L. Faust, ed., *Historical Times Illustrated Encyclopedia of the Civil War* (hereafter cited as *Encyclopedia*), pp. 268–69, 401. John Horace Forney and William Henry Forney were the grandsons of Daniel Hoke, brother of Robert's grandfather John Hoke. Robert Daniel Johnston was a first cousin to the Forney brothers, his mother and their father being siblings. In addition to the five Confederate generals born in Lincoln County, three other Confederate generals married three Lincoln County sisters, the daughters of Dr. Robert Hall Morrison, a well-known Presbyterian minister and a founder of Davidson College. Lieutenant General Thomas J. "Stonewall" Jackson married Mary Anna Morrison; Major General Daniel Harvey Hill married Isabelle Morrison; and Brigadier General Rufus Barringer married Eugenia Morrison. Sherrill, *Annals of Lincoln County*, pp. 111, 158–59, 252.

21. Lawson Henderson to Beverly Daniel, December 8, 1837, William Henderson Papers, NCDAH; Sherrill, *Annals of Lincoln County*, p. 119; *Gaston Observer*, May 5, 1994. James Pinckney Henderson, a schoolmate of Michael Hoke's, left North Carolina in 1835. In Texas, he became a confidant of Sam Houston and was subsequently selected by Houston as

the attorney general and European agent for the republic of Texas. Powell, ed., *North Carolina Biography*, 3:101.

22. Sherrill, *Annals of Lincoln County*, pp. 451–52; Leedy and Stroup, eds., *Pictorial Walk*. Indicative of the local interest in education in the first quarter of the nineteenth century was the establishment of Lincolnton Female Academy on December 21, 1821. Nixon, "The History of Lincoln County," pp. 139–43.

23. Sherrill, *Annals of Lincoln County*, pp. 452–53; "The Teacher's Certificate" of Robert Hoke, June 13, 1845, in possession of Southern Stars Chapter, United Daughters of the Confederacy, Lincolnton, North Carolina.

24. Clarence Clifford Norton, *The Democratic Party in Ante-bellum North Carolina, 1835–1861*, p. 148.

25. Graham was born in eastern Lincoln County at Vesuvius, the elegant plantation of his father, Joseph Graham, a successful iron entrepeneur. Powell, ed., *North Carolina Biography*, 2:337–39.

26. Alfred Nixon was an eminent historian of Lincoln County. Leedy and Stroup, eds., *Pictorial Walk*.

27. Samuel A. Ashe, *History of North Carolina*, 2:440.

28. Leedy and Stroup, eds., *Pictorial Walk*; Powell, ed., *North Carolina Biography*, 3:165; *Raleigh Register*, November 27, 1843.

29. Ashe, *History of North Carolina*, 2:440; George H. Gibson, "Opinion in North Carolina Regarding the Acquisition of Texas and Cuba, 1835–1855," *North Carolina Historical Review* 37: 7, 8 (hereafter cited as "Opinion in North Carolina"); Norton, *The Democratic Party in Ante-bellum North Carolina*, p. 149; Wheeler, *Historical Sketches of North Carolina*, 2:246.

30. D. Thompson to Michael Hoke, May 21, 1844, collection of Harold Ford, Lincolnton, North Carolina.

31. Norton, *The Democratic Party in Ante-bellum North Carolina*, p. 149; Gibson, "Opinion in North Carolina," p. 7, 8; Powell, ed., *North Carolina Biography*, 3:165, 2:337–39; Thomas E. Jeffrey, "'Free Suffrage' Revisited: Party Politics and Constituional Reform in Ante-bellum North Carolina," *North Carolina Historical Review* 59: 33–36, 46. While Hoke carried Lincoln County, most of the twenty-seven counties he won were in the eastern half of the state. Graham took thirty-five counties, finding his heaviest support in the Piedmont and mountain counties. Support was about the same for the Democratic presidential candidate in November. Polk polled 39,287 votes to Clay's 43,232. John L. Cheney, Jr., ed., *North Carolina Government, 1585–1974*, pp. 1330–31, 1396–97.

32. Powell, ed., *North Carolina Biography*, 3:165; Gibson, "Opinion in North Carolina," p. 11.

33. Ashe et al, eds., *Biographical History*, 1:310; Sherrill, *Annals of Lincoln County*, pp. 138–39; Leedy and Stroup, eds., *Pictorial Walk*; Frances Burton Pollock, "A Confederate Veteran I Know," Robert F. Hoke Papers, NCDAH. A longstanding tradition in North Carolina holds that Peter Ney escaped death by firing squad in Paris on December 7, 1815, when sympathetic French guards used blank cartridges in their guns. Ney subsequently made his way to Charleston, South Carolina, and then to Piedmont North Carolina, where he made his home until he died in 1846. Powell, ed., *North Carolina Biography*, 4:368.

34. Powell, ed., *North Carolina Biography*, 3:165; Sherrill, *Annals of Lincoln County*, p. 133, 138; Ashe et al, eds., *Biographical History*, 1:311.

35. Powell, ed., *North Carolina Biography*, 3:166; *Raleigh News and Observer*, July 9, 1912.

36. Swope, ed., *Swope*, p. 188. John Hoke bequeathed to Michael a "negro boy Randel" and a "negro girl Doug." As to the slaves not specifically bequeathed to his children, John pro-

vided, "Where my black families have small children I should wish them to be sold with their parents." Last Will and Testament of John Hoke, Will Book 2, p. 241, Office of the Clerk of Superior Court, Lincoln County, North Carolina. Because Michael's vocation was law and politics, he owned few slaves. Local records reveal that he purchased only two slaves in Lincoln County. Bills of Sale from Robert H. Burton to Michael Hoke, December 24, 1835, and November 25, 1837, Lincoln County, North Carolina, Public Registry. Sherrill, *Annals of Lincoln County*, p. 138.

37. David Schenck Diary, September 10, 1849, and August 28, 1852, David Schenck Papers, SHC. Schenck became a noted attorney, judge, historian, and author. His most notable book, *North Carolina, 1780–1781*, reflected his abiding interest in the Revolutionary War. He was the guiding force behind the establishment of Guilford Courthouse National Park. Sherrill, *Annals of Lincoln County*, pp. 290–92; Gallagher, *Stephen Dodson Ramseur*, p. 7.

38. William A. Graham, "The Battle of Ramsaur's Mill," *North Carolina Booklet* 4 (June 1904): 5–23. This battle was actually a civil war, as there was not a British soldier among the nearly two thousand combatants. No uniforms were worn; the Whigs pinned white paper to their hats, while the Tories pinned green twigs to theirs. William L. Carpenter, "The Battle of Ramsour's Mill," LCL.

39. Powell, ed., *North Carolina Biography*, 2:247.

40. *Lincoln Courier*, September 13, 1845; Sherrill, *Annals of Lincoln County*, p. 155.

41. Swope, ed., *Swope*, p. 188, Brown and York, *Our Enduring Past*, p. 251. Ironically, the United States Senate seat Revels filled had been vacated at the beginning of the Civil War by Jefferson Davis. Revels attempted to hide his Lincoln County past because, while in Lincolnton, he had lived with his brother, Elisha, a free black who owned slaves. Fearful that his past would ruin his career in the ministry and politics, Revels chose to omit any reference to his six-year stay in Lincolnton. R. C. Lawrence, "The Strange Case of Hiram Revels," LCL.

42. David Schenck Diary, June 8, 1851, September 5, 1852, and October 17, 1852, David Schenck Papers, SHC; Gallagher, *Stephen Dodson Ramseur*, p. 8.

43. Ashe et al, eds., *Biographical History*, 1:311; Frances Burton Hoke to Robert F. Hoke, September 5, 1852, Robert F. Hoke Papers, NCDAH. Kentucky Military Institute remained in operation until 1971, when financial difficulties and declining enrollment caused it to close. When it shut its doors, it was the oldest private military school in the country. John E. Kleber, Jr., ed., *The Kentucky Encyclopedia*, p. 506; Garvin F. Davenport, *Ante-Bellum Kentucky*, p. 62; Leland Hathaway Journal (1852–55), Leland Hathaway Papers, SHC.

44. Frances Burton Hoke to Robert F. Hoke, September 5, 1852, Robert F. Hoke Papers, NCDAH.

45. Kleber, ed., *The Kentucky Encyclopedia*, p. 506; Ashe et al, eds., *Biographical History*, 1:311.

46. Hamilton, "General Robert F. Hoke," Robert F. Hoke Papers, SHC; Ashe et al, eds., *Biographical History*, 1:311; David Scheck Diary, July 31, 1851, David Schenck Papers, SHC; Sherrill, *Annals of Lincoln County*, p. 133, 157.

47. Josephus Daniels, untitled manuscript, Robert F. Hoke Papers, NCDAH; Pollock, "A Confederate Veteran I Know," Robert F. Hoke Papers, NCDAH. Following the Civil War, Miles felt the wrath of many people both in the South and the North while he served as the jailer of Jefferson Davis. When he died in 1925, Miles was the last surviving full-rank major general of the Civil War. Ezra Warner, *Generals in Blue*, pp. 322–23; Faust, ed., *Encyclopedia*, p. 492; Trevor N. Dupuy, Curt Johnson, and David L. Bongard, eds., *The Harper Encyclopedia of Military Biography*, p. 506.

48. C. B. Edwards, "The Man Who Shook Hands with Lincoln," Robert F. Hoke Papers, SHC; Richard W. Iobst and Louis H. Manarin, *The Bloody Sixth*, p. 111; Adjutant General's Roll of Honor Scrapbook, NCDAH.

49. Edwards, "The Man Who Shook Hands with Lincoln", Robert F. Hoke Papers, SHC.

50. Ibid.

CHAPTER 2
Sabers Rattle: The First Lifeblood Is Spilled

1. David Schenck Diary, March 11, 1861, SHC.

2. Barrett, *The Civil War in North Carolina*, p. 10; Ethel S. Arnett and W. C. Jackson, *Greensboro, North Carolina*, pp. 390–91; Ellis, John Willis, *The Papers of John Willis Ellis* (hereafter cited as *John Willis Ellis*), 2:612.

3. Clement Dowd, *Life of Vance*, p. 441; Ashe, *History of North Carolina*, 2:588–90, 601; R. D. W. Connor, *North Carolina: Rebuilding an Ancient Commonwealth*, 2:146. The regiment was not organized as directed in Hoke's letter of April 19 because of problems related to mobilization and the inability of some companies to meet the required troop strength. Walter Clark, ed., *Histories of the Several Regiments and Battalions from North Carolina in the Great War, 1861–65* (hereafter cited as *Regiments*), 1:124.

4. Ashe, *History of North Carolina*, 2:590; Barrett, *The Civil War in North Carolina*, p. 18; Ellis, *John Willis Ellis*, 2:655, 664; Hugh Talmage Lefler, ed., *North Carolina History Told by Contemporaries*, pp. 286–88; Robert Frederick Hoke Diary (hereafter cited as Hoke Diary), April 22–29, 1861, LCL.

5. Hoke Diary, April 22–29, 1861, LCL; Ellis, *John Willis Ellis*, 2:664.

6. Hoke Diary, April 24, 28, and 29, 1861, LCL; *Lincolnton Star*, May 3, 1861; Sherrill, *Annals of Lincoln County*, p. 169.

7. *Lincolnton Star*, May 3, 1861. The railroad had come to Lincolnton in late 1860. Sherrill, *Annals of Lincoln County*, p. 168.

8. Hoke Diary, May 1, 1861, LCL; Barrett, *The Civil War in North Carolina*, p. 14; *Charlotte Democrat*, May 1, 1861.

9. Manly Wade Wellman, *Rebel Boast*, p. 22, 33; Hoke Diary, May 2–17, 1861, LCL; Louis H. Manarin, ed., *North Carolina Troops*, 3:1; Clark, ed., *Regiments*, 1:125.

10. Manarin, ed., *North Carolina Troops*, 3:1. Lee died at Fraser's Farm, Virginia. Weymouth T. Jordan, Jr., and Louis H. Manarin, eds., *North Carolina Troops*, 9:468; Wellman, *Rebel Boast*, p. 37.

11. Manarin, ed., *North Carolina Troops*, 3:1; Wellman, *Rebel Boast*, p. 39.

12. Glenn Tucker, *Front Rank*, p. 10; Clark, ed., *Regiments*, 1:73–74, 116; *Charlotte Observer*, July 21, 1912.

13. Wellman, *Rebel Boast*, p. 40; Manarin, ed., *North Carolina Troops*, 3:1; John G. Barrett, *North Carolina As a Civil War Battleground*, p. 11; Barrett, *The Civil War in North Carolina*, p. 22; Hoke Diary, May 18, 1861, LCL.

14. Clark, ed., *Regiments*, 1:79; Tucker, *Front Rank*, p. 11; *Petersburg Express*, May 20, 1861.

15. Manarin, ed., *North Carolina Troops*, 3:1; Clark, ed., *Regiments*, 1:79; Hoke Diary, May 18, 1861, LCL; Wellman, *Rebel Boast*, p. 41.

16. Ashe, *History of North Carolina*, 2:610–15; Gallagher, *Stephen Dodson Ramseur*, pp. 3–4.

Endnotes

17. Clark, ed., *Regiments*, 1:76; Barrett, *The Civil War in North Carolina*, p. 22. After observing the remainder of the First North Carolina, a writer for the *Petersburg Express* reported, "Without drawing invidious distinctions, we must say this is the best equipped regiment which has yet made its route through our city." *Petersburg Express*, May 22, 1861; Hoke Diary, May 21, 1861, LCL; Wellman, *Rebel Boast*, pp. 42–43.

18. Clark, ed., *Regiments*, 1:80–81; *Fayetteville Observer*, May 27, 1861.

19. Clark, ed., *Regiments*, 1:81–82; Wellman, *Rebel Boast*, p. 43; Hoke Diary, May 24–31, June 1–5, 1861, LCL; Patricia Faust, ed., *Historical Times Illustrated Encyclopedia of the Civil War* (hereafter cited as *Illustrated*), p. 468; William C. Davis et al, eds., *First Blood*, p. 79.

20. Clark, ed., *Regiments*, 1:82.

21. Hoke Diary, May 25–26, 1861, LCL; Sherrill, *Annals of Lincoln County*, p. 252; Wellman, *Rebel Boast*, p. 44.

22. Hoke Diary, May 27–31, 1861, LCL; Wellman, *Rebel Boast*, p. 47.

23. Wellman, *Rebel Boast*, pp. 48–49; Hoke Diary, June 1–5, 1861, LCL.

24. Hoke Diary, June 6, 1861, LCL; Clark, ed., *Regiments*, 1:83–89; Wellman, *Rebel Boast*, p. 49; Benjamin R. Huske, "Account of the Battle of Bethel," Military Collection (Civil War), Box 70, Folder 73, NCDAH.

25. *O.R.* I, 2, pp. 77, 93–94; Clark, ed., *Regiments*, 1:84–85; Hoke Diary, June 7–8, 1861, LCL; "Recollections of an Unknown Officer of the 1st North Carolina Volunteers," Military Collection (Civil War), Box 72, Folder 36, NCDAH; Huske, "Account of the Battle of Bethel," Military Collection (Civil War), NCDAH; Wellman, *Rebel Boast*, pp. 50–51.

26. *O.R.* I, 2, p. 94; Clark, ed., *Regiments*, 1:83, 86; Wellman, *Rebel Boast*, pp. 50–51; Hoke Diary, June 9, 1861, LCL.

27. The Union movement toward Little Bethel began as early as 10 P.M. on June 9. *O.R.* I, 2, p. 83, 94; Wellman, *Rebel Boast*, p. 51; C. Whit Lloyd, "Orange Light Infantry," Military Collection (Civil War), Box 71, Folder 23, NCDAH; Hal Bridges, *Lee's Maverick General: Daniel Harvey Hill*, p. 28; Clark, ed., *Regiments*, 1:89; Hoke Diary, June 10, 1861, LCL.

28. *O.R.* I, 2, pp. 76–79; Clark, ed., *Regiments*, 1:88.

29. Huske, "Account of the Battle of Bethel," Military Collection (Civil War), NCDAH. General Butler complained about the leak of information in his official report on Big Bethel. *O.R.* I, 2, p. 81, 94; Clark, ed., *Regiments*, 1:90–91.

30. Wellman, *Rebel Boast*, p. 52; Whit, "Orange Light Infantry," Military Collection (Civil War), NCDAH; Clark, ed., *Regiments*, 1:90–91; *O.R.* I, 2, p. 88, 95; Huske, "Account of the Battle of Bethel," Military Collection (Civil War), NCDAH; Hoke Diary, June 10, 1861, LCL.

31. Clark, ed., *Regiments*, 1:93–97; Wellman, *Rebel Boast*, p. 53; Bridges, *Daniel Harvey Hill*, p. 29.

32. Huske, "Account of the Battle of Bethel," Military Collection (Civil War), NCDAH.

33. Ashe, *History of North Carolina*, 2:627–28. Wyatt, a native of Virginia, had moved to North Carolina with his parents in 1856. Clark, ed., *Regiments*, 1:98, 100–102; Tucker, *Front Rank*, p. 14.

34. Ashe, *History of North Carolina*, 2:628–29; *O.R.* I, 2, p. 95.

35. Clark, ed., *Regiments*, 1:105–6; Huske, "Account of the Battle of Bethel," Military Collection (Civil War), NCDAH.

36. Clark, ed., *Regiments*, 1:102–5.

37. Clark, ed., *Regiments*, 1:105; "Recollections of an Unknown Officer of the 1st North

Carolina Volunteers," Military Collection (Civil War), NCDAH; *O.R.* I, 2, p. 97.

38. *O.R.* I, 2, p. 96; Wellman, *Rebel Boast*, p. 57; George Wills to "Pa," June 16, 1861, Wills Papers, SHC; Whit, "Orange Light Infantry," Military Collection (Civil War), NCDAH.

39. Hoke Diary, June 10, 1861, LCL; Henry E. Shepherd, "Gallant Sons of North Carolina," *Confederate Veteran* 27:413; Clark, ed., *Regiments*, 1:111.

40. Hoke Diary, June 11, 1861, LCL; *O.R.* I, 2, p. 97; Wellman, *Rebel Boast*, p. 60; Clark, ed., *Regiments*, 1:110.

41. Wellman, *Rebel Boast*, pp. 61–62.

42. Powell, ed., *North Carolina Biography*, 1:374; Wellman, *Rebel Boast*, pp. 65–66; Hoke Diary, July 14, 23–31, and August 1–16, 1861, LCL.

43. Hoke Diary, August 22–31 and September 1–3, 1861, LCL; Manarin, ed., *North Carolina Troops*, 3:1; Clark, ed., *Regiments*, 1:111; Wellman, *Rebel Boast*, p. 67.

44. Hoke Diary, September 5, 1861, LCL; Manarin, ed., *North Carolina Troops*, 3:2. The flag-presentation ceremony was marred by John W. Baker, the young man sent from Fayetteville to deliver an address on the occasion. Before the time for his speech came, Baker was treated to some local whiskey. He subsequently made such a spectacle of himself that he cried after his speech was over. Wellman, *Rebel Boast*, p. 68.

45. Hoke Diary, October 7–17, 1861, LCL; Manarin, ed., *North Carolina Troops*, 3:2.

46. Hoke Diary, October 20–30, 1861, LCL; Manarin, ed., *North Carolina Troops*, 3:2.

47. Hoke Diary, October 31 and November 1–14, 1861, LCL; Wellman, *Rebel Boast*, p. 71.

48. Hoke Diary, November 12–14, 1861, LCL; Manarin, ed., *North Carolina Troops*, 3:1–2; Clark, ed., *Regiments*, 1:76, 114–23.

49. Hoke Diary, November 15–30 and December 1–31, 1861, LCL; Jordan and Manarin, eds., *North Carolina Troops*, 9:118.

CHAPTER 3
A Rising Star

1. Clark, ed., *Regiments*, 2:541; Barrett, *The Civil War in North Carolina*, pp. 36–47, 66–69. Of the victory at Hatteras Inlet, Union admiral David D. Porter wrote, "This was our first naval victory, indeed our first victory of any kind, and should not be forgotten . . . and ultimately proved one of the most important events of the war." David D. Porter, *Naval History of the Civil War* (hereafter cited as *Naval History*), p. 47; J. G. D. Hamilton, *History of North Carolina since 1860*, p. 17; William R. Trotter, *Ironclads and Columbiads*, p. 70.

2. Three companies of the Thirty-third North Carolina had been dispatched to Hyde County in October 1861. They subsequently joined the regiment upon its arrival in New Bern. Jordan and Manarin, eds., *North Carolina Troops* 9:112; Clark, ed., *Regiments*, 2:537–41; Ashe et al, eds., *Biographical History*, 7:56–57.

3. While leading the Thirty-third North Carolina at the Battle of the Wilderness on May 5 and 6, 1864, Avery was seriously wounded; he died of the injuries six months later. Powell, ed., *North Carolina Biography*, 1:67–68; Jordan and Manarin, eds., *North Carolina Troops*, 9:118.

4. Jordan and Manarin, eds., *North Carolina Troops*, 9:118; Clark, ed., *Regiments*, 1:5, 8.

Endnotes

5. Barrett, *The Civil War in North Carolina*, p. 84, 95–100; *O.R.* I, 9, p. 241; Daniel H. Hill, *Bethel to Sharpsburg*, 1:219–21; Ashe, *History of North Carolina*, 2:684; Trotter, *Ironclads and Columbiads*, pp. 105–6; Clark, ed., *Regiments*, 2:308–9.

6. Barrett, *The Civil War in North Carolina*, p. 96; *O.R.* I, 9, p. 242; Alan D. Watson, *A History of New Bern and Craven County* (hereafter cited as *New Bern*), p. 375.

7. Barrett, *The Civil War in North Carolina*, pp. 98–99; Clark, ed., *Regiments*, 2:310–11, 542; *O.R.* I, 9, p. 209, 223–24, 243, 255, 262; Trotter, *Ironclads and Columbiads*, pp. 109–16; Ashe, *History of North Carolina*, 2:685; Clement A. Evans, *Confederate Military History: North Carolina* (hereafter cited as *North Carolina*), p. 40.

8. *O.R.* I, 9, p. 244, 259; Clark, ed., *Regiments*, 2:310, 541–42; Barrett, *The Civil War in North Carolina*, pp. 91–100; Ashe, *History of North Carolina*, 2:685–86; Hill, *Bethel to Sharpsburg*, 1:222; Trotter, *Ironclads and Columbiads*, pp. 110–11.

9. Clark, ed., *Regiments*, 2:542; Watson, *New Bern*, p. 375; *O.R.* I, 9, p. 259; Hill, *Bethel to Sharpsburg*, 1:221.

10. Barrett, *The Civil War in North Carolina*, p. 100; Hill, *Bethel to Sharpsburg*, 1:223. As to the time the battle began, contemporary accounts vary from 7:00 A.M. to 7:30 A.M. Branch put it between these two times. Colonel Campbell noted that it started at 7:20 A.M. *O.R.* I, 9, p. 240, 244, 250; Trotter, *Ironclads and Columbiads*, p. 114.

11. Evans, ed., *North Carolina*, p. 40; Ashe, *History of North Carolina*, 2:686; Barrett, *The Civil War in North Carolina*, p. 100; Trotter, *Ironclads and Columbiads*, p. 114; Clark, ed., *Regiments*, 2:542–43; Watson, *New Bern*, p. 376; *O.R.* I, 9, p. 212, 220; Hill, *Bethel to Sharpsburg*, 1:225–26.

12. Hill, *Bethel to Sharpsburg*, 1:226; Clark, ed., *Regiments*, 2:543; Barrett, *The Civil War in North Carolina*, p. 102; *O.R.* I, 9, p. 229, 267.

13. *O.R.* I, 9, p. 245, 250, 255, 259–60; Hill, *Bethel to Sharpsburg*, 1:226; Clark, ed., *Regiments*, 2:315, 543; Barrett, *The Civil War in North Carolina*, p. 103; Trotter, *Ironclads and Columbiads*, p. 116.

14. *O.R.* I, 9, p. 260.

15. Ibid.

16. *O.R.* I, 9, p. 229, 246, 255, 260.

17. Hill, *Bethel to Sharpsburg*, 1:229–30; Barrett, *The Civil War in North Carolina*, p. 104; *O.R.* I, 9, p. 245.

18. *O.R.* I, 9, p. 226, 245; Clark, ed., *Regiments*, 2:543; Hill, *Bethel to Sharpsburg*, 1:231.

19. *O.R.* I, 9, p. 260.

20. Ibid, p. 256, 260–61; W. G. Lewis to "Cousin William," March 20, 1863, Battle Family Papers, SHC. In addition to Vance, a number of the retreating Confederates swam the creek. Clark, ed., *Regiments*, 2:323.

21. *O.R.* I, 9, p. 256, 261; Clark, ed., *Regiments*, 2:323–24.

22. *O.R.* I, 9, p. 261; *Raleigh News and Observer*, May 11, 1921; Clark, ed., *Regiments*, 2:545.

23. Barrett, *The Civil War in North Carolina*, p. 107; Watson, *New Bern*, p. 380; Evans, ed., *North Carolina*, p. 41; *O.R.* I, 4, pp. 578–79; *O.R.* I, 51, part 2, p. 512; *O.R.* I, 9, p. 205.

24. Jordan and Manarin, eds., *North Carolina Troops*, 9:112; Clark, ed., *Regiments*, 2:544.

25. Hill, *Bethel to Sharpsburg*, 1:232–33; Clark, ed., *Regiments*, 2:544; Trotter, *Ironclads and Columbiads*, pp. 116–19; Charles F. Walcott, *History of the Twenty-first Massachusetts Volunteers*, p. 75.

26. *Raleigh News and Observer*, May 11, 1921; Robert Dollard, *Recollections of the Civil War*,

p. 53; Powell, ed., *North Carolina Biography*, 2:337–39; Clark, ed., *Regiments*, 2:327; Barrett, *The Civil War in North Carolina*, p. 104; Trotter, *Ironclads and Columbiads*, pp. 115–18; Graham, William Alexander, *The Papers of William Alexander Graham, 1857–1863*, 5:373–74.

27. Powell, ed., *North Carolina Biography*, 1:68; Jordan and Manarin, eds., *North Carolina Troops*, 9:112; Clark, ed., *Regiments*, 2:545.

28. Clark, ed., *Regiments*, 2:21, 469, 545; Jordan and Manarin, eds., *North Carolina Troops*, 9:112.

29. *O.R.* I, 11, part 1, p. 741; James Hagemann, *The Heritage of Virginia*, p. 320; Clark, ed., *Regiments*, 2:545–46; Evans, ed., *North Carolina*, pp. 57–58.

30. Clark, ed., *Regiments*, 2:545–46; *O.R.* I, 11, part 1, pp. 741–42.

31. Ashe, *History of North Carolina*, 2:725; *O.R. Supplement*, 2:453; *O.R.* I, 11, part 1, p. 743; Clark, ed., *Regiments*, 2:23–24, 546.

32. Jordan and Manarin, eds., *North Carolina Troops*, 9:112; Clark, ed., *Regiments*, 2:546.

33. *O.R.* I, 11, part 2, p. 881, 894; Jordan and Manarin, eds., *North Carolina Troops*, 9:112; Clark, ed., *Regiments*, 2:547.

34. Clark, ed., *Regiments*, 2:547; *O.R. Supplement*, 2:453; Richard F. Epps to "My Dear sweet little Wife & children," July 13, 1862, Confederate Papers (Letters), SHC; *O.R.* I, 11, part 2, pp. 881–82, 894.

35. *O.R.* I, 11, part 2, p. 895. That the Federals had been routed was everywhere in evidence to the Confederates. Epps wrote that they had left "eve[r]y thing behind." Richard Epps to "My Dear sweet little Wife & children," July 13, 1862, Confederate Papers (Letters), SHC. General Branch observed that "the evidence of a rout and precipitate fight were most striking." *O.R.* I, 11, part 2, p. 883.

36. *O.R. Supplement*, 2:453; *O.R.* I, 11, part 2, p. 895; Ashe, *History of North Carolina*, 2:729–30; Clark, ed., *Regiments*, 2:25, 547.

37. Ashe, *History of North Carolina*, 2:729; Faust, ed., *Encyclopedia*, p. 295. After the battle, the flag that Campbell had waved at his death bore the marks of thirty-two bullets. When Lane was hit by the minie ball, he turned to his colorbearer, leaned down, and asked, "Sergeant, is my scalp cut?" The young officer responded, "No, Colonel, it is only scorched a little." Clark, ed., *Regiments*, 1:368, 2:548.

38. *O.R.* I, 11, part 2, p. 895; Clark, ed., *Regiments*, 2:27; Richard F. Epps to "My Dear sweet little Wife & children," July 13, 1862, Confederate Papers (Letters), SHC.

39. Ashe, *History of North Carolina*, 2:731–32; Clark, ed., *Regiments*, 2:27, 548; Richard F. Epps to "My Dear sweet little Wife & children," July 13, 1862, Confederate Papers (Letters), SHC; Faust, ed., *Encyclopedia*, p. 821; *O.R.* I, 11, part 2, p. 895.

40. Faust, ed., *Encyclopedia*, p. 821; *O.R.* I, 11, part 2, p. 883, 895; Clark, ed., *Regiments*, 2:548; Ashe, *History of North Carolina*, 2:735.

41. Jordan and Manarin, eds., *North Carolina Troops*, 9:113; Ashe, *History of North Carolina*, 2:732; Edwards, "The Man Who Shook Hands with Lincoln," Robert F. Hoke Papers, SHC.

42. *O.R.* I, 11, part 2, p. 895; Clark, ed., *Regiments*, 2:27, 2:548; Jordan, ed., *North Carolina Troops*, 9:113. Although Ramseur would recover and return to duty, his right arm was rendered virtually useless by the ball he took at Malvern Hill. Gallagher, *Stephen Dodson Ramseur*, p. 44.

43. Edwards, "The Man Who Shook Hands with Lincoln," Robert F. Hoke Papers, SHC.

44. Ashe, *History of North Carolina*, 2:728; Jordan and Manarin, eds., *North Carolina Troops*, 9:113; Richard F. Epps to "My Dear sweet little Wife & children," July 13, 1862, Confederate Papers (Letters), SHC.

45. Richard F. Epps to "My Dear sweet little Wife & children," July 13, 1862, Confederate Papers (Letters), SHC; *O.R.* I, 11, part 2, p. 894; *O.R. Supplement*, 2:453.

46. Clark, ed., *Regiments*, 2:548–49; *O.R.* I, 11, part 2, pp. 895–96; Jordan, ed., *North Carolina Troops*, 9:113; *O.R. Supplement*, 2:454.

47. Clark, ed., *Regiments*, 1:370–71, 2:472, 549–51; Jordan and Manarin, eds., *North Carolina Troops*, 9:113, 118; *O.R.* I, 12, part 2, p. 183, 220–23.

48. *O.R.* I, 12, part 2, p. 223; Clark, ed., *Regiments*, 2:472, 550–51; Jordan and Manarin, eds., *North Carolina Troops*, 9:113; Tucker, *Front Rank*, p. 32.

49. Jordan and Manarin, eds., *North Carolina Troops*, 9:113; Clark, ed., *Regiments*, 1:370, 2:551; *O.R.* I, 12, part 2, p. 223.

50. Clark, ed., *Regiments*, 1:370, 2:29–30, 551–52; *O.R.* I, 12, part 2, p. 675; Jordan and Manarin, eds., *North Carolina Troops*, 9:113.

51. *O.R.* I, 12, part 2, pp. 675–76; Clark, ed., *Regiments*, 1:371, 2:552; Jordan and Manarin, eds., *North Carolina Troops*, 9:113.

52. Clark, ed., *Regiments*, 1:371, 2:30–31, 473, 552; *O.R.* I, 12, part 2, pp. 676–77.

53. Clark, ed., *Regiments*, 1:372, 2:473, 552, 656; Jordan and Manarin, eds., *North Carolina Troops*, 9:113–14; Shelby Foote, *The Civil War: Fort Sumter to Perryville*, p. 644; Ashe, *History of North Carolina*, 2:744.

54. Jordan and Manarin, eds., *North Carolina Troops*, 9:114; Clark, ed., *Regiments*, 2:32, 552–53; *O.R.* I, 19, part 1, p. 985.

55. Jordan and Manarin, eds., *North Carolina Troops*, 9:114; Clark, ed., *Regiments*, 1:575, 2:32; Faust, ed., *Encyclopedia*, pp. 18–19; Tucker, *Front Rank*, p. 29; Stephen W. Sears, *Landscape Turned Red: The Battle of Antietam*, pp. 284–85; John Cannan, *The Antietam Campaign*, p. 197.

56. Ronald H. Bailey et al, eds., *The Bloodiest Day: The Battle of Antietam*, p. 129; Clark, ed., *Regiments*, 2:553; Jordan and Manarin, eds., *North Carolina Troops*, 9:114; Cannan, *The Antietam Campaign*, p. 197.

57. Bailey et al, eds., *The Bloodiest Day: The Battle of Antietam*, p. 129; Clark, ed., *Regiments*, 2:553; *O.R.* I, 19, part 1, pp. 985–86. Brigadier General Maxcy Gregg was wounded by the same bullet that killed Branch. Faust, ed., *Encyclopedia*, p. 325.

58. *O.R.* I, 19, part 1, p. 986; Clark, ed., *Regiments*, 2:33, 474, 555; Jordan and Manarin, eds., *North Carolina Troops*, 9:114.

59. Foote, *The Civil War: Fort Sumter to Perryville*, p. 703; *O.R.* I, 19, part 1, p. 984; Clark, ed., *Regiments*, 2:474, 555; Jordan and Manarin, eds., *North Carolina Troops*, 9:114.

60. Clark, ed., *Regiments*, 2:555; Jordan and Manarin, eds., *North Carolina Troops*, 9:114.

CHAPTER 4
"How Are You, General Hoke?"

1. Hamilton, "General Robert F. Hoke," Robert F. Hoke Papers, SHC; Jordan, ed., *North Carolina Troops*, 6:533–34. Trimble would recover in time to lead one of the three prongs of the climactic charge on the afternoon of July 3, 1863, at Gettysburg. Wounded again in

the leg during that assault, he was taken prisoner, and his limb was amputated. William Davis, ed., *The Confederate General*, 6:60–61; *O.R.* I, 21, p. 543; James Cooper Nisbet, *4 Years on the Firing Line*, pp. 113–15; Henry W. Thomas, *History of the Doles-Cook Brigade*, pp. 208–24, 350–56; Clark, ed., *Regiments*, 4:233–36.

2. Nisbet, *4 Years on the Firing Line*, pp. 113–15; Ashe, *History of North Carolina*, 2:765; William J. Jones, *Christ in the Camp*, pp. 283–84; W. W. Bennett, *The Great Revival in the Southern Armies*, pp. 204–10.

3. Evans, ed., *North Carolina*, p. 133; *O.R.* I, 21, p. 550; Nisbet, *4 Years on the Firing Line*, p. 115, 117.

4. Jordan and Manarin, eds., *North Carolina Troops*, 6:534; Thomas, *History of the Doles-Cook Brigade*, p. 356; *O.R.* I, 21, p. 543; Jubal Early, *Jubal Early's Memoirs* (hereafter cited as *Memoirs*), pp. 166–67.

5. *O.R.* I, 21, p. 552; Early, *Memoirs*, p. 167, 169.

6. Early, *Memoirs*, p. 167; *O.R.* I, 21, p. 552; Nisbet, *4 Years on the Firing Line*, pp. 122–23.

7. *O.R.* I, 21, p. 552; Evans, ed., *North Carolina*, p. 133; Jay Luvaas and Harold W. Nelson, eds., *The U. S. Army War College Guide to the Battles of Chancellorsville and Fredericksburg*, (hereafter cited as *Chancellorsville and Fredericksburg*), p. 41; Early, *Memoirs*, p. 170; *O.R.* I, 21, p. 672.

8. Early, *Memoirs*, pp. 171–72; *O.R.* I, 21, p. 552, 672; Nisbet, *4 Years on the Firing Line*, p. 123; Clark, ed., *Regiments*, 4:236.

9. *O.R.* I, 21, p. 553, 672; Early, *Memoirs*, pp. 172–73.

10. Early, *Memoirs*, pp. 173–74; Freeman, *R. E. Lee*, 2:467; William C. Oates, *The War Between the Union and the Confederacy and Their Lost Opportunities* (hereafter cited as *Lost Opportunities*), p. 374; *O.R.* I, 21, p. 632, 647, 657, 672; Nisbet, *4 Years on the Firing Line*, p. 124.

11. Oates, *Lost Opportunities*, p. 374; *O.R.* I, 21, p. 665, 672–73.

12. Early, *Memoirs*, p. 177. According to one North Carolina officer, Lee was convinced by a group of officers, over Jackson's objections, to call off the night assault. Clark, ed., *Regiments*, 2:557–58; *O.R.* I, 21, p. 634.

13. Thomas, *History of the Doles-Cook Brigade*, p. 226; Early, *Memoirs*, p. 179; *O.R.* I, 21, p. 589, 634, 666, 672; Evans, ed., *North Carolina*, p. 139.

14. Early, *Memoirs*, p. 179; Nisbet, *4 Years on the Firing Line*, p. 125; *O.R.* I, 21, p. 554, 633, 667; Clark, ed., *Regiments*, 2:135.

15. Early, *Memoirs*, p. 179; Clark, ed., *Regiments*, 4:236; Hamilton, "General Robert F. Hoke," Robert F. Hoke Papers, SHC.

16. Hamilton, "General Robert F. Hoke," Robert F. Hoke Papers, SHC; *O.R.* I, 21, p. 1099; clipping from unidentified newspaper, Robert F. Hoke Papers, NCDAH.

17. Jordan, ed., *North Carolina Troops*, 13:179; Faust, ed., *Encyclopedia*, pp. 97–98, 370; Early, *Memoirs*, p. 188; Bartlett Yancey Malone, *Whipt 'Em Everytime*, pp. 70–71; Iobst and Manarin, *The Bloody Sixth*, p. 111.

18. Iobst and Manarin, *The Bloody Sixth*, pp. 110–11; Isaac E. Avery to his sister, January 23, 1863, Waightstill Avery Papers, SHC.

19. William J. Pfohl to Christian Thomas Pfohl, February 5, 1863, Christian Thomas Pfohl Papers, SHC.

20. Adjutant General's Roll of Honor Scrapbook, NCDAH.

21. Malone, *Whipt 'Em Everytime*, p. 71; Jordan, ed., *North Carolina Troops*, 13:179; Iobst and Manarin, *The Bloody Sixth*, p. 111; Ashe et al, eds., *Biographical History*, 1:313.

22. Jordan, ed., *North Carolina Troops*, 13:179–80; Iobst and Manarin, *The Bloody Sixth*, p. 112; Malone, *Whipt 'Em Everytime*, p. 73; Early, *Memoirs*, pp. 190–91.

23. Jordan, ed., *North Carolina Troops*, 13:179–81; Malone, *Whipt 'Em Everytime*, p. 74; William J. Pfohl to Christian Thomas Pfohl, March 6, 1863, Christian Thomas Pfohl Papers, SHC; Iobst and Manarin, *The Bloody Sixth*, p. 116.

24. Iobst and Manarin, *The Bloody Sixth*, p. 116; Jordan, ed., *North Carolina Troops*, 13:181; Malone, *Whipt 'Em Everytime*, pp. 75–76.

25. Jordan, ed., *North Carolina Troops*, 13:182–83; Foote, *The Civil War: Fredericksburg to Meridian*, pp. 262–67.

26. In his official report of the Battle of Chancellorsville, Lee recorded that the Union crossing at Fredericksburg began on the morning of April 28. Private Malone noted the same date in his diary. Malone, *Whipt 'Em Everytime*, p. 76. However, most other sources indicate that the crossing was effected on the morning of April 29. Early, *Memoirs*, p. 193; Luvaas and Nelson, eds., *Chancellorsville and Fredericksburg*, p. 126; O.R. I, 25, part 2, p. 268; O.R. I, 25, part 1, p. 557, 796; Jordan, ed., *North Carolina Troops*, 13:183; Samuel W. Eaton Diary (hereafter cited as Eaton Diary), April 29, 1863, Samuel W. Eaton Papers, SHC.

27. Early, *Memoirs*, pp. 193–96; Eaton Diary, April 29, 1863, Samuel W. Eaton Papers, SHC; Malone, *Whipt 'Em Everytime*, p. 76; Jordan, ed., *North Carolina Troops*, 13:183.

28. Eaton Diary, April 29 and 30, 1863, Samuel W. Eaton Papers, SHC; Malone, *Whipt 'Em Everytime*, p. 76; Early, *Memoirs*, pp. 195–97.

29. Early, *Memoirs*, pp. 197–98.

30. Malone, *Whipt 'Em Everytime*, p. 77; Eaton Diary, May 1, 1863, Samuel W. Eaton Papers, SHC; Early, *Memoirs*, p. 199; Freeman, *Lee's Lieutenants*, 2:605.

31. Malone, *Whipt 'Em Everytime*, p. 78; Early, *Memoirs*, pp. 201–3; Eaton Diary, May 2, 1863, Samuel W. Eaton Papers, SHC; Freeman, *Lee's Lieutenants*, 2:607–12.

32. Early, *Memoirs*, pp. 204–6; Iobst and Manarin, *The Bloody Sixth*, p. 118; Jordan, ed., *North Carolina Troops*, 13:184; Ernest B. Furgurson, *Chancellorsville 1863*, pp. 258–61; Charles C. Osborne, *Jubal*, p. 151; Freeman, *Lee's Lieutenants*, 2:616; Eaton Diary, May 3, 1863, Samuel W. Eaton Papers, SHC; Jordan and Manarin, eds., *North Carolina Troops*, 6:534.

33. Iobst and Manarin, *The Bloody Sixth*, p. 118; Jordan, ed., *North Carolina Troops*, 13:185; Early, *Memoirs*, p. 206, 220; Eaton Diary, May 3, 1863, Samuel W. Eaton Papers, SHC.

34. Jordan, ed., *North Carolina Troops*, 13:185; Early, *Memoirs*, pp. 221–24; Eaton Diary, May 4, 1863, Samuel W. Eaton Papers, SHC; E. A. Patterson, "Story of the War," Military Collection (Civil War), Box 71, Folder 42, NCDAH; Furgurson, *Chancellorsville 1863*, p. 292.

35. Early, *Memoirs*, p. 228; Jordan, ed., *North Carolina Troops*, 13:186; O.R. I, 25, part 1, p. 869; *Spirit of the Age*, May 25, 1863.

36. Early, *Memoirs*, pp. 228–29.

37. *Salisbury Watchman*, June 1, 1863; Clark, ed., *Regiments*, 3:410; Iobst and Manarin, *The Bloody Sixth*, p. 119; *Spirit of the Age*, May 25, 1863. Jubal Early recorded in his memoirs that Lee was not present at the charge, but Lee's biographer, Douglas Southall Freeman, noted that Lee was on hand for the Confederate offensive. Early, *Memoirs*, pp. 227–29; Freeman, *R. E. Lee*, 2:554.

38. Early, *Memoirs*, pp. 230–31.

39. Ibid, pp. 233–34; Wagner, William, *Letters of William Wagner*, p. 50; Jordan, ed., *North Carolina Troops*, 13:187; Jack D. Welsh, *Medical Histories of Confederate Generals*, p. 103; author's personal interview with Robert Frederick Hoke Pollock (grandson of Robert F.

Hoke) at Southern Pines, North Carolina, July 11, 1993; Eaton Diary, May 4, 1863, Samuel W. Eaton Papers, SHC.

40. Hoke Family Papers in possession of Van Wyck Webb (grandson of Robert F. Hoke), Raleigh, North Carolina.

CHAPTER 5
Frustration and Heartbreak

1. Malone, *Whipt 'Em Everytime*, p. 79, 85–86, 92–93; Iobst and Manarin, *The Bloody Sixth*, p. 120, 123, 165–66.

2. Jordan, ed., *North Carolina Troops*, 13:187–88; Iobst and Manarin, *The Bloody Sixth*, pp. 120–22; Malone, *Whipt 'Em Everytime*, pp. 79–80; William J. Pfohl to Christian Thomas Pfohl, May 29, 1863, Christian Thomas Pfohl Papers, SHC; *Spirit of the Age*, June 1, 1863.

3. Early, *Memoirs*, p. 237; Hamilton, "General Robert F. Hoke," Robert F. Hoke Papers, SHC; Ashe et al, eds., *Biographical History*, 1:314, 7:14–15; Powell, ed., *North Carolina Biography*, 1:66–72. Prior to the war, Avery and Fisher were principals in the Western North Carolina Railroad, an enterprise designed to bring the railroad from Salisbury to Morganton. Clark, ed., *Regiments*, 1:293–308; Evans, ed., *North Carolina*, p. 194.

4. Iobst and Manarin, *The Bloody Sixth*, p. 122; Jordan, ed., *North Carolina Troops*, 13:188; Early, *Memoirs*, p. 237; *Raleigh Standard*, June 3, 1863.

5. Jordan, ed., *North Carolina Troops*, 13:189; Iobst and Manarin, *The Bloody Sixth*, pp. 123–24; Early, *Memoirs*, pp. 240–53; Clark, ed., *Regiments*, 1:310, 2:135.

6. Iobst and Manarin, *The Bloody Sixth*, p. 127; Early, *Memoirs*, pp. 253–54; Eaton Diary, June 22 and 23, 1863, Samuel W. Eaton Papers, SHC; Malone, *Whipt 'Em Everytime*, p. 83.

7. Malone, *Whipt 'Em Everytime*, p. 84; Clark, ed., *Regiments*, 3:412; Terry Jones, *Lee's Tigers*, p. 165.

8. Early, *Memoirs*, p. 266; Iobst and Manarin, *The Bloody Sixth*, p. 133; Evans, ed., *North Carolina*, p. 176; Clark, ed., *Regiments*, 3:413.

9. Glenn Tucker, *High Tide at Gettysburg* (hereafter cited as *High Tide*), pp. 156–59; Iobst and Manarin, *The Bloody Sixth*, pp. 133–35, 139; Early, *Memoirs*, p. 267; Clark, ed., *Regiments*, 1:311, 3:413–14; *O.R.* I, 27, part 2, p. 475; John A. McPherson to I. T. Avery, August 3, 1863, Robert F. Hoke Papers, NCDAH.

10. Ashe et al, eds., *Biographical History*, 7:15; John A. McPherson to I. T. Avery, August 3, 1863, Robert F. Hoke Papers, NCDAH; Clarence E. Hatton, "Gen. Archibald Campbell Godwin," *Confederate Veteran* 38:134; Clark, ed., *Regiments*, 3:414.

11. William J. Seymour, *The Civil War Memoirs of Captain William J. Seymour* (hereafter cited as *Seymour*), p. 73; Clark, ed., *Regiments*, 3:414, 2:136, 313; Tucker, *High Tide*, p. 291; Malone, *Whipt 'Em Everytime*, p. 85; John A. McPherson to I. T. Avery, August 3, 1863, Robert F. Hoke Papers, NCDAH.

12. Iobst and Manarin, *The Bloody Sixth*, p. 136; Tucker, *High Tide*, p. 180; Clark, ed., *Regiments*, 2:136, 1:313, 4:517, 3:415; Harry Pfanz, *Gettysburg: Culp's Hill and Cemetery Hill* (hereafter cited as *Culp's Hill*), p. 240; John A. McPherson to I. T. Avery, August 3, 1863, Robert F. Hoke Papers, NCDAH; clipping from unidentified newspaper, Robert F. Hoke Papers, SHC; Pollock, "A Confederate Veteran I Know," Robert F. Hoke Papers, NCDAH. According to General Hoke's great-grandson, "Old Joe" lost a portion of his ear in the

Endnotes

attack on Cemetery Hill. Author's interview with Hoke Kimball (great-grandson of Robert F. Hoke) in Raleigh, North Carolina, February 27, 1993.

13. *O.R.* I, 27, part 2, p. 470; Tucker, *High Tide*, pp. 292–93; Iobst and Manarin, *The Bloody Sixth*, p. 137; Clarence E. Hatton, "Gen. Archibald Campbell Godwin," *Confederate Veteran* 28:135; Seymour, *Seymour*, p. 35; Pfanz, *Culp's Hill*, p. 237, 250–53; Clark, ed., *Regiments*, 2:136, 5:607, 1:313, 3:415.

14. Pfanz, *Culp's Hill*, pp. 252–55; *O.R.* I, 27, part 2, p. 484; Iobst and Manarin, *The Bloody Sixth*, pp. 137–39; Clark, ed., *Regiments*, 1:313; John A. McPherson to I. T. Avery, August 3, 1863, Robert F. Hoke Papers, NCDAH; Ashe et al, eds., *Biographical History*, 7:15–16.

15. Tucker, *High Tide*, pp. 284–92; Pfanz, *Culp's Hill*, pp. 252–62; *O.R.* I, 27, part 2, p. 480, 482–87; Iobst and Manarin, *The Bloody Sixth*, p. 137; Clark, ed., *Regiments*, 1:313, 2:136–37; Ashe et al, eds., *Biographical History*, 7:16.

16. Iobst and Manarin, *The Bloody Sixth*, p. 140; *O.R.* I, 27, part 2, p. 485; Clark, ed., *Regiments*, 1:314, 2:138–39, 5:607; Carl Schurz, *The Reminiscences of Carl Schurz*, 3:24.

17. *O.R.* I, 27, part 2, p. 485; Iobst and Manarin, *The Bloody Sixth*, p. 141; Malone, *Whipt 'Em Everytime*, p. 86; Clark, ed., *Regiments*, 1:317.

18. Iobst and Manarin, *The Bloody Sixth*, p. 141, 143; Early, *Memoirs*, pp. 281–83; Malone, *Whipt 'Em Everytime*, p. 86. Although there was heavy skirmishing at times during the movement back to Virginia, the brigade was not involved in any serious engagements. Jordan, ed., *North Carolina Troops*, 13:192; John Paris Diary (hereafter cited as Paris Diary), July 10, 12, and 14, 1863, John Paris Papers, SHC; Clark, ed., *Regiments*, 1:317, 3:416.

19. Iobst and Manarin, *The Bloody Sixth*, pp. 143–44; Eaton Diary, July 29, 30, and 31 and August 1 and 2, 1863, Samuel W. Eaton Papers, SHC; Paris Diary, July 22, 24, 25, 26, and 29, 1863, John Paris Papers, SHC; Jordan, ed., *North Carolina Troops*, 13:192–93; William F. Wagner, *Letters of William F. Wagner, Confederate Soldier* (hereafter cited as *Wagner*), pp. 60–61.

20. *Charlotte Observer*, July 21, 1912.

21. Early, *Memoirs*, p. 276; Clark, ed., *Regiments*, 2:137; Iobst and Manarin, *The Bloody Sixth*, p. 151; *O.R.* I, 29, part 2, p. 676.

22. *O.R.* I, 29, part 2, p. 676; *O.R.* I, 18, p. 998; *O.R.* IV, 2, p. 786; Wagner, *Wagner*, p. 65.

23. *O.R.* IV, 2, p. 674, 783–85; Barrett, *The Civil War in North Carolina*, pp. 190–91; William Trotter, *Silk Flags and Cold Steel*, p. 16; Glenn Tucker, *Zeb Vance: Champion of Personal Freedom* (hereafter cited as *Zeb Vance*), p. 145.

24. James M. McPherson, *Battle Cry of Freedom*, pp. 695–96; Archibald Henderson, *North Carolina: The Old North State and the New*, 2:266; *O.R.* IV, 2, p. 784; Iobst and Manarin, *The Bloody Sixth*, p. 146. Born in Hillsborough, North Carolina, in 1818, Holden was a political ally of Robert F. Hoke's father, Michael. Holden was defeated by Vance in the gubernatorial campaign in 1864 but was elected governor in 1868. However, less than three years later, he was impeached and banned forever from political office in the state. Powell, ed., *North Carolina Biography*, 3:169–71; Ashe et al, eds., *Biographical History*, 3:184–206.

25. *O.R.* IV, 2, pp. 783–85; *O.R.* I, 29, part 2, p. 676.

26. *O.R.* I, 29, part 2, p. 676, 692; *O.R.* I, 27, part 3, pp. 1058–68.

27. Campbell's statement was made in response to Lieutenant Colonel Lay's distressing report about conditions in North Carolina. *O.R.* IV, 2, p. 786; Iobst and Manarin, *The Bloody Sixth*, p. 151.

28. Mary to "My dearest Rufus," September 9, 1863, Patterson Papers, SHC; *O.R.* I, 29, part 2, p. 692.

29. David Schenck Diary, September 11, 1863, SHC; Peter Mallett to Zebulon Vance, September 9, 1863, Zebulon B. Vance Papers, NCDAH; Zebulon Vance to Robert F. Hoke, September 7, 1863, Zebulon B. Vance Papers, NCDAH; W. T. Auman, "Neighbor against Neighbor: The Inner Civil War in the Central Counties of Confederate North Carolina" (hereafter cited as "Neighbor against Neighbor"), pp. 260–61.

30. Jordan, ed., *North Carolina Troops*, 13:554–55; Calvin J. Cowles to Jas. M. Sanders, September 17, 1863, Calvin J. Cowles Papers, NCDAH; Doran L. Cart, "A Soldier's Conscience, Part I: The Letters of Thomas F. Price," *Camp Chase Gazette* 14, p. 21.

31. Robert F. Hoke to S. A. Sharpe, September 25, 1863, S. A. Sharpe Papers, SHC; J. Gwyn to his mother, September 25, 1863, Lenoir Family Papers, SHC; Calvin J. Cowles to "Publisher *Richmond Examiner*," September 25, 1863, Calvin J. Cowles Papers, NCDAH; P. F. Faison to Col., October 21, 1863, S. A. Sharpe Papers, SHC.

32. J. A. Parks to Zebulon B. Vance, November 16, 1863, Zebulon B. Vance Papers, NCDAH; Rhoda Ledder to Zebulon B. Vance, November 29, 1863, Zebulon B. Vance Papers, NCDAH; Barrett, *The Civil War in North Carolina*, p. 194; Trotter, *Silk Flags and Cold Steel*, p. 155; Jesse Kinley to Zebulon B. Vance, October 17, 1863, Zebulon B. Vance Papers, NCDAH; Rebecca Varner to Zebulon B. Vance, November 16, 1863, Zebulon B. Vance Papers, NCDAH; E. B. Crawford to Zebulon B. Vance, November 16, 1863, Zebulon B. Vance Papers, NCDAH; W. H. Greene to Zebulon B. Vance, November 21, 1863, Zebulon B. Vance Papers, NCDAH; William Alexander Graham, *The Papers of William Alexander Graham* (hereafter cited as *William Alexander Graham*), 5:538.

33. S. C. James to C. T. Pfohl, November 8, 1863, Christian Thomas Pfohl Papers, SHC; E. B. Cranford to Zebulon B. Vance, November 16, 1863, Zebulon B. Vance Papers, NCDAH; L. S. Wright to B. and E. Wright, November 27, 1863, Wright Family Papers, DU; Graham, *William Alexander Graham*, 5:539; John W. Graham to Z. B. Vance, December 6, 1863, Zebulon B. Vance Papers, NCDAH; Auman, "Neighbor against Neighbor," p. 266; Peter W. Hairston, "The Civil War Diary of Peter W. Hairston" (hereafter cited as "Hairston"), *North Carolina Historical Review* 67:82.

34. Iobst and Manarin, *The Bloody Sixth*, pp. 151–58; Jordan, ed., *North Carolina Troops*, 13:194–95; Malone, *Whipt 'Em Everytime*, pp. 89–91.

35. Iobst and Manarin, *The Bloody Sixth*, p. 153, 158; Robert F. Hoke to Zebulon B. Vance, October 21, 1863, Zebulon B. Vance Papers, NCDAH.

36. Jordan, ed., *North Carolina Troops*, 13:196; Clark, ed., *Regiments*, 3:272, 1:318; Iobst and Manarin, *The Bloody Sixth*, p. 153, 159.

37. Malone, *Whipt 'Em Everytime*, p. 92; *O.R.* I, 29, part 1, p. 629; Clark, ed., *Regiments*, 1:319; Iobst and Manarin, *The Bloody Sixth*, pp. 163–64; Seymour, *Seymour*, p. 92; Jordan, ed., *North Carolina Troops*, 13:198.

38. Jordan, ed., *North Carolina Troops*, 13:198; Iobst and Manarin, *The Bloody Sixth*, pp. 164–65; Jones, *Lee's Tigers*, p. 183; Freeman, *Lee's Lieutenants*, 3:266; Frank Moore, ed., *Rebellion Record*, 8:165; Osborne, *Jubal*, p. 207.

39. *O.R.* I, 29, part 1, p. 613, 623–24, 630; Freeman, *Lee's Lieutenants*, 3:266; Freeman, *R. E. Lee*, 3:191; Clark, ed., *Regiments*, 1:319–20, 3:417–18; Jordan, ed., *North Carolina Troops*, 13:199–200. Some historians have concluded that the bayonet charges at Rappahannock Station were two of the true such charges during the war. Jones, *Lee's Tigers*,

Endnotes

pp. 184–85; Osborne, *Jubal*, p. 207; Iobst and Manarin, *The Bloody Sixth*, p. 165; Hairston, "Hairston," pp. 70–73; Malone, *Whipt 'Em Everytime*, p. 92; Moore, ed., *Rebellion Record*, 8:166; Ashe, *History of North Carolina*, 2:831; Early, *Memoirs*, p. 315.

40. Moore, ed., *Rebellion Record*, 8:166; *O.R.* I, 29, part 1, pp. 624–25, 629–30; Clark, ed., *Regiments*, 3:418; Early, *Memoirs*, p. 315; Iobst and Manarin, *The Bloody Sixth*, p. 167, 169; Freeman, *R. E. Lee*, 3:192.

41. Early, *Memoirs*, p. 316; Jordan, ed., *North Carolina Troops*, 13:201; Iobst and Manarin, *The Bloody Sixth*, pp. 169–72; Freeman, *R. E. Lee*, 3:193; Moore, ed., *Rebellion Record*, 8:166; Hairston, "Hairston," p. 71.

42. Hairston, "Hairston," p. 81; Robert F. Hoke to Zebulon B. Vance, November 11, 1863, Zebulon B. Vance Papers, NCDAH; *O.R.* I, 29, part 2, p. 833.

43. Paris Diary, November 22, 1863, John Paris Papers, SHC; Hairston, "Hairston," pp. 81–82.

44. Paris Diary, November 24 and 26 and December 12, 1863, John Paris Papers, SHC; Hairston, "Hairston," p. 83; Jordan, ed., *North Carolina Troops*, 13:201–2.

45. Paris Diary, November 28, 1863, John Paris Papers, SHC; R. F. Hoke to Dr. Hackett, December 8, 1863, Gaden Hackett Papers, SHC.

CHAPTER 6
The Promise of a New Year

1. Royce Singleton, *John Taylor Wood: Sea Ghost of the Confederacy* (hereafter cited as *Wood*), p. 90; Freeman, *R. E. Lee*, 3:218; *O.R.* I, 33, p. 1061.

2. Henderson, *North Carolina*, 2:270; Barrett, *The Civil War in North Carolina*, pp. 164–68.

3. Ashe, *History of North Carolina*, 2:863; Hamilton, "General Robert F. Hoke," Robert F. Hoke Papers, SHC; Moore, *North Carolina*, 2:251; Barrett, *The Civil War in North Carolina*, p. 174; Henderson, *North Carolina*, p. 270; W. A. Willoughby to wife, January 22, 1863, W. H. Noble Papers, DU; W. G. MacRae to "Dear Don," August 2, 1872, Hugh MacRae Papers, DU.

4. Ashe, *History of North Carolina*, 2:863; Hamilton, "General Robert F. Hoke," Robert F. Hoke Papers, SHC; *O.R.* I, 33, p. 1101; Barrett, *The Civil War in North Carolina*, p. 203; Connor, *North Carolina: Rebuilding an Ancient Commonwealth*, 2:246; Trotter, *Ironclads and Columbiads*, 223–24; Dave Page, *Ships versus Shore: Civil War Engagements along Southern Shores and Rivers* (hereafter cited as *Ships*), p. 76; Henderson, *North Carolina*, 2:270.

5. *O.R.* I, 33, p. 1099; Thomas, *History of the Doles-Cook Brigade*, p. 358.

6. General Foster was replaced by Major General Benjamin Butler as commander of the Department of Virginia and North Carolina in November 1863. Barrett, *The Civil War in North Carolina*, p. 131, 152–53, 177; statement of W. Wilson, July 2, 1862, H. Briggs Papers, SHC.

7. Jordan, ed., *North Carolina Troops*, 13:203, 206; Barrett, *The Civil War in North Carolina*, p. 203, 209; *O.R.* I, 33, p. 1102; Ashe, *History of North Carolina*, 2:865; Clark, ed., *Regiments*, 4:486; Singleton, *Wood*, p. 94.

8. *O.R.* I, 33, p. 1102.

9. Ibid, pp. 1102–3.

10. Ibid, pp. 1099–1100, 1103–4; Jordan, ed., *North Carolina Troops*, 13:203; Paris Diary,

General Robert F. Hoke

January 20, 1864, John Paris Papers, SHC.

11. *O.R.* I, 33, p. 95; Iobst and Manarin, *The Bloody Sixth*, pp. 176–77.

12. *O.R.* I, 33, p. 95; Iobst and Manarin, *The Bloody Sixth*, pp. 176–77; Robert F. Hoke to John Whitford, January 23, 1864, Whitford Papers, NCDAH.

13. Clark, ed., *Regiments*, 3:131–32, 5:326; Iobst and Manarin, *The Bloody Sixth*, p. 177; Robert F. Hoke to John Whitford, January 23, 1864, Whitford Papers, NCDAH; Paris Diary, January 29, 1864, John Paris Papers, SHC. In advance of his movement from Wilmington, General Martin had consulted with Hoke at Goldsboro. Singleton, *Wood*, p. 92.

14. Iobst and Manarin, *The Bloody Sixth*, p. 177; William H. S. Burgwyn, *A Captain's War: The Letters and Diaries of William H. S. Burgwyn* (hereafter cited as *Burgwyn*), p. 119; Jordan, ed., *North Carolina Troops*, 13:203; Paris Diary, January 30, 1864, John Paris Papers, SHC.

15. Burgwyn, *Burgwyn*, p. 119; Iobst and Manarin, *The Bloody Sixth*, p. 177. Batchelder's Creek is referred to as Bachelor's Creek in some reports and is now known by that name. Barrett, *The Civil War in North Carolina*, p. 204; Powell, *Gazetteer*, p. 18; Clark, ed., *Regiments*, 3:333; Paris Diary, January 31, 1864, John Paris Papers, SHC; Ashe et al, eds., *Biographical History*, 1:315.

16. Barrett, *The Civil War in North Carolina*, p. 205; *O.R.* I, 33, pp. 97–98.

17. Iobst and Manarin, *The Bloody Sixth*, pp. 177–78; Paris Diary, February 1, 1864, John Paris Papers, SHC; *O.R.* I, 33, p. 67, 93–94; Barrett, *The Civil War in North Carolina*, p. 204; Jordan, ed., *North Carolina Troops*, 13:204; Clark, ed., *Regiments*, 3:7.

18. Paris Diary, February 1, 1864, John Paris Papers, SHC; *O.R.* I, 33, pp. 93–94; Jordan, ed., *North Carolina Troops*, 13:204; Barrett, *The Civil War in North Carolina*, p. 204; William J. Pfohl to Christian Thomas Pfohl, February 9, 1864, Christian Thomas Pfohl Papers, SHC; Clark, ed., *Regiments*, 3:7–8, 333–34, 4:486–87.

19. Clark, ed., *Regiments*, 4:487; Thomas, *History of the Doles-Cook Brigade*, p. 359.

20. *O.R.* I, 33, p. 95; *New York Herald*, February 4, 1864; Iobst and Manarin, *The Bloody Sixth*, p. 178.

21. *O.R.* I, 33, pp. 96–99; Trotter, *Ironclads and Columbiads*, p. 229; Barrett, *The Civil War in North Carolina*, p. 205; Henry A. Chambers, *Diary of Captain Henry A. Chambers* (hereafter cited as *Chambers*), pp. 171–72; Clark, ed., *Regiments*, 3:133.

22. *Richmond Dispatch*, February 8, 1864; Singleton, *Wood*, p. 98.

23. Clark, ed., *Regiments*, 4:487–88.

24. Clark, ed., *Regiments*, 5:325–33. The Confederates were disappointed to find but one enemy ship in the river. Lieutenant George Gift, one of the raiders, recalled, "The original design was to attack and cut out some four or five vessels that were accustomed to lay in the river, but unfortunately, this one was all that could be found." *O.R.N.* I, 9, pp. 451–53; Singleton, *Wood*, pp. 100–104.

25. Barrett, *The Civil War in North Carolina*, pp. 211–12; *O.R.* I, 33, pp. 85–86; Clark, ed., *Regiments*, 3:133.

26. Clark, ed., *Regiments*, 3:133; Ashe, *History of North Carolina*, 2:866; Barrett, *The Civil War in North Carolina*, p. 206; *O.R.* I, 33, p. 93; Iobst and Manarin, *The Bloody Sixth*, p. 179; Jordan, ed., *North Carolina Troops*, 13:205; Trotter, *Ironclads and Columbiads*, p. 230; Hamilton, *History of North Carolina since 1860*, pp. 23–24.

27. *O.R.* I, 33, pp. 92–94, 98–99; Barrett, *The Civil War in North Carolina*, p. 206; Jordan, ed., *North Carolina Troops*, 13:204; Trotter, *Ironclads and Columbiads*, p. 230.

28. Clark, ed., *Regiments*, 3:133; Iobst and Manarin, *The Bloody Sixth*, p. 179; Chambers, *Cham-*

Endnotes

bers, p. 173; Barrett, *The Civil War in North Carolina*, p. 207.

29. *O.R.* I, 33, pp. 92–94, 96, 99, 1187. Following continued criticism by Pickett, Barton was temporarily relieved of command by General Robert Ransom at Drewry's Bluff. Warner, *Generals in Gray*, p. 19.

30. Singleton, *Wood*, p. 106; Porter, *Naval History*, p. 472; Clark, ed., *Regiments*, 3:133, 334.

31. *Raleigh Daily Confederate*, February 14, 1864; *Wilmington Journal*, February 6, 1864; Trotter, *Ironclads and Columbiads*, p. 230; *O.R.* I, 33, pp. 1160–61; Moore, *History of North Carolina*, 2:257.

32. Barrett, *The Civil War in North Carolina*, p. 207; Hamilton, "General Robert F. Hoke," Robert F. Hoke Papers, SHC; Ashe, *History of North Carolina*, 2:868; W. R. Burwell to brother, May 10, 1864, Edmund Burwell Papers, SHC; Clara Boyd to Mrs. Carter, February 23, 1864, D. M. Carter Papers, SHC.

33. Iobst and Manarin, *The Bloody Sixth*, p. 179; Paris Diary, February 4, 1864, John Paris Papers, SHC; Jordan, ed., *North Carolina Troops*, 12:12, 13:205; *O.R.* I, 33, p. 94, 96; Barrett, *The Civil War in North Carolina*, p. 207.

34. *O.R.* I, 33, p. 1103, 1160–61.

35. *O.R.* I, 33, p. 94, 97, 1101; Barrett, *The Civil War in North Carolina*, p. 214; Jordan, ed., *North Carolina Troops*, 13:205; Iobst and Manarin, *The Bloody Sixth*, pp. 179–80.

36. Iobst and Manarin, *The Bloody Sixth*, p. 181; *Raleigh News and Observer*, September 20, 1953; Richard Randolph, "Confederate Dilemma: North Carolina Troops and the Deserter Problem," *North Carolina Historical Review* 66:205; Rush C. Hawkins, *An Account of the Assassination of Loyal Citizens of North Carolina* (hereafter cited as *Loyal Citizens*), p. 16.

37. Paris Diary, February 5, 1864, John Paris Papers, SHC; *Raleigh News and Observer*, September 20, 1953; W. R. Burwell to brother, March 10, 1864, Edmund Burwell Papers, SHC; "A Sermon Preached before Brig. Gen. Hoke's Brigade by Rev. John Paris," John Paris Papers, SHC.

38. Hawkins, *Loyal Citizens*, p. 19.

39. *Raleigh News and Observer*, September 20, 1953; Barrett, *The Civil War in North Carolina*, p. 208; U.S. Congress, *Murder of Union Soldiers in North Carolina*.

40. Hamilton, "General Robert F. Hoke," Robert F. Hoke Papers, SHC.

CHAPTER 7
"Heaven Has Crowned Our Efforts with Success"

1. Trotter, *Ironclads and Columbiads*, p. 230; Barrett, *The Civil War in North Carolina*, p. 213; Herbert M. Schiller, *The Bermuda Hundred Campaign* (hereafter cited as *Bermuda Hundred*), p. 18; *O.R.* I, 33, pp. 1244–45.

2. *O.R.* I, 51, part 2 supplement, pp. 808–9, 818–20; Ashe, *History of North Carolina*, 2:878–79; Wayne K. Durrill, *War of a Different Kind: A Southern Community in the Great Rebellion*, pp. 186–87. Much of Davis's concern about Raleigh centered around the potential arrest of Holden. William T. Auman and David D. Scarboro, "The Heroes of America in Civil War North Carolina," *North Carolina Historical Review* 58:350, 360.

3. Edwin G. Moore, "Ransom's Brigade," *Southern Historical Society Papers*, 36:363.

General Robert F. Hoke

4. Iobst and Manarin, *The Bloody Sixth*, pp. 181–89; Jordan, ed., *North Carolina Troops*, 13:208; Trotter, *Ironclads and Columbiads*, p. 239.

5. In response to General Wessells's desperate plea for manpower on April 15, just three days before Hoke attacked Plymouth, Major General John Peck at New Bern offered little assistance, remarking about the impending Confederate attack, "Under all the circumstances I think their spring demonstrations will be light." *O.R.* I, 33, p. 877; Barrett, *The Civil War in North Carolina*, p. 214. Frequent delays in the receipt of construction materials for the *Neuse* caused idle workmen to dub her the CSS *Neus-ance*. Trotter, *Ironclads and Columbiads*, p. 236; W. R. Burwell to brother, March 10, 1864, Edmund Burwell Papers, SHC; William N. Still, Jr., *Iron Afloat: The Story of the Confederate Ironclads* (hereafter cited as *Iron Afloat*), p. 91.

6. James Carson Elliott, *The Southern Soldier Boy: A Thousand Shots for the Confederacy* (hereafter cited as *Soldier Boy*), p. 61; *Charlotte Observer*, May 14, 1905; C. Vann Woodward, ed., *Mary Chesnut's Civil War* (hereafter cited as *Chesnut*), pp. 585–86.

7. *Charlotte Observer*, May 14, 1905.

8. Iobst and Manarin, *The Bloody Sixth*, pp. 181–82; Jordan, ed., *North Carolina Troops*, 13:208; William Beavans Diary (hereafter cited as Beavans Diary), April 5 and 6, 1864, William Beavans Papers, SHC; George W. Wills to sister, April 2, 1864, George Whitaker Wills Papers, SHC; W. R. Burwell to brother, March 10, 1864, Edmund Burwell Papers, SHC.

9. John K. Walker to Lucinda Walker, March 14, 1864, John K. Walker Papers, DU; Iobst and Manarin, *The Bloody Sixth*, p. 181; Paris Diary, March 9, 12, 13, 16, 21, 22, and 23, 1864, John Paris Papers, SHC; Jordan, ed., *North Carolina Troops*, 13:207.

10. Freeman, *Lee's Lieutenants*, 3:336; Iobst and Manarin, *The Bloody Sixth*, p. 180; Joseph Blount Cheshire, *Nonnulla*, pp. 146–47; Clark, ed., *Regiments*, 5:318; *Charlotte Observer*, May 14, 1905; Robert Elliott, *Ironclad of the Roanoke: Gilbert Elliott's* Albemarle (hereafter cited as *Albemarle*), p. 166.

11. Barrett, *The Civil War in North Carolina*, p. 215; Gilbert Elliott, "The Career of the Confederate Ram *Albemarle*," *Century Magazine* (May-October 1888):420. The cornfield in which the ship was constructed was owned by William Ruffin Smith, Jr., whose son, Peter, supervised much of the day-to-day work and provided badly needed tools and blacksmith facilities. Elliott, *Albemarle*, pp. 88–89. Each of the guns was mounted on a carriage, enabling it to fire through portholes located fore and aft on either side. Trotter, *Ironclads and Columbiads*, pp. 234–36.

12. *O.R.* I, 33, p. 1266, 1273; *O.R.* I, 51, part 2 supplement, p. 855, 857.

13. Paris Diary, April 12, 1864, John Paris Papers, SHC. While in Virginia, Hoke was in attendance when Governor Vance made his last speech during his tour of the North Carolina troops' camps. It occurred at a grand review of Lee's army near Orange Court House. According to one observer, Hoke gazed upon Vance "with mingled pride and affection." Tucker, *Zeb Vance*, p. 346; "Address of Mr. Stedman, of North Carolina," *Statue of Zebulon Baird Vance*, pp. 74–75; Beavans Diary, April 13 and 14, 1864, William Beavans Papers, SHC; Paris Diary, April 13, 1864, John Paris Papers, SHC.

14. *O.R.* I, 51, part 2 supplement, pp. 857–58.

15. Jordan, ed., *North Carolina Troops*, 13:208, 563; Clark, ed., *Regiments*, 3:419; Charles N. Branham, ed., *Register of Graduates and Former Cadets of the United States Military Academy, 1802–1965*, pp. 242–43; Thomas, *History of the Doles-Cook Brigade*, p. 366.

16. Jordan, ed., *North Carolina Troops*, 13:563; Singleton, *Wood*, p. 113; Clark, ed., *Regiments*, 5:175.

17. Clark, ed., *Regiments*, 5:176; Cheshire, *Nonnulla*, p. 145; Wayne Mahood, *The Plymouth Pilgrims: A History of the Eighty-fifth New York Infantry in the Civil War* (hereafter cited as *Pilgrims*), p. 160; Iobst and Manarin, *The Bloody Sixth*, p. 189. Conaby Creek was a deep waterway which wound its way to the river from the southeast side of town. Ashe, *History of North Carolina*, 2:882.

18. Clark, ed., *Regiments*, 5:176; Mahood, *Pilgrims*, p. 159; Iobst and Manarin, *The Bloody Sixth*, p. 189; Ezra Warner, *Generals in Blue*, pp. 551–52.

19. Iobst and Manarin, *The Bloody Sixth*, p. 189; Clark, ed., *Regiments*, 5:176; Mahood, *Pilgrims*, pp. 160–61.

20. Barrett, *The Civil War in North Carolina*, p. 214; Clark, ed., *Regiments*, 5:175, 321. Some of the sunken boats were filled with stones. Mahood, *Pilgrims*, p. 166.

21. On March 21, Butler suggested to Rear Admiral S. P. Lee and General Peck that a land expedition be used to destroy the *Albemarle*. *O.R.* I, 33, p. 296, 707, 711, 740, 748, 749, 769; Still, *Iron Afloat*, p. 159; William A. Smith, "The Siege and Capture of Plymouth," *Personal Recollections of the War of the Rebellion: Addresses Delivered before the New York Commandery of the Loyal Legion of the United States* (hereafter cited as *Personal Recollections*), pp. 322–43; Wilfred W. Black, "Civil War Letters of E. N. Boots from New Bern and Plymouth," *North Carolina Historical Review* 36:206, 220, 222.

22. Mahood, *Pilgrims*, p. 164; J. W. Whitehill to Robert F. Hoke, April 17, 1894, Robert F. Hoke Papers, NCDAH.

23. Barrett, *The Civil War in North Carolina*, pp. 217–18; Trotter, *Ironclads and Columbiads*, p. 241; Still, *Iron Afloat*, p. 161; Mahood, *Pilgrims*, p. 166; Smith, "The Siege and Capture of Plymouth," *Personal Recollections*, p. 334. As Hoke was approaching Plymouth, Flusser's tone grew more ominous: "The ram will be down to-night or to-morrow. I fear, for the protection of the town, I shall have to abandon my plan of fighting. . . . The army ought to be reinforced at once." *O.R.N.* I, 9, p. 637.

24. *Raleigh Daily Confederate*, April 17, 1864.

25. Iobst and Manarin, *The Bloody Sixth*, p. 190; Beavans Diary, April 15, 1864, William Beavans Papers, SHC; Graham, *William Alexander Graham*, 6:70–71; William Gaston Lewis to his wife, April 16, 1864, William Gaston Lewis Papers, SHC.

26. Graham, *William Alexander Graham*, 6:71; Still, *Iron Afloat*, p. 158; Iobst and Manarin, *The Bloody Sixth*, p. 190; Beavans Diary, April 16, 1864, William Beavans Papers, SHC.

27. Iobst and Manarin, *The Bloody Sixth*, p. 190; Beavans Diary, April 17, 1864, William Beavans Papers, SHC; Smith, "The Siege and Capture of Plymouth," *Personal Recollections*, p. 328; Graham, *William Alexander Graham*, 6:72; W. A. Croffut and John M. Morris, *The Military and Civil History of Connecticut*, pp. 480–87; *O.R.* I, 33, p. 296; Mahood, *Pilgrims*, p. 168; Clark, ed., *Regiments*, 5:177.

28. Mahood, *Pilgrims*, p. 169; Jordan, ed., *North Carolina Troops*, 13:209; *O.R.* I, 33, p. 288.

29. Elliott, *Soldier Boy*, p. 13. Captain John W. Graham noted that Hoke's batteries offered no return to the Union artillery fire; however, it is apparent that the Union garrison at the forts in Plymouth was startled by the few well-placed shells at the opening of hostilities. Graham, *William Alexander Graham*, 6:73; Smith, "The Siege and Capture of Plymouth," *Personal Recollections*, p. 328; Mahood, *Pilgrims*, p. 168; *Fayetteville Observer*, May 2, 1864; *Raleigh Daily Confederate*, April 30, 1864.

30. Iobst and Manarin, *The Bloody Sixth*, p. 191; Mahood, *Pilgrims*, p. 170.

31. Elliott, *Albemarle*, pp. 167–68; Still, *Iron Afloat*, p. 158.

General Robert F. Hoke

32. Iobst and Manarin, *The Bloody Sixth*, p. 191; Mahood, *Pilgrims*, p. 171; Elliott, *Soldier Boy*, p. 13.

33. Graham, *William Alexander Graham*, 6:73–74; Iobst and Manarin, *The Bloody Sixth*, p. 191; Jordan, ed., *North Carolina Troops*, 13:565.

34. One Confederate soldier who witnessed the dangerous advance of the Eleventh Virginia on Fort Gray opined that it was a result of a "fool order" from Colonel Terry. William H. Morgan, *Reminiscences of the War of 1864–1865* (hereafter cited as *Reminiscences*), pp. 183–85; Joseph E. Fiske, *War Letters of Capt. Joseph E. Fiske*, p. 57; Mahood, *Pilgrims*, p. 172; Jordan, ed., *North Carolina Troops*, 13:565; *Raleigh Daily Confederate*, April 30, 1864; Graham, *William Alexander Graham*, 6:74–75.

35. Clark, ed., *Regiments*, 5:178; Jordan, ed., *North Carolina Troops*, 13:565.

36. Clark, ed., *Regiments*, 5:178–79, 3:338; Jordan, ed., *North Carolina Troops*, 13:565; Iobst and Manarin, *The Bloody Sixth*, p. 192; Elliott, *Soldier Boy*, pp. 13–14; Graham, *William Alexander Graham*, 6:74–75; Luther Dickey, *History of the 103rd Pennsylvania Regiment, 1861–1865*, p. 262; *Richmond Examiner*, April 24, 1864.

37. *O.R.* I, 33, pp. 301–2; *Raleigh Daily Confederate*, April 30, 1864; Clark, ed., *Regiments*, 5:180, 3:8, 339. Colonel Mercer's body was transported from Plymouth to Tarboro, where it was buried beside that of a West Point classmate, Major General William Dorsey Pender, who had died a year earlier from wounds sustained at Gettysburg. Iobst and Manarin, *The Bloody Sixth*, pp. 193–94; Thomas, *The History of the Doles-Cook Brigade*, p. 346.

38. *O.R.* I, 33, pp. 302–3.

39. Iobst and Manarin, *The Bloody Sixth*, p. 194; Graham, *William Alexander Graham*, 6:75.

40. Elliott, *Albemarle*, pp. 168–69; J. Thomas Scharf, *The Confederate States Navy from Its Organization to the Surrender of Its Last Vessel* (hereafter cited as *Confederate States Navy*), p. 405; *O.R.N.* I, 9, p. 656; Still, *Iron Afloat*, p. 158.

41. On the thirty-two-hour trip from Hamilton to Plymouth, the *Albemarle* was accompanied by another Confederate vessel, the *Cotton Plant*. Little is known about the ship, although it is believed to have carried Confederate riflemen protected by screens. Elliott, *Albemarle*, pp. 170–71; Clark, ed., *Regiments*, 5:319; Elliott, "The Career of the Confederate Ram *Albemarle*," *Century Magazine* (May-October 1888): 422–23.

42. Elliott, *Albemarle*, pp. 176–77, 182–83; Elliott, "The Career of the Confederate Ram *Albemarle*," *Century Magazine* (May-October 1888): 423; Joseph E. Fiske, "An Involuntary Journey through the Confederacy," *Civil War Papers Read before the Commandery of the State of Massachusetts Military Order of the Loyal Legion of the United States* 2 (hereafter cited as "Involuntary Journey," *Civil War Papers*): 514; Barrett, *The Civil War in North Carolina*, pp. 217–18; Mahood, *Pilgrims*, p. 179; Trotter, *Ironclads and Columbiads*, pp. 246–47; Roy F. Nicols, ed., "Fighting in North Carolina Waters," *North Carolina Historical Review* 40:79; N. Lanpheur, "Fall of Plymouth," N. Lanpheur Papers, DU.

43. Morgan, *Reminiscences*, p. 189; Elliott, *Albemarle*, pp. 183–84; Iobst and Manarin, *The Bloody Sixth*, pp. 194–95; Clark, ed., *Regiments*, 5:182.

44. Clark, ed., *Regiments*, 5:182.

45. Barrett, *The Civil War in North Carolina*, p. 218; Clark, ed., *Regiments*, 5:182; E. A. Wright, "Capture of Plymouth, N.C.," *Confederate Veteran* 24:200; Iobst and Manarin, *The Bloody Sixth*, pp. 194–95.

46. Beavans Diary, April 20, 1864, William Beavans Papers, SHC; Clark, ed., *Regiments*, 3:340; Elliott, *Soldier Boy*, p. 14; Graham, *William Alexander Graham*, 6:75–77; Mahood, *Pil-*

Endnotes

grims, p. 180; B. F. Blakeslee, *History of the Sixteenth Connecticut Volunteers*, p. 70.

47. Barrett, *The Civil War in North Carolina*, p. 219. During the approach from the west by Hoke's (Lewis's) brigade, Battery Worth was captured by the Confederates. Clark, ed., *Regiments*, 3:342, 1:401–2; Jordan, ed., *North Carolina Troops*, 13:567; *Raleigh Daily Confederate*, April 30, 1864; Graham, *William Alexander Graham*, 6:75–77.

48. Barrett, *The Civil War in North Carolina*, p. 219; *O.R.* I, 33, p. 299; Cheshire, *Nonnulla*, p. 148; *Polkton Ansonian*, July 12 and 19, 1876; *Raleigh Daily Confederate*, May 3, 1864; Henry T. Guion Journal, April 20, 1864, William Alexander Graham Papers, SHC; J. W. Whitehill to Robert F. Hoke, April 17, 1894, Robert F. Hoke Papers, NCDAH.

49. Henry T. Guion Journal, April 20, 1864, William Alexander Graham Papers, SHC; *Raleigh Daily Confederate*, April 30, 1864; *O.R.* I, 33, p. 299.

50. *O.R.* I, 33, p. 299; *Raleigh Daily Confederate*, April 30, 1864; *Polkton Ansonian*, July 19, 1876.

51. E. A. Wright, "Capture of Plymouth, N.C.," *Confederate Veteran* 24:200; *Polkton Ansonian*, July 19, 1876; Arnold C. Wright, "After the Battle of Plymouth, N.C.," *Confederate Veteran* 25:16.

52. Clark, ed., *Regiments*, 3:345; Mahood, *Pilgrims*, pp. 182–83; Dickey, *History of the 103rd Pennsylvania Regiment, 1861–1865*, p. 268; Trotter, *Ironclads and Columbiads*, p. 248; *New York Sun*, July 5, 1912.

53. *New York Sun*, July 5, 1912.

54. Morgan, *Reminiscences*, p. 186.

55. Peter M. Chaitin et al, eds., *The Coastal War*, p. 96; Trotter, *Ironclads and Columbiads*, p. 249; Singleton, *Wood*, p. 114; Jordan, ed., *North Carolina Troops*, 13:568–69; *Raleigh Daily Confederate*, May 3, 1864; Barrett, *The Civil War in North Carolina*, p. 220; Ashe, *History of North Carolina*, 2:887.

56. *O.R.* I, 51, part 2 supplement, p. 870; *Raleigh Daily Confederate*, April 23, 1864. As the Confederates saw it, Plymouth would become the home port for the *Albemarle*, which would be used to chase enemy naval forces from the North Carolina sounds. Barrett, *The Civil War in North Carolina*, p. 220; *Tarboro Southerner*, April 30, 1864.

57. *Petersburg Daily Register*, April 23, 1864; *Richmond Examiner*, April 24, 1864; J. B. Jones, *Rebel War Clerk's Diary*, 2:189–90.

58. *O.R.* I, 51, part 2 supplement, p. 874. Robert E. Lee's son, W. H. F. Lee (born four days after Hoke in 1837), was promoted to major general on April 23, three days after the effective date of Hoke's promotion. However, Hoke's promotion was confirmed by the Confederate Senate on May 11, while Lee's was not confirmed until June 9. *Southern Historical Society Papers* 2:341–42; Hamilton, "General Robert F. Hoke," Robert F. Hoke Papers, SHC; *O.R.* I, 33, p. 1321; Clark, ed., *Regiments*, 2:618; Gallagher, *Stephen Dodson Ramseur*, p. 97.

59. Mahood, *Pilgrims*, p. 184; *O.R.* I, 33, p. 968; *O.R.* I, 51, part 1 supplement, p. 1288; *New York Tribune*, April 26, 1864.

60. Charles Loehr, "Plymouth Campaign," p. 6, NCC; Elliott, *Soldier Boy*, p. 15; Morgan, *Reminiscences*, p. 180; Clark, ed., *Regiments*, 2:140; Lawson Harrill, *Reminiscences, 1861–1865*, p. 20. Hoke subsequently donated the flag to the North Carolina Hall of History, the precursor of the North Carolina Museum of History. *Orphan's Friend and Masonic Journal*, June 4, 1920.

61. Loehr, "Plymouth Campaign," p. 7, NCC; Graham, *William Alexander Graham*, 6:69;

Clark, ed., *Regiments*, 2:618; John K. Walker to Garrison Walker, April 21, 1864, John K. Walker Papers, DU.

62. Beavans Diary, April 23, 1864, William Beavans Papers, SHC; *Charlotte Observer*, May 14, 1905.

63. As might be expected, Ransom's brigade suffered the highest number of Confederate casualties—more than 470. Weymouth T. Jordan, Jr., and Gerald W. Thomas, "Massacre at Plymouth: April 20, 1864," *North Carolina Historical Review* 72:146; Wright, "Capture of Plymouth, N.C.," *Confederate Veteran* 24:200; Mahood, *Pilgrims*, pp. 187–88.

64. The "Plymouth Massacre" has been a source of debate for historians since the war ended. Richard Iobst, William Trotter, and Luther Dickey concluded that no massacre took place. Iobst and Manarin, *The Bloody Sixth*, p. 199; Trotter, *Ironclads and Columbiads*, pp. 417–19; Dickey, *History of the 103rd Pennsylvania Regiment, 1861–1865*, p. 270. Without question, the most complete, most authoritative, and best study ever made of controversy is Weymouth T. Jordan, Jr., and Gerald W. Thomas, "Massacre at Plymouth, April 20, 1864," *North Carolina Historical Review* 72:158, 184, 191–92. *Richmond Daily Examiner*, April 30, 1864.

65. Hamilton, "General Robert F. Hoke," Robert F. Hoke Papers, SHC.

CHAPTER 8
From Triumph to Disappointment

1. Beavans Diary, April 24, 1864, William Beavans Papers, SHC; *O.R.* I, 33, p. 1303.

2. *O.R.* I, 33, p. 1303. The official title of Beauregard's command was the Department of North Carolina and Cape Fear. Alfred Roman, *The Military Operations of General Beauregard* (hereafter cited as *General Beauregard*), 2:195–96; Beavans Diary, April 24, 1864, William Beavans Papers, SHC.

3. Clark, ed., *Regiments*, 3:349; *O.R.* I, 51, part 2 supplement, p. 879; Beavans Diary, April 25, 1865, William Beavans Papers, SHC; *Polkton Ansonian*, July 12, 1876. The West Point class of 1846 counted among its graduates Stonewall Jackson, George McClellan, A. P. Hill, George Pickett, Cadmus Wilcox, and George Stoneman. John C. Waugh, *The Class of 1846 from West Point to Appomattox*, xiv–xxi. Peck was likewise a West Point graduate, finishing eighth in a class that included U. S. Grant. Faust, ed., *Encyclopedia*, p. 567.

4. Beavans Diary, April 26, 1864, William Beavans Papers, SHC; Roman, *General Beauregard*, 2:197; *O.R.* I, 33, p. 311, 990–91; Barrett, *The Civil War in North Carolina*, pp. 122–23.

5. Beavans Diary, April 27, 1864, William Beavans Papers, SHC; *O.R.* I, 51, part 2 supplement, p. 880; Roman, *General Beauregard*, 2:542; Still, *Iron Afloat*, pp. 162–63; *O.R.* I, 33, p. 1002.

6. Barrett, *The Civil War in North Carolina*, p. 221; *O.R.* I, 33, pp. 310–11; Beavans Diary, April 28, 1864, William Beavans Papers, SHC. Davis maintained hopes that the *Neuse* might be refloated in time to assist with the New Bern campaign. Roman, *General Beauregard*, 2:197.

7. Beavans Diary, April 29, 1864, William Beavans Papers, SHC; *Polkton Ansonian*, July 26, 1876; Roman, *General Beauregard*, 2:197; *O.R.* I, 51, part 2 supplement, p. 880.

8. Roman, *General Beauregard*, 2:197, 544; *O.R.* I, 51, part 2 supplement, p. 882, 884; Still,

Iron Afloat, p. 163.

9. *O.R.* I, 33, p. 1329; Clark, ed., *Regiments*, 3:349; Barrett, *The Civil War in North Carolina*, pp. 220–21, Jordan, ed., *North Carolina Troops*, 13:210, 569.

10. *O.R.* I, 33, p. 312, 1031; Barrett, *The Civil War in North Carolina*, p. 221.

11. Barrett, *The Civil War in North Carolina*, p. 221; *O.R.* I, 33, pp. 310–11, 991; Ursula Loy and Pauline Worthy, *Washington and the Pamlico*, pp. 43–45.

12. *O.R.* I, 33, pp. 310–11; Loy and Worthy, *Washington and the Pamlico*, p. 44. Among the buildings claimed by the inferno were the Presbyterian, Methodist, and Roman Catholic churches. *Fayetteville Observer*, May 16, 1864.

13. *O.R.* I, 36, part 2, p. 940; James Evans, Jr., to James Evans, Sr., May 3, 1864, James Evans Papers, SHC.

14. Iobst and Manarin, *The Bloody Sixth*, pp. 199–200; Barrett, *The Civil War in North Carolina*, p. 221; Clark, ed., *Regiments*, 3:349; *O.R.N.* I, 9, p. 810; *O.R.* I, 51, part 2 supplement, p. 883; J. C. Long to Sarah MacKay, May 30, 1864, McKay-Stiles Papers, SHC.

15. Beavans Diary, May 2, 1864, William Beavans Papers, SHC; Clark, ed., *Regiments*, 3:349; Iobst and Manarin, *The Bloody Sixth*, p. 200; *O.R.* I, 36, part 2, pp. 940–41, 943.

16. Beavans Diary, May 2 and 3, 1864, William Beavans Papers, SHC; *Polkton Ansonian*, July 26, 1876; *O.R.* I, 51, part 2 supplement, p. 886; *O.R.N.* I, 9, p. 811; James Evans, Jr., to James Evans, Sr., James Evans Papers, SHC.

17. Not only was Hoke's plan of attack almost identical to the one outlined for the Pickett expedition, but it varied very little from that suggested by Beauregard on May 1. Ashe, *History of North Carolina*, 2:897; *O.R.* I, 51, part 2 supplement, pp. 882–84; Barrett, *The Civil War in North Carolina*, p. 203.

18. *O.R.* I, 51, part 2 supplement, p. 889; Barrett, *The Civil War in North Carolina*, p. 224; Jordan, ed., *North Carolina Troops*, 13:210, 569; *Polkton Ansonian*, July 26, 1876; Beavans Diary, May 4, 1864, William Beavans Papers, SHC; *Raleigh Daily Confederate*, May 11, 1864.

19. *Charlotte Observer*, May 14, 1905; Roman, *General Beauregard*, 2:199; *Raleigh Daily Confederate*, May 11, 1864.

20. Clark, ed., *Regiments*, 4:84–85, 3:349; *O.R.* I, 36, part 2, p. 5; Barrett, *The Civil War in North Carolina*, p. 224; *Raleigh Daily Confederate*, May 11, 1864.

21. *Raleigh Daily Confederate*, May 11, 1864; Iobst and Manarin, *The Bloody Sixth*, p. 201.

22. *Raleigh Daily Confederate*, May 11, 1864; Henry L. Wyatt Camp, "'Tarheels' to 'Yellow-Hammers,'" *Confederate Veteran* 21:59.

23. *O.R.N.* I, 9, pp. 770–71. On the expedition, the *Bombshell* acted as a tender, carrying provisions and coal, while the *Cotton Plant* served as a troop transport. Elliott, *Albemarle*, p. 194; Barrett, *The Civil War in North Carolina*, p. 222; Still, *Iron Afloat*, p. 162.

24. Trotter, *Ironclads and Columbiads*, pp. 249–51; Scharf, *Confederate States Navy*, p. 406; *O.R.N.* I, 9, p. 768, 770–71; Clark, ed., *Regiments*, 5:321–22; Elliott, *Albemarle*, pp. 193–210; Barrett, *The Civil War in North Carolina*, pp. 222–23.

25. Singleton, *Wood*, p. 115; Barrett, *The Civil War in North Carolina*, p. 224; Clark, ed., *Regiments*, 3:350, 2:619; *Raleigh Daily Confederate*, May 11, 1864.

26. Clark, ed., *Regiments*, 4:85; *Raleigh Daily Confederate*, May 11, 1864.

27. Clark, ed., *Regiments*, 3:349; Thomas, *History of the Doles-Cook Brigade*, p. 361.

28. Roman, *General Beauregard*, 2:199; Clark, ed., *Regiments*, 3:350; Jordan, ed., *North Carolina Troops*, 13:210.

29. *Raleigh Daily Confederate*, May 11, 1864; *O.R.* I, 36, part 2, pp. 3–4, 809.

30. Thomas, *History of the Doles-Cook Brigade*, p. 361; *Raleigh Daily Confederate*, May 11, 1864; Hamilton, "General Robert F. Hoke," Robert F. Hoke Papers, SHC; Clark, ed., *Regiments*, 3:356; Blair Burwell to Robert F. Hoke, September 6, 1904, Robert F. Hoke Papers, SHC; *Masonic Journal*, March 7, 1919.

31. Trotter, *Ironclads and Columbiads*, p. 252; Jones, *Rebel War Clerk's Diary*, 2:196; *Charlotte Observer*, July 21, 1912.

CHAPTER 9
Spring Bloodbath

1. Elliott, *Soldier Boy*, p. 16; Jordan, ed., *North Carolina Troops*, 13:570; Faust, ed., *Encyclopedia*, p. 57; William Glenn Robertson, *Back Door to Richmond* (hereafter cited as *Back Door*), p. 16, 21–22.

2. Faust, ed., *Encyclopedia*, p. 57; T. Harry Williams, *P. G. T. Beauregard: Napoleon in Gray* (hereafter cited as *Beauregard*), pp. 210–11; Robertson, *Back Door*, p. 77.

3. The citizens of Petersburg credited Hagood's brigade with saving the city during the skirmish on May 6 and 7. Ministers praised the South Carolinians from pulpits, and local merchants refused to accept payment for purchases made by the soldiers. Roman, *General Beauregard*, 2:198; P. G. T. Beauregard, "The Defense of Drewry's Bluff" (hereafter cited as "Drewry's Bluff"), *Battles and Leaders of the Civil War*, 4:196; Ashe, *History of North Carolina*, 2:907; *O.R.* I, 36, part 2, p. 964.

4. Jordan, ed., *North Carolina Troops*, 13:570; *O.R.* I, 36, part 2, p, 972; Paris Diary, May 7, 1864, John Paris Papers, SHC.

5. Jordan, ed., *North Carolina Troops*, 13:570; *O.R.* I, 51, part 2 supplement, p. 902, 903; Freeman, *Lee's Lieutenants*, 3:467; Robertson, *Back Door*, p. 108; Schiller, *Bermuda Hundred*, pp. 124–25.

6. *O.R.* I, 51, part 2 supplement, p. 903; Robert F. Hoke to James W. Cooke, May 7, 1864, Charles V. Peery Collection (private), Charleston, South Carolina.

7. Diary of Cary Whitaker, May 9, 1864, Cary Whitaker Papers, SHC; Clark, ed., *Regiments*, 1:402; Jordan, ed., *North Carolina Troops*, 13:210; Beauregard, "Drewry's Bluff," *Battles and Leaders of the Civil War*, 4:196; Paris Diary, May 9, 1864, John Paris Papers, SHC; Schiller, *Bermuda Hundred*, p. 137.

8. Clark, ed., *Regiments*, 3:350; Jordan, ed., *North Carolina Troops*, 13:570; *O.R.* I, 36, part 2, p. 244; Elliott, *Soldier Boy*, p. 17.

9. Robertson, *Back Door*, p. 122; Williams, *Beauregard*, p. 211. Sources disagree as to the exact time of Hoke's arrival; at any rate, it was sometime between 1:30 P.M. and 2:30 P.M. Don Lowry, *No Turning Back*, p. 289; Schiller, *Bermuda Hundred*, p. 150; *O.R.* I, 51, part 2 supplement, p. 915; Clark, ed., *Regiments*, 2:4, 3:350; Elliott, *Soldier Boy*, p. 17.

10. Robertson, *Back Door*, p. 128; *O.R.* I, 51, part 2 supplement, p. 915; Schiller, *Bermuda Hundred*, p. 150; *O.R.* I, 36, part 2, p. 987. Pickett's temporary division included the brigades of Corse, Kemper, Matt Ransom, and James G. Martin. Lowry, *No Turning Back*, p. 291; Ashe, *History of North Carolina*, 2:908; Beauregard, "Drewry's Bluff," *Battles and Leaders of the Civil War*, 4:197.

Endnotes

11. Ashe, *History of North Carolina*, 2:908; Faust, ed., *Encyclopedia*, p. 57; Schiller, *Bermuda Hundred*, p. 160; Lowry, *No Turning Back*, p. 298; Robertson, *Back Door*, p. 140.

12. *O.R.* I, 51, part 2 supplement, p. 921, 980; Robertson, *Back Door*, pp. 139–40; Lowry, *No Turning Back*, p. 296; Johnson Hagood, *Memoirs of the War of Secession*, p. 231; Elliott, *Soldier Boy*, p. 17.

13. *O.R.* I, 51, part 2 supplement, p. 919; Robertson, *Back Door*, p. 140; *O.R.* I, 36, part 2, p. 986, 992; Roman, *General Beauregard*, 2:555–56.

14. *O.R.* I, 36, part 2, p. 992; Roman, *General Beauregard*, 2:556; Robertson, *Back Door*, p. 142; Schiller, *Bermuda Hundred*, pp. 164–65; *O.R.* I, 51, part 2 supplement, pp. 921–22.

15. Robertson, *Back Door*, p. 142; Elliott, *Soldier Boy*, p. 17; Schiller, *Bermuda Hundred*, pp. 164–65; *O.R.* I, 36, part 2, p. 991; Lowry, *No Turning Back*, p. 299; Hagood, *Memoirs of the War of Secession*, p. 232.

16. Robertson, *Back Door*, pp. 143–46; Elliott, *Soldier Boy*, p. 17; Freeman, *Lee's Lieutenants*, 3:474; Schiller, *Bermuda Hundred*, p. 182; Beavans Diary, May 11, 1864, William Beavans Papers, SHC; Roman, *General Beauregard*, 2:556; *O.R.* I, 36, part 2 supplement, p. 691, 997.

17. Jordan, ed., *North Carolina Troops*, 13:570; Robertson, *Back Door*, pp. 145–46. Johnson Hagood described the lines at Drewry's Bluff as "in the nature of an entrenched camp." Hagood, *Memoirs of the War of Secession*, p. 232; *O.R.* I, 36, part 2, pp. 994–96; Beavans Diary, May 12, 1864, William Beavans Papers, SHC; *O.R.* I, 51, part 2 supplement, p. 924.

18. Robertson, *Back Door*, p. 145; Lowry, *No Turning Back*, p. 304; *O.R.* I, 36, part 2, p. 114, 994–96; Beauregard, "Drewry's Bluff," *Battles and Leaders of the Civil War*, 4:209.

19. Jordan, ed., *North Carolina Troops*, 13:570; Elliott, *Soldier Boy*, p. 18; Schiller, *Bermuda Hundred*, p. 192; Robertson, *Back Door*, p. 148; Clark, ed., *Regiments*, 2:285, 4:490, 575, 3:136, 351.

20. Schiller, *Bermuda Hundred*, pp. 193–94; Clark, ed., *Regiments*, 3:136; Robertson, *Back Door*, pp. 148–49.

21. Theo. F. Klutz, Jr., "The Boy Who Saved Richmond," *Confederate Veteran* 6:213–14.

22. Wood was born on July 20, 1846, at Prince Edward Courthouse, Virginia. Klutz, Jr., "The Boy Who Saved Richmond," *Confederate Veteran* 6:213–14; Jordan and Manarin, eds., *North Carolina Troops*, 6:554; Manarin, ed., *North Carolina Troops*, 3:76.

23. Klutz, Jr., "The Boy Who Saved Richmond," *Confederate Veteran* 6:213–14; Freeman, *Lee's Lieutenants*, 3:476; Schiller, *Bermuda Hundred*, pp. 193–94.

24. Klutz, Jr., "The Boy Who Saved Richmond," *Confederate Veteran* 6:214; *O.R.* I, 51, part 2 supplement, p. 928; *O.R.* I, 36, part 2, p. 999; Schiller, *Bermuda Hundred*, p. 192; Robertson, *Back Door*, p. 149; Lowry, *No Turning Back*, p. 345; Hagood, *Memoirs of the War of Secession*, p. 232.

25. Klutz, Jr., "The Boy Who Saved Richmond," *Confederate Veteran* 6:214. Conventional wisdom is that reports of Gillmore's success against Hoke's right were received too late in the day for Butler and Smith to attack on May 13. Robertson, *Back Door*, p. 149.

26. Robertson, *Back Door*, p. 149; *O.R.* I, 51, part 2 supplement, p. 925; *O.R.* I, 36, part 3, p. 850, 857.

27. Robertson, *Back Door*, pp. 149–50; Beauregard, "Drewry's Bluff," *Battles and Leaders of the Civil War*, 4:197–99; Freeman, *Lee's Lieutenants*, 3:478–80; Lowry, *No Turning Back*, pp. 345–46; Roman, *General Beauregard*, 2:202.

28. Hagood, *Memoirs of the War of Secession*, p. 234; Robertson, *Back Door*, p. 153; Schiller,

Bermuda Hundred, p. 199; George M. LaLane Diary, May 14, 1864, Museum of the Confederacy; Jordan, ed., *North Carolina Troops*, 13:570–71; Clark, ed., *Regiments*, 3:353.

29. Robertson, *Back Door*, p. 153; Clark, ed., *Regiments*, 4:490, 575, 3:352–53; Elliott, *Soldier Boy*, p. 20; Jordan, ed., *North Carolina Troops*, 13:571. Some accounts indicate that Ransom was wounded on May 13; however, most contemporary diaries report that the event occurred a day later. Edward X. Phifer to his mother, May 29, 1864, Phifer Family Papers, SHC; Chambers, *Chambers*, p. 196.

30. Elliott, *Soldier Boy*, pp. 19–20; Robertson, *Back Door*, p. 154; Jordan, ed., *North Carolina Troops*, 13:571; Beauregard, "Drewry's Bluff," *Battles and Leaders of the Civil War*, 4:200; *O.R.* I, 36, part 2, p. 199.

31. *O.R.* I, 36, part 2, pp. 199–201, 207–8, 236–39, 1004; Robertson, *Back Door*, p. 174, 261; Schiller, *Bermuda Hundred*, pp. 340–42. Of the three division commanders at Drewry's Bluff, Beauregard was most familiar with Colquitt. Beauregard, "Drewry's Bluff," *Battles and Leaders of the Civil War*, 4:200–201; Roman, *General Beauregard*, 2:203; Hagood, *Memoirs of the War of Secession*, p. 236; Freeman, *Lee's Lieutenants*, 3:483.

32. *O.R.* I, 36, part 2, pp. 200–201; Beauregard, "Drewry's Bluff," *Battles and Leaders of the Civil War*, 4:201; Robertson, *Back Door*, p. 174; Clark, ed., *Regiments*, 3:353; Jordan, ed., *North Carolina Troops*, 13:571; Schiller, *Bermuda Hundred*, p. 224; Hagood, *Memoirs of the War of Secession*, p. 235; Cary Whitaker Diary, May 15, 1864, Cary Whitaker Papers, SHC.

33. Hagood, *Memoirs of the War of Secession*, p. 236; Robertson, *Back Door*, p. 178; *O.R.* I, 36, part 2, p. 199.

34. Robertson, *Back Door*, p. 182; *O.R.* I, 36, part 2, p. 201, 212, 237; *O.R.* I, 51, part 2 supplement, p. 938; Beauregard, "Drewry's Bluff," *Battles and Leaders of the Civil War*, 4:201.

35. *O.R.* I, 36, part 2, pp. 202–3, 237; Schiller, *Bermuda Hundred*, p. 224; Hagood, *Memoirs of the War of Secession*, p. 245.

36. *O.R.* I, 36, part 2, p. 202, 237; Beauregard, "Drewry's Bluff," *Battles and Leaders of the Civil War*, 4:202–3; Clark, ed., *Regiments*, 1:403.

37. Schiller, *Bermuda Hundred*, p. 276; *O.R.* I, 36, part 2, p. 202; Beauregard, "Drewry's Bluff," *Battles and Leaders of the Civil War*, 4:203; Williams, *Beauregard*, p. 219; Freeman, *Lee's Lieutenants*, 3:488.

38. Williams, *Beauregard*, p. 219; Hagood, *Memoirs of the War of Secession*, p. 249; *Charlotte Observer*, July 21, 1912; Clark, ed., *Regiments*, 3:354.

39. *O.R.* I, 36, part 2, pp. 203–4; Beauregard, "Drewry's Bluff," *Battles and Leaders of the Civil War*, 4:203. Corse and Clingman were called upon for the late-afternoon pursuit because they had not been heavily engaged during the day. Hagood, *Memoirs of the War of Secession*, pp. 249–50; Robertson, *Back Door*, p. 206.

40. Elliott, *Soldier Boy*, p. 20; Roman, *General Beauregard*, 2:209; Beauregard, "Drewry's Bluff," *Battles and Leaders of the Civil War*, 4:204; *O.R.* I, 36, part 1, p. 20; Williams, *Beauregard*, p. 220; *O.R.* I, 36, part 2, pp. 202–5, 238; Hagood, *Memoirs of the War of Secession*, p. 236, 249–50.

41. *O.R.* I, 36, part 2, p. 202, 205; Hagood, *Memoirs of the War of Secession*, p. 245.

42. *O.R.* I, 36, part 2, p. 1018, 1022; Hagood, *Memoirs of the War of Secession*, p. 251; Clark, ed., *Regiments*, 3:355; *O.R.* I, 51, part 2 supplement, p. 948; Robertson, *Back Door*, pp. 221–22; letters, May 21 and 25, 1864, Asa Biggs Papers, DU; Schiller, *Bermuda Hundred*,

p. 308; Jordan, ed., *North Carolina Troops*, 13:571–72.

43. *O.R.* I, 36, part 3, p. 818, 821, 842. Martin's father, a planter and shipbuilder, represented northeastern North Carolina in the state legislature. At West Point, Richard Ewell and George Thomas were classmates of Martin's. During his tenure in the United States Army, Martin met his future wife, Marian M. Read, the great-granddaughter of a signer of the Declaration of Independence. Powell, ed., *North Carolina Biography*, 4:226–28; Faust, ed., *Encyclopedia*, p. 477; Clark, ed., *Regiments*, 4:531.

44. Prior to the Civil War, Clingman maintained a running feud with Dr. Elisha Mitchell of the University of North Carolina over the highest peak in the Black Mountain range of western North Carolina. Dr. Mitchell fell to his death in 1857 attempting to validate his claim; the highest summit east of the Mississippi was later named Mount Mitchell. Another peak on the same ridge was named for Clingman. Powell, ed., *North Carolina Biography*, 1:387–88; *Asheville Citizen-Times*, January 23, 1949; *Raleigh News and Observer*, September 29, 1957.

45. Faust, ed., *Encyclopedia*, p. 331; Davis, ed., *The Confederate General*, 3:48–49; Warner, *Generals in Gray*, pp. 121–22.

46. Faust, ed., *Encyclopedia*, p. 151; Davis, ed., *The Confederate General*, 2:9–10; Warner, *Generals in Gray*, p. 58.

47. Hagood, *Memoirs of the War of Secession*, p. 253; *O.R.* I, 42, part 3, p. 1108.

48. Hagood, *Memoirs of the War of Secession*, p. 253; Faust, ed., *Encyclopedia*, p 149; *O.R.* I, 36, part 3, p. 206.

49. Freeman, *R. E. Lee*, 3:362–66; Wayne R. Maney, *Marching to Cold Harbor* (hereafter cited as *Cold Harbor*), pp. 66–69, 75–76; Freeman, *Lee's Lieutenants*, 3:498–99.

50. Freeman, *R. E. Lee*, 3:368; Freeman, *Lee's Lieutenants*, 3:500–501; Robertson, *Back Door*, p. 236; Maney, *Cold Harbor*, p. 80.

51. *Charlotte Observer*, July 21, 1912.

52. Freeman, *R. E. Lee*, 3:371–73; Freeman, *Lee's Lieutenants*, 3:503; Roman, *General Beauregard*, 2:563; *O.R.* I, 36, part 3, p. 850.

53. Freeman, *R. E. Lee*, 3:372; Freeman, *Lee's Lieutenants*, 3:503; *O.R.* I, 36, part 3, p. 857.

54. Freeman, *Lee's Lieutenants*, 3:505; Hagood, *Memoirs of the War of Secession*, pp. 254–55.

55. Hagood, *Memoirs of the War of Secession*, pp. 254–55; Freeman, *Lee's Lieutenants*, 3:505; *O.R.* I, 36, part 3, p. 858.

56. Maney, *Cold Harbor*, pp. 85–86; Jaynes et al, eds., *The Killing Ground*, p. 151; Freeman, *Lee's Lieutenants*, 3:505–6; *O.R.* I, 36, part 3, p. 817; Clark, ed., *Regiments*, 5:198.

57. Freeman, *Lee's Lieutenants*, 3:505; *O.R.* I, 36, part 3, p. 411; Maury Klein, *Edward Porter Alexander* (hereafter cited as *Alexander*), p. 118.

58. *O.R.* I, 51, part 2 supplement, p. 974; Ashe, *History of North Carolina*, 2:913; Hagood, *Memoirs of the War of Secession*, p. 255; Paris Diary, May 31, 1863, John Paris Papers, SHC.

59. Freeman, *Lee's Lieutenants*, 3:505; Freeman, *R. E. Lee*, 3:375. Anderson had replaced Longstreet as corps commander on May 6 after Longstreet was wounded at the Wilderness. Warner, *Generals in Gray*, p. 9, 193; Maney, *Cold Harbor*, p. 86.

60. Maney, *Cold Harbor*, p. 96; Hagood, *Memoirs of the War of Secession*, p. 255; Freeman, *R. E. Lee*, 3:377.

61. Freeman, *Lee's Lieutenants*, 3:506; Maney, *Cold Harbor*, p. 95; Lowry, *No Turning Back*, p. 444; Noah Trudeau, *Bloody Roads South*, p. 267; Hagood, *Memoirs of the War of Secession*, pp. 255–57.

62. Freeman, *Lee's Lieutenants*, 3:506; Maney, *Cold Harbor*, p. 99; Hagood, *Memoirs of the*

War of Secession, p. 257.

63. Hagood, *Memoirs of the War of Secession*, pp. 257–58; Freeman, *Lee's Lieutenants*, 3:507; Clark, ed., *Regiments*, 2:798.

64. Trudeau, *Bloody Roads South*, p. 269; Hagood, *Memoirs of the War of Secession*, pp. 258–59; Clark, ed., *Regiments*, 5:201; Edward Porter Alexander, *Fighting for the Confederacy*, p. 400; Alfred Seeyle Roe, *The Ninth New York Heavy Artillery*, p. 400; *Raleigh Standard*, June 15, 1864.

65. Clark, ed., *Regiments*, 5:202; Trudeau, *Bloody Roads South*, p. 273; Hagood, *Memoirs of the War of Secession*, p. 259.

66. Alexander, *Fighting for the Confederacy*, p. 401; Trudeau, *Bloody Roads South*, p. 278.

67. Freeman, *R. E. Lee*, 3:378–83.

68. Maney, *Cold Harbor*, pp. 116–17; Freeman, *R. E. Lee*, 3:383; Alexander, *Fighting for the Confederacy*, p. 401.

69. Freeman, *R. E. Lee*, 3:386; Jordan, ed., *North Carolina Troops*, 13:12; Ashe, *History of North Carolina*, 2:913; Ashe et al, eds., *Biographical History*, 1:317. Lee was still suffering from ill health on the morning of June 3. The previous day, he had been able to mount a horse for the first time in ten days. Maney, *Cold Harbor*, p. 118.

70. Jordan, ed., *North Carolina Troops*, 13:32; Freeman, *R. E. Lee*, 3:386; Hagood, *Memoirs of the War of Secession*, p. 259; Ashe, *History of North Carolina*, 2:913; Maney, *Cold Harbor*, p. 94; Dickert, *History of Kershaw's Brigade*, p. 371.

71. Klein, *Alexander*, p. 119; Freeman, *R. E. Lee*, 3:387; Alexander, *Fighting for the Confederacy*, p. 411; Hagood, *Memoirs of the War of Secession*, pp. 259–60; Martin T. McMahon, "Cold Harbor," *Battles and Leaders of the Civil War* 4:217; Clark, ed., *Regiments*, 4:533.

72. Hagood, *Memoirs of the War of Secession*, p. 260; Paris Diary, June 3, 1863, John Paris Papers, SHC; Clark, ed., *Regiments*, 2:5.

73. Walter Taylor, *Four Years with General Lee*, p. 135; *O.R.* I, 36, part 3, p. 869.

74. E. M. Law, "From the Wilderness to Cold Harbor," *Battles and Leaders of the Civil War*, 4:142; McMahon, "Cold Harbor," *Battles and Leaders of the Civil War* 4:218; Hagood, *Memoirs of the War of Secession*, p. 260; Clark, ed., *Regiments*, 2:5, 517; William Swinton, *Campaigns of the Army of the Potomac*, p. 487; Taylor, *Four Years with General Lee*, p. 135.

75. Hagood, *Memoirs of the War of Secession*, p. 262; U. S. Grant, *Personal Memoirs of U. S. Grant*, 2:226; Evans, ed., *North Carolina*, p. 251, 255; Dickert, *History of Kershaw's Brigade*, p. 373.

76. Ashe, *History of North Carolina*, 2:913; Ashe et al, eds., *Biographical History*, 1:317; Freeman, *R. E. Lee*, 3:391.

77. Maney, *Cold Harbor*, p. 177; *O.R.* I, 36, part 3, p. 600, 638, 874; *O.R.* I, 51, part 2 supplement, pp. 982–83; Edward S. Ellis, *Low Twelve*, n.p.

78. Clark, ed., *Regiments*, 4:533.

79. Clark, ed., *Regiments*, 4:533; Maney, *Cold Harbor*, pp. 202–3; *O.R.* I, 36, part 1, p. 1035; Freeman, *R. E. Lee*, 3:402–3.

Endnotes

CHAPTER 10
Summer Siege

1. Hagood, *Memoirs of the War of Secession*, pp. 263–65; Clark, ed., *Regiments*, 2:799; Freeman, *R. E. Lee*, 3:397–98; Jordan, ed., *North Carolina Troops*, 12:270.

2. Hagood, *Memoirs of the War of Secession*, p. 265; Clark, ed., *Regiments*, 2:799, 3:212; James I. Robertson, *General A. P. Hill*, pp. 281–82; Evans, ed., *North Carolina*, p. 262; Roman, *General Beauregard*, 2:229; Jordan, ed., *North Carolina Troops*, 12:270; Freeman, *R. E. Lee*, 3:404–5; Robert E. Lee, *Lee's Dispatches*, pp. 227–32.

3. A. A. Humphreys, *Campaigns of the Civil War: The Virginia Campaign of '64 and '65*, p. 209; Thomas J. Howe, *The Petersburg Campaign: Wasted Valor* (hereafter cited as *Wasted Valor*), p. 18; Lee, *Lee's Dispatches*, p. 232; Robert E. Lee, *The Wartime Papers of Robert E. Lee* (hereafter cited as *Wartime Papers*), p. 779; Hagood, *Memoirs of the War of Secession*, p. 265. Some Confederate officers believed that Lee acted too cautiously. Among them was Brigadier General Edward Porter Alexander, who thought Lee should have moved Hoke closer to Petersburg. Alexander, *Fighting for the Confederacy*, p. 420, 423.

4. *O.R.* I, 40, part 2, p. 652; Roman, *General Beauregard*, 2:229.

5. *O.R.* I, 40, part 2, p. 653.

6. Freeman, *R. E. Lee*, 3:407; Howe, *Wasted Valor*, pp. 23–24; *O.R.* I, 40, part 2, p. 655; Evans, ed., *North Carolina*, pp. 262–63; W. Gordon McCabe, "Defence of Petersburg," *Southern Historical Society Papers* 2:266–67.

7. *O.R.* I, 40, part 2, pp. 654–56.

8. Hagood, *Memoirs of the War of Secession*, p. 265; *Charleston News*, July 25, 1897; Howe, *Wasted Valor*, p. 24, 26; Clark, ed., *Regiments*, 2:6.

9. Howe, *Wasted Valor*, p. 29; Dickert, *History of Kershaw's Brigade*, p. 379; *O.R.* I, 40, part 1, p. 801; Hagood, *Memoirs of the War of Secession*, p. 266.

10. *Charleston News*, July 25, 1897; *O.R.* I, 40, part 1, p. 801; Hagood, *Memoirs of the War of Secession*, p. 266; Howe, *Wasted Valor*, p. 37; Henry Kershaw Dubose, *The History of Company B, Twenty-first Regiment South Carolina Confederate States Provisional Army* (hereafter cited as *Twenty-first Regiment*), p. 73.

11. Jordan, ed., *North Carolina Troops*, 12:270; Howe, *Wasted Valor*, pp. 29–36.

12. *O.R.* I, 40, part 1, p. 801; Hagood, *Memoirs of the War of Secession*, p. 267; Howe, *Wasted Valor*, pp. 37–38.

13. Hagood, *Memoirs of the War of Secession*, p. 267; Howe, *Wasted Valor*, pp. 37–38; Clark, ed., *Regiments*, 3:689, 2:6; "Narrative of Captain S. B. Alexander," Military Collection (Civil War), Box 70, Folder 1, NCDAH.

14. Clark, ed., *Regiments*, 4:534; Freeman, *R. E. Lee*, 3:410; *O.R.* I, 40, part 2, p. 657; Roman, *General Beauregard*, 2:231; Howe, *Wasted Valor*, p. 38; *Charleston News*, July 25, 1897; Dubose, *Twenty-first Regiment*, p. 74.

15. *Charleston News*, July 25, 1897; Hagood, *Memoirs of the War of Secession*, p. 267; *O.R.* I, 40, part 1, p. 801; Clark, ed., *Regiments*, 2:6, 1:405; 4:494–95; Evans, ed., *North Carolina*, pp. 263–64; Roman, *General Beauregard*, 2:231–32; Howe, *Wasted Valor*, pp. 52–55; Jordan, ed., *North Carolina Troops*, 12:270.

16. Roman, *General Beauregard*, 2:232; Hagood, *Memoirs of the War of Secession*, p. 268; Clark, ed., *Regiments*, 1:406, 4:495; Evans, ed., *North Carolina*, p. 265.

17. Howe, *Wasted Valor*, pp. 93–94, 100–101; Evans, ed., *North Carolina*, p. 265; *O.R.* I, 40,

part 2, p 141; Clark, ed., *Regiments*, 2:7.

18. Howe, *Wasted Valor*, pp. 96–97; Clark, ed., *Regiments*, 1:406, 3:212; Jordan, ed., *North Carolina Troops*, 12:270.

19. Howe, *Wasted Valor*, pp. 96–97; Hagood, *Memoirs of the War of Secession*, p. 268. From the outset of the battle, Beauregard had urgently requested that the War Department dispatch the twelve hundred men in Gracie's brigade from Chaffin's Bluff to Petersburg. Roman, *General Beauregard*, 2:232; McCabe, "Defence of Petersburg," *Southern Historical Society Papers* 2:271.

20. McCabe, "Defence of Petersburg," *Southern Historical Society Papers* 2:270–71; Howe, *Wasted Valor*, p. 107; Evans, ed., *North Carolina*, p. 265; Jordan, ed., *North Carolina Troops*, 12:270; *O.R.* I, 40, part 1, p. 802; Hagood, *Memoirs of the War of Secession*, pp. 268–69; *Charleston News*, July 25, 1897.

21. *O.R.* I, 40, part 2, p. 120; Howe, *Wasted Valor*, pp. 112–13; McCabe, "Defence of Petersburg," *Southern Historical Society Papers* 2:271.

22. Howe, *Wasted Valor*, p. 115; Clark, ed., *Regiments*, 1:406.

23. Hagood, *Memoirs of the War of Secession*, p. 269; *O.R.* I, 40, part 1, p. 802; Howe, *Wasted Valor*, pp. 123–24; W. P. Derby, *Bearing Arms in the Twenty-seventh Massachusetts Regiment of Volunteer Infantry during the Civil War*, p. 338; *Charleston News*, July 25, 1897; Jordan, ed., *North Carolina Troops*, 12:270.

24. Howe, *Wasted Valor*, pp. 133–36. Estimates of Union losses during the Battle of Petersburg range from 8,150 to 12,000, while estimates put Confederate losses between 2,970 and 4,700. Evans, ed., *North Carolina*, p. 265; Hagood, *Memoirs of the War of Secession*, p. 270.

25. *O.R.* I, 40, part 2, p. 157; Howe, *Wasted Valor*, p. 136; Dickert, *History of Kershaw's Brigade*, pp. 382–85.

26. Hagood, *Memoirs of the War of Secession*, p. 281; McCabe, "Defence of Petersburg," *Southern Historical Society Papers* 2:272.

27. Hagood, *Memoirs of the War of Secession*, pp. 270–71, 281; *O.R.* I, 40, part 2, p. 678. According to D. A. Dickert of Kershaw's brigade, the townspeople soon grew accustomed to the shelling and ignored it "as long as one did not drop in their immediate vicin[i]ty." Dickert, *History of Kershaw's Brigade*, p. 388; Noah Andre Trudeau, *The Last Citadel: Petersburg, Virginia, June 1864–April 1865* (hereafter cited as *Citadel*), pp. 82–83; *O.R.* I, 40, part 1, pp. 797–99.

28. Trudeau, *Citadel*, pp. 82–83; *O.R.* I, 40, part 1, p. 797, 804–5; C. W. Field, "Campaign of 1864 and 1865," *Southern Historical Society Papers* 14:549–50.

29. *O.R.* I, 40, part 1, p. 797, 803; Hagood, *Memoirs of the War of Secession*, p. 278.

30. *O.R.* I, 40, part 1, p. 797, 803; Trudeau, *Citadel*, p. 84; Hagood, *Memoirs of the War of Secession*, p. 277.

31. *O.R.* I, 40, part 1, pp. 797–98; Hagood, *Memoirs of the War of Secession*, p. 278.

32. Field, "Campaign of 1864 and 1865," *Southern Historical Society Papers* 14:550; *O.R.* I, 40, part 1, p. 798; Hagood, *Memoirs of the War of Secession*, p. 276.

33. *O.R.* I, 40, part 1, pp. 798–99; Freeman, *R. E. Lee*, 3:454.

34. *O.R.* I, 40, part 1, p. 798, 804. Twenty years after the incident, Hagood reconsidered the punishment he felt was due Anderson, noting, "This looks pretty harsh." Hagood, *Memoirs of the War of Secession*, pp. 276–77.

35. Freeman, *R. E. Lee*, 3:454; Hagood, *Memoirs of the War of Secession*, p. 278.

36. Clark, ed., *Regiments*, 2:800; Hagood, *Memoirs of the War of Secession*, p. 286.

37. Evans, ed., *North Carolina*, p. 266; Clark, ed., *Regiments*, 2:800, 3:689–90, 1:407, 4:535.

38. Clark, ed., *Regiments*, 2:8, 800–801, 3:689; Hagood, *Memoirs of the War of Secession*, p. 284, 286; John Cherry to his sister, July 21, 1864, Lucy Cherry Crisp Papers, ECU.

39. Hagood, *Memoirs of the War of Secession*, p. 284.

40. Hagood, *Memoirs of the War of Secession*, pp. 285–86; Clark, ed., *Regiments*, 1:407, 2:800, 4:535; A. T. Graham, "Capt. J. G. Morrison," *Confederate Veteran* 14:279–80.

41. Clark, ed., *Regiments*, 4:535, 2:8; Powell, ed., *North Carolina Biography*, 4:226–28; *O.R.* I, 40, part 2, p. 699; Hagood, *Memoirs of the War of Secession*, p. 284.

42. M. W. Venable, "In the Trenches at Petersburg," *Confederate Veteran* 34:59; Clark, ed., *Regiments*, 3:213, 689–90, 1:407; *Charleston News*, July 25, 1897.

43. *O.R.* I, 40, part 2, p. 707; *O.R.* I, 37, part 1, pp. 766–68; Singleton, *Wood*, pp. 116–17; Lee, *Lee's Dispatches*, p. 270; Hamilton, "General Robert F. Hoke," Robert F. Hoke Papers, SHC.

44. Hagood, *Memoirs of the War of Secession*, p. 287; Evans, ed., *North Carolina*, p. 263; John Cherry to "My dear sister," July 6 and 21, 1864, Lucy Cherry Crisp Papers, ECU; Clark, ed., *Regiments*, 2:801.

45. Evans, ed., *North Carolina*, pp. 267–68; Hagood, *Memoirs of the War of Secession*, p. 283; Jordan, ed., *North Carolina Troops*, 12:271. Martin's brigade of Hoke's division had been positioned on the site of "the Crater" just two days before the mine was blown. Clark, ed., *Regiments*, 2:801; Official Report of August 6, 1864, General Order and Letter Book of Major General Robert F. Hoke, Robert F. Hoke Papers, NCDAH; *O.R.* I, 40, part 1, p. 791; Faust, ed., *Encyclopedia*, p. 190.

46. Venable, "In the Trenches at Petersburg," *Confederate Veteran* 34:59–60; Hagood, *Memoirs of the War of Secession*, p. 283.

47. Hagood, *Memoirs of the War of Secession*, p. 286, 290–98; *O.R.* I, 42, part 2, p. 437, 1158, 1166; Evans, ed., *North Carolina*, p. 269; Clark, ed., *Regiments*, 1:407, 4:495, 3:213.

48. Hagood, *Memoirs of the War of Secession*, p. 298, 301–2.

49. Richard J. Sommers, *Richmond Redeemed*, p. 10; Hagood, *Memoirs of the War of Secession*, p. 303; E. J. Williams to his sister, September 20, 1864, Williams Papers, SHC.

50. Hagood, *Memoirs of the War of Secession*, pp. 303–4; Sommers, *Richmond Redeemed*, p. 11.

CHAPTER 11
The Autumn of the Confederacy

1. Freeman, *R. E. Lee*, 3:501; James Morris Morgan, *Recollections of a Rebel Reefer* (hereafter cited as *Rebel Reefer*), p. 208; Hagood, *Memoirs of the War of Secession*, p. 305.

2. *O.R.* I, 42, part 2, p. 1302; Freeman, *R. E. Lee*, 3:500; William Davis et al, eds., *Death in the Trenches*, p. 145; Klein, *Alexander*, p. 126; Hagood, *Memoirs of the War of Secession*, p. 305; Jordan, ed., *North Carolina Troops*, 12:271; Sommers, *Richmond Redeemed*, p. 111.

3. Sommers, *Richmond Redeemed*, p. 112; Freeman, *R. E. Lee*, 3:501; Morgan, *Rebel Reefer*, p. 205; Burgwyn, *Burgwyn*, p. 151; Clark, ed., *Regiments*, 4:495.

4. Freeman, *R. E. Lee*, 3:501; Sommers, *Richmond Redeemed*, pp. 114–15, 118. Upon being informed by Brigadier General John Gregg just after dark on September 29 that Lee had decided to attack that night, Field marched three brigades toward Fort Harrison. At 1 A.M. on September 30, he called on his immediate commander, Lieutenant General Richard Ander-

son. To Field's surprise, Anderson was asleep, and upon being awakened, he declared that Field was mistaken about a night assault. Field, "Campaign of 1864 and 1865," *Southern Historical Society Papers* 14:556.

5. Burgwyn, *Burgwyn*, p. 151; Sommers, *Richmond Redeemed*, pp. 112–13, 137; Hagood, *Memoirs of the War of Secession*, pp. 305–6; Field, "Campaign of 1864 and 1865," *Southern Historical Society Papers* 14:556.

6. Clark, ed., *Regiments*, 4:495–96, 3:213, 1:408; Davis et al, eds., *Death in the Trenches*, pp. 144–48; Ashe et al, eds., *Biographical History*, 1:318; Alexander, *Fighting for the Confederacy*, p. 478.

7. Ashe et al, eds., *Biographical History*, 1:318; Clark, ed., *Regiments*, 4:495, 1:408; Freeman, *R. E. Lee*, 3:502; Burgwyn, *Burgwyn*, p. 151; Field, "Campaign of 1864 and 1865," *Southern Historical Society Papers* 14:557.

8. Sommers, *Richmond Redeemed*, pp. 135–38; Burgwyn, *Burgwyn*, p. 151; Alexander, *Fighting for the Confederacy*, p. 478; Klein, *Alexander*, p. 127; Clark, ed., *Regiments*, 4:496.

9. Clark, ed., *Regiments*, 4:496; Sommers, *Richmond Redeemed*, pp. 135–42; Field, "Campaign of 1864 and 1865," *Southern Historical Society Papers* 14:557; Freeman, *R. E. Lee*, 3:502; James R. Hagood Memoirs, p. 181, South Carolina State Library.

10. Sommers, *Richmond Redeemed*, p. 137, 145; Clark, ed., *Regiments*, 1:408, 3:214, 4:496–97; Burgwyn, *Burgwyn*, p. 153.

11. Clark, ed., *Regiments*, 3:214.

12. Freeman, *R. E. Lee*, 3:503–4. According to Bratton, "General Hoke assaulted, but so feebly, was so quickly repulsed, that I did not put my regiments in again." *O.R.* I, 42, part 1, p. 880; Morgan, *Rebel Reefer*, p. 210.

13. Edward Porter Alexander to his wife, October 3, 1864, Alexander Papers, SHC; Klein, *Alexander*, p. 127; Freeman, *R. E. Lee*, 3:504.

14. Clark, ed., *Regiments*, 4:496–97, 1:408; E. J. Williams to his sister, October 2, 1864, Williams Papers, SHC. Some of the brigade flags, including banners belonging to the Eighth North Carolina, were captured by the enemy, while others were destroyed by Hoke's troops when their capture appeared imminent. Sommers, *Richmond Redeemed*, p. 148.

15. Clark, ed., *Regiments*, 1:409, 3:214–15, 691; Hagood, *Memoirs of the War of Secession*, p. 307.

16. Hagood, *Memoirs of the War of Secession*, pp. 307–8; *O.R.* I, 42, part 3, p. 108, 116; Field, "Campaign of 1864 and 1865," *Southern Historical Society Papers* 14:557–58.

17. Field, "Campaign of 1864 and 1865," *Southern Historical Society Papers* 14:558; Hagood, *Memoirs of the War of Secession*, p. 308.

18. Alexander, *Fighting for the Confederacy*, p. 483; Hagood, *Memoirs of the War of Secession*, p. 308.

19. Freeman, *Lee's Lieutenants*, 3:xxviii, 592–93. Sommers was much more harsh in his criticism of Hoke, contending that Hoke was promoted to major general "not because of any sustained excellence" but because of his performance at Plymouth. According to Sommers, Hoke's failure to cooperate "constantly underscored the unwisdom of promoting him." Sommers, *Richmond Redeemed*, pp. 116–17.

20. Clark, ed., *Regiments*, 3:691, 4:536; unidentified letter to John A. Ray, July 29, 1864, Nevin Ray Papers, DU.

21. *Masonic Journal*, March 7, 1919.

22. Ibid.

Endnotes

23. Ibid.

24. Hagood, *Memoirs of the War of Secession*, p. 309; *O.R.* I, 42, part 1, p. 876; *O.R.* I, 42, part 3, p. 1148, 1156; Clark, ed., *Regiments*, 1:409; Welsh, *Medical Histories of Confederate Generals*, p. 143; Donald Bridgeman Sanger and Thomas Robson Hay, *James Longstreet*, p. 281; H. J. Eckenrode and Bryan Conrad, *James Longstreet: Lee's War Horse*, p. 321; Sommers, *Richmond Redeemed*, p. 44, 509.

25. Gallagher, *Stephen Dodson Ramseur*, pp. 155–65; Welsh, *Medical Histories of Confederate Generals*, p. 180; Sherrill, *Annals of Lincoln County*, p. 180; William R. Cox, "Major-General Stephen Dodson Ramseur," *Southern Historical Society Papers* 18:257–59.

26. *Masonic Journal*, March 7, 1919.

27. Ibid.

28. Clark, ed., *Regiments*, 3:691–92; *Masonic Journal*, March 7, 1919.

29. Jeffrey D. Wert, *General James Longstreet*, p. 395; Hagood, *Memoirs of the War of Secession*, p. 309, 312–14; Clark, ed., *Regiments*, 4:536.

30. Davis, ed., *The Confederate General*, 4:14–15; Faust, ed., *Encyclopedia*, pp. 419–20; Powell, ed., *North Carolina Biography*, 3:371–72.

31. Hagood, *Memoirs of the War of Secession*, p. 310, 312; *O.R.* I, 42, part 3, p. 1186.

32. Gallagher, *Stephen Dodson Ramseur*, p. 166; Cox, "Major-General Stephen Dodson Ramseur," *Southern Historical Society Papers* 18.257–59; Schenck Diary, October 22, 1864, David Schenck Papers, SHC. Following his funeral at the Presbyterian church in Lincolnton, Ramseur was laid to rest in the cemetery of the local Episcopal church. His wife and daughter were later buried beside him. Sherrill, *Annals of Lincoln County*, pp. 180–81.

33. Hagood, *Memoirs of the War of Secession*, pp. 312–13.

34. Eckenrode and Conrad, *James Longstreet: Lee's War Horse*, p. 323; *O.R.* I, 42, part 3, p. 1227, 1232–33; Clark, ed., *Regiments*, 3:691–92.

35. Hagood, *Memoirs of the War of Secession*, pp. 314–15; *O.R.* I, 42, part 3, p. 1262, 1265, 1280.

CHAPTER 12
The Fate Is Sealed

1. Clark, ed., *Regiments*, 3:692; Hagood, *Memoirs of the War of Secession*, p. 315.

2. *London Times*, November 15, 1864; Barrett, *The Civil War in North Carolina*, pp. 261 63; A. M. Waddell, *An Address before the Association, Army of Northern Virginia, October 28, 1887*, NCC (hereafter cited as *Address*); Freeman, *Lee's Lieutenants*, 3:618; Hagood, *Memoirs of the War of Secession*, p. 329; C. B. Denson, *An Address Containing a Memoir of the Late Major-General William Henry Chase Whiting* (hereafter cited as *Whiting*), pp. 30 31; R. E. Lee to Z. B. Vance, August 29, 1864, Zebulon B. Vance Papers, NCDAH.

3. Barrett, *The Civil War in North Carolina*, p. 245; Page, *Ships*, p. 83; Chris Fonvielle, "The Last Rays of Departing Hope" (hereafter cited as "Last Rays") *Blue and Gray Magazine* (December 1994): 11–12.

4. Barrett, *The Civil War in North Carolina*, pp. 245–47; Page, *Ships*, p. 83. The design of Fort Fisher was based upon a study of the original Malakoff Tower, the Russian earthwork fortification at Sebastopol that withstood the attacks of the combined forces of France and Great

Britain during the Crimean War. Fonvielle, "Last Rays," *Blue and Gray Magazine* (December 1994): 13–14.

5. Lamb, a native of Norfolk, came to the Cape Fear in 1861 as a twenty-six-year-old major with no experience as a soldier and no formal engineering training. A Phi Beta Kappa scholar at William and Mary, he had graduated with a law degree but was too young to practice. Rod Gragg, *Confederate Goliath*, pp. 14–17; Barrett, *The Civil War in North Carolina*, p. 265; Fonvielle, "Last Rays," *Blue and Gray Magazine* (December 1994): 15; Mrs. J. A. Fore, "What Fort Fisher Meant to the Confederacy," *Confederate Veteran* 37:178; William Lamb, *Colonel Lamb's Story of Fort Fisher* (hereafter cited as *Lamb's Story*), p. 2; Faust, ed., *Encyclopedia*, pp. 374–75; Waddell, *Address*, p. 16.

6. Clark, ed., *Regiments*, 5:218–21; Gragg, *Confederate Goliath*, pp. 19–21; Lamb, *Lamb's Story*, pp. 2–4; William Lamb, "The Defense of Fort Fisher," *Battles and Leaders of the Civil War*, 4:642–43.

7. Welles, *The Diary of Gideon Welles*, 2:127; Porter, *Naval History*, pp. 691–92; Barrett, *The Civil War in North Carolina*, pp. 263–64; Gragg, *Confederate Goliath*, pp. 34–37.

8. *O.R.N.* I, 10, pp. 784–85; Gragg, *Confederate Goliath*, pp. 26–27; *Wilmington Journal*, October 31, 1864; Porter, *Naval History*, p. 712.

9. Barrett, *The Civil War in North Carolina*, pp. 264–66; Gragg, *Confederate Goliath*, pp. 44–49; Lamb, *Lamb's Story*, p. 14.

10. Freeman, *Lee's Lieutenants*, 3:617–18; *O.R.* I, 42, part 3, pp. 1278–80; Mrs. J. A. Fore, "What Fort Fisher Meant to the Confederacy," *Confederate Veteran* 37:179; *O.R.N.* I, 11, p. 620; James Longstreet, *From Manassas to Appomattox*, p. 580; Hamilton, "General Robert F. Hoke," Robert F. Hoke Papers, SHC; Jefferson Davis, *Rise and Fall of the Confederate Government*, 2:549.

11. Hagood, *Memoirs of the War of Secession*, p. 315; Gragg, *Confederate Goliath*, p. 60; Clark, ed., *Regiments*, 3:692, 4:538–39; *O.R.* I, 42, part 3, p. 1282.

12. *O.R.* I, 42, part 3, p. 1283, 1284; Clark, ed., *Regiments*, 3:692.

13. Robert C. Black III, *The Railroads of the Confederacy* (hereafter cited as *Railroads*), pp. 228–29; Trotter, *Silk Flags and Cold Steel*, p. 59; Freeman, *Lee's Lieutenants*, 3:618; Clark, ed., *Regiments*, 4:539, 2:802; Hagood, *Memoirs of the War of Secession*, pp. 315–16.

14. Hagood, *Memoirs of the War of Secession*, pp. 315–16.

15. Black, *Railroads*, p. 228; Hagood, *Memoirs of the War of Secession*, p. 316; Trotter, *Silk Flags and Cold Steel*, p. 59; Lee, *Lee's Dispatches*, p. 326.

16. *O.R.* I, 46, part 2, pp. 1026–27; Black, *Railroads*, p. 335.

17. Clark, ed., *Regiments*, 3:692.

18. *O.R.* I, 42, part 3, p. 1056, 1060, 1067, 1298–99; *Richmond Examiner*, December 22, 1864; Clark, ed., *Regiments*, 3:693; *O.R.N.* I, 11, pp. 360–61.

19. Barrett, *The Civil War in North Carolina*, pp. 266–67; William A. Wright to Charles Phillips, December 21, 1864, Kemp P. Battle Papers, SHC; *O.R.* I, 46, part 2, pp. 1026–27; *O.R.* I, 42, part 1, pp. 1020–22; Clark, ed., *Regiments*, 2:9, 802, 3:693, 4:539.

20. Clark, ed., *Regiments*, 2:9; *O.R.* I, 42, part 1, p. 1020; Barrett, *The Civil War in North Carolina*, p. 268; Trotter, *Ironclads and Columbiads*, p. 355; Lamb, *Lamb's Story*, p. 14.

21. *O.R.* I, 42, part 1, pp. 1020–21; Clark, ed., *Regiments*, 4:539; Barrett, *The Civil War in North Carolina*, p. 268; Gragg, *Confederate Goliath*, pp. 63–64; Lamb, *Lamb's Story*, p. 17.

22. *O.R.* I, 42, part 1, p. 1021; Daniel W. Barefoot, *Touring the Backroads of North Carolina's Lower Coast*, p. 229; *O.R.* I, 42, part 3, p. 1303; Gragg, *Confederate Goliath*, pp. 71–72;

Clark, ed., *Regiments*, 4:539.

23. Barrett, *The Civil War in North Carolina*, p. 268; *O.R.* I, 42, part 1, p. 967; Gragg, *Confederate Goliath*, p. 72.

24. Clark, ed., *Regiments*, 4:541–42.

25. Weitzel had been Grant's choice to be the supreme army commander on the expedition, but Weitzel's superior, Benjamin Butler, chose to take part in the operation. Gragg, *Confederate Goliath*, pp. 35–37; Faust, ed., *Encyclopedia*, p. 812; J. A. Mowris, *A History of the One Hundred and Seventeenth Regiment, N. Y. Volunteers*, p. 154; *O.R.* I, 42, part 3, pp. 1308–9; *O.R.* I, 42, part 1, p. 1022; Clark, ed., *Regiments*, 2:802.

26. Barrett, *The Civil War in North Carolina*, p. 269; Gragg, *Confederate Goliath*, pp. 88–89; *O.R.* I, 42, part 1, pp. 968–69, 980; *O.R.N.* I, 11, p. 262. A congressional investigation subsequently concluded that Butler's decision "not to assault the fort seems to have been justified by all facts and circumstances then known or afterwards ascertained." U.S. Congress, "Fort Fisher Expedition," Report of the Joint Committee on the Conduct of the War (38th Cong., 2d sess.), 2:259.

27. *O.R.* I, 42, part 1, p. 999, 1020; *O.R.* I, 42, part 3, pp. 1317–18, 1320; W. H. C. Whiting to Braxton Bragg, December 26, 1864, W. H. C. Whiting Papers, SHC; Clark, ed., *Regiments*, 3:215, 693; Hagood, *Memoirs of the War of Secession*, p. 317.

28. Barrett, *The Civil War in North Carolina*, p. 271; Trotter, *Ironclads and Columbiads*, pp. 383–86; Gragg, *Confederate Goliath*, pp. 96–100; Clark, ed., *Regiments*, 2:9; Judith Lee Hallock, *Braxton Bragg and Confederate Defeat* (hereafter cited as *Confederate Defeat*), 2:231–32; *O.R.* I, 42, part 3, p. 1328, 1344, 1359; Ashe et al, eds., *Biographical History*, 1:319; Don C. Seitz, *Braxton Bragg: General of the Confederacy* (hereafter cited as *Bragg*), p. 483, 485; Lamb, *Lamb's Story*, p. 22.

29. *O.R.* I, 42, part 3, pp. 1335–36; Ashe, *History of North Carolina*, 2:939.

30. Clark, ed., *Regiments*, 4:540; Gragg, *Confederate Goliath*, pp. 81–82; *O.R.* I, 42, part 1, pp. 968–69; *O.R.* I, 42, part 3, p. 1108.

31. Clark, ed., *Regiments*, 2:9, 802, 3:215, 693, 4:497, 541; Hagood, *Memoirs of the War of Secession*, p. 317; Barrett, *The Civil War in North Carolina*, p. 271; James Sprunt, *Chronicles of the Cape Fear River* (hereafter cited as *Chronicles*), p. 492; *Raleigh State*, November 19, 1895.

32. *O.R.* I, 42, part 3, pp. 1359–60, 1362; Clark, ed., *Regiments*, 4:541; Ashe, *History of North Carolina*, 2:940; *Raleigh State*, November 19, 1895.

33. *O.R.* I, 46, part 1, p. 43; Trotter, *Ironclads and Columbiads*, pp. 387–88; Gragg, *Confederate Goliath*, pp. 106–7; Porter, *Naval History*, p. 711; Grant, *Personal Memoirs of U. S. Grant*, 2:395–96.

34. *O.R.* I, 46, part 2, p. 29; Hagood, *Memoirs of the War of Secession*, p. 323; Gragg, *Confederate Goliath*, p. 107; Trotter, *Ironclads and Columbiads*, p. 388; Porter, *Naval History*, p. 711.

35. *O.R.* I, 46, part 2, p. 74; Barrett, *The Civil War in North Carolina*, p. 271; Clark, ed., *Regiments*, 3:215; Sprunt, *Chronicles*, p. 492.

36. *Raleigh Daily Confederate*, January 24, 1865; Hagood, *Memoirs of the War of Secession*, p. 323. Sprunt was born in Scotland in 1846, but he grew up in the Wilmington area. During the Civil War, he served aboard blockade runners and a Confederate steamer. Sprunt, *Chronicles*, p. xv, xvi, 4, 492; *O.R.* I, 46, part 2, p. 1044; Clark, ed., *Regiments*, 4:497; Barrett, *The Civil War in North Carolina*, p. 271; Lamb, *Lamb's Story*, p. 22.

37. *O.R.* I, 46, part 2, p. 1044; Ashe, *History of North Carolina*, 2:941; *O.R.* I, 46, part 1, p. 396; Lamb, *Lamb's Story*, pp. 22–23; Clark, ed., *Regiments*, 3:223–24; Gragg, *Confederate Goliath*, pp. 110–12.

38. *O.R.* I, 46, part 2, p. 1048; *O.R.* I, 46, part 1, p. 396; Clark, ed., *Regiments*, 3:694; Hagood, *Memoirs of the War of Secession*, p. 323; *Raleigh Daily Confederate*, January 24, 1865; Porter, *Naval History*, p. 712.

39. *O.R.* I, 46, part 2, pp. 1047–48; Hagood, *Memoirs of the War of Secession*, p. 323; *Raleigh Daily Confederate*, January 24, 1865; *O.R.* I, 46, part 1, p. 432; Gragg, *Confederate Goliath*, pp. 115–17; Page, *Ships*, p. 91; Lamb, *Lamb's Story*, p. 23.

40. Gragg, *Confederate Goliath*, p. 109, 116–17; Joseph J. Wescoat Diary, January 13, 1865, Joseph J. Wescoat Papers, DU; Barrett, *The Civil War in North Carolina*, p. 273; *O.R.* I, 46, part 1, p. 396.

41. *O.R.* I, 46, part 1, p. 432; *O.R.* I, 46, part 2, p. 1046, 1048; "Braxton Bragg to Thomas Bragg, January 20, 1865," *Southern Historical Society Papers* 10:346–47.

42. *O.R.* I, 46, part 2, p. 1044; *Raleigh Daily Confederate*, January 24, 1864; *O.R.* I, 46, part 2, p. 432; Hagood, *Memoirs of the War of Secession*, p. 323; Barrett, *The Civil War in North Carolina*, p. 273; Clark, ed., *Regiments*, 2:802; Gragg, *Confederate Goliath*, pp. 126–27; "Braxton Bragg to Thomas Bragg, January 20, 1865," *Southern Historical Society Papers* 10:347; William Lamb, "Account of Colonel William Lamb," *Southern Historical Society Papers* 10:354.

43. *O.R.* I, 46, part 1, pp. 432–37; "Braxton Bragg to Thomas Bragg, January 20, 1865," *Southern Historical Society Papers* 10:347; Seitz, *Bragg*, p. 496; Gragg, *Confederate Goliath*, pp. 126–27; *Raleigh Daily Confederate*, January 24, 1865; *O.R.* I, 46, part 2, p. 1051, 1055, 1056, 1057. Problems with steamer transportation prevented a significant portion of Hagood's soldiers from reaching the fort. Hagood, *Memoirs of the War of Secession*, pp. 324–25.

44. Gragg, *Confederate Goliath*, pp. 136–37; Lamb, *Lamb's Story*, p. 26; *O.R.* I, 46, part 2, p. 1064.

45. *O.R.* I, 46, part 2, p. 1064; "Braxton Bragg to Thomas Bragg, January 20, 1865," *Southern Historical Society Papers* 10:348; *O.R.* I, 46, part 1, p. 433; Lamb, *Lamb's Story*, pp. 26–27; Clark, ed., *Regiments*, 5:227; Gragg, *Confederate Goliath*, p. 154.

46. Gragg, *Confederate Goliath*, pp. 154–55; Barrett, *The Civil War in North Carolina*, pp. 276–77; Trotter, *Ironclads and Columbiads*, p. 395; Porter, *Naval History*, p. 716; Lamb, *Lamb's Story*, pp. 26–27; Clark, ed., *Regiments*, 5:228; Page, *Ships*, p. 94.

47. *O.R.* I, 46, part 2, p. 399, 433; "Braxton Bragg to Thomas Bragg, January 20, 1865," *Southern Historical Society Papers* 10:348; Clark, ed., *Regiments*, 2:10, 802, 4:542; Ashe, *History of North Carolina*, 2:943.

48. Lamb, *Lamb's Story*, p. 24, 27–33; Clark, ed., *Regiments*, 5:229; Gragg, *Confederate Goliath*, pp. 179–80, 192–95; Barrett, *The Civil War in North Carolina*, pp. 277–78; *O.R.* I, 46, part 2, pp. 1064–65.

49. Clark, ed., *Regiments*, 5:233. In fairness to Colquitt, it should be pointed out that Lamb refused to be evacuated, choosing instead "to share the fate of my garrison." Lamb, *Lamb's Story*, p. 37; Clark, ed., *Regiments*, 5:223, 233–35; Trotter, *Ironclads and Columbiads*, pp. 398–99; Gragg, *Confederate Goliath*, pp. 224–25; "Braxton Bragg to Thomas Bragg, January 20, 1865," *Southern Historical Society Papers* 10:348–49; Hallock, *Confederate Defeat*, 2:239; *O.R.* I, 46, part 1, pp. 444–47.

Endnotes

50. Barrett, *The Civil War in North Carolina*, p. 7, 278–79; Gragg, *Confederate Goliath*, p. 202, 223, 226; *O.R.* I, 46, part 1, p. 417, 440; J. Reilly, "Report on the Battle of Fort Fisher," DeRossett Papers, NCDAH.

51. *O.R.* I, 46, part 2, p. 1065, 1069, 1078.

52. Porter, *Naval History*, p. 726; Barrett, *The Civil War in North Carolina*, p. 279; Gragg, *Confederate Goliath*, p. 221; Clark, ed., *Regiments*, 3:694, 4:542.

53. Porter, *Naval History*, pp. 716–17; Alexander H. Stephens, *A Constitutional View of the Late War Between the States*, 2:619.

54. Schenck Diary, January 1865, David Schenck Papers, SHC; Hagood, *Memoirs of the War of Secession*, p. 328; Clark, ed., *Regiments*, 3:694; William Lamb, "Account of Colonel William Lamb," *Southern Historical Society Papers* 10:359.

55. W. Buck Yearns and John G. Barrett, eds., *North Carolina Civil War Documentary*, p. 90; Denson, *Whiting*, p. 47, 50; *Wilmington Daily Journal*, January 17, 1865; John Paris, "Campaign of 1865: The Fall of Fort Fisher," John Paris Papers, SHC.

56. Clark, ed., *Regiments*, 4:542; Charles E. Pearce to N. M. Curtis, February 22, 1897, Newton M. Curtis Papers, Chicago Historical Society. Curtis was so badly wounded that the soldiers who pulled him to the rear believed he was dead. Gragg, *Confederate Goliath*, p. 211, 267–68.

57. John D. McGeachy to Catherine McGeachy, January 17, 1865, McGeachy Papers, DU; Charles A. Hill to his wife, January 20, 1865, quoted in Richard Everett Wood, "Port Town at War: Wilmington, North Carolina, 1860–1865," NCC; Clark, ed., *Regiments*, 4:542.

58. Lamb, "Account of Colonel William Lamb," *Southern Historical Society Papers* 10:356; *Wilmington Daily Journal*, January 18, 1865; *Raleigh Weekly Conservative*, January 25, 1865.

59. Gragg, *Confederate Goliath*, p. 117; *O.R.* I, 46, part 2, pp. 1043–47; Clark, ed., *Regiments*, 3:215, 694.

60. Porter, *Naval History*, p. 712; *Raleigh News and Observer*, August 10, 1881.

CHAPTER 13
"We Will Dispute Every Point"

1. Hagood was of the opinion that immediately after the fall of Fort Fisher, Hoke's forces should have been sent to South Carolina to make a stand. Hagood, *Memoirs of the War of Secession*, pp. 330–31.

2. *O.R.* I, 46, part 2, p. 1078, 1081; Gragg, *Confederate Goliath*, pp. 243–44; Barrett, *The Civil War in North Carolina*, p. 280; Evans, ed., *North Carolina*, p. 283.

3. John M. Schofield, *Forty-six Years in the Army* (hereafter cited as *Forty-six Years*), pp. 345–46; T. M. Eddy, *The Patriotism of Illinois*, 2:365; Barrett, *The Civil War in North Carolina*, p. 281; *O.R.* I, 46, part 2, p. 1087, 1115, 1123, 1132.

4. *O.R.* I, 46, part 2, p. 1085, 1095, 1104–5, 1120; *Richmond Daily Examiner*, January 19, 1865; Clark, ed., *Regiments*, 2:10, 802, 3:694–95.

5. In response to Hoke's request for river "torpedoes," Confederate navy lieutenant Pembroke Jones was sent down from Wilmington to place the explosives. *O.R.* I, 46, part 2, p. 1095, 1104 5, 1107, 1115, 1138; Ashe, *History of North Carolina*, 2:955.

6. *O.R.* I, 46, part 2, p. 1115, 1117.

General Robert F. Hoke

7. *O.R.* I, 46, part 2, p. 1087, 1096, 1137–38; "Braxton Bragg to Thomas Bragg, January 20, 1865," *Southern Historical Society Papers* 10:349.

8. *O.R.* 46, part 2, p. 1109, 1138–39.

9. *O.R.* I, 46, part 2, p. 263, 1030, 1037, 1136, 1138, 1141, 1154, 1160, 1168, 1186; Faust, ed., *Encyclopedia*, p. 434.

10. Schofield, *Forty-six Years*, p. 346; *O.R.* 47, part 1, p. 910, 927; *O.R.* I, 47, part 2, p. 1130.

11. *O.R.* I, 47, part 2, p. 1138, 1139; Henry Little, *The 7th Regiment of New Hampshire Volunteers in the War of Rebellion* (hereafter cited as *7th New Hampshire*), p. 406; Isaiah Price, *History of the Ninety-Seventh Regiment, Pennsylvania Volunteer Infantry*, p. 358; Hagood, *Memoirs of the War of Secession*, p. 334; David Buie to Catherine McGeachy, February 13, 1865, McGeachy Papers, DU.

12. R. F. Hoke to Zebulon B. Vance, February 10, 1865, Zebulon B. Vance Papers, NCDAH; *O.R.* I, 47, part 1, p. 910, 927–28; Barrett, *The Civil War in North Carolina*, p. 281; Ashe, *History of North Carolina*, 2:956; Sprunt, *Chronicles*, p. 495; *O.R.* I, 47, part 2, p. 1171; *O.R.* II, 8, p. 217.

13. *O.R.* I, 47, part 1, p. 910, 959; Barrett, *The Civil War in North Carolina*, p. 281; Hagood, *Memoirs of the War of Secession*, pp. 335–36; *O.R.* I, 47, part 2, p. 1214, 1215, 1216. With a major crisis developing around him, Hoke was urged to arrange transportation to Wilmington for the prisoners of war. *O.R.* II, 8, p. 244; *O.R.* I, 46, part 2, p. 575.

14. Hagood, *Memoirs of the War of Secession*, pp. 338–39; *O.R.* I, 47, part 1, p. 929; Fonvielle, "Last Rays," *Blue and Gray Magazine* (December 1994): 59.

15. Hagood, *Memoirs of the War of Secession*, pp. 339–42; Zaccheus Ellis to his mother, March 1, 1865, Z. Ellis Papers, SHC; *O.R.* I, 47, part 1, p. 962.

16. Ashe, *History of North Carolina*, 2:956; Barrett, *The Civil War in North Carolina*, p. 283; Clark, ed., *Regiments*, 3:695, 4:497; *O.R.* I, 47, part 1, p. 911; Daniel Eldredge, *The Third New Hampshire and All about It* (hereafter cited as *Third New Hampshire*), p. 634; John L. Swain to Richard L. Wills, February 19, 1865, William J. Wills Papers, SHC; *O.R.* I, 47, part 2, p. 1227; *O.R.* II, 8, p. 268.

17. *O.R.* II, 8, p. 276; *O.R.* I, 47, part 2, p. 1233, 1241–42. Johnson Hagood reported that Bragg estimated the number of Federal prisoners in Wilmington at ten thousand. Hagood, *Memoirs of the War of Secession*, p. 343.

18. Hagood, *Memoirs of the War of Secession*, pp. 342–43.

19. *O.R.* I, 47, part 2, p. 1233; Hagood, *Memoirs of the War of Secession*, pp. 343–44; Clark, ed., *Regiments*, 4:427; R. F. Hoke to Maj. Parker, February 1865, Robert F. Hoke Papers, NCDAH.

20. Ashe, *History of North Carolina*, 2:956; *O.R.* I, 47, part 1, p. 911; Fonvielle, "Last Rays," *Blue and Gray Magazine* (December 1864): 64; Eldredge, *Third New Hampshire*, pp. 634–35; *Wilmington Morning Star*, August 10, 1993; Clark, ed., *Regiments*, 3:695.

21. Breckinridge had only recently been appointed secretary of war to replace John A. Seddon, a victim of the political fallout from the loss of Fort Fisher. Gragg, *Confederate Goliath*, p. 242; *O.R.* I, 47, part 1, p. 930, 1077; Clark, ed., *Regiments*, 4:428; Eldredge, *Third New Hampshire*, p. 635.

22. *O.R.* I, 47, part 1, p. 1077; Hagood, *Memoirs of the War of Secession*, p. 348; Barrett, *The Civil War in North Carolina*, p. 283; Zaccheus Ellis to his mother, March 1, 1865, Z. Ellis Papers, SHC.

23. Barrett, *The Civil War in North Carolina*, p. 283; Hagood, *Memoirs of the War of Secession*, p. 348; Clark, ed., *Regiments*, 2:10, 802, 4:428, 543; *O.R.* I, 47, part 2, p. 1249; Andrew J. Howell, *The Book of Wilmington*, p. 145; *Raleigh Weekly Confederate*, March 1, 1865; W. McKee Evans, *Ballots and Fence Rails: Reconstruction on the Lower Cape Fear*, p. 22.

24. Hagood, *Memoirs of the War of Secession*, pp. 348–49; *Raleigh Weekly Conservative*, March 1, 1865.

25. Clark, ed., *Regiments*, 2:11, 518, 802, 3:215, 695, 4:428–29, 542; Hagood, *Memoirs of the War of Secession*, p. 349; Ashe, *History of North Carolina*, 2:957.

26. Lieutenant Washington's horse had temporarily escaped while the officer was dismounted just after crossing the pontoon. Clark, ed., *Regiments*, 4:429.

27. Clark, ed., *Regiments*, 3:215; Hagood, *Memoirs of the War of Secession*, p. 349; *O.R.* II, 8, p. 290, 296, 297.

28. Hagood, *Memoirs of the War of Secession*, p. 349; Clark, ed., *Regiments*, 2:696; *O.R.* I, 47, part 2, pp. 1263–64, 1270; Klutz, "The Boy Who Saved Richmond," *Confederate Veteran* 6:214.

29. *O.R.* I, 47, part 2, p. 1292.

CHAPTER 14
The Last Grand Stand of the Confederacy

1. John G. Barrett, *Sherman's March through the Carolinas* (hereafter cited as *Sherman's March*), p. 113, 146; Jay Luvaas, "Johnston's Last Stand—Bentonville" (hereafter cited as "Last Stand") *North Carolina Historical Review* 33:332, 337; John Gibson, *Those 163 Days*, p. 186, 221.

2. Craig L. Symonds, *Joseph E. Johnston: A Civil War Biography* (hereafter cited as *Johnston*), pp. 340–42; Barrett, *The Civil War in North Carolina*, p. 290; *O.R.* I, 47, part 2, p. 1247, 1274; Gibson, *Those 163 Days*, pp. 186–87; Woodward, ed., *Chesnut*, pp. 715–52; Weymouth T. Jordan, Jr., *The Battle of Bentonville* (hereafter cited as *Bentonville*), pp. 2–3; Faust, ed., *Encyclopedia*, p. 400; Louise Wigfall Wright, *A Southern Girl in '61: War-Time Memories of a Confederate Senator's Daughter*, p. 240.

3. Jordan, *Bentonville*, pp. 7–8.

4. Hallock, *Confederate Defeat*, 2:248–50; Symonds, *Johnston*, p. 344, 346; *O.R.* I, 47, part 2, p. 1318, 1328; Seitz, *Bragg*, p. 513; Trotter, *Ironclads and Columbiads*, p. 406; Barrett, *The Civil War in North Carolina*, p. 285.

5. Hagood, *Memoirs of the War of Secession*, p. 349; Clark, ed., *Regiments*, 3:215–16. Although the rail service was superior to that in Virginia, Hagood's brigade was delayed by a train accident on the trip to Kinston. *O.R.* I, 47, part 2, p. 912, 1341.

6. Symonds, *Johnston*, p. 346; *O.R.* I, 47, part 2, p. 1334, 1338. For information on the Bragg-Hill dispute, see Hal Bridges, *Lee's Maverick General: Daniel Harvey Hill*, pp. 225–31, 234–38, 240–45, 267–68.

7. *O.R.* I, 47, part 2, p. 724, 1341; Barrett, *The Civil War in North Carolina*, pp. 285–86; Hagood, *Memoirs of the War of Secession*, p. 352.

8. J. D. Cox, *The March to the Sea*, pp. 156–58; Barrett, *The Civil War in North Carolina*, p. 286; *O.R.* I, 47, part 1, p. 912; *O.R.* I, 47, part 2, p. 722.

9. *O.R.* I, 47, part 2, p. 1339.

10. A. M. Waddell Chapter, United Daughters of the Confederacy, "What Happened at South-

General Robert F. Hoke

west Creek in the Spring of 1865"; *Kinston Daily News*, June 6, 1915; *O.R.* I, 47, part 1, p. 1086; Barrett, *The Civil War in North Carolina*, pp. 286–89.

11. *O.R.* I, 47, part 2, pp. 1350–51; Clark, ed., *Regiments*, 4:543; Hagood, *Memoirs of the War of Secession*, pp. 353–55; Sheldon B. Thorpe, *The History of the Fifteenth Connecticut Volunteers* (hereafter cited as *Fifteenth Connecticut*), pp. 93–94; A. M. Waddell Chapter, United Daughters of the Confederacy, "What Happened at Southwest Creek in the Spring of 1865"; *Kinston Daily News*, June 6, 1915; Barrett, *The Civil War in North Carolina*, p. 287.

12. Barrett, *The Civil War in North Carolina*, p. 287; Thorpe, *Fifteenth Connecticut*, p. 93, 112; Clark, ed., *Regiments*, 4: 543–44.

13. Thorpe, *Fifteenth Connecticut*, p. 95, 112; *O.R.* I, 47, part 1, p. 1087; Hagood, *Memoirs of the War of Secession*, p. 353; Barrett, *The Civil in North Carolina*, p. 288.

14. H. J. H. Thompson to his wife, March 11, 1865, and March 1865 (n.d.), H. J. H. Thompson Papers, DU; *Raleigh News and Observer*, December 11, 1903. Estimates of the total number of prisoners taken by Hoke and Hill on March 8 range between a thousand and fifteen hundred. Hagood, *Memoirs of the War of Secession*, p. 354; Clark, ed., *Regiments*, 2:803; *O.R.* I, 47, part 2, p. 743, 1350; *Kinston Daily News*, June 6, 1915.

15. *O.R.* I, 47, part 1, p. 1045, 1078; Graham, *William Alexander Graham*, 6:274; Barrett, *The Civil War in North Carolina*, p. 291, 300; Jordan, *Bentonville*, p. 7.

16. *O.R.* I, 47, part 2, p. 724, 732; *O.R.* I, 47, part 1, p. 912, 932; Barrett, *The Civil War in North Carolina*, p. 288; Cox, *The March to the Sea*, p. 159; Hagood, *Memoirs of the War of Secession*, p. 355.

17. *O.R.* I, 47, part 1, p. 1087; *O.R.* I, 47, part 2, p. 1360; Barrett, *The Civil War in North Carolina*, p. 288; Hagood, *Memoirs of the War of Secession*, p. 354; Clark, ed., *Regiments*, 3:708, 4:544.

18. Barrett, *The Civil War in North Carolina*, pp. 289–90; *O.R.* I, 47, part 2, p. 1360; Trotter, *Ironclads and Columbiads*, p. 407; Hagood, *Memoirs of the War of Secession*, p. 354; *O.R.* I, 47, part 1, p. 956; Thomas Kirwan and Henry Splaine, *Memorial History of the 17th Massachusetts Regiment, Massachusetts Volunteer Infantry*, pp. 346–47; Clark, ed., *Regiments*, 4:544–46.

19. Clark, ed., *Regiments*, 4:546, 1:411–12; Hagood, *Memoirs of the War of Secession*, pp. 354–55; Barrett, *The Civil War in North Carolina*, p. 290; William Calder Diary, March 10, 1865, William Calder Papers, DU; *O.R.* I, 47, part 2, p. 789, 1366–67.

20. Barrett, *The Civil War in North Carolina*, p. 290; Davis, *Rise and Fall of the Confederate Government*, 2:539.

21. Hagood, *Memoirs of the War of Secession*, p. 355; *O.R.* I, 47, part 2, pp. 1366–67, 1379. After being at anchor for more than a year, the *Neuse* was not used in the battle at Southwest Creek. Bragg ordered the ram to be sacrificed after it provided cover for Hoke. The crew obeyed his orders. Barrett, *The Civil War in North Carolina*, p. 290; Trotter, *Ironclads and Columbiads*, pp. 409–10.

22. Symonds, *Johnston*, pp. 347–48; Ashe, *History of North Carolina*, 2:979; Luvaas, "Last Stand," *North Carolina Historical Review* 33:332; Barrett, *The Civil War in North Carolina*, p. 311; *O.R.* I, 47, part 1, p. 23; Jordan, *Bentonville*, p. 7; *O.R.* I, 47, part 2, p. 800, 1373; Hagood, *Memoirs of the War of Secession*, p. 356.

23. *O.R.* I, 47, part 1, p. 23; Calder Diary, March 12, 1865, William Calder Papers, DU; Hagood, *Memoirs of the War of Secession*, p. 355; *O.R.* I, 47, part 2, p. 1367, 1462; Clark, ed., *Regiments*, 4:584, 588; Trotter, *Silk Flags and Cold Steel*, pp. 289–90; Tucker, *Zeb*

Endnotes

Vance, pp. 371–74; Tucker, *Front Rank*, p. 74.

24. *O.R.* I, 47, part 2, p. 1395; Jordan, *Bentonville*, p. 7.

25. Hagood, *Memoirs of the War of Secession*, pp. 355–56; Jordan, *Bentonville*, pp. 13–14; Barrett, *The Civil War in North Carolina*, pp. 323–25; Gibson, *Those 163 Days*, pp. 210–18; Mark L. Bradley, *Last Stand in the Carolinas: The Battle of Bentonville* (hereafter cited as *Last Stand*), pp. 119–32.

26. Hagood, *Memoirs of the War of Secession*, pp. 355–56; Joseph E. Johnston, *Narrative of Military Operations during the Civil War* (hereafter cited as *Narrative*), pp. 384–85; Jordan, *Bentonville*, pp. 7–8; *O.R.* I, 47, part 2, p. 1424; Barrett, *The Civil War in North Carolina*, pp. 325–26.

27. Wade Hampton, "The Battle of Bentonville," *Battles and Leaders of the Civil War*, 4:701; Barrett, *Sherman's March*, pp. 159–62; Johnston, *Narrative*, p. 385; *Fayetteville Observer*, April 19, 1970; Gibson, *Those 163 Days*, p. 218, 220.

28. Hampton, "The Battle of Bentonville," *Battles and Leaders of the Civil War*, 4:701; Gibson, *Those 163 Days*, p. 218; Barrett, *Sherman's March*, p. 159; *O.R.* I, 47, part 2, p. 1427, 1428, 1429, 1435.

29. Hagood, *Memoirs of the War of Secession*, p. 358; *O.R.* I, 47, part 2, pp. 885–86; Barrett, *Sherman's March*, pp. 160–61.

30. Hagood, *Memoirs of the War of Secession*, p. 358; Clark, ed., *Regiments*, 4:547; Gibson, *Those 163 Days*, pp. 219–20. Williams was captured during the fighting at Bentonville the following day. Hiram Smith Williams, *This War So Horrible: The Civil War Diary of Hiram Smith Williams*, p. 127; *O.R.* I, 47, part 2, p. 1428; Barrett, *Sherman's March*, p. 160.

31. Barrett, *Sherman's March*, p. 163; Jordan, *Bentonville*, p. 15; Hagood, *Memoirs of the War of Secession*, p. 358; Luvaas, "Last Stand," *North Carolina Historical Review* 33:335–37; Gibson, *Those 163 Days*, pp. 219–21; Hampton, "The Battle of Bentonville," *Battles and Leaders of the Civil War*, 4:702; *O.R.* I, 47, part 1, p. 25, 423; Symonds, *Johnston*, p. 350.

32. Barrett, *Sherman's March*, p. 163; *O.R.* I, 47, part 1, p. 1056; Alexander C. McClurg, "The Last Chance of the Confederacy," *Atlantic Monthly* 50 (September 1882): 390; Luvaas, "Last Stand," *North Carolina Historical Review* 33:335; Jordan, *Bentonville*, p. 16.

33. Jordan, *Bentonville*, p. 7, 16; Barrett, *Sherman's March*, p. 164; Gibson, *Those 163 Days*, pp. 220–21; Hagood, *Memoirs of the War of Secession*, p. 358; Clark, ed., *Regiments*, 3:698, 4:547; Symonds, *Johnston*, p. 350; Johnston, *Narrative*, p. 386. Hardee broke camp on March 19 at 3 A.M. and set his army in motion for Bentonville. *O.R.* I, 47, part 2, p. 1428; Bradley, *Last Stand*, p. 161.

34. Jordan, *Bentonville*, p. 17; Faust, ed., *Encyclopedia*, p. 207; Trotter, *Silk Flags and Cold Steel*, p. 262; Barrett, *Sherman's March*, p. 163; Luvaas, "Last Stand," *North Carolina Historical Review* 33:337, 340; Gibson, *Those 163 Days*, p. 221.

35. *O.R.* I, 47, part 2, p. 906; *O.R.* I, 47, part 1, p. 423; Hagood, *Memoirs of the War of Secession*, p. 358; Hampton, "The Battle of Bentonville," *Battles and Leaders of the Civil War*, 4:704.

36. Luvaas, "Last Stand," *North Carolina Historical Review* 33:335, 344; Gibson, *Those 163 Days*, p. 220; Hampton, "The Battle of Bentonville," *Battles and Leaders of the Civil War*, 4:705; Johnston, *Narrative*, pp. 386–87; Hagood, *Memoirs of the War of Secession*, p. 360; Barrett, *Sherman's March*, pp. 166–67; Nathaniel Cheairs Hughes, Jr., *General William J. Hardee: Old Reliable* (hereafter cited as *Hardee*), p. 287; Symonds, *Johnston*, p. 350; Clark, ed., *Regiments*, 3:195; Dickert, *History of Kershaw's Brigade*, p. 523; Bradley, *Last Stand*, p.

180; Joseph E. Johnston to R. F. Hoke, January 27, 1871, Robert F. Hoke Papers, NCDAH.

37. Luvaas, "Last Stand," *North Carolina Historical Review* 33:340–41; Jordan, *Bentonville*, p. 17; Barrett, *Sherman's March*, pp. 166–67; *O.R.* I, 47, part 2, pp. 903–4; Trotter, *Silk Flags and Cold Steel*, pp. 264–65.

38. Tucker, *Front Rank*, pp. 70–71; Manly Wade Wellman, *Giant in Gray: A Biography of Wade Hampton of South Carolina*, p. 175; Barrett, *Sherman's March*, p. 160; Trotter, *Silk Flags and Cold Steel*, p. 258; Luvaas, "Last Stand," *North Carolina Historical Review* 33:333.

39. Barrett, *Sherman's March*, p. 168; Gibson, *Those 163 Days*, p. 223; Jordan, *Bentonville*, pp. 18–19; Symonds, *Johnston*, p. 350; Luvaas, "Last Stand," *North Carolina Historical Review* 33:343; Clark, ed., *Regiments*, 4:21.

40. Gibson, *Those 163 Days*, p. 224; Barrett, *Sherman's March*, pp. 168–69; Luvaas, "Last Stand," *North Carolina Historical Review* 33:343; Charles S. Brown to his family, April 26, 1865, Charles S. Brown Papers, DU.

41. Jordan, *Bentonville*, p. 19; Barrett, *Sherman's March*, p. 171; Hagood, *Memoirs of the War of Secession*, p. 360; Luvaas, "Last Stand," *North Carolina Historical Review* 33:344–45; Bradley, *Last Stand*, pp. 222–23; Gibson, *Those 163 Days*, p. 224; McClurg, "The Last Chance of the Confederacy," *Atlantic Monthly* 50 (September 1882): 393–94; Trotter, *Silk Flags and Cold Steel*, p. 271; L. P. Thomas to R. F. Hoke, March 18, 1901, Robert F. Hoke Papers, NCDAH.

42. Barrett, *Sherman's March*, pp. 173–74; Clark, ed., *Regiments*, 2:651; Samuel W. Ravenel, "Ask the Survivors of Bentonville," *Confederate Veteran* 18:124; McClurg, "The Last Chance of the Confederacy," *Atlantic Monthly* 50 (September 1882): 395; Luvaas, "Last Stand," *North Carolina Historical Review* 33:345; *O.R.* I, 47, part 1, p. 497, 504.

43. Johnston, *Narrative*, p. 388; Barrett, *Sherman's March*, p. 174; Gibson, *Those 163 Days*, pp. 225–27; Luvaas, "Last Stand," *North Carolina Historical Review* 33:346–48.

44. Luvaas, "Last Stand," *North Carolina Historical Review* 33:348; Jordan, *Bentonville*, p. 21; Barrett, *Sherman's March*, pp. 174–75; *O.R.* I, 47, part 1, p. 1080; Hagood, *Memoirs of the War of Secession*, p. 361.

45. Gibson, *Those 163 Days*, pp. 227–28; Barrett, *Sherman's March*, pp. 177–78. As to the time Sherman received the report of the first day's events at Bentonville, estimates range from 9:30 P.M. on March 19 to 2:00 A.M. on March 20. Jordan, *Bentonville*, pp. 20–21; Hughes, Jr., *Hardee*, p. 290; Johnston, *Narrative*, pp. 389–90; Hagood, *Memoirs of the War of Secession*, p. 361.

46. Luvaas, "Last Stand," *North Carolina Historical Review* 33:349, 351; Hughes, Jr., *Hardee*, p. 291; *O.R.* I, 47, part 2, p. 919; Gibson, *Those 163 Days*, pp. 228–29; Jordan, *Bentonville*, p. 21; Barrett, *Sherman's March*, pp. 176–78; Clark, ed., *Regiments*, 3:197, 698–99, 4:21; Johnston, *Narrative*, p. 390; Bradley, *Last Stand*, pp. 330–31, 332, 338, 340–41.

47. Clark, ed., *Regiments*, 3:698–99; Johnston, *Narrative*, p. 390.

48. Mrs. John H. Anderson, "North Carolina Boy Soldiers at the Battle of Bentonville," *Confederate Veteran* 35:174–76; Barrett, *Sherman's March*, p. 179. Following the war, Clark studied law on Wall Street and returned to North Carolina to open a practice. In 1902, he was elected chief justice of the North Carolina Supreme Court. A distinguished historian, Clark compiled and edited the *Histories of the Several Regiments and Battalions from North Carolina in the Great War, 1861–1865*. Since the publication of the monumental five-volume work in 1901, it has remained the most outstanding study of its kind. Powell, ed., *North Carolina Biography*, 1:378–79; R. F. Hoke to F. H. Busbee, April 7, 1890, Robert F.

Hoke Papers, SHC.

49. Jordan, *Bentonville*, p. 23; Barrett, *Sherman's March*, pp. 179–80; Gibson, *Those 163 Days*, pp. 228–29; Luvaas, "Last Stand," *North Carolina Historical Review* 33:351.

50. Gibson, *Those 163 Days*, pp. 228–29; Hagood, *Memoirs of the War of Secession*, p. 361; Barrett, *Sherman's March*, pp. 180–82.

51. Barrett, *Sherman's March*, p. 182; Jordan, *Bentonville*, p. 26; *O.R.* I, 47, part 1, p. 27; Hagood, *Memoirs of the War of Secession*, p. 363; Clark, ed., *Regiments*, 1:412, 3:217, 699.

52. Luvaas, "Last Stand," *North Carolina Historical Review* 33:354; Barrett, *Sherman's March*, pp. 182–83; Gibson, *Those 163 Days*, p. 231; Hagood, *Memoirs of the War of Secession*, p. 363, 412; William Calder Diary, March 22, 1865, William Calder Papers, DU.

CHAPTER 15
"But It Is All Over Now"

1. Clark, ed., *Regiments*, 1:412, 3:699, 4:498; Jordan, ed., *North Carolina Troops*, 12:148; Barrett, *The Civil War in North Carolina*, p. 368; *O.R.* I, 47, part 2, pp. 1453–54.

2. Barrett, *Sherman's March*, p. 184, 195, 203; Hagood, *Memoirs of the War of Secession*, p. 363; *O.R.* I, 47, part 3, pp. 732–33. Although he abdicated his field command, Bragg retained nominal command of the Department of North Carolina. He set up temporary headquaters in Raleigh, where he despaired over the ever-worsening Confederate cause. Hallock, *Confederate Defeat*, 2:254.

3. Clark, ed., *Regiments*, 3:699; Hagood, *Memoirs of the War of Secession*, p. 364.

4. Hagood, *Memoirs of the War of Secession*, pp. 365–66.

5. Ibid, pp. 364–66; Barrett, *Sherman's March*, p. 201; Walter Clark, *The Papers of Walter Clark*, 2:149–50.

6. A combined return on the same day for the corps of Lee, Cheatham, and Stewart of the Army of Tennessee indicated a total infantry strength of 6,823. *O.R.* I, 47, part 3, p. 748, 754; Hagood, *Memoirs of the War of Secession*, p. 367; Clark, ed., *Regiments*, 4:498–99; Lewis Shore Brumfield, "Thomas Lanier Clingman and the Shallow Ford Families," p. 120, NCC.

7. Barrett, *Sherman's March*, p. 201; B. L. Ridley, "Last Battles of the War," *Confederate Veteran* 3:70; Clark, ed., *Regiments*, 4:498–99; William Calder Dairy, April 7, 1865, William Calder Papers, DU; Hagood, *Memoirs of the War of Secession*, p. 367.

8. Barrett, *Sherman's March*, p. 201; *O.R.* I, 47, part 3, p. 129, 768; Hagood, *Memoirs of the War of Secession*, p. 367.

9. Barrett, *Sherman's March*, p. 198, 203, 210; *O.R.* I, 47, part 3, p. 150.

10. *O.R.* I, 47, part 3, p. 154; Barrett, *Sherman's March*, pp. 200–201, 209; Hagood, *Memoirs of the War of Secession*, pp. 367–68.

11. Cornelia Phillips Spencer, *The Last Ninety Days of the War*, p. 72, 143. Swain was greatly interested in protecting the library and other buildings of the first state university to open its doors in the United States. Although the long war had robbed North Carolina of resources and many promising young men, Swain now had the university in session with a few students. Clement Dowd, *Life of Vance*, p. 483; Tucker, *Zeb Vance*, p. 393; Gibson, *Those 163 Days*, pp. 242–43; Barrett, *Sherman's March*, p. 210, 259.

12. Johnston, *Narrative*, p. 396; Hagood, *Memoirs of the War of Secession*, p. 368; Clark, ed.,

Regiments, 3:200; *O.R.* I, 47, part 3, p. 789.

13. Barrett, *Sherman's March*, p. 204, 211.

14. *O.R.* I, 47, part 3, p. 177, 178. It was not Vance's intention to reach a separate peace with Sherman, but his letter and entreaties were so construed by Jefferson Davis and some Confederate military officers. Ashe, *History of North Carolina*, 2:997; Tucker, *Zeb Vance*, pp. 394–95; Dowd, *Life of Vance*, p. 483.

15. *O.R.* I, 47, part 3, p. 178, 180; Barrett, *Sherman's March*, p. 207, 210.

16. Gibson, *Those 163 Days*, p. 242; Clark, ed., *Regiments*, 1:412, 4:499, 594; Ridley, "Last Battles of the War," *Confederate Veteran* 3:70; Hagood, *Memoirs of the War of Secession*, p. 368; Robert F. Hoke to F. H. Busbee, April 7, 1890, Robert F. Hoke Papers, SHC; *O.R.* I, 47, part 3, p. 186.

17. Barrett, *Sherman's March*, p. 216; Trotter, *Silk Flags and Cold Steel*, p. 307; Tucker, *Zeb Vance*, p. 399; Dowd, *Life of Vance*, p. 484.

18. Clark, ed., *Regiments*, 4:32; Ashe, *History of North Carolina*, 2:999; Kemp P. Battle, *Memories of an Old-Time Tar Heel* (hereafter cited as *Memories*), p. 192; narrative of J. J. Laughinghouse, Robert F. Hoke Papers, NCDAH.

19. Narrative of J. J. Laughinghouse, Robert F. Hoke Papers, NCDAH.

20. Elements of Joseph Wheeler's cavalry commands remained in and about Raleigh until April 13. Ashe, *History of North Carolina*, 2:999; Clark, ed., *Regiments*, 3:200, 4:22, 31–32.

21. Barrett, *Sherman's March*, pp. 216–17, 220; Tucker, *Zeb Vance*, p. 399; Dowd, *Life of Vance*, pp. 484–85; Z. B. Vance to Cornelia P. Spencer, February 17, 1866, D. L. Swain Papers, SHC.

22. Barrett, *Sherman's March*, p. 216; Tucker, *Zeb Vance*, p. 399; Franklin Ray Shirley, *Zebulon Vance: Tarheel Spokesman*, p. 59; narrative of J. J. Laughinghouse, Robert F. Hoke Papers, NCDAH.

23. Hagood, *Memoirs of the War of Secession*, p. 368; Clark, ed., *Regiments*, 1:412–13; Ashe, *History of North Carolina*, 2:1000; Barrett, *Sherman's March*, pp. 221–22.

24. Hagood, *Memoirs of the War of Secession*, p. 368; Barrett, *Sherman's March*, p. 226, 229; *O.R.* I, 47, part 3, p. 207; Gibson, *Those 163 Days*, p. 259.

25. Hagood, *Memoirs of the War of Secession*, p. 368; Clark, ed., *Regiments*, 3:200, 1:412.

26. Clark, ed., *Regiments*, 4:22, 1:413, 3:200–201; Hagood, *Memoirs of the War of Secession*, p. 368.

27. Clark, ed., *Regiments*, 3:200–201.

28. Clark, ed., *Regiments*, 3:201; Hagood, *Memoirs of the War of Secession*, p. 368.

29. Clark, ed., *Regiments*, 4:22, 32.

30. Hagood, *Memoirs of the War of Secession*, p. 368.

31. Hagood, *Memoirs of the War of Secession*, p. 369; Clark, ed., *Regiments*, 4:32.

32. Each general went into the meeting at Bennett House with a different purpose in mind. Johnston was interested in an armistice so that civil authorities could negotiate an end to the war. Sherman, cognizant that his government did not acknowledge the existence of the Confederate States of America, was anxious for Johnston to surrender on the same terms agreed upon between Lee and Grant. Johnston, *Narrative*, p. 402; Gibson, *Those 163 Days*, pp. 262–63; *O.R.* I, 47, part 3, p. 808; B. L. Ridley, "Captain Ridley's Journal," *Confederate Veteran* 3:99; Hagood, *Memoirs of the War of Secession*, p. 369.

33. Palmer's soldiers liked Lincolnton and found its residents to be refined and intelligent. Ina W. Van Noppen, "The Significance of Stoneman's Last Raid," *North Carolina Historical*

Review 38:503–4; Sherrill, *Annals of Lincoln County*, pp. 181–82.

34. Symonds, *Johnston*, p. 356; Hagood, *Memoirs of the War of Secession*, p. 369.

35. Hagood, *Memoirs of the War of Secession*, pp. 369–70.

36. Hagood, *Memoirs of the War of Secession*, p. 370; Ridley, "Captain Ridley's Journal," *Confederate Veteran* 3:99, 204.

37. Hagood, *Memoirs of the War of Secession*, p. 370; *O.R.* I, 47, part 3, p. 839.

38. Barrett, *Sherman's March*, p. 267; *O.R.* I, 47, part 3, pp. 293–94; Hagood, *Memoirs of the War of Secession*, pp. 370–71; *New Bern Times*, April 25, 1865.

39. Johnston, *Narrative*, pp. 411–12; Hagood, *Memoirs of the War of Secession*, p. 371.

40. Clark, ed., *Regiments*, 1:413, 2:804, 3:217, 700, 4:22, 32; Johnston, *Narrative*, pp. 412–14; Barrett, *Sherman's March*, pp. 270–71.

41. Hagood, *Memoirs of the War of Secession*, p. 371; Johnston, *Narrative*, pp. 415–16.

42. Hagood, *Memoirs of the War of Secession*, pp. 371–72. When Davis made his request for the shipment of the silver, the treasury contained thirty-nine thousand dollars, but it had been considerably depleted by the time the distribution was made to the soldiers. Gibson, *Those 163 Days*, pp. 277–78; Clark, ed., *Regiments*, 4:22, 32; Christopher Losson, *Tennessee's Forgotten Warriors: Frank Cheatham and His Confederate Division*, p. 248.

43. Hagood, *Memoirs of the War of Secession*, p. 392.

44. Hagood, *Memoirs of the War of Secession*, p. 372; Tucker, *Front Rank*, p. 82; Clark, ed., *Regiments*, 4:33–34; "General Hoke's Farewell Address to His Division," Robert F. Hoke Papers, NCDAH.

45. Hagood, *Memoirs of the War of Secession*, p. 372; Clark, ed., *Regiments*, 1:413, 3:217, 700, 4:549, 2:764; Jordan, ed., *North Carolina Troops*, 12:275.

46. Hagood, *Memoirs of the War of Secession*, p. 372.

47. Ashe et al, eds., *Biographical History*, 1:320.

48. Ridley, "Captain Ridley's Journal," *Confederate Veteran* 3:99, 204.

CHAPTER 16
Picking up the Pieces: A Half-Century of Reconstruction

1. Barrett, *The Civil War in North Carolina*, pp. 350–66; Hugh Talmage Lefler and Albert Ray Newsome, *North Carolina: The History of a Southern State*, p. 460; Hamilton, "General Robert F. Hoke," Robert F. Hoke Papers, SHC.

2. Sherrill, *Annals of Lincoln County*, p. 83; Barrett, *The Civil War in North Carolina*, pp. 360–61; *Raleigh Weekly Conservative*, February 13, 1865; "Proceedings of Stockholders, North Carolina Railroad Company," July 1912, Robert F. Hoke Papers, NCDAH.

3. Josephus Daniels, "Two Illustrious Roberts of the Southern Confederacy," *Confederate Veteran* 36:291; Ashe, *History of North Carolina*, 2:1011; Ashe et al, eds., *Biographical History*, 1:320; Sherrill, *Annals of Lincoln County*, p. 330; "Proceedings of Stockholders, North Carolina Railroad Company," July 1912, Robert F. Hoke Papers, NCDAH.

4. Clarence Poe, *True Tales of the South at War*, p. 204; *The Uplift*, December 1909; *Masonic Journal*, March 7, 1919; *Charlotte Observer*, July 21, 1912; unidentified newspaper clipping, Robert F. Hoke Papers, SHC; H. H. Cunningham, *Doctors in Gray: The Confederate Medical Service*, p. 7.

General Robert F. Hoke

5. "The Unveiling of the Statue of General Robert E. Lee," *Southern Historical Society Papers* 17:266; "Build the Davis Monument," *Confederate Veteran* 1:121; "National Confederate Memorial," *Confederate Veteran* 3:276.

6. Hamilton, "General Robert F. Hoke," Robert F. Hoke Papers, SHC; *Charlotte Observer*, January 17, 1907; *Masonic Journal*, March 17, 1919; R. F. Hoke to Miss Lida Perry, March 29, 1876, Robert F. Hoke Papers, NCDAH; R. F. Hoke to Miss Lida Thackery, April 30, 1887, Robert F. Hoke Papers, NCDAH; George F. Towle to Robert F. Hoke, May 24, 1871, Robert F. Hoke Papers, NCDAH; J. E. Johnston to R. F. Hoke, January 27, 1871, and September 23, 1871, Robert F. Hoke Papers, NCDAH; G. T. P. Beauregard to "Dear General," December 2, 1874, Robert F. Hoke Papers, NCDAH; R. F. Hoke to F. H. Busbee, April 7, 1890, Robert F. Hoke Papers, SHC; Robert F. Hoke to C. B. Edwards, October 17, 1905, Robert F. Hoke Papers, SHC; *Raleigh News and Observer*, December 11, 1903; author's interview with Ann Pollock West (granddaughter of Robert F. Hoke) and her husband, Robert West, in Warsaw, North Carolina, October 20, 1989.

7. Victor S. Bryant, "R. F. Hoke, Soldier and Good Citizen," *North Carolina Review* (February 1913).

8. Bryant, "R. F. Hoke, Soldier and Good Citizen," *North Carolina Review* (February 1913); *Charlotte Observer*, July 21, 1912; *The Uplift*, December 1909; "Resolution of Respect," Henry L. Wyatt Camp, United Confederate Veterans, July 12, 1912, Robert F. Hoke Papers, NCDAH; *Raleigh News and Observer*, May 11, 1921; "Proceedings of Stockholders, North Carolina Railroad Company," July 1912, Robert F. Hoke Papers, NCDAH.

9. Longstreet would reciprocate the hospitality in later years when Hoke visited Longstreet at the latter's hostelry in Gainesville, Georgia. Sanger and Hay, *James Longstreet*, p. 318, 396; Military Service Record of Robert F. Hoke, National Archives.

10. Connor, *North Carolina: Rebuilding an Ancient Commonwealth*, 3:495; Ashe et al, eds., *Biographical History*, 1:320–21; Edward G. Longacre, *Pickett: Leader of the Charge*, pp. 172–73; *O.R.* II, 8, pp. 903–4; U.S. Congress "Murder of Union Soldiers in North Carolina"; James A. Padgett, "Reconstruction Letters from North Carolina," *North Carolina Historical Review* 19:402; Cheshire, *Nonnulla*, pp. 150–51.

11. Ashe et al, eds., *Biographical History*, 1:320–21; Connor, *North Carolina: Rebuilding an Ancient Commonwealth*, 3:495; Cheshire, *Nonnulla*, pp. 150–51.

12. Jordan and Manarin, eds., *North Carolina Troops*, 6:539, 9:119; Special Orders No. 4, Adjutant and Inspector General's Office, January 6, 1864, original in possession of author; "Turner" to George M. Hoke, July 16, 1864, original in possession of author; Sherrill, *Annals of Lincoln County*, p. 189.

13. Military Service Record of Robert F. Hoke, National Archives; untitled narrative of Josephus Daniels, Robert F. Hoke Papers, NCDAH.

14. Frances Burton Hoke Pollock, "A Confederate Veteran I Know," Robert F. Hoke Papers, NCDAH.

15. Unidentified newspaper obituary of Lydia A. Hoke, Robert F. Hoke Papers, NCDAH; Pollock, "A Confederate Veteran I Know," Robert F. Hoke Papers, NCDAH. Lydia Van Wyck's grandfather, Samuel Maverick, was a Revolutionary War hero. His fleet of seventeen ships was captured by the British navy. Unidentified newspaper clipping entitled "Forgotten Men Who Made Brooklyn History," Hoke Family Papers in possession of Hoke Kimball (great-grandson of Robert F. Hoke), Raleigh, North Carolina; Maury Maverick to Lydia Hoke Webb, March 19, 1938, Robert F. Hoke Papers, NCDAH.

16. Pollock, "A Confederate Veteran I Know," Robert F. Hoke Papers, NCDAH; unidentified newspaper clipping entitled "Forgotten Men Who Made Brooklyn History," Hoke Family Papers in possession of Hoke Kimball (great-grandson of Robert F. Hoke), Raleigh, North Carolina; Battle, *Memories,* p. 53.

17. Pollock, "A Confederate Veteran I Know," Robert F. Hoke Papers, NCDAH; author's interview with Ann Pollock West (granddaughter of Robert F. Hoke) and her husband, Robert West, in Warsaw, North Carolina.

18. Account of the Grand Masque Ball, White Sulphur Springs, Virginia, August 28, 1868, Robert F. Hoke Papers, NCDAH; gravestone of Frances Burton Hoke, Old White Church Cemetery, Lincolnton, North Carolina.

19. Unidentified newspaper obituary of Lydia A. Hoke, Robert F. Hoke Papers, NCDAH; *Fayetteville Observer*, January 2, 1983; Jefferson Davis to Robert F. Hoke, January 8, 1870, January 19, 1870, and May 3, 1870, Robert F. Hoke Papers, NCDAH; Wade Hampton to R. F. Hoke, May 19, 1872, May 24, 1872, July 2, 1872, and October, 1, 1872, Robert F. Hoke Papers, NCDAH.

20. Anne Van Wyck, *Descendants of Cornelius Barentse Van Wyck*, n.p.; Jefferson Davis to R. F. Hoke, August 7, 1871, Robert F. Hoke Papers, NCDAH; Varina Davis to "My dear Genl. Hoke," n.d., Robert F. Hoke Papers, NCDAH; *Raleigh News and Observer*, September 13, 1949; Leedy and Stroup, eds., *Pictorial Walk*, n.p.; author's interview with Robert Frederick Hoke Pollock (grandson of Robert F. Hoke) in Lincolnton, North Carolina, September 24, 1995.

21. Powell, ed., *North Carolina Biography*, 3:165–66; *Raleigh News and Observer*, January 28, 1934.

22. Powell, ed., *North Carolina Biography*, 3:165–66; *Raleigh News and Observer*, January 28, 1834, September 26, 1944, and September 25, 1944; *Atlanta Constitution*, October 18, 1846; J. Hiram Kite, "Michael Hoke," *Clinical Orthopaedics* 14 (1959): 1–4.

23. *Raleigh News and Observer*, January 28, 1934, and November 7, 1931.

24. Van Wyck, *Descendants of Cornelius Barentse Van Wyck*, n.p.; *Raleigh News and Observer*, November 17, 1968, November 17, 1959, and September 1, 1963; *Wilson Daily Times*, May 1, 1961; Talmage C. Johnson and Charles R. Holloman, *The Story of Kinston and Lenoir County*, p. 138.

25. Mallory Hope Ferrell, *Tweetsie Country: The East Tennessee and Western North Carolina Railroad* (hereafter cited as *Tweetsie Country*), pp. 1–2; North Carolina Board of Agriculture, ed., *North Carolina: Land of Opportunity*, p. 63; Opening Proceedings of Cranberry Iron Coal Company, February 23, 1873, Robert F. Hoke Papers, NCDAH; Carolyn Sakowski, *Touring the Western North Carolina Backroads*, pp. 204–5; *North Carolina Standard*, May 26, 1863; Horton Cooper, *History of Avery County, North Carolina* (hereafter cited as *Avery County*), pp. 19–20.

26. Ferrell, *Tweetsie Country*, pp. 2–5; Robert F. Hoke to Lydia Van Wyck, September 17, 1902, Robert F. Hoke Papers, NCDAH; *Raleigh News and Observer*, May 18, 1940.

27. Ina W. Van Noppen and John J. Van Noppen, *Western North Carolina since the Civil War*, p. 351; William Sharpe, *A New Geography of North Carolina*, 2:554–55; Robert F. Hoke to Thomas Graham, June 6, 1890, Robert F. Hoke Papers, SHC. Interest in the Cranberry Mine revived in 1960 when estimates placed the amount of economically recoverable ore in the vein at 7.5 million tons. *Asheville Citizen-Times*, February 7, 1960; *Greensboro Daily News*, May 14, 1960.

General Robert F. Hoke

28. The East Tennessee and Western North Carolina Railroad was affectionately known as "Tweetsie" because of the shrill blasts from its engines as they came around the mountains. *Raleigh News and Observer*, May 18, 1940, and July 5, 1992; *Charlotte Observer*, August 2, 1992.

29. Cooper, *Avery County*, p. 37.

30. Hamilton, "General Robert F. Hoke," Robert F. Hoke Papers, SHC; *Raleigh Times*, July 3, 1912; *Raleigh News and Observer*, July 9, 1912; "Proceedings of Stockholders, North Carolina Railroad Company," July 1912, Robert F. Hoke Papers, NCDAH.

31. As early as 1866, Hoke and A. C. Avery, the brother of Colonel Issac Erwin Avery and Colonel Clark M. Avery, had discussed a possible railroad line from western North Carolina into Tennessee. R. F. Hoke to "Dear Maj.," June 6, 1866, Robert F. Hoke Papers, NCDAH; A. C. Avery to R. F. Hoke, May 23, 1867, Robert F. Hoke Papers, NCDAH; "Proccedings of Stockholders, North Carolina Railroad Company," July 1912, Robert F. Hoke Papers, NCDAH.

32. Kemp P. Battle, *History of the University of North Carolina* (hereafter cited as *University*), 2:136–37.

33. Battle, *University*, 2:246–47; card entry for Chapel Hill Iron Mountain Company, Robert F. Hoke Papers, SHC; Robert F. Hoke to E. W. Lyon, January 8, 1891, Robert F. Hoke Papers, SHC; Powell, ed., *North Carolina Biography*, 1:224; Ashe et al, eds., *Biographical History*, 1:321.

34. Hoke's wartime comrade Thomas Jordan Jarvis served as governor of North Carolina while the railroad was being built and provided much support for the project. Battle, *University*, 2:245–47; Thomas Jordan Jarvis, *The Papers of Thomas Jordan Jarvis*, 1:385.

35. *The Uplift*, December 1909; *Masonic Journal*, March 7, 1919; Robert F. Hoke to "My Dear Daughter," August 18, 1902, Robert F. Hoke Papers, NCDAH; *Salmagundi*, June 1896.

36. Various newspaper obituaries of Robert F. Hoke, Robert F. Hoke Papers, NCDAH; Robert F. Hoke to Hoke Smith, February 10, 1890, Robert F. Hoke Papers, SHC.

37. Undated clipping from *Raleigh News and Observer*, Robert F. Hoke Papers, SHC.

38. *Raleigh News and Observer*, December 11, 1903.

39. Daniels, "Two Illustrious Roberts of the Southern Confederacy," *Confederate Veteran* 36:290; *Raleigh News and Observer*, June 20, 1928; *Richmond Virginian*, July 5, 1912.

40. *Raleigh Times*, November 15, 1967; *Masonic Journal*, March 7, 1919; Henry E. Shepherd, "Gallant Sons of North Carolina," *Confederate Veteran* 27:413.

41. *Charlotte Observer*, July 21, 1912.

42. *Charlotte Observer*, July 21, 1912.

43. Ironically, Hoke's father had been in the first legislature to convene in the State Capitol building that stood just blocks from the general's home. *Raleigh Times*, November 15, 1967; *Raleigh News and Observer*, November 27, 1961; Elizabeth Culbertson Waugh, *North Carolina's Capital, Raleigh*, p. 116.

44. Leedy and Stroup, eds., *Pictorial Walk*, n.p.; *The Uplift*, December 1909; *Charlotte Evening Chronicle*, July 3, 1912; Sherrill, *Annals of Lincoln County*, p. 433; Alton B. Claytor, "Lincoln Lithia Inn," *The State* (March 20, 1937): 38; *Salmagundi*, June 1896; Robert F. Hoke to W. H. Lacey, February 11, 1890, and November 22, 1890, Robert F. Hoke Papers, SHC; Brown and York, *Our Enduring Past*, p. 144.

45. *The Uplift*, December 1909; *Salmagundi*, June 1896; unidentified newspaper clipping entitled "Lincoln County Has Only Tin Mine in U.S.," clipping file, NCC.

46. Brown and York, *Our Enduring Past*, p. 144; Robert F. Hoke to "My Dear Daughter," August 18, 1902, Robert F. Hoke Papers, NCDAH; Robert F. Hoke to "Dear mr. Webb," August 25, 1902, Robert F. Hoke Papers, NCDAH; Robert F. Hoke to "My Dear Daughter," August 29, 1902, Robert F. Hoke Papers, NCDAH; Robert F. Hoke to Lydia Van Wyck, September 17, 1902, Robert F. Hoke Papers, NCDAH; Robert F. Hoke to "My Dear Grand Daughters," December 3, 1911, Robert F. Hoke Papers, NCDAH; Connor, *North Carolina: Rebuilding an Ancient Commonwealth*, 3:495; *Raleigh Times*, July 3, 1912; Ashe et al, eds., *Biographical History*, 1:321.

47. *The Uplift*, December 1909; Brown and York, *Our Enduring Past*, p. 144; Plat Book A, p. 216, Lincoln County Public Registry, Lincolnton, North Carolina; Hoke Family Papers in the possession of Hoke Kimball (great-grandson of Robert F. Hoke), Raleigh, North Carolina.

48. *Lincoln County News*, July 5, 1912.

49. *Raleigh News and Observer*, July 4, 1912.

50. *Lincoln County News*, July 5, 1912; *Raleigh News and Observer*, July 4, 1912; *Charlotte Observer*, July 2, 1912, and July 4, 1912; *Baltimore Sun*, July 4, 1912.

51. *Raleigh News and Observer*, July 4, 1912, and July 5, 1912; *Lincoln County News*, July 5, 1912; various newspaper obituaries of Robert F. Hoke, Robert F. Hoke Papers, NCDAH; "Proceedings of Stockholders, North Carolina Railroad Company," July 1912, Robert F. Hoke Papers, NCDAH.

52. *Carolina and Southern Cross*, May 1913; *Raleigh Times*, July 3, 1912; *Raleigh News and Observer*, July 4, 1912; *Baltimore Sun*, July 4, 1912; *Charlotte News*, July 6, 1912; various newspaper obituaries of Robert F. Hoke, Robert F. Hoke Papers, NCDAH; Raleigh Cemetery Association, ed., *Historic Oakwood Cemetery*, n.p.

53. *Lincoln County News*, July 26, 1912.

54. Ibid.

CHAPTER 17
Requiem for a Modest Man

1. Not only did North Carolina supply more troops than any other Confederate state, but it suffered the most casualties as well. Over forty thousand North Carolina troops died during the war, more than twice as many as from any other state of the Confederacy. Barrett, *The Civil War in North Carolina*, pp. 28–29; Ashe, *History of North Carolina*, 2:1010. Of Pender, the splendid warrior who died from a wound sustained at Gettysburg, Robert E. Lee said, "If General Pender had remained on his horse half an hour longer we would have carried the enemy's position." Tucker, *Front Rank*, p. 53. Matthew F. Maury described General Pettigrew as "the most promising young man of the South," and eminent North Carolina historian Stephen B. Weeks termed him "one of the brightest men" ever born in the state. Powell, ed., *North Carolina Biography*, 5:79; Ashe et al, eds., *Biographical History*, 6:409.

2. Ashe et al, eds., *Biographical History*, 1:309; Powell, ed., *North Carolina Biography*, 3:166; Daniels, "Two Illustrious Roberts of the Southern Confederacy," *Confederate Veteran* 36:290–92.

3. "Resolution of Camp Hardee, No. 39, United Confederate Veterans," Robert F. Hoke Papers, NCDAH.

General Robert F. Hoke

4. Tucker, *Front Rank*, p. 78; Ashe, *History of North Carolina*, 2:990; *Raleigh News and Observer*, July 5, 1912; Hagood, *Memoirs of the War of Secession*, p. 253.

5. Undated clipping from *Atlanta Journal*, Robert F. Hoke Papers, NCDAH; Clark, ed., *Regiments*, 4:537, 5:4.

6. Clark, ed., *Regiments*, 5:325, 2:558.

7. Clark, ed., *Regiments*, 4:526; Elliott, *Soldier Boy*, p. 61; *Raleigh News and Observer*, July 5, 1912.

8. Powell, ed., *North Carolina Biography*, 4:392–93; *Masonic Journal*, March 7, 1919.

9. *O.R.* I, 43, part 3, p. 1108.

10. Powell, ed., *North Carolina Biography*, 3:17–18; Hamilton, "General Robert F. Hoke," Robert F. Hoke Papers, SHC. The Reverend Cheshire, a licensed attorney and an author, served for many years as bishop of the Episopal Diocese of North Carolina. Cheshire, *Nonnulla*, p. 150.

11. Tucker, *Front Rank*, p. 10, 70; Tucker, *Zeb Vance*, p. 346; Freeman, *Lee's Lieutenants*, 2:391.

12. Bryant, "R. F. Hoke, Soldier and Good Citizen," *North Carolina Review* (February 1913): 5; *The Uplift*, December 1909.

13. *Raleigh News and Observer*, May 11, 1921.

14. *New York Sun*, July 4, 1912; *The Uplift*, December 1909.

15. *Charlotte Observer*, July 22, 1912.

16. *The Uplift*, December 1909.

17. *Charlotte Observer*, July 4, 1912; *Lincoln County News*, July 26, 1912; *Masonic Journal*, March 7, 1919; Hamilton, "General Robert F. Hoke," Robert F. Hoke Papers, SHC; *Greensboro Daily News*, July 5, 1912.

18. *Masonic Journal*, March 7, 1919; Hamilton, "General Robert F. Hoke," Robert F. Hoke Papers, SHC; unpublished narrative of Josephus Daniels, Robert F. Hoke Papers, NCDAH.

19. *Masonic Journal*, March 7, 1919; *The Uplift*, December 1909; Unidentified newspaper clipping, Robert F. Hoke Papers, NCDAH.

20. *The Uplift*, December 1909; *Masonic Journal*, March 7, 1919; *Raleigh News and Observer*, May 11, 1921; *Raleigh News and Observer*, December 11, 1903.

21. *Raleigh New and Observer*, December 11, 1903; *Raleigh News and Observer*, May 11, 1921; *Richmond Virginian*, July 5, 1912; "Proceedings of Stockholders, North Carolina Railroad Company," July 1912, Robert F. Hoke Papers, NCDAH; *Orphans' Friend and Masonic Journal*, June 4, 1920. In his article, Ashe compared Hoke to Marshal Ney, Napoleon's lieutenant, and suggested to readers that the legislature request General Hoke to sit for a portrait. *Raleigh News and Observer*, November 23, 1902.

22. *Raleigh News and Observer*, July 9, 1912; *Richmond Virginian*, July 5, 1912; Powell, ed., *North Carolina Biography*, 3:165; Van Wyck, *Descendants of Cornelius Barentse Van Wyck*, n.p.

23. *Charlotte Observer*, July 9, 1912; Powell, ed., *North Carolina Biography*, 3:165, 166; *Raleigh News and Observer*, May 11, 1921, and July 9, 1912.

24. Hamilton, "General Robert F. Hoke," Robert F. Hoke Papers, SHC; telegram from J. C. Pritchard to R. F. Hoke and telegram from Robert F. Hoke to J. C. Pritchard, June 8 (no year), Robert F. Hoke Papers, SHC; *Raleigh News and Observer*, June 20, 1928.

25. North Carolina General Assembly, *Joint Resolution Inviting General Robert F. Hoke to Attend the General Assembly* (H.R. 543, S.R. 344), Robert F. Hoke Papers, SHC; *Charlotte*

Observer, July 21, 1912.

26. R. F. Hoke to Fanny McNeely, March 15, 1899, Hoke Family Papers in possession of Hoke Kimball (great-grandson of Robert F. Hoke), Raleigh, North Carolina.

27. Harris Harrison to R. F. Hoke, June 8, 1885, Robert F. Hoke Papers, SHC.

28. *Fayetteville Observer-Times*, January 2, 1983; *Raleigh News and Observer*, February 23, 1907; Robert C. Lawrence, *Here in Carolina*, p. 96; Powell, *Gazetteer*, p. 178.

29. Powell, *Gazetteer*, p. 231.

30. *Raleigh News and Observer*, June 20, 1928; *Kinston Daily Free Press*, May 10, 1920; *Raleigh News and Observer*, September 11, 1927; Wilie Jones to Bennehan Cameron, February 16, 1924, Bennehan Cameron Papers, SHC; Charles Reagan Wilson and William Ferris, eds., *Encyclopedia of Southern Culture*, p. 703; Storer P. Warer to Van Wyck Hoke, April 27, 1943, Hoke Family Papers in the possession of Van Wyck Webb (grandson of Robert F. Hoke), Raleigh, North Carolina; *Raleigh News and Observer*, May 2, 1943. The S.S. *Robert Hoke* was severely damaged by, but survived, a torpedo attack in the Arabian Sea while bound for East Africa in December 1943. Press release of the War Shipping Administration, March 28, 1944, Robert F. Hoke Papers, NCDAH.

31. Freeman, *R. E. Lee*, 3:379; *Charlotte Observer*, July 21, 1912; *New York Tribune*, July 4, 1912; *Boston Evening Herald*, July 3, 1912; *Boston Record*, July 4, 1912; *Boston Journal*, July 4, 1912; *Philadelphia Public Ledger*, July 4, 1912; *Pittsburgh Dispatch*, July 4, 1912; *Newark Evening News*, July 3, 1912; *Baltimore Sun*, July 4, 1912; *Washington Evening Star*, July 3, 1912; *Norfolk Virginian-Pilot*, July 4, 1912; *Raleigh News and Observer*, July 4, 1912; *Greensboro Daily News*, July 4, 1912; *Charlotte Evening Chronicle*, July 3, 1912; *Charlotte News*, July 3, 1912; *Charlotte Observer*, July 4, 1912; *Atlanta Journal*, July 3, 1912; *Jacksonville Times Union*, July 4, 1912; *New Orleans Picayune*, July 4, 1912; *Montgomery Adventurer*, July 4, 1912; *Nashville Banner*, July 4, 1912; *St. Louis Globe*, July 4, 1912; *Indianapolis Star*, July 4, 1912; *Chicago Inter Ocean*, July 4, 1912; *San Francisco Bulletin*, July 3, 1912; *San Francisco Evening Post*, July 3, 1912.

32. Hamilton, "General Robert F. Hoke," Robert F. Hoke Papers, SHC; Michael Hoke to Bennehan Cameron, April 8, 1924, Bennehan Cameron Papers, SHC; Trevor N. Dupuy et al, eds., *The Harper Encyclopedia of Military Biography*, pp. 428–29.

33. Hamilton, "General Robert F. Hoke," Robert F. Hoke Papers, SHC; Michael Hoke to Bennehan Cameron, April 8, 1924, Bennehan Cameron Papers, SHC. J. Bryan Grimes was a popular lecturer on North Carolina history. He was the featured speaker at the dedication of the marker to General Hoke at Southwest Creek in May 1920. For many years, Grimes was a member of the North Carolina Historical Commission. Powell, ed., *North Carolina Biography*, 2:376; *Kinston Free Press*, May 10, 1920.

34. Michael Hoke to Bennehan Cameron, April 8, 1924, Bennehan Cameron Papers, SHC.

35. Augustus Van Wyck to R. F. Hoke, March 4, 1907, Robert F. Hoke Papers, SHC.

36. Hamilton, "General Robert F. Hoke," Robert F. Hoke Papers, SHC.

37. "Maj. Gen. Robert Frederick Hoke," *Confederate Veteran*, 20:437–38.

38. Freeman, *R. E. Lee*, 3:379.

39. Tucker, *Front Rank*, p. 19; *Raleigh News and Observer*, July 9, 1912; *Masonic Journal*, March 7, 1919; Ashe, *History of North Carolina*, 2:951; Hamilton, "General Robert F. Hoke," Robert F. Hoke Papers, SHC.

40. Michael Hoke to Bennehan Cameron, April 8, 1924, Bennehan Cameron Papers, SHC.

41. Hamilton, "General Robert F. Hoke," Robert F. Hoke Papers, SHC; Dupuy et al, eds., *The*

General Robert F. Hoke

Harper Encyclopedia of Military Biography, pp. 428–29.

42. Hamilton, "General Robert F. Hoke," Robert F. Hoke Papers, SHC.

43. *Masonic Journal*, March 7, 1919.

Bibliography

Manuscripts and Miscellaneous Papers

A. M. Waddell Chapter, United Daughters of the Confederacy. "What Happened at Southwest Creek in the Spring of 1865." In possession of the author.

Alexander Papers. Southern Historical Collection, Wilson Library, University of North Carolina at Chapel Hill.

Auman, W. T. "Neighbor against Neighbor: The Inner Civil War in the Central Counties of Confederate North Carolina." Ph.D. diss., University of North Carolina at Chapel Hill, 1988.

Avery, Waightstill. Papers. Southern Historical Collection, Wilson Library, University of North Carolina at Chapel Hill.

Battle Family Papers. Southern Historical Collection, Wilson Library, University of North Carolina at Chapel Hill.

General Robert F. Hoke

Battle, Kemp P. Papers. Southern Historical Collection, Wilson Library, University of North Carolina at Chapel Hill.

Beauregard Papers. Library of Congress.

Beavans, William. Papers. Southern Historical Collection, Wilson Library, University of North Carolina at Chapel Hill.

Biggs, Asa. Papers. Perkins Library, Duke University.

Biggs, H. Papers. Southern Historical Collection, Wilson Library, University of North Carolina at Chapel Hill.

Brown, Charles S. Papers. Perkins Library, Duke University.

Brumfield, Lewis Shore. "Thomas Lanier Clingman and the Shallow Ford Families." North Carolina Collection, Wilson Library, University of North Carolina at Chapel Hill.

Buie Papers. Southern Historical Collection, Wilson Library, University of North Carolina at Chapel Hill.

Burgwyn Family Papers. Southern Historical Collection, Wilson Library, University of North Carolina at Chapel Hill.

Burton Family Papers. Southern Historical Collection, Wilson Library, University of North Carolina at Chapel Hill.

Burwell, Edward. Papers. Southern Historical Collection, Wilson Library, University of North Carolina at Chapel Hill.

Calder, William. Papers. Perkins Library, Duke University.

Calder, William. Papers. Southern Historical Collection, Wilson Library, University of North Carolina at Chapel Hill.

Cameron, Bennehan. Papers. Southern Historical Collection, Wilson Library, University of North Carolina at Chapel Hill.

Carpenter, William. "The Battle of Ramsour's Mill." Lincoln County Museum.

Chaves, Rachel Susan "Bee." Papers. Perkins Library, Duke University.

Confederate Papers (miscellaneous). Southern Historical Collection, Wilson Library, University of North Carolina at Chapel Hill.

Confederate Pension Papers. North Carolina Division of Archives and History.

Cowles, Calvin J. Papers. North Carolina Division of Archives and History.

Crisp, Lucy Cherry. Papers. Joyner Library, East Carolina University.

Bibliography

Curtis, Newton M. Papers. Chicago Historical Society.

DeRossett Papers. North Carolina Division of Archives and History.

Eaton, Samuel W. Papers. Southern Historical Collection, Wilson Library, University of North Carolina at Chapel Hill.

Ellis, Z. Papers. Southern Historical Collection, Wilson Library, University of North Carolina at Chapel Hill.

Evans, James. Papers. Southern Historical Collection, Wilson Library, University of North Carolina at Chapel Hill.

Gibson, S. J. Papers. Library of Congress.

Gift, Ellen S. Papers. Southern Historical Collection, Wilson Library, University of North Carolina at Chapel Hill.

Goldsborough, L. M. Papers. Library of Congress.

Hackett, Gaden. Papers. Southern Historical Collection, Wilson Library, University of North Carolina at Chapel Hill.

Hagood, James R. Memoirs. South Carolina Library.

Harding, Ezekiah, and John Harding. Papers. Perkins Library, Duke University.

Hathaway, Leland. Papers. Southern Historical Collection, Wilson Library, University of North Carolina at Chapel Hill.

Henderson, William. Papers. North Carolina Division of Archives and History.

Hoke Family Records. In possession of Hoke Kimball, Raleigh, North Carolina.

Hoke Family Records. In possession of Van Wyck Webb, Raleigh, North Carolina.

"Hoke House, The (Inverness)." Lincoln County Library.

Hoke, Michael. Letters. Harold Ford Collection (private), Lincolnton, North Carolina.
Hoke, Robert F. Diary. Lincoln County Library.

Hoke, Robert F. Papers. North Carolina Division of Archives and History.

Hoke, Robert F. Papers. Southern Historical Collection, Wilson Library, University of North Carolina at Chapel Hill.

Hoke, Robert F. Papers. Southern Stars Chapter, United Daughters of the Confederacy, Lincolnton, North Carolina.

Hoke, William Alexander. Papers. Southern Historical Collection, Wilson Library,

General Robert F. Hoke

University of North Carolina at Chapel Hill.

Hooper, Aurelia. Papers. Perkins Library, Duke University.

Iobst, Richard William. "Fort Fisher: A Study." Master's thesis, University of North Carolina at Chapel Hill, 1962.

Joyner, Clinton, Jr. "Major General Robert Frederick Hoke and the Civil War in North Carolina." Master's thesis, East Carolina University, 1974.

LaLane, George M. Papers. Museum of the Confederacy.

Lanpheur Papers. Perkins Library, Duke University.

Lenoir Family Papers. Southern Historical Collection, Wilson Library, University of North Carolina at Chapel Hill.

Lewis, William Gaston. Papers. Southern Historical Collection, Wilson Library, University of North Carolina at Chapel Hill.

Low, Thomas. Papers. Perkins Library, Duke University.

MacRae, Hugh. Papers. Southern Historical Collection, Wilson Library, University of North Carolina at Chapel Hill.

Mangum, Adolphus Williamson. Papers. Southern Historical Collection, Wilson Library, University of North Carolina at Chapel Hill.

McGeachy Papers. Perkins Library, Duke University.

McKay-Stiles Papers. Southern Historical Collection, Wilson Library, University of North Carolina at Chapel Hill.

Military Collection (Civil War). North Carolina Division of Archives and History.

Nixon, Alfred. "Address of August 27, 1908." Lincoln County Library.

Noble, W. H. Papers. Perkins Library, Duke University.

Paris, John. Papers. Southern Historical Collection, Wilson Library, University of North Carolina at Chapel Hill.

Patterson Papers. Southern Historical Collection, Wilson Library, University of North Carolina at Chapel Hill.

Peery, Charles V., Collection (private). Charleston, South Carolina.

Pettigrew Papers. Southern Historical Collection, Wilson Library, University of North Carolina at Chapel Hill.

Phifer, Edward W., Jr. Papers. North Carolina Division of Archives and History.

Bibliography

Phifer Family Papers. Southern Historical Collection, Wilson Library, University of North Carolina at Chapel Hill.

Pfohl, Christian T. Papers. Southern Historical Collection, Wilson Library, University of North Carolina at Chapel Hill.

Schenck, David. Papers. Southern Historical Collection, Wilson Library, University of North Carolina at Chapel Hill.

Sharpe, S. A. Papers. Southern Historical Collection, Wilson Library, University of North Carolina at Chapel Hill.

Swain, D. L. Papers. Southern Historical Collection, Wilson Library, University of North Carolina at Chapel Hill.

Thompson, H. J. H. Papers. Perkins Library, Duke University.

Tyson, Bryan. Papers. Perkins Library, Duke University.

Vance, Zebulon B. Papers. North Carolina Division of Archives and History.

Walker, John K. Papers. Perkins Library, Duke University.

Walker Papers. North Carolina Division of Archives and History.

Wells, William J. Papers. Southern Historical Collection, Wilson Library, University of North Carolina at Chapel Hill.

Wescoat, Joseph J. Papers. Perkins Library, Duke University.

Whitaker, Cary. Papers. Southern Historical Collection, Wilson Library, University of North Carolina at Chapel Hill.

Whitford Papers. North Carolina Division of Archives and History.

Whiting, W. H. C. Papers. Southern Historical Collection, Wilson Library, University of North Carolina at Chapel Hill.

Will Papers. Southern Historical Collection, Wilson Library, University of North Carolina at Chapel Hill.

Williams Papers. Southern Historical Collection, Wilson Library, University of North Carolina at Chapel Hill.

Wills, George Whitaker. Papers. Southern Historical Collection, Wilson Library, University of North Carolina at Chapel Hill.

Wood, Richard Everett. "Port Town at War: Wilmington, North Carolina 1860–1865." Ph.D. diss., Florida State University, 1974.

Wright Family Papers. Perkins Library, Duke University.

General Robert F. Hoke

Articles and Pamphlets

Anderson, Mrs. John H. "North Carolina Boy Soldiers at the Battle of Bentonville." *Confederate Veteran* 35 (1927): 174 76.

Auman, William T., and David D. Scarboro. "The Heroes of America in Civil War North Carolina." *North Carolina Historical Review* 58 (1981): 327–63.

Black, Wilfred W., ed. "Civil War Letters of E. N. Boots." *North Carolina Historical Review* 36 (1959): 205–23.

Bryant, Victor S. "R. F. Hoke, Soldier and Good Citizen." *North Carolina Review* (February 1913): 5.

Cabell, W. L. "Build the Davis Monument." *Confederate Veteran* 1 (1893): 121–25.

Cart, Doran L. "A Soldier's Conscience, Part I: The Letters of Thomas F. Price." *Camp Chase Gazette* 14 (1987): 21–29.

Claytor, Alton B. "Lincoln Lithia Inn." *The State* (March 20, 1937): 38.

Cox, William R. "Major-General Stephen Dodson Ramseur." *Southern Historical Society Papers* 18: 255–60.

Daniels, Josephus. "Two Illustrious Roberts of the Southern Confederacy." *Confederate Veteran* 36 (1928): 290–92.

Elliott, Gilbert. "The Career of the Confederate Ram *Albemarle*." *Century Magazine* (May-October 1888): 419–23.

Field, C. W. "Campaign of 1864 and 1865." *Southern Historical Society Papers* 14: 542–54.

Fiske, Joseph E. "An Involuntary Journey through the Confederacy." *Civil War Papers Read before the Commandery of the State of Massachusetts Military Order of the Loyal Legion of the United States* 2 (1900): 514.

Fonvielle, Chris. "The Last Rays of Departing Hope." *Blue and Gray Magazine* (December 1994): 10–21, 48–62.

Fore, Mrs. J. A. "What Fort Fisher Meant to the Confederacy." *Confederate Veteran* 37 (1929): 178–80.

Gibson, George H. "Opinion in North Carolina Regarding the Acquisition of Texas and Cuba, 1835–1855." *North Carolina Historical Review* 37 (1960): 1–21, 185–201, 477–87.

Graham, William A. "The Battle of Ramsaur's Mill." *The North Carolina Booklet* 4 (1904): 5–23.

Bibliography

Hairston, Peter W. "The Civil War Diary of Peter W. Hairston." Edited by Everard H. Smith. *North Carolina Historical Review* 67(1990):59–86.

Hatton, Clarence R. "Archibald Campbell Godwin." *Confederate Veteran* 28 (1920): 133–36.

Henry, L. Wyatt Camp. "'Tarheels' to 'Yellow-Hammers.'" *Confederate Veteran* 21 (1913): 59.

Hickey, John M. "Confederate National Monument." *Confederate Veteran* 3 (1895): 276.

Jeffrey, Thomas E. "'Free Suffrage' Revisited: Party Politics and Constitutional Reform in Antebellum North Carolina." *North Carolina Historical Review* 59 (1982): 24–48.

Jordan, Weymouth, Jr., and Gerald W. Thomas. "Massacre at Plymouth, April 20, 1864." *North Carolina Historical Review*, 72 (1995): 125–97.

Kite, J. Hiram. "Michael Hoke." *Clinical Orthopaedics* 14 (1959): 1–4.

Klutz, Theo. F., Jr. "The Boy Who Saved Richmond." *Confederate Veteran* 6 (1898): 213–14.

Luvaas, Jay. "Johnston's Last Stand—Bentonville." *North Carolina Historical Review* 33 (1956): 332–58.

Maffitt, Emma M. "The Confederate Navy." *Confederate Veteran* 25 (1917): 157–60, 217–21, 264–67, 315–17.

McCabe, W. Gordon. "Defence of Petersburg." *Southern Historical Society Papers* 36: 257–73.

McClurg, Alexander C. "The Last Chance of the Confederacy." *Atlantic Monthly* 50 (September 1882): 389–400.

Moore, Edwin G. "Ransom's Brigade." *Southern Historical Society Papers* 36: 363–67.

Nichols, Roy F. "Fighting in North Carolina Waters." *North Carolina Historical Review* 40 (1963): 75–84.

Nixon, Alfred. "History of Lincoln County." *North Carolina Booklet* 9 (1910): 111–86.

Padgett, James A. "Reconstruction Letters from North Carolina." *North Carolina Historical Review* 19 (1942): 59–94, 187–208, 280–302, 381–404.

Randolph, Richard. "Confederate Dilemma: North Carolina Troops and the Deserter Problem." *North Carolina Historical Review* 66 (1989): 61–86.

General Robert F. Hoke

Ravenel, Samuel W. "Ask the Survivors of Bentonville." *Confederate Veteran* 18 (1910): 124–26.

Ridley, B. L. "Captain Ridley's Journal." *Confederate Veteran* 3 (1895): 99, 203–5.

———. "Last Battles of the War." *Confederate Veteran* 3 (1895): 20, 36–37, 70–71.

Shepherd, Henry E. "Gallant Sons of North Carolina." *Confederate Veteran* 27 (1919): 413–14.

Van Noppen, Ina W. "The Significance of Stoneman's Last Raid." *North Carolina Historical Review* 38 (1961): 19–44, 149–72, 341–61, 500–526.

Venable, C. S. "The Campaign from the Wilderness to Petersburg." *Southern Historical Society Papers* 14: 535–42.

Venable, M. W. "In the Trenches at Petersburg." *Confederate Veteran* 34 (1926): 59–61.

Wright, Arnold C. "Capture of Plymouth, N.C." *Confederate Veteran* 24 (1916): 200.

———. "After the Battle of Plymouth, N.C." *Confederate Veteran,* 25 (1917): 16.

Books and Official Records

Alexander, Edward Porter. *Fighting for the Confederacy: The Personal Recollections of General Edward Porter Alexander.* Edited by Gary Gallagher. Chapel Hill: University of North Carolina Press, 1989.

Anderson, Jean Bradley. *The Kirklands of Ayr Mount.* Chapel Hill: University of North Carolina Press, 1991.

Arnett, Ethel S., and W. C. Jackson. *Greensboro, North Carolina.* Chapel Hill: University of North Carolina Press.

Ashe, Samuel A. *History of North Carolina.* 2 vols. Raleigh, N.C.: Edwards and Broughton, 1925.

Ashe, Samuel A., Stephen B. Weeks, and Charles L. Van Noppen, eds. *Biographical History of North Carolina.* 8 vols. Greensboro, N.C.: Charles L. Van Noppen, 1905–17.

Bailey, Ronald H., et al. *The Bloodiest Day: The Battle of Antietam.* Volume in *The Civil War* series. Alexandria, Va: Time-Life Books, 1984.

Barefoot, Daniel W. *Touring the Backroads of North Carolina's Lower Coast.* Winston-Salem, N.C.: John F. Blair, Publisher, 1995.

Bibliography

Barrett, John G. *Sherman's March through the Carolinas.* Chapel Hill: University of North Carolina Press, 1956.

———. *The Civil War in North Carolina.* Chapel Hill: University of North Carolina Press, 1963.

———. *North Carolina As a Civil War Battleground, 1861–1865.* Raleigh: North Carolina Division of Archives and History, 1975.

Battle, Kemp P. *Memories of an Old-Time Tar Heel.* Chapel Hill: University of North Carolina Press, 1945.

———. *History of the University of North Carolina.* 2 vols. Spartanburg, S.C.: Reprint Company, 1974.

Bennett, W. W. *The Great Revival in the Southern Armies.* Harrisonburg, Va.: Sprinkle Publications, 1989.

Black, Robert C., III. *The Railroads of the Confederacy.* Wilmington, N.C.: Broadfoot Publishing, 1987.

Blakeslee, B. F. *History of the Sixteenth Connecticut.* Hartford, Conn.: Case, Lockwood and Brainard Company, Printers, 1875.

Boatner, Mark M., III. *Encyclopedia of the American Revolution.* Mechanicsburg, Pa.: Stackpole Books, 1994.

Branham, Charles N., ed. *Register of Graduates and Former Cadets of the United States Military Academy, 1802–1965.* West Point, N.Y.: West Point Alumni Foundation, 1965.

Bridges, Hal. *Lee's Maverick General: Daniel Harvey Hill.* New York: McGraw-Hill, 1961.

Brown, Marvin A., and Maurice C. York. *Our Enduring Past.* Lincolnton, N.C.: Lincoln County Historic Properties Commission, 1986.

Burgwyn, William H. S. *A Captain's War: The Letters and Diaries of William H. S. Burgwyn, 1861–1865.* Edited by Herbert Schiller. Shippensburg, Pa.: White Mane Publishing, 1994.

Cannan, John. *The Antietam Campaign: August-September 1862.* Conshohocken, Pa: Combined Books, 1994.

Chaitin, Peter M., et al. *The Coastal War.* Volume in *The Civil War* series. Alexandria, Va.: Time-Life Books, 1984.

Chambers, Henry A. *Diary of Captain Henry A. Chambers.* Edited by T. H. Pearce and Selby A. Daniels. Wendell, N.C.: Broadfoot's Bookmark, 1983.

Cheney, John L., Jr., ed. *North Carolina Government, 1585–1974: A Narrative and Statistical History*. Raleigh: North Carolina Department of the Secretary of State, 1981.

Cheshire, Joseph Blount. *Nonnulla*. Chapel Hill: University of North Carolina Press, 1930.

Clark, Walter. *The Papers of Walter Clark*. Edited by A. L. Brooks and H. T. Lefler. Chapel Hill: University of North Carolina Press, 1948.

Clark, Walter, ed. *Histories of the Several Regiments and Battalions from North Carolina in the Great War, 1861–1865*. 5 vols. Raleigh: State of North Carolina, 1901.

Connor, R. D. W. *North Carolina: Rebuilding an Ancient Commonwealth, 1584–1925*. Chicago: American Historical Society, 1929.

Cooper, Horton. *History of Avery County, North Carolina*. Asheville, N.C.: Biltmore Press, 1964.

Cope, Robert F., and Manly Wade Wellman. *The County of Gaston: Two Centuries of a North Carolina Region*. Baltimore: Gateway Press, 1997.

Cox, J. D. *The March to the Sea: Franklin and Nashville*. New York: Charles Scribner's Sons, 1882.

Croffitt, W. A., and John Morris. *The Military and Civil History of Connecticut, 1861–1865*. New York: 1868.

Davenport, Garvin F. *Antebellum Kentucky: A Social History, 1800–1860*. Oxford, Ohio: Mississippi Valley Press, 1943.

Davis, Archie K. *Boy Colonel of the Confederacy: The Life and Times of Henry King Burgwyn, Jr*. Chapel Hill: University of North Carolina Press, 1985.

Davis, Jefferson. *Rise and Fall of the Confederate Government*. 2 vols. Richmond: Garrett and Massie, 1938.

Davis, William, et al. *First Blood*. Volume in *The Civil War* series. Alexandria, Va.: Time-Life Books, 1983.

Davis, William, et al. *Death in the Trenches*. Volume in *The Civil War* series. Alexandria, Va.: Time-Life Books, 1986.

Davis, William, ed. *The Confederate General*. 6 vols. Harrisonburg, Pa.: National Historical Society, 1991.

Denson, C. B. *An Address Containing a Memoir of the Late Major-General William Henry Chase Whiting*. Raleigh, N.C.: Edwards and Broughton, 1895.

Derby, W. P. *Bearing Arms in the Twenty-seventh Massachusetts Regiment of Volun-*

Bibliography

teer Infantry during the Civil War. Boston: Wright and Potter Printing Company, 1883.

Dickert, D. Augustus. *History of Kershaw's Brigade.* Wilmington, N.C.: Broadfoot Publishing, 1990.

Dickey, Luther. *History of the 103rd Pennsylvania Regiment, 1861–1865.* Chicago: 1910.

Dollard, Robert. *Recollections of the Civil War, and Going West to Grow Up with the Country.* Scotland, S.D.: 1906.

Dowd, Clement. *Life of Vance.* Charlotte, N.C.: Observer Printing and Publishing House, 1897.

Dubose, Henry Kershaw. *The History of Company B, Twenty-first Regiment South Carolina Confederate States Provisional Army.* Columbia, S.C.: 1909.

Dupuy, Trevor N., Curt Johnson, and David L. Bongard, eds. *The Harper Encyclopedia of Military Biography.* New York: HarperCollins Publishers, 1992.

Durrill, Wayne K. *War of a Different Kind: A Southern Community in the Great Rebellion.* New York: Oxford University Press, 1990.

Early, Jubal Anderson. *Jubal Early's Memoirs: Autobiographical Sketch and Narrative of the War Between the States.* Baltimore: Nautical and Aviation Publishing Company of America, 1989.

Eckenrode, H. J., and Bryan Conrad. *James Longstreet: Lee's War Horse.* Chapel Hill: University of North Carolina Press, 1986.

Eddy, T. M. *The Patriotism of Illinois: A Record of the Civil and Military History of the State in the War for the Union.* 2 vols. Chicago: Clarke and Company, 1865–1866.

Edmondston, Catherine Ann Devereux. *"Journal of a Secesh Lady": The Diary of Catherine Ann Devereux Edmondston, 1860–1866.* Edited by Beth G. Crabtree and James W. Parton. Raleigh: North Carolina Division of Archives and History, 1979.

Eldredge, Daniel. *The Third New Hampshire and All about It.* Boston: E. B. Stillings and Company, 1893.

Elliott, James Carson. *The Southern Soldier Boy: A Thousand Shots for the Confederacy.* Raleigh, N.C.: Edwards and Broughton, 1907.

Elliott, Robert. *Ironclad of the Albemarle: Gilbert Elliott's Albemarle.* Shippensburg, Pa.: White Mane Publishing, 1994.

Ellis, Edward S. *Low Twelve.* New York: Macoy Publishing and Masonic Supply Company, 1913.

General Robert F. Hoke

Ellis, John Willis. *The Papers of John Willis Ellis*. Edited by Noble J. Tolbert. 2 vols. Raleigh: North Carolina Division of Archives and History, 1964.

Evans, Clement A., ed. *Confederate Military History: North Carolina*. Atlanta: Confederate Publishing Company, 1899.

Evans, W. McKee. *Ballots and Fence Rails: Reconstruction on the Lower Cape Fear*. Chapel Hill: University of North Carolina Press, 1966.

Farrell, Mallory Hope. *Tweetsie Country: The East Tennessee and Western North Carolina Railroad*. Boulder, Colo.: Pruett Publishing Company, 1976.

Faust, Patricia, ed. *Historical Times Illustrated Encyclopedia of the Civil War*. New York: Harper and Row, 1986.

Foote, Shelby. *The Civil War: A Narrative*. 3 vols. New York: Vintage Books, 1986.

Freeman, Douglas Southall. *R. E. Lee*. 4 vols. New York: Charles Scribner's Sons, 1934.

———. *Lee's Lieutenants*. 3 vols. New York: Charles Scribner's Sons, 1942–43.

Furgurson, Ernest B. *Chancellorsville 1863*. New York: Alfred A. Knopf, 1992.

Gallagher, Gary. *Stephen Dodson Ramseur*. Chapel Hill: University of North Carolina Press, 1985.

Gibson, John. *Those 163 Days*. New York: Coward-McCann, 1961.

Gragg, Rod. *Confederate Goliath: The Battle of Fort Fisher*. New York: HarperCollins Publishers, 1991.

Graham, William Alexander. *The Papers of William Alexander Graham, 1864–1865*. Vols. 5 (edited by Max R. Williams and J. G. Hamilton) and 6 (edited by Max R. Williams). Raleigh: North Carolina Division of Archives and History, 1976.

Grant, U. S. *Personal Memoirs of U. S. Grant*. 2 vols. New York: Charles L. Webster and Company, 1885.

Hagemann, James. *The Heritage of Virginia: The Story of Place Names in the Old Dominion*. West Chester, Pa.: Whitford Press, 1986.

Hagood, Johnson. *Memoirs of the War of Secession*. Camden, S.C.: J. J. Fox, 1989.

Hallock, Judith Lee. *Braxton Bragg and Confederate Defeat*. Vol. 2. Tuscaloosa: University of Alabama Press, 1991.

Hamilton, J. G. D. *History of North Carolina since 1860*. Vol. 3. Spartanburg, S.C.: Reprint Company, 1973.

Bibliography

Hatch, Charles E., Jr. *Yorktown and the Siege of 1781.* Washington: GPO, 1954.

Hawkins, Rush C. *An Account of the Assassination of Loyal Citizens of North Carolina.* New York: 1897.

Henderson, Archibald. *North Carolina: The Old North State and the New.* 2 vols. Chicago: Lewis Publishing Company, 1941.

Hill, Daniel H. *Bethel to Sharpsburg: North Carolina in the War Between the States.* 2 vols. Wilmington, N.C.: Broadfoot Publishing, 1992.

Howard, O. O. *Autobiography of Oliver Otis Howard, Major General, United States Army.* 2 vols. New York: Baker and Taylor Company, 1907.

Howe, Thomas J. *The Petersburg Campaign: Wasted Valor, June 15–18, 1864.* Lynchburg, Va.: H. E. Howard, 1988.

Howell, Andrew J. *The Book of Wilmington.* Wilmington, N.C.: 1930.

Hughes, Nathaniel Cheairs, Jr. *General William J. Hardee: Old Reliable.* Wilmington, N.C.: Broadfoot Publishing, 1987.

Hyde, Thomas Worchester. *Following the Greek Cross.* Boston: Houghton Mifflin, 1911.

Iobst, Richard W., and Louis H. Manarin. *The Bloody Sixth: The Sixth North Carolina Regiment, Confederate States of America.* Gaithersburg, Md.: Butternut Press, 1987.

Jarvis, Thomas Jordan. *The Papers of Thomas Jordan Jarvis, 1869–1882.* Edited by Wilfred Buck Yearns. Raleigh: North Carolina Division of Archives and History, 1969.

Jaynes, Gregory, et al. *The Killing Ground.* Volume in *The Civil War* series. Alexandria, Va.: Time-Life Books, 1986.

Johnson, Robert Underwood, and Clarence Clough Buel, eds. *Battles and Leaders of the Civil War.* 4 vols. Secaucus, N.J.: Castle.

Johnson, Talmage C., and Charles R. Holloman. *The Story of Kinston and Lenoir County.* Raleigh, N.C.: Edwards and Broughton, 1954.

Johnston, Henry P. *The Yorktown Campaign and the Surrender of Cornwallis, 1781.* New York: Harper and Brothers, 1881.

Johnston, Joseph E. *Narrative of Military Operations during the Civil War.* New York: Da Capo Press, 1959.

Jones, J. B. *Rebel War Clerk's Diary.* Philadelphia: J. B. Lippincott, 1866.

Jones, J. William. *Christ in the Camp.* Harrisonburg, Va.: Sprinkle Publications, 1986.

Jones, Terry. *Lee's Tigers: The Louisiana Infantry in the Army of Northern Virginia.* Baton Rouge: Louisiana State University Press, 1987.

Jordan, Weymouth T., Jr. *The Battle of Bentonville.* Wilmington, N.C.: Broadfoot Publishing, 1990.

Kirwan, Thomas, and Henry Splaine. *Memorial History of the 17th Massachusetts Regiment, Massachusetts Volunteer Infantry, 1861–1865.* Salem, Mass.: Salem Press, 1911.

Kleber, John E., ed. *The Kentucky Encyclopedia.* Lexington: University of Kentucky Press, 1992.

Klein, Maury. *Edward Porter Alexander.* Athens: University of Georgia Press, 1971.

Lamb, William. *Colonel Lamb's Story of Fort Fisher.* Carolina Beach, N.C.: Blockade Runner Museum, 1966.

Lawrence, Robert C. *Here in Carolina.* New York: J. J. Little and Ives Company, 1939.

Lee, Robert E. *Lee's Dispatches: Unpublished Letters of General Robert E. Lee, C.S.A., to Jefferson Davis.* Edited by Douglas Southall Freeman. Baton Rouge: Louisiana State University Press, 1957.

————. *The Wartime Papers of Robert E. Lee.* Edited by Clifford Dowdey and Louis H. Manarin. New York: Da Capo Press, 1961.

Leedy, Guy M., and Carolyn M. Stroup, eds. *A Pictorial Walk through Lincoln County.* Lincolnton, N.C.: Lincoln Times-News, 1969.

Lefler, Hugh Talmage, and Albert Ray Newsome. *North Carolina: The History of a Southern State.* Chapel Hill: University of North Carolina Press, 1973.

Leonard, Thomas. *The Story of Fort Fisher.* Ocean City, N.J.: 1915.

Little, Henry. *The 7th Regiment of New Hampshire Volunteers in the War of Rebellion.* Concord, N.H.: 1886.

Longacre, Edward G. *Pickett: Leader of the Charge.* Shippensburg, Pa.: White Mane Publishing, 1995.

Longstreet, James. *From Manassas to Appomattox.* Bloomington: Indiana University Press, 1960.

Losson, Christopher. *Tennessee's Forgotten Warriors: Frank Cheatham and His Confederate Division.* Knoxville: University of Tennessee Press, 1989.

Lowry, Don. *No Turning Back: The Beginning of the End of the Civil War, March–June 1864.* New York: Hippocrene Books, 1992.

Bibliography

Loy, Ursula, and Pauline Worthy. *Washington and the Pamlico*. Washington-Beaufort Bicentennial Commission, 1976.

Luvaas, Jay, and Harold W. Nelson, eds. *The U. S. Army War College Guide to the Battle of Antietam: The Maryland Campaign of 1862*. Carlisle, Pa.: South Mountain Press, 1987.

————. *The U. S. Army War College Guide to the Battles of Chancellorsville and Fredericksburg*. Carlisle, Pa.: South Mountain Press, 1988.

Mahood, Wayne. *The Plymouth Pilgrims: A History of the Eighty-fifth New York Infantry in the Civil War*. Highstown, N.J.: Longstreet House, 1989.

Malone, Bartlett Yancey. *Whipt 'Em Everytime: The Diary of Bartlett Yancey Malone*. Edited by William W. Pierson. Wilmington, N.C.: Broadfoot Publishing, 1987.

Maney, R. Wayne. *Marching to Cold Harbor: Victory and Failure, 1864*. Shippensburg, Pa.: White Mane Publishing, 1995.

McMurry, Richard M. *Two Great Rebel Armies: An Essay in Confederate Military History*. Chapel Hill. University of North Carolina Press, 1989.

McPherson, James M. *Battle Cry of Freedom*. New York: Oxford University Press, 1988.

Moore, Frank, ed. *Rebellion Record*. 12 vols. New York: G. P. Putnam, 1862–69.

Moore, John W. *History of North Carolina*. 2 vols. Raleigh, N.C.: Alfred Williams and Company, 1880.

Morgan, James Norris. *Recollections of a Rebel Reefer*. Boston: 1917.

Morgan, William H. *Reminiscences of the War of 1861–1865*. Lynchburg, Va.: 1911.

Mowris, J. A. *A History of the One Hundred and Seventeenth Regiment, N.Y. Volunteers*. Hartford, Conn: Case, Lockwood, and Company, 1866.

Nichols, George Ward. *The Story of the Great March: Reminiscences of the Civil War*. New York: Harper and Brothers, 1865.

Nisbet, James Cooper. *4 Years on the Firing Line*. Wilmington, N.C.: Broadfoot Publishing, 1991.

Norton, Clarence Clifford. *The Democratic Party in Antebellum North Carolina, 1835–1861*. Chapel Hill: University of North Carolina Press, 1930.

Oates, William C. *The War Between the Union and the Confederacy and Their Lost Opportunities*. Dayton, Ohio: Morningside Bookshop, 1985.

Official Records of the Union and Confederate Navies in the War of the Rebellion. 30 vols. in 2 series. Washington: GPO, 1894–1922.

General Robert F. Hoke

Osborne, Charles C. *Jubal: The Life and Times of General Jubal A. Early, CSA.* Chapel Hill, N.C.: Algonquin Books, 1992.

Page, Dave. *Ships versus Shore: Civil War Engagements along Southern Shores and Rivers.* Nashville, Tenn.: Rutledge Hill Press, 1994.

Pender, William Dorsey. *The General to His Lady: The Civil War Letters of William Dorsey Pender to Fanny Pender.* Edited by William W. Hassler. Chapel Hill: University of North Carolina Press, 1962.

Pfanz, Harry. *Gettysburg: Culp's Hill and Cemetery Hill.* Chapel Hill: University of North Carolina Press, 1993.

Poe, Clarence. *True Tales of the South at War.* Chapel Hill: University of North Carolina Press, 1961.

Porter, David D. *Naval History of the Civil War.* Secaucus, N.J.: Castle, 1984.

Powell, William S. *The North Carolina Gazetteer.* Chapel Hill: University of North Carolina Press, 1968.

————. *North Carolina through Five Centuries.* Chapel Hill: University of North Carolina Press, 1989.

Powell, William S., ed. *Dictionary of North Carolina Biography.* 5 of a projected 6 vols. Chapel Hill: University of North Carolina Press, 1979–94.

Price, Isaiah. *History of the Ninety-Seventh Regiment, Pennsylvania Volunteer Infantry, during the War of the Rebellion, 1861–1865.* Philadelphia: 1875.

Purcell, L. Edward. *Who Was Who in the American Revolution.* New York: Facts on File, 1993.

Raleigh Cemetery Association, ed. *Historic Oakwood Cemetery.* Raleigh, N.C.: Edwards and Broughton, 1990.

Robertson, James I. *General A. P. Hill: The Story of a Confederate Warrior.* New York: Random House, 1987.

Robertson, William Glenn. *Back Door to Richmond: The Bermuda Hundred Campaign, April–June 1864.* Baton Rouge: Louisiana State University Press, 1987.

Roe, Alfred Seeyle. *The Ninth New York Heavy Artillery.* Worchester, Mass.: F. S. Blanchard and Company, 1899.

Roman, Alfred. *The Military Operations of General Beauregard.* 2 vols. New York: Da Capo Press, 1994.

Sakowski, Carolyn. *Touring the Western North Carolina Backroads.* Winston-Salem, N.C.: John F. Blair, Publisher, 1990.

Bibliography

Sanger, Donald Bridgeman, and Thomas Robson Hay. *James Longstreet*. Baton Rouge: Louisiana State University Press, 1952.

Scharf, J. Thomas. *History of the Confederate States Navy from Its Organization to the Surrender of Its Last Vessel*. New York: Fairfax Press, 1977.

Schiller, Herbert. *The Bermuda Hundred Campaign*. Dayton, Ohio: Morningside House, 1988.

Schofield, John M. *Forty-six Years in the Army*. New York: Century Company, 1897.

Schurz, Carl. *The Reminiscences of Carl Schurz*. 3 vols. New York: McClure Company, 1907–8.

Sears, Stephen. *Landscape Turned Red: The Battle of Antietam*. New York: Warner Books, 1983.

Seitz, Don C. *Braxton Bragg: General of the Confederacy*. Columbia, S.C.: The State Company, 1924.

Seymour, William J. *The Civil War Memoirs of Captain William J. Seymour: Reminiscences of a Louisiana Tiger*. Edited by Terry L. Jones. Baton Rouge: Louisiana State University Press, 1991.

Sharpe, William. *A New Geography of North Carolina*. 4 vols. Raleigh, N.C.: Sharpe Publishing Company, 1954–65.

Sherrill, William L. *Annals of Lincoln County, North Carolina*. Baltimore: Regional Publishing Company, 1972.

Shirley, Franklin Ray. *Zebulon Vance: Tarheel Spokesman*. Charlotte, N.C.: McNally and Loftin, Publishers, 1962.

Singleton, Royce. *John Taylor Wood: Sea Ghost of the Confederacy*. Athens: University of Georgia Press, 1979.

Sommers, Richard J. *Richmond Redeemed: The Siege at Petersburg*. Garden City, N.Y.: Doubleday and Company, 1981.

Spencer, Cornelia Phillips. *The Last Ninety Days of the War*. Wilmington, N.C.: Broadfoot Publishing, 1993.

Sprunt, James. *Chronicles of the Cape Fear River, 1660–1916*. Wilmington, N.C.: Broadfoot Publishing, 1992.

Stephens, Alexander H. *A Constitutional View of the Late War Between the States*. Chicago: National Publishing Company, 1868.

Stiles, Robert. *Four Years under Marse Robert*. New York and Washington: Neale Publishing, 1903.

Still, William N., Jr. *Iron Afloat: The Story of the Confederate Ironclads*. Columbia: University of South Carolina Press, 1985.

Supplement to the Official Records of the Union and Confederate Armies. 32 of a projected 100 vols. Wilmington, N.C.: Broadfoot Publishing, 1994–.

Swinton, William. *Campaigns of the Army of the Potomac*. New York: Charles Scribner's Sons, 1887.

Swope, Gilbert Ernest, ed. *History of the Swope Family and Their Connections*. Lancaster, Pa.: T. B. and H. B. Cochran, Printers, 1896.

Symonds, Craig L. *Joseph E. Johnston: A Civil War Biography*. New York: W. W. Norton and Company, 1992.

Taylor, Walter H. *Four Years with General Lee*. New York: Bonanza Books, 1962.

Thomas, Henry W. *History of the Doles-Cook Brigade, Army of Northern Virginia, C.S.A.* Dayton, Ohio: Morningside House, 1988.

Thorpe, Sheldon B. *The History of the Fifteenth Connecticut Volunteers*. New Haven, Conn.: Price, Lee, and Adkins Company, 1893.

Thwaites, Reuben Gold. *Travels West of the Alleghenies*. Cleveland: Arthur H. Clark Company, 1904.

Trotter, William. *Silk Flags and Cold Steel*. Vol. 1 of *The Civil War in North Carolina*. Greensboro, N.C.: Signal Research, 1988.

———. *Ironclads and Columbiads*. Vol. 3 of *The Civil War in North Carolina*. Greensboro, N.C.: Signal Research, 1989.

Trudeau, Noah Andre. *Bloody Roads South: The Wilderness to Cold Harbor, May–June 1864*. Boston: Little, Brown and Company, 1989.

———. *The Last Citadel: Petersburg, Virginia, June 1864–April 1865*. Boston: Little, Brown and Company, 1991.

Tucker, Glenn. *High Tide at Gettysburg*. Indianapolis: Bobbs-Merrill Company, 1958.

———. *Front Rank*. Raleigh: North Carolina Confederate Centennial Commission, 1962.

———. *Zeb Vance: Champion of Personal Freedom*. Indianapolis: Bobbs-Merrill Company, 1965.

Underwood, Adin B. *The Three Years' Service of the Thirty-third Massachusetts Infantry Regiment*. Boston: 1881.

Bibliography

U.S. Congress. *Murder of Union Soldiers in North Carolina: Letter from the Secretary of War, May 3, 1866.* 39th Cong., 1st sess., 1866. House Executive Doc. 98.

———. *Statue of Zebulon Baird Vance.* Washington: GPO, 1917.

Van Noppen, Ina W., and John J. Van Noppen. *Western North Carolina since the Civil War.* Boone, N.C.: Appalachian Consortium, 1973.

Van Wyck, Ann. *Descendants of Cornelius Barentse Van Wyck.* New York: Tobias A. Wright, Printer and Publisher, 1912.

Waddell, Alfred M. *An Address before the Association, Army of Northern Virginia, October 28, 1887.* Richmond: William Ellis Jones, 1888.

———. *Some Memories of My Life.* Raleigh, N.C.: Edwards and Broughton, 1908.

Walcott, Charles F. *History of the Twenty-first Massachusetts Volunteers.* Boston: 1882.

War of the Rebellion: A Compilation of the Official Records of the Union and Confederate Armies. 70 vols. in 128. Washington: GPO, 1880 1901.

Warner, Ezra. *Generals in Gray: Lives of the Confederate Commanders.* Baton Rouge: Louisiana State University Press, 1959.

———. *Generals in Blue: Lives of the Union Commanders.* Baton Rouge: Louisiana State University Press, 1964.

Watson, Alan D. *A History of New Bern and Craven County.* New Bern, N.C.: Tryon Palace Commission, 1987.

Waugh, Elizabeth Culbertson. *North Carolina's Capital, Raleigh.* Chapel Hill: University of North Carolina Press, 1967.

Waugh, John C. *The Class of 1846 from West Point to Appomattox: Stonewall Jackson, George McClellan and Their Brothers.* New York: Warner Books, 1994.

Welles, Gideon. *The Diary of Gideon Welles.* Edited by Howard Beale. 3 vols. New York: W. W. Norton and Company, 1960.

Wellman, Manly Wade. *Giant in Gray: A Biography of Wade Hampton of South Carolina.* New York: Charles Scribner's Sons, 1949.

———. *Rebel Boast: First at Bethel—Last at Appomattox.* New York: Henry Holt and Company, 1951.

———. *They Took Their Stand.* New York: G. P. Putnam's Sons, 1959.

Welsh, Jack D. *Medical Histories of Confederate Generals.* Kent, Ohio: Kent State University Press, 1995.

General Robert F. Hoke

Wert, Jeffrey. *General James Longstreet: The Confederacy's Most Controversial Soldier*. New York: Simon and Schuster, 1993.

Wheeler, John Hill. *Historical Sketches of North Carolina from 1584 to 1851*. Baltimore: Regional Publishing Company, 1964.

Whitener, Daniel Jay. *North Carolina History*. Oklahoma City: Harlow Publishing, 1958.

Williams, Hiram Smith. *This War So Horrible: The Civil War Diary of Hiram Smith Williams*. Edited by Lewis N. Wynne and Robert T. Taylor. Tuscaloosa: University of Alabama Press, 1993.

Williams, T. Harry. *P. G. T. Beauregard: Napoleon in Gray*. Baton Rouge: Louisiana State University Press, 1955.

Wilson, Charles Reagan, and William Ferris, eds. *Encyclopedia of Southern Culture*. Chapel Hill: University of North Carolina Press, 1989.

Wilson, James Grant, and Titus Munson Coan, eds. *Personal Recollections of the War of the Rebellion: Addresses Delivered before the New York Commandery of the Loyal Legion of the United States*. 4 vols. New York: J. J. Little and Company, 1863–91.

Woodward, C. Vann, ed. *Mary Chesnut's Civil War*. New Haven, Conn.: Yale University Press, 1981.

Wright, Louise Wigfall. *A Southern Girl in '61: War-Time Memories of a Confederate Senator's Daughter*. New York: Doubleday and Page, 1905.

Yearns, W. Buck, and John G. Barrett, eds. *North Carolina Civil War Documentary*. Chapel Hill: University of North Carolina Press, 1980.

Index

Index

Index

Index

Index